INTERNATIONAL STUDIES

of the
Committee on International Relations
University of Notre Dame

INTERNATIONAL STUDIES

of the
Committee on International Relations
University of Notre Dame

The Representative Republic
FERDINAND A. HERMENS

Catholicism, Nationalism, and Democracy in Argentina
JOHN J. KENNEDY

Why Democracies Fail: A Critical Evaluation of the
Causes for Modern Dictatorship
NORMAN L. STAMPS

The Fate of East Central Europe: Hopes and
Failures of American Foreign Policy
Edited by STEPHEN D. KERTESZ

German Protestants Face the Social Question
WILLIAM O. SHANAHAN

Diplomacy in a Whirlpool:
Hungary Between Nazi Germany and Soviet Russia
STEPHEN D. KERTESZ

Soviet Imperialism: Its Origins and Tactics
Edited by WALDEMAR GURIAN

Pan-Slavism: Its History and Ideology
HANS KOHN

The Foreign Policy of the British Labour Government
M. A. FITZSIMONS

Christian Democracy in Italy and France
MARIO EINAUDI *and* FRANCOIS GOGUEL

Bolshevism: An Introduction to Soviet Communism
WALDEMAR GURIAN

(Out of Print)

The Soviet Union: Background, Ideology, Reality
Edited by WALDEMAR GURIAN

The Catholic Church in World Affairs
Edited by WALDEMAR GURIAN *and*
M. A. FITZSIMONS

Europe Between Democracy and Anarchy
FERDINAND A. HERMENS

THE
REPRESENTATIVE
REPUBLIC

FERDINAND A. HERMENS

UNIVERSITY OF NOTRE DAME PRESS

1958

Library of Congress Catalog Card Number 57-14969

© 1958, University of Notre Dame Press

Notre Dame, Indiana

PREFACE

This book is a protest against the fallacy that constitutional government is necessarily weak, and that it must be on the defensive in the struggle against subversion by either the extreme Right or the extreme Left. Constitutional government can be strong enough to carry the battle into the camp of the enemy. If it avoids what Alexander Hamilton called "improper channels of government" it will, if certain pre-political conditions are granted, make it possible for the state to carry out its proper functions. In this case it will satisfy the average citizen, attract doubters to its side, and isolate the hard core of its opponents to such an extent that they will be only a nuisance rather than a danger.

This, at any rate, is the view of those who founded our "representative republic." It is as vigorously enunciated in *The Federalist* papers as it is in Jefferson's first inaugural address. James Madison, in the opening sentence of the often quoted (and misunderstood!) No. 10, held it to be the principal advantage of a "well constructed Union" that it could "break and control the violence of faction"; what he says about "faction" applies fully to the Communists, Fascists and Nazis of our time. Madison was well aware of the economic, and other, elements of division which encourage political conflict. He differed from Karl Marx, however, by going a step farther and showing, as pointed out in more detail below, how the devices of constitutional government could be employed to control the effects of these divisions.

Likewise, in our day, we should not just be content to relate the existence of political difficulties to such factors as the class structure. It is the task of political science to go beyond that point and to show how the devices of integration contained in the arsenal of constitutional government can marshall what is sound within a nation and allow it to act on behalf of the whole, strengthening (rather than passively presupposing) the basis for political consensus in the process.

This function cannot be fulfilled unless we recognize its existence and realize its nature. That is what the framers of the Constitution did when, to use again the words of Madison (No. 48 of *The Federalist*), they felt that certain defects of the "critical period in American history" might be "imputable to peculiar circumstances connected with the war," but that "the greater part of them may be considered as the spontaneous shoots of an ill-constituted government."

Of "ill-constituted government" we have had a great deal since the end of the First World War, and from its "spontaneous shoots" we suffer grievously. In the pages that follow an attempt will be made to identify them as far as that can be done in one volume and by one writer. It is, of course, a never-ending task, requiring a constant re-evaluation of general principles in the light of concrete facts. Besides, the working of political institutions should always be examined in relation to the economic, social, and political problems of time and place, and it would be desirable that in future considerations of these problems economists and sociologists should cooperate closely with political scientists.

The author wishes to acknowledge with grateful appreciation the generous assistance of colleagues and friends in connection with the work on the manuscript. Mr. D. C. Holland, of University College in London, has read the chapter on parliamentary government in Britain. Professor François Goguel of the *Institut d'Etudes* of the University of Paris, who, for years, has provided me with information on French political developments, made thorough and detailed comments concerning both chapters on France. In addition, Professor Yves R. Simon, of the University of Chicago, examined the one on the Third Republic, and Professor Roger Pinto, of the University of Paris, the one on the Fourth Republic. The *Service de Presse et d'Information* of the French Embassy to the United States has always been willing to help, no matter how difficult it was to comply with my numerous requests. The chapter on the Bonn Republic was read by Professor John Brown Mason of Georgetown University. Dr. Helmut Unkelbach of the University of Bonn, Dr. Guenther Willms of the Federal Supreme Court in Karlsruhe, Dr. Joseph Bollig, a member of the Diet of North Rhine-Westphalia, and Mr. Leo Sarlette, are among those who provided me with information on various aspects of German political developments. Professor Mario Einaudi of Cornell University read the chapter on Italy, much of which is based upon material provided by Professor Giuseppe D. Ferri until his untimely death in 1953, and subsequently by Dr. Elio Caranti, of the University of Rome. I am also indebted for assistance to Professor Giovanni Schepis of the University of Rome, and to Dr. Guglielmo Negri of the staff of the Italian Chamber of Deputies. Dr. Edward O'Connor of Washington, D.C. offered valuable suggestions concerning Chapter XIX.

Needless to say, the responsibility for the facts stated and views expressed in this book is entirely the author's. He is also responsible for translations from French, German, Italian and Spanish publications, unless otherwise indicated.

At the University of Notre Dame, my colleagues of the Committee on International Relations have always given assistance in many ways. This applies particularly to its chairman, Professor Stephen Kertesz, who, like the Rev. Stanley Parry, C.S.C., Head of the Department of Political Science, has been most encouraging and most helpful. Mr. Louis Tondreau, my assistant during the time the book was written, has patiently secured material, taken care of numerous files, and rearranged the footnotes. Mr. John Lipinski has gone over the entire manuscript, and made useful suggestions of a stylistic nature. As on previous occasions, Mrs. Hermens has given unstintingly of her time to the preparation and editing of the manuscript.

Ferdinand A. Hermens

South Bend, Indiana
September 1, 1957.

CONTENTS

ix

Section I

‸‸

FORM, FORCES,

AND POLICY

IN GENERAL

Chapter 1

SOCIETY AND THE STATE

◣◤

PLAN AND PURPOSE.

"For forms of government let fools contest—
That which is best administered is best."

When Alexander Hamilton quoted these words of Pope's in No. 68 of *The Federalist* he called them a "political heresy." Immanuel Kant, the German philosopher, in his tract on *Perpetual Peace,* agreed with this evaluation of the then already famous dictum, adding, rather angrily, that a good administration proved nothing in favor of a good government, and that the presence or the absence of the latter could be of vital significance to the life of a nation.[1]

In our day Hamilton's "political heresy" has advanced to the rank of orthodoxy. It virtually suffices to recite Pope's rhymes to predispose the listener toward acceptance of whatever point one wants to make. In the pages that follow we shall try, however, to reverse the process. We shall not hesitate to commit ourselves in favor of the orthodoxy of yesterday, and the heresy of today. It will, in fact, be argued that political form is a vital ingredient of political action. It has much to do, for example, with the channels of selection which determine who is to rise into the ranks of a country's political elite, and no less with what the "elect," once they have reached their places, can or cannot do. Different types of "elites," equipped with different tools of action, will affect the fate of a nation in entirely different ways. In our day the Communist "elites" governing Russia and China have, in the course of a few years, been able to overturn the social structure of their countries, whereas, in the case of China in particular, the structure of society had for thousands of years proved stronger than the actions of any government.

Political form, then, may mean much for the domestic life of a country, and this book will be devoted to an attempt to show how, in that field, the interaction of political form and of social forces leads

2

to results which social factors could never have by themselves. On a later occasion the author hopes to show also that the political processes which govern a nation's domestic life determine, to a significant extent, its actions in the field of international relations. Different men act differently in the field of foreign as well as domestic politics; the habits which they acquire in the domestic struggle for power—on which depends their initial and ultimate success or failure—will, subconsciously, but all the more decisively, be transferred to the modes of thought and action guiding them in their dealings with other nations.

JAMES MADISON, POLITICAL FORM, AND SOCIAL FORCES.

Where the burden of proof is as great as it is bound to be in such an undertaking, it is necessary to reduce, from the outset, the danger of misunderstandings. Let us, then, state forthwith that whoever emphasizes one particular aspect of reality need not, for that reason, ignore others. Our model should be the writers of the constitutional period, in particular the authors of *The Federalist*. They were, from the first to the last sentences they wrote, concerned with the problems of political form. Thus Madison in No. 10, writing of certain shortcomings of "pure democracy," meaning, in particular, the proneness to mob psychology resulting from the gathering of thousands of people in a public square, said that they flowed "from the form of government itself." Similarly, dealing in No. 48 with certain abuses prevalent during the "Critical Period of American History," [2] he concluded: "Some of them, it will be found, may be imputable to the peculiar circumstances of the war; but the greater part of them may be considered as the spontaneous shoots of an ill-constituted government." [3]

Madison clearly implied that a particular type of political form was not, as it was argued in his day as well as in ours, an inevitable result of existing social forces but that, to some extent at least, it was subject to free choice. The exercise of this choice was the meaning of the movement for a new Constitution, which was to establish a "representative republic" on a federal basis. No one can deny that this deliberate use of a change in political form as an instrument of "social control," was highly successful in large areas of the nation's political life, even if it did not succeed in *all* respects, the founders of the American Republic having had to pay their inevitable toll to human fallibility. It will be seen, however, that where we come to the methods with which to ascertain political reality, we can hardly do better than to turn back to their way of thinking. The agreement on method, in fact, extends to the evaluation of those parts of their work in regard to which their success fell short of being complete.

It is a part of this methodological soundness that the same Madison who laid such stress on the dynamism of political form was quite specific in his references to the dynamism of social forces. He did this so strongly that Charles A. Beard [4] put him (and those who expressed similar views before or after him, including Alexander Hamilton, Chief Justice John Marshall and, in a later day, Woodrow Wilson) into a line of reasoning which culminated in the economic interpretation of history as formulated by Karl Marx. Madison, however, referred to the divisive forces of society [5] merely in order to show how the institutions of the "representative republic," supplemented by the large size of the country, could be expected to *"break and control* the violence of faction." (Italics added.) In other words, where Beard, clearly influenced by Marx and his followers, listed the forces of society and attributed political action to them directly and exclusively, for Madison their enumeration was only the first step; he proceeded to show that they meant one thing if left to themselves, and something else again when diverted into the channels provided by the proper type of political form.

In order to make clear that the rejection of one type of one-sidedness does not, indeed, mean sponsoring another, let us list the factors involved in political action: 1) form, 2) forces, 3) policy. The first two terms are self-explanatory. By "policy" we mean political actions insofar as they are not determined by political form and social forces. The use made of this latitude may, in periods of rapid change, such as occurred during and after World War II, go far toward shaping the fate of a country, or of a continent. Besides, the three groups of factors are mutually interdependent: Not only can political form exert an active influence on social forces, but the latter can influence political form, not in the sense of ever being able to dispense with it, but by substituting one type of political form for another. The policy decisions of political leaders, finally, can influence the fate of both social forces and of political form; in some cases, as happened in France, Italy, Germany and Japan after the Second World War, a country's political institutions have to be rebuilt from the ground up, and in this process free policy decisions may account for much. Occasionally, there is reason to recall the part played by pure accident in the course of history, as was done by Oscar Handlin in his book, *Chance or Destiny: Turning Points in American History.*[6] We must add that it is one of the purposes of the proper type of political form to narrow down the range within which accidents acquire significance.

Political form will, however, occupy the center of the stage in our discussions. According to an old English rule there usually exists, in a complicated situation, a key problem, the solution of which facilitates an orderly approach to the rest. It will be seen that political form does constitute the key problem in the tangle of factors involved in the recent past. We shall, therefore, focus our attention upon political form, always ready to shift it in the direction of social forces, or of political decision, where the facts call for such a course.

FORM AND HUMAN SOCIETY.

When we speak of political form we naturally do not have in mind what might be called the "paper form" of those written constitutions which have sprung up since the end of the eighteenth century, and mushroomed during the twentieth. They are characterized much more by witless verbosity than by the awareness of the concrete problems to be solved which distinguishes the American Constitution. To illustrate the nature of these problems, it will be well to refer to Aristotle's use of the term "form." For the Greek philosopher, "form" is not, as it is taken to be in our day, the opposite, but an essential ingredient of "substance." The two complementary terms are "form" and "matter." In Aristotle's words: "In everything which is generated matter is present, and one part of the thing is matter and the other form." [7] To take an example: For a sculptor the block of marble on which he works is his "matter," and what he adds (assisted by the proper tools) is "form." One of these two elements is as important as the other. Without the sculptor the marble would remain mere stone; without suitable material (and the proper tools) the greatest artist would be helpless; he could do little, for example, with a pile of dry sand.

It will help to elucidate the nature of the relationship between form and matter in political life if we refer to what Winston Churchill said in a debate held in the House of Commons in 1931: "We are now at a time when the metal of politics is fluid, is molten. The various molds are ready, and we have now, perhaps, a chance in this year or two to decide into which molds that metal should be guided." [8] This statement must be corrected both by widening and by narrowing its meaning. It must be widened because "the metal of politics" is always dependent upon molds to give it shape; that dependence is not limited in time. The statement must be narrowed because political life is never as plastic as molten metal. Political form deals not with individuals who, in the language of the schoolmen, constitute the *materia prima*—prime matter—of political society, but with a variety of social groups which constitute *materia secunda*—secondary matter. Most of the "forming" to which human beings can be subjected has been accomplished by the time political form comes into play; thus, social forces have been created which can be "formed" only to a limited extent.

Still, the molding effect of political form on both social groups and individuals can go far; what happened under the totalitarian dictatorships of the twentieth century is a case in point. It will be easier to understand this process if, for a moment, we recall that our "prime matter," (individual human beings), has an almost unlimited capacity for being "formed." The human child differs fundamentally from the young animal. The latter is largely "formed" as soon as it is born. Its "instincts" are the major manifestation of this "formation"; they are a reliable, and at a comparatively early stage a sufficient guide in its struggle for self-preservation. Human beings are in a different position. Their instincts are developed only in a rudimentary fashion, and their minds need to be "formed" in the most elementary respects. By way of compensation they can be formed in a great many different directions; whereas the animal goes straight ahead in the way prescribed by its nature and can rarely be taught to do much else, human beings may develop along a variety of lines. Most of the choices open to them are made for them by their families, and by the other social groups of which they become members, but there does remain a substantial range of free decisions to be made by the individual.

The fact that individuals can be molded to such a large extent by social groups implies that the latter's work need not be final. Political form does, primarily, act on social groups, but it always has the possibility of acting directly upon individuals as well. Characteristically, where political form generates as much pressure as it does under modern totalitarian dictatorships, one of its aims is to destroy all social groups standing between itself and the individual. The individual, of course, is helpless when unsupported by social formations against a concentration of power in the state. In such cases, the characteristics of individuals as well as of social groups may be altered under the impact of political form.

The further question arises whether, if social groups can do so much to form individuals, this formation is sufficient. Social groups do provide a substantial measure of coordination, and their action may be favorable to the attainment of the goals proper to the state,[9] in particular to that unity of action which is the primary characteristic of the state. Only the anarchist will, however, assume either that this will always be the case, or that it will ever be sufficient. Commonsense compels us to agree with John Locke when he speaks of "the variety of opinions and the contrariety of interests which unavoidably happen in all collections of men"; [10] it further suggests that if these social forces are left to themselves anarchy will be the result.

This was also the view of Thomas Aquinas. He deserves to be quoted at some length because the times in which he lived were, as are our own, characterized by a large-scale disintegration of democracy. In fact, modern democracies, incapable of mastering the different, and divergent, forces of society have yielded to tyranny in a manner quite similar to that of so many Italian city republics during the thirteenth century. Confronted with such results, Thomas wrote:

> For where there are many men together and each one is looking after his own interest, the multitude would be broken up and scattered unless there were also an agency to take care of what appertains to the commonweal. In like manner, the body of a man or any other animal would disintegrate unless there were a general ruling force within the body which watches over the common good of all members.—With this in mind, Solomon says: "Where there is no governor, the people shall fall."
>
> Indeed it is reasonable that this should happen, for what is proper and what is common are not identical. Things differ by what is proper to each: they are united by what they have in common. But diversity of effects is due to diversity of causes. Consequently, there must exist something which impels towards the common good of the many, over and above that which impels towards the particular good of each individual.[11]

For Thomas the goal was "unity of peace"—coherent government action strong enough to ban the ever latent danger of anarchy. Where unity was the goal, he concluded that it could best be reached by something which had unity in itself; from this point of view, he preferred monarchy.[12] Let us recall that he lived in a time when historical circumstances favored such a conclusion, as city republics were collapsing, and yielding to tyrannies, all over Italy; only orderly monarchies seemed capable of guaranteeing man's basic rights together with the principle of authority. The preference for monarchy has, however, a permanent significance from the point of view of method: It indicates that political form must be something that stands, by its very nature, over and above society and its natural divisiveness; it must constitute a unifying force in itself.

It is hardly necessary to repeat that the founders of the American Republic agreed as much with Thomas whom they did not know as with John Locke, whom they knew so well. This is clearly implied in Madison's listing of the divisive forces of society. He would have been willing to apply to social groups what Alexander Hamilton, in the Constitutional Convention, said about individuals: "We must take man as we find him; and if we expect him to serve the public, must interest his passions in doing so. A reliance on pure patriotism had been the source of many of our errors." [13] "A reliance on pure patriotism" was frequently advocated by the opponents of the new Constitution. In their opinion, if only the states, a vital part of the *materia secunda* so far as the Federal Government was concerned, would act upon what was their clear duty under the Articles of Confederation, they would provide the general government with the necessary tools of action. This approach to the problem is similar to the one displayed by many observers in the political crises of our time, such as the one in the France of the Fourth Republic. It is emphasized time and again that if only the parties constituting the French National Assembly would act in concord, the measures required for the salvation of the country would be taken. Hamilton realistically reminds us that if we want people to work for the common good we must place them in such a position that they are, to a reasonable extent, able to serve their own good simultaneously. If we demand too much from them we engage in what the theologian calls "counsels of perfection"; we expect man, and, in particular, political man, to live and work for the common good exclusively while he is engaged in competitive struggle which pushes him in the direction of self-preservation. Hamilton knew that times may come when we must expect people and groups to rise above their own immediate interests, and work for the general welfare directly regardless of sacrifices; he also knew that, as a rule, times of crises are the only ones in which such an appeal can be expected to be successful, and that even then its impact may not be strong enough. In the end, then, all depends upon the creation of institutions which permit the selfishness of both individual human beings and social groups to act in a reasonable measure of harmony with the requirements of the general welfare—institutions which, by their very nature, lead from the divisiveness of society to the unity of action characteristic of the state.

MARX, ENGELS, AND THE STATE.

This realization compels us to return to the economic interpretation of history which will, in fact, dog every step we are trying to take. It is part and parcel of the intellectual atmosphere in which we live; as "good children of our age" [14] we are all inclined to accept, *prima facie*, what accords with the economic interpretation [15] and to frown upon anything that contradicts it. It does not matter that this attitude is, as a rule, subconscious, and that most of those who are guided by it would, if challenged, deny that they adopt it systematically. To the economic interpretation of history there applies what Max Weber said about the Christian ethic: It is not a taxi which one may enter and leave at will. It has a logic of its own, part of which is its exclusiveness. Were the purpose merely to analyze the economic aspects of political life with the admission that others might be of fundamentally equal importance, we would have returned from Marx to Madison. For we would no longer be confronted with "materialism" which is essentially monism, and loses not just its exclusiveness, but its essence, when other factors are admitted on an equal footing.

Marx and Engels themselves left no doubt that there is no room for compromise so far as the relationship between the economic interpretation of history and the problem of political form (which, basically, is identical with that of the state) is concerned. Friedrich Engels has developed the Marxist view of these matters more fully than his friend, in particular in his classic work on *The Origin of the Family, Private Property, and the State.*[16] Basically, three points are made:

First, the state has not always existed; there have been societies in the past which were able to do without it; this implies, of course, that the state (and the elements of political form through which it is constituted) are not essential to human society.

Second: When the state did develop, this was the result of the cleavage in mutually antagonistic social classes. The state is a by-product of the class struggle; it is an instrument of the ruling class for the suppression, and exploitation, of the ruled.

Third: The time will come when the division into social classes becomes a hindrance to production. The classes will fall. "Along with them, the state will inevitably fall." It will be replaced by a "society . . . that will organize production on the basis of a free and equal association of the producers." This will "put the whole machinery of the state where it will then belong: into the Museum of Antiquities, by the side of the spinning wheel and the bronze axe."

This last point, of course, clearly aligns Engels with the anarchists. As it is utopian, it cannot be checked against practical experience. The first point presents a different problem, however; if human society has actually, for extended periods, existed without the intervention of political form, it might conceivably do so again.

STATE, VIRTUE, AND INTELLIGENCE.

If we are to examine this point we encounter a semantic obstacle; much depends on what we mean by "state." Few would want to use the term as extensively as those for whom it is coterminous with society; we can, however, avoid the dangers lurking, in this case as in others, behind the "tyranny of words" by stating the problem in its most general aspects: The question is whether human society could ever exist without authority, and whether authority could be generated from society without the intervention of political form.

It will facilitate this discussion if we proceed from Marxian sociology to Marxian theology. Evidently, the division into social classes occupies, in the thought of Marx and Engels, much the same place as does the Fall in the minds of Christian writers. Thus, it will help us evaluate the views of the founders of "scientific socialism" as well as the general nature of the problem, if we recall that, according to a widespread opinion, the need for the authority, and the organs by which authority is made effective, arises from the sinful nature of man. During the constitutional period, no one contradicted Thomas Paine when he wrote: "Society is produced by our wants and government by our wickedness; the former promotes our happiness *positively* by uniting our affections, the latter *negatively* by restraining our vices . . . The first is a patron, the last is a punisher." [17]

A few words will suffice to indicate that human depravity cannot be the only reason for the existence of political authority. To begin with, we can all agree with Aristotle that human beings are not only "social" but also "political beings." They must live in society, but if this society is to be orderly it has to be "political," which means that there is a need for an effective authority transcending social divisions. The need for such an authority arises from the fact that even perfectly intelligent and perfectly virtuous beings might not always be able to agree on the concrete means to be used to attain the ends which, we can assume, would be unanimously agreed upon. There would be no difficulty if only one means were available to reach a certain end; perfectly intelligent beings would realize its nature.[18] Several means might, however, serve the same purpose. Thus, to take a modern example: Street traffic could move just as well on the left as on the right side of the road, but it has to move on one side or the other. A choice has to be made, and it must be complied with. Perfectly virtuous beings would agree with a choice once it is made; force would not be needed to secure their compliance. Still, there has to be a choice, and to make it would be the function of the organs of authority.

To this extent the need for such an authority is not the result of any "wickedness." Where such "wickedness" exists (and is supplemented by imperfect intelligence) it adds, of course, to the reasons why authority is needed; it also requires the presence of the means of coercion adequate to the task of securing compliance, where necessary, by force. It is interesting, however, to note that Thomas Aquinas insists on being specific on the point that government is not the result of the Fall, as Augustine, among others, had assumed. He gives the rational explanation set forth above but adds, as an "argument from authority," that, according to the Bible, one of the orders among the angels was called "Powers." [19]

When we introduce the element of human "wickedness," care has to be taken to avoid that thorough pessimism in regard to human nature which is characteristic of Machiavelli and Hobbes. If men are so utterly depraved that one will always do all he can to take advantage of the other, using the cunning of the "fox" if nature has not endowed him with the strength of the "lion," human society ceases to be human. Nothing but physical force remains to keep such beasts from continuously devouring each other. Little room exists for constitutional government, and none for democracy.

Taking a more realistic view,[20] we might observe that, wherever a framework of order has been provided, the average human being is willing to "live and let live." The danger that a different situation might develop, in which this basic human tendency cannot manifest itself, arises from that minority of human beings which is willing to follow the path of criminality. It is a minority: otherwise, order, in human society, could not be maintained with a comparatively small number of men; a small police force can be efficient because the vast majority of the people are willing to comply with the law of the land and, in fact, to assist in its enforcement. Minorities can, however, upset the pattern according to which majorities prefer to live. If but a few carry a gun and use it, the time will come when everyone has to do the same, and the behavior of the majority will tend to follow the pattern set by the minority.

The basic problem is what Goetz Briefs,[20a] speaking primarily in regard to modern economic life, has called "marginal morality." The economists of the Austrian school assumed that the market price was determined by the "marginal utility" of a good. Likewise, those with the lowest moral standards in social life can force their own law of action upon the rest. Public authority, on the other hand, made effective by the proper instruments of coercion, is the organ of the majority to keep in check this standard-shattering minority. The purpose is to secure a "common good" which includes that of the minority. The task is to make the actual and potential members of the minority accept the pattern of orderly society; they will benefit from it once it has been established.

MARX, ENGELS, AND MORGAN.

We must now turn from Christian theology (and the rational arguments which supplement, and largely replace [21] it) to Marxian theology, for which the acquisition of private property in the means of production, and the division into social classes which follows it, constitutes the fall from the state of original innocence. At first, the founders of "scientific socialism" assumed, as they put it in "The Communist Manifesto," that "The history of all hitherto existing society is the history of class struggles." Later, Engels added [22] that this statement held only for all *written* history. When, in 1847, the Communist Manifesto was issued, little was known about the social organization of primitive societies. More became known later, and Marx and Engels were particularly impressed with Lewis H. Morgan's *Ancient Society*.[23] Marx prepared an extensive abstract of this work with the intention of writing a treatise on its bearing upon the interpretation of social development. When death overtook him, his friend Engels undertook this task, the result being the book on *The Origin of the Family, Private Property, and the State*. Engels placed Morgan's work on as high a plane as Marx's *Das Kapital*, even if he mentioned that "important additional material" might necessitate "material alterations." [24] Since that time anthropological research has accumulated a vast amount of "additional material," [25] but the points on which Morgan has been challenged effectively do not affect those which guided Engels in his analysis of the origin of the state. Morgan had done extensive field work in one particular case: his survey of the political institutions of the seven tribes of the Iroquois confederation (inhabiting parts of the Eastern United States and Canada) is, to this day, unchallenged in its more important descriptive features, and unrivalled in its use of interpretative principles not yet deterred by behaviorism from seeing the forest as well as the trees. Engels is right when he accepts Morgan's findings as the proof for the existence of a classless society, and, as we shall see on a later occasion, we can also follow him in his emphasis on the absence of private property as the basic reason for this fact. It is the characteristic feature of a social class that groups of families have a fixed position in society; to be born into a certain family means that the individual, regardless of his own ability, shares its high, or low, position, although there has always been a limited possibility for the individual to move up or down the social ladder. Social classes are possible only when those who have secured a comparatively elevated position for themselves are able to barricade themselves within it. When individual success, based on personal accomplishment, which stood at the beginning of this social differentiation, begins to "harden," [26] it becomes hereditary. This "barricading" is possible only when the materials are available from which social barricades can be built. They do not exist among the most primitive groups, which live from the proceeds of hunting and collecting. Under those conditions, private property of land makes no sense, food is perishable, and whatever tools the individual uses can be fashioned without too much difficulty. Nothing, then, can be accumulated which would make it possible for a group of people who have secured an elevated position to entrench themselves within it. A basic equality prevails and, as long as it does, there are no social classes.

Differences arise in the interpretation of the primitive political organization. If we digress a little and follow Morgan and Engels in their description of primitive, in particular Iroquois, life in some detail, we do so on account of the principle involved. The time has come, not only for history, but also for political science, to "enlarge its horizon." [27] Traditionally, political scientists have limited themselves to written history; even in the twentieth century they have rarely progressed beyond Aristotle in a field where progress was imperative. As will be seen later, this procedure has kept important problems from being seen in their proper focus.

The basis of Iroquois political life was the clan, which Morgan designates by its Latin name *gens*. Its members were united by the bond of common descent, although adoption into a clan was possible. Descent was in the female line, not because this was a universal feature of primitive society, as Morgan erroneously assumed, but because he encountered the Iroquois in one of several alternative phases [28] of development. The peace-time officers who took care of the government of the clan were the sachems. This office was elective, the male candidates usually being taken from the same family, even if the rule of descent in the female line was followed, brother succeeding brother, or the nephew the uncle. Every adult member of the clan, male or female, took part in the election. Among the Seneca-Iroquois, for example,[29] two candidates had to be voted upon, and the one with the largest number of votes was elected; he could not, however, take office until he was approved by the remaining clans of the tribe, and accepted by the confederacy. The military officers were called chiefs. They were also elected, but apparently to a larger extent on the basis of personal qualities, such as bravery, than were the sachems. The number of chiefs was larger than that of sachems. The tribe of the Seneca-Iroquois, with about 3,000 persons, had eight sachems—one for each of the clans—and about 60 chiefs. Both sachems and chiefs were nominally elected for life, but could be deposed by either their clan or by the council of the tribe. The assembly of the clan had to be convoked for all important decisions; there was thus no danger of usurpation on the part of the elected officers. Furthermore, in the words of Morgan:

> All the members of an Iroquois gens were personally free, and they were bound to defend each other's freedom; they were equal in privileges and in personal rights, the sachem and chiefs claiming no superiority; and they were a brotherhood bound together by the ties of kin. Liberty, equality, and fraternity, though never formulated, were cardinal principles of the gens.[30]

Above the clan there was the brotherhood of clans.[31] It served mostly social functions. The next, and in most cases highest, form of organization was the tribe, uniting the clans inhabiting a certain area, and speaking the same dialect. The tribe was governed by a council, consisting of the sachems, and chiefs, of the clans. About the latter Morgan says: "Called together under circumstances known to all, held in the midst of the people, and open to their orators, it was certain to act under popular influence." [32]

The Iroquois, like the Aztecs in Mexico, represented one of the few cases where there existed a confederacy uniting a number of tribes, originally five and later six in number. The origin of the Iroquois confederacy is obscured by legend, although we may readily accept the tradition that tremendous obstacles had to be overcome before a union so obviously beneficial to all could be established. This is said to have been done between 1400 and 1450 A.D., the "Hiawatha" of Longfellow's famous poem being the guiding force, even though the Hiawatha of the poet was far removed from the Deganawida of history.[33] The exclusive purpose of the confederacy was the maintenance of peace among the component tribes and common defense against outsiders. The supreme organ of government was a council of 50 sachems, apportioned among the tribes and clans according to their strength. Two permanent war chiefships were created, both assigned to the Seneca tribe. The confederacy could, however, go to war as a unit only if the decision was unanimous; otherwise each tribe was free to act on its own.

The question is what to conclude from this type of organization in regard to the origin of authority and of government. Not unnaturally, Morgan says about the council of the clan:

> It was a democratic assembly because every adult male and female member had a voice upon all questions brought before it. It elected and

deposed its sachem and chiefs, it elected Keepers of the Faith, it condoned or avenged the murder of a gentilis (a clansman), and it adopted persons into the gens (clan).[34]

Speaking of the council of the tribe, Morgan says:

> Although oligarchical in form, the government was a representative democracy; the representative being elected for life, but subject to deposition. The brotherhood of the members of each gens, and the elective principle with respect to office, were the germ and the basis of the democratic principle. Imperfectly developed, as other great principles were in this early stage of advancement, democracy can boast a very ancient pedigree in the tribes of mankind.[35]

Similar considerations apply to the government of the confederacy.

Engels, who is concerned with the origin of the state, believes himself to be in agreement with Morgan's evaluation. He is able to do so because for Morgan the government of these primitive communities does not constitute a *state*. For him, "all forms of government are reducible to two general plans." The first "is founded upon persons, and upon relations purely personal"; it "may be distinguished as a society (*societas*)." The second, on the other hand, "is founded upon territory and upon property, and may be distinguished as a state (*civitas*)." [36] The basic unit is territorial; it deals with property as well as with persons, whereas personal relationship constituted the only basis of "gentile society."

We may well agree with Morgan that there is an important difference between the two types of organization which he describes. Once again, however, we must be on our guard against "the tyranny of words." Morgan does not distinguish between "society" and "state" in the customary manner. The primitive society which he portrays so vividly does not lack political organization. In fact, Morgan repeatedly speaks of "government," and characterizes it, using the modern term without hesitation, as "democratic." Certainly there existed among the Iroquois (as more or less among all primitive tribes) organs of authority which transcended the family, and all types of mere blood relationship. The clan maintained peace and order among its members, the tribe did so among the clans; the confederacy was instituted to perform the same service among the tribes, and put a stop to the internecine warfare among them, a task in which, incidentally, it succeeded admirably. All these units claimed, and defended, a certain territory.

There existed, then, among these primitives what we call "political form." In some respects it had a modern touch, such as in the election of officers by a majority, or in the custom of the Seneca to limit the candidates in an election to two, a process which has effects not dissimilar to some of those characteristic of a modern two-party system.[37] These organs of political form were of a rudimentary nature, but they existed. They existed because they had to exist; unity of action as well as defense against internal and external enemies were vital needs; without adequate provision for them there could have been no orderly society.[38]

To return to Engels: He accepts Morgan's factual premises, but does not realize what they imply, namely, that political organization, and with it, political power, are as old as mankind. For Engels, of course, *everything* changes when private property becomes more important, and social classes make their appearance—and not just *something*, even if this something is very important. It is interesting to note how Engels describes the change. Like Morgan, he is bound to view it as progress; civilization could not have followed barbarism without the accumulation of private property, even if this made possible the division into social classes. Both Marx and Engels were proud of the cool detachment—the "freedom from value judgments," as we would say—with which they viewed social change; both of them allow, however, on occasion, their manner of description to become so sentimental as to refute their claim to objectivity. Thus Engels writes:

> The power of these primordial communities had to be broken, and it was broken. But it was broken by influences which from the outset appear to us as a degradation, a fall from the simple moral grandeur of the ancient gentile society. The lowest interests—base greed, brutal sensuality, sordid avarice, selfish plunder of common possessions—usher in the new, civilized society, class society; the most outrageous means— theft, rape, deceit and treachery—undermine and topple the old, class-less, gentile society. And the new society, during all the 2,500 years of its existence, has never been anything but the development of the small minority at the expense of the exploited and oppressed great majority; and it is so today more than ever before.[39]

RULING CLASSES AND POLITICAL FORM.

No one would deny that when social classes developed, there was antagonism between them, and there existed the opportunity for the more powerful to exploit the less powerful. Furthermore, the organs of political form, more strongly developed in their external aspects (such as police and army), could with comparative ease be monopolized by one class, and used by it to the detriment of others. Karl Marx has given us a telling example for this in the twenty-fourth chapter of the first volume of *Das Kapital,* dealing with "original accumulation": [40] The English nobility, beginning in the fifteenth century, used its control of parliament for the purpose of destroying, with the sanction of the law, the British yeomanry and taking their land away from them, not hesitating to act with the utmost brutality.

The question is, however, in the first place, whether, when such domination of the organs of the state by one class exists, the state itself ceases to be a social necessity. The British peasantry suffered great harm from the way British state power was used, but would not it, and all other social classes, have suffered even greater harm from the absence of all state power? The civil war of the seventeenth century gave the English their last taste of the depredations bound to follow when the state no longer has an effective "monopoly of the legitimate use of force" (to use Max Weber's famous term); a multitude of atrocities were visited upon the inhabitants of the areas affected by hostilities. Merely the fact that political form was only partially ineffective, that it survived, in particular, in local government, kept matters from getting unbearable. As it was, sensitive persons, such as Hobbes, recoiled from the horrors caused by the absence of adequate power to such an extent that they were willing to take refuge in absolute power. Government, then, has its social function even if a particular group uses it for its own benefit. Besides, there are limits to such behavior: No ruling class (no foreign conqueror even) has ever been able to maintain itself in power for long without paying its respects to the existence of common interests between itself and the ruled; to the extent that this is done, the use of physical force [41] against the ruled can be replaced by the voluntary (even if subconscious, and grudging) consent of the latter.

In this connection it is important to bear in mind the implications of the fact that no social class ever dominates the political life of a country merely as a class. It must act through the medium of (a particular) political form. This medium has its own dynamism, which may carry the rulers beyond their original intentions. Thus, the British nobility had to act through the institution of parliament. For Marx and Engels this was a mere sham, just as "bourgeois democracy," in a later day, was in their view a thin veil hiding the fact that one class ruled, and oppressed, all others. Britain's aristocratic rulers found, however, that when they defended their own freedom against the King they were, to an ever-increasing extent, compelled to defend the freedom of all citizens, be they "bourgeois" or, later, "proletarians." Besides, they had to divide into political parties. This meant that the ruling party was always opposed by another. In the contest between them the outsider was, to use one of Marx's favorite terms, the *tertius gaudens,* the "joyful third." The "outsider" means, in the first place, the undecided voter who, standing between them, hands the palm of victory to one or the other; it also means those outside the active electorate of the time. The latter, while they did not have the franchise, did share in the general advantages of constitutional government, including the right of petition, of free speech, and of free organization. With the "Great Reform" of 1832 the nobility found itself constrained to abandon its near-monopoly [42] of political power; within a generation universal manhood suffrage became virtually a fact. The members of the old families continued to provide a substantial portion of their country's leaders, but, as was demonstrated by the Churchills and Edens of our day, they had to follow the trend of the times. They could, during the twentieth century, no longer serve either the prejudices, or the interests, of the classes from which they sprang.

Thus, while for Engels the oppression of the ruled majority by the ruling minority was bound to become ever more acute, in Britain the mechanism through which the minority was ruling forced it to admit the majority to power. The latter, beginning with the Liberal government of 1906, inaugurated more and more measures for the benefit of the people. The process was completed under Attlee, and it was so thorough that the succeeding Conservative governments did not dare challenge its fundamental features. The high taxes on incomes and estates which began with Lloyd George's 1909 budget struck back forcefully against the descendants of those who, utilizing the power of the state, had deprived the peasant of his land; their holdings began to dwindle. The worm had turned indeed. While, for the period before the First Electoral Reform we had to argue that even if the ruling minority did utilize the instrumentalities of the state to promote its class interests, it could not help serving the community at the same time, it might, since 1945, have been argued that although the ruling Labour party enacted measures intended primarily for the benefit of its constituents, and financed them largely by taxing its opponents, it also served the interests of the whole. It not only maintained law and order, but in certain fields, such as the granting of self-government to India, Pakistan and Burma, it took measures which its opponents might have found difficult to take, but which they soon admitted to have been in the interest of all. Such "de-colonization" Marx and Engels would have welcomed with particular warmth. Would they, seeing the power of the state used for such purposes, have continued to hold that it was merely the instrument of the ruling class for the oppression, and exploitation, of the ruled?—

Marxian theory logically culminates in the conclusion that the state, being a by-product of the class struggle, will "wither away" when the dictatorship of the proletariat has succeeded in establishing the "classless society." Marx did not go into any details; it was part of his belief in "scientific socialism" that all developments would be determined by the course of events, so they could not be "blueprinted" in advance. Still, the prediction of a classless society, in which the state would "wither away," was definite.

In this connection the question arises whether the Russian experience since the Bolshevist revolution does not assume the significance of experiment which puts the Marxian theory to the acid test.[43] The private ownership of the "produced means of production" ceased to exist in Russia more than a generation ago. Vlacheslav Molotov, then still Foreign Minister, was taken to task when, early in 1956, he claimed that only the "foundations" of a Socialist society had been laid; this society itself, he implied, did not as yet exist. The rebuke was natural, but one wonders whether Molotov was not led to his views by the observation that, while in a Socialist society there should at least be indications of a "withering away" of the state, reality showed no signs of it. If this is the case and if, in fact, the concentration of state power is greater now in a "Socialist society" than it ever has been in "bourgeois democracies," must we not conclude that something is wrong with the theory from which the opposite conclusions had been drawn? Has it not been proven that human society cannot do without political form? It is interesting to note that a beginning, at least, has now been made with the modification of the Communist theory of the state,[44] but this is one of the cases where there cannot be a half-way house solution; as long as the conclusions drawn from certain premises are found to be in fundamental contradiction to the facts the premises themselves should be abandoned. If the voice of experience joins that of theoretical reflection in demonstrating that we cannot do without the state, and without political form, frankness compels us to admit it. We should then realize that, while "socio-economic forces" are important, they must always act through the medium of a certain type of political form, which modifies their action, and often these forces themselves, in the process. We must, to repeat it, return from Marx to Madison, and make room for both political form and social forces—ever being mindful of the range of free choice left to the makers of policy by the various possible combinations of these two groups of factors.

Chapter 11

THE MEANING OF DEMOCRACY

If political form is, once again, to be accorded its proper place in political analysis, this can be done only on the basis of a realism which is not afraid of consequences. Such realism has, in recent generations, been frequently absent in regard to forms of government in general, and in the discussion of democracy in particular. We shall, for that reason, first concentrate on democracy. A critical review of its ideological interpretation will be followed by an attempt to demonstrate that, if we examine the facts as they are, there still remains a substantial difference between this form of government and its rivals. References to democratic reality will, for the time being, be limited to those countries where there is reason to assume that there exists a reasonable degree of *con*formity between social forces and political form; this means the United States, Britain, the older Commonwealth nations, Switzerland, Scandinavia and the Benelux countries.

About the ideological proponents of democracy it can certainly be said that they have made that form of government appear in the light of an unsurpassable ideal. The outstanding proponent of this school of thought is Rousseau, and his field of observation is the "pure democracy" of the city state. "Democracy" is interpreted literally to mean "the rule of the people" or, as Carl Schmitt,[1] in his precise juridical diction has phrased it, "identity of the ruler and the ruled." All important questions must be submitted to a popular assembly consisting of the adult citizens. The election of representatives constitutes a step in the direction of aristocracy, for, in the words of Rousseau:

> Sovereignty cannot be represented for the same reason that it cannot be alienated; it consists essentially of the general will, and the general will does not lend itself to representation: it is the same or it is different. . . . The English people think that they are free, but they

20

deceive themselves grievously; they are free only during the election
of the members of Parliament: As soon as these are elected they are
slaves, they are nothing.[2]

Rousseau is, of course, right when he concludes that if the term
democracy, as defined by him, were interpreted rigorously, there
could never have been such a government. "If there were a people of
gods, it could govern itself democratically. A government so perfect
is not fit for men."[3] The proper conclusion would, of course, have
been that, as long as we want to deal with political reality, rather
than to waste our time with speculations about impossible forms of
government, there is something radically wrong with this interpretation; an entirely new start should have been made. Instead, both
Rousseau and those guided by him entered that path of uneasy compromise between irreconcilables, which has been the bane of democratic theory ever since. Thus, it is held, there may be "commissars"
of the people, who conduct its affairs according to its mandates and
its directions. Public officials are an evil, if a necessary one. Wherever
possible, they are to be selected by everybody being given his turn,
or by lot. If they are elected, their term of office must be brief, and
they must be subject to recall.[4] The sole task of these officials is to
apply the laws voted by the popular assembly to specific cases. If the
equality of political knowledge, political interests and political energy,
which is required by the functioning of this mechanism does not exist,
its lack is the result of an unfavorable environment: Democratic institutions, once created, will in the end themselves create the material
which they need.

Where this view is developed consistently democracy is held
possible only in small communities. The well-known formulation of
Aristotle sees its limits where the voice of a herald is no longer able
to reach all those gathered for a popular assembly. The leaders of
modern democratic revolutions had to accept as democracies large
modern states, which were necessarily governed with the help of parliamentary institutions. They justified this by the claim that the members
of these parliaments were true "representatives," doing no more than
to express the will of the people.

This conception of democracy must be rejected for reasons of
method. It has been abstracted from the consciousness of those who
call themselves democrats, and if it is to claim validity it presupposes
the identity of thought and action. This identity, however, does not
exist. It is "an old truth, that the persons and choirs who appear in
the drama of history, hardly ever understand and even more rarely

desire what actually happens and is accomplished over all the heads by the unmerciful logic of events." [5]

There are various reasons for this discrepancy between that which is, and that which is thought to be. Some are to be found in the fact that the individual simply does not see the context within which he is acting. He weaves, after all, only a few threads into the texture of his time, the final pattern of which he does not know. Ignorance is supplemented by bias; ideological preferences and material interests exert pressure even upon those who strive the hardest to adhere to objective truth. Political interpretation is, therefore, in reality, if not by necessity, *standortsbedingt*—conditioned by the place man holds in the world of interests and ideologies. [6] This danger is particularly great for the opponents of existing institutions. Those who defend what exists cannot deny its obvious defects, but whoever proposes something new is able to idealize it, without exposing himself as much to the danger of refutation as does his conservative opponent. The temptation to paint a rosy picture of plans to be realized in the future is so great because to do so helps in the difficult task of tearing people away from their traditional moorings.

If the social scientist is aware of these facts, he will base his evaluation of institutions, wherever possible, on their actual functioning rather than upon the arguments advanced by their theoretical exponents. Objective facts are not subject to the interests and prejudices of the observer; if we do make a serious effort, in full awareness of the pitfalls threatening us, we can come reasonably close to seeing them as they are. We should rely on factual analysis in particular when institutions have existed as long as is now the case with those of modern democracy. The present-day political scientist no longer has to look for the future in his crystal ball if he wants to know what democracy means; all he has to do is to assess an experience now extending over generations.

The interpretation of democracy sketched above is vitiated by just about all the defects inherent in an ideological view of history. Its proponents stood at the beginning of a great movement, the practical results of which they could not foresee; besides men like Rousseau were sufficiently French not to let the splendor of their theoretical constructions be marred by any close attention to reality. They also were men of the opposition, and the defects of the *Ancien Régime,* while often exaggerated, were substantial enough to call forth man's best efforts to bring it down. Where there is too little liberty the temptation exists to insist on nothing *but* liberty and to deny authority in the process, overlooking the complementary nature of the two concepts. The type of freedom demanded by some of these writers was, in the terminology of Max Weber,[7] freedom *from* the state rather than freedom *within* the state. It is, to be sure, unlikely that the "ideas of 1789" could have achieved their propagandistic effect without being borne on the wings of fantasy, but this makes it all the more necessary for us to find a more realistic basis for our concept of democracy.

DEMOCRATIC REALITY: THE FUNCTIONS OF LEADERSHIP.

The first fact of political life to be observed in the countries where democratic revolutions were victorious is the need for political leadership. The fiction of the "rule of the people" had to retreat into political oratory. The positions which the absolute ruler and his officials had been forced to leave were not allowed to remain vacant; they were occupied immediately by the protagonists of "popular sovereignty" who defended them successfully against all comers.

This came to be because it had to be. In the first place, there is the need for division of labor. The direction of large social groups requires a complicated apparatus which even in the case of otherwise equal ability those who have specialized in this work are best qualified to run. A need for such men existed, if in rudimentary fashion, even in the ancient city-state, though Plato knew that these "serviceable officials" do not constitute the core of the problem. When the question was asked "who are they, and what services do they perform?" the answer was: "There are heralds and scribes, perfected by practice, and divers others who have great skill in various sorts of business with the government of States—what shall we call them?" To this query the answer was: "They are the officials and servants of the rulers, as you just called them, not themselves rulers." [8]

In our day, the division of labor is becoming ever more extensive, and the successors of the "heralds and scribes" perform some rather important functions. Obviously experience and training count for more than they did in the past, and this accentuates the anti-egalitarian consequences of the need for public officials. Still, the real problem arises with those whom Plato calls "the rulers" rather than with "the servants of the rulers," no matter how highly qualified, trained and influential. Let us call them political leaders, and in order to clarify the nature of leadership let us list the tasks which these men have to perform: innovation, integration, and limitation.

Innovation means the willingness and the ability to tackle new tasks. This function differentiates the political leader most clearly from the bureaucrat. We have accustomed ourselves to consider states and governments as static entities. Actually, the state constitutes, as do all other social organizations, a *realer Willensverband* [9]—"in reality an association of wills." The wills of the individual, of the families, and of all the social groups constituting it are constantly in action; they change in the process, and tend to diverge in all directions. They must be integrated for the purpose of uniting them for common action; the state is, in Renan's famous formulation "a plebiscite daily repeated." In this process much can be taken for granted, as established processes renew themselves, even if their nature may change gradually and imperceptibly. Still, situations arise constantly which, even in the framework of stable institutions, require decisions which cannot be based on any pre-established rule. Plato was constantly preoccupied with the question whether there should be a "government of men" or a "government of laws"; the answer, of course, is that there must be both. The laws should establish an orderly framework to regulate everyday routine, but there are always cases which no law can foresee, and which must be handled on the basis of a discretionary and prudential decision. Actions in the field of foreign policy represent the best illustration; they not only have domestic implications which may not be too difficult to assess, but they also lead to reactions by foreign nations, which, as many an American Secretary of State has realized to his dismay, even the best informed cannot always anticipate. In such a case rules may determine how a decision is to be reached; they cannot indicate the decision itself.

Typical examples of innovation develop also when a country's patterns of thought and action require change. The political leader may, at the bottom of his heart, be as much attached to the patterns of the past as are his followers; he may have to struggle hard to convince himself before he sets out to convince others. This latter task is, at times, harrowing; honest misunderstandings will mingle with the dust stirred up, and the denunciations produced, by the vested interests connected, or believing themselves to be connected, with what is to be modified. To brave this witches' brew is not given to everyone, for, while the troubles involved in the shouldering of such a task are a certainty, final success in the venture is no more than a possibility. It is small wonder that the minority capable of taking the lead in such enterprises is small, and that the average person prefers conformity to the patterns of the present.

Courage, then, as well as imagination, resourcefulness, and persuasiveness, set the leader apart in the task of innovation. Attributes of intellect must join these qualities of character. If the political leader is to be successful in the long run, he must have an adequate grasp of the political realities of his time. Whoever wants to change what has been inherited from the past will do well to know it first; by that way alone can he learn what it is possible to learn about the effects likely to be produced by attempts at modification. The essence of political action, after all, lies in the employment of forces already in existence for the purpose of creating something new. Therefore, the better we know that which is—and this, of course, includes what Montesquieu called "the necessary relationships which derive from the nature of things" [10]—the more likely we are to anticipate that which *will be*. Whether the attainable degree of knowledge is achieved and utilized has much to do with both the success and the failure of political action; we shall, when we survey some of the critical decisions of the immediate past, have to discuss examples for both.

The kind of knowledge required is, however, not that of the expert. No glorification of the expert, rightly resisted by political scientists from Aristotle [11] to Harold Laski,[12] can do away with the fact that his knowledge and his skill have been acquired in dealing with the problems of the past; he is always inclined to allow the experience which he has gained in that manner to congeal into hard and fast rules. His very virtues turn into vices when new and unprecedented problems arise. The best illustrations arise in the field of military life. Public opinion tends to accord military commanders a prestige not easily given to the statesman, or to the expert in general; yet, military men are experts with all of the latters' essential attributes. Their conservatism has lost many a war. Thus Walter Bagehot [13] recalls a saying current in the Great Britain of the early nineteenth century, to the effect that "Frederic the Great lost the Battle of Jena." Near that city, in 1806, the famed Prussian army crumbled before the onslaught of Napoleon's men. King Frederic had been a great military leader, and the officers whom he trained took pride in following his precepts to the letter. As a result time passed them by. The soldiers of the French Revolution led by Napoleon were of a different stripe, operating under a different system of tactics and requiring changes which the Prussian generals were neither willing nor able to make. It took a complete revamping of the entire Prussian state, undertaken by a new group of *political* leaders, to make it possible for Prussia's armies to be a useful ingredient in the forces which were to defeat Napoleon at Leipzig and Waterloo.

In our day, who does not recall the French generals of the period between the wars, and their belief in the Maginot Line? They could not forget that, in 1916, the battle of Verdun had been won by a well-entrenched army, decimating the attacker with the machine gun, the weapon typical of World War I. The latter was, however, no

match for Hitler's tanks and dive-bombers, to the power of which
men with imagination, including Charles DeGaulle, had tried to draw
attention, only to be ridiculed by the majority of the "experts." In England, on the other hand, the rise of Winston Churchill brought a
typical political "amateur" to the helm who was keenly aware of the
need for modernity. For years he had discussed some of its aspects
with a physicist, Professor Frederick Lindemann.[14] When Goering's
Luftwaffe embarked on the "Battle of Britain" a radar system, better
developed than those used in any other country, served to warn the
defenders and to mislead the invaders, helping mightily to turn the
tide of battle.

So far as American military history is concerned, suffice it just to
mention the case of the then Colonel Billy Mitchell, whose emphasis
on airpower as against seapower was ridiculed by the military leaders
of his day, and which was vindicated with such calamitous results for
ourselves at Pearl Harbor.

If innovation is of such a nature that the expert is, as a rule, not
qualified to originate it, the true political leader will be. In the struggle
which has brought him to the top, he has encountered difficulties and
attacks from all sides. He has survived them only on account of his own
resourcefulness. He seems to be endowed with a kind of "sixth sense."
Thucydides somewhat overstates this case in his praise of Themistocles,
and, of course, not every political leader is a Themistocles. Still, it is
worth quoting what the Greek historian wrote about the Greek statesman:

> By his own native capacity, alike unformed and unsupplemented by
> study, he was at once the best judge in those sudden crises which admit
> of little or of no deliberation, and the best prophet of the future, even
> to its most distant possibilities. An able theoretical expositor of all that
> came within the sphere of his practice, he was not without the power
> of passing an adequate judgement in matters in which he had no
> experience. He could also excellently divine the good and the evil which
> lay hid in the unseen future. In fine, whether we consider the extent
> of his natural powers, or the slightness of his application, this extraordi-
> nary man must be allowed to have surpassed all others in the faculty
> of intuitively meeting an emergency.[15]

Integration is another vital political task which the average citizen finds as hard to solve as the average expert. Political problems are
complex; whatever is done in one field has repercussions in a thousand
others. Unless we see the "big picture" and grasp simultaneously as
many of the various aspects of a problem as possible, we shall not find
a solution which does not create more difficulties than it eliminates.

Suppose, in a country like the United States, we are in favor of political isolation; no effort is made to secure allies. To compensate for this deficiency we should, unless we want to run the risk of aggression, develop a substantial measure of military strength. That, in turn, requires conscription as well as heavy taxation, unless large-scale deficit financing, with the concomitant danger of inflation, is accepted. Conscription is never popular, and whichever tax is adopted, it hurts somebody; other adjustments may be needed in many fields. These complications the average person is no more able to face than the typical expert. Expertness is based upon specialization; this creates a tendency to view one's own limited field in terms of absolutes, and to develop an aversion to all others. On the other hand, the political leader is confronted early in his career with all the ramifications of political decision; he will not long survive, unless he is able to give an answer acceptable to at least most of the interests involved. He is comparable to the trial lawyer who may at any time be called upon to acquaint himself, in short order, with highly technical details—such as ballistics, chemistry or accounting. The testimony of the experts is likely to be contradictory, and it always has to be evaluated. The good lawyer will, after relatively short study, be able to give the proper answers; in the process he has not seldom confounded the experts. Similarly, the political leader, while he cannot specialize in anything sufficiently to rival the expert in the mastery of detail, will be able to go "to the heart of the matter," wherever this is necessary, after a compartively short examination.[16]

Finally, the task of limitation. As Walter Bagehot said a century ago: "Not only does a bureaucracy tend to undergovernment, in point of quality; it tends to overgovernment, in point of quantity." [17] Trained officials come to believe that what they do is of such great importance to the public that there cannot be enough of it. Along with this, there is the tendency to "empire-building" which is inherent in any office— its chief knows that the more people he employs the higher, the more powerful, and perhaps the better paid, his own position will be. It is, again, the task of the political leader to be sufficiently in contact with overall reality to be able to see, and establish, the proper limits to governmental activity. If matters are overdone, the blame will, after all, come to rest on him.

THE NEED FOR LEADERSHIP EXPLAINED AWAY.

It would seem, then, that political leaders have tasks to fulfill which are both vital and beyond the capacity of the average citizen. Various efforts have been made, however, to explain these facts away, or to make them less damaging to the ideological concept of democracy. This applies, in the first place, to the possibility of a "direct" democracy. Even now, political literature abounds with nostalgic references to the time when the "sovereign people" transacted the business of government in person; indirect democracy appears as a substitute which may be necessary, but cannot rival the qualities of the original. Attempts are made to come as close, through a variety of devices, to the ideal as possible; initiative, referendum, and recall, for example, owe their origin to such endeavors. In fact, however, the "identity between rulers and ruled" existed no more in the city-state than it does in modern, "indirect," democracy.

In the "direct democracies" of history, to begin with, only a minority of those entitled to it used to attend the popular assembly. Thus, in Athens, the resident citizen population (adult males) numbered from 35,000 to 45,000, but an attendance of 6,000 in the popular assembly was considered good.[18] Nor did this minority constitute a "representative sample." In Athens there were constant complaints that the more shiftless elements of the population, including the sailors from the Piraios, were as likely to attend as the more stable elements were likely to be absent.[19] Likewise, in the Swiss *Landsgemeinde,* the subject of so much romantization, the number of those participating has again more often than not constituted a minority of the citizens and, while New England town meetings have, in many respects, done well, still they, too, have suffered from the defect of minority attendance, and consequent minority vote. At times, troublemakers have been rather assiduous in their attendance. Thus Thomas Jefferson complained that, when towards the end of his second term, town meetings were held to protest the embargo and the non-intercourse acts (which had produced much unemployment in New England) every neighborhood drunk would appear, together, of course, with the representatives of the interests most directly affected, whereas the average citizen was likely to be absent.

It is more significant yet, from the point of view of our discussions, that "direct" democracy has never been able to live up to the requirements of its name and to get along without either elected officials, or leaders in the assembly. Athens had, among others, a large parliamentary elective body, the Council of 500, whose members were elected by lot, and which had the task of preparing and, through one of its committees, of guiding the affairs of the assembly. The most important officials were the ten generals, elected by majority vote. They spoke frequently in the assembly; while every citizen had the same right there was little time available in an assembly which, even at the peak of its power, met less frequently than once a week, and for possibly no longer than a day. The resolutions voted upon might have been drafted by the Council of 500. If they were, they could be changed and others substituted for them. However, every such formulation had to be undertaken by an individual or, at the most, by a small group. The people at large were limited to voting "Yes" or "No." Actually, when the leading men of the state were as strong as Themistocles and Pericles were in their prime, they controlled the assembly, and the entire government, with as firm a hand as a British Prime Minister controls his parliament and cabinet. Still, it was easier for a rabble-rouser to influence the Athenian popular assembly than it would be for his modern counterpart to sway the House of Commons; Aristophanes, in his comedy, *The Knights,* has provided us with telling, if exaggerated, illustrations. The disorders which might result incidentally, were not limited to Athens. They occurred even in Switzerland and were the reason why the popular assembly was abolished in the cantons Schwyz (which gave the country its name) and Unterwalden.[20]

If, then, leaders are necessary both in a "direct" and in an "indirect" democracy, it might yet be argued that in both cases their function is merely to follow public opinion. The latter is said to be the decisive factor in a democracy and, as we shall see, this statement has a strong element of truth in it. We should, however, not overlook the results of modern public opinion analysis. There is no *public* opinion before the *private* opinions of a great many individuals have been fused. In this process of fusion, political leaders play their part. They establish a common denominator between the opinions of "all sorts and conditions of men," which has to be created, and always re-created, in a long and arduous process.

Nor does the formation of opinions take place exclusively on the basis of persuasion by arguments. Actions always speak louder than words. When a statesman in charge of a large country does something which is bound to have considerable political repercussions, the people will be inclined to rally to his decision and to accept, and thereby morally sanction, the accomplished fact. The request for a declaration of war, made by McKinley in 1898 or by Woodrow Wilson in 1917, is a case in point; once it is made many who opposed that step previously will fall in line. Similarly, when President Roosevelt enunciated the formula of "unconditional surrender" during the Casablanca Conference, he not only reflected certain tendencies existing in war-time public opinion, but he strengthened them immeasurably.

Another objection to the existence of democratic leadership is raised by Marxists, who believe that a particular social environment is responsible for the type of inequality reflected in political leadership. When, for example, Robert Michels' study on *Political Parties* [21] was published, Konrad Haenisch, a leading German Social Democrat, answered that perhaps Michels discussed the conditions of the present correctly, but that the situation would be different in the future; socialism was a doctor capable of curing all ills, including those resulting from human psychology.[22] Haenisch was following the major lines of arguments as laid down by Karl Marx himself. In the latter's words:

> The individual . . . has no real existence outside the milieu in which he lives, and in order to understand the true nature of man it is necessary to integrate him in society, in social life . .
>   All history is nothing but a continual transformation of human nature.[23]

Since Marx wrote those lines, research has combined with experimentation to refute them. So far as the problem of leadership is concerned, psychologists have discovered its existence under circumstances which could not possibly be affected by the class structure, for example, among groups of children with an identical social background; in their play, leadership asserts itself immediately, as most children are as ready to "follow the leader" as a few are anxious to lead. Reference has also been made to the animal world.[24] Thus among a brood of baby chicks, a day old, one or two will show characteristics of leadership absent among the rest.

So far as experimentation is concerned, we need only apply to the specific case of leadership what has been said above about the relationship between the economic interpretation of history and the continued existence of the state in Russia. In the first days after the Bolshevist revolution, Lenin and his associates were embarrassed by the question whether, having assumed the functions of the old council of ministers, they should assume the title of ministers. For a party which had always glorified "the masses of the toilers" this seemed impossible. Trotsky, by a stroke of genius, suggested the name "commissar." Its adoption solved a serious propagandistic problem but, as the years passed, reality conflicted so strongly with pretense that, eventually, the old titles made their reappearance, not only so far as the government was concerned, but also in the army, where the old officers' uniforms made their reappearance, more resplendent than ever. All of this marks a departure from what was for Lenin, as it had been for Marx and Engels, a point of principle. Lenin assumed that "capitalist culture" had simplified the problems of government so much that they "can be reduced to such simple operations of registration, filing and checking" that they were "in reach of every literate person" and could be performed for "'workingmen's wages,' which circumstance can (and must) strip those functions of every appearance of 'official grandeur.'"[25] Stalin performed miracles in bringing "capitalist culture" to Russia, meaning, specifically, the "large-scale production, factories, railways, the postal service, telephones, etc." which Lenin had in mind. Yet, he found that the problems of both industrial and administrative management grew only more complex as a result, necessitating ever more care in the selection and training of those to whom these tasks were entrusted, and culminating in an income differentiation greater than in the "capitalist" countries.[26] Nor has the specific need for political leadership shown signs of abating. One of Stalin's titles was "Leader," and while his successors have been more careful in the choice of words which betray too clearly the basic identity between the Russian, Italian, and German versions of totalitarianism, they have left no doubt that "leadership" would continue; only, it would be "collective."

LEADERSHIP AND RULERSHIP.

Thus it does seem that the active conduct of the affairs of organized society will always lie in the hands of a minority. The time has now come, however, to look at the other side of the coin and to ask ourselves whether it follows that we can properly speak of an "iron law of oligarchy," and conclude that no form of government exists which deserves to be called democratic. To this writer it has always seemed that a negative reply to that question is indicated. Since leadership, to be defined more definitely in the succeeding pages, is the major characteristic of democracy, we might simply say that democracy is government by leadership. All other forms of government, differ as they may among themselves, have the one feature in common that they do not select the guardians of public authority in the competitive process which is an essential ingredient of true leadership. For the time being, they might all be grouped together under the designation of "government by rulership."

When the author developed this view for the first time, Robert Michels, in an otherwise generous evaluation of what was obviously a beginner's effort,[27] stated that the differentiation between governments by leadership and governments by rulership was a distinction without a difference. In the spring of 1933 I discussed the matter with him in Rome, and suggested that our disagreement be put to a simple test. I had come to Italy from Paris, traversing Switzerland. Was there not a substantial difference between the governments of France and Switzerland on the one hand, and that of Fascist Italy on the other? Was it not possible to determine this difference in the ordinary process of abstraction, and call what resulted for France and Switzerland democracy, and what resulted for Italy something different? [28]

The difference between government by leadership and government by rulership is real, indeed. In the first place, it consists in the fact that the "elite" of the former constitutes an "open group," and that of the latter a "closed group." When, for example, Venice became finally an aristocratic city, the names of 450 families were entered into the "golden book"; their members had a share in the government of the city, and the others did not. The ranks of a democratic elite, on the other hand, are open to all comers—not so much in practice as in theory, since human reality never confronts us with a "pure type," but in terms sufficiently clear to be convincing to anyone who is willing to apply standards to political life which are no more perfectionist than are commonly applied to human affairs.

The very concept of leadership implies free competition. In a "direct" democracy this competition expresses itself in the possibility of any one orator's challenging the proposals of any other. In an "indirect democracy" the challenge takes place in periodical elections. The newcomer may, to be sure, have the odds against him. Michels has reminded us that the old leaders are not without means of defending their positions. That, however, is a vital necessity for the orderly conduct of business. Those elected to democratic office do need a certain amount of time, and a measure of tenure and stability, if they are to carry out any kind of political plan. Still, wherever democratic institutions function properly, the established leaders are constantly on the lookout for new talent. There is work to be shared; young men may be inclined to shoulder the more tedious, and more onerous, burdens. The mere necessity of facing periodical elections encourages the voluntary retirement of older men. The campaign may be arduous, and its result uncertain; it seems best to let a younger man take over. Where the success of the latter is not assisted by their elders, they will not hesitate to take the law into their own hands. What they lack in reputation, they make up in virility; their success is facilitated by the constant change in the nature of the tasks confronting a community, as those who were well qualified to tackle the problems of one day may be baffled by those of the next, and betray uncertainty and hesitation. Here again the young men will see and, if necessary take, their chances.

Changes in the democratic elite are, as a rule, gradual. There are however, cases where a wholesale turnover took place; history records political "earthquakes" and political "landslides." When, for example, the Democratic party took over in the United States in 1933 and the Labour party in Britain in 1945, the leading positions in the government were manned by entirely new teams. Besides, a thoroughgoing renovation took place in the ranks of the defeated. When, eventually, in 1953, the Republicans came to power again, they were as different from those who had left Washington twenty years earlier as the Conservatives whom Churchill led back to power in London in 1951 were different from those with whom he had been defeated in 1945. In both cases it had been realized that a mere piecemeal renovation of political leadership, guided by those who had held office in the past, would not do; there had to be new blood all along the line if there was to be a reasonable chance of success.

From this flexibility of the democratic elite it follows that it cannot be separated by any deep gulf from the led. The various layers of leadership blend into one another gradually. The group at the top, including, in the United States, the President, the members of the National Security Council and the Cabinet, and the presidential assistants and advisers, numbers a few dozen. There follow the 531 members of Congress; their work is supplemented by the expert staffs both in their own offices and in those of the committees to which they belong. Next come the thousands of men and women associated with the top levels of state governments; these are, at the same time, the medium levels of national government. To those concerned with political life directly we must add those whose part is indirect: newspaper editors and publishers, writers, lecturers, and the whole, and often unholy, host of pressure group leaders. As we get to the lowest layer we discover the hundreds of thousands of precinct workers employed by both major political parties; their views and actions will be influenced by the people at large with whom they are in daily contact and to whom they pay the closest attention.

Thus, the closer we look at the reality of democratic leadership, the more complex, and the less romantic, it becomes. Unfortunately, the word "leader" carries psychological connotations which may cause us to view history in Carlylian terms; a close look at the drab, and at times dreary, reality of democratic leadership at work provides a patent antidote. Also, of course, true leadership has little in common with what is called by that name in totalitarian countries. The Nazi slogan, "leadership principle," constitutes a contradiction in terms. Leadership must be spontaneous; a group of people must realize, freely and instinctively, that a particular person can conduct their common affairs better than they could themselves. Men (and women) appointed from above are not leaders; they are rulers.

Finally, we should not ignore the influence exerted by those who, for ordinary intents and purposes, may be called politically indifferent. Their numbers are legion. Whoever takes it upon himself to discuss politics with his acquaintances will soon discover that, unless something of a dramatic nature is happening a political topic will sadden them. Shift the conversation to the latest star in the movies, on the baseball diamond or on the football field, and their eyes begin to brighten. Nine-tenths of those entitled to vote in democratic countries—including the oldest, and most admired, such as Britain and Switzerland—belong in this category. Yet, this vast majority does have political notions, and political instincts, of its own. These can be guided, and the established political leadership will try every resource at its command to take advantage of this fact. In the end, however, the millions of voters will go (or not go) to the polling booths and, as in the American elections of 1932, they may in a single day bury a whole generation of political leaders under an avalanche of ballots.

Public opinion, indeed, may be fluid; it is always useful to refer to its analysis by writers as critical as Ferdinand Toennies.[29] Still, on occasion it does become firm, and then, like a hurricane, it sweeps away everything in its path. Such hurricanes are not manufactured at will. Rival elites, assisted by their supporters in the modern "media of mass communication," take the field at the same time. Both do their best, but, for one side, it will not be enough. Clearly, the initiative for substantial changes lies with those whom we must classify as the led rather than as the leaders.

These aspects of contemporary political reality make it somewhat difficult for us to understand Rousseau's above-quoted statement that the English were free only at a time of parliamentary elections, and slaves afterwards. He overlooked what John Locke had written a good deal earlier: Whoever is elected once, wants, as rule, to be re-elected. He has, therefore, to pay close attention to what his voters want him to do. These were the times before the First Electoral Reform. Even then, Edmund Burke, presenting himself to the Electors of Bristol, was flanked by a colleague (Bristol then electing two members to the House of Commons) who considered it expedient to announce that he would always be glad to submit his actions in Westminster to their every wish. Burke, in his classic reply,[30] indicated that he would always be most respectful of the opinions of those who elected him, but that he might, on occasion, have to differ. Burke's views have, to this day, found more admirers than followers, even if Senator Kennedy was able to point out that there have always been outstanding examples of the latter.[31] Burke himself had to pay for his independence by the loss of his seat at Bristol.

With the forward march of "mass democracy" the dependence of the leader upon his followers has increased to the extent of reminding one constantly of that leader of the French Revolution who, seeing a crowd move outside, exclaimed: "I am their leader; therefore I must follow them." This attitude has not been without its effects even among the men deemed autocratic by their contemporaries. President Coolidge, in one of the few jokes he permitted himself, told this story on the oft-decried "Czar" of the House of Representatives, Speaker Cannon: "Uncle Joe has his ear so close to the ground that it is always full of grasshoppers." Realistic complaints against the democratic leaders of our day express regret that, affected, and infected, by the tenets of "Gallup poll democracy" they are so anxious to please that, at times, they are unwilling to lead, a plaint which Walter Lippmann has made rather effectively in his *Public Philosophy*.[32] Whatever the merits of this charge, it constitutes a far cry from the claim that democratic leaders cannot be distinguished from autocrats.

FORCE AND CONSENT.

On the other hand, the elites which constitute the reality of government by rulership differ from their democratic counterparts both in their constitution and in their relations to the ruled. The two factors are interrelated. When, in 1923, the Italian Chamber of Deputies debated an election law which was intended to assure the Fascists of victory in the elections of 1924 by giving the strongest party two-thirds of the seats even if it should have only one-fourth of the votes, Mussolini was accused of wanting to perpetuate a government by force. His answer was blunt: "We have left many dead on the road to Rome, and, naturally, whoever makes himself illusions, is a fool. The power we have and we hold. We shall defend it against anyone. Here is the revolution: in this firm will to hold the power!" [33] Il Duce clearly implied that he was not only determined to hold on to power by force, but that he had taken it by force; this was incorrect only insofar as in that process he had—to use Machiavelli's metaphor—mixed the attributes of the fox with those of the lion, tricking the King and his Nationalist advisers into placing him into a position from which he did not intend to retreat.

In a democracy, those who aspire to power cannot use the methods of physical force. They must present themselves to the people—figuratively, and at times literally—"hat in hand." Door to door canvassing by the candidates themselves may no longer be feasible, although Senator Kefauver has used similar methods extensively. Not infrequently, however, rival candidates appear on the same platform, presenting themselves, and explaining their policies to the same audience. Thus, any voter who wants to secure information about the aspirants to office is given every opportunity to do so. It is interesting that among those who express the view that the people as a rule do know whom they choose there is Machiavelli, who said that "in the election of their magistrates they make far better choices than princes." [34]

The different origin of the two types of elites has inevitable consequences on their respective relationships with the ruled. In the above-mentioned speech in the Italian Chamber of Deputies, Mussolini—echoing views previously expressed by Pareto [35]—taunted his opponents by stating the obvious fact that all types of government contain in themselves elements of both force and consent. Consent, Mussolini added, would never reach one hundred per cent; to make everybody happy would be "squaring the circle." He continued: "What is the state? All your legal codes, all your doctrines and laws are null unless, at a given moment, the policeman with his physical force makes the indestructible weight of the laws felt." [36]

Mussolini overlooked some rather important differences: Whereas under government by leadership, *consent* precedes, accompanies, and modifies force, under a government by rulership (of whatever type), *force* precedes, accompanies, and modifies consent. To take the democratic case first: Most officeholders, once elected (in a process in which consent precedes the access to the use of force), want to be reelected. They will, for this reason alone, do their best to comply with the wishes of the voters, even if they are not always aware of the way in which their actions are shaped. Thus, a man as steeped in the traditions of a great democracy as Sir Eyre Crowe could comment in conversation on the fact that the British Foreign Office was only once during his tenure as permanent under-secretary disturbed by expressions of popular disapproval; he concluded that, as a rule, he and his associates made British foreign policy as they deemed best. Professor Friedrich [37] rightly adds that British officials have always been careful to consider what the public would and would not freely accept. Democratic leaders, and their subordinates, are, as he puts it, guided by the "rule of anticipated reactions." As long as these reactions are, in the main, correctly anticipated, it matters little that officials are not constantly subjected to questions about details which the people cannot possibly judge. Even then the power wielded by public officials is constantly affected by the anticipated need of popular approval. Sometime, free and competitive elections must be held; the sum total of the government's acts goes into the balance, and it had better not be found wanting.

A non-democratic elite, which has power not granted by the voters in a free choice, will, if its members are prudent, certainly bear in mind the need for popular consent. A different type of consent is, however, involved. Potential dissent is limited by the fact that, in the last resort, it can be met by physical force. To brave such force is a risk which few are inclined to take, even if Aristotle was overstating his case a little when he said that "no one attempts what is impossible." [38] Such a situation sets up important psychological reactions. Human beings constantly try to make the best of what they cannot help. In a political situation of the kind described, the first step, on the part of many potential opponents of the government, will be to put out of their minds all types of action which are impractical. As William James has told us, however, convictions tend to follow action —or, in this case, *inaction*. It does not promote a man's peace of mind if he finds himself in violent opposition to conditions which he cannot change. He will try—subconsciously, to be sure—to make himself accept them. In that type of effort the average person succeeds rather well for the simple reason that the affairs of government are rather remote from his own personal interests, and beyond his personal horizon. What, in such a case, has, in the end, all the characteristics of genuine consent, constitutes, therefore, to a large extent a passive adjustment to a substantial measure of constraint.

The political class of a rulership has another great advantage over the ruled: In the possession of executive power, it can, to a much larger extent than its counterparts in a democracy, create accomplished facts which discourage any manifestation of dissent. Thus, the Western world was surprised when, in August, 1914, the German *Reichstag* met and the appropriations for the war were voted unanimously, even by the Social Democrats who had, up to that time, been expected to place international above national solidarity. A decision, however, had been taken by that time which no member of the opposition could reverse. The armies were marching; blood was being shed; any manifestation of dissent—certain to be branded as treason by the government—might have been exploited ruthlessly on the other side of the border where there were some people whose intentions were no more peaceful than those of the German militarists. Besides, the Chancellor, von Bethmann-Hollweg, had calculated that, if hostilities were to begin against Czarist Russia, with its record for persecuting opposition groups, the Social Democrats would consider the war a measure of defense against absolutism. For these reasons a majority of the Social Democrats did go along voluntarily, a strong minority yielding to the wishes of the majority.

The situation was entirely different in countries like England and France, which had parliamentary government. In these nations the makers of foreign policy were identical with the leaders of the majority; thus, they had no reason to commit any actions designed to place this majority face to face with accomplished facts. Besides, there was the constant supervision by the opposition, supported, in the country, by a press which was aware that the creation of any definite popular trend against the government would affect the behavior of the latter. Such a situation does not mean that democratic leaders can never create accomplished facts, nor that, on occasion, they have had both reason and opportunity to do so. It does mean that both incentive and opportunity are greatly lessened even if, as will be discussed later, the situation existing under an independent executive as it does exist in the United States is not identical with that prevailing under the parliamentary system.

Consent, then, tends to be "the genuine article" in a democracy; it changes its nature in rulerships to such an extent that it may be denatured to the point of perversion. Perverted consent has been highly developed by modern dictatorships. This applies, in particular, to the plebiscites which they organize with such monotonous success. If, on such occasions, the ruled are, in theory, called upon to decide on the dictator's tenure of power, their consultation always comes after the dictatorship exists as a matter of fact.[39] There is no real alternative: Those who favor the dictatorship may say "Yes" and feel happy but, for its opponents, the "No" means choosing a vacuum. Where the "Yes" is given voluntarily, it is done in ignorance of at least some of the facts on which such a decision ought to be based. Freedom of the press, and of assembly, have been absent for some time before the plebiscite takes place. Besides, the preparations for the vote are usually characterized by violent propaganda, full of threats for those who should dare vote "No," or not vote at all. After all of this has been done, it may not be necessary to resort to an open violation of the secrecy of the ballot; when the voter enters the booth, the fears instilled in him so insistently are right by his side. Actually, the ballot may not be secret even if it is so in appearance; where those in charge of the polling stations are all on the side of the "powers that be" they do have ways to find out how people voted, and, not infrequently, they make no bones about it. Actually, the mere possibility that this *might* be the case has its intimidating effects.

Lastly, there are always the possibilities of fraud. Victor Hugo [40] described them in classical terms when he analyzed the plebiscite through which Napoleon III had the people of France ratify his *coup d'état*: ". . . . baseness has counted, platitude has scrutinized, trickery has controlled, falsehood has done the adding, venality has verified, the lie has proclaimed."

It is strange that, when governments report that more than 90 per cent of the votes cast in a plebiscite or in an election are favorable to them, their claims are still so widely taken at face value. Charles E. Merriam gave what should have been considered the final verdict when he wrote: "Where there is no freedom of speech, of press, of assembly and organization, where force and intimidation are at hand or standing in the background, the action of the electors is in no sense an electoral choice. It measures not voting, but the intimidating power of those in authority." [41]

To sum up: If Mussolini was right in stating that there is a mixture of force and consent in all governments he overlooked, in the first place, that there are differences of quantity. In well-established democracies physical force is relegated to its minimum; it is needed only for the control of the comparatively small minority of actual or potential law-breakers which, as mentioned above, if allowed to go unchecked, would force its own, lawless, action upon the majority. In any type of rulership, however, physical force is, in addition, needed to defend the form of government itself against attack from within; its extent varies according to the type of rulership in question and according to the type of social forces confronting it from below. The aim is, in all cases, a stable equilibrium between force and consent, but even the most traditional and most widely accepted type of rulership needs elements of physical force with which a democracy can dispense.

The differences of quality are even more important than those of quantity. Only in a democracy is the claim to consent ever put to the one test which is meaningful: The people are periodically, in free and competitive elections, given an opportunity of expressing both consent and dissent, the latter involving the replacement of the elite in power by a competing one. This process establishes a relationship between the rulers and the ruled within which, when we speak of "Governments . . . deriving their just powers from the consent of the governed" the words mean exactly what they say. On the other hand, totalitarian dictatorships—the type of rulership Mussolini had in mind

—claim all kinds of consent, but never put it to the test of a free choice between alternatives. That even frantic expressions of consent, as they appear so frequently in parades and demonstrations, are not genuine becomes obvious when, in countries such as Eastern Germany, Poland or Hungary, after years of totalitarian rule the reins are but lightly relaxed. The result is an outburst of popular dissent which, unless checked by the most concentrated application of physical force, would sweep the existing political system away almost literally overnight.

Chapter III

DEMOCRACY IN HISTORY

▄▗

DEMOCRACY IN PRIMITIVE HISTORY.

The problems of democracy, like those of governments by ruler-ship, can be seen in their proper perspective only by discussing them in the context of historical reality. In this chapter we shall, therefore, begin by returning briefly to primitive democracy, to which reference has been made in our discussion of the economic interpretation of history. There will follow an equally brief review of certain aspects of the democratic city-state, both in antiquity and during the Middle Ages; its tumultuous history constitutes the background against which the institutions of the "representative republic" were established, and against which the thought of its founders must be understood.

When, in our day, attention is given to the problems of political organization in primitive society, the conclusions reached tend to be cast in the mold of certain patterns of thought originating in nineteenth century evolutionism. It is still taken for granted by some that, in the beginning of human history, there was no government at all, and that, when government did develop, it arose in its simplest form, as "the rule of one." The ancient classification into monarchies, aristocracies, and democracies may have fostered this view, as it suggests a sequence in time so far as the development of government is concerned, starting with what appeared as the most simple, and the most primitive.

As mentioned above, modern anthropological research leaves no doubt that democracy is the oldest form of government.[1] As such it has existed for a period which some estimate at tens of thousands and others at hundreds of thousands of years, but which, in either case, greatly exceed in length those covered by other forms of government. Three conclusions follow from this fact. In the first place, proponents of democracy will find their hand strengthened if they claim that the requirements of democracy conform closely to those of human nature.

41

They will, by the same token, see their task made more difficult because they cannot say that the shortcomings of modern democracy should be excused because democracy is so recent as to be necessarily beset with "infantile disorders." Finally, the props are knocked from under one of the premises upon which the attempt rests to explain government in terms of psychoanalysis. The talk about the *"oedipus complex,"* which is supposed to explain so many features of modern political life, is idle for the simple reason that political organization, in the beginnings of mankind, did not follow the authoritarian pattern assumed.

So far as the details of anthropological research into a primitive political organization are concerned, reference has been made to the bold generalizations of Lewis H. Morgan,[2] as corrected (and over-critically corrected) by Robert H. Lowie,[3] and to the conclusions of the Viennese school of anthropologists, headed by Schmidt and Koppers and summarized so ably by Sylvester A. Sieber and Franz H. Mueller,[4] as well as to the monumental survey by Richard Thurnwald.[5] To sum up, let us quote from an anthropologist who had the gift of presenting the results of the painstaking research of a lifetime in simple and popular terms. Julius E. Lips writes: "Are we justified in speaking of law and legal norms even with reference to the most ancient primitive tribes in the earliest stages of civilization? Indeed we are, because there is no chaos, but law and order." [6]

The cave-man then, who, thanks to science fiction, comic-strips and movies, still holds a potent sway over people's minds, is a figment of the imagination. Man was never a law unto himself; he lived in a society, and this society had its rules. Compared with more recent developments, "society" was infinitely stronger than "political organization"; the latter entered into play in a rather supplementary fashion. Social groups had, however, means of coercion at their command which were hardly less effective than those of the modern state. Robert H. Lowie, speaking specifically of the conditions typical of North America, refers to the "tremendous, not to say terrific, force of established custom and public opinion." He continues:

> To meet with universal reprobation on the part of one's neighbors; to have derisive songs sung in mockery of one's transgressions; to be publicly twitted with disgraceful conduct by joking relatives—these were eventualities to which no Indian lightly exposed himself. They made it possible to dispense largely with a powerful executive and with penal institutions; while the customary law sufficed, rendering new legislation unnecessary.[7]

Friedrich Engels was impressed by the fact that, during this period, those characteristics of the state, which were his *bête noire,* such as armies, police and prisons, did not exist. They were, as a rule, not needed; their functions were, at a time when division of labor had hardly begun, exercised by society in the normal course of its functioning. Instruments of restraint might, however, be required on special occasions, when they were promptly created.[8]

There was government, then, as much of it as was needed at any time. In essence, it was not so different from the government of our day. In the words of Julius Lips: "Legally and socially, the purposes and aims of government in a primitive society are the same as in modern society; to regulate life within and without the community, to hold the group together, to safeguard their food supply, to keep up the established order, and to maintain peace inside and outside of the borders." [9]

The bulk of the available evidence indicates that it is permissible to speak of "government by leadership"; this certainly applies to the truly primitive groups, which derived their living from hunting and collecting. As to the reasons, we can, as mentioned above, agree with the Marxists: The technique of production left little room for the acquisition of private property. Of land there was enough for all; the items of food secured through collecting or hunting were too perishable to be stored; the tools and weapons required were simple enough to make it possible for nearly everyone to produce them. There was, then, a basic equality in regard to the material conditions of life, a factor that was promptly reflected in political life. Such inequality as did assert itself in the latter, was, in the main, due to personal characteristics: prudence and eloquence in council, bravery in battle, skill in the hunt. If, in the election to offices, members of certain families had an advantage over others, the power of all officials was limited. This the first explorers, and the conquerors, who came after them, sometimes discovered to their grief. They took it for granted that, in conditions so primitive, there must exist chiefs with absolute power. Thus, as late as in the 1890's, the Germans assumed that they could make valid agreements with the "chiefs" of the Herrero tribe in Africa for the ceding of tribal lands. In the eyes of the natives the chiefs did not have such power; they refused to accept the transfer, and the bloody "Herrero-war" was the result.

As the basic cause of this "equality of opportunity" vanished, so did its social and political "superstructure." When hunting and collecting yielded to horticulture, and the latter to agriculture, the private property of land became natural, simply because someone "mixed his labor" with it.[10] After cattle had been domesticated, the same tendency asserted itself even more strongly; large herds could be owned by one man who might be able to secure better average yields than if the same number had been in the hands of many others. Under such conditions, the atmosphere is prepared for a definite social stratification. As Joseph Schumpeter [11] has put it, the success of an individual, based upon his personal accomplishments, "hardens": He has property which can be left to his descendants, and the latter wield a position of some special, and inevitably also political, prominence on account of the power which goes with these possessions. This means "power derived from wealth" (*Reichtumsmacht*), and it is invariably associated with its opposite, "wealth derived from power" (*Machtreichtum*): those who wield political power (derived from the exercise of community functions) may, and often do, use it to increase their wealth, and strengthen their political power in the process. The position which they acquire is held by families rather than by individuals. These families constitute the element of continuity which leads to the rise of social classes.

The transition from primitive "government by leadership" to a more definite "government by rulership" was, necessarily, slow, and it assumed many forms. When the early versions of aristocracy and monarchy [12] developed, they were close to the people; institutions for the control of the rulers existed which were, at times, remarkably similar to those of modern constitutionalism. The change could, of course, be hastened by military conquest; Alexander Ruestow, in his monumental work designed to establish the place which contemporary events occupy in the course of history,[13] has laid great stress on the fact that the great empires of the near and far East owed their origin to the overrunning of peaceful, and still comparatively democratic, agriculturists, by more warlike, and much less democratic, nomads. That, however, is a comparatively minor detail. To unite large areas under democratic rule was impossible, given the primitive means of communication; government by rulership was, for a time, a historical necessity.

CITY DEMOCRACY.

Democracy did get its chance again in the ancient city-state. Within its borders communication was simple and, at the same time, a state was powerful enough to ward off the attacks of its enemies. In both Greece and Rome, when these countries entered the light of recorded history, government was aristocratic. The Athens of the seventh century (700–600 B.C.), for example, was ruled by the heads of aristocratic families whose political power had, evidently, arisen in connection with their social and economic prominence. The period in question was, however, one of unrest and challenge. Not abstract ideas, but concrete grievances, lay at the origin of the demand for a change. The wealthy families were said to have exploited those who depended upon them; they demanded too large a part of the crop from the share-croppers; the rates of interest which they charged were exorbitant. In the evaluation of these complaints as recorded by contemporary historians we must bear in mind that when revolutionary changes take place, they are hardly ever the result of oppression alone. By the time they occur the worst is usually over. Those excluded from political power have, more often than not, succeeded in improving their economic and social position, and demand a share in political rule both for its own sake and as a lever for further progress in their material well-being. It is always good to remember the truth contained in the saying that, if you already have power you may, among other things, also make a revolution.

Greek, and in particular Athenian, economic and social life developed rapidly during the sixth century. Money economy took root; the division of labor and foreign trade expanded; many artisans became comparatively wealthy. Urban life developed on a substantial scale. Cities have, throughout history, been the natural breeding place of democracy. Where many people live in close proximity they discuss matters of common concern, and it becomes possible for a kind of public opinion to crystallize. This opinion is ready to challenge the rulers of the state, if they are believed to act in a manner inimical to the public interest. From such criticism it is only a step to resistance and rebellion; in cities men can easily band together and offer collective resistance against their rulers. In the case of Athens these developments were favored by military technique. The infantry, called the *Hoplitai,* took the place of the cavalry. The latter had consisted of knights, who were aristocrats able to own their own horses and bring their own attendants. The infantryman did not need more than his shield and spear, weapons which the members of the middle classes could afford. It soon developed that the men who had become vital for the defense of the state could no longer be excluded from a share in its government.

The first reforms, enacted by Draco in 624, were limited to the economic and social field. The laws were codified. They were harsh, giving rise to the term "draconian," but, probably, at that time any definite legislation had the purpose, and the result, of setting limits to the discretionary decisions of aristocratic judges.[14] Draco's measures, however, did not satisfy anyone. After a generation of turmoil Solon, whose moral authority was accepted by both sides, was entrusted with further reforms,[15] promulgated in 594. These tackled both the economic and the political side of the problem. The position of the debtors was lightened—some say by the cancellation of their debts, others by their reduction. A monetary reform was instituted. In the fundamental change of the political structure of the state the aristocratic and the democratic elements were mixed. The citizens were, as before, divided into three classes, according to their wealth. The highest group, the Knights, continued to constitute the military and political aristocracy; the *Zeugitai* (owners of mule teams) may, more or less, be identified with the middle classes, the *Thetes* with the daily laborers. The only right of the latter was to vote in the popular assembly which became, however, more important in the course of time. There continued to exist the Council in the Areopagos, the most aristocratic body of the city, consisting of past and present office-holders; its power diminished as that of the assembly increased. The Council of 400 (its membership to be raised to 500 later) consisted of members elected, some say entirely by lot, others in a process combining regular election with selection by lot. As Plutarch relates, it was Solon's intention that this council should operate as a brake upon the popular assembly, which it did to some extent.

Solon thought that he had constructed a tailor-made Constitution, adapted to the concrete needs of time and place. Still, he had, apparently, gone too far and too fast. The people were not yet able to use their new rights effectively; antagonisms developed which the democratic process was not yet strong enough to resolve. A generation of unrest was followed, in 560, by the dictatorship of Pisistratos who, together with his sons, ruled, with two interruptions, between 560 and 510.

At the end of this period the Solonian Constitution was revised, in a democratic sense, by Clisthenes. It may be well to speak of an Athenian democracy only for the subsequent period lasting, with two relapses into oligarchy caused by the Peloponnesian War, until 338, when the Macedonians conquered Athens in the battle of Chaironaia. (We may disregard the period of municipal autonomy enjoyed by Athens under Macedonian rule until 102 B.C., when the Roman conquest took place.) This stretch covers a period of 170 years, comparable to American history between the establishment of the Federal Constitution and the present time. In discussing the events of this period, we limit ourselves to a few problems significant from a more general point of view.

The first question is whether the government of Athens deserved the name of democracy. Two groups of residents were excluded from citizenship: the slaves, whose numbers are estimated at from 75,000 to 100,000, and the resident aliens, numbering with their families 96,000.[16] The total number of resident citizens including their family members, lay between 140,000 and 176,000. The citizens did, then, constitute the numerically strongest group. Still, many have said that the existence of the remaining two groups destroys the claim that Athens was democratic. They overlook, in the first place, that democracy may, as happened more recently in the cases of countries with colonies, such as England and France, live in a non-democratic relationship with others, although the processes by which its own internal government is carried on cannot be termed other than democratic. Certainly, where 6,000 people might appear at a popular assembly, and where elections of a more local character attracted an even larger number of people, the resulting processes were bound to be entirely different from, for example, the deliberations of a small body of aristocrats, or from those in which the decisions of a monarch are made. In Athens there did exist the right of free speech, called *parrhesia*,[17] and it was limited only slightly during the Peloponnesian War. Equally, there was free competition for political power among groups of political leaders, the decision lying, as is the case in modern democracies, in the hands of those citizens who cared to participate in their making.

Wherever the democratic process operates some of the features develop which, in our day, we characterize as "the democratic way of life." Pericles, in his Funeral Oration,[18] intended to contrast the free and easy intercourse among Athenians with conditions of a different type in non-democratic Sparta when he said:

> The freedom which we enjoy in our government extends also to our ordinary life. There, far from exercising a jealous surveillance over each other, we do not feel called upon to be angry with our neighbour for doing what he likes, or even to indulge in those injurious looks which cannot fail to be offensive, although they inflict no positive penalty.

The democratic process, as it operated in Athens, affected non-citizens as well as citizens. In their daily pursuits they mingled freely; citizens might work side by side with slaves in the erection of public buildings. The slaves had more freedom in Athens than in other Greek cities. The death penalty was reserved to the courts; a slave who complained of cruel treatment might seek refuge in a temple and demand that he be sold to a different master. In the great trials which Athens had to endure during the Peloponnesian Wars (431–04) the loyalty of her non-citizen population was never in doubt. The resident-aliens served as a regular part of the armed forces, providing infantrymen as well as rowers for the fleet, and considerable numbers of slaves had to be called upon after heavy losses had been sustained. Many of these slaves were subsequently freed. The general condition of the slaves in democratic Athens is best illustrated by the observation that in Athens the slave felt freer than the citizen did in oligarchic Sparta; also, when Plato, in his indictment of democracy as contained in the eighth book of *The Republic*,[19] says that democratic license was carried to such a point that slaves became "insolent," he clearly meant to imply that in his native city the relationship between master and slave did not follow too harsh a pattern. In the same manner, the writer, commonly referred to as "The Old Oligarch," complains about "the extraordinary amount of license granted to slaves and resident aliens at Athens." He adds that the reason why it is illegal to beat a slave or a resident alien is that an Athenian citizen might be mistaken for either, as they were clothed in the same way and did not differ in personal appearance.[20]

Athenian government, then, was democratic, both in its procedures and in its effects. It had its Achilles heel, however, in the popular assembly. As mentioned above, the existence of that institution did not dispense it from the need of leadership. The latter was so much a part of it that Thucydides, writing about Pericles, adds that "what was nominally a democracy became in his hands government by the first citizen."[21] Pericles had, however, as Thucydides declares, unusual gifts of leadership, and he lived at a time propitious to their exercise. The period of his preëminence was followed immediately by one characterized by men of lesser stature, who were not able, and often not willing, to save the popular assembly from its inherent weaknesses.

POPULAR ASSEMBLIES AND CROWD PSYCHOLOGY.

These weaknesses were seen clearly by the founders of our "representative republic." Thus, Madison, in No. 10 of *The Federalist*, was able to write:

> . . . a pure democracy, by which I mean a society consisting of a small number of citizens, who assemble and administer the government in

person, can admit of no cure for the mischiefs of faction. A common passion or interest will, in almost every case, be felt by a majority of the whole; a communication and concert result from the form of government itself; and there is nothing to check the inducements to sacrifice the weaker party or an obnoxious individual. Hence it is that such democracies have ever been spectacles of turbulence and contention; have ever been found incompatible with personal security or the rights of property; and have in general been as short in their lives as they have been violent in their deaths.[22]

When Madison wrote these lines, he did not merely argue as a conservative interested in defending the rights of property. The target of his criticism was that sheer irrationality of mob rule which so many writers have proclaimed to be an inevitable characteristic of democratic government. This practice begins with Herodotus according to whom a speaker who advanced the cause for aristocracy, expressed himself in these terms: "The mob . . . . rushes wildly into state affairs with all the fury of a stream swollen in the winter, and confuses everything. Let the enemies of the Persians be governed by democracies . . ."[23] On the other hand, Madison and his associates meant to establish, once and for all, that it was a characteristic of what they called "pure" democracy and what more current terminology calls "direct" democracy.

The term "mob rule," of course, carries psychological connotations which make it unfit for scientific discussion. Sociological literature has dealt with the subject under the heading of "the psychology of the crowd." Gustave Le Bon wrote a book under this title,[24] which had a sensational success in Continental Europe, although Le Bon, a gifted writer, was not the originator of the theory which he developed, and which owes so much of his success to the facile generalizations in which he indulged. Still, the subject is important and its analysis is vital from the point of view of both political theory and comparative government.

The basic fact is the psychological contagion which may develop among a number of people gathered in the same spot. A crowd milling in a public square does not constitute a problem; it remains a haphazard gathering of individuals. The situation changes as soon as something happens to establish a psychological contact among these individuals. This may be the result of an accident which results in a panic; in this case the laws of crowd psychology assert themselves in striking terms, but the absence of a leader excludes any unified direction of the resulting effort. Where the psychological fusion is the result of leadership, it may take the most divergent forms: the call for a lynching or for a crusade, a summoning to penitence in a church or to heroic efforts for the common good in a political meeting. The required psychological communication will not develop unless the number of those gathered is substantial. In a small group, people may exchange their views, but they will not be fused into a psychological whole. In a large crowd, this can easily happen, and Madison was right when he emphasized that the mere fact of thousands of people gathering in a public square was liable to lead to the results which he deplored in such forceful language. If the laws of crowd psychology may lead to positive as well as to negative results, the latter are more likely to develop, at any rate in a popular assembly. Reason and responsibility tend to become the casualties of the processes involved. They are attributes of the individual and, in a "psychological" crowd, the individual is submerged. While reason is weakened, emotions are strengthened. Under their sway, people in a crowd have done things of which they would not have been capable as individuals, and of which they were ashamed when they were released from the laws of crowd psychology and became thinking and responsible individuals again.

The Athenians were aware of the dangers inherent in the institution of the popular assembly. An elaborate set of rules,[25] quite comparable to those governing the actions of a modern parliament, had been drawn up to guard against these dangers; as long as these rules were obeyed, there was a substantial measure of orderliness and responsibility. When the crowd became excited, however, the rules could be swept away. Thus, in 406 B.C., six of the victorious generals returned to the city after the naval battle of the Arginusae, feeling certain that they would be received in triumph. They had accomplished much; the Athenian forces, so utterly depleted by a series of reversals that they seemed hardly capable of another great effort, had won a magnificent victory which, if properly exploited, would have enabled the city to end a disastrous war with an honorable peace. Instead, eight generals (including two who had not returned to Athens) were accused of having failed to save the shipwrecked and bury the dead, and the matter was referred to the popular assembly. There, the generals stated, in the brief period of time alloted to them, that, while they had taken the main body of the fleet to attack the part of the Spartan navy which had not been involved in the engagement, they had dispatched an adequate number of vessels on the errands mentioned; unfortunately, the captains of the ships sent to the rescue were forced back by a violent storm. These arguments appeared to impress the assembly when it had to be adjourned for a festival.

Meanwhile, however, various artifices were used to stir up popular passions against the accused, and the Senate was prevailed upon to propose that the assembly take one vote on the guilt or innocence of the eight instead of having each of them tried separately, and that, if the verdict be guilty, the penalty be death. When this resolution was introduced in the assembly it was charged that it was illegal, a separate vote being required for each individual. This only produced a more ugly mood in the crowd; it was demanded that if the objection were not withdrawn, its authors should be tried in the same vote as the generals, "a proposition to which the mob gave vociferous assent." [26] The intimidation accomplished its purpose, although one opponent of the illegal procedure employed could not be silenced. Socrates happened to be a member of the presiding body at that time and, in his *Apology*, Plato reports him as having said the following:

> The only office of state which I ever held, O men of Athens, was that of senator: the tribe Antiochis, which is my tribe, had the presidency at the trial of the generals who had not taken up the bodies of the slain after the battle of Arginusae; and you proposed to try them all together, which was illegal, as you all thought afterwards; but at the time I was the only one of the Prytanes who was opposed to the illegality, and I gave my vote against you; and when the orators threatened to impeach and arrest me, and have me taken away, and you called and shouted, I made up my mind that I would run the risk, having law and justice with me, rather than take part in your injustice because I feared imprisonment and death.[27]

Socrates failed in his protest; the eight accused were sentenced to death in one vote and the six present executed forthwith. Thus a blow was struck at the morale of the Athenian armed forces from which there was to be no recovery.

This incident was extreme, but the effects of crowd psychology, as manifested in the popular assembly, affected Athenian policy, in particular foreign policy, on more than one occasion. It made Athenian democracy—as it more or less made all "direct" democracy, at any rate the urban variety of this species—rather warlike. Democratic Athens entered the Peloponnesian War with much more alacrity than oligarchic Sparta. Opportunities to make an honorable peace were repeatedly destroyed by the effects of unbridled oratory on unorganized masses. The Athenians, as individuals, might realize that the war was disastrous; Aristophanes' gibes in his *Lysistrata* at those forcing the continuation of the war apparently found a powerful echo in the hearts of his fellow-citizens. The popular assembly was, however, a law unto itself, always more likely to be swayed by those preaching the glories of conquest or the sweetness of revenge than a reasonable composition of existing differences.

With all its defects, the Athenian popular assembly was not as destructive as were the comparable bodies of other city-states. Athens recovered her liberty, after a brief lapse, at the end of the Peloponnesian War, in 403. Her democracy, at first chastened, soon hurried back into some of the old mistakes, although there was no longer enough military power left to encourage further large-scale military adventures.

When viewing Athenian democracy as a whole, we must emphasize its defects, but we should not overlook the simple fact that Athens has never been greater than when it enjoyed a democratic form of government. Although many obstacles were put into the way of the development of a responsible leadership, Athenian democracy is distinguished by as many brilliant statesmen as there were in contemporary autocracies. Democratic Athens took the lead in the defense of Greece against the Persians (although at that time the "pure" or almost "pure" democracy of later years did not yet exist); the city was twice the metropolis of a large empire. Arts and sciences flourished as never before or after. To be sure, there was partisan struggle and partisan hatred. Even this does not weigh too heavily, however, if Athenian democracy is compared not with what an ideal rulership might have been, but with the reality as exemplified by rulerships of the time. The best instance is Sparta, regarding which Thucydides, who does not favor democracy, says that "she was torn by internal dissensions more than any other Greek city." In addition, Athens had her liberty to compensate her for whatever material defects were connected with her democracy; even then there were undoubtedly many who, if called upon to choose, would have preferred free government to good government. They knew that when democratic government is bad, it at least allows its citizens to say so and to do their best to improve existing defects and overcome apparent evils.

The political developments in Ancient Rome followed lines so different from those of the Greek city-state that they need not be discussed. Rome was never a "pure democracy" even to the limited extent that this held true for Athens. The Roman Senate was, throughout the period of the Republic, a rather aristocratic body, and its powers were great. The two consuls formed an executive much more powerful than that of the ten generals elected in Athens. There were popular meetings, *comitia,* but never one great popular assembly for the city as a whole. Power was, in fact, so carefully divided that the Greek writer, Polybius,[28] described it in a manner suggesting the separation of powers doctrine as developed by Montesquieu and applied in the Constitution of the United States. This, of course, does not mean that the Roman experience has no bearing upon the history of democracy. There did exist a substantial measure of government based upon the active consent of the governed, and when the empire was established, there occurred a marked change in the nation, proud self-reliance and free self-expression being replaced by a system which placed a premium upon subservience. However, the specific problems of "pure" democracy, which we have discussed in the case of Athens, do not arise in that of Rome, whose history, therefore, has no immediate bearing upon our problems.

THE MEDIEVAL CITY-STATE.

Medieval city democracy, on the other hand, developed features similar to those of Ancient Athens. These features occupy a place of even more immediate significance as a part of the background against which the thought of the Founders of the "representative republic" took shape. Once again democratic institutions arose for reasons of a practical order. The cities developed an economic and social life quite different from that of the surrounding countryside, and this placed them in opposition to the feudal lords of the time. Their economy was based on money rather than barter. Their early leaders were merchants who wanted specific guarantees from their feudal overlords, such as guarantees of personal freedom, special commercial tribunals, freedom from restrictions upon their business, and a "peace" of the city, meaning a legal code adapted to their needs. Eventually, the accumulation of these concrete demands crystallized into a movement for independence from feudal overlordship. In 1057 the citizens of Milan were successful in their bid for freedom; twenty years later Cambrai, in France, was the first northern town to revolt. Setbacks occurred, but in the course of time the more important towns had secured, over a large part of Western Europe, a more or less comprehensive degree of freedom from feudal rule. The militant manner in which freedom was won, in many cases had its consequences for the form of government which developed. In most French and Belgian towns, the citizens banded together in a "commune," a voluntary association which organized popular meetings in which the people took an oath of allegiance implying willingness to share in the common defense. The need to rely upon every adult male citizen capable of bearing arms for the city's protection assured, for a time, the democratic character of the new government.

During the early period of urban independence, popular assem-

blies were a part of the city government even in towns as far north as Magdeburg and Speyer in Germany. For obvious geographic reasons, to which perhaps reasons of popular psychology may be added, they were more frequent in Southern France, and constituted the rule in Italy. The powers of these assemblies were less extensive and their use less well regulated than those of their Athenian predecessor. The citizens might be limited to expressing consent or dissent; the position of elected officials was strong. In not a few cases, oligarchy developed in fact while the city was, in theory, still democratic. Certain officials, or members of their families, were again and again elected to the leading positions in their city until, in the end, a hereditary right had been established.

The democratic current continued, however, to be strong in a number of Italian cities in which political life was turbulent indeed. In the Italian city-states (not only the democratic ones) there occurred, between 1000 and 1500 A.D., according to one writer, no fewer than 7,000 revolutions and 300 massacres. Where the popular assembly (*Parlamento*) existed, it had its share in these disturbances. There is no case in which its part in the city government was as well regulated as it had been in Athens. The reputation which it acquired as a result is best illustrated by this passage, taken from a law which Savonarola had passed in Florence in 1495 after that city had shaken off the rule of the Medici and regained, for the time being, its republican status:

> . . . it is also known that in no way can our liberty be so easily subverted and this new and good rule be overthrown as by means of the Parlamento (as the popular assembly was known in Italian cities) . . . The Magnificent Signory and Gonfalonier do hereby provide and ordain that no Parlamento shall be held in the future—that henceforth the Signory shall swear never again to convoke one and that whoever shall plot to do so shall be put to death and 3000 florins be awarded to his denouncer.[29]

To the extent, then, that medieval city democracy relied upon the popular assembly it was a failure. The representative principle was, during this period, rarely applied in a democratic way. Oligarchies, particularly in the form of merchant aristocracies, were successful over long periods, but their method of rule had little in common with the active consent of the governed postulated by the democratic principle; membership in their ruling class was definitely limited to certain families.

GUILD DEMOCRACY.

Medieval democracy developed another significant feature when, during the thirteenth and fourteenth centuries, it gave birth to a form of guild democracy. Where this stage was reached it had been preceded by generations of aristocratic rule, exercised by wealthy merchants. The merchants had become separated from the rest of the people soon after independence had been won. They had the advantage of early organization; their guilds had been powerful already during the final period of feudal overlordship, when they were allowed to assume such public functions as administering the laws pertaining to their operations, or providing for certain public expenditures. The political power of the merchant guilds increased in proportion to the wealth of their members. They were elected to public office time and again and, in the end, cooptation in the sense of filling vacancies by the officeholders of the day supplanted elections. A formal revision of the constitution was not always required to effect this change. Protests against the political ascendancy of the merchant patriciate were, at first, rather rare because it distinguished itself as much by a spirit of public service as by a desire for power. The achievements of many of the cities ruled by merchant aristocracies are well known; suffice it to refer to the towns which were members of the Hanseatic League.

During the second half of the thirteenth and throughout the fourteenth centuries, this patrician rule was challenged by the craftsmen and gave rise, where the challenge was successful, to a new period of democratic rule. When historians, such as Carl Lamprecht, deal with these developments, they are inclined to concentrate on symptoms rather than on causes. They refer to incidents between members of the ruling families, their young sons in particular, and the remainder of the population; the insolence of the young patricians is said to have led to riots and revolutionary upheavals. Obviously, in some cases the "political class" of this aristocracy had degenerated; its membership became rather restricted, and the leading families prevented the infusion of new blood, thereby destroying the "circulation of the elite" so indispensable to their own continued biological and intellectual vigor. In not a few cases, probably the patricians despised the artisans without making any effort to conceal their scorn. In such cases, they might also be inclined to sacrifice the common good to their own private or group interests.

The basic cause for the challenge to patrician rule was, however, the disturbance of the hitherto existing equilibrium between the social and the political order. Dozens of craft guilds had been formed, and not a few of their members were more wealthy than were many of the patricians. In the aggregate they represented more wealth than the merchants, and they were certainly more numerous. Clearly, they would have challenged the patrician rule even if it had been above reproach. Their immediate demands were concrete and modest. The administration of their own economic affairs was the first right they wanted and won. They obtained public privileges, which meant that the guild ceased to be merely a private economic association and assumed a political character. This, in turn, resulted in a considerable measure of training in the exercise of public duties, which encouraged the guild members to feel competent to take the government of their city into their own hands. Their earliest triumphs were achieved in Italy in the second half of the thirteenth century; at the beginning of the fourteenth the guild members were victorious in The Netherlands, and gradually most of the German towns likewise capitulated to guild rule. Holdouts of aristocratic rule, however, existed everywhere.

The new constitutions varied widely in particulars. They had one significant feature in common: political power was based upon groups rather than upon individuals. The groups had been established to represent economic interests, even if this was not their only function, and even if they differed greatly from modern pressure groups. Advocates of a "corporate state," as well as of guild socialism, have claimed that these constitutions represented "organic" democracy, entrusting political control to the "natural" units of social life rather than to such "artificial" and "inorganic" entities as modern political parties.

If, in our evaluation of these claims, we recall what has been said above about the difference between society and the state, these constitutions mean simply that an attempt was made to avoid political form in the proper sense of that term. There was to be no "transformer" standing between the formations of society, with their natural diversity, and the unity of action required for the existence of the state. A study of the actual results of these constitutions reveals in practice all of the differences which this theoretical consideration makes us expect. Even during the Middle Ages, when competition was not nearly as keen as it became later, economic interests were a disintegrating rather than an integrating force. The individual guilds were much more inclined to look after the welfare of their members than after that of the community. "Members" means masters; it must be borne in mind that admission of new masters soon came to be limited in the interests of those who held that rank at a particular

time. Above all, the question arose as to which guilds were to participate in the governments of the cities, and what numerical weight was
to be allotted to them in the city council. No solution of this problem
ever seemed natural. In the words of Professor Pirenne: "We find the
civic constitutions subject, during the fourteenth century, to perpetual
fluctuation. They were continually revised; 'members' were added or
suppressed; the classification of crafts was modified and still there was
dissatisfaction." [30]

The example of Ghent, the most powerful of the democratic cities
of The Netherlands, is instructive in this regard. There the weavers
and fullers, who had borne the brunt of the battle against the patriciate, constituted two of the three "members," i.e., combinations of
guilds to which the city government was entrusted. They had obtained
this dominating influence because they were able to seize and defend it. There was no peace between the two guilds. In 1345 the
weavers crushed the fullers and annulled their power; four years later
the weavers were defeated by an alliance of the fullers and the lesser
crafts. In 1359 the weavers again obtained the upper hand, and in the
following year inflicted great losses upon their old enemies, the fullers,
in the famous battle of the Friday Market.

Nor were conditions satisfactory in the following decades. A lesson of general validity may be drawn from this experience: while
the method of the quantitative yardstick, i.e., counting heads, adopted
by modern democracies, to ascertain the extent of political power to
be assigned certain groups, may not be ideal from every point of
view, it nevertheless constitutes at least a simple formula which makes
for the peaceful settlement of all claims to political power. The same
holds true with regard to the second difficulty of a government based
upon the representation of interests: one interest is as good as another; there is no common denominator for them; the organized group
interests have no direct relationship to an ideal binding on all. On the
basis of these facts the the guilds in Ghent quite naturally refused to
submit to majority rule. Each guild formed a little world of its own.
Account had to be taken of its susceptibilities in distributing public
offices and care exercised not to disturb the balance of power. The
guilds submitted every important matter to their members and frequently refused to yield in the city council when they were in the
minority. As a last resort, a decision was more than once sought in
the streets, where guildsmen assembled under their banners and engaged in bloody battles.

While this guild rule lasted it was always suspected of ignoring the
interests of the community. The patrician city council of the past had

been accepted as an authority standing above the interests of the various crafts and capable of curbing their excesses. Once the craft guilds had supreme authority, they acted as they pleased. Each guild was inclined to set the prices of its products as high as possible; outside competition was sharply restricted without regard for the sacrifices imposed upon the consumer.

When it became increasingly difficult for a journeyman to set himself up as a master, a new problem arose; there developed the beginnings of a modern proletariat. In some cases a master might employ large numbers of help. This applied, in particular, to the textile industry of Lombardy and Flanders, where the conditions of life and labor were rather bad for the workers, in addition to their being excluded from any participation in the rule of their city.

It is significant that when an attempt was made in Florence to organize the proletarians—called *ciompi*—into guilds and grant them a share in the government of the city, the experiment promptly failed. Following a popular uprising, three new guilds were set up, in 1378, to encompass these workers who were henceforth to appoint three of the nine priors of the city. No fairer attempt to give all citizens a share in municipal government was made during the Middle Ages. However, it soon became apparent that the new guilds differed fundamentally from the old organizations. Their prime objective could not be the regulation of a trade; they were employees of the masters organized in the *arti maggiori* and were obliged to leave the direction of trade to their employers. Hence their interests were different from those of the older guilds and peaceful cooperation proved an impossibility. Open conflict broke out; the craft guilds (*arti minori*) combined with the merchant guilds (*arti maggiori*), and the workers' guilds were crushed and dissolved. Such difficulties were the exception during the Middle Ages only because mass production was limited.

Thus, where urban democracy during the Middle Ages gave the public assembly of the citizens a prominent place in city government, it failed on account of the irrationality of the latter; in the cities in question there was a tendency for tyranny to take the place of a disintegrating democracy. Where the craft guilds took over the city government on the basis of a representation of (selected) interests, they were not able to resist the rising power of the princes who, beginning in the fifteenth century, set out to organize the modern state, which is characterized by the direct rule over the individual citizen through the organs of the government, that dispenses with intermediaries either in the form of feudal vassals or corporate entities such as guilds.

Again, economic changes were a basic factor in this transition. Trade and commerce expanded; a national economy was beginning to replace the municipal economy of the Middle Ages. The protectionism of the cities obstructed economic progress, particularly in the cities ruled by the craft guilds. When the final struggle for the independence of the cities took place, the attempt to organize political power on the basis of interest groups did not prove a source of strength. In Ghent, for example, different crafts fought one another even while they were facing the common enemy. The radicals beheaded the leader of the wealthy boatsmen's guild, and secured the appointment of a shoemaker as captain general of the city. When, in 1492, Ghent lost her independence, many of her citizens welcomed the change as implying the end of a narrow restrictionism as well as a guarantee for a return to law and order.

Medieval democracy was, of course, rural as well as urban, although in rural areas it never succeeded in organizing a fairly large territory. The exception is Switzerland. In the valleys of the Alps feudalism never took more than a tenuous hold. The difficulties of the terrain were a powerful equalizer and, when the inhabitants of the original three *cantons* banded together to ward off the Hapsburg attempt to establish an effective subjection to feudal rule, the mountains facilitated the defense to such an extent as to provide them with the margin of victory. The democratic character of the government had, even in the case of these original *cantons*, its limitations. The popular assembly did not, and could not, meet often enough to become as powerful as it was in the city-state; as mentioned above, its disorderly character led to its abolition in Schwyz and Zug. In the election of officials certain aristocratic tendencies appeared early; in this case also there was a tendency for members of the same family to be elected and reelected. No formal oligarchy ever developed as it did, for example, in Venice, or in a city like Berne (which became a part of the Swiss confederation) which were clearly ruled by merchant aristocrats. The extent, then, to which medieval Switzerland was democratic, was limited, and so was the extent of rural democracy in general. We shall return, on a later occasion, to those areas where, if the government could not be called democratic, it did develop forms of constitutional government coming fairly close to such a result.

Chapter IV

GOVERNMENT BY RULERSHIP

▀▄

THE REALITY OF MONARCHY.

The various types of government by rulership have one feature in common with government by leadership: Ideology clashes with reality. The traditional classification [1] lists monarchies and aristocracies—the rule of one and the rule of the best. Actually, no form of government is ever "monarchy" in the sense that only one man rules; nor has there ever been a government which could truly have been called "government by the best."

Monarchy is never the rule of one man because the monarch needs a large number of people—even as he needs his arms and his eyes. He must have officials willing and capable of carrying out his commands and, equally, he depends on them to inform him on conditions in his realm; he can no more see everything than can he do everything. Theoretically, the monarch might draw his intermediaries from all groups among the people. Practically, there is a tendency for him to entrust this task to a social class, the nobility, of which the monarch is at the same time a member and the head. With the nobility he engages freely in social intercourse; a selection of its members comes to constitute the royal court. For these reasons, Montesquieu was able to write:

> The intermediate, subordinate, and dependent powers constitute the nature of monarchical government; I mean of that in which a single person governs by fundamental laws. . . .
>
> The most natural, intermediate, and subordinate power is that of the nobility. This in some measure seems to be essential to a monarchy, whose fundamental maxim is, no monarch, no nobility; no nobility, no monarch; . . .[2]

In recent literature, the point made by Montesquieu is usually associated with the name of Gaetano Mosca, who set out to develop

60

a realistic theory of forms of government as early as 1884.[3] For Mosca, the active conduct of political affairs in all forms of government lay, as mentioned above, in the hands of an active minority. About monarchy, he says:

> But the man who is at the head of the state would certainly not be able to govern without the support of a numerous class to enforce respect for his orders and to have them carried out; and granting that he can make one individual, or indeed many individuals, in the ruling class feel the weight of his power, he certainly cannot be at odds with the class as a whole or do away with it. Even if that were possible, he would at once be forced to create another class, without the support of which action on his part would be completely paralyzed.[4]

It is interesting to note, in passing, that Mosca speaks of "political class" rather than "ruling class," whereas the English translation uses the latter term in its very title. Mosca was willing to accept this but, obviously, by selecting the term "political class" he meant to stress a point of principle: the primacy of the political, which Aristotle emphasized so strongly. When, on the other hand, we speak of "ruling class" we are, subconsciously, paying tribute to the economic interpretation of history—certainly, the term accords better with the basic implications of the views of Karl Marx than with those of Aristotle. Mosca did not accept the Marxian view that a social class as such can be a "ruling" class. In the political field there is a specific function to be fulfilled, and this function acts as a selector of those who are to fulfill it even if, in the main, they are taken from a particular social class. Besides, in the case of traditional monarchy, this class does not owe its origin to economic considerations; it developed because those who exercised certain political functions made these hereditary in their families.

ARISTOCRACIES.

At any rate, if the above analysis is correct, "aristocracies," even if, in fact, they constitute oligarchies (meaning a hereditary rule based on wealth and power rather than on the individual excellence of the rulers), represent the only case in which basic facts are in accord with the implications of traditional classification. Since the aristocratic principle has, historically, been so much less important than the monarchic, it can be dealt with briefly, and it will be best to treat it first.

According to both Plato and Aristotle, it is a basic characteristic of aristocracy that it faces two kinds of dangers: those implied in the conflict between rulers, and those resulting from possible dissension among the rulers themselves. All aristocracies have been apprehensive lest one man make himself superior to the rest. It was felt necessary to take elaborate precautions against such a contingency. Thus, there was in Venice the "Council of Ten," which met at night and whose absolute and discretionary power extended to the city's leading officials as well as to all citizens. On two occasions the *Doge,* the city's chief magistrate, had been accused, sentenced to death, and executed before the light of the new day dawned.

Only in urban areas has it been possible to combine an effective executive with basic equality among the aristocrats. In cities, the ruling families, living in close proximity, were able to fashion reliable tools for both action and supervision. When the aristocratic principle was extended to large rural areas the concern for equality obscured the need for authority. It is, perhaps, not improper to regard the governments of the German Empire after the Treaty of Westphalia (1648), and of the Kingdom of Poland as approximations of rural aristocracies. The result was failure in both cases. In Poland, the noblemen's insistence on equality made them act almost like anarchists. Each of them had his own local area in which he maintained his own authority. The nobles were unwilling to establish a central government with power sufficient to provide even for the common defense. Each nobleman was a member of the Diet, where he enjoyed the right of *liberum veto,* which made it possible for him to veto acts of the entire body. Sir Walter Scott, in his *Life of Napoleon,*

> recounts on the authority of John Sobieski, afterwards King of Poland, the following story. To get round the opposition of an obstinate individual the rest of the diet agreed to meet before the usual time, and shut and bolted the door. The excluded dissentient climbed in through the chimney and hid in the stove. It was summer and the chamber was unheated. "Here he lay *perdu,* until the vote was called, when, just as it was about to be recorded as unanimous, he thrust his head out of the stove and pronounced the fatal *veto.* . . . One of the nobles who stood by unsheathed his sabre and severed at one blow the head of the dissentient from his body." [5]

An aristocratic political class, then, does well if it does not try to govern a large area on the basis of an "aristocratic" constitution. The group as a whole benefits if it accepts one head, the monarch, connected with the rest by social intercourse and, not infrequently, by intermarriage. There were, to be sure, periods of history when the nobility did see in the King its enemy, and fought him without quarter —unsuccessfully in Continental Europe, but successfully in England, where the result was that, in the end, it was not the aristocracy that won out but that the democratic principle gradually supplanted oligarchic rule.

MONARCHY AS A SYMBOL.

The institution of monarchy is useful to an aristocratic ruling class not only on account of its capacity for integration, but also because of its strong appeal as a symbol. The role of symbolism belongs to those facts of political life which academic writers have been inclined to neglect, although the two chapters on monarchy in Walter Bagehot's *English Constitution* should have made its analysis an integral part of political science long ago.[6] Symbols appeal to the irrational in man. In all of us the rational element represents, perhaps, as small a part of our total motivation as does the visible part of an iceberg represent the whole. For the great mass of mankind symbols are so important because the average person is neither qualified nor desirous of making a rational analysis of the actual workings of his government. It is so much easier to let the imagination construct a simple and, if possible, an attractive picture.

Monarchic symbolism fits these requirements ideally. The "rule of one" is the most simple and, as Bagehot emphasized, for that reason the most "intelligible government." [7] Bagehot continues: ". . . the action of a single will, the fiat of a single mind, are easy ideas: anybody can make them out, and no one can ever forget them." Monarchy has, in addition, the advantage of bringing family life into politics. Of this Bagehot says: "It brings down the pride of sovereignty to the level of petty life." Such matters as a royal marriage can claim more popular attention than does the most important business of government. To quote Bagehot again: "The women—one half the human race at least—care fifty times more for a marriage than a ministry. All but a few cynics like to see a pretty novel touching for a moment the dry scenes of the grave world." [8] That monarchy means the reign of a family rather than a person makes it possible, at the same time, to multiply its personal appeal. The King's relatives can represent him where he cannot go himself. This again reflects strength on the institutions as a whole, and on the country which enjoys its advantages.

Pomp and ceremony form, in addition, a more natural part of monarchy than of a republic. A gun salute for a King appears more appropriate than one for a President; royal marriages, royal journeys of all kinds, royal jubilees, and royal burials all call for glamor and pomp. The average person may not be aware of the intricate details behind the splendor of those occasions but, even in our day, he enjoys them thoroughly [9]—witness the large number of Americans who flocked to Britain for the coronation of Queen Elizabeth II, or the large number of other foreign visitors anxious to take pictures of the changing of the guards at Buckingham Palace.

Monarchy, furthermore, has a tendency to lift itself above the business of government. It can perform the task of symbolizing national unity in a manner unrivalled by an elective President. People tend to consider a monarch untainted by political decisions, to which they object even where he is clearly involved in their making as well as in their execution. They want their sovereign to be something different from, and higher than, the business of ordinary government; they want to place him on a pedestal and keep him there. In Czarist Russia there was a saying: "The heavens are high and the Czar is far away." The implication was that whatever concrete grievances existed were not to be imputed to the Czar; if he knew of them he would certainly apply the remedy. The Czar, of course, might know very well about these conditions, and he might clearly have decided that he could not, or would not, remedy them, but the feeling existed nonetheless. This tendency can go so far that people want to idolize their princes. Not a few monarchs have taken advantage of the fact in order to claim divine status, or at least divine sanction for their rule.

MONARCHY AS AN ACTIVE PRINCIPLE OF GOVERNMENT.

These advantages can serve the purposes of a nobility well. The institution of monarchy, in such cases, acts, in the formulation of Walter Bagehot, "as a disguise." [10] The people might not look with favor upon being governed by a "political class" of noblemen; they might readily accept the substance of that rule when presented to them in the form of monarchy. Inevitably, however, the King is more than a disguise for the rule of noblemen. He does need his "intermediate powers," but, then, intermediate powers are intermediate. In the first place, the King has always enjoyed the privilege of raising new men to the rank of the nobility. Extensive use has been made of this right, in particular when the old nobility had been depleted by war. In the second place, the monarch has one right, in particular: he is what Sieyès, in one of the happy formulations which sprang from his fertile brain, called "the Grand Elector." Much as the King depends upon the nobility as a group, he can select from among its members those with whom he intends to share his powers. It is customary for monarchs—or for those who make up their minds for them —to select one overall coordinator, or rather to permit such a man (a Richelieu, a Mazarin, or a Bismarck) to emerge in a process in which court intrigues play their part.

There were exceptions to this rule; Charlemagne directed his government himself, as did William the Conqueror, and so did Henry VIII after Cardinal Wolsey fell from grace. The monarch who can afford the attempt to be his own effective head of government, however, has always been the exception. The principle of heredity, aggravated by inbreeding, rarely produces men with the necessary qualifications. Matters need not be as bad as they were around 1800, when it was said that every one of the reigning monarchs of Europe had shown at least occasional signs of insanity. In a later day, Lord Bryce observed that of all of the reigning princes he had come to know not one would, had he been born a commoner, achieved a higher status in life than that of a subordinate army officer or of a bank clerk. When such monarchs do allow one man to become the key factor in their government, they need not become mere figureheads. There exists, in such a case, something parallel to the "rule of anticipated reactions" in a democracy. What the King's favorite does, or fails to do, must at least have the tacit approval of the monarch; this necessity sets limits to the discretionary powers of the King's chief aide. Some monarchs have tried to assert themselves more fully by relying upon a group of men, rather than upon a single person, which gave them the opportunity to play one against the other. This possibility—exemplified so well by George III—has its drawbacks; government may become erratic, and intrigue exceed even generously drawn bounds. No matter, however, in what way this particular problem is decided, the existence of the monarchy provides for a hierarchical order in the political class which is entirely different from the conditions characteristic of an "aristocracy." This order is arranged from above, rather than being established in a series of decisions made by equals for strictly limited periods.

DESPOTISM.

Monarchy is, however, not always the same thing. We must, in particular, distinguish "despotism" from the traditional type of absolute monarchy. It is the characteristic of absolute rule that the one person formally in power is not checked by any legal rules. In addition to checks which are covered by the written or unwritten law of the land, there may be, of course, checks arising from reality. Thus, it is customary to consider the period between 1614, when the last Estates General met in France, and 1789, the year of the Great Revolution, as one of absolutism. Yet, throughout this period the powers of the

King were not legally absolute in every respect: even a Louis XIV
and XV were unable to touch the privileges enjoyed by certain corporate bodies. In addition, the King lacked the devices of communication so vital to the enforcement of a ruler's will, devices which the
modern dictator has at his disposal. Thus, the French King's control
over large parts of his country was always indirect, and at times remote. As a result, the traditional pattern of society was protected
from royal interference. Custom, furthermore, forced the King's actions into certain channels even where the affairs of the central government were involved.

In regard to all of these matters there exists a marked difference
between the absolute monarchs of the Western world and the despots
of the Orient. Aristotle brings out the salient points of the difference
when he discusses what he calls the second form of monarchy. In
his words:

> There is another sort of monarchy, not uncommon among the bar-
> barians, which nearly resembles tyranny. But this is both legal and
> hereditary. For barbarians being more servile in character than Hellenes
> and Asiatics than Europeans, do not rebel against a despotic govern-
> ment. Such royalty has the nature of tyrannies because the people
> are by nature slaves; but there is no danger of their being overthrown
> for they are hereditary and legal. Wherefore also their bodyguards
> are such as a king and not as a tyrant would employ, that is to say,
> they are composed of citizens whereas the guards of tyrants are mer-
> cenaries. For kings rule according to law over voluntary subjects, but
> tyrants over involuntary; and the one are guarded by their fellow
> citizens, the others are guarded against them.[11]

Aristotle's discussion contains a point which one can accept only
with some difficulty: the primary reason for the difference between
monarchy in countries such as Greece and despotism in Asia is seen
in differing national characteristics. So far as the latter are concerned,
it is always good to bear in mind the objections to terms such as national character, which Professor Friedrich, using modern examples,
has formulated as follows:

> Assertions concerning *the* British, *the* French, and *the* Germans have
> been among the most potent weapons of propaganda. Nations have,
> in the age of nationalism, been readily personalized and their char-
> acter has been set forth with assurance by travelers, journalists and
> scholars alike. It is not too much to say that this entire literature is,
> from a scientific viewpoint, worthless. Though some have written of
> these matters with learning, the argument usually focuses either upon
> selected personal experiences from which generalizations are drawn

to fit the author's preconceived notions or political prejudices, or a selection is made from the particular country's literature to prove a preconceived idea or point of view. As might be expected, the particular author's own nation (with some notable exceptions) is depicted as possessing a most desirable character, while one or more others are proclaimed as bad. That the age of nationalism should have produced such mental constructs is probably natural enough; that these constructs do not stand critical analysis is certainly clear.[12]

To be sure, there have been more serious attempts of late to analyze national differences than those referred to by Friedrich, but all of them suffer from the defect that political form is treated as if it did not exist. National characteristics operate, for the writers in question, as much in a political vacuum as do social classes for the Marxians. Still, if this onesidedness is corrected, we may accept the influence of national characteristics as a part of the social "matter" which operates in conjunction with political form. It is baffling, though, that despotism seems limited to Asia and Africa (Russia, in this connection, counting more as a part of Asia than as a part of Europe). Various reasons could be given for this geographic limitation of a form of government, for which there is no parallel. We must, of course, shy away from any and all "racial" interpretations; Aristotle's view that the "barbarians" in question were "by nature slaves" is one of them. An oppressive climate, in most of these countries, however, seems to have contributed to the fatalism which is, or has been in the past, such a well-known characteristic of these peoples, although this explanation holds only partially so far as Russia is concerned. By the same token, of course, it might be said that Czarist Russia exhibited, even before the abolition of its "absolute" character in 1905, only a part of the characteristics of despotism.

All of these phenomena appear, however, in a different light if we accept Professor Wittfogel's well-documented theory of the "hydraulic society." [13] Wherever regular rainfall was lacking, but an adequate water supply could be secured by means of irrigation, cultural yields could be vastly increased. If this was done, the control over the necessary installations provided instruments of political power not otherwise available, and political opposition was bound to be reduced if it had to be attempted against those who controlled the people's livelihood. This explanation does not apply to all cases of despotism, but it covers most of them.

Whatever the reason, in the case of despotism the area of physical force at the top expanded because it encountered so little resistance from below. A government based more strongly upon the "consent of the governed" was out of the question as long as the dull apathy existed which is so characteristic of the conditions under discussion. For the modern reader, a popular book such as *Anna and the King of Siam* [13a] does much better in providing a general introduction into conditions so totally foreign to his experience than could a learned treatise, although Professor Wittfogel has shown us what can be done along those lines. Clearly the despot enjoys a much wider range of arbitrary power than the European monarchs did even if they were "absolute." The French monarchy might use *lettres de cachet* to silence actual or potential opponents (and to jail or exile people for a number of other, not necessarily political, reasons), but this process aroused opposition which set limits to its use. The Oriental despot would, in such cases, be more likely to avail himself of the services of the executioner. Such behavior was taken for granted as long as the ruler did not attempt any wholesale interference with the lives and the customs of his people, and as long as he was not manifestly incompetent,[14] and also if no major calamity arose, such as a famine, for which the despot would be held responsible.

Aristotle was right, however, in saying that, in spite of the substantial range of arbitrary actions available to the despot, the form of government itself was "legal and hereditary." What he meant to convey can, perhaps, be best understood by using the term "legitimate." Such a government differs from tyranny by being accepted as natural; it is not opposed by a substantial part of the population. Repression from above, for that reason, never did reach the proportions characteristic of tyranny. Still, Montesquieu could say that "The principle of despotic government is fear," to which a "timid, ignorant, and faint-spirited people" [15] rather readily submitted. Arbitrary action from above, always revolting to any high-minded person,[16] inevitably encourages arbitrary reaction from below, which it cannot altogether suppress. The government of Czarist Russia has been called by a French observer *absolutisme modéré par l'assassinat*—"absolutism moderated by assassination."

Such assassinations are always a possibility. They have led to little moderation in the daily affairs of the government; rather, they have been accepted as a necessary risk. This state of affairs leads to an atmosphere of its own. Thus Prince Bülow, German Chancellor from 1900–1909, relates in his memoirs an encounter which he had, in July 1914, with his successor, von Bethmann-Hollweg. Bülow asked whether there would be a general war. "No," Bethmann answered, it was inconceivable that Russia should come to the assistance of the "Serbian murderers"—the heir to the Austrian throne, and his wife, having been assassinated at Sarajevo under conditions which led both the Austrian and the German governments to assume the complicity of the Serbian government. Bülow then told the following story. The last French Ambassador in St. Petersburg before the War of 1812 was General Savary, Duke of Rovigo by the grace of Napoleon, of whom Bülow writes that: "In certain rather delicate circumstances he had managed to retain the Czar's confidence, thanks to his tact, good nature, and exceptional distinction of manner." When, in 1814, Czar Alexander entered Paris together with his victorious allies, he sent immediately for Savary, who, when asked which position he now held, answered "None." The Czar sent at once for a close friend of the French King to inform him that he was most anxious to see Savary in a position fitting his talents and his "noble character." The Frenchman shrugged his shoulders, and declared that this was impossible because Savary had been the president of the court martial which had condemned the Duke of Enghien to death, "the cousin of his Very Christian Majesty." The Czar was amazed, and exclaimed: "What! That is all? And I dine every night with Bennigsen and Oncharov, who strangled my father." [17]

If such occurrences are extreme, their possibility is characteristic of despotism. They seem so remote to us because there hardly exists any modern variety of this species; even the states in the southern half of the Arab peninsula, which were not so long ago thoroughly despotic, show a few signs of change. It is necessary, however, to emphasize the differences between despotism and tyranny. The latter arises in a totally different social setting and has characteristics which, in spite of all similarities, vary essentially from those of despotism. As it will be discussed later, tyranny is always the answer to a failure of democracy. Where, however, democratic government is even attempted, there is bound to be a much more widespread and active interest in the affairs of government than there is in the nations subjected to despotism. Tyranny must resort to wholesale use of force from the top because there is so much pressure from below.

We may, then, accept a substantial difference among the three major types of the "rule of one"—legitimate monarchy, despotism and tyranny. The term "legitimate" is used not in the sense of nineteenth century conservatives, such as the Austrian Chancellor Metternich, for whom it meant the continuation of the pre-revolutionary constitutional pattern, but in the sense of the Italian historian, Guglielmo Ferrero. [18] This means that the government rests upon the consent of the people to an extent sufficient to dispense with the need for a wholesale suppression of actual or potential opposition. The type of consent implied is, however, in the case of monarchy and aristocracy, passive rather than active; the existing government is accepted as a matter of course. Where, as in a democracy, the government rests on active consent, its actions are constantly and critically observed in order to decide whether a particular government is—within the framework of the same constitutional order—to be replaced by a new one or not. "Legitimate" rulership is, however, at least in the case of monarchy and aristocracy, based on a type of consent which is real enough to make it possible for the rulers to accept generally promulgated laws as "the rule of action," and this feature does make such governments "voluntary" in Plato's [19] sense.

In the case of monarchy, we must further distinguish between absolute and limited monarchy. The latter type is represented by the Constitution of the German and Austro-Hungarian empires before 1918. The Emperor, and the political classes connected with him, were flanked by a popularly elected parliament, which had the task of legislation. The executive was, however, the sole preserve of the monarch, who retained the right to appoint and dismiss the government. In a parliamentary monarchy of the British type, of course, the executive emanates from parliament, and parliamentary monarchy represents, for that reason, a special type of *democracy*. The substantial powers which the sovereign retains in a limited monarchy make the latter share in the more significant aspects of the general dynamics of one-man rule.

THE DYNAMICS OF PERSONAL POWER.

The first discussion of these dynamics is to be found in Herodotus, who makes Otanes, one of the Persians presented as discussing the various forms of government, express himself in these terms:

To me it seems advisable, that we should no longer have a single man rule over us—the rule of one is neither good nor pleasant. Ye cannot have forgotten to what lengths Cambyses went in his haughty tyranny, and the haughtiness of the Magi ye have yourselves experienced. How indeed it is possible that monarchy should be a well-adjusted thing, when it allows a man to do as he likes without being answerable? Such licence is enough to stir strange and unwonted thoughts in the heart of the worthiest of men. Give a person this power, and straightway his manifold good things puff him up with pride, while envy is so natural to human kind that it cannot but arise in him. But pride and envy together include all wickedness; both leading on to deeds of savage violence. True it is that kings, possessing as they do all that heart can desire, ought to be void of envy, but the contrary is seen in their conduct towards the citizens. They are jealous of the most virtuous among their subjects, and wish their death; while they take delight in the meanest and basest, being ever ready to listen to the tales of slanderers. A king, besides, is beyond all other men inconsistent with himself. Pay him court in moderation, and he is angry because you do not show him more profound respect—show him profound respect, and he is offended again, because (as he says) you fawn on him. But the worst of all is, that he sets aside the laws of the land, puts men to death without trial, and subjects women to violence.[20]

Evidently, Otanes fails to see the differences between the various types of one-man rule. He charges the absolute monarch, who may govern according to the laws (and customs) of the land, with all the excesses which history ascribes to despots and tyrants. We can, however, agree with Otanes in regard to his basic assumption: the one-man ruler finds himself in a situation which will induce him to act in a special manner. This "situation" represents the influence of political form.

The condition which confronts the one-man ruler arises for Otanes, in the first place, from the fact that he is "not answerable" or, as we would put it, not responsible to someone else for his actions. The consequences are stated in Lord Acton's famous saying: "Power tends to corrupt, and absolute power corrupts absolutely." [21] Men are subject to temptation. Power multiplies temptations, and the wielder of absolute power does not see himself confronted with any immediate check. Little wonder, then, if he is inclined to satisfy urges which the average person has learned to suppress.

Otanes means to make a second, and perhaps more important point. The one-man ruler is elevated high above the level of his fellowmen. No one is available to him for a genuine discussion among equals. We all stand in need of such discussion; unless there is someone who can tell us the unvarnished truth we may allow our imagination to carry us away from the realities of life. What psychologists call "the test of reality" is essentially linked to this possibility of a frank and free discussion among equals. It is difficult for the one-man ruler to achieve it. No one likes to hear unpleasant truths and the absolute ruler does not *have* to hear them. Those who come into contact with him are always tempted to tell him what he would like to hear. Records of this tendency to flatter absolute rulers are as old as recorded history. In some cases efforts were made to find a remedy for this evil; thus the court jester might be given the right to say anything he wanted, and he was used by others to say what they did not dare say. The artificial nature of such a device is the measure of its practical limitations. The same goes for attempts by certain monarchs to escape the dangers of flattery when they tried to mingle with their people incognito in order to ascertain their true feelings.

The mere fact, however, that such steps were taken, indicates that the tendencies resulting from the political form of one-man rule never have the field to themselves. As mentioned above, the effects of social forces and of free policy decisions go hand in hand with those of political form. In the case of one-man rule the impact of social forces has already been mentioned; it depends on them whether there develops absolute monarchy of the traditional type or Oriental despotism, the latter, in turn, being more favorable to the irrational effects of one-man rule. When we speak of "policy" we should, in this case, specify it to mean personality. It always depends on a man's character whether, and to what extent, he will yield to pressure of any kind. To clarify this point we might, for a moment, return to "pure democracy." Alexander Hamilton wrote:

> In all very numerous assemblies, of whatever character composed, passion never fails to wrest the scepter from reason. Had every Athenian citizen been a Socrates, every Athenian assembly would still have been a mob.[22]

Hamilton intended to say that the political form, as represented by the popular assembly was everything and character nothing. His mistake becomes obvious in the reference to Socrates who, after all, in 406 did assume the risk of braving the assembly in one of its ugliest moods. Had, in reality, "every Athenian been a Socrates" this particular assembly would *not* have been "a mob." The point, of course, is that men of the caliber of Socrates are exceptional; the average human being does succumb to crowd psychology, and he does so all the more easily because he is not aware of its existence.

PERSONAL POWER IN TOTALITARIAN RULE.

In the case of the one-man ruler only one person is directly involved. A great deal, then, depends on his character. Some will readily succumb to the impact of the situation in which they find themselves; others will put up a battle, even if they do not escape from it without scars. The institution as a whole must be judged by its long-run effects. Where, in particular, monarchy is hereditary, the chances are that a fair proportion of those who come to the throne will lack the special stamina needed to see the world as it is. This means that, to the extent that policy decisions are made by the ruler, their rationality is as much in jeopardy as is the rationality of decisions made by a popular assembly.

The recent history of totalitarian dictatorship indicates, however, that one-man-rule presents its problems even where it is not hereditary. Mussolini, Hitler and Stalin were, of course, subjected to the special influence of tyranny as well as to the general impact of one-man rule. Tyranny is permeated by the all-corroding influence of fear. No tyrant has ever been safe in his position,[23] and to counter actual, potential, or even imaginary opposition he has felt constrained to set up an elaborate apparatus of suppression. In a tyranny everyone is suspected by the man at the top, even his closest collaborators. Obviously, such an atmosphere renders discussion among equals especially difficult.

To consider a few examples of the totalitarian trinity of the recent past: Mussolini brought the strongest mental stamina to the task of resisting the situation in which he found himself. Flattery did not deceive him easily, and he maintained his contacts with the outer world with comparative success. Furthermore, while his was the strongest power center in Rome, it was not the only one. The monarchy continued to exist—relegated into the shadows, to be sure, but, as events were to demonstrate, it was ready to emerge from them whenever the opportunity presented itself. In the meantime, it formed the rallying point for the more conservative critics of Fascist policies. Nor must we overlook the existence of the Vatican, and the influence which it retained in combination with the Catholic Church in Italy, which fascism partly subdued and tried to subvert, but never controlled. That the open conflict between fascism and the Church, which took place in 1931, ended with a compromise, showed that with the Catholic Church Mussolini found himself in the presence of limitations of which he could never be entirely unaware. On at least one occasion, Pius XI used his opportunity to bring matters to Mussolini's attention about which he might not have been otherwise told in such straightforward terms. As Attalio Tamaro relates the incident:

> One day the Pope was engaged in conversation with the first Italian ambassador to the Holy See, de Vecchi, of whom he was rather fond. Suddenly, he interrupted the conversation and asked him whether he would be willing to transmit to Mussolini a personal message, even if this required personal courage. The ambassador agreed. Thereupon, Pius XI expressed himself as follows: "Tell Signor Mussolini that the deification of which he is the object does not please me and does harm to him. He must not place himself between heaven and earth in such a manner that his feet hardly remain on the ground any longer.

Please, in my name, make him reflect that there is only one God. Signor Mussolini, therefore, could be only a false god, an idol or a false prophet. Please induce him—in my name—to reflect that peoples at the end always despise their graven images. If he does not change, he, too, will take an evil end."

De Vecchi called on Mussolini and was received by him. The dictator listened to what the ambassador had to say, and asked him whether he had transmitted everything correctly and not added anything. Then (after having been assured that the ambassador had merely related the Pope's message), he answered: "Very well. Transmit my answer forthwith. Tell the Pope that he is right." An ironic smile was visible on the lips of Mussolini.[24]

It is impossible to say whether this conversation had any practical results. Certainly, the outward symptoms of the developments against which the Pope had tried to warn continued unabated, and with them presumably, their psychological effects. So far as important policy decisions are concerned, the negative influence of the situation in which Mussolini found himself can hardly be discounted in the case of the determination to enter the Second World War on Nazi Germany's side. Hitler, to be sure, did everything to dazzle Mussolini with the spectacle of Germany's armed might. But, if the *Duce* really had been the disciple of Machiavelli that he claimed to be, nothing that the *Fuehrer* told him or showed him could have caused him to yield. Machiavelli enunciated an obvious truth when he said that the little prince must never ally himself with a big one. If the alliance lost both would be lost, but if it won, the little prince would become the satellite of the big one. Therefore, rationality, as defined by his own mentor, should have compelled Mussolini to remain neutral, whatever the risk. There was, in June 1940, no lack of balanced and experienced men in Rome who endeavored to keep *Il Duce* from committing his fatal blunder; in addition to the court and the Vatican, American diplomatic pressure was exerted to the fullest. Mussolini made the final decision without subjecting it to serious discussion with anyone.

Hitler is the one in the recent crop of totalitarian dictators who offered the least personal resistance to the deceptive effects of both absolute and tyrannical rule. He wanted, and apparently needed, flattery in large doses. It soon became a matter of general knowledge that he had no liking for unfavorable news, and those who reported to him endeavored to color their information to please him. The peak of the mood of unreality which was the consequence was reached during the last weeks of his life when he was holding out in the bunker of his chancellory in Berlin, with Russian shells exploding overhead. For days he expected relief from armies which had long since ceased to exist.[25] What happened in these climactic hours represented, however, only the culmination of a long sequence of events. An interesting fact was brought to light when, after the collapse of the Third *Reich,* Allied investigators came to read the reports in which Hitler's advisers seemed to have incriminated themselves, coloring their information in such a manner that they appeared to be trying to encourage Hitler in his evil ways. When questioned, these men attempted to exculpate themselves by stating that reports made to Hitler were always made for a purpose and, therefore, discounted by everyone "in the know." The investigators asked how they were supposed to ascertain what represented a man's real opinion and what was merely manufactured for Hitler's consumption. The answer was that whatever was intended for Hitler's eyes was typed in large characters. He needed glasses to read, and it seemed improper for *Der Fuehrer* to acknowledge such a human weakness.

Stalin differed significantly from both Hitler and Mussolini. He was not a schizophrenic like Hitler, and his general mental makeup predestined him for rationality to a much greater extent than his German counterpart. There is nothing in his record which could be compared to Hitler's putting to death millions of people for no other reason than that they happened to be of Jewish ancestry; this was done during the war years when they could have been made to serve his purposes in urgently needed work, just as other unwilling millions were made to do. This particular type of insanity is not to be encountered in Stalin's case, not at least in the pre-war period.

Stalin's record immediately before, and during the war is something else again. According to Khrushchev [26] he did not believe in the imminence of Hitler's attack simply because he did not want to believe it. In this respect, at least, he had managed to shield himself from reality,[27] and Russian military and diplomatic sources found it difficult to transmit to him the information which they possessed. In Khrushchev's words: "Because the leadership was conditioned against such information, such data was dispatched with fear and assessed with reservation." [28] As a result, necessary defense measures were not taken.

Nor did Stalin's military leadership escape the charge of irrationality. Until Khrushchev's speech became known, there had existed in the Western countries a widespread view that Stalin was, during the war, in constant telephonic communication with his generals at the front, and that his final decisions tended to constitute the consensus of expert opinion. As Isaac Deutscher [29] put it: "His role seems to have been that of the cool, detached and experienced arbiter of his own generals."

Khrushchev presents us with a different picture. According to him Stalin, after the outbreak of hostilities, fell victim to "nervousness and hysteria." [30] He was "very far from an understanding of the real situation which was developing at the front." [31] On one occasion, Khrushchev claims that he tried insistently to warn Stalin against continuing a military operation which was bound to fail and which, when Stalin— who would not answer the telephone personally—persisted in having it continued, did cost "hundreds of thousands of our soldiers." [32]

If this interpretation is correct, there were, indeed, striking similarities between Hitler's and Stalin's conduct of the war. That Stalin's mistakes, compounded by the effects which the slaughter of large numbers of competent and loyal officers in the years before the war were bound to produce,[33] did not lead to defeat, is in good part to be credited to geography, the large size of the country, and the severity of the Russian winter which presented Hitler with difficulties akin to those encountered by Napoleon. Besides, of course, lend-lease enabled Stalin to replace much of the equipment which his mistakes had caused to be lost in the early part of the war, and provided him with types of weapons which the German generals did not expect to face.

The field in which the irrationality of Stalin's acts is most obvious is, however, in that of domestic politics, in particular the great purges. A totalitarian ruler, to be sure, must use a heavy hand, and his followers as well as his enemies have to know that his will is the law. Still, only a feeling of panic can explain the way in which Stalin sacrificed hundreds of thousands of lives in situations where a Mussolini would simply have shuffled his supporters around, promoting some and demoting others. Nor can the odium which Stalin imposed upon Communist rule through some of the pre-war anti-religious campaigns be explained rationally; in this case as in others less radical means would have given him all he really wanted. The same applies to the treatment of certain nationality groups which amounts to genocide.

Many of these drawbacks were overcompensated by the fact that the effects of tyrannical one-man rule were so much greater on the other side of the front. Even old and reliable Nazis, such as Rosenberg, might warn Hitler that he must not treat the Russians quite as much as "racial inferiors" as he did; others might emphasize the desirability of restoring their land to the Russian farmers. Utter blindness prevented Hitler from capitalizing on the wholesale disaffection which existed both in the Russian army and among the Russian people during the first months of the war. Clearly, Stalin was saved from the results of his own irrationality by someone whose irrationality exceeded his own.

It is quite possible that definite symptoms of Caesaromania developed during the last years of Stalin's life, and that, as Khrushchev declared,[34] had he lived a little longer, measures of wanton severity against his closest collaborators might once again have been taken on a large scale. Some rather serious observers, not inclined to accept mere rumor for fact, consider it possible that the anticipation of such a possibility caused some of the top men in the party to assassinate him.[35]

WILLIAM II AND PERSONAL POWER.

It is now time that we leave the totalitarian rulers of the immediate past. We enter a totally different atmosphere if we go back far enough in history to come to William II, the famous "Kaiser" of World War I days. The German Empire was proud of being a *Rechtsstaat*. The rule of the law did prevail, and impartial courts enforced it. In the *Reichstag* matters of policy could always be freely debated, although it must be repeated that this could be done only after crucial and irreversible decisions had been taken.

The Emperor, then, and the government appointed by him, retained a substantial margin for discretionary decisions, particularly in the field of foreign affairs.[36] The situation is best characterized by an edict of William I, in which Bismarck caused the latter to say:

> It is My determination that in Prussia no less than in the legislative bodies of My realm there shall be no question of the constitutional right possessed by Me and My successors to the personal direction of the policy of My Government, and that no colour shall be given to the opposite opinion, which holds that the . . . inviolability of the King's person, or the counter-signature required by My Royal Ordinances, has any bearing upon the independent nature of the Royal decisions.[37]

In the Prussian parliament Bismarck commented on his edict as follows:

> If the Emperor has a Chancellor who feels unable to countersign whatever represents the Imperial policy, he can dismiss him any day. The Emperor has a much freer hand than the Chancellor, who is dependent on the Imperial will, and can take no step without the Imperial sanction . . . In this place I can put forth no expression of opinion in which I do not know the Emperor to agree, and for which I have not his authority . . . In the Constitution, the Minister is merely an almost negligible stop-gap.[38]

This was not, and was not meant to be, absolute rule but it implied a substantial amount of what the French called *pouvoir personnel*—"personal power."

It is necessary to discuss in some detail the results of this "personal power," as demonstrated by William II. In the first place, they constitute one of the clearest demonstrations of what the lack of the proper "test of reality" can come to mean in political life. In addition, these events had an important bearing on the turn which the affairs of mankind took with the outbreak of the First World War. Until then, there had been every indication of a gradual, but irreversible, progress toward civilization which, to an increasing extent, was also a progress towards democracy. In the wake of the First World War these tendencies were decisively weakened and, in certain ways, reversed. Tyranny, to which the major countries of the Western world seemed to have developed an immunity, arose in the aggravated form of the totalitarian one-party state, first in Russia and subsequently in Italy and Germany. Thus, a chain of events was initiated which the best efforts of the (comparatively few) farsighted men whom this period produced were not able to break. The effects of political form were crucial both in starting this chain, and in adding to it some of its strongest links. They begin with William II and the policies which he, or underlings chosen by him, initiated, the mere possibility of which a modicum of rationality would have excluded, even if other factors developed later and made it impossible for the effects of the original mistakes to be brought under control.

To avoid misunderstandings, it must be emphasized that the personality of Germany's last Emperor was as important as were the results of "personal power"; had these personality defects not existed, political form could not have produced the effects that it did—just as these personality defects, without the effects of political form, would not have sufficed to bring about the results from which the world has suffered ever since. To evaluate William's particular, and peculiar, traits we need not resort to Sigmund Freud; his own father, who was dying of cancer of the throat, and was to reign for only 100 days in 1888, has given us a clear enough estimate of what Germany, and the world, was soon to be confronted with. Bismarck, who relates the story in the first pages of the third volume of his memoirs, had made observations of his own, as a result of which he deemed it imperative that William be removed from the exclusive company of the officers of his regiment in Potsdam, and he shifted to a civilian task. The Chancellor failed in this effort, but he was glad when the Prince himself requested that documents on foreign affairs be made available to him. Bismarck, in fact, secured the fulfillment of this wish over the objections of Frederic, who wrote to Bismarck, on September 28, 1886, less than two years before William was to ascend the throne: "In view of the lack of maturity and of experience of my oldest son, connected with his tendency to overbearing and exaggeration, I consider it definitely dangerous to bring him in contact with foreign affairs at this time."

There is, of course, a remedy for such personality defects. When the letters of William's grandmother, Queen Victoria, were published,[39] they showed a remarkable resemblance between grandparent and grandchild in personal characteristics, such as the tendency to scribble marginal notes on documents, at times in unprintable language. In England, the institution of parliamentary government took care of the situation; in the last resort all significant decisions were made by the Prime Minister and the cabinet rather than by the Queen. In this process, the Queen might exert considerable influence,[40] but she had no real power of her own. In Germany the situation was reversed; the power was the monarch's, and his advisers were limited to mere influence. This influence might still represent the actual power of decision, as it often did in Bismarck's case. It is significant that, in fact, the Chancellor could express himself about William I in rather critical terms. Carl Schurz reports that the monarch was aware of this criticism and merely chuckled when it was mentioned to him.[41] William II, however, was extremely sensitive to criticism, and he intended to be "his own Chancellor." As Bismarck was to formulate it:

> Emperor William II does not feel the need to have collaborators with opinions of their own, who, in the fields involved, could confront him with the authority of life and experience.[42]

Bismarck added:

> The Emperor prefers second-rate men as ministers, and the situation is insofar not the correct one, as the ministers do not provide the monarch with council and suggestions, but expect and receive both from His Majesty.[43]

William II, appearing as a magnificent figure to those who were overawed by the splendor of the German Empire,[44] was recognized as an erratic amateur by those close enough to him to know the truth. As Professor M. J. Bonn, who was well acquainted with the German political life of the period, at one time put it in conversation with this writer: "*Was der Kaiser, tat war kein Regieren sodern ein Hineinregieren*"—"What the Emperor did was not to govern but to meddle with the government." This indiscriminate meddling was possible because William selected those who occupied the more important positions in the country; he chose men willing to accept his constant interference.

Inevitably, the Emperor's actions were based on information in which flattery had its part. William asked for it; one of the many slogans in the coining of which he was so proficient, was "*Schwarzseher dulde ich nicht*"—"I do not tolerate people who see black." The most telling testimony for this tendency dates from the First World War. Thus, Grand Admiral von Tirpitz writes:

> And here we are, landed in a desperate war; and . . . yet they all keep a furtive eye on the Emperor, who is surrounded by triflers . . . The Emperor sat there, filled up with news of victories—nothing else may be conveyed to him; and they talk, among other things, of "a gigantic upheaval in India," whereupon everyone sings Hosanna . . . It may be that he purposely deceives himself.[45]

Emil Ludwig, from whom this quotation is taken (and who gives several others which are equally telling), follows it with a similar one from Count Stürgkh, the liaison officer of the Austrian Chief of Staff with the German High Command, and a frequent guest of the Emperor's:

"To keep up this mood, he [the Emperor] was told innumerable stories of the trenches, in which the German soldier always appeared in the best light towards the enemy. . . . When he visited the troops, care was taken that he got only the most favourable impressions." [46]

This is not the place to trace the cases in which German policy was influenced by a man elevated so high that no one could, if necessary, *force* him to listen to the truth. Certainly, a sense of reality had no part in the abrupt change in German foreign policy which followed Bismarck's dismissal. The "Iron Chancellor" had accomplished much, but he was keenly aware of the limitations of German power. He felt that, while the enmity of France must be taken for granted, everything had to be done to safeguard Germany against le cauchemar des coalitions—"the nightmare of coalitions"—of a simultaneous attack by several major powers, in particular France and Russia. The "reinsurance treaty" with Russia served that purpose; it provided that if either partner were attacked the other would assume an attitude of friendly neutrality. William allowed the treaty to lapse after Bismarck's dismissal, and the alliance between France and Russia followed in 1894. Bismarck had kept on good terms with England by refusing to challenge the maritime supremacy so vital to the island realm. William reversed gears completely; Germany embarked on the construction of a large navy of her own. The Emperor personally aggravated the situation by violating British sensitivities on more than one occasion—and in 1904 England and France, "hereditary enemies" for centuries, reached an agreement. German "encirclement" was all but completed, but too many Germans overlooked that a German foreign policy based upon a sense of reality would have excluded the very possibility of such a result.

William's erratic actions, then, did much to bring about the constellation of powers which made the First World War possible. When, during the crisis of July 1914, the existence of this constellation should have been the primary consideration of German policy, impelling it to explore every avenue leading to a peaceful solution, William, his dynastic feelings outraged by the assassination of the heir to the Austrian throne, at first made matters worse by egging his Austrian allies on to war against Serbia. When, at last, he saw the text of the Serbian reply to the Austrian ultimatum, he immediately reached the conclusion that a war between Austria and Serbia was no longer justified, but it was too late. By that time the Russian Czar had been forced by the Russian nationalists and militarists into ordering complete mobilization against Germany as well as against Austria; this led to the German ultimatum, and the beginning of the World War.

As long as mere rationality is our criterion, much could be said about William's influence on the military conduct of the war during its first phase. It culminated in the so-called "Battle of the Marne" which was no "battle" but a German withdrawal. William, and his protégé and Chief of Staff, the younger von Moltke, had first, led astray by over-optimistic reports, decisively weakened the German armies advancing on Paris, and then allowed a 29-year old lieutenant colonel to go to the front and to order, in the name of his chief, a withdrawl at a time when the men in the field would have preferred to continue a struggle in which they enjoyed the advantage of the initiative. William's influence on military decisions subsided when von Moltke was succeeded by von Falkenhayn; he was completely pushed aside when von Hindenburg and Ludendorff took over. The Emperor remained, however, the key to the diplomatic conduct of the war.[47] In that field, suffice it to mention just one example for his reluctance to face facts; it is particularly impressive because it comes from as strange a source as von Papen, so well known in this country through his exploits as German military attaché in Washington, and so little suspected of any anti-monarchical feelings. Von Papen claims that when he returned to Germany he was thoroughly convinced that the resumption of unlimited submarine warfare would lead to America's entering the war and to the defeat of the Central Powers. He reports that the Chief of Staff of the period, von Falkenhayn, listened to him sympathetically, and von Bethmann-Hollweg, the Chancellor, even more so; the latter had reached the conclusion that the war had to be terminated as early as it could be done on reasonable terms. In the final resort, all depended again on the Emperor. William did, at last, receive von Papen, with whom he had had a cordial conversation prior to his leaving for the United States in 1913. Papen expected the Emperor to be keenly interested in the changes which had taken place since that time, but he had to report:

> My disappointment was all the greater when the Emperor, after a brief salutation, gave me a lecture himself about developments over there, which I could interrupt only in rare moments with brief remarks. It was his opinion that all the pressure of the Allies would not succeed in bringing the United States into the war: "You can be certain, the American people and their Congress will never permit themselves to be driven into a war against us!" [48]

William, then, pushed reality away whenever an attempt was made to bring it close to him. His case, to repeat it, was extreme, and it has frequently been claimed that the German environment, as well as his own personality, provided ideal conditions for the tendencies of one-man rule with which we are dealing. These tendencies are, however, universal; example after example could be quoted, from country after country, and covering widely differing periods of history, to make the point. The problem was well enough known for Machiavelli to take an interest in it. In Chapter 23 of *The Prince* [49] he discusses "how flatterers must be shunned," and he begins by saying that succumbing to flattery is "a mistake which princes can with difficulty avoid." They face the dilemma that "there is no other way of guarding oneself against flattery than by letting men understand that they will not offend you by speaking the truth; but when everyone can tell you the truth you lose their respect." Machiavelli recommends a third course: the Prince is to select certain wise men who are to tell him the truth, whereas a free expression of opinion by others is not tolerated. That, of course, is a difficult rule to follow, and Machiavelli rightly concludes: "It is an infallible rule that a prince who is not wise himself cannot be well advised, unless by chance he leaves himself entirely in the hands of the one man who rules him in everything, and happens to be a very prudent man." Even accepting this last solution [50] presupposes, of course, certain qualifications which not every ruler possesses, and in which William II certainly was deficient. When such men come to the throne they are not likely to resort to any course of action which might provide for their salvation. A few men may, under such conditions, still speak their minds. There were such men in Germany and the writings of two of them, in particular, were impressive. Professor Quidde wrote his *Caligula*,[51] and, with somewhat greater chances of success, a conservative, Count Ernst Reventlow, wrote his *Kaiser Wilhelm II und die Byzantiner* [52]—"Emperor William II and the Byzantines." Where Quidde, a man of known liberal convictions, had had to content himself with writing ostensibly only about Caligula, leaving it to the reader to draw his own conclusions about the contemporary scene, Count Reventlow fully and frankly discussed the situation in Germany as it developed under William II. The result was, however, utter futility, just as it was in the case of sensational writers, such as the journalist Maximilian Harden, who relentlessly exposed certain abuses which had developed at the court.

What we are concerned with is, in fact, what Nikita Khrushchev called "the cult of the individual." Men placed into the kind of position held by Stalin and, to an extent so surprisingly similar in the face of all institutional and national differences, William II,[53] simply have no remedy for the personality defects which they may bring into their exalted station. They are surrounded by flatterers. To quote St. Thomas: "For, as Augustine says, it is very difficult for rulers 'not to be puffed up amid flattering and honouring tongues and the obsequiousness of those who bow too humbly, but to remember that they are men.' " [54]

If such flattery is inevitable, so are its effects on not a few men. As Khrushchev said about Stalin: "Such a man supposedly knows everything, sees everything, thinks for everyone, can do anything, is infallible in his behaviour." [55] The very fact that rulers are surrounded by people who tell them such things tends to nullify responsible criticism. He who encounters so many flatterers (even if he is oblivious of the fact that he has something to do with the selection of those whom he encounters) is bound to form a low opinion of his fellow-men, which, in turn, will make him less inclined to permit any free and frank discussion of his policies by people willing to provide it.

It is, of course, a long road from Stalin to William II, and it must be repeated that examples like those represented by William II are extreme; it does indeed, take a William II for them to occur. Still, what we must emphasize is that the tendency is created by the institution. There applies to such a case what Thomas Paine said in a somewhat different connection: ". . . instead of seeking to reform the individual the wisdom of a nation should apply itself to reform the system." [56] The

Germans might have mitigated the situation when, in November 1908, the Emperor considered, as a result of the disastrous *Daily Telegraph* [57] interview, the possibility of his abdication. They could have remedied the evil for good only if they had forced the adoption of the parliamentary system, which would have taken care of any future William II as well as the one they were confronted with at the time. Bismarck, in the final years of his life, did not seem too far removed from that view, when he wrote: "In forty years I have seen many parliaments come and go, and I have regarded them as less damaging for our overall development than the errors of a monarch might become . . ." [58] Before him the Italian Bismarck, Camillo Cavour, when told that his task might have been simpler had he not been constantly harassed by parliament, answered:

> You forget that under an absolutist government I would not have wanted to be a minister, and in addition I could not have become one. I am what I am because I have the opportunity of being a constitutional minister . . . Parliamentary government has its inconveniences, as other governments do, but it is still the best. I may get impatient with certain types of opposition and may reject them spiritedly; but, when I think it over, I congratulate myself that I have to combat them, because they force me to explain my ideas better, and to double my efforts to convince public opinion. An absolutist minister commands; a constitutional minister has to persuade in order to be obeyed. Believe me, the worst chamber is still preferable to the best anti-chamber. [59]

The above remarks will have served their purpose if they have demonstrated that the value of monarchy depends not alone on the personal qualities of the monarch. It will not do to say that if the ruler is wise and prudent the monarchy will successfully serve the common good. There are tendencies inherent in the institution which represent a danger to even the best of men, and which constitute a trap for the weaker ones. In the course of time there will be some of the latter, and if they come to power under conditions as crucial as those which confronted William II, the result may be fatal. This does not mean that there were not periods of history during which the balance of the pros and cons tipped the scales in favor of monarchy. Under modern conditions, however, which have limited so drastically the usefulness of kings who "rule" as well as "reign," the negative implications of the institution should be considered carefully—although there are few cases left where there exists a free choice which could be resolved in favor of a type of monarchy in which the sovereign has real "power." Meanwhile, there remains the task of writing and, if necessary, rewriting history with the proper regard for the effects of an institution such as "personal power." The historian may be reluctant to do so because these effects of an institution cannot be "documented"; they must be ascertained in a process of abstract analysis. They are nonetheless real, and if we are ever to profit by the lessons of history we must be able to depend upon the proper diagnosis of historical reality.

Chapter V

LEGITIMATE RULERSHIP
IN HISTORY:

*its conflict with the requirements
of modern society*

~~~~~~

URBAN ARISTOCRACIES.

Government by rulership, no less than government by leadership, has presented different problems in different periods of history. The only way to do it justice would be to discuss its variations in their historical setting. To do so extensively would require a substantial volume of its own. This chapter will be limited to discussing some of the major historical problems of the two stable versions of government by rulership, monarchy and aristocracy. Both have substantial historical achievements to their credit; still, the question to which most of this chapter will be devoted is whether, confronted with the realities of modern society, they could display the strength which they have displayed in the past.[1]

Little has to be said about aristocracy. While, in reality, it never constituted the rule of the best which the name postulates, it has provided a highly successful type of city government, flourishing, in not a few cases, for centuries. The best-known examples are those of merchant aristocracies, in particular in cities connected with maritime trade. In Germany all the members of the Hanseatic League were ruled by such merchant aristocracies; in 1417 the League's Diet passed a resolution forbidding the member cities to allow their councils to be elected by the citizens. The League itself reached the peak of its strength in the fourteenth century and began to decline in the fifteenth; most of the ninety cities which belonged to it at one time became subject to territorial princes. Hamburg, Bremen, and Lübeck, however, retained their independence long enough to join, in 1871, Bismarck's empire as independent entities—the only republics in a country in which the monarchic principle was strongly entrenched.

Among the aristocratic cities of Italy, Venice rose to a splendor unknown to any other city or combination of cities. It grew out of a combination of little island republics, which were governed by elected tribunes. In 697 a union of these independent towns was established, and a *Doge* became their head. As in other aristocratic cities, the wealthy merchants who set the tone wanted neither a monarchy nor a democracy. More and more power came gradually into their hands; about 1172 the Great Council, composed of 480 magnates, was substituted for the popular assembly. In 1223 there appeared the Senate, consisting of all officials and 120 members of the Great Council. The Senate was the main organ of legislation; its deliberations were governed by elaborate rules of procedure, which gave great weight to expert knowledge. The *Doge* had a cabinet consisting of 26 department heads, but in 1178 a "Little Council" of six was established for the dual purpose of watching him and of constituting an "inner cabinet" capable of rapid action. In 1296 the Great Council was definitely closed to the people; in the end the election of all officers was limited to the 450 families whose names were entered into the Golden Book. In 1310 the above-mentioned "Council of Ten" was created. First intended to act as a check against any attempt to set up a monarchy, it also became a substitute for the Senate, able to take its place in emergencies.—The Republic of Venice lasted over a thousand years; its Constitution provided for the proper balance between executive authority and legislative supervision, and did, therefore, lead to real stability. The city retained its independence until, in 1796, it was conquered by Napoleon.

The fact that, in this case as in others, merchant oligarchies were able to last has something to do with their nature. The members of the ruling group were not just businessmen in the modern sense of the term; they were frequently, and often deservedly, called "royal merchants." One of the reasons why they found it easy to dominate the cities in which they lived was the ownership of ships which, at that time, gave them military as well as economic power. They were not inclined to use either shortsightedly; they knew how to take the long-run view of their own interests. Nor did they have either the reasons, or the opportunity, for exploiting people dependent upon them the way England's landed aristocracy exploited the peasants when it virtually expropriated them. Seafaring merchants had to employ people, but also to keep working with them under conditions demanding their constant loyalty. Furthermore, the biological vitality of the aristocratic ruling class was promoted by the large size of their families, which made possible a substantial degree of natural selection in the recruitment of the future rulers. There were, not infrequently, a dozen or so children in one family, more of whom in wealthy families than in others had a chance to survive the high rate of infant mortality so characteristic of the time. If ten children reached maturity and five of them were sons, one of them was likely to have the qualifications needed to carry on actively the traditions of the family. The training of the young was begun early, and took place under a system of rigid discipline; a sense of *noblesse oblige* was imparted to them as much as a knowledge of the business which they had to pursue. These factors go far to explain the success of the oligarchic principle in cities. A city like Venice might, of course, annex and dominate much of the neighboring, and even some distant, territories; still, for the reasons mentioned above, the aristocratic principle could not be extended successfully to rural areas.

MONARCHY IN HISTORY.

Monarchy represents the successful application to large areas of the principle of government by rulership. In the Western world, monarchy first confronts us in the form of the heroic monarchy, as described in the *Iliad* and the *Odyssey*. The King was, in this case as in others, the supreme commander in war; he was also the high priest and the highest judge. This combination of religious and political tasks made royalty semi-religious; kings were "sacred" early in history. The monarchs whom we encounter in the *Iliad* were, of course, not absolute rulers. The nobility was closely associated with them, and the assembly of the warriors represented the popular element. In fact, even the lowliest warrior was able to address this meeting, although the treatment of Thersites by Odysseus in the *Iliad* shows that if a commoner did not hold to what was considered his proper place, a member of the aristocracy might step in and correct him.

In the *Odyssey* we notice a receding of the royal influence; the noblemen behaved as if they were the sole masters of the realm. Obviously, in times of peace the King lost much of the importance which he derived from his position as the commander of the army. Furthermore, as city life developed the prestige of monarchy was bound to suffer. It is difficult for a man to claim descent from the gods when daily contacts with the people show him to be an ordinary mortal. Besides, the complications of city life led to the rise of additional magistrates, a certain division of labor becoming necessary in the government. As specialized officials arose, they took away more and more of the King's power. Ultimately, the King was dispossessed by the nobles; the latter, several centuries later, had to accept gradual transition to democracy.

In the trend of Western history monarchy becomes significant again when we encounter the Germanic tribes. Their type of monarchy exhibited many of the features characteristic of heroic monarchy in Greece. Most Germanic tribes were republican, even if the differences between the "princes" of the republics and the "kings" of the monarchies was not great. If we may follow Tacitus,[2] such monarchy as there was was elective. This election was limited to the members of certain families, but still it was an election, and the active consent of the leading men of the tribe was apparently needed as much for the selection of the King as for his actual rule. The elective feature was to become permanent for the German kingship, while it soon became shadowy in France.

The subsequent history of monarchy developed in three distinct phases, that of feudal monarchy, estates monarchy, and feudal-bureaucratic monarchy. The needs for political organization on the basis of feudalism arose from the difficulties of communication, and from the barter economy characteristic of the time. Roads never reached the condition in which they had been maintained during the Roman Empire; no system of communication comparable to that of the Incas in Peru, who sent messages by relay runners, was ever developed in the Western world. It was natural, therefore, for the King to entrust the administration of a certain area to one of his liege-men. The latter was the King's appointee and was to carry out the government in the name of the King. Still, royal control was rather remote. In the end, most of these men succeeded in making their offices hereditary. The Normans might, in the comparatively small area of England, use feudalism as a means of a—comparatively—centralized government, as Charlemagne had done before in his much larger realm. Those were exceptions, however, rather than the rule; ordinarily the King's vassals governed their own areas largely to suit themselves.

Economic and social changes were slow during the Middle Ages, but they were never absent. Still, Werner Sombart[3] assigns the beginning of modern capitalism only to the sixteenth century. Even before this economic change took place there were not insignificant changes in the social structure. A higher degree of centralized government became necessary than the old feudal system could provide. Princes all over Europe realized both the need for a more effective government and the necessity of enlisting the voluntary aid of their vassals to bring it about: they began to summon parliaments. These were not yet the antagonists of the royal power, but constituted devices employed by its holders to accomplish its purposes. The members of the Estates parliaments at first resigned themselves reluctantly to the request for meeting in one place and for sanctioning measures, in particular taxes, applying to the entire country. They would, for the most part, have preferred to be left alone in the enjoyment of their separate rights.[4] They were particularly reluctant to accept majority decisions.

It did not take long, of course, before the assembled Estates realized that they could wield considerable power and secure otherwise unobtainable concessions from the prince. In this process, they did manage to set limits to arbitrary decisions of the ruler, and never neglected the opportunity to secure economic advantages for themselves. Still, with all their accomplishments these parliaments exhibited the fundamental weakness of all aristocratic gatherings: they knew how to limit the existing executive, but it was to take centuries before they learned how to replace it. Meanwhile, whenever these parliaments were able to assert themselves as much as they wished, they invariably weakened executive power so much as to promote near-anarchy. For this reason, more often than not, power simply slipped out of their hands without there being any need for a prince to take violent measures against them.

With the establishment of the modern state feudalism gave way to the feudal-bureaucratic monarchy. Once gunpowder had been invented and mercenary armies developed on a large scale the King's dependence upon his vassals had been weakened decisively. Where in the past it had been necessary to lay siege to any castle in which a nobleman offered resistance (a process which might require months), cannons could now, in short order, breach any wall, be it that of a castle or a city. At the same time, the King, thanks to the rising money economy, found it easier to finance the salaries of his military and civilian employees. Men whose economic fate he controlled he could, of course, engage and dismiss at will.

The transition to the modern state was gradual; the name "feudal-bureaucratic monarchy" indicates that it took the form of a compromise. The nobility eventually came to find it practical to abandon its resistance to centralized royal government. The monarch, in turn, realized the advantages of making the nobility a partner in his rule. The social ties connecting him with the aristocracy made for mutual understanding and adjustment. As mentioned above, the symbolic functions of monarchy could be shared more easily with a nobility of old standing than with officials recruited from the outside, or the representatives of the new wealth. Therefore, monarchy, nobility, bureaucracy and army were, for centuries, to constitute a united and effective political class.

Still, the same economic forces which had made the more centralized state possible eventually operated in opposition to feudal-bureaucratic rule. The economic position of the ruling class was undermined, slowly at first, but to an ever-larger extent later and, in the end, the political "superstructure" had to give way.

MODERN SOCIETY VERSUS MONARCHY.

In making this point, we are not taking a leaf from the Marxian book although there is, of course, no reason not to agree with Marx where he has the facts on his side. The classical statement for what we have to say is, in fact, contained in Sieyès: "What is the Third Estate?" His views could be summarized by saying that when a condition is reached where the old political class represents only a fraction of the total economic and intellectual potential of a country, but still tries to monopolize political power, the disproportion is too great to be tolerable in the long run.

Before we take up the change in the social position of the old political class, it will be well to recall, however, that economic change also had its effects so far as the direct needs, particularly the financial requirements, of the government are concerned. This is the point with which both the British and the French monarchies ran into the difficulties which led to their undoing. In England, James I had managed to have his own way, but his successor paid for the conflict with his head as well as with his crown. When the monarchy was restored this had to be done in the form of a compromise; parliament was willing to vote the necessary appropriations but only at the price of a considerably enhanced power of its own, which was eventually to lead to cabinet government, out of which, in turn, democracy grew by natural and organic steps. In France Louis XVI found himself saddled with debts which he could no longer master by traditional means. It became necessary to levy direct taxes upon the clergy and the nobility. Their shortsighted resistance to this long overdue step led to the convocation of the Estates General of 1789, the Revolution and the end of the monarchy.

With the fall of Napoleon the House of Bourbon won, in appearance, a complete victory. It was forced to leave the field a decade and a half later, to be followed by Louis Philippe who, between 1830 and 1848 tried to give the country a modernized version of monarchy. Further east, and on the Iberian peninsula, the principle of monarchy remained a potent political force well into the twentieth century. Still, it encountered increasing pressures which led first to its transformation and then to its termination.

The factors which made for the basic change in the social position of the old political class as a whole, and its head, the monarch, in particular, can be listed briefly. So far as the position of the King rested on economic strength, this had its origin in non-economic sources; to use Werner Sombart's term, it was *Machtreichtum*— "wealth derived from power." This wealth was nonetheless real, and greatly served to enhance the prince's political position. For centuries there was no distinction between the ruler's personal possessions and those of the state; more or less all public revenue was available to bolster the King's personal purse. As time progressed, however, the opposite happened; when the modern state developed, the financial needs of the government rose faster than the income from which they were traditionally met. The King found it increasingly necessary to use his personal means for the purposes of government. This not only left him with less money for himself but reduced his ability to reward his supporters with land or pensions. In this respect, the Reformation had been a last great windfall for the princes, enabling them to appropriate the possessions of the Church. This development had much to do with the growth of personal power in England as well as in Continental Europe, but only where absolutism could be formally established was it possible to solve the King's financial worries and this rule also had its exceptions. Even in France the King could find himself under enough of a financial strain to make him willing to engage in questionable financial activities. Thus, Louis XV had a share in the so-called "pact of famine," a company which acquired a monopoly of the grain supply, using it to exact extortionate prices in periods of shortage. To take a rather recent, but no less significant example: When King Farouk of Egypt was deposed, his enemies accused him of having been a beneficiary of certain transactions by which the Egyptian army was provided with inferior weapons and supplies during the war against Israel. In the seventeenth and eighteenth centuries public opinion might hold the individual monarch to account for such transactions without questioning the institution itself; in the twentieth century Naguib and Nasser had no difficulty using them to rally popular support for the proclamation of the republic.

Another point: As long as the financial resources of monarchy remained adequate, royal and princely courts were the centers of culture. They attracted poets, sculptors, painters and musicians; the art produced by these men served the purposes of monarchist propaganda effectively. The development of modern economic life not only limited the resources of the ruler available for such purposes but brought about a disproportionate rise in the income of those standing outside the ruling class. The merchants and manufacturers of the industrial age might not always be discerning patrons of the arts, but they did have financial resources which overshadowed those of King and nobility. Besides, to the extent that the government continued to patronize the arts, this was done by the agencies of a rather abstract and anonymous state. When a "royal" museum bought a painting, the result was no longer what it had been when the artist was commissioned by the King himself and paid from the latter's private purse.

Art itself changed under the impact of the new social forces. A painting by Michelangelo could not but enhance the prestige of the prince who had ordered it, admired by connoisseur and people alike, but when King Edward VIII bought a drawing by Toulouse-Lautrec the best he could hope for was acceptance by a limited group. By the same token the music of a Brahms or Beethoven would fit in as naturally with the splendor, and the prestige, of a court whereas the music of a modern composer might succeed in doing nothing but to create controversy wherever it is performed. Even more abrupt changes took place when the legitimate theater, again so well suited to the life of a court, found itself all but submerged by movies and television, the offerings of which were governed by the tastes of the multitude.

Science always had a rather "bourgeois" character even if, as during the early twentieth century, the monarchs of Prussia and Germany succeeded in dazzling scholars with the splendor of their reign, and in making devoted servants of most of them, and servile flatterers of a few. Such developments were exceptional, however, and the social sciences, in particular, were producing results critical of the principles of government by rulership.

The cities in which princes resided during the Middle Ages, and in the first centuries thereafter, found in the court their economic as well as their cultural center. Their population was comparatively small, and they tended to take pride in the court and monarchy. To this day some of these towns in Germany (the country which for so long had so many more princes than any other) retain the charm which princely rule bestowed upon them. Large cities such as Paris, London and Berlin never managed to fit into the atmosphere of monarchy. The multitudes of their inhabitants might become as critical of hereditary authority as were the citizens of the ancient Greek city-state. In France, Louis XIV followed a sound instinct when he transferred his court to Versailles. When, during the French Revolution, his successor was forced to return to Paris he became the prisoner of forces which could no longer be controlled, including the mobs of the city. The Kings of Prussia developed Potsdam to escape from Berlin at least part of the time. In the latter city the royal castle formed a *Gutsbezirk*, a large estate enjoying administrative and judicial autonomy on the model of the estates of Eastern Germany, in order to create at least a buffer between the King and "his" capital city.

Mechanization and equalization also played their part in regard to the position of the monarch. The princes of past centuries were attired in splendid uniforms; they travelled in gold-covered coaches which were marvels of the art of carriage-making, representing a substantial fortune. In later years, monarchs took refuge in army uniforms, but, to an increasing extent, they and the members of their families found it practical to appear in ordinary civilian clothes, in which they might not be easily distinguished from their subjects. So far as modern travel is concerned, the railroads still offered the possibility of special royal trains and royal carriages. When the automobile arrived on the scene no attempt to set the King's car apart from those of his subjects succeeded. Oil-rich princes and sheiks in Arabia might take pleasure in riding in their diamond-studded gold Cadillacs, but the bad taste of it all was obvious, apart from the fact that, within a few years, the most splendid vehicle of this type was sure to lag in performance behind any low-priced car just off the assembly line.

NOBILITY AND MODERN SOCIETY.

Many of the changes affecting the King pertained to the nobility [5] as well. Its traditions of magnificence, of splendor and, at times, of devoted public service were entirely opposed to those characteristics of an economy, and a society, dominated by modern business. The capitalistic entrepreneur engages in economic activity for the immediate purpose of financial gain. Profits, to be sure, may not constitute in his motivation any more than tokens by which the score is kept in a fascinating game, but he can rarely sit back in order to enjoy his gains in an atmosphere of culture and refinement, even if that would suit his tastes. The slogan, "Three generations from overalls to overalls," exaggerates the speed with which "the circulation of the elites" takes place in the business world, but enough of it is true to indicate the vital difference between the new world and the old.

The old aristocracy was not interested in such frenzied activity; their wealth and social position had come down to its members from generation to generation. They were inclined to look down on the businessmen—even if they might have more tact than that French nobleman who invited a wealthy commoner and his wife to dinner and made them eat with the servants. Members of the nobility, however, could never keep an element of envy out of their contempt for the businessman; their taste for luxurious living created a demand for funds which they had to meet in some way or other.

Aristocrats might, of course, attempt to secure a share in the new wealth. Where the land they owned increased in value because it became a part of urban real estate, or on account of the mineral wealth which it contained, the solution was simple, but it was available only to a minority. On the other hand, men with titles might find easy entrance into prominent and remunerative positions as directors of industrial corporations; they were given such opportunities on a substantial scale in Britain as well as in the Germany of the nineteenth century, where Bismarck gave the feudal-bureaucratic monarchy a new lease on life by the splendor of his military victories. Those who succeeded in taking advantage of such opportunities would find it easier to continue "Living as a Lord." [6] In this respect as in others, the British aristocracy benefited from its lack of rigidity; even so, lords with directorships in corporations are more numerous among those with recent than among those with older titles. Certainly, the group as a whole came under severe pressure during the twentieth century.

Service in the army and in the administration were more suitable to the tastes, and the aptitudes, of aristocrats. The advantages which accrued to them from these sources were for generations both substantial and indispensable. Still, even this kind of activity led to conflicts. Administrative work requires competent specialists; not all aristocrats were inclined to undergo the rigors of the necessary training, for which, in addition, they did not always possess the intellectual prerequisites. It was not uncommon to allow commoners to do the work, and let the prestige, and the revenue, go to the aristocrats. A titled official's ability to lend social prestige to his position might, to some extent, compensate for his deficiencies, but as the technical nature of the work kept growing commoners had to be accepted more and more.[7] Comparatively few noblemen qualified for judicial, and hardly any for engineering, positions. On the other hand, few fields were as suitable for men with the upbringing and the training of aristocrats as diplomacy. Still, when, as happened in Imperial Germany, the foreign service became a virtual monopoly of noblemen, the disadvantages were obvious. Thus, in the four years preceding American entry into the First World War, the titled members of the German

Embassy in Washington were hardly a match for their British and French colleagues. They had found it easy enough to make contacts with a New York and Washington society whose members were largely Republican, but when the Wilson administration took over, contacts between its leading members, and supporters, and the German Embassy were few and far between.[8] Even so, Count Bernstorff and his associates absorbed enough of the free air of Washington to make their judgment superior to that of their employers in Berlin. The latter, of course, had to live with the handicap of their Emperor's erraticism, but the fact that the Chancellor, the Foreign Secretary, and all the top men in the Foreign Office, were noblemen hardly helped them to equal the efficiency of their French and English counterparts.

In the military service the nobility found, for generations, positions germane to its ability, to its training, and to its habits. Noblemen did well in simple command, being accustomed to handling people. Still, historians of the French Revolution have painted a vivid picture of the contrast arising in the French army of the Ancient Regime between the pretence of the noblemen who were given every substantial position of command and the reality which made it necessary to have an underpaid commoner do the work for them. Matters never went that far in the Prussian army; still, there are such cases as a Gneisenau and Scharnhorst in the Napoleonic wars doing Field Marshal von Blücher's work, and in the First World War a Ludendorff deputizing, and, in fact, acting, for von Hindenburg. The position of noblemen in the army became more difficult as the technical character of modern armies became more pronounced. Aristocrats enjoyed service in the infantry a great deal less than that in the cavalry; they were hardly to be encountered in the engineering corps and even ill at ease in the artillery. In the navy, which was to attain such vital (and fatal) importance in the Germany of William II, they might still be given a fair share of the places at the very top, but they were a minority among a battleship's officers and their names can hardly be found among the commanders of submarines.[9]

FORCES PROMOTING DEMOCRACY.

For all of these reasons, whether they concern specifically the monarch or the nobility, the entire system of feudal-bureaucratic monarchy found itself in growing conflict with the requirements of the times. Its position was challenged even more directly by those forces which made for the ultimate victory of a government based on the active consent of the governed, and constituted of leaders recruited from a very large reservoir extending all over the country, easily changed without the institutions themselves being affected. Popular education ranks first among the factors to be considered. It became possible with the availability of comparatively inexpensive books, one of the results of the printing press. Besides, a growing part of the population flocked into urban areas, where the fixed cost of operating a school could be distributed over a larger number of pupils. A larger national income provided resources from which the necessary revenue could be derived through taxation. Last but not least, in modern economic life popular education is necessary as well as possible. When, for example, the English endeavored to spread popular education in an India where the economy remained static, they discovered that it would not "take"; the children returned to their village where they had no use for reading and writing, and forgot what they had learned. Where, however, economic life is modern, it is difficult for the illiterate to hold a job; he will be taken advantage of in so many ways that the inducement to overcome this handicap is great. Such compulsion from below is stronger than all efforts made from above.

The royal rulers of Continental Europe might be proud of having instituted popular education, and they were not unmindful of the advantages of having literate conscripts for their armies. They overlooked, however, that people with an adequate education will take a more active interest in political affairs than did their illiterate ancestors. Schools might, of course, be used, and to a considerable extent were used, for the purpose of dynastic propaganda. It depended, however, upon the pupils how they would react to it; the more active and more intelligent ones could not fail to notice its artificial nature. Both the information and the propaganda which the opponents of the existing order were not slow to provide found a fertile ground both among the educated and among the discontented.

Ultimately, the press came to be the major vehicle for both information and propaganda. Its active role, to be sure, can be largely discounted before the nineteenth century. Prior to that time the pamphlet was the product of the printing press which had the strongest impact upon public affairs. It played an important part in the German Reformation and in the American Revolutionary War, where Tom Paine's *Commonsense* is credited by many, including George Washington, with having turned a protest against "taxation without representation" into a war of independence. The Wenger case in the United States and the Wilkes case in England showed, however, in the closing phases of the eighteenth century, what the press was destined to become a few generations later. Eventually, of course, the press came to be *the* instrument of "mass communication"; it held an uncontested monopoly for over a century, until the advent of radio and television broke it. Governments did not neglect such opportunities as the press might offer to them; in all of the countries still ruled by monarchies, but subject to the impact of industrialization, newspapers were founded to enable the government to convey its message to the people. Their popular appeal, however, was all but insignificant; their circulation figures were unimpressive when compared with those of the large, independent, and usually opposition, press. In addition to the Socialist press, which more than offset the influence of official journals, there were the independent papers in such capital cities as Berlin and Vienna. They followed, for the most part, a liberal line, more or less openly opposed to a type of monarchy which attempted to safeguard a substantial degree of power for a political class whose days were numbered. If these papers advocated the parliamentary system of government, the Social-Democratic press was, of course, openly republican.

The independent press could not have reached its importance without the rise of the modern intelligentsia. The latter had become a power of its own in the France of the Ancient Regime, where the *philosophes* did so much to prepare the climate for the revolution. To the extent that the intellectuals did not make their living as writers, which at first hardly any were able to do, they were lawyers, doctors and teachers. Gradually, the group as a whole became important for the formulation of public consciousness. Attempts were made, to be sure, to attach it to the old political order, but they succeeded fully only in countries like England, where a truly democratic government developed. In all other nations a substantial number of these men proved unassimilable. Standing outside the existing political order they provided all types of opposition groups, including socialist parties, with effective leadership. England's political class, on the other hand, was as hospitable to intellectuals as it was to others; a writer like Disraeli could be easily transformed from a critic of the existing order into its staunch defender. Entrusted with a share of political power these men had to face its responsibilities. If they had any practical sense the utopian schemes which so easily fill the mind of the intellectual would vanish; intellectual reflection and political action would enter an organic union.

This absorption and assimilation of the intellectuals was, however, possible only to a government which was willing to change. Otherwise, the critical minds of those men could not have been satisfied; besides, intellectuals do not constitute a stable and, above all, a hereditary group. In their ranks the "circulation of the elites" is even more rapid than it is among the industrial entrepreneurs, social mobility being called for by the functions to be fulfilled. A democracy, or a government moving in its direction, could adapt itself to this mobility; a government by leadership calls for changes at the top as much as does the nature of intellectual work. It is still possible for nuclei of intellectuals to stand outside a democratic political order, viewing it from the position of the critic and the "debunker." About them Walter Bagehot was able to write: "The 'too clever by half' people, who live in 'Bohemia,' ought to have no more influence in Parliament than they have in England, and they can scarcely have less." [10] At any rate, in democracies with a "well-regulated system of government," this situation lacks any revolutionary potential.

Nationalism is another democratic force. Absolute monarchy might be able to claim the credit for creating the national state, as is the case in France, but even French nationalism has, ever since the Great Revolution, had a democratic tinge. In 1870, the proclamation of the Third Republic began with these words: "The Republic has defeated the invasion of 1792; the Republic is proclaimed." Resistance to the advancing German army was led by Left-wingers such as Gambetta; when the elections to the National Assembly [11] took place, those who wanted to resume the war voted for the Republicans, and the "defeatists" voted for the Monarchists. In later decades, to be sure, both Boulangism and the Dreyfus affair tended to make nationalism appear as the preserve of the Right. What Barrès propagated was, however, a pseudo-conservatism just as the monarchism of the *Action Française* was a pseudomonarchism.[12] Certainly, during the First World War, the Leftist Clemenceau handled France's national aspirations in a manner to which the proponents of the old order soon had to give grudging admiration.

Other examples could be cited to show the conflict between the monarchic principle and the idea of the national state. Both monarchy and nobility considered themselves a part of an international order, united by the same language (even the Prussian King, Frederick the Great, while fluent in French, was unable to speak or write German properly) and by the same social customs. Kings and princes intermarried in disregard of national boundaries, and then found themselves caught in nationalistic conflicts. It did not help Marie Antoinette that she was born an Austrian, nor did the same fact make the position of Napoleon's second wife, Marie Louise, more pleasant. During the First World War, the monarchs of the two most powerful belligerent countries, Britain and Germany, were cousins; the British royal family had, on this occasion, to accept a thoroughgoing, and somewhat humiliating process of nationalization. The Hohenzollern dynasty of Roumania was compelled to lead that country's war against Germany and Austria, and the heir apparent of the German principality of Mecklenburg-Strelitz fought as a Russian general against his own future subjects. Even the comic element was not lacking; members of some Scotch regiments had qualms about fighting against troops commanded by the Bavarian Crown Prince Rupprecht, whom they considered their legitimate ruler.

Even armies have been, in modern times, a more reliable tool of democracy than of monarchy. During the Middle Ages the members of the ruling class did not merely lead the army, they were the army. Since that time they have had to content themselves with attempts to provide the army with officers, all large armies, ever since the French Revolution, having been recruited by conscription. Thus, in case of war, the army constituted "the people in arms." In the long run it is, however, difficult to induce a people to fight for any but its own interests—or what it considers its own interests. Monarchs of a more remote past followed a natural instinct when, where possible, they employed aliens as soldiers (not infrequently Swiss), or when they tried to form groups of professional warriors, whose interests were closely connected with their own, such as the Russian Cossacks. During the First World War, the conscript armies of Germany, Austria and Russia became a fertile breeding-ground for revolutionary propaganda, which, incidentally, proved particularly effective in the navy. Navies have, since the days of ancient Athens, provided an especially strong democratic influence, and both the Russian and German revolutions of 1917 and 1918 were greatly assisted by active support from the sailors.

MONARCHY IN TRANSITION.

A large variety of factors, then, worked to undermine the social position of the political class of the feudal-bureaucratic monarchy. Against an array so formidable, a retreat was in order. The new position behind which the forces of old barricaded themselves, and which they held for more or less extended periods, was the constitutional monarchy. Its practical aspects have been mentioned above. Its theory had been developed in France and Belgium. When Louis XVIII ascended the throne of France, he was considered to have absolute sovereignty, but to share it, of his own volition, with a freely-elected parliament. This legal fiction was, of course, without practical value. With the introduction of the elective principle—even if the franchise was at first narrowly restricted—a new force had been introduced into the constitutional system; it was not to relent until it had deprived the monarchy of its independent power. In this struggle parliament had an adequate supply of weapons at its command. No law could be passed without parliamentary sanction. There was to be a separation of powers, with the executive reserved to the government, but time and again the executive found itself hamstrung even in its own domain, because parliament refused to approve a law without which a particular course of executive action was difficult. In addition, the principle of annual appropriations provided the "representatives of the people" with an opportunity for a critical survey of the entire field of government and of administration. When the British parliament began to enter the road which was to be climaxed in the recognition of parliamentary supremacy and the establishment of parliamentary government, its only right had been to refuse appropriations demanded by the King, but the use of this right, in the end, swept everything else aside.

Actually, the political situation of constitutional monarchy was replete with anomalies. Its defenders tried to secure for it a measure of popularity by exploiting the popular prejudice against political parties and political leaders. The latter were portrayed as amateurish and irresponsible. It was held to be meretorious for a King to appoint "experts" rather than "politicians" to his cabinet. For the prime ministership this claim could never be maintained; the political functions of this office were so obvious that the King had to take a man deemed capable of leadership wherever he could find him, from members of the court, from higher army officers, from the diplomatic service—at times from foreign countries. At any rate, it was obvious that there was no definite career which would lead a man to this position by way of expert training. The theory of the system would have required the Prime Minister to come from the administrative bureaucracy, but it is interesting to note that Bismarck, perhaps the most successful Prime Minister to operate under a constitutional monarchy, gave up rather soon in his attempt to make headway in the Prussian bureaucracy, which did not have much use for a man with originality. Bismarck was "rediscovered" after having been elected to the Prussian Diet.

The system of constitutional monarchy was, of course, one of dualism. The Duc de Broglie, the leader of the French Monarchists in the 1870's, said rightly that if a government and parliament, standing side by side, were not to paralyze one another it was, in the long run, necessary that either the government "make" the parliamentary majorities or that these majorities "make" the government.[13] As long as the second possibility was to be eliminated, there remained only the alternative of mutual paralysis or of the creation of parliamentary majorities by the executive.[14] This has been attempted time and again. Thus, when Napoleon III tried to convert his dictatorship into a constitutional monarchy, he secured its parliamentary position by the device of *candidature officielle*—"the official candidacy"—the government presenting its own candidate to the voters and using all of the resources at its command to have a majority of the ballots cast, or at any rate counted, in his favor. In Prussia, which was not a dictatorship, such crude devices could not be used, but others were available. Thus, for a long time, many of the Diet members consisted of civil servants; in 1855, no fewer than 285 of 352 members were government employees who, for the most part, were only too much inclined to do the government's bidding. The situation changed when, in 1862, the Progressive party established a firm political framework for the Liberal forces, but then Bismarck succeeded in breaking its backbone by charting the course which was to lead to victory in three successive wars. Nor was the "Iron Chancellor's" bag of tricks depleted when the effects of these victories began to wear off. When, as a result of the depression of 1873, he turned from free trade to protection, one of his reasons was the wish to promote the formation of economic interest parties which might make any clearcut parliamentary majority of one party, or even a group of related parties, impossible.[15]

The existence of parties with majorities of their own was, of course, a thorn in the side of any monarch willing to retain his power, be he George III in England or William II in Germany. For all of them, if they wanted to rule, it was necessary to divide, and, while in theory monarchy was a unifying force, it had to become the opposite so far as the country's political structure was concerned. When the means by which the latter could be influenced had become limited, the right of parliamentary dissolution was always available, ready to be used to curb the power of any parliamentary majority. Bismarck as well as his successors used it extensively and, at times, successfully; that Germany had a multiple-party system, rather than a two-party system, was, in part, due to this fact.

The most important device, however, which was used in Germany as well as in other countries to bolster the position of the feudal-bureaucratic ruling class presented itself as a result of an historical accident. When, in 1873, Alsace-Lorraine was included within Germany, 397 districts were laid out, each of which was to return one

Deputy to the *Reichstag*, which was elected on the basis of universal manhood suffrage. These constituencies were apportioned on the approximate basis of one Deputy for each 100,000 inhabitants. The country's population increased from about 41 million at that time to close to 68 million in 1914. During this period the number of voters in the industrial areas increased by leaps and bounds whereas it remained stationary in the rural districts. The latter were the strongholds of the Conservatives, whereas Socialists, Progressives and Catholics dominated the urban areas. Thus, there developed a tremendous discrepancy between the number of voters in constituencies which elected Conservatives and those which elected centrist or Left-wing Deputies. This situation led to severe criticism, but no change took place until the end of the First World War, when the monarchy was about ready to capitulate, anyway, and to permit the adoption of the parliamentary system.

Thus, practically all of the methods to give the executive a parliamentary majority available to the supporters of constitutional monarchy, were questionable. They might do for a while but were bound to create enough antagonism to make them unworkable in the long run. It was natural, therefore, that the supporters of this government tried to bolster its position by more straightforward, democratic, means. Reference has already been made to attempts to use the press for this purpose. The result was a rather colorless type of paper edited, as Professor Dovifat expressed it, by "a journalistic civil service" which never showed the initiative and the resourcefulness without which a successful newspaper is impossible. Furthermore, the official, or semi-official, character of these papers was known, and whatever views were expressed in them were discounted in advance.

Conservative political parties were another and, on the whole, more effective means to give a constitutional monarchy a firm foothold in the contest for popular favor. If they were more successful than official newspapers they were also more dangerous. A government might, at any time, stop the publication of an official newspaper or change its editors. Political parties, however, had ideas, and a life of their own. In a way even organized monarchists are enemies of monarchy. One could apply to them what Tertullian has expressed in these words: "I consider it audacity to dispute over the goodness of the Divine command, because we must not accept it because it is good but because God has issued it." [16] People who really believe in absolute monarchy do not try to give many reasons for it. If they do, and if, at the same time, they found political parties to propagate these reasons, they will soon discover that their faith in the King tends to limit itself to the cases in which they approve of his policies. As their liberal opponents lampooned the attitude of the Prussian monarchists:

> Unser Koenig absolut
> Wenn er unsern Willen tut.

"Our King is absolute if he does what we want him to do." Thus, the approval of a King's policies by a Conservative party always includes the possibility of disapproval. In fact, all Conservative parties have, on occasion, refused to follow their monarch. During the Napoleonic Wars, the Prussian nobility obstinately opposed the reforms proposed by Prime Ministers von Stein and von Hardenberg, which represented the only way to revitalize the Prussian state. Similarly, a century later, the Prussian Conservatives fought to the bitter end against any attempt to reform the indirect and plutocratic system of voting to the Prussian Diet. Nor did, for that matter, Bismarck and the Conservative party of his day always see eye to eye.

Still, Bismarck has emphasized rather strongly,[17] that a constitutional monarchy is not possible if the government cannot rely upon at least one major political party which is willing to support it, even where it does not agree with it. To some extent, in fact, Conservative parties tend to supplement the old "intermediate powers" of constitutional monarchy; after the nobility has lost ground they try to rally support in new quarters. Conservative parties are a contradiction in terms, however. While their goals are those of the past, the means employed belong to the present. In such a contest the means have a habit of defeating the ends. Conservative parties never accomplished much by appealing to the voters on the basis of their claim for hereditary authority. If they wanted to succeed, they had to appeal to free convictions; for them, too, the motto was "Persuade or Perish." If Conservative parties followed this road to its logical end the result was what Disraeli called "Tory democracy," or, in other words, the acceptance of that democratic order which they had set out to fight. As long as there was no intention to surrender, obstacles appeared everywhere. Thus, opposition parties would develop which, on account of their rejection of the existing system, could never be saddled with any political responsibility. This situation allowed them to exploit all kinds of discontent, in particular the misery resulting from depressions. If such parties are too successful under a parliamentary system they have to take over the responsibility for running the government; thus they find themselves transformed into supporters of authority. For this reason, a fully democratized system—if certain conditions exist which will be taken up shortly—is crisis proof and, in particular, depression proof. All a major misfortune does in a stable democratic country is to bring about the ouster of one government and its replacement by another. A different, and perhaps more vigorous, team takes over, but it operates under the same political system whereas under a constitutional monarchy the growth of opposition parties always jeopardizes the existing political order.

This happens although constitutional theory absolves the King from blame; responsibility is supposed to rest on the shoulders of the Prime Minister and his colleagues, who formally assume it by countersigning every political act of the monarch. Actually, carried to its logical conclusion, the rule that "The King can do no wrong" means that he can do nothing; this, with some modifications, is the case under the parliamentary system. In a constitutional monarchy, the King (or whoever makes up his mind for him) appoints and dismisses the Prime Minister and the cabinet. Therefore, he makes major policy decisions indirectly where he does not make them directly. Ultimately, then, criticism of the King's ministers is bound to become criticism of the King himself and of the institution which he represents.

Sooner or later, the logic of events brought out this implication in one country after the other. Thus, in France, the revolution of 1830 swept away the regular line of the House of Bourbon and with it the principle of constitutional monarchy. Louis Philippe essayed a version of parliamentary monarchy which was, however, far removed from its British model. He payed the penalty in the revolution of 1848, one of the results of the world economic crisis of 1847. The latter, at the same time, swept away what there remained in the way of absolute governments in Europe (with the exception of Russia which was only partly European, anyway).

Unsuccessful wars had similar effects upon constitutional monarchy. Napoleon III, by that time a constitutional monarch in theory, if not in reality, did not survive his defeat at Sedan. No major wars occurred afterwards until the beginning of the First World War. When it was about to break out there were men who knew of the dangers which it entailed for the monarchic principle. Thus, before Czar Nicholas II finally committed his country to complete mobilization against Germany as well as against Austria which, as the English had warned him, was likely to lead to war, he was told that this was folly. A Russian victory would be won in an alliance led by the major democratic countries of the world and thus promote democracy in Russia as well. An Allied defeat, on the other hand, would mean revolution. The Czar was too weak to act upon this advice, and was to lose his life as well as his crown. While Russia, in 1914, might not have represented a proper type of constitutional monarchy, Germany and Austria did, and yet the defeat swept both emperors, and all the kings, grand dukes, and princes of Germany, off their thrones, denying them an opportunity to stay as parliamentary monarchs.

Something might, in addition, be said for the contention that if the democratic countries, hard-pressed as they were at times, won the war, this was, in part, due to the nature of their government. They were, to begin with, free from the irrationality which the principle of "personal power" had introduced into German foreign and military policy. Their institutions were flexible, allowing, in both Britain and France, prime ministers who had failed to be replaced by men like Lloyd George and Clemenceau, who did measure up to the emergency, and who could take over without jeopardizing the basic nature of their country's institutions. These men, in the end, did manage to marshall the material resources of their countries at least as well as did the monarchies, and they added moral resources to them which the latter lacked.

In most cases, wars and depressions have operated as the final test of the "survival of the fittest" in the political order. Constitutional monarchy has failed this test; at any rate, in the older democratic countries, democracy has passed it. Where it lost out, as in France in 1799, 1852 and 1940, powerful forces arose to work for its restoration.

We might, with qualifications to be added forthwith, state that under the type of social conditions created by modern industrial life, democracy represents a condition of stable equilibrium. Where it can be made to take root, it weathers both depressions and wars in a manner which traditional monarchy has not been able to rival during the twentieth century. Monarchies not only collapsed one after the other but, where they were overthrown, they were more likely to leave a few nostalgic regrets in their wake than to lead to any serious attempt at restoration. What has been done in the latter field since the end of World War I is not impressive. Thus, when the last Austrian Emperor, Charles II, dramatically tried to regain the Hungarian part of his realm, his failure was almost as comic as it was tragic. Admiral Horthy might officially declare that Hungary was a monarchy, but he was in no hurry to establish a monarch on the throne. Neither was Franco when, in theory, he restored monarchy to Spain. Both men were, in fact, dictators, although Horthy less so than Franco, and the peaceful transition from dictatorship to any "legitimate" form of government implies problems which no one has as yet been able to solve.

What has been said about monarchy applies, with certain modifications, to the patrician oligarchy in the cities. It bowed out more gracefully; the guardians of patrician rule knew how to bend before they had to break. In the city states of Hamburg, Lübeck and Bremen, for example, they left a more affectionate memory of their rule than did the monarchies in the neighboring German principalities, but then the guardianship of these memories came to rest in the hands of mayors who, more often than not, belonged to the Social-Democratic party— firm republicans, even if they knew how to temper their political convictions with respect for a great and glorious past.

THE TWILIGHT ZONE OF GOVERNMENT.

If we survey these facts [18] we can only agree with what Tocqueville said more than a century ago in these words:

> The various occurrences of national existence have everywhere turned to the advantage of democracy: all men have aided it by their exertions, both those who have intentionally labored in its cause and those who have served it unwittingly; those who have fought for it and even those who have declared themselves its opponents have all been driven along in the same direction, have all labored to one end; some unknowingly and some despite themselves, all have been blind instruments in the hands of God.[19]

Toqueville's conclusions require modification in one important respect. He took it for granted that the forces which undermined the position of the old rulership would also create a workable democracy. It did not occur to him that a power vacuum might develop, the old authority being destroyed without a new one taking its place. This happened on a large scale. Two groups of factors operated, singly and jointly, in that direction. First, under the impact of ideological forces, modern democracy has, outside the Anglo-Saxon orbit, tended to allow the natural preoccupation with liberty to obscure the need for effective authority. This attitude has found its institutional embodiment in various versions of what Madison called "an ill-constituted government"; the details will be discussed later.

Democracy can, on the other hand, fail to take root because the social "matter" of a particular country is, at a particular time, not adapted to the requirements of the democratic version of political "form." If the active consent of the governed is the characteristic feature of government by leadership, the governed must be able to inform themselves about the actions of the government which it is their task either to support or to replace. Here the simple criterion of literacy provides a good part of the answer. Before the advent of radio and television the press had a virtual monopoly of political information. Illiterates had no access to it, not only because they were unable to

read, but also because they could not have afforded to subscribe. Illiteracy is, in fact, but a symptom of a general social condition which
conflicts with the requirements of democracy. It means that the bulk
of the people not only live in ignorance of the world around them but
that they cannot hold their own in social and economic life except
under rather primitive conditions. Not capable of taking the initiative
in the fields which directly concern their daily lives, they are as much
destined to be manipulated—if not openly coerced—in the political, as
they are destined to be exploited in the economic field.

Under such conditions we are confronted with what Italian writers
call "the absentee masses." If the law bestows the franchise upon
these illiterate and backward people, they do not know how to use
it. Fraud and coercion play an important part in elections, casting
doubt upon the moral claims of those who had been declared victors.
If it was said that "Christ stopped at Eboli," so did democracy. Such
conditions were, and still are, more pronounced in Latin America
(and now in Asia and Africa) than they were in Southern Italy.
Writers inclined to substitute psychological generalizations for sound
social and institutional analysis complain that Latin Americans are
"bad losers" when, in fact, the official losers have good reason to doubt
that they were the real losers. A willingness to revolt naturally results from such conditions. So do, not infrequently, the means for
such action. A Mexican writer [20] has given us a vivid description of
the ease with which "these horribly malleable masses" can be manipulated: "The 'leader' assembles them on a ranch, or in a most miserable
little village. He distributes among them their rations of 'pulque'
(cheap liquor), gives them instructions as to what to do, what they
have to say, and whom they are to greet with the shout 'vivas' [21] and
whom with shouts of 'death.'"

Ultimately, democracy can be a reality only if it is rooted in the
people in the sense that the pyramid of leadership reaches to the very
bottom of the population. A local leadership, based on active consent
in the sense that it is always tested by a rival leadership in free and
competitive elections must exist in the smallest unit; national leadership must recruit itself from such local (and provincial) leadership.
Where that stage has been reached, there will be no "absentee masses,"
or, as a former Mexican President, Portes Gil,[22] says, "anonymous
masses." The majority of the people will still leave the political initiative to their leaders, but these leaders will be in close contact with
the people who, on election day, have an effective choice of either
retaining them or of replacing an entire group of leaders by their
rivals. Such a result, no matter how radical, will be respected and,
therefore, accepted. In time it will be understood that in a democratic

country the opposition has as vital a part to play in the constitutional pattern as does the government; the leaders of both will cooperate in warding off any attempt from the outside at an overthrow of the Constitution. Revolutionary elements will, at the same time, be starved for leaders; most of those qualified for that task will prefer to work within the ranks of one or the other of the leading democratic parties.

We need not repeat that these conditions are absent in large parts of the world. They have been absent ever since the French Revolution which, in its later, and more radical, stages was made in Paris, where the effects of crowd psychology intervened at every critical moment, and was imposed by force upon the provinces which might not learn for weeks what had happened in the capital. The practical part played by the *philosophes* of the period of enlightenment in these events may have been overestimated, but it was real. Edmund Burke [23] was right when he spoke of "the clumsy subtilty of their political metaphysics." [24] Those who acted under the impact of such ideas believed that "the rights of man" would be secured by proclaiming them. Burke, on the other hand, emphasized that one of man's greatest needs is effective government; he was also right when he added that this can be secured only by building on structures already existing in a country.

Burke did, on occasion, overemphasize his points, unduly generalizing in his turn, and provoking the answer which Thomas Paine (not lax himself when it comes to overstatements) gave in his *Rights of Man*. Burke also overlooked the tragic element in these events when, discussing the members of the Third Estate in the National Assembly, he said: "Among them, indeed, I saw some of known rank, some of shining talents; but of any practical experience in the state, not one man was to be found. The best were only men of theory." [25] The factual observations are correct, but Burke failed in his analysis to note that, whereas England did give such men (including himself) the opportunity of proving themselves in government, the feudal-bureaucratic monarchy of France did not. It is small wonder that these leaders, having been unable to develop practical ideas of government, surrendered to impractical ones.

The French experience has been repeated again and again. In the countries recently freed from colonial rule there has existed a group of intellectuals at the top who had been educated in the leading universities of the West, and who saw no reason why their peoples should not enjoy both national independence and free government. Yet, at the bottom of the political pyramid of these nations millions of people lived in conditions which, in some cases, were literally those of the stone age. The gap was too great, even where much progress had been made. We shall see later, in the case of India, that it still made a difference whether, under these unfavorable conditions, a Constitution is adopted which acknowledges the principle of authority, or whether, as in Indonesia, the libertarian pattern of democratic thought, characteristic of Continental Europe, finds its embodiment in the new political system. Even the best Constitution cannot, however, eliminate the basic cleavage between the political form of democracy and a society not ready for it.

For such cases Burke, and many a political doctor following him, ordered a judicious mixture of the old and the new. In theory, it had everything in its favor, but it was found wanting in practice. Thus in Mexico, in 1822, Iturbide made the attempt to set up a native monarchy after having led the country to freedom from Spain during the preceding year. He was much ridiculed when he set up a native nobility, but he was instinctively aware of the need for what Montesquieu had called "the intermediate powers." His "Knights of Guadalupe," however, were not, as had been the European nobility of an earlier period, the natural rulers of society; their obvious and immediate failure was also Iturbide's, who was overthrown in 1823 and executed in 1824. Nor were the results any better when, in 1863, French troops enabled Maximilian to have himself proclaimed Emperor; when foreign support was withdrawn he was defeated in 1867, and followed Iturbide to execution. In Brazil, a branch of the Portuguese royal house maintained itself until 1889. About Dom Pedro II (1840–89) Karl Loewenstein says that his reign "represented monarchy at its best." [26] The country derived many advantages from a monarchy that became more and more similar to that of England; yet, the monarchy was abolished, and is now only the subject of memories.

Or, to take an example from an entirely different environment: When, in 1915, the then President of China, Yüan Shik-k'ai, tried to make himself Emperor he had the backing of one of America's most outstanding political scientists, Dr. Frank J. Goodnow.[27] He took all possible precautions, but his failure was both rapid and final.

Much, then, as we might agree with Burke that every attempt should be made to provide for a general transition from the old to the new, this has, in many cases, proven impossible. In recent years the invention of radio made it somewhat easier to establish contacts between a country's leaders and its people, but such contacts are precarious. We are, in these cases, confronted by a "twilight zone" of government, the social basis for traditional rulership having collapsed without society as yet being ready for democracy. Wherever the latter failed, not "legitimate" monarchy, but dictatorship, to be discussed in the next chapter, stood ready to take its place.

Chapter VI

THE PATTERN OF TYRANNY

THE MEANING OF DICTATORSHIP.

In the world in which we live legitimate rulership is, indeed, limited to a few areas, consisting of hardly more than Ethiopia, the Arab monarchies, and Thailand, and in most of these countries substantial concessions have been made to the spirit of democratic constitutionalism. Everywhere else the only government capable of contesting the ground with democracy is dictatorship.

When speaking of dictatorship, we must exclude from our discussions the very phenomenon which gave rise to the use of the term, namely, the dictatorship of republican Rome. As Professor Watkins has shown,[1] it has nothing in common with dictatorship in the proper sense of the term. The Roman Constitution was replete with checks and balances; in a time of crisis it seemed obvious that prompt and proper action would not be forthcoming unless someone were placed in the position to cut the Gordian knots with which the government of the country was tied down. Thus, absolute power was given for a limited period, but experience shows that this institution operated as intended. While normal constitutional limitations were suspended temporarily, they became effective again in short order. The anticipation of this fact had much to do with the conduct of the dictators; they, too, were guided by the "rule of anticipated reactions." Republican government was strengthened rather than perverted in the process.

If, then, a grant of temporary emergency powers under the name of dictatorship is no more than the application of the democratic principle of leadership to conditions where the power of the leader has to be maximized, it follows that we shall not, as Carl Schmitt[2] did, distinguish between "commissary" and "sovereign" dictatorship. "Commissary" dictatorship, i.e., a grant of emergency powers, is part and parcel of the *democratic* pattern; it not only has nothing to do with "sovereign" dictatorship, but is its mortal enemy. To take a recent

111

example: Democracy in Germany was not overthrown because the government of Dr. Bruening assumed certain powers. It was not Bruening who overthrew the republic, but his arch foe, Hitler. Bruening's trouble was not that he was too strong, but that he was too weak. As will be mentioned below, the particular form in which Bruening assumed his emergency powers placed them outside the normal constitutional pattern, and weakened them in the process. Constitutional forms are, however, available within which such powers arise organically, and without any detraction from their moral strength.

If we limit ourselves to using the term dictatorship in its generally accepted sense, it requires a further distinction. On the one hand we have tyranny, as recent history has produced it in the case of the totalitarian dictatorships of Russia, Italy and Germany. On the other hand, there is what, for lack of a better name, we might call "authoritarian" dictatorship. It is, in many ways, similar to tyranny, but there remains a substantial difference of origin, structure and operation between the two which requires a different evaluation. For the time being our observations will, in the main, be limited to tyranny.

Tyranny clearly follows a pattern of its own; it is governed by what Hegel would have called its "objective spirit." What has been done by Lenin, Stalin, Mussolini and Hitler was not simply a result of their own decisions. They may have felt that they were acting of their own free will, but the institutional framework within which they were working was governed by certain imminent necessities of its own which (in spite of all leeway in detail, some of which was important), they could disregard only by bringing the entire political structure down upon themselves. Herbert Agar[3] has reminded us of the law stated by Herbert Spencer: "The Assyrian conqueror, leading a slave by a chain, is himself attached to the chain." Who would want to deny that this is the way in which the German *Fuehrer*—or the Italian *Duce*, from whom, after all, Hitler copied the term—"led" his people through the depths of moral and material degradation to war and defeat?

THE ORIGIN OF TYRANNY.

The pattern of tyranny was woven more than 2000 years ago. Plato gave us a comprehensive description of it in the eighth and ninth books of *The Republic;*[4] Aristotle added details in the third book of his *Politics*, and St. Thomas Aquinas systematically rearranged the basic facts in his treatise, *On Kingship.*[5] Other writers have ably dealt with the same subject,[6] but we shall, in the main, confine ourselves to the writings of the men mentioned above, who have given what might be called the classical theory of tyranny. The factual history of dictatorship has found much less favor with prominent writers than has its theory. To this day, no satisfactory treatise on the subject as a whole exists.[7] However, there is no lack of excellent studies on individual tyrants and on waves of tyranny in certain periods of history. In the following remarks it will suffice to make a few references to practical developments; the similarity of tyrannical policies pursued in different ages, and in the most different national climates, is great, indeed. Professor Sherman, limiting himself to Aristotle, rightly says that: "It at first seems incredible that such complete parallels should exist between political theory of the fourth century B.C. and the political history of the twentieth. The correspondences are not chance or occasional. One can read almost consecutively in Aristotle's account and match detail to detail."[8] The reasons why more than "chance or occasional" correspondence is involved lies in the simple fact that certain basic aspects of human action have not changed over the centuries; fundamental patterns do repeat themselves from period to period and from one environment to the other.

Let us first consider the origin of tyranny. The form of government which, Plato insists, precedes it, is democracy; as he puts it: "that it [tyranny] has a democratic origin is evident."[9] This is also the view of Aristotle and St. Thomas. The former draws attention to the fact that the dictator usually is a demagogue; he pretends (as Plato has also emphasized)[10] to be the protector of the poor and is more often than not the leader of the popular party. For St. Thomas the democratic origin of tyranny is, in most instances, so evident that he is inclined to reject democracy for that very reason.

In the case of all of these writers we must bear in mind that their opposition to democracy was caused by the unsatisfactory kind of democracy with which they were acquainted. Plato lived at a time when, after the death of Pericles, Athenian democracy had lost its original strength and degenerated into the much less satisfactory condition which it developed during the fourth century before Christ. St. Thomas lived during a time which was similar to that of Plato. During the thirteenth century, in one Italian city-state after the other, there was a fight of factions which led to a renascence of tyranny. St. Thomas, whose opposition to democracy was by no means as systematic as that of Plato, doubted, and for his times quite rightly, that democracy could be strong enough to prevent those factional fights which, again and again, led to the rise of tyranny. As mentioned above, he endorsed monarchy for that reason as the best device for the purpose of securing a law-abiding government.

Let us return to Plato, for whom all forms of government disintegrate in the same manner, that is, they push their characteristic features to the logical limit, and thereby provoke a swing of the pendulum toward the opposite extreme: ". . . the excessive increase of anything often causes a reaction in the opposite direction; and this is the case not only in the seasons and in vegetable and animal life, but above all in forms of government . . ."[11]

More specifically he says:

> Democracy has her own good, of which the insatiable desire brings her to dissolution.
> What good?
> Freedom, I replied . . . I was going to observe, that the insatiable desire of this and the neglect of other things introduces the change in democracy, which occasions a demand for tyranny.[12]

The same argument is later presented as follows:

> The excess of liberty, whether in states or individuals, seems only to pass into excess of slavery. . . .
> And so tyranny naturally arises out of democracy, and the most aggravated form of tyranny and slavery out of the most extreme form of liberty.[13]

It will be seen that Plato's theory of the origin of tyranny is quite different from those held most frequently at the present time. The ultimate cause is to be found in the weakness of democracy,[14] rather than in the strength of external factors. Plato insists strongly on the point that tyranny arises out of the internal weakness of the democracy preceding it:

> And, as in a body which is diseased the addition of a touch from without may bring on illness, and sometimes even when there is no external provocation a commotion may arise from within—in the same way wherever there is weakness in the state there is also likely to be illness, of which the occasion may be very slight, the one party introducing from without their oligarchical, the other their democratical allies, and then the state falls sick, and is at war with herself; and may be at times distracted, even when there is no external cause.[15]

Those who, beginning with Aristotle,[16] have analyzed revolutions systematically, have been aware that the internal factors stressed by Plato may be either replaced, or supplemented by external ones; when discussing above why traditional rulerships lost their strength in the course of modern history, we had to stress external factors exclusively. Plato's onesidedness has, however, distinct advantages when he deals with the transition from democracy to tyranny. Here his analysis stresses a point which is crucial even if he fails to see that a democracy may fail to provide for the proper balance between liberty and authority not only because no adequate provision is made for authority but also because the social conditions of the time may go far toward defeating any step taken in that direction.

Whatever the details, Plato's analysis, so far as the rise of tyranny is concerned, is correct in every essential. In probably every historical case [17] developments took the following course: A fight between parties (or, in the past, between factions) develops, and this struggle brings the country to a state of near anarchy. People will tire of such a state of affairs and become willing to tolerate almost any government which promises "order." One of the parties, with the "tyrant" as its leader, then takes over all the power into its own hands. This party must establish a tyrannical rule for the very reason that it destroys a democracy. As mentioned above, people exposed, even briefly and tentatively, to democratic experience, are more intensely aware of political events than they would be under an "absolute" monarchy. Where so many more take an active interest in politics, a larger number have to be forcibly overcome. Tyrannical pressure from above is so great, therefore, because it has to suppress so much democratic pressure from below.

We could almost summarize these points by defining tyranny as "oppressed democracy," or, with Ferrero, as "inverted democracy." [18] The social atmosphere makes for democracy, and this tendency toward democracy can be crushed only by the various terroristic devices of tyranny. Yet, tyranny must combine many of the trappings of democracy with an extreme concentration of physical force in order to simulate the genuine consent which it lacks. The fact that tyranny is mainly a reaction to a democracy degenerating into anarchy is, however, so important that it may be well to digress for a moment and consider its historical verification.

In ancient Greece, for instance, the dictatorship of Pisistratos was established in 560 B.C. after a full generation of partisan struggles which had made it clear that the people were not yet able to live peacefully under the Constitution which Solon had given them in 590 B.C. Pisistratos was the leader of one of the three factions of Athens (the people living in the hills of Attica, the "mountaineers" as we might say) and with him his faction assumed power.—In the case of ancient Rome, the fact that the establishment of the Empire followed upon the partisan struggles of the first century before Christ is so obvious that no details need be mentioned.

Or let us take the tyranny of medieval and renaissance Italy. In the "direct" democracy of the medieval city-state, it had never been possible to establish the proper relationship between the majority and the minority; the struggle between principal "factions," for the most part called Ghibellines and the Guelfs, exceeded in bitterness and duration anything which has happened before or since. According to Ferrari, this partisan warfare in Italy, between 1000 and 1500 A.D., led to 300 massacres and 7,000 revolutions.[19] What Sismondi [20] has to say about the time when a "podestà" was appointed to help Italian cities escape from the fights among the nobles, characterizes the entire period: "The podestà . . . needed also a hand of iron to maintain order among nobles, so turbulent and so vindictive; he was accordingly invested with almost unlimited authority, the republics preferring rather to submit to his despotic sway than to anarchy." [21] A podestà was expected to prevent a dictatorship, but not infrequently he became a dictator himself; if he did not another might step in and make up for the omission.

In modern history conditions have not been different from what they were in the more remote past. Cromwell's rise to power followed long years of party strife and, according to an English observer: "The Protectorate of Oliver Cromwell . . . was grudgingly accepted by the people in preference to utter anarchy." [22] When Napoleon made himself the First Consul, people still remembered the years of The Terror, and they were aware that if the Directory would ever call free elections, civic strife would flare up anew. Napoleon III was elected President of France in the same year which witnessed bloody clashes between the Republicans of the Right and of the Left.

The rule that dictatorship follows upon a state of near anarchy is confirmed by the totalitarian dictatorships of the twentieth century. With regard to Russia, Professor Gurian succinctly expresses a view shared by all competent observers:

> Thus the anarchy grew continually worse. It only needed a comparatively small organized group to overthrow Kerensky and his government. The army fell increasingly to pieces, and the majority of the population adopted an entirely passive attitude, living only for the moment . . . Its leaders were neither numerous nor endowed with any great military capacity. But they were the active element in the universal anarchy.[23]

Turning to pre-Fascist Italy one need only read Balbo's Diary for the year 1922,[24] in order to see that the authority of the legitimate government was non-existent in large areas. The Fascists were able to occupy entire cities and fight it out in the streets with their opponents.

In regard to pre-Nazi Germany, we may quote Emil Ludwig (making allowances for his customary exaggerations), who describes the chaos of the early 30's as follows:

> Through Germany's streets there roared anarchy. Four armies, armed at least with knives, daggers, fighting rings, howled through the squares, droned through the cities, beat their drums throughout the country. No one knew exactly with which one of these armies the masses held themselves, nor did the masses themselves know . . .[25]

In the Greece of the middle 1930's, the proponents of democracy hopelessly paralyzed one another. C. M. Woodhouse comments: "The deadlock precipitated his [General Metaxas'] *coup d'état* and left in the hearts of many Greeks the feeling that it was about time too." [26] The feeling that it was "about time" is characteristic of countries in which dictatorship emerges. The average person's instinctive demand for conditions under which he can lead his life in peace is so strong that, for the moment, he will accept almost anything in preference to a permanent threat to law and order. The degree of consent which is evident in the first stages of dictatorships follows from this fact.

THE METHODS OF TYRANNICAL RULE.

The pattern of tyranny also applies to the methods used by tyrants in their rise to power. Plato repeats that the tyrant first secures for himself a following by posing as the "protector of the poor," and continues: "Then comes the famous request for a body guard, which is the device of all those who have got thus far in their tyrannical career—'Let not the people's friend' as they say 'be lost to them.' " [27] Plato was evidently referring to Pisistratos, who obtained a bodyguard from the Athenian popular assembly by claiming a self-inflicted wound as proof that his life was threatened by his opponents. That bodyguard soon grew and proved to be an excellent instrument for the intimidation of political opponents, and for the seizure of power; it was expanded into a weapon of systematic terror afterwards. In our day, the private armies of the Nazi and Fascist parties served the same purpose as did the "club-bearers" of Pisistratos.

It is not necessary to quote Aristotle and St. Thomas in detail on the subject of the instruments of tyrannical terror, but it may be interesting to recall in passing the reasons which St. Thomas gives for the maintenance of such a force: "Because the government of tyrants is displeasing to the multitude subject to it, tyrants must have a great many satellites to safeguard themselves against their subjects." [28]

Both the tyrant and his active supporters must be men who, even if they did not plan a policy of systematic cruelty from the outset, are willing to practice it. Plato opens the ninth book of *The Republic* with a description of the "tyrannical man," in the course of which he makes remarks which have caused him to be called a precursor of psychoanalysis:

> Certain of the unnecessary pleasures and appetites I conceive to be unlawful; everyone appears to have them, but in some persons they are controlled by the laws and by reason, and the better desires prevail over them—either they are wholly banished or they become few and weak; while in the case of others they are stronger, and there are more of them.
> I mean those which are awake when the reasoning and human and ruling power is asleep; then the wild beast within us, gorged with meat or drink, starts up and having shaken off sleep, goes forth to satisfy his desire; and there is no conceivable folly or crime which at such a time, when he has parted company with all shame and sense a man may not be ready to commit.[29]

We need not discuss whether all men have such "appetites"; suffice it to recall that criminologists tell us that in every country there is a certain percentage of people with criminal tendencies, which is higher than the percentage of those who actually commit crimes. Civil government, when it is "law-abiding" in Plato's sense, represses the active manifestation of such tendencies, and this is the reason why actual criminality is lower than potential criminality. The opposite happens under tyranny: Criminality is needed to maintain the regime, and so it is encouraged, and thereby developed. As Plato puts it:

> And the more detestable his [the tyrant's] actions are to the citizens, the more satellites and the greater devotion in them he will require?
> Certainly.
> And who are the devoted band, and where will he procure them?
> They will flock to him, he said, of their own accord, if he pays them.[30]

In another passage Plato is rather outspoken about the men who will serve the tyrant as instruments of terror: "For example, there are the thieves, burglars, cut-purses, foot-pads, robbers of temples, man stealers of the community; or if they are able to speak they turn informers, and bear false witness, and takes bribes." [31] This passage reminds one of the criminal records which so many Fascists and Nazis proved to have when brought to court as a result of some of the street brawls in which they had been involved. Also, it is interesting to read Sismondi on the kind of supporters which some of the renaissance dictators attracted:

> That the protection against the law extended to the guilty was one of the great means of seduction. The law threatened criminals with the most terrible punishment: prosecutions began with torture, and ended with the wheel. Nevertheless every village festival produced a murder; and those who committed it were exactly the sort of determined men whom the tyrant most desired to have about him. By shielding them from justice, he obtained from them and their families a grateful attachment, proportioned to the cruelty of the punishment which they escaped. These men. the most dangerous leaders of a rabble, were therefore all devoted to the prince.[32]

Care must be taken, however, to recall that if dictators need gangsters, and therefore attract them, tyranny is not simply gangsterism. Its origin may well lie in a perverted kind of idealism which becomes criminal because it is perfectionist. A goal is contemplated which is deemed desirable in the interests of, be it the nation, be it of the social class, or be it, in the end, humanity as a whole. Aspirants to totalitarian rule are impatient with the limitations which human nature places in the way of those who respect it. Their ends are so important to them that they are indifferent to the means used to reach them. In Lenin's words: "Everything that helps the Revolution is right, and everything that hinders it is wrong." [33] As mentioned above, whoever is guided by such considerations overlooks that, in the formulation of Ralph Waldo Emerson, "means determine the end"; wherever means are used indiscriminately to reach a good end they have soon to be employed so extensively that they are the sole remaining reality, the ideal end receding more and more into the shadows.

The relationship between utopian idealism and actual barbarism was seen clearly by Nietzsche, who wrote in his *Will to Power:*

> My thoughts do not revolve around the degree of freedom which is to be granted to one or the other or to all, but around the degree of power, which one or the other is to wield over all. In other words, the question is to what extent a sacrifice of freedom, even an enslavement, will provide the basis for developing a higher type. To express it most crudely: how could one sacrifice the development of mankind in order to bring into existence a type higher than man? [34]
>
> The most powerful man . . . would have to be the most evil one insofar as he forces his ideals on all men against their ideals and re-creates them in his image. To be evil means here: hard, painful, forced upon.[35]

In the last paragraph, Nietzsche attempts to mitigate his earlier characterization of the mightiest man as the "most evil" man, who is "evil" simply because he is hard and is willing to inflict pain on others in the pursuit of his own deals. Most of us, having witnessed the practical application of the Nietzschen prescription, are more impressed with the barbarism of the means than with the "ideals" of the end. Yet, an attempt to see both sides of the picture is a necessary ingredient to any application of the study of the pattern of tyranny to the problems of the Cold War. Otherwise, Plato's brilliant analysis might be turned into additional grist for the mills of the moralizers. This would mean more sand in the machinery of a diplomacy which has to handle the obstacles by which it is confronted, obstacles which are a result of a war in which the true lessons to be derived from a proper understanding of tyranny were so systematically disregarded.

If we now consider the policies with the help of which tyrants secure control of their peoples, we might well borrow the title "Step by Step," under which Winston Churchill [36] assembled speeches and articles dealing with the way in which aggressors were inching their way forward in order to secure a favorable position for the final assault on the democracies. Had Hitler [37] and the Japanese militarists shown their plans from the beginning they would have been stopped; in the same way, had any tyrant ever shown from the outset where he was ultimately to lead his people, means might have been found to block his path.

In speaking about the tyrant, Plato says: ". . . in the early days of his power, he is full of smiles, and he salutes everyone whom he meets;—he to be called a tyrant who is making promises in public and also in private! liberating debtors, and distributing land to the people and his followers, and wanting to be so kind and good to everyone!" [38] When Plato speaks of a tyrant "distributing land to the people" who does not think of the Bolshevists who gained the favor of the peasants by letting them take the land held by the nobles and by the state? They won the support of added millions by promising and, for the time being, bringing them peace. Hitler held out the hope of work to the millions of the unemployed and of the "end of the bondage of interest" to indebted farmers. Mussolini developed the pattern of lulling the opponents of totalitarianism into sleep by making some of them his temporary allies in a coalition government in which he and his followers constituted a minority—a tactic later employed with equal success by Hitler, and by the Communists in some of the "Peoples Democracies" where they also started out by "distributing land to the people." All of these governments, indeed, at first tried to be "all things to all men."

The early smiles of the tyrant do not last long. As Plato puts it: And the protector of the people is like him; having a mob entirely at his disposal, he is not restrained from shedding the blood of kinsmen; by the favorite method of false accusation he brings them into court and murders them, making the life of man to disappear, and with unholy tongue and lips tasting the blood of his fellow citizens; some he kills and others he banishes, at the same time hinting at the abolition of debts and partition of lands: and after this, what will be his destiny? Must he not either perish at the hands of his enemies, or from being a man become a wolf—that is, a tyrant? [39]

This catalogue of tyrannical terror is almost complete. The tyrant does not hesitate to kill, as Plato says, but before he does so, he discredits his victims. The results, fully intended, are described as follows by St. Thomas:

Therefore this kind of government is to be avoided as the Wise man admonishes (Eccli. IX, 18): "Keep thee far from the man who has the power to kill, because forsooth he kills not for justice's sake but by his power, for the lust of his will." Thus there will be no safety; everything is uncertain when there is a departure from justice nor can anything be made stable when it depends upon the will of another, much less of his caprice. [40]

This terror is so effective because all the means of the state are at its disposal. As Sismondi remarks: "Social organization, founded for the common good, was directed by an usurping hand for the oppression of all." [41]

It is important to note that terror rules the active supporters of the tyrant as well as the rest of the people. Again Plato has anticipated some rather recent developments:

Then some of those who joined in setting him up, and who are in power, speak their minds to him and to one another, and the more courageous of them cast in his teeth what is being done.

Yes, that may be expected.

And the tyrant, if he means to rule, must get rid of them; he can not stop while he has a friend or an enemy who is good for anything.

He can not.

And therefore he must look about him and see who is valiant, who is high-minded, who is wise, who is wealthy; happy man, he is the enemy of them all, and must seek occasion against them whether he will or not, until he has made a purgation of the State.

Yes, he said, and a rare purgation.

Yes, I said, not the sort of purgation which the physicians make of the body; for they take away the worse and leave the better part, but he does the reverse.

If he is to rule, I suppose that he can not help himself.

What a blessed alternative, I said: —to be compelled to dwell only with the many bad, and to be by them hated, or not to live at all! [42]

When Plato mentions people who speak their minds to the tyrant after having at first supported him, one thinks of some of the early supporters of Hitler, such as Pastor Niemöller, Hermann Rauschning and the industrialist, Fritz Thyssen. These men escaped with their lives, but others, in particular the victims of the "purgation" which began on June 30, 1934, and entailed the execution of as many leading Nazis as anti-Nazis, did not. Hitler's success in ridding himself of so many actual and potential opponents in one blow is said to have inspired Stalin to conduct the great purges which fill the late 1930's. Stalin's excesses have been exposed by his collaborators, but has their source been eliminated? A well-ordered constitutional government possesses safeguards in that respect which tyranny lacks. Besides, were not Stalin's deficiencies—his "rudeness," his "over-bearing," his "capriciousness"—definite qualifications for the political infighting which precedes the rise of a new man to power in a totalitarian system? Can the accession of a man like Stalin to the type of position which he held and within which, as Khrushchev himself admits, his negative characteristics became more pronounced in the course of time [43] be prevented as long as the system itself is allowed to stand?

When we speak of the attempts of the modern dictators to become totalitarian, i.e., to secure a monopoly of organization for themselves, we might be inclined to believe that this feature, at least, is recent. Yet, its basic elements existed more than 2000 years ago. For their most complete catalogue we are indebted to Aristotle:

The tyrant . . . must not allow common meals, clubs, education, and the like; he must be on his guard against anything which is likely to inspire either courage or confidence among his subjects; he must prohibit literary assemblies or other meetings for discussion, and he must take every means to prevent people from knowing one another (for acquaintance begets mutual confidence). Further he must compel the inhabitants to appear in public and live at his gates; then he will know what they are doing: if they are always kept under, they will learn to be humble. In short he should practice these and the like Persian and barbaric arts which all have the same object. A tyrant should also endeavor to know what each of his subjects says or does, and should employ spies, like the "female detectives" of Syracuse, and the eavesdroppers whom Hiero was in the habit of sending to any place of resort or meeting; for the fear of informers prevents people from speaking their minds, and if they do, they are more easily found out. Another art of the tyrant is to sow quarrels amongst the citizens; friends should be embroiled with friends, the people with the notables, and the rich with one another.[44]

While this passage deals with the tyrant's devices for keeping the bulk of the population under control, Aristotle also refers to the special treatment accorded to actual or potential leaders of the opposition. Periander of Corinth is reputed to have developed this and many other devices of tyranny. When a tyrant from some other city sent an emissary to him for advice on how to maintain his rule, Periander took a sheaf of wheat and cut off all protruding ears. As Aristotle remarks: "the tyrant should lop off those who are too high; he must put to death men of spirit." [45] St. Thomas makes a similar observation and relates it to the potential leadership by the victims of such acts. According to him:

> . . . tyrants hold the good in greater suspicion than the wicked, and to them the valour of others is always fraught with danger.
>
> So the above-mentioned tyrants strive to prevent those of their subjects who have become virtuous from acquiring valour and high spirit in order that they may not want to cast off their iniquitous domination. They also see to it that there be no friendly relations among these so that they may not enjoy the benefits resulting from being on good terms with one another, for as long as one has no confidence in the other, no plot will be set up against the tyrant's domination. Wherefore they sow discords among the people, foster any that have arisen, and forbid anything which furthers society and co-operation among men, such as marriage, company at table and anything of like character, through which familiarity and confidence are engendered among men.[46]

"Bread and circus" is another of the time-honored devices by which tyrants have maintained their ascendancy. So far as "bread" is concerned, we have mentioned how greatly Hitler's hands were strengthened by the abolition of unemployment in Germany. The tyrants of the ancient world, and of medieval and renaissance Italy, did not have modern mass unemployment to cope with, but such jobs as they were able to give always created good will for them, and of "circuses" there was, of course, no end. The two elements were combined as much as possible, although Aristotle was aware of the fact that the kind of public works which the tyrant was likely to build might not increase the living standards of the people, and in fact be calculated to do the opposite:

> Also, he (the tyrant) should impoverish his subjects; he thus provides money for the support of his guards, and the people, having to keep hard at work, are prevented from conspiring. The Pyramids of Egypt afford an example of this policy; also the offerings of the family of Cypselus, and the building of the temple of Olympian Zeus by the Pisistratidae, and the great Policratean monuments at Samos: all these works were alike intended to occupy the people and keep them poor.[47]

If Aristotle lived today, he would risk being accused of being a "neo-classical economist"; let it be mentioned then, that there is a difference between public works of genuine usefulness and those which serve, in the main, the propagandistic needs of a ruler. The erection of public buildings has, at any rate, played a part in the policies of all dictators. Napoleon I and III must be mentioned in this connection as well as Mussolini and Hitler, and some of the gigantic industrial works built under Stalin—not to mention the Moscow subway—served the same purpose. If the economic results were not beneficial, the atmosphere in which dictatorship operates makes it always possible to secure the kind of popular reaction desired. Thus it was said about one of the ancient dictators that he earned the gratitude of his people by taking all their money away from them and then giving them half of it back. Also, there is again Sismondi, who has this to say: "Galeazzo Sforza, the more to excite the attachment of the people, moved more by the senses than by reflection, surrounded himself with the magnificence of the richest monarch. The Milanese people were grateful to him for the spectacle, without considering that they paid for it themselves."[48]

A warlike character is another common, and often fatal, characteristic of tyrannies. Again Plato has given a catalogue which is almost complete. He says:

> But when he has disposed of foreign enemies by conquest or treaty, and there is nothing to fear from them then he is always stirring up some war or other, in order that the people may require a leader.
>
> To be sure.
>
> Has he not also another object, which is that they may be impoverished by payment of taxes, and thus compelled to devote themselves to their daily wants and therefore less likely to conspire against him?
>
> Clearly.
>
> And if any of them are suspected by him of having notions of freedom, and of resistance to his authority, he will have a good pretext

for destroying them by placing them at the mercy of the enemy; and for all these reasons the tyrant must be always getting up a war. He must.[49]

The second reason given by Plato may appear rather strange, but the first and the third have always been among the motives which inspired wars on the part of dictatorships. The absolute control of a country required during a war does indeed provide apparent justification for many of the oppressive acts of dictatorship. So far as Plato's third reason is concerned, Reinhold Schairer relates the following:

> A new report has come through that in certain parts of Germany 90 per cent of all members of the Catholic and Protestant youth organizations are now killed. They report that in the battle of Stalingrad at the most dangerous point a death battalion was put in action which was entirely annihilated. This battalion comprised, among others, 250 young Protestant ministers and Catholic priests. They died according to Hitler's wishes together with their friends and companions.[50]

But there are two more motives which push a tyrant toward war and which Plato omits; they are perhaps more potent than the others taken together. Sismondi indicates the first when he says that the Visconti (the rulers of Milan) "had resolved not to suffer any free state to subsist in Italy, lest their subjects should learn that there was a better government than their own." [51] This is indeed a powerful consideration with tyrants. Mussolini and Hitler have never left any doubt that they were chafing under the fact that the "decadent democracies" were among their neighbors, demonstrating by their mere existence that the evils of dictatorship were not necessary.

The other reason for the wars of tyranny, which escaped the attention of Plato, has been expressed by Napoleon in the single sentence: "We must give the French people something new every three months." After quoting these words, Constant adds that they were "said (by) a man who understands these things well. He has kept his his word." [52] People living under a tyranny are, indeed, always restless and it is necessary, at repeated intervals, to do something spectacular in order to divert their attention from their real problems.

Some of the methods by which modern dictators conduct their wars also have their precedents. When Plato says that tyrants make war after having "disposed of foreign enemies by conquest or treaty," he evidently implies that these treaties serve the purpose of later conquest and are to be broken once they have served their ends. What Plato implies, Sismondi makes explicit in his reference to Archbishop John Visconti, who was then the tyrant of Milan, and who, incidentally, terrorized the Pope as well as everyone else.[53] As Sismondi puts it, in speaking of Florence: "She was at peace with him, it was true; but she well knew that the Viscontis neither believed themselves bound by any treaty, nor kept any pledge."[54] Nor should we assume that fifth column tactics have been employed only by recent dictators. What we now call fifth column will always spring up spontaneously in an ideological war. It played a large part in some of the wars of antiquity and in those of the medieval city-state; also, what the Bolshevists called "partisans" during the Russian civil war was the same thing by a different name. Tyrants, of course, stir up fifth columns for their own benefit. Again we may quote Sismondi in reference to the Viscontis: "They liberally recompensed their partisans, and won over traitors in every state inimical to them."[55] By doing so, they only transferred to other countries the tactics of stirring up distrust and animosity among different groups, tactics which, according to Plato, Aristotle and St. Thomas, are part and parcel of their rule in their own lands.

With regard to wars, the subservience of the tyrant to the general pattern of tyranny is particularly obvious. Ferrero[56] has drawn our attention to the large part which fear—*la grande peur*—plays in tyrannical aggression. The same consideration applies to all of their acts. As Plato says:

> And must not such a state and such a man be always full of fear?
> Yes, indeed.
> He who is the real tyrant, whatever men may think, is the real slave, and is obliged to practice the greatest adulation and servility, and to be the flatterer of the vilest of mankind . . . all his life long he is beset with fear and is full of convulsions and distractions, even as the state which he resembles.
> He has to be master of others when he is not master of himself.[57]

St. Thomas carries the same point farther when he quotes Job (XV, 21) as follows in regard to the tyrant: "The sound of dread is always in his ears: and when there is peace (that is when no one is attempting to harm him) he always suspecteth treason."[58] This fear explains the terror used against the tyrant's domestic opponents. As Sismondi expresses it: "The despot, even when he has silenced by terror the people whom he has oppressed and disarmed, always feels at war with them; he has too much to fear from every class, to hope, with any chance of success, to attach any of them to his cause."[59]

The realization that fear governs the foreign policy of the tyrant in as great a degree as it governs his other acts may explain many recent developments, which it would otherwise be difficult to understand. A dictator suffers from a persecution complex, so that when he speaks of forestalling somebody else's attack in a case where he himself is the aggressor, perhaps he only means what he says. According to former Ambassador Davies, there were highly-placed people in Moscow who on the day of the Nazi invasion of Russia expected a simultaneous English attack through the Baltic. Only in a government which is constantly at war with its own people can such lack of mental balance be explained. One is reminded of the fact that when reporting on the "purges" Mr. Davies had this to say: "There were and are many indications of a condition bordering on 'panic' in government circles." [60] Some of the decisions taken by Hitler and Mussolini may well have had a similar background.

FORCE AND CONSENT IN A PEOPLE.

If these are the policies of the tyrant, how do the people react to them? For those who have never lived under a tyranny, this reaction is difficult to understand. They see the many instances of self-humiliation and self-degradation which occur in every dictatorship. What George Kennan says about Germany under Nazi rule applies to all countries in a similar position:

> Our experiences with Germany have demonstrated that we have not succeeded very well, as a nation, in understanding the position of the man who lives under the yoke of modern despotism. Totalitarianism is not a national phenomenon; it is a disease to which all humanity is in some degree vulnerable. To live under such a regime is a misfortune that can befall a nation by virtue of reasons purely historic and not really traceable to any particular guilt on the part of the nation as a whole. Where circumstances weaken the powers of resistance, to a certain degree, the virus triumphs.[61]

Actually, the victims of tyranny have often been blamed as much as the tyrant himself; de la Boëtie's *Discourse on Voluntary Servitude* [62] is the classical example, and the immediate popularity which followed upon its publication in this country during the Second World War is typical of the sentiments of those who have not seen those things happen to their own people.[63] A more realistic and, therefore, much fairer attitude is taken by Plato and those who followed his guidance on the analysis of tyranny. In the following passages, Plato almost exhausts the subject:

> Beginning with the State, I replied, would you say that a city which is governed by a tyrant is free or enslaved?

No city, he said, can be more completely enslaved.

And yet, as you see, there are freemen as well as masters in such a State?

Yes, he said, I see that there are—a few; but the people, speaking generally, and the best of them are miserably degraded and enslaved.

Then if the man is like the State, I said, must not the same rule prevail? His soul is full of meanness and vulgarity—the best elements in him are enslaved; and there is a small ruling part, which is also the worst and maddest. . . .

And the State which is enslaved under a tyrant is utterly incapable of acting voluntarily?

Utterly incapable.[64]

The last passage contains in itself all that is needed for the proper evaluation of the charge of "voluntary servitude," but so far as responsibility for crimes of tyrants is concerned, it may be useful to quote Sismondi:

Italy might justly glory in the fact, that wherever she was free, she was always found constant in the road to virtue: she is not answerable for the crimes with which she was sullied by her tyrants. Several thousand citizens had always contributed, by their vote, to all that Florence did that was grand and noble; while about fifty princes, distributed in as many palaces, with the few wretches which it belongs to tyrannical governments always to bring forward, sufficed to commit, in spite of a whole population, all the crimes which affrighted Italy.[65]

Sismondi would be wrong, of course, if he blamed those fifty rulers and "a few wretches" alone, but that was not his intention. He was aware of the fact that tyranny always demands cooperation by an active and substantial minority. The passivity on the part of most of the others is partly forced upon them, and partly the result of their own inclinations. In regard to the latter group, Sismondi says: ". . . the usurper finds himself supported by the inert part of the nation—by those who, incapable of thinking, or of investigating for themselves, must be contented with borrowed ideas, and with blindly assenting to every doctrine which the government may promulgate." [66] Sismondi expresses this view in reference to the time when the dictatorship has already become established, but the same condition obtains from the outset. His further remarks could have been made in regard to the propaganda efforts of the latter-day tyrannies:

If any memory of the period of liberty is preserved amongst the ignorant classes, it only refers to unhappiness and pain. They have heard of efforts, the sacrifices, made by their fathers in defence of the people's rights; but they see only the evils of the struggle, while the result, because it is not of a material nature escapes their imagination. They conclude that bread was as dear, and labour as painful, in the days of liberty as in their times; and to the privations they endure were then added dangers and violent catastrophes, of which fathers transmitted to their children some terrible details. Slavery, it is said, so debases man as to make him love it; and experience confirms the maxim.[67]

This is one of the points on which Sismondi almost sounds like de la Boëtie, but one might refer to Rousseau [68] who said that if there ever were "natural slaves," the reason was that at one time people had been made slaves against their nature. Let us also bear in mind what Constant had to say on the matter:

No people ever forsook true freedom. To say that men do so is to say that they prefer humiliation, sorrow, destitution and misery; it is to pretend that they can submit without regret to parting from those they love, to having their lives disrupted, their property seized, their opinions and their most private thoughts controlled, and even their persons thrown into prison, and led to the scaffold.[69]

The truth contained in these remarks will, perhaps, be more appreciated after the uprisings which took place in the Russian-occupied zone of Germany in 1953 and in Poland and Hungary in 1956. They showed that, as soon as the reigns of totalitarian rule were, in the wake of the crisis following Stalin's demise, slackened the least little bit, the people's will to freedom burst forth, even if their wishes were completely defeated in the cases of Germany and Hungary and only partly fulfilled in that of Poland.

In this connection we must recall that tyranny is oppressed democracy. That dictatorship arises in an environment pointing to democracy means not only that more repressive measures have to be taken than traditional rulerships have found necessary, but also that it is opportune to use more extensively the outward forms of democracy the more their spirit has been perverted. Reference has already been made to the plebiscites employed by modern dictators since the days of Napoleon I. They are useful instruments of both foreign and domestic propaganda. Domestic opponents who would have liked to vote for an alternative will find themselves frustrated; those who were maneuvered into voting "for" will often find that their self-abasement has interfered with their self-respect sufficiently to reduce their ability to employ such means of effective opposition as might be available. This applies even more strongly to the more explicit expressions of consent which Constant had in mind when he wrote:

> A despot puts an end to all outward forms of freedom; to justify overthrowing institutions and substituting others, a usurper needs to retain these forms; but in possessing himself of them, he defiles them. Since it is dangerous for a usurper to allow true public opinion to exist but necessary for him that it should appear to function, he must first so terrorize the people that true public opinion is stifled and then so terrorize them that they express false opinions which they do not have.[70]

The perversion of free opinion reaches its climax when totalitarian rulers deem fit to bring people to trial rather than to "liquidate" them without formality. To quote again Constant:

> When a despot of old sent his executioner to lead a disgraced favorite to the scaffold, victim and executioner acted their part in silence; when a usurper prosecutes an innocent man, he orders a campaign of defamation against the victim, so that the slander, repeated often enough, may seem to be a sentence passed by the nation.[71]

The Communists rulers of Russia and China have gone a step beyond Constant's model Napoleon: they have made people confess to crimes which they never committed, a practice now, so far as it applies to Stalin, confessed for him by Khrushchev.[72] If such people escape with their lives, as Cardinal Mindszenty [73] did, they will find it difficult to be effective leaders of such resistance as might be possible in their country. Yet, these confessions (extracted, to quote again the First Secretary of the Communist Party of the USSR, "with the help of cruel and inhuman tortures") [74] will be taken at face value by many in a position to know better.

These manifestations of pseudo-consent go far to explain the widespread willingness to give credit to the claim that dictatorship is, as Mussolini put it, at one time, "authoritarian democracy." We can only repeat that while in a government by leadership consent precedes, accompanies, and modifies force, in a government by rulership force precedes, accompanies, and modifies (in the case of tyranny: perverts) consent.

TYRANNY AND REVOLT.

When dealing with the fact that there is not more active resistance to dictatorships, one can again turn to Sismondi, who gives the reasons in a passage, part of which has been quoted above: The best people, he says, "could not resign themselves to the loss of liberty, which they knew would be followed by the loss of virtue. They would willingly have resisted; but soldiers, paid with their own money, shielded the tyrant within walls which their fathers had raised to protect their freedom. Social organization, founded for the common good, was directed by an usurping hand for the oppression of all." [75] This passage bases the difficulties of serious resistance upon the fact that the tyrant keeps the people disarmed, something which Plato had also intimated.[76] Disarmament of their people is indeed the first preoccupation of any tyranny; few offenses are as grave in a totalitarian country as the unauthorized possession of weapons. Aristotle has given the reason: "The tyrant desires that his subjects shall be incapable of action, for no one attempts what is impossible, and they will not attempt to overthrow a tyranny, if they are powerless." [77]

Action against a tyrant is, of course, never *entirely* impossible, and, as a result, there have always been people who attempted it. Still, it may be useful to consider some of the difficulties which they have to face. First, as St. Thomas remarks: "It may happen that those who act against the tyrant are unable to prevail and the tyrant, thus provoked, rages the more." [78] Innocent people may be made to suffer. One thinks of the assassination of Kirov which was followed by the Russian "purges," and of the assassination of a German diplomat in Paris in 1938—who apparently was not even a Nazi—which was followed by the slaying of thousands of Jewish people in Germany.

Second, St. Thomas holds that even if the opponents of tyranny succeed, "the multitude may be broken up by factions either during their revolt against the tyrant, or, concerning the organization of the government, after the tyrant has been overthrown." [79] Fears that events might take such a course were of considerable importance in Italy and Germany; they existed in Argentina even during the period immediately preceding Peron's overthrow,[80] and what happened later went far toward justifying them. In Italy, during the Matteotti crisis of 1924, the opponents of the Fascists had to emphasize that they were united only in regard to the "moral fact": they jointly opposed a government guilty of terror, but did not intend to form a common government capable of replacing it. However, as Danton puts it: *"On ne détruit que ce qu'on remplace"*—"One does not destroy except what one replaces." Fear that it might not be possible to replace dictatorship by something better was, indeed, a great handicap to the proponents of democratic government in both Italy and Germany.

Third, St. Thomas adds that the old tyranny may be followed by a new one which might be worse. As he expresses it:

For this is wont to happen in tyranny, namely, that the second becomes more grievous than the one preceding, inasmuch as, without abandoning the previous oppressions, he himself thinks up fresh ones from the malice of his heart: whence, in Syracuse, when there was a time that everybody desired the death of Dionysius, a certain old woman kept constantly praying that he might be unharmed and that he might survive her. When the tyrant learned this he asked why she did it. Then she said, "When I was a girl we had a harsh tyrant and I wished for his death; when he was killed, there succeeded him one who was somewhat harsher: I was very eager to see the end of his dominion also: then we began to have a third ruler still more harsh—that was you. So if you should be taken away a worse would succeed in your place." [81]

This may well be applied to modern conditions by referring to the fear held by many Italians under Mussolini and so many Germans under Hitler that the existing dictatorship might be replaced by Bolshevism. The fear might have been unfounded (which it did not prove to be for the Russian-occupied part of Germany), but while it existed it was effective, and the official propaganda machine lost no opportunity to nourish it.

Dictators, of course, have always known how to protect themselves. As Aristotle told us: ". . he who would kill a tyrant must be prepared to lose his life if he fail." [82] Besides, all modern dictators have developed some rather intricate techniques for the prevention of attempts at assassinations.[83] The tyrants of the past, not aware of such methods, felt it necessary to resort to the means employed by Filippo Maria Visconti (who ruled Milan from 1412–1427): [84] He locked himself up in his castle, without setting foot in the city for years. His only excursions were into his castles in rural districts; he went there in a flotilla of barges, drawn by fast horses over canals specifically built for this purpose. People were carefully investigated before being admitted to his presence. An elaborate system of spies and counter spies precluded the possibility of organizing a plot against him. As Burckhardt puts it: "His security was based upon the fact that no one [of his collaborators] trusted the other"—their master always stirred up antagonisms among them.[85]

One of the methods of self-protection used by modern dictators consists in the fact that their public appearances are rarely known beforehand. Difficulties of that kind confronted their most determined opponents in the past as well as they do in the present. In renaissance Italy, for example, when a plot was formed against the Medici in Florence,[86] the conspirators had to wait a long time before the two

Medici brothers would both appear on one occasion; this was necessary because survival of one of them made success impossible. In the end it was decided to kill them at a Mass in the cathedral, the signal to be the elevation of the Host. Only one of the brothers was actually killed, and so the tyranny continued. For similar reasons, Galeazzo Sforza, the ruler of Milan, whose misdeeds, if Sismondi's catalogue is correct, even Hitler could not easily have exceeded, was for the same reason also killed in church; [87] in this case the goal of the conspirators was not reached because the people failed to rally to the call for freedom. Modern dictators evidently have a great advantage over their renaissance precursors: They don't go to church, so the occasions when a public appearance could be predicted are rare!

Last but not least, dictators have always known how to protect themselves by means of terror against both domestic and foreign opponents. Whoever makes an attempt upon the life of a dictator will not simply be tried and executed, as would be the case in a democratic state; he will be tortured, and all his relatives and friends are threatened by the same treatment. Again, what is done today in that regard can hardly exceed the historic precedent. Sismondi reports to us that when the Visconti brothers were the rulers of Milan "their own subjects trembled under frightful cruelties. They shamelessly published an edict by which the execution of state criminals was prolonged to the period of forty days. In it the particular tortures to be inflicted, day by day were detailed, and the members to be mutilated designated, before death was reached." [88] This, incidentally, they called "the Lent."

Foreign opponents, no matter who they might be, were dealt with by these tyrants in as terroristic a manner. Let us again quote Sismondi:

> Urban V., on his arrival in Italy, endeavoured also to oppose the usurpations of the Viscontis, who had just taken possession of San Miniato, in Tuscany, and who, even in the states of the church, were rendering themselves more powerful than the pope himself. Of the two brothers, Barnabas Visconti was more troublesome to him, by his intrigues. Urban had recourse to a bull of excommunication, and sent two legates to bear it to him; but Barnabas forced these two legates to eat, in his presence, the parchment on which the bull was written, together with the leaden seals and silken strings. The pope, frightened at the thought of combating men who seemed to hold religion in no respect, and wearied, moreover, with his ill successes, was glad to return to the repose of Avignon, where he arrived in the month of September, 1370, and died the November following.[89]

Consider the treatment which Hitler gave to Neville Chamberlain. His outburst of rage was fully calculated to make the peaceful British Prime Minister "frightened at the thought of combating" such a man. Hitler's fits of rug-chewing were evidently staged for similar purposes; Napoleon followed a like procedure when he shouted at Talleyrand in the most uncivilized manner at a party. Khrushchev has, apparently, done the same repeatedly with foreign visitors. The average person does, indeed, shrink from the task of fighting such men—which is the intention.

AUTHORITARIAN AND TOTALITARIAN DICTATORSHIP.

These, then, are the major aspects of tyranny so far as its origin, its methods of rule, its relation to its own people, and to other nations, are concerned. Our illustrations have been taken from cases separated by centuries, and by all conceivable differences in national environments. Still, it has resulted in pointing out that whatever is essential to one tyranny (which means that it is a typical part of its internal power structure) applies to all others. The most important conclusion to be drawn has been expressed in the above-quoted words of George Kennan: "Totalitarianism is not a national phenomenon; it is a disease to which all humanity is in some degree vulnerable." [90] Yet, to this day, learned treatises appear which explain Communism in terms of Russian history, Fascism in terms of Italian history, and, now, Chinese Communism in terms of Chinese history. The national environment in which a tyranny operates has, of course, much to do with details, and some of these are very important. Much of the confusion existing in the analysis of our subject arises, however, from the identification of despotism with tyranny. Their outward manifestations may be quite similar and their reflections in political literature—so often quoted during the past generation—may sound alike, but, then, those who cannot see the difference, for example, between the rule of Czar Nicholas II and of Lenin (let alone Stalin) simply do not want to see.

Important, and in some respects essential, differences do, however, exist between the two types of dictatorships referred to as "authoritarian" and "totalitarian." We use the term "authoritarian dictatorship" reluctantly. It is misleading not only on account of the psychological connotation that democracy does not permit the establishment of an effective authority, but also because the term "authority," when applied to any kind of dictatorship, comes close to being an abuse. If freedom and authority are complementary terms,[91] it is as true to say that, where there is no genuine freedom, there is no true authority, as it is to say that where there is no genuine authority, there is no true freedom. Therefore, if it were possible to replace the term "authoritarian dictatorship" by a better one, we would do so with alacrity. Meanwhile, the inevitable surrender to current terminology will lose its sting if the dangers accompanying it are made sufficiently apparent to prevent us from succumbing to them inadvertently.

The first difference between the two types of dictatorship concerns their origin. A totalitarian dictatorship arises from below; its authoritarian counterpart is instituted from above, by people at, or close to, the top of the political pyramid. Modern totalitarian leaders have invariably founded demagogic mass parties, which enrolled thousands,[92] and in some cases hundreds of thousands of members before they achieved power. These parties have to work in competition with other parties, and in this process they develop a leadership thoroughly trained in the arts of demagoguery. The type of persuasion in which they specialize is not attractive to most people with even limited intellectual pretensions; in compensation, they do attract those who are willing to commit, or condone, acts of violence, plus those who are "down and out" and feel that they have nothing to lose from a violent upheaval.

The personnel resulting from such a struggle differs fundamentally from that characteristic of the political class of an authoritarian dictatorship. The latter, to begin with, is numerically small; as a rule, a few men set out to obtain power in a more or less conspirational manner, without any previous mass backing. Men like Franco in Spain, Trujillo in the Dominican Republic, or, to go farther back in history, Díaz in Mexico, did not start by founding a political party with mass support in order to use it as their tool for the seizure of power; their jumping off place was a high position in the government or, more frequently, in the army. The aim of such men is always to secure power in a more or less bloodless *coup;* if, as in the case of Franco, the old-fashioned type of *pronunciamiento* does not suffice and a civil war develops which makes mass support necessary, this is something unanticipated, and not comparable to the type of mass support attracted by totalitarian leaders.

Such differences have important consequences. That leaders of totalitarian movements are not part of the old ruling class means that, being closer to the people, they are able to acquire a grasp of propaganda which, in spite of all efforts, escapes their authoritarian colleagues, much to the latters' chagrin. What applies to the men at the top holds even more strongly for the "intermediate powers" just below them, on whom dictators have to rely as much as anyone else. Authoritarian dictators rely primarily on the army and the police. The army of a country subject to dictatorial rule is, to be sure, not the mere technical instrument for the fulfillment of protective functions which it has become in the older democracies. It may have come to include a strong political element, and a Latin American general may originally have been a politician. Still, in most cases, the bulk of the officers, and the non-commissioned officers on whom authoritarian dictators have to rely are likely to be more interested in their professions than in any political tasks.

This means, in the first place that, while the power of this "intermediate group" may be adequate for the negative task of suppressing open manifestations of opposition, it will not be "totalitarian" in the positive results achieved. Mussolini has defined "totalitarian" to mean "everything of the State, nothing against the State, nothing outside the State." [93] For "State" we must substitute "Party"; if the Fascists avoided formulations as provocative as the Nazi slogan, *Die Partei befiehlt dem Staat*—"The party gives orders to the state"—this omission was but a matter of "public relations." It sounded better to speak of "the state" rather than of "the party," which Fascists, however, were quite willing to do when the occasion demanded it.[94]

What any totalitarian dictator needs is close control of every manifestation of social activity. Contrary to a wide-spread impression, dictators have never succeeded in replacing the spontaneous thinking of their subjects by an indoctrination leading to a system of "conditioned reflexes." In the uprisings of 1953 in the Russian zone of Germany and in 1956 in Poland, and, in particular, in Hungary, young people who could not remember any educational influence except the one to which they had been subjected under totalitarian rule clearly saw through its pretenses, and they did not lack the courage to revolt, which they did as soon as there was even a flicker of a chance to succeed. Dictators do, of course, go as far as they can to win the consent of the ruled; what Mosca called the "formula"—a set of beliefs designed to make the domination of a particular ruling class acceptable to those subjected to it—is amplified into an elaborate set of tenets which are drummed into the people day and night. In this respect, once again, the totalitarian dictatorship does very much better than its authoritarian counterparts; of its highly trained propagandists, incidentally, not a few may sincerely believe what they say,[95] although there is never a lack of cynics in their ranks.

No dictator, however, has ever had the same confidence in the effectiveness of this propagandistic effort as those observers in the

Western countries who, during the Second World War, were of the opinion that German youth, having grown up under Hitler, must have become completely nazified in its thinking. Dictators never fail to build up a control system likely to work where all persuasion fails. Their basic views are well expressed in Caligula's favored slogan: *Oderint dum metuant*—"Let them hate me while they fear me." They might be inclined to modify this to read: "Let them hate me while they are not organized." The opposition of individuals, no matter how numerous, has never hurt a dictatorship. Organized opposition is something else again, and totalitarian rulers know that any free organization, established for no matter what purpose, can snowball overnight into the kind of avalanche which passed over Eastern Germany in June 1953 and over Hungary in November 1956; it would have buried the Communist system completely had it not been rescued by Russian armed might.

What totalitarian rulers do, and have to do, to ward off such dangers is illustrated, both in its brutal and in its comic aspects, by the policy of *Gleichschaltung* instituted by the victorious Nazis in 1933. Nazi party members were present in most existing organizations and institutions; they had been grouped, wherever possible, in a "cell." The meaning of *Gleichschaltung* was that these Nazi cells were to assume control, with the party member having the membership card with the lowest number, indicating seniority, to become "leader." Political organizations other than the Nazi party and its subsidiaries were, of course, liquidated, but everything else was to be "coordinated." People could understand this demand so far as organizations with a direct or indirect political connotation were involved; they were flabbergasted by the Nazi demand that even such non-political organizations as an artisans' guild, a students' fraternity, or a rabbit-breeders' association be included. Nazis knew, however, what they were doing. The members of student fraternities, for example, in the crucial elections of 1932 and 1933 might have overwhelmingly voted for the Nazis or their Nationalist allies, but friction between them and their—clumsily anti-intellectual—Nazi rulers was not slow to develop. At an early stage of the game an incident in Heidelberg illustrated what might be expected; the members of a strongly Rightist fraternity gathered for the usual purpose of imbibing beer, but soon some of them expressed themselves in rather unflattering terms about *Der Fuehrer* and did this so lustily that others had to share their secret whether they wanted to or not. Clearly, the Third *Reich* was safer without such activities. The members of a rabbit-breeder's association —frequent in a country where these animals provide both an inexpensive supply of meat and an interesting hobby—might be a bit more conservative but, in the end, might still be inclined to "let the fur fly" at the expense of others than their animals. Therefore, the Nazis rightly insisted on "coordinating" everything. They did run into trouble where they could not find enough people in their own ranks able to maintain their sway over these groups—a task requiring a minimum of brains even where there was no lack of brawn to back them up. In that case—which soon came to include all student fraternities—they simply disbanded the organization in question.

A totalitarian system would, however, not be totalitarian if such results were accepted as final. If certain organizations must be disbanded their members must not be allowed to go their own way; they must be forced into organizations which party members could control. Therefore, in all totalitarian countries both the ruling party and its many subsidiaries mushroomed, taking in new members by the hundred thousand. All organizations with economic or social purposes (such as employers associations and trade unions) were brought under party domination. When Mussolini established the "corporative state" in Italy, he knew that he might not be able to perform the economic miracles claimed by the propaganda accompanying this step, but that, at least, one more instrument of regimentation had become available. Besides, whoever was not, or not sufficiently, covered by such organizations (and who could escape them entirely?) was—at any rate, in the cases of Germany and Russia—taken care of by the organization of his city block. There was a special block warden; periodically, all people living in his domain had to gather in order to listen to party speeches or to sing party songs. They might be bored to death, but, as long as they were assembled under party auspices they were unable to gather by themselves and to engage in conspirational activities.

Thus totalitarian rulers assure themselves a virtual omnipresence in all forms of social organization, even the smallest. Time and again authoritarian dictators have tried to do the same, only to accept failure in the end. The members of their "intermediate group," mostly professional soldiers and policemen, are, in the first place, never numerous enough to undertake all of the tasks involved in totalitarian control, and they are deficient in quality as well as in quantity. In a way, they are a contradiction in terms: a non-political political class. They may be able to smash an existing organization, but few of them know how to replace it with one that they could lead themselves. In the majority of the cases they lack the propagandistic ability which is an outstanding characteristic of so many members of a totalitarian party. Nor do they—again with exceptions—have a stomach for the methods of terror and torture which accompany totalitarian rule on wholesale scale. A substantial number of them, at least, have enough of a sense of professional pride to recoil from the methods of deceit and coercion—if not outright slaughter—inseparable from totalitarian rule; when, during the Budapest uprisings, units of the regular Russian army ceased fighting they simply declared that they had no stomach for fighting women and children—a weakness no one could ever have charged the Gestapo or its Russian, or for that matter its Hungarian [96] counterparts. Lastly, while members of a totalitarian party can be relied upon to act, if necessary, on their own when encountering opposition, soldiers and policemen usually wait for orders to come from above, which, when received, may come too late and be carried out halfheartedly.

The difference between the totalitarian and the authoritarian dictatorship is, in fact, most clearly illustrated by the special agencies of terror which form an adjunct to all totalitarian parties and to all types of totalitarian rule. Thus, in Germany, Hitler created, in the form of the storm troops and the SS, a special party army which was, after his seizure of power, supplemented by a special police, the Gestapo. These agencies were, of course, established for the purpose of doing the dirty work which the regular army and the regular police were reluctant to undertake, even if, as early as in 1933, the storm troops were increased so much in size [97] that many of their units ceased to be suitable for such ends. Their place was largely taken by the SS. The mere existence of these forces, however, which invariably entered into open rivalry with the regular army and the regular police, demonstrates the difference between the two types of dictatorship. It is no less significant that in the Communist countries political commissars were attached to army units, making it plain to them that they were as much under totalitarian control (and subjected to totalitarian terror) as anyone else. During the war, both Germany and Russia had large army units serving the special purposes of the secret police.

The fact that authoritarian dictatorships lack these special instruments of terror makes them less repulsive, but it also constitutes one of the reasons why they invariably fail in their attempts to fill every void created by the suppression of organized centers of resistance. They may try hard enough, and some of them, such as Perón in Argentina, may be fairly successful in attracting support from outside the army and the police. The result is, however, a hybrid. What Perón won through a type of labor organization which he (and his wife) dominated, he lost in the army which, as events were to prove, had final word in the struggle for power. Most authoritarian dictators are aware of their limitations, and they are content with a power structure resting more or less on the surface of social life. Opposition may, for that reason, express itself much more freely, for example, in Franco's Spain than it ever did in Nazi Germany or Communist Russia; people who have lived under these totalitarian systems never cease to marvel at what appears to them as the "liberality" of the Franco regime.

In regard to a major aspect of these differences the authoritarian dictatorship is comparable to despotism: It may set limits to the open (and in particular organized) manifestations of dissent, but having made it impossible for people to express their own views, it does not force them to express views which they do not have. Thus it does leave its opponents "the dignity of silence." Besides, it makes it possible for them to put forth their true feelings among their associates— even among casual acquaintances—much more freely than could ever be expected under totalitarian rule. In this respect, matters go farthest with people such as Dollfuss and Schuschnigg in Austria and Batista in Cuba, who have been called dictators against their will although this designation is more apt for Dollfuss and Schuschnigg than for Batista. Rightly or wrongly, they feel that they must step in and rule with methods implying a substantial measure of physical force, but they clearly do this with a bad conscience, and with moderation wherever it appears possible.[98]

Authoritarian dictatorships such as the one of Dollfuss and Schuschnigg in Austria became possible, to quote Hamilton again, because "improper channels of government" had been chosen in a country where the economic and social conditions for democratic government did exist.[99] In virtually every other case, however, the primary reason for the rise of authoritarian dictatorships has been the lack of the social soil in which democracy could have taken root. If this were not likely to lead to misunderstandings, one might be inclined to say that they serve a historical function: they may provide for the political stability needed to allow economic and social progress to advance and establish the conditions out of which, in the end, the democratic process may be able to sprout. To the extent that this assumption is correct, it would warrant a more reserved attitude towards these dictatorships than can be encountered among those proponents of democracy who are ready to embark on a "crusade" against any and all deviations from the democratic pattern. What is, for example, the use of promoting the overthrowing of a dictatorship such as the one which was headed by Ubico in Guatemala—and there are many Guatemalans who insist that American encouragement had something to do with its fall—when it brings such Communist-dominated leaders as Arevalo and Arbenz to the top?

The conclusions which might be drawn from such considerations cannot, on this occasion, be discussed fully. The proper place for them would be in a volume on "Ethics and Politics," which would have to begin by making a careful distinction between morality and moralizing in political life, and to add a more detailed analysis of the essence of authoritarian dictatorships than is possible within this volume. It would also have to be brought out that any classification is dangerous [100] and that, ultimately, after all applicable general categories have been applied, it is always necessary to discuss each case on its own merits. It would, of course, have to be taken into account that even an authoritarian dictatorship remains a dictatorship; this means that there is an interference with the lives of the people as well as with their liberty. Also, some authoritarian dictators, to a rather substantial extent, give in to the temptations of self-enrichment which absolute rule offers, and they are less considerate of the lives of their opponents than they could afford to be. In this connection, as well as in others, it is obvious that they, too, are subjected to the absence of the "test of reality" which applies to all one-man rulers. This fact may influence policy decisions [101] as well as the treatment of political opponents.

Furthermore, if an authoritarian dictatorship may provide a measure of stability which encourages economic progress it is never certain whether this progress will go in the right direction. Thus, during Díaz' long rule in Mexico much of what remained of the efforts of the colonial government to protect the land of the Indians was destroyed, and a concentration of the ownership in land took place which aggravated the social tensions which came into the open after the revolution of 1911. Lastly, it hardly needs to be mentioned that the proper handling of democratic processes requires practical experience; this experience is—at any rate, in its genuine version—lacking even under the most "benevolent" dictatorship.

DICTATORSHIP AND SUCCESSION.

The Achilles heel of all types of dictatorship is the problem of succession. It is more acute in the authoritarian than in the totalitarian version because in the former the person of the dictator constitutes the driving force of the entire government; everything is geared to it, and everything is likely to collapse when he is removed by death or revolt. An orderly succession is impossible. As Walter Bagehot wrote when the dictatorship of Napoleon III was at the height of its power: "France elects its ruler in the streets of Paris. Flatterers may suggest that the democratic empire (of Napoleon III) will become hereditary, but close observers know that it cannot . . . The representative despot must be chosen by fighting, as Napoleon I and Napoleon III were chosen." [102]

One reason for this need is that a dictatorship requires a man with unusually strong personal characteristics. No dictator is likely to choose and train a successor who would have the necessary qualifications; such a man might be unwilling to wait his turn and reach for power before his time. Therefore, dictators will either ignore the problem of succession, or try to pass on their mantle to people whom it does not fit. Thus the demise of an authoritarian dictator usually means the end of the dictatorship. If a new dictator arises he will have to fight his way to the top, such experimental selection constituting the only method likely to produce the kind of man required.

In a modern totalitarian dictatorship, on the other hand, the totalitarian party represents an element of continuity; it will attempt to provide for orderly succession. This cannot be done in the same manner in which, for example, in the United States, the Vice-President follows the President in case of the latter's death. Even a totalitarian dictatorship is too personal to permit power to be shifted from one man to another without a hitch. After people have been told for decades that a Stalin is endowed with godlike qualities, it is difficult for them to believe the next day that a Malenkov or a Khrushchev, or a "collective leadership" possess similar attributes. Therefore, there will be, even in a totalitarian dictatorship, a struggle for succession; this struggle will decide the issue, rather than any fixed rule, or any preference expressed by a dead man.

In this connection it is important to bear in mind that there exists a strong tendency for the dictatorship of a party to be associated with the dictatorship of one man within the party. A totalitarian ruling class is comparable to an army; having to confront, by its very nature, numerous enemies (arising from the desire of the average person not to be dictated and lied to) it will be strongest if the principle of unity of command is followed. When, after the death of Stalin, Khrushchev and his associates made a serious effort to establish "collective rule," this meant, in the first place, that having cast doubt upon the validity of one man's claim to absolute rule they cast doubt upon the claim of the party as well. In the second place, they incurred the danger of indecision which is inseparable from the absence of unity of command. Both facts became apparent as a result of the developments which took place in Poland and Hungary in 1956. As Joseph and Stewart Alsop commented:

In this absolutely unexpected situation, the "committee system" in the Kremlin, which had worked well enough before, began to display the indecision and internal division which are characteristics of committee systems. The experts, while they lack solid evidence, have no doubt at all that a fierce internal conflict has developed within the Kremlin's "collective leadership." [103]

In spite of these difficulties Russia's totalitarian dictatorship has, after the death of both Lenin and Stalin, shown a potentiality for survival which its authoritarian counterpart lacks. The party did provide an element of continuity; its leading members realized only too well that they were "riding a tiger" and, as a result, "could not let go." Too many of their fellow-citizens had grievances against them to permit a peaceful transition from dictatorship to democracy; besides, few people who have power, or even a share in power, are anxious to abandon it. Therefore, the apparatus built up in a totalitarian dictatorship has a tendency to maintain itself by its own momentum. Its members may even resign themselves to the likelihood that a particular individual will secure more or less absolute control of the party and use it to "purge" his opponents within its ranks. This is a "calculated risk" which the active party members feel they have to take.

Thus, while the problem of succession presents its difficulties in all kinds of dictatorship, these are, in the totalitarian version, mitigated by the existence of the party. That the authoritarian dictatorship is more likely to fall is, in the long run, an advantage to the country concerned. Ultimately, a more truly stable form of political existence than any dictatorship provides must be found, and a process of trial and error may be required before the proper solution is obtained. The very instability of an authoritarian dictatorship facilitates this development.

Chapter VII

CONSTITUTIONALISM AND
THE MEANING OF THE
REPRESENTATIVE REPUBLIC

CONSTITUTION AND POLITICAL FORM IN GENERAL.

The discussion of dictatorships, then, whether authoritarian or totalitarian, leads to the conclusion that they are a failure. They are a failure in the first place for reasons of transcendental criticism: They violate the standards of a value system based upon the fundamental rights of the human person. The cause does not simply lie in the personal inclinations of the individual dictator, but in the fact that these men could not maintain their power in any other way.

Dictatorships are, in the second place, unable to satisfy the requirements of immanent criticism. Established as a cure for political instability, they may accomplish that purpose in the short run. Incapable, however, of solving the problem of succession, they fail to achieve stability in the long run.

Dictatorships are, finally, fully subjected to the irrational tendencies inherent in all types of "personal power." In fact, they aggravate these tendencies through the feeling of insecurity from which they suffer. Basic aspects of their policies can be explained only against a background of fear which has, at times, degenerated into panic.

These defects of dictatorship must not allow us to overlook that the basic reason for their rise is the weakness of democracy; this weakness leaves a vacuum which dictators fill. Ultimately, all depends upon whether the development of such a vacuum can be prevented. As we have seen, democracy may fail either because the general social conditions of a country do not permit the democratic process to take root, or because political life has been "made to operate in an improper channel." Wherever this second possibility is involved, we are con-

144

fronted with the problems of democratic constitutionalism which, in turn, is best discussed in connection with a brief reexamination of the general problem of political form.

CONSTITUTION AND CONSTITUTIONALISM.

We must begin by distinguishing between "constitution" and "constitutionalism." In the most general sense of the term, "constitution" is identical with "political form." As Professor Wittfogel has put it: "All governments that persist over time—and many others as well— have a certain pattern (constitution)." [1] This pattern is real, even if it does not include any devices for the purpose of restraining the ruler. We have defined political form as the sum total of devices which, in reality, fulfill the task of acting as the transformer which has to stand between the differing, and diverging, forces of society and the unity of action characteristic of the state. This means that there is political form wherever there is a state. The state must, in some way or other, be "constituted" from the raw material of society; it is the task of a "constitution" [2] to do so.

We revolt instinctively at the thought of using either the term constitution or political form in connection with a dictatorship. It is interesting to note that, in this respect, we find ourselves in agreement with a writer with as little appreciation of the specific democratic version of constitutional government as Oswald Spengler. The author of *The Decline of the West* [3] saw the need for political form more clearly than most modern writers. He emphasized that a people can never act as such or, for that matter, as a cultural unit—it has to be "in form," and it is "in form" as a state. [4] Spengler uses the analogy of the athlete; before rigorous training has caused him to be "in form," he may be potentially outstanding, but actually a failure. Similarly, all the great potentialities which a people possesses have to be actualized before they can be brought into play; this is the task of political form. Spengler realizes, however, that not every type of "forming" a society into a state does justice to the deeper implications of the term "form"; he is explicit in regard to what he calls "Caesarism," about which he says:

> By the term "Caesarism" I mean that kind of government which, irrespective of any constitutional formulation that it may have, is in its inward self a return to thorough formlessness . . . It does not matter that Augustus in Rome, and Hwang-ti in China, Amasis in Egypt and Alp Arslan in Baghdad disguised their position under antique forms. The spirit of these forms was dead, and so all institutions, however carefully maintained, were thenceforth destitute of all meaning

and weight. Real importance centred in the wholly personal power exercised by the Caesar, or by anybody else capable of exercising it in his place. It is the *recidive* of a form-fulfilled world into primitivism, into the cosmic-historyless. Biological stretches of time once more take the place vacated by historical periods.[5]

Spengler would not deny, of course, that "Caesarism" follows a pattern of its own. It is comparable to a mountain stream, swollen by spring rains and sending its turbulent waters across its banks, spreading havoc and destruction, even if it follows the "pattern" imposed upon it by the law of gravitation. When we speak of political form in the more proper sense of the term, we have in mind a well-channeled river, the course of which is clearly foreseen and controlled. What this means in political life is, perhaps, best expressed by the difference between what Latin American writers call "institutionalism" and "personalism." In the former case, the institutions are more important than the men who serve them; in the second, the man at the top means everything and the institution nothing.

The practical difference between the two types becomes most clearly apparent in the problem of succession. In pre-revolutionary France it used to be said, *Le roi est mort; vive le roi*—"The king is dead; long live the (new) king." Similarly, when, in the United States, a President dies, the Vice-President is sworn in as President within a few hours. Rules known to all and accepted by all have been laid down well in advance of the event; everybody automatically transfers to the new President the loyalty and the respect due to his office. It is interesting to note that, in the midst of the struggle between President Johnson and the Senate, Carl Schurz made this point, in his previously mentioned conversation with Bismarck. According to Schurz:

> He [Bismarck] said that he looked upon that struggle as a test of the conservative element in our political fabric. Would the impeachment of the President and, if he were found guilty, his deposition from office, lead to any further conflicts dangerous to the public peace and order? I replied that I was convinced that it would not; the executive power would simply pass from the hands of one man to the hands of another according to the constitution and the laws of the country without any resistance on the part of anybody; and, on the other hand, if President Johnson were acquitted, there would be general submission to the verdict as a matter of course, although popular excitement stirred up by the matter ran very high throughout the country.[6]

In the case of Johnson the Secretary of State, as the law governing presidential succession required at that time, would have had to succeed him, and the situation was by no means normal. Yet, Schurz was able to be quite sure of himself on the point he was trying to make.

We need not repeat that matters are entirely different in a dictatorship; for that reason we must, when speaking either of political form, or of constitution in the more proper sense of the term, exclude all "illegitimate" government. There are important differences even within the range of "legitimate" governments. While, for example, absolute monarchy encounters, in the framework of Western society, many obstacles which prevent its rule from being as "absolute" in fact as it may be in theory, this limit to princely power does not prevent "autocratic," and, at times, downright arbitrary decisions. The reason is the lack of effective checks by "intra-governmental forces." [7] Wherever such checks are absent, there is again *pouvoir personnel*— "personal power"—depending, for its exercise, upon the person of the ruler and not subjected to effective institutional channeling and control. The element of genuine political "form" is, in such cases, rudimentary; to some extent we are again confronted with a mere biological fact.[8]

Constitutional monarchy implies a more substantial degree of institutional rule, although the extent of personal power remains considerable. In the case of full-fledged democratic constitutionalism, the situation changes radically. Persons become subordinated to the rule of the institution; no simple biological fact (such as the accident of heredity) brings anyone to the top of the political pyramid. That position is reached by virtue of having gone through a strictly regulated process of election. The mere fact that this process must be repeated after a few years has as deep an influence on the nature of such rule as does the fact that the manner of its exercise is, in its turn, subject to detailed rules, such as, in a parliamentary system, the need to retain the confidence of a parliamentary majority.[9]

POLITICAL STRUCTURE AND POLITICAL VALUES.

Thus, it would seem that the two terms, political form and constitution, cannot, in their more specific meaning, be applied to dictatorship. To other forms of government they apply more properly the more the superiority of the constitutional rule over the personal element—which can never be entirely avoided—is established. There arises the further question whether the terms "constitution" and "political form" should be given a more limited or a more extended meaning. If we want to restrict, as much as possible, the area to be covered we can say with Aristotle that "A constitution is the arrangement of magistracies in a state, especially the highest of all." [10] Most writers dealing with the subject, including Plato, Thomas Aquinas and John Locke, start their discussion of constitutions in this simple and practical manner, no matter how many related elements they subsequently introduce into the discussion.

The alternative apparently is to consider, with Montesquieu, everything pertaining to "The Spirit of the Laws," including a variety of factors taken from the physical and social environment, the social structure, and mental attitudes. This approach,[11] if used indiscriminately, could lead to utter diffusion; where everything is introduced at once, nothing remains specific. Montesquieu himself avoids this danger; even though he does not speak of the method of successive approximations, he uses it. His analysis begins with the simpler elements as referred to in Aristotle's above-mentioned definition, and he takes up additional points by introducing whatever new elements the situation requires. This procedure makes it possible to do justice to the dynamics of political form. These dynamics may be supplemented, or modified, by a particular environment, but they always exist and are an active force in regard to that environment, important consequences resulting, to recall Madison's expression, "from the form of government itself." The conclusion, then, is that there is no conflict between these two types of approach to the task of defining the twin terms, "constitution" and "political form"; they belong together, the proper procedure being to start with the term in its most limited sense and to extend the analysis as a particular situation demands it.

It might seem, however, that the "values" which are connected with a particular form of government constitute an exception to this rule, and that they must be introduced into the discussion from the outset. Values, of course, pertain to ends, and forms of government are means. Any discussion of values is, however, likely to go astray unless it is combined with an analysis of the means to be used for their realization. Max Weber,[12] in his very first examination of the relationship between value judgments and the requirements of objectivity in the social sciences, made the point that we do not really know our ends unless we have a thorough understanding of the means which we propose to use. Means are not often neutral in regard to values. Reference has frequently been made to the implications of the choice of means made, for example, by such utopian perfectionists as modern Communists; the questionable means which they use are an all-pervasive reality, and the lofty ends which they profess to serve seem by now to have evaporated even from their consciousness. If, then, we believe in certain values, a mere reiteration of this fact will not bring them to life. If we limit ourselves to declamatory statements, the world passes us by. If we proceed to act, but choose our means haphazardly we risk accomplishing the opposite of what we set out to do. On the other hand, as long as we choose the right means we cannot fail to reach the goal we set for ourselves.

These simple considerations have an important bearing on the modern discussion of constitutional government. Those who want constitutional government in the form of democracy do so because they place the values of human dignity and human freedom above all; democracy is an essential means for the realization of those ends. In democratic thought there is, however, a tendency to ignore the essential nature of the means which must be applied if the end sought is to be reached. Since the days of the French Revolution European constitution-makers, in particular those outside the Anglo-Saxon world, seem to have been guided by the assumption that it suffices to proclaim "The Rights of Man and of the Citizen" in order to enjoy them. When this did not turn out to be the case, the remedy was sought in an even longer catalogue of human rights. The latest batch of written constitutions has added a variety of social rights which, although highly desirable in themselves, simply cannot be secured by constitutional enactment.

What matters is not the endless repetition of aspirations common to most of us, but the discernment, and the application, of the means likely to realize these aspirations. In this regard, the founders of this country saw clearly. James Madison emphasized that constitutional guarantees of human rights constitute, by themselves, mere "parchment barriers." [13] In the same vein, George Washington said in his Farewell Address: "Liberty . . . is indeed, little else than a name, where the government is too feeble to withstand the enterprises of faction, to confine each member of the society within the limits prescribed by the laws, and to maintain all in the secure and tranquil enjoyment of the rights of person and property." In view of the prominent part played by Thomas Jefferson in the enunciation of the rights of man, it is interesting to note what he said about the writers of ancient Greece: "They had just ideas of the value of personal liberty, but none at all of the structure of government best calculated to preserve it." [14] If personal liberty does mean something to us, we, too, would do well to concentrate our attention on "the structure of government best calculated to preserve it."

This implies that, when discussing constitutional government we should not simply define it in terms of restraint. Before we can restrain power there must *be* power. As Alexander Hamilton put it before the New York Ratifying Convention: "Power must be granted, or civil society cannot exist." [15] Hamilton rightly warned that too little power was as dangerous as too much power. Rigid limitations could, therefore, defeat their own purposes. As Lynton K. Caldwell summarizes his ultimate conclusion: "Power was best controlled, not by rigid limitations, but by the provision of channels for its responsible operation." [16]

THE ELEMENTS OF CONSTITUTIONAL GOVERNMENT.

If these considerations guide our definition of constitutional government, we might say that its requirements are, first, the establishment of an effective organization of political power; second, guiding it into channels which will make a body of objective rules superior to the persons who act in their framework; and, third, the limitation of power for the purpose of guaranteeing the "inalienable" rights of the citizen. These three requirements (tailored, of course, to the requirements of *democratic* constitutionalism) may appear contradictory, but they are supplementary. So far as the relation between the granting and the channeling of power is concerned, government is, in the long run, the more effective the more it is institutionalized. Properly channeled power is, at the same time, the best guarantee for human rights which, in such a case, possess what we might call a "built-in" character. This guarantee results, on the one hand, from the restraints inherent in a properly channeled organization of political power, which makes a government willing to respect fundamental rights. It equally results from the fact that such a government will be strong enough to make these rights respected by others. How important this can be is readily ascertained from the conditions which arose in country after country after the First World War. The Weimar Constitution, for example, was exemplary in its enumeration of fundamental rights. When, however, the democratic governments formed in accordance with its specifications were no longer strong enough to impose their will on the extremists, the people's rights to "life, liberty and the pursuit of happiness" were more and more in jeopardy.

Effectively guaranteed human rights, on the other hand, can contribute to the vigor of democratic government as much as that vigor is needed to guarantee their implementation. Such rights are not just a "bourgeois" [17] institution, intended to provide everyone with a *laissez-faire* preserve of his own. Democratic government derives its ultimate source of strength from persons who, in the formulation applied by Pope Pius XII in his Christmas allocution of 1944, constitute a true people, rather than being mere parts of "a shapeless multitude, or, as it is called, 'the masses,'" [18] subject to easy manipulation. It is, indeed, erroneous to regard the individual and society as in conflict; Thomas Aquinas has warned against that error,[19] and, more recently, Rudolph Smend [20] has directed the shafts of his irony against that "mechanical" view of this relationship which, instead of recognizing its essential mutuality, divides a given area between the two, the share of the one going at the expense of that of the other.

A constitution, then (at any rate, in this era of ours in which the applicability of this term becomes more and more limited to the countries where effective democracy is possible),[21] means that body of rules which establishes, regulates and limits the organs of public power. We need not repeat that we are dealing with those rules which perform these functions in reality, whether they are a part of a written constitution or not. The framers of such documents have been inclined to overlook that all they could do was to "suggest processes of integration." [22] Where a written constitution is largely absent, the body of rules and procedures which we call "constitution" has been able to adapt itself organically to the requirements of the social processes involved. Rules laid down in writing introduce a measure of clarity and stability; they will, however, be successful only to the extent that they do justice to the dynamism of the social relations involved.

Again, we must recall Ernest Renan's definition of the state as *un plebiscite de tous les jours*—"a plebiscite daily repeated." By the same token, those elements of political form which constitute [23] the state are constantly in action; they are real only to the extent that they renew themselves in this process. Some of the most important of these factors are not even mentioned in written constitutions. In other cases, rules are enunciated which are so unrealistic that they remain confined to paper. Or again, a provision contained in a written constitution may be effective but yield results quite different from those intended. At any rate, no constitutional document has ever exhausted the area of actual constitutional government. It has had to be supplemented by additional rules, whether these owe their existence to mere practice or to enactments which lack the status of constitutional law. Likewise, every constitution has been changed in the course of its application; at times, it has been perverted.

For these reasons we shall, for the time being, ignore written constitutions even when they make important, and effective, decisions, such as those implied in the choice between the British type of parliamentary government and the American type of a presidential executive. It is more important that all democratic governments have certain procedures in common. These relate to the manner in which a constitution confronts, and channels, the living forces of society in order to extract from them that measure of unity which is needed to make the state a reality.

THE REPRESENTATIVE REPUBLIC AND DEMOCRACY.

Once again we must turn to the thought of those who established our "representative republic," as there is no better guide to a realistic analysis of the living processes of modern democratic constitutionalism. We may disagree with them in regard to certain aspects of the organization of authority which they initiated. In regard to the way, however, in which they specified the task of the democratic constitution-maker, they are without peers in constitutional history. If, in the second half of the twentieth century, we want to regain a measure of political control over discordant social forces we shall, indeed, achieve progress only if we return to the methodological approach developed on these shores nearly two centuries ago.

It will be asked, however, whether the founders of the "representative republic" were really proponents of *democratic* constitutionalism? It may be well to digress for a moment in order to elaborate on what has been said on this subject above. We need not repeat that Madison, in No. 10 of *The Federalist,* used the term "representative republic" where we would say "indirect democracy." It is interesting to note, however, that in support of this identification, no one can be quoted more explicitly than Alexander Hamilton. His views are important not only on account of his conservatism, which should protect him against any charge that he might not really have wanted a "representative republic," but also on account of the position which he occupies in the movement for the new constitution; Charles A. Beard has rightly called him "the colossus" of that movement. His identification of what we call "indirect democracy" and what Madison termed "the representative republic" occurs in a letter written to Gouverneur Morris in 1777, parts of which we have previously quoted:

> That instability is inherent in the nature of popular governments I think very disputable; unstable democracy, is an epithet frequently in the mouths of politicians; but I believe that from a strict examination of the matter—from the records of history, it will be found that the fluctuations of governments in which the popular principle has borne a considerable sway, have proceeded from its being compounded with other principles;—and from its being made to operate in an improper channel. . . . But a representative democracy, where the right of election is well secured and regulated, and the exercise of the legislative, executive, and judiciary authorities is vested in select per-

sons, chosen really and not nominally by the people, will, in my opinion, be most likely to be happy, regular, and durable.[24]

Hamilton, then, does use the term "representative democracy" to denote exactly what Madison termed "the representative republic." Besides, his letter contains an effective defense of democracy against a charge made against it as much in our day as it was made in his. Thomas Paine and Thomas Jefferson—to go to the opposite end of the political scale—defined the term "representative republic" basically in the same sense as Madison or Hamilton. Paine wrote in his *Rights of Man:*

> Simple democracy was society governing itself without the use of secondary means. By ingrafting representation upon democracy, we arrive at a system of government capable of embracing and confederating all the various interests and every extent of territory and population; . . .
> It is on this system that the American government was founded. It is representation ingrafted upon democracy. . . .
> It [the system of "representation ingrafted upon democracy"] is preferable to simple democracy even in small territories. Athens, by representation, would have surpassed her own democracy.[25]

Paine, then, speaks of "simple democracy" where Madison says "pure democracy," but the slight variation in language merely serves to underline the identity of thought. Similar considerations apply to Jefferson, who saw so little difference between the terms "republican" and "democratic" that he came to be the founder of a party which was to link the two in its name. He defined the content of both terms when, in a letter to Samuel Kercheval, written in 1816, he said:

> For let it be agreed that a government is republican in proportion as every member composing it has his equal voice in the direction of its concerns (not indeed in person, which would indeed be impracticable beyond the limits of a city, or a small township), but by representatives chosen by himself, and responsible to him at short periods, and let us bring the test of this canon to every branch of our constitution.

Republican government is for Jefferson, then, based upon what we have called "the active consent" of the governed; it had been similarly defined by Madison in No. 39 of *The Federalist*.[26] Jefferson rejected "pure democracy," however, because it was "impracticable" in a large territory, rather than because of its intrinsic defects. His letter to Isaac H. Tiffany, written in 1816, a sentence of which was quoted above, suggests the same trend of thought as the letter to Kercheval, but seems at the same time to imply a greater awareness of the possibilities of social control inherent in the representative principle.[27] When Jefferson says that "the introduction of this new principle of representative democracy has rendered useless almost everything written before on the structure of government" he overstates his case. He is right, however, insofar as many of the charges advanced against democracy in our day, plucked so indiscriminatingly from the pages of history, do ignore what is peculiar to a "pure democracy" where, indeed, the people may become a "mob" which, in the words of Herodotus,[28] "rushes wildly into state affairs with all the fury of a stream swollen in the winter, and confuses everything." That particular aspect of the "Menace of the Herd"[29] can, with the (not unimportant) exceptions, be disregarded within the confines of a "representative republic."

Quoting Jefferson in order to show that the Constitution is not based upon the assumption of an essential difference between the principles of a democracy and those of a republic might appear onesided. Let us add, then, what, a good generation later, the great Conservative, John C. Calhoun, had to say on the subject:

> The Government of the United States was formed by the Constitution of the United States;—and ours is a democratic, federal republic.
> It is democratic in contradistinction to aristocracy and monarchy. It excludes classes, orders and all artificial distinctions. To guard against their introduction, the constitution prohibits the granting of any title of nobility by the United States or by any State . . . The whole system is, indeed, democratic throughout. It has for its fundamental principle the great cardinal maxim, that the people are the source of all power; that the governments of the several states and of the United States were created by them, and for them . . .[30]

Finally, in order to round the corner into the twentieth century, let us recall that in 1913 William Howard Taft quoted Bluntschli, whom he calls "the great Heidelberg publicist," and with whom he is in evident agreement, to the effect that: "Representative Government and self-government are the great works of the English and American people. The English have produced representative monarchy with parliamentary legislation and parliamentary politics. The Americans have produced the representative republic."[31]

THE REPRESENTATIVE REPUBLIC AND THE CONTROL OF
DISRUPTION.

Terminology, then, need not stand in our way when we turn to the founders of the "representative republic" for guidance in the analysis of the principles of democratic constitutionalism. The substance of what we want to achieve, and what Hamilton, Madison, and their associates tried to and, to a large extent, did achieve, is the same: the harnessing of the forces of society into channels which receive streams from different sources and unite them all freely in one mighty and constructive current. These social sources are not only economic in origin, but, to quote Madison again in No. 10, they also arise from "different opinions concerning religion, concerning government, and many other points, as well of speculation as of practice . . ." as well as from "an attachment to different leaders ambitiously contending for preëminence and power." When Madison comprises the effects of all of these factors under the heading of "faction" he fails to do justice to the difference between the elements of violence and passion inherent in that term and the more restrained manner in which, as a rule, what we call pressure groups and political parties manifest themselves, but this does not affect the trend of the argument.

Certainly, Madison moves safely on the path of democratic constitutionalism when he says about the apparently most natural remedy for such differences (which consists in eliminating their causes by imposing unity upon them from above):

> It could never be more truly said than of the first remedy, that it was worse than the disease. Liberty is to faction what air is to fire, an aliment without which it instantly expires. But it could not be less folly to abolish liberty, which is essential to political life, because it nourishes faction, than it would be to wish the annihilation of air, which is essential to animal life, because it imparts to fire its destructive agency.[32]

At this point Madison rejects "pure democracy" because it not only does not permit of a remedy for faction, but encourages its most violent manifestations. The problem then is how a "representative republic" solves our problem. For Madison the first weapon available in its armory by which it can "break and control the violence of faction" is majority rule. In his words:

> If a faction consists of less than a majority, relief is supplied by the republican principle, which enables the majority to defeat its sinister views by regular vote. It may clog the administration, it may convulse the society; but it will be unable to execute and mask its violence under the forms of the Constitution.[33]

This passage enunciates only one of the several aspects of majority rule, but it is a vital one. Professor Zurcher has formulated what is perhaps the most disturbing feature of latterday democracy: "In far too many instances, the decision-making process in a democracy is slowed and even blocked in the very organs set up to articulate the popular will." [34] This result Madison meant to prevent by the application of majority rule; it will be seen later that this principle, if consistently applied in the election of parliamentary assemblies, will go far toward accomplishing what Madison wanted it to accomplish. On the other hand, the disregard of this principle under the heading of "proportional representation" invites exactly what Madison was determined to prevent.

One more implication of Madison's statement is clear: When he took it for granted that recourse must be had to majority rule, he took an affirmative stand on the use of power within a democracy. He did, after all, set out to *"break and control* the violence of faction." "Factions" were to be dealt with not merely by moral exhortation; they were to be countered with all the weapons of public power consistent with the purposes of a government which "derived its just powers from the consent of the governed." In this regard, he was, as we shall see below, guided by considerations which Jefferson and Lincoln were to state explicitly. That both of these men were most mindful of the need to safeguard human rights only goes to show that orderly majority rule entails that channeling of public power which is conducive to the protection of the rights of the individual, whether he belongs to the majority or to the minority. Before returning to that point, let us, in all brevity, list the other weapons which, according to Madison, are at the disposal of a "representative republic" for the purpose of dealing with factional divisions.

The first of these weapons is the very principle of government constituted on the basis of representation. It makes it possible "to refine and enlarge the public views, by passing them through the medium of a chosen body of citizens, whose wisdom may best discern the true interests of their community, and whose patriotism and love of justice will be least likely to sacrifice it to temporary or partial considerations."

This passage has two implications. The one which has been brought out by all commentators (and criticized by most) concerns the possibility that representatives might take care of the *res publica* better than the people themselves. It has led to the charge that Madison was an "elitist," a charge which will not trouble us if we recall that democracy is government by leadership and that Jefferson defended a "natural aristocracy," based on talent and performance. A full evaluation of that problem will, however, lead us back to the problem of majority rule; we shall see that representative government not only makes it possible to "refine and enlarge the public views" (Madison, incidentally, was realistic enough to see that the opposite might also happen) but that it also comprises the methods by which "public" opinion is formed in the first place, as it never exists by itself.

Madison's remarks further make it clear that the number of those to whom the conduct of public affairs is entrusted in a "representative republic" has a bearing upon the nature of their actions. As mentioned in No. 55 of *The Federalist*, it must lie below a certain level "in order to avoid the confusion and intemperance of a multitude," in other words, in order to exclude the dangers associated with a popular assembly. There must be, on the other hand, at least enough "to secure the benefits of free consultation and discussion, and to guard against too easy a combination for improper purposes." [35] This number needs, at the same time, "to be derived from the great body of the society, not from an inconsiderable proportion, or a favored class of it; otherwise a handful of tyrannical nobles, exercising their oppressions by a delegation of their powers, might aspire to the rank of republicans, and claim for their government the honorable title of a republic." [36]

This passage states the difference between the political processes operating in an aristocracy and those in a "representative republic." Madison found it necessary to protest against applying the term "republican" to them and, speaking of Venice, he said: ". . . absolute power over the great body of the people is exercised, in the most absolute manner, by a small body of hereditary nobles." [37] While this statement is an exaggeration, it does point out that the number of those endowed with the rights of active citizenship at the bottom matters no less than that of those who exercise power at the top. At a certain point a change of quantity becomes one of quality; the process of integration becomes essentially different. Madison, then, does not simply want the representative feature as an instrument to guarantee "order." He wants it to rest on a sufficiently wide popular basis, and to secure the advantages of an orderly deliberation, which include the presence of an effective "test of reality" based upon free and frank decision among equals.

Madison sees the final reason why a representative republic may succeed in the control of dissent, even in cases where a "pure democracy" is likely to fail, in the "greater number of citizens and extent of territory which may be brought within the compass of republican than of democratic government." In his words:

> Extend the sphere, and you take in a greater variety of parties and interests; you make it less probable that a majority of the whole will have a common motive to invade the rights of other citizens; or if

such a common motive exists, it will be more difficult for all who feel
it to discover their own strength, and to act in unison with each other.
Besides other impediments, it may be remarked that, where there is
a consciousness of unjust or dishonorable purposes, communication is
always checked by distrust in proportion to the number whose concurrence is necessary.[38]

This passage has, again, a number of implications, some of which will
be considered later. At this juncture it is interesting to note that Madison provides an added defense of majority rule. Where elections are
held under the majority system of voting the number of those who
must be won over constitutes a larger percentage of the total than is
the case under any system of proportional representation; the more
people that have to be brought together the less likely it will be that
passion and fanaticism, which so often animate a minority, will
prevail.

A common thread, then, unites the three factors which, according to Madison, enable a "representative republic" to face the danger
of disruptive divisions with a prospect of success. Majority rule in a
small area, government by elected, and responsible, representatives,
and the large size of the country each constitute a particular aspect
of the process of integration characteristic of the democratic state. We
must add, however, that Madison's arguments are incomplete. Political parties in the modern, democratic sense of the term, are also
needed to establish that measure of political control over the discordant forces of society which was Madison's goal; they will form the
subject of the next chapter.

Chapter VIII

POLITICAL PARTIES

~~~~~~

PARTIES AND FACTIONS.

If Madison failed to realize that political parties must be the channel through which the actions of the citizens must flow if a representative republic is to be both orderly and free, other observers shared in his deficiency both in his own time and during subsequent generations. Political parties are, indeed, subjected to almost as formidable a barrage of criticism in our day as they were in the days of George Washington and James Madison. It is charged that their divisions divide the country against itself. They are said to make it impossible for the government to avail itself of the best talent in a nation, since the members of the opposition are excluded from the public service. In the United States, the point is frequently made that the major parties are no longer justified because they have ceased to stand for any "real" difference of opinion. More than a generation ago it was said that: "The party term Republican isn't definitive any more. It isn't even descriptive. No more so is the party term Democrat. They are labels on empty bottles, signs on untenanted houses, cloaks that cover but do not conceal the skeletons beneath them." The logical conclusion was "Why Not Scrap Them Both?" [1] There follows the charge that parties, instead of responding to issues, create them. They would be justified as long as they serve the specific purpose for which they were founded; after that they ought to disband rather than to perpetuate their existence. It has been suggested that parties be replaced by "leagues" whose purpose would be to respond to one particular issue, and whose existence would be terminated once that issue is settled.[2]

The answers to these charges have rarely been given in a manner commensurate with their importance.[3] Misunderstandings concerning the nature of party continue and this is a field where the misconceptions of theory lead to continued demand for changes in practice, which, if adopted, might jeopardize the very essence of that combination of freedom and order which the representative republic was to provide, and has provided, with such a substantial measure of success.

When trying to analyze political parties we must, however, avoid the mistakes to which an uncritical empiricism is bound to lead. Not everything called a political party deserves that name. In this case as in others we cannot simply pile detail upon detail without making a selection from among them guided by a working hypothesis as to the nature of the problem with which we are to deal. It must, in the first place, be emphasized that political parties are one thing, and "factions" another. To clarify this issue we might, for the time being, limit ourselves to a purely descriptive definition: Political parties are voluntary and permanent organizations for the conquest of political power in free and competitive elections. The factions of the past, such as the Guelphs and the Ghibellines in the cities of medieval Italy, have one feature in common with modern democratic parties: both fight for political power. They are separated from them by a wide gulf in all other respects.

Factions, in particular, were not voluntary. Modern political parties, as Max Weber has put it, are based on "formally free recruiting." [4] That political parties are put to the test in free and competitive elections means that, in order to win, they must go out into the highways and the byways inviting everyone, including members of the opposite party, to join their fold. This the factions of old did not do. They were of a rather clannish type, consisting of families, and not of individuals. These families were held together by the force of tradition, supported by the ever-present danger of retaliation which threatened anyone who might want to exercise a choice of his own. Factional claims extended to the personal lives of their members as well as to their political allegiance, as history's most famous lovers, Romeo and Juliet, were to realize; the fact that their families had been lined up with different factions by remote ancestors meant tragedy for their young lives.

That factions did not secure success by "free recruiting" implied the need of resorting to the physical violence with which the annals of the medieval Italian city-states are filled. There was no possibility of a peaceful coexistence between the rival groups. One of them was the "good" party—*buona parte*—Napoleon Bonaparte's ancestors evidently having had the wisdom of choosing the right group. The opposite was the "bad" party—*mala parte*—a name which Curzio Malaparte has endeavored to perpetuate in the appelation under which he chose to write.

In consideration of such features, it naturally follows that factions could not, as do modern political parties, maintain open and above-board organizations.[5] Cohesion among them was conspirational, and this contributed to the many irresponsible acts committed by their leaders. Considering all of these facts, it was natural for George Washington to make himself, in his Farewell Address, the spokesman for the anxieties which the nature and the history of faction inspired among the founders of the new republic. The factions of the city-state did "design to direct, control, counteract or awe the regular delibera-tion and action of the constituted authorities." Thus, when a popular assembly was to be held, they would endeavor to fill the meeting place with their own followers, preventing others from being present, or from expressing their views. Their "alternate domination . . . sharp-ened by the spirit of revenge" was, indeed, regarded by the people of their respective cities as an affliction. Washington was equally right when he said that "the disorders and miseries" which resulted from such factional fights gradually inclined "the minds of men to seek security and repose in the absolute power of an individual": a dicta-torship was established giving the people the "peace" they wanted, but at the price of freedom.

Washington was wrong, however, when he applied what he be-lieved to be the lessons of history to the division into political parties of those who had established the new Constitution. When Jefferson left the fold of the "patriots" and founded the "Republican-Demo-cratic" party, those who remained in the government naturally had to set up a party of their own, even if these "Federalists" hardly ever succeeded in doing successfully what they would have preferred not to do at all. When Professor Schattschneider asks why Jefferson's res-ignation from Washington's cabinet, which initiated this development, "is not marked by a national holiday," [6] he aptly emphasizes that "the representative republic" could, in the final analysis, be a success only because political parties arose and succeeded in breathing life into a constitutional mechanism which, without them, would have degen-erated either into disorder or into dictatorship.

The political parties of American history, and of the history of all other democratic countries, turned out, in fact, to have charac-teristics exactly opposite those of medieval factions. That they were, in the first place, based on "free recruiting," and that they had to go out into the highways and byways of political life in order to secure power, did cause them certainly to resort to all the tricks of propaganda and deception with which their record is replete. But it also infused into them respect for the freedom of those to whose free decision they had to appeal, and it forced them to be tolerant of one another. If the voter was free to like a party, he must also be free to leave it, and if he was free in this one important respect, he must be allowed to be free in others. Intolerance,[7] then, had no more place in party life than did violence; there was need for more than one party if the very purpose of a party was to be served.

PARTIES AND FUNCTIONS.

None of this was, nor could be, foreseen during the eighteenth century. Therefore, parties were not called into existence by a theoretical analysis. They arose haphazardly; at first, nearly everyone opposed them and no one really understood them—not even Jefferson who, as late as in 1803, discussed the possibility of a "Reconciliation with the Federalists," [8] unaware of the fact that the very concept of party presupposes a party *system* with at least two members. Still, whatever arises from an objective need has the advantage of being free to follow its own logic, regardless of the feelings experienced by those who are its unwitting instruments. It will, if left alone, render services which no device sprung from the fertile brain of a Sieyès could have provided.

The nature of these services becomes obvious when we remember that democratic constitutions place power into the hands of hundreds of thousands, if not millions, of individual voters. If these remain isolated from one another, no coherent political action will result. Charles Maurras, the famous "Master" of the Action Française, and one of the modern world's most famous opponents of democracy, states categorically: "A democracy is necessarily amorphic and atomistic . . ." [9] For him, this implies that democracy must degenerate into anarchy if it is to remain true to itself.

In reality, political parties are the institution which stands between democracy and anarchy. This realization makes it possible for us to progress from the descriptive definition given above to a functional one: Political parties are the instruments of democratic government. They provide, in the first place, for the mechanism of that government. On the one hand, this includes a majority able to govern and an opposition free to criticize and able to replace it, and, on the other, the personnel which is necessary for the operation of the government, an elite being just as vital for a democracy as it is for a rulership.

The practical necessity for party organization becomes obvious wherever elections are held. Individual voters realize that they are powerless unless they band together with others in order to promote the success of a candidate and of the policies for which they want him to stand. The immediate effects of this compulsion to unite are limited to the area in which a candidate is to be elected. (For the time being, we assume that elections take place in single-member districts, and that the rules of the majority system apply.) The issues confronting a country, however, rarely differ essentially from one constituency to another. There is, therefore, a tendency for nationwide organizations [10] to arise and to promote the success of candidates willing to combine in a joint effort to conquer political power. To the extent that this tendency prevails [11] in the process of elections, we have, instead of a guerilla warfare of individuals without aim and purpose, a battle between large armies, the major ones of which fight for victory in the country as a whole.

Victory means power, and power means responsibility. As to details, the manner in which public power is organized in a democracy differs significantly, depending on whether it is the parliamentary system as developed in Britain, or the presidential system provided by the Constitution of the United States. In the first case, the formation of a government is treated as a party matter. Whichever party, or group of parties, secures a majority in the popular branch of the legislature, forms the government. In the United States and the countries which have followed its example, a chief executive is elected in a process different from, and independent of, the elections to the Congress. The basic problems are the same, however, to the extent that political organization is as much needed to elect a president as it is to secure a parliamentary majority.

PARTIES AND MAJORITIES.

The primary problem, then, is the winning of majorities. Its very nature is ignored when it is approached in the terms of static thinking. The latter assumes that, if there are majorities, the electoral process will reflect them, and if there are none electoral systems will not alter this result. What is overlooked, however, is that, while marriages may be made in heaven, political parties are not. Their raw material consists in thousands, if not millions, of individuals, many of whom might go in one direction or another. Reference has been made to Winston Churchill's statement that in 1931 the metal of British politics was molten, ready to be guided into definite molds. Not only must we repeat that the basic relationship indicated by Sir Winston is of a permanent and universal nature, but also that the material to be molded is "secondary" rather than "primary" matter. Yet the experience of all democratic countries indicates that the political attitudes of voters are more flexible than it would appear on the surface. Their allegiance to any one party is, indeed, "a plebiscite daily repeated." Under most conditions, the political line-up may be conservative in the sense that those who vote for a particular party usually continue to do so, but change the basic conditions under which they have been voting, and the result will be substantially different.[12]

Countries with a two-party system have, invariably, used the simplest, and most effective type of political channeling: The plurality system in single-member constituencies. This means that the candidate with the largest number of votes is declared elected even if he does not have more than 50 per cent of the total. No candidate is, of course, *certain* of success unless he does obtain more than 50 per cent. All candidates want to win if they possibly can, and for this reason the absolute majority is their goal even where it is not necessarily required. Only two candidates can, however, expect either to get 50 per cent or come reasonably close to it, the simple reason being that 100 over 50 is 2. Strong pressure will be brought to bear on weaker candidates to withdraw from the race, or rather not to enter it from the outset. Once the results are announced they are final, and if the presence of a third or fourth candidate has taken enough votes away from a major candidate to allow his principal opponent to be elected with a mere plurality, vain regrets will not alter the result.

This system has revolutionary results simply because it maximizes the incentive to political fusion. All kinds of social differences must be overcome; "all sorts and conditions of men" must meet on the basis of a common *political* denominator. They must do so immediately; there is no second chance if, when the votes are counted, it develops that someone else has been more efficient at this task. For the time being, suffice it to refer to the fate of minor parties which stand in the way of the powerful current towards the integration which the plurality system initiates. Experience proves that the followers of such a party are, as a rule, drawn into this current rather quickly and do not resent it. On the other hand, political "elites," on the middle as well as on the higher level, may offer a substantial and prolonged resistance. Thus, in England, it was always rather clear, ever since the formation of the first Labour government in 1924, that the Liberal party with all its great and glorious history did not have a political future, and that the votes cast for it would, for the most part, be "thrown away." The bulk of the party's former followers drew this conclusion almost immediately. A substantial number of the party's elite did join either the Conservative or the Labour party, sharing in the leadership of both, but an organizational framework was maintained which continued to hold the loyalty of some of the best minds in the party or, for that matter, in the country. However, it was powerless so far as the formation of the country's political consciousness and the conduct of its government were concerned.

The United States has never experienced such an extended period of loyalty to a lost political cause. Minor parties have repeatedly arisen and, at times, demonstrated substantial strength, such as the anti-Masonic party, the Know-Nothings, the Populists, and the Progressives, led by political figures as outstanding as Theodore Roosevelt and the elder LaFollette. The movements headed by the two last-named men are characteristic of the nature of their political demise. Theodore Roosevelt garnered a larger percentage of the votes than any third-party candidate had done before or after him. Yet the result was defeat. The organization created by "T.R." was allowed to lapse almost immediately. The two groups in the Republican party had fought one another without mercy in 1912, but they presented a common candidate in 1916, former Supreme Court Justice (and later Chief Justice) Hughes, who came so close to victory that, on the evening of election day, he retired in the belief that he was the next President of the United States.

Similarly, when in November of 1924 Robert LaFollette secured 16.2 per cent of the total popular vote he was evidently leading a substantial group. By way of comparison let it be mentioned that in countries with proportional representation (subsequently referred to as P.R.) parties with a lower percentage of the total have played, and continue to play, a decisive part in their nation's history; thus, the French Socialists polled 15 per cent of the votes in the elections of 1956, and on this basis, their leader, Guy Mollet, became Prime Minister. In the United States, LaFollette secured only the electoral votes of his native state of Wisconsin, 2.4 per cent of the total. The day after the elections, the impressive coalition which he had led collapsed; few thought any longer of founding the new party which had been planned in case a more substantial vote had been secured. By 1928 the bulk of LaFollette's followers had been reabsorbed by the Republican and Democratic parties; LaFollette himself continued to be elected to the Senate as a Republican.

Experiences such as these demonstrate the dynamic character of any two-party system. The major parties constitute channels within which there moves a variety of different, and often discordant, currents. Some of them are turbulent enough to be constantly attempting to open up a new channel for themselves but, as a rule, the embankment proves high enough for their containment. In the exceptional case that the opening of a new major channel does take place, the currents pouring into it are strong enough to carry the bulk of the waters from one of the old channels along; where, as in the United States in the case of the Republican party, or in Britain in the case of the Labour party, a third group establishes itself it soon becomes one of the leading parties, dispossessing one of its predecessors. The result, of course, is not a type of unity which would imply uniformity. The remaining differences, however, are subjected to a constant process of adjustment, with the result that the parties are able to perform their functions, even though it might be noted that, in this respect, there is considerable variation between two major parties under the parliamentary system, as in Britain and Canada, and their equivalent under the separation of powers, as in the United States. This problem will be discussed later.

There exists an even greater contrast between the two-party system of the Anglo-Saxon type and the multiple-party system of most other countries. Whatever its ultimate causes may be, the difference is invariably associated with a divergence from the plurality system of voting; Georges Vedel,[13] following Maurice Duverger,[14] has emphasized that, in regard to the effect upon the party system, the plurality system is in a class all by itself, as it encourages integration while all other types encourage multiplication.

There remains, nonetheless, a difference between systems which retain the principle of election by majority and those which adopt that of P.R. Of the former, there are three major variations. There is first the case of run-off elections, in which the two candidates with the highest vote in the first ballot appear in a second if no one has obtained an overall majority in the first. The second type, the French *scrutin de ballotage,* is more liberal. If no candidate obtains more than 50 per cent in the first ballot a second ballot is held in which every candidate can present himself again, even new ones, and the plurality decides. The third system is that of the alternative vote. Where more than two candidates are in the field—which almost invariably happens under this system—the voter may indicate a second choice. If no candidate secures an overall majority of the first choice votes, the candidate with the lowest number of first choices is eliminated, and his second choices are transferred to those for whom they were marked. This process is continued until one candidate does have more than 50 per cent of the votes.

So far as the effects of these systems are concerned, there applies to all of them, with minor modifications, what Woodrow Wilson had to say about the *scrutin de ballotage* characteristic of the France of the Third Republic:

> The result is, that the multiplication of parties, or rather the multiplication of groups and factions within the larger party lines, from which France naturally suffers overmuch, is directly encouraged. Rival groups are tempted to show their strength on the first ballot in an election, for the purpose of winning a place or exchanging favor for favor in the second. They lose nothing by failing in the first; they may gain concessions or be more regarded another time by showing a little strength; and rivalry is encouraged, instead of consolidation. France cannot afford to foster factions.[15]

If "France cannot afford to foster factions" neither can any other country, and yet this is what all the systems listed above will do to a greater or lesser degree. The system of run-off elections is most conservative. A candidate who fails to place either first or second is automatically eliminated; his votes are "wasted," and there is no chance to use them for bargaining purposes. Still, where this system was adopted in American primaries, it has led to a substantial increase in the number of candidates.[16] The alternative vote is similarly conservative; yet, its introduction in Australia was followed immediately by the establishment of a third party, the Country party, which has introduced certain, not unimportant, modifications into the Australian political system. The unlimited second ballot as practiced in France fosters, more than any of the other systems, the multiplication of parties.

This multiplication does change the picture for the worse when compared with a two-party system. If there are, within any of the British or American parties, groups which differ appreciably from one another they are at least flexible. The line-up may vary from occasion to occasion and, as long as it does not harden, compromises are not too difficult to obtain.[17] The situation changes when there are separate party organizations, all with loyalties and interests of their own. In such cases there comes into play what Goetz Briefs has called the "organized interest of associations," meaning that any organization has interests of its own which are different from those of its individual members and which may, in fact, enter into conflict with the very purposes for which the association was founded. Above all, the organization wants to perpetuate its existence and to increase its power. Thus, in a country like France the various parties of the Right may have broadly similar purposes, and those who vote for them may (and usually are) more interested in these common purposes than in the shades of differentiation existing between them. However, party leaders and, in particular, party bureaucrats do feel differently; it has become almost second nature to them that everything pertaining to their separate group is of primary importance, and everything else of secondary importance.

Still, as long as majority voting is retained in some form or other there are limits to the process of differentiation. In the first place, not all minor parties have the same chance. Ultimately, in an election the decisions as to whether a candidate of the Right or of the Left is to be chosen depends not upon the convinced partisans of either, but upon the undecided voters whose place is in the center of the political spectrum. They may constitute the "driftwood" that party leaders often call them, or they may deserve the praise bestowed upon them by Disraeli, who spoke of them as "conscientious men" and "deeply meditative individuals," distinguished not only by their "sensitive turn of mind" but by a "charitable vein that seems to pervade their being." [18] At any rate, standing in the center of the political line-up they are farther removed from all extremists than from the more moderate groups. The following diagram, representing roughly the condition existing in France between the two world wars, illustrates the situation:

Extreme Right	Right	Moderate Right	Marginal Voters	Radicals	Socialists	Communists
—→	—→	—→	←—	←—	←—	

The extreme Right and the extreme Left, farthest removed from the undecided voter, are under the greatest handicap. Whenever in France, for example, the Communists presented, under majority voting, their candidates without previous arrangements with other parties —and the nature of an extremist party makes such arrangements difficult—the percentage of seats which they obtained was around one-fifth of their share in the votes.[19] Usually, when such a process continues for long, the party in question loses votes as well as seats, its supporters being unwilling to "throw their votes away."

A multiple-party system, then, as it develops under systems of majority voting which deviate from the simple rules of the plurality system, differs from one under P.R., in the first place by the fact that extremist parties are under constant pressure. It is no less important that, so far as the other groups are concerned, the result is a multiplicity of *related*, rather than of unrelated, parties. In France the various groups of the Right and Left might all present their own candidates in the first ballot but, in the second, usually two serious candidates, one supported by the entire Right and the other by the entire Left, would remain. Thus, a measure of agreement on both "men" and "measures" had to be reached before victory could be achieved, and the splits caused during the first ballot were healed, to some extent, during the second. This process makes a substantial difference when we compare such parties to those which arise under P.R. In that case any group of any size (the details depend upon the concrete characteristics of the type of P.R. used) can elect its own candidates with its own votes, with the result that everyone can develop his peculiarities to his heart's content.

These differences have their effect upon the parties' ability to serve their function of being instruments of democratic government. At this juncture suffice it to recall that the two-party system, as conditioned by the plurality system of voting, does its part with commendable regularity. In Britain this means an overall parliamentary majority for one party, and in the United States, primarily a majority in the electoral college, and secondarily, the Congress. The American President does derive great benefits from a cooperative House and Senate which, in most cases, are more likely to be forthcoming from a body controlled by his own party than by the opposition. John Quincy Adams and Andrew Johnson during their entire tenure, and Woodrow Wilson and Herbert Hoover during the final two years of their administrations, provide examples of the futility which tends to be associated with the coexistence of a President and a Congress systematically hostile to presidential policies. Dwight D. Eisenhower presents, perhaps, the only case of a President who could look forward to as much cooperation from a Congress organized by the opposition as from one controlled by his own party; however, he later declared himself "tremendously disappointed" in the record of the first session of the Eighty-fifth Congress, which was controlled by his opponents.

GOVERNMENT AND OPPOSITION.

Much as democratic government is a majority government, it does need an opposition. Elections would not be free if there were no opposition. In that case, there would be no choice for the voter. Nor would the issues of a campaign be properly presented. Woodrow Wilson [20] quotes aptly from a letter to the editor of *The* (London) *Times:* "In party government party life becomes like a court of justice. The people are the judges, the politicians the advocates, who 'he adds caustically rather than justly,' only occasionally and by incident speak their real opinion." Parties must, indeed, present issues the way advocates do, and Wilson was right in implying that in that process they are more likely than their critics assume to present opinions which have become their own.

To be fully effective, opposition must be expressed in parliamentary bodies as well as in the country. It is not enough to say with Cobden: "If the minority are discontented with the existing state of things, let them set to work and exert themselves until they become the majority," [21] even if this rule constitutes an important part of the truth. The minority should be given the satisfaction of knowing that if they are out of office for some years in the sense that they do not control the executive, they are at least a recognized part of a parliament in which they can contribute towards controlling the executive. This will avoid the feeling of frustration which might otherwise follow upon their failure to obtain a majority, and it will also make the leaders of the opposition more responsible. In a parliamentary body they possess a platform from which they can reach the public more effectively than they can from any other; they will also be forced to express themselves, in debate with their opponents, on the concrete merits of proposals made by the majority, being constantly under pressure to produce constructive alternatives.

The government itself will benefit from a situation in which its supporters have to discuss governmental policies constantly with its opponents. As Pericles put it in his Funeral Oration: "We decide or debate, carefully and in person, all matters of policy, holding not that words and deeds go ill together, but that acts are foredoomed to failure when undertaken undiscussed." [22] Government of which discussion is a vital part has, above all, the advantage of having, so to speak, a "built-in" test of reality by free and frank discussion; its leaders must listen to the "other side," whether they want to or not. If this promotes the rationality of political decision, it also fosters the democratic character of the government. Rulers can be forced more easily to reveal the background of a particular decision during the course of a parliamentary debate, as in England, or during the course of committee hearings and committee investigations, as in the United States, rather than by any discussions in the press or on the platform.

The efficiency with which an opposition can fulfill its functions depends on a variety of factors. It must, in the first place, have a case. In 1857 five opposition candidates opposed to the Empire of Napoleon III had managed to get themselves elected in Paris (in addition to four in the provinces) in spite of very formidable official pressure brought to bear against them. Their arguments resounded not only through the halls of the Chamber, but throughout the country, and had much to do with the progressive weakening of the Empire. As a rule, however, the opposition needs a minimum of members. Generally speaking, it is adequate if a majority controls around 60 per cent of the seats—enough to give it leeway to account for the accidental absence of some of its members, and to allow for occasional open dissent in its own ranks without jeopardizing its existence.

Any majority party exceeding such a relation of strength will run into difficulties. Substantial dissent will develop in its own ranks as its constituent parts are no longer held together tightly by the need of preventing a parliamentary victory of the opposition; they will start fighting each other. The most recent example in the United States is the Supreme Court controversy of 1937 which followed so closely on the heels of the overwhelming Democratic victory of 1936 and was characterized by one group of Democrats fighting another. Benjamin Disraeli rightly said: "There is nothing like a good small majority," and he states the reasons as follows:

> No government can be long secure without a formidable opposition. It reduces their supporters to that tractable number which can be managed by the joint influence of fruition and hope. It offers vengeance to the discontented and distinction to the ambitious; and employs the energies of aspiring spirits, who otherwise may prove traitors in a division, or assassins in a debate.[23]

Political practice has left it to accident to provide for a reliable majority along with a strong opposition. When parliamentary bodies developed, it was the simplest method to elect their members in local, usually single-member, constituencies. Experience was to show that in such a fashion—as long as the plurality system was used—one party did, as a rule, have an adequate overall majority, while another party, or several other parties, constituted an adequate opposition. A party which had a majority in one part of the country, such as the cities, usually found itself a minority in another, such as the rural areas. Exceptionally, as the American elections of 1932, 1934 and 1936, and the British elections of 1918, 1931 and 1945 have demonstrated, the accidents of plurality elections in single-member constituencies may lead to an overly strong majority. Similarly, though this happens less frequently, they may lead, as they did in Britain in 1950, to weak and indecisive majorities. Both defects could, of course, be prevented, though in Britain, as well as in the United States, most people would probably feel that they occur too infrequently to require major adjustments.[24]

PARTIES AND THE PEOPLE.

Not all parties provide in equal measure for a majority and a minority sufficiently coherent to fulfill their functions. Where parties exist in little more than name, as was the case in the French *Convention*, they may be organized in such a rudimentary fashion as to constitute little more than a mob, subject to all the dangers of crowd psychology. In the end, the members of the *Convention* lost control over their actions to such an extent that, after having sanctioned the execution of thousands of innocent people, they started sentencing each other to death. Recent French parliaments were more prudent in this regard. Rather than apply the death penalty to themselves they inflicted it upon one government after the other. This could happen only because there was no party organization strong enough to restrain them from acts which they themselves often regretted shortly after they had been committed.

We may follow Max Weber in stating that party organization has proceeded through three stages: Parties of aristocrats, parties of "notables," and mass parties. The English parties of the period between the Glorious Revolution and the first electoral reform (1689–1832) are an illustration for the first possibility. At the nucleus of each there was an aristocratic clique. This was supported, of course, by a popular element (such as the clergy of the Church of England in the case of the Tories, and much of the rising business community in the case of the Whigs). The aristocrats were still firmly enough in command of the parties because of the large number of "pocket" boroughs from which members of the House of Commons were virtually nominated by a landowner. Family ties were the basis on which cohesion was maintained in these parties. When, in Disraeli's *Coningsby* [25] an old aristocrat is confronted by a rebellious nephew who would like to act in accordance with his convictions he tells him: "You go with your family, Sir, like a gentleman; you are not to consider your opinions like a philosopher or a political adventurer."

The first electoral reform deprived the aristocracy of enough influence to change the character of British parties and with it the character of the British political system. There was, for the time being, no substitute for the type of cohesion which the aristocracy had provided. The middle class element was dominant, and the principal characteristic of the period was instability. One hesitates to apply to a country such as England the term "party of notables"; the lawyer, the doctor and the teacher never quite played the part they did in France. Yet, certain basic characteristics of "parties of notables" did develop. A substantial number of House of Commons members had been elected primarily with the help of locally prominent people, and there was nothing to establish effective cooperation among them. Therefore, the period from 1832 to 1867 is one of relative instability. The two leading parties were each split in two, and there were minor groups in the House. The formation of governments was—comparatively [26]—difficult; it might take a couple of weeks, and coalitions and minority cabinets proved necessary on occasion. In a substantial number of cases more than 10 per cent of a party's members failed to vote in accordance with party directions.[27]

This situation was corrected by a step which everyone expected to achieve the opposite result: The second and third electoral reforms broadened the franchise which was given, for the first time, to many industrial workers. There were many illiterates among them, and this produced apprehensions which came to be expressed in more memorable phrases than were called forth perhaps by any other single event in British political history. Thus Lord Derby called the Reform Act of 1867 "a leap in the dark," Carlyle spoke of "shooting Niagara," and Robert Lowe proclaimed: "We must educate our masters." As it happened, the objects of this educational solicitude were to "educate" their would-be educators. Both parties faced the task of attracting the new vote. The Liberals, under the leadership of Joseph Chamberlain and Schnadhorst set out to register voters on a precinct to precinct basis. The Conservatives, at first, disdainfully called this organization a "caucus," but soon realized that it was efficient, and proceeded to imitate it. Thus the popular party organization was born, and it revolutionized the British political system. The thousands of new party members were not interested in the sophisticated political differentiations prevalent among their elite; as one spokesman put it: "We now think in battalions." Clearcut and simple issues had to be presented, and political dissension at the top proved to be unpopular with the rank and file. When, in 1877, Joseph Chamberlain addressed a convention of Liberal delegates in Birmingham, who were about to set up the national organization of the Liberal party, he said: "Our association will be founded upon the belief that the Liberals in the country are more united than their leaders." [28] The bulk of the party members preferred to think in the more personal terms of the party's leader— the actual or the potential Prime Minister—rather than in terms of either abstract "principles" or even concrete issues; a vote for the Conservatives was a vote for Disraeli, and a vote for the Liberals was one for Gladstone.

Thus a plebiscitary feature was introduced in British political life;

it gave the Prime Minister a position of strength incomparably greater than that enjoyed by his counterpart in countries which have the parliamentary system without a two-party system. This means that in England and in the countries comparable to her political structure—such as Canada—political parties finally and truly became instruments of *democratic* government; through their medium the people secured a direct part in selecting the government of their country. Of course, mass parties have also arisen since that time in countries lacking a two-party system, but wherever coalitions must be formed at the discretion of party leaders, they lack the basis of direct popular sanction. In addition, the strength which these parties derive from their mass support may become a negative factor; it has, at times, merely helped one party to frustrate the efforts of all others. Such features are primarily a concomitant of the system of *unrelated* multiple parties typical of P.R.

PARTIES AND LEADERS.

If, then, political parties with strong roots among the people do establish an effective mechanism of government by creating both a strong government and a strong opposition, they will also be able to provide for the proper political personnel. While the need for an "elite" is something which appears to be shameful to the proponents of the ideological concept of democracy, it is yet both obvious and fully compatible with the requirements of "government by leadership." The functions of political leaders have been discussed above. Suffice it to say that the combination of political parties and elections under the majority system tends to provide leaders, even in the case of "mass parties" which some have held to be unsuited to this purpose. It is true enough that when the British and Canadian voter goes to the polls, he is primarily interested in the party for which he votes and in its national leader, rather than in the individual member of parliament. Yet, party leaders know that if the bulk of their followers is ready to cast its ballots for virtually any bearer of the party label, the undecided voter may take a good long look at the candidate for whom he votes, and he may provide the margin of victory. Care is taken, therefore, to present the best possible candidate.

This is even more obvious in the United States than in countries with a parliamentary system. Most observers would agree that the Republican victories of 1952 and 1956 were due to the fact that Dwight D. Eisenhower was heading the ticket. Similarly, in the state of Ohio Robert A. Taft and Frank Lausche have proven repeatedly that their personal popularity could carry them to victory even when their party was losing, and such examples from all over the country could be multiplied. In these cases it is, at the same time, obvious that a democracy is not simply, as Hobbes said, "an aristocracy of orators." Taft had to make a considerable effort to attain forensic ability even if he did attain it in the end. The voter is frequently as much impressed by character and accomplishments as by any oratorial artistry.

The existence of political parties entails, however, another stage in the selection of political leaders. In parliamentary bodies, in particular, a test is made of "the capacity for effective statement, for framing legislation, for mastery in parliamentary debate, for teamwork, cooperation, and successful compromise." [29] There is, where the parliamentary system obtains, also the testing ground of executive ability where some, beginning with minor offices, may rise to the top in a process which is both slow and methodical. Thus, those who may have been elected to parliamentary bodies primarily on the basis of oratorical ability will have to pass the judgment of their peers before they can advance beyond the first stage. Their colleagues will hardly be satisfied with anything except what their rather critical judgment reveals to them as the best, as their own political future may depend on the performance of these men. The final result of the democratic mechanism of selection may still not always be excellent, but in two world wars the leaders of the democratic nations certainly proved the equals of the non-democratic rulers whom they had to confront.

PARTIES AND POLITICAL AGREEMENT.

In addition to providing for the mechanism and the personnel of democratic government, political parties also help to establish that area of fundamental agreement which their rule seems to presuppose. This statement may, at first sight, appear paradoxical. In political campaigns much effort is concentrated on finding a "winning issue"; in this process, matters are made a subject of controversy which should not be, and there are invariably attempts to stir up enthusiasm by painting the opposition in the darkest possible colors. Reference has often been made to what Lord Balfour (speaking of England, but having in mind the conditions governing party government the world over) expressed in these terms:

> Our alternating Cabinets, though belonging to different Parties, have never differed about the foundations of society. And it is evident that our whole political machinery pre-supposes a people so fundamentally at one that they can safely afford to bicker; and so sure of their own moderation that they are not dangerously disturbed by the never-ending din of political conflict. May it always be so.[30]

England herself has, of course, not always been "fundamentally at one." The civil war of the seventeenth century was accompanied by as many atrocities as such periods of discord have seen in any country,[31] and the memory rankled for a long time. After the Glorious Revolution there was, for generations, a lack of complete popular acceptance of the new dynasty; it appeared only with the ascension of George III in 1760. The rule of this monarch, in turn, led to a great deal of dissent, and there was to be more in the first half of the nineteenth century, culminating in the battles for Catholic emancipation, the first electoral reform, and in the Chartist movement.

In reality party government, instead of presupposing agreement on fundamentals, tends to create it. In the British case it was, of course, always accompanied by the plurality system of voting which caused parties to be large, and if they were large they had to be tolerant because they contained members of all major social and religious groups in their own ranks. We might call this process "intraparty integration," and reemphasize, in passing, that the maintenance of any large party is a never-ending task, as the various elements which compose it must again and again be reconciled with one another on the basis of a common denominator which is bound to shift in the process.

In addition to intra-party integration there is inter-party integration; it results from the need to reconcile the undecided voter who stands between the major parties. Most of the campaign ammunition fired by both camps is aimed in his direction and, from the fact that the same type of voter has to be won over by both sides there follows a tendency on the part of both to make concessions to him, which, in turn, set in motion a process of mutual assimilation. Details of that process will be discussed in the next chapter. At this juncture suffice it to refer, as sufficient proof for the point under consideration, to the claim, made so frequently in the United States, that there is no "real" difference between the two major parties, and that they are as much alike as "tweedledum and tweedledee." Certainly, if they are that much alike they cannot, at the same time, fail to help establish that "unity on fundamentals" which Lord Bryce considered a pre-condition for their alternation in power.

There do remain, however, enough differences between the two leading exponents of a two-party system to justify their existence. This would be the case, as a matter of fact, even if the difference were merely one between the "ins" and the "outs." Parties could not perform their services were it not for the existence of competition between them; if the freedom of the voter consists in the possibility of choosing between alternatives, more than one party is needed. A "mere" struggle between two groups of rival elites does give the people a chance to confirm its old leaders or to choose new ones; if one particular team is worn out it is, indeed, essential that another take its place.

Thus, as long as we realize the vital need for the mechanism of partisan warfare to operate if "government by leadership" is to be a reality we shall not be inclined to blame parties for any failure to develop greatly different "principles" and "programs." Both terms usually rest upon a misunderstanding of the nature of politics in general and of democratic politics in particular. When "principles" are taken as seriously as some people want to take them, they become "isms." Parties develop into political sects and, instead of "bickering" with one another in comparative safety, they lead a kind of holy war against each other.

Actually, the demand for "principles" breaks down simply because "principles" of the kind involved have little substance in real life. Even the most carefully outlined principles are, by the force of circumstance, based on conclusions drawn from the observation of the past. Political life is, however, concerned with the new and unexpected developments which history creates as it unfolds itself from day to day. If we stick to the letter of our "principles" then, like the German Social-Democrats after the First World War, we shall be so fascinated by the notions of the past that we do not realize what happens in the present and thereby exclude ourselves from the opportunity to mold the trends of history as best we can. The sense in which practical politics should be directed has been aptly characterized— though not lived up to—by the unfortunate General von Schleicher, who, when he formed his government in Germany, declared it to be his intention "to do the right thing at the right time." The attempt to do this indicates the possibilities as well as the limitations of what we can do to influence the course of events. Political parties in their attitude toward these problems need not and will not be identical; when trying to cope with them a party may, indeed, as André Siegfried has put it, exhibit a definite political tendency, "a certain manner to conceive society and the state, to take things, to feel them, to react or not to react under the action of these or those exterior circumstances." [32] Such tendencies the ordinary voter is quite well able to discern among the parties which solicit his vote, and this gives him a sufficient basis for his decision.

If parties are distinguished by flexible tendencies rather than by rigid principles it follows that their alternation in power need not interfere with political continuity. Every election campaign is, of course, characterized by a fair measure of verbal excesses but, as soon as a party takes over the reins of government it will be practical and pragmatic enough to take over existing institutions and existing policies as they are and try to modify them gradually, as conditions permit, rather than to tear up everything root and branch. Party leaders would rarely be able to do the latter if they wanted to, and they will lose any such desire when they become acquainted with the actual operation of what they have been rejecting and realize that it was not what they had imagined it to be.

Ample historical proof could be cited for this contention. It begins with the first time in the history of modern democracy when a free election produced a complete change: the victory of Jefferson's "Republican-Democrats" over the "Federalists" in 1800. Jefferson had vigorously opposed what appeared to him as the building up of an overlarge apparatus of federal power. Yet, when he came into office he continued all of these policies, except that he reduced military (in particular naval) expenditures sharply, with results which he himself soon had reason to regret. The same has happened ever since, not excluding the elections of 1952 when the Republicans took over after twenty years of Democratic government and not only retained the reforms instituted by the "New Deal" and the "Fair Deal" but expanded them. They did approach this task with a different philosophy, placing, wherever they felt this to be possible, their main reliance upon private rather than public initiative; they hoped that, in the course of the years, they might be able to shift the currents of history into channels substantially different from those in which the Democrats preferred to operate. If so, the latter would, when resuming power in their turn, once again be likely to make the change-over gradual, and to interfere with the requirements of continuity no more than their rivals.

FUNCTIONAL AND NON-FUNCTIONAL EXPLANATIONS OF PARTY.

More points could be treated, but the time has now come to elucidate the functional view of political parties as set forth above [33] by comparing it with other theories. If our interpretation is correct it contains what might be called the "pure theory" of political parties—a theory explaining their nature under the most general, if at the same time most abstract, conditions, even though political reality approximates them under a two-party system. As long as parties are required by the operation of democratic government this basic need underlies their existence in all democratic countries, whatever the differences between the nations, and the parties, in question; it also explains the more important aspects of any kind of party, except totalitarian parties which are essentially different and will be dealt with later.

This implies, in the first place, that not all characteristics of parties operating within a democratic environment have the same significance. Some of them may be the typical symptoms of a transitory stage, such as the lack of popular roots. Others may explain why a particular party arose without explaining the essentials of party as such. This applies, for example, to all attempts to give an "historical" analysis of the origin of the British two-party system. Historical factors have played their part in its rise, but they led to the result they did because the developing parliamentary system was bound to give birth to political parties in the same way in which in the biological organism the function creates the organ, and because the plurality system directed these historical forces into two major channels.

We should, for that reason, never look for mere manifestations of dissent as the explanation for the existence of political parties; parties arose because democracy needed them, and the concrete type of dissent which may have created one party or the other is incidental. This does not mean that all parties will develop into the "pure type" characteristic of Anglo-Saxon democracy; thus, Social-Democratic and Christian-Democratic parties do exhibit certain characteristics of their own. These characteristics are, however, superimposed upon the more general features of political parties, and the question is whether, in the long run, these general features will not assert themselves more strongly than any particular ones—which they might have done long since had the plurality system of voting been used and exerted the influence towards a fusion of the most disparate elements on a purely political basis which is its major characteristic.

It is, in particular, necessary not to be obsessed with what is assumed to be the economic "basis" of a particular party system. The social stratification of a party's members is, of course, always interesting, and it may be of great importance for a specific problem. Social classes belong, however, to the dimension of *society*, and political parties to that of *politics* which, as mentioned repeatedly, essentially transcends whatever is merely "social," including the division into social classes. If empirical observation shows that the supporters of a political party are, in the main, derived from a certain social class, the decisive element lies in that minority which does not come from that class. Thus, in the United States there has, since the advent of the New Deal, been a strong tendency for industrial workers to support the Democratic party. A number of workers has, however, always voted the Republican ticket and, whenever the Republicans won, this percentage has been substantial. As a result neither the Democratic, nor the Republican, party could afford to be a class party; the former always had enough members not belonging to the lower income groups to induce it to pursue policies calculated to be acceptable to all, and the latter must rely upon enough voters from the lower income groups to force it to present its policies in terms appealing to them.

That such tendencies are not accidental has been realized for some time. G. De Ruggiero [34] summarizes the views of an Italian writer of the late eighteenth century, Vittorio Alfieri, in these words: "The conflict of social classes compromised the power of Rome; the conflict of parties nourishes the strength of England." American party history could, from its very beginnings, easily be rewritten in Alfieri's terms. Certainly, when Beard in his "Economic Interpretation" discussed the Federalists (as the instruments of "the moneyed interests") and the Republican-Democrats (as the political expression of "small farmers and debtors") in terms of social classes he was expressing a half-truth, overlooking what he himself came to recognize as the more important part of the truth when, in the chapter on "Political Parties As Agents and Motors" in his book, *The Republic*,[35] he stressed the integrating effects of party. There were enough representatives of the wealthier element in the Republican-Democratic party to induce it to pursue a policy agreeable to a large number of them. In the crucial election of 1800 Jefferson, not unsuccessfully, wooed the wealthy as well as the poor. After he had come to power, he expressed himself as follows in a letter to Albert Gallatin: "It is material to the safety of Republicanism to detach the mercantile interest from its enemies and to incorporate them into the body of its friends. A merchant is naturally a Republican, and can be otherwise only from a vitiated state of things." [36] The purpose of this letter was to discuss how bankers (certainly the most characteristic representatives of the "moneyed interests"!) could be torn away from their Federalist moorings. Jefferson, then, did not think that "the natural history" [37] of American political parties lay in social divisions; while, of course, he never developed a clear-cut theory of political parties, his sound instinct kept him away from one-sided interpretations as much as from one-sided appeals.

As long as political parties are understood in the context of the work they have to do, it will be realized that they are, indeed, in all major respects agents of integration rather than of disintegration. It will also be seen that if they tend to be similar in their basic tenets they again merely heed the call of the functions which they exist to fulfill.

It only need be added that if they are to serve their purpose they cannot depend upon any one issue. The need for a government is a permanent feature of a democracy. So is the need for political parties designed to provide for both the mechanism and the personnel of the government and for the basis of popular consent upon which they have to rest. "Leagues," as proposed by Ostrogorski, could not assure the needed continuity and stability. Nor could they solve the task of integration. They would be concerned with one particular issue, and the government has to meet a number of related issues at the same time. Finally, Leagues could not secure responsible government. As they would come and go the voters would not know whom to hold to account if something went wrong. The "representative republic," in fact, needs the type of parties which the logic of its institutions has produced, and reproduced, beginning with the first decade of its existence.

Chapter IX

THE TYRANNY OF THE MAJORITY

▄▄

MAJORITY RULE AS A POLITICAL PROCESS.

Democratic and representative government have been confronted, throughout their history, by two major charges. The one is that democracy knows of no effective way to establish authority, in the absence of which liberty leads to license and, in the end, democracy to tyranny. The basic aspects of this matter have been discussed in the preceding chapter. It has been demonstrated that representative government, combined with an effective party organization, provides the means by which liberty and authority can be combined to the lasting advantage of both.

The second charge is the opposite of the first. It is held that democratic government is too strong rather than too weak, and this fear has found expression in the popular term, "tyranny of the majority." A great many writers, some of them prominent in the history of political thought, have used this term, thereby endorsing the warning which it conveys. It will be sufficient, however, to enlarge briefly upon the true implications of majority rule, as set forth above, in order to show that, both in the assumptions underlying it, and in the results which it produces, it is not properly subject to the charges leveled against it.

In the past, when majority rule was defended, it would be referred to as that admirable rule of "counting heads in order to save the trouble of breaking them." This generation, having witnessed the efficiency of the totalitarian dictatorships in "breaking" heads appreciates the strength of this argument. Still, it is negative, and majority rule should stand or fall upon the basis of its positive aspects. Majority rule, to be sure, means that, in the selection of a candidate or in the determination of an issue, there prevails the will of those who cast fifty per cent plus one of the valid votes. We should, however, go beyond this result and study the process by which it is achieved. This process, with exceptions too few to be considered at this juncture, is one of persuasion. It is necessary to convince thousands, and often millions, of voters that a particular candidate deserves to be preferred to his rivals. No matter how powerful the appeal of organized propaganda may be, in the end the individual voter enters the polling booth and makes his own decision, which is based upon a considerable degree of independence in the case of the undecided voter. We may say, therefore, that government by majority is government by persuasion. The reason why a particular candidate prevails is that he and his supporters have done a better job of persuading voters than their rivals.

Before we proceed we may note one of the implications of majority rule which is more easily overlooked than all others, that is, that majority rule is based upon a deeper respect for the human person than can be found in any other way of making political decisions. All non-democratic forms of government must assume that the people are not able to judge the affairs of their community. Some kind of an elite, selected by means other than the free choice of the governed, and often self-perpetuating without regard for any criterion relating to its social usefulness, makes decisions *for* the people. At best this is done in the manner in which parents and guardians act on behalf of minors. Democracy, by placing decisions in the hands of the majority, assumes that people are of age and able to act on their own. The Christian might well remember that while St. Paul speaks of the time when, in his youth, even the future master is subject to the authority of servants and tutors, he adds that, ultimately, he reaches "man's estate" and makes his own decisions. Democracy is "man's estate" in government.

Majority rule not only presupposes a relative maturity of the people, but it also protects their individual rights. This is most clearly seen when we consider individuals as members of the various minority groups which compose a modern state, be they of a religious, racial, social or political character. Thomas Woodlock said at one time that "Democracy is the protection of minorities through the rule of the majority." The reason is to be found in the simple fact that it takes members of many a minority to make up a majority. In the United States no political group can aspire to the status of a major party unless it is willing to accept in a prominent position within its ranks Protestant, Catholic and Jew. In communities with large groups of unassimilated citizens of foreign descent, it has become a fine art to establish a balance between candidates of different national origins.

If any mistake is made in a campaign, disaster may be the result. The classical illustration is provided by the elections of 1884, in which Grover Cleveland was opposed by James G. Blaine. A few days before election day a Republican rally was held in New York. A speaker said, in the presence of Blaine, and without being rebuked by him, that the Democratic party consisted of a combination of "rum, romanism and rebellion." Blaine lost the electoral vote of New York, and thereby the presidency, by 1,100 out of a total of about a million votes. Other factors entered the picture, but observers are generally agreed that a last-minute swing of Catholic votes toward Cleveland was larger than his margin of victory.

The implication is that any minority, no matter how small, may be large enough to turn the scales in an election. To the members of the minority itself we must add that part of the majority group that resents discrimination no matter against whom it is directed. This part may be large. In England, for example, Catholic emancipation was voted by a parliament which had no Catholic members, at a time when the electorate consisted entirely of non-Catholics. In the United States, Negroes would not have accomplished nearly as much as they did in recent years had it not been for the support of white people the country over. In all democratic countries there now exist organized groups for the purpose of fighting movements that preach intolerance. These groups are composed for the most part of people who belong to the majority and work for tolerance because they are repelled by intolerance.

There is, of course, a difference between the country at large and a particular part of it. In certain periods in American history, majorities have, in municipalities or even in states, supported intolerance. The Klan of the 1920's is the best example. However, such "factious" local majorities never have succeeded in the nation at large. When, in 1924, the Klan attempted to dominate both the Democratic and Republican national conventions, it failed, and it soon went into eclipse. Eventually, it became a political necessity for national party leaders to rebuke people reputed to be advocates of intolerance who might try to identify themselves with their party. Thus, in 1936, Mr. John B. Hamilton, the chairman of the Republican National Committee, disavowed Mr. Winrod, who was running for the Republican nomination for Governor of Kansas. In 1944, Mr. Dewey used the most stinging words in his vocabulary to ward off the support of Mr. Gerald L. K. Smith. In such matters the influence wielded by national party leaders tends to increase. National government now possesses more power and patronage than ever before, and those who are in control of practical politics are more determined than ever to elect, not just local office-holders, but a President and a Congressional majority.

Concessions forced upon party leaders by minorities and the friends of these minorities within the majority group, are not worthless even if they are at first insincere. Practical concessions have their value regardless of the motive inspiring them. It is of particular importance that no party has been able to gain or retain power that was not willing to place the power of the law enforcement agencies behind the rights of all. This makes it difficult for any group to use violence against a minority. Besides, it does not promote a man's success if he does not believe what he professes. As William James has told us, convictions tend to follow actions. Those people, therefore, who, for reasons of political convenience, ask for tolerance in their campaign speeches are likely to convince themselves at the same time that they are trying to persuade others.

It is of equal importance that a political campaign forces people to work together. Instead of merely preaching tolerance they have to practice it. Intolerance is a prejudice, and a *praejudicium* is a judgment which is made before the evidence has been examined. A political campaign throws leading members of all groups together in an association which at times becomes rather close. An all-out effort is demanded. It soon becomes obvious that it is a luxury to regard people within a party primarily as belonging to a certain group, and to evaluate them on the basis of the qualities ascribed to that group. Members of a campaign team will either be judged on the basis of their personal efficiency or the work will suffer. Thus intolerance is subjected, throughout the length and breadth of a country's "political class," to the kind of test which it can stand the least. Intolerance, to be sure, may find among the people at large a kind of breeding ground which the country's responsible leaders are in no immediate position to reach. A lost war, an inflation, a depression, or any other national misfortune may be seized upon to stir up group antagonisms. However, as long as the majority system of voting prevails, advocates of intolerance can but rarely elect candidates with their own votes. They would need the independent vote and, in a nation like the United States, they will not get it. Therefore, comparatively level-headed people are apt to remain at the levers of political control. They can generally prevent the worst during the crisis, and afterwards get to work in order to heal the wounds which popular passion has inflicted upon community life in times of stress.

If majority voting does not lead to the oppression of religious, racial and social minorities, it is even less apt to lead to the suppression of a large minority party. People who are afraid that the majority may be able to act tyrannically towards its defeated rival attribute too much weight to some of the more passionate arguments which develop during a political campaign. Such arguments are cherished by the convinced partisans of both sides, some of whom engage in a "whispering campaign" in which there will be indeed "no holds barred." Let it be repeated, however, that regulars and partisans do not win elections, and that the undecided voter is more likely to be repelled than to be attracted by campaign exaggerations. For the party leaders it is often difficult to steer a middle course between the zeal of their convinced followers and the skepticism of the independent voter. Once a campaign is over, the more passionate arguments will evaporate; if they are at all remembered, the reason is likely to be that members of one party will use them to taunt those of the other with the nonsense that they or their leaders have emitted while the struggle was hot.

MAJORITIES AND THE GENERAL WILL.

The very nature of the contest between parties tends, in fact, to frustrate any attempt of one group to tyrannize the other. As mentioned above, their attempts to persuade the independent voter will result in a desire to persuade each other. In this process, they are more likely to establish a measure of a "common will" than they are to divide the country against itself. The term, "common will," of course, evokes all the dubious connotations with which Rousseau burdened it. It would be a mistake, however, simply to discard it as a matter of metaphysical speculation. In any country which is not actually on the verge of civil war, there will be found, at any time, large areas of both objective and subjective agreement, to which much of what Rousseau said about the "common will" applies.

The objective area of agreement is based upon the realization, subconscious rather than conscious, that there is a wide measure of common interests for the people living in a country. Most of them want to "live and let live," and they cannot do so unless law and order are preserved. As Aristotle puts it: "One citizen differs from another, but the salvation of the community is the common business of all." [1] On a later occasion he adds that "for the sake of mere life . . . mankind meet together and maintain the political community." [2] The desire, then, to protect "mere life" is at the root of the factors which comprise the objective part of the common will; because people affirm life, they must affirm order within the community, and this fact sets limits to the practical manifestations of whatever differences separate them.

Agreement upon the need for law and order means that we "agree to disagree," or rather, agree to disagree in peace. The devices of the democratic process are relied upon to settle the differences that remain. These devices have, as mentioned above, the further advantage of enlarging the area of agreement, and of reducing the area of disagreement. Before we proceed, it may be well to remember that, in judging the extent of actual disagreement, we may be misled, as we so often are, by taking a metaphysical approach to what is essentially an empirical problem. It is simple enough to construct systems of values profoundly at odds with one another, and to find apparent justification for them in what people say—and even more, in what some people write. There is, indeed, in modern society a wide measure of disagreement on important problems, but the basic needs of human beings in general, and of human beings living in certain historical forms of social life in particular, are still there to impose their superior claims. A great many people bow in fact to these needs who, in theory, accept one of those "isms" which would turn the world upside down. Most anarchists, for example, have been rather quiet citizens in their private lives, their devotion to their professed political creed, to some extent, being a form of escapism from the routine of their daily existence. George Sorel, the most famous modern advocate of violence, was one of them. In times of stress, to be sure, a large number of people may be brought to support, in appearance at least, some of the competing "isms," although in reality they would be quite satisfied if a workable solution could be found to the practical problems confronting them. One in inclined to say that, in modern society, the extent of disagreement upon fundamentals would be very much reduced if people who actually agree on ends could only find the means most suitable to accomplish those ends. Confusion as to means is a much more important source of social conflict than disagreement as to ends. It is the task of the instruments of "social control" to reduce the effects of this confusion to a level where society can stand it. The contest between parties, when based upon the rule of the majority, is one of the devices which serve this purpose.

This service of majority rule becomes plain when we consider how it tends to create and enlarge the area of subjective agreement, which is such an effective supplement to the area of objective agreement. The average person is not only willing to adapt himself to social necessity, but also to those views which the great majority of his fellow-citizens hold at any particular time. Majority rule serves to spread such views. As a result, certain tenets come to be accepted by society in the sense that most people do not question them, and that action can be based upon them without producing major friction.

The best illustration is the change in the United States from the atmosphere of the "New Era" in the 1920's to that of the "New Deal" in the 1930's and 1940's. Economic conditions may well be accepted as the primary basis of the two different social and political climates. In the 1920's, post-war unemployment was quickly absorbed by what soon became the biggest boom of all time. Luxuries and semi-luxuries, such as automobiles, radios and the movies became available to large population groups which previously had been confronted with difficulties in securing the essentials of life. Wages were high, and long-time unemployment so limited that it no longer entered the consciousness of the average worker as a real possibility. It was assumed that these conditions would last. A mood of optimism spread over the country, and the influence of radical political groups, whose demands were based upon assumptions opposed to this optimism, declined to the lowest point in the modern history of the country.[3] The Socialists, who looked so impressive in the presidential elections of 1912, had difficulties keeping their party alive. So did all groups of anarchist inspiration. The Communists, whose party became so influential in Continental Europe in the 1920's, hardly got a foothold in the United States. During this period even trade unions lost in membership, and trade union thought and policy was under the leadership of Samuel Gompers, who was willing to accommodate himself to the spirit as well as to the practices of the time.

The social basis of this development must not make us overlook the share which political conditions had in widening it. A great many people, for example, ceased to be Socialists because it had become obvious that votes cast for this party would be wasted. These potential Socialists did not go underground and prepare a revolution; they were assimilated by the two-party system.

There were changes even in the major parties. The Democratic party, under Bryan, had absorbed the major elements of Populist radicalism. Under Wilson it had held most of them in its ranks and, in 1916, added to them millions of people of progressive tendencies from all over the country. The 1928 standard-bearer, Alfred E. Smith, was certainly a determined advocate of reform wherever reform could be expected to operate within the framework of existing institutions, but he was also willing to make concessions in a field where few Democratic leaders had made concessions before. The most significant development was his endorsement of the protective tariff. He caused some of the country's outstanding industrial and financial leaders, with whom William Jennings Bryan would hardly have wanted to be seen, to join his party. The basic explanation for Smith's course of action was to be found in the simple fact that the Democrats could not, at that time, expect to attract enough of the independent voters unless they were ready to accept the social tenets held by most of them. What party leaders did for pragmatic reasons became part and parcel of their party's new creed. The party's propaganda helped to spread this creed—the country's creed—in groups which no other agency could have reached.

The depression which began in 1929 reached the dimensions of a social upheaval when, in 1931, the credit structure of the country collapsed and nothing seemed safe and secure any longer. The elections of 1932 showed a large protest vote. When the new President was inaugurated in March, 1933, far-reaching reform measures were proposed under the most dramatic circumstances. Public opinion rose spontaneously in their favor. Few of the remaining Republican members of Congress opposed administration measures, no matter how much they might be at variance with what had been for so long their —and their country's—basic views. The one attempt at organized opposition made by the "Liberty League" was soon to result in a failure which became proverbial.

Public feeling in regard to the relationship between government and business had changed fundamentally. More government regulation was demanded, and, as the ultimate success of the TVA shows, direct government operation was accepted to an extent undreamed of a few years earlier. Social security legislation, as well as federal regulation of wages and hours and collective bargaining came to be taken for granted. Norman Thomas complained that the "New Deal" had "stolen" his 1932 platform; if this is correct, leading Republicans soon came to have a share in the larceny.

The fact that some of the basic elements within the subjective area of agreement can change so fast makes it obvious that objective social necessity may have comparatively little to do with the matter. This is one of the reasons why the acceptance of majority rule, even in its wider ramifications, does not imply the assumption that the majority is necessarily right. Majorities, in fact, like kings, may be either right or wrong, although it has been argued above that, in this day and age at least, decisions by majorities are "safer" than those made by kings or dictators.

Before we proceed it may be interesting to note that while democratic writers have often blundered when trying to explain the nature of majority rule, a scholar with monarchist leanings has made a substantial contribution toward presenting the correct view of the problem. Rudolf Smend [4] calls decision by a majority "a struggle with the tendency of integration." He compares the process of voting to an athletic contest. In both cases the outcome is accompanied by "a beneficial discharge of tensions, a catharsis." The deeper reason for this feeling, he adds, is completely independent of whether or not the result is objectively right. The decision in itself is "an essentially integrating act in the life of the community and, therefore, at the same time it constitutes an intensification of the feeling of vitality on the part of the individual, regardless as to whether he belongs to the majority or to the minority."

The average person is, indeed, ordinarily inclined to accept the results of a majority decision. He seems to agree with Rousseau's remark that those who failed to agree with the views of the majority did so because they "erred." To some extent, people feel that way. Whoever has advised friends on how they should vote in a certain election will have found that voters who have no strong opinions of their own will think that the advice was bad if the candidate did not win. They seem to feel that there is something morally wrong in being on the losing side. Even those who take a more rational view of politics may share this feeling to a certain degree. They conclude that perhaps the arguments of the other side were stronger than they appeared to be during the campaign; at any rate, the winning candidate is to be given a chance, and the benefit of the doubt is to be accorded to him, for some time at least. The general insistence that those who engage in politics must be "good losers" is related to this fact; it is symptomatic of the psychology of majority decision that the defeated candidate is expected to be among the first to congratulate the victor.

THE CLASSICAL ARGUMENT ON THE "TYRANNY OF THE MAJORITY."

It would seem therefore, that the people at large fully understand and accept majority rule. Our arguments in this respect would not be complete, however, without a specific answer to the claim that there is "a tyranny of the majority," a claim made by such outstanding men as Jefferson, de Tocqueville, and Calhoun. In justice to these writers it should be recalled that they lived at a time when orderly majority rule was in its infancy. When Jefferson wrote that "One hundred and seventy-three despots would surely be as oppressive as one . . . An elective despotism is not the government we fought for," [5] he thought of the Virginia legislature with which he came into contact during the earlier part of his career. Professor Nevins says about it: "Debate became less formal, the contempt for deliberative dignity would have shocked stately pre-Revolutionary leaders like Peyton Randolph, and some members were palpably illiterate. But this rampant democracy in exterior traits did not carry with it an intelligent progressivism in legislation." [6] Jefferson was elected governor by this legislature for two terms of one year each, one of which, according to Nevins, "was the blackest in his life." Difficulties abounded; positive achievements were rare. Worse things happened in other states. When the Federal Constitution later forbade bills of attainder, the reason was that some of the riotous state legislatures had passed them.

So far as de Tocqueville is concerned, his impressions were formed during the most turbulent part of Jacksonian democracy, when the French nobleman's wealthy friends were terrified at the thought of what "King Andrew" would do next. Besides, it is interesting to note that when de Tocqueville feels compelled to give a practical illustration for the tyranny of the majority, he mentions a lynching which occurred during the war of 1812.[7] Such developments belong to the field of crowd psychology and are obviously very much outside the normal functioning of majority rule in a "representative republic."

Turning now to the specific arguments upon which rests the identification of the rule of the majority with the tyranny of the majority, it would be almost possible to summarize them in the one sentence of Jefferson that "One hundred and seventy-three despots would surely be as oppressive as one." It is clearly implied that the absolute power of a number of men is no different from the absolute power of one man. De Tocqueville adds the supporting arguments that the interests of the majority are opposed to those of the minority, and that a victorious party may act tyrannically toward the defeated party in the same way in which a victorious nation may act tyrannically toward a defeated nation.[8]

We may readily agree with the basic assumption that the absolute power of one man is susceptible to tyrannical abuse, but majorities as they operate within the framework of political parties in a "representative republic" are something else again. In the first place, there *is* a difference between absolute power in the hands of one man and a similar power in the hands of a number of men. As soon as supreme power is held by a multiplicity of people, they act as a check upon each other. The leaders of the majority party in a democratic country certainly do not lack people who tell them the unvarnished truth, and so much of their time is spent in listening to the arguments of such people and trying to answer them that some critics hold that it is *too* much.

In the second place, majority government is not, as is tyranny, based upon usurpation; it has, in fact, the clearest moral title to authority possessed by any form of government. Its mandate is from the people, whom those in power need not fear, and from the people there also comes its organic strength. As Jefferson said in his first inaugural address: ". . . . I believe this . . . the strongest government on earth. I believe it is the only one where every man, at the call of the laws, would fly to the standard of the law, and would meet invasions of the public order as his own personal concern." [9] Such inherent power dispenses with the need of resorting to any act of petty tyranny.

Finally, it is not true that the interests of a majority are different from those of the minority, and that the two can be compared to a conquering and a conquered nation, as de Tocqueville assumed. There is never a clear line of division between majority and minority. Voters who were with the majority yesterday and gave it its power, may leave it tomorrow and turn it into a minority. The undecided voters are, indeed, quite likely to do so if they think that acts of injustice have been committed, and no one can ever tell who belongs to a particular voting group and who does not. The only safe procedure for a victorious party is to treat nearly all of its supporters as potential opponents and the opposition voters as potential friends, rather than as defeated enemies. If members of the opposition can be won over, as is often the case, they may be needed in order to make up for losses from the ranks of the majority's followers.[10]

It would seem, therefore, that the time has now come to do what Josiah Phillips Quincy [11] advised us to do more than two generations ago: Put "that venerable bugbear, the tyranny of majorities," to rest. Orderly majority rule is, in its very essence, the opposite of tyranny. The events of the last generation should have taught us that whenever real tyranny exists it is exercised by a minority. The protagonists of the totalitarian rulers of our times have indeed boldly proclaimed the right of an organized minority (the members of the totalitarian party), to rule over their country. Modern technology has come to their assistance, and William Henry Chamberlin has rightly said: "Because of the appalling concentration of power in the totalitarian state there has, perhaps, never been an age in history when so few could inflict so much suffering on so many." [12] The task which confronts us, then, is indeed "the protection of majorities." [13] All we can do, and all we have to do to accomplish this purpose, is to make genuine majority rule a reality.

Chapter x

REPRESENTATIVE GOVERNMENT MISREPRESENTED:

vocational and proportional representation

The French Revolution seems to have finally established the principle that representation is a form of integration. The deputy was to represent the nation as a whole, not a particular locality or a particular interest, and he was to be elected with this primary function in view. However, some of the important implications of this concept of representation—which an Italian scholar [1] has called the "classical concept"—are being overlooked to this day. This applies especially to those who demand vocational and proportional representation. In both cases the essential difference between society and the state is ignored; the unity of the state is, by some miracle, to result from a juxtaposition of mere parts. The advocates of the two schemes might be reminded of what Goethe expressed in the following words:

> Die Teile hab ich in der Hand,
> Leider fehlt nur das einigende Band.

—"The parts I have in my hand; unfortunately, the tie to hold them together is missing."

CORPORATIVISM OF THE RIGHT AND OF THE LEFT.

So far as the movement in favor of vocational representation is concerned, a double distinction must be made. First there is the difference between the Right wing and the Left wing of the corporative movement. The Rightists are inspired by the medieval guild. Organizations are to be formed which contain employers as well as employees; they are to settle their economic differences among themselves and, at the same time, they are to govern the state. Views of this kind are more likely to be held by employers than by employees, and are usually sponsored by conservative political parties. On the other end of the political spectrum, we have the anarcho-syndicalists (to use the term most popular in the Romanic countries) and the guild socialists (the term popularized by G. D. H. Cole and others in England after the First World War). They are trade unionists. For them the "guild" is to be one big union in which employers, if at all tolerated, would be but a minor factor. Theirs, therefore, is the corporatism of the Left.

In their basic assumptions the views of the Rightists and Leftists are so similar that no distinction need be made in detail. The two groups, in fact, inspire one another, both in their negation of the democratic state and in the few steps of an affirmative nature which have ever been taken. The favorite objects of their criticism are political parties, which are rejected on account of their "inorganic" nature. The literature of French syndicalism (let us mention only the name of Sorel) is replete with such charges, and the Rightists, less original in their thought, have borrowed from it freely. In Italy, there have, indeed, been quite a number of syndicalists who joined the ranks of the Fascists, without feeling in the least disturbed in the comfortable use of their old slogans.

The question arises how much validity we can accord to the corporatist-syndicalist criticism of political parties. Parties are based upon an *idem sentire de re publica*—upon a "feeling the same way about the public matter." This "feeling the same way" may be of a very general nature. All that is needed is enough unity to make it possible that those who follow the same banner fight for the joint conquest and the joint retention of political power. That much unity, as it is obvious from their history, parties do possess. How much unifying, and, therefore, integrating capacity is there in vocational groups?

VOCATIONALISM AND INTEGRATION.

First, it would be a mistake to assume that modern vocational groups are "organic" in the sense that they owe their existence to spontaneous growth. They must be organized by somebody, and if their organizations are to be capable of fulfilling public functions, they must be established by an act of authority emanating from above. Let us consider but a few of the practical problems involved. Thus, experience shows that, as long as there is a free choice, some workers will join a trade union and some will not. In the United States union members are still a minority of the total number of those employed for wages and salaries, even though several decades of legislation intended to facilitate the growth of unions have now elapsed. Furthermore, as long as organizations are established on a voluntary basis alone, there may be more than one for a particular trade. In the United States the American Federation of Labor has found itself confronted, since 1936, by the Committee for Industrial Organization (later called the Congress of Industrial Organizations). When the two were, at last, reunited, the fusion long remained rather superficial, and powerful unions remained outside. Nor did the merger mean the end of jurisdictional disputes.

There are no clearly drawn "natural" lines of division on the side of the employers either. If they were ever to be given the kind of public authority which the proponents of a corporative state would like to confer upon them, each group would likely covet as much territory as possible. Economic activities are interrelated. Whoever wants complete control of a part of them, must control them all. An illustration was provided in Germany when the Nazis tried to establish a "corporative" organization in the field of agriculture, placing it in charge of Walter Darré. Of course, he took his farmers first. But then he wanted the grist millers, because they grind the farmer's grain. There followed those merchants who either bought from or sold to the farmer. Ultimately Darré wanted the merchant marine, because some of its ships carried the farmer's products. Here he was stopped. However, this could be done, only because over and above him there remained a political organization. Without such an organization, would not the farmers, the merchants, the shipowners, and all others, have constantly fought for territory?

For the sake of argument let us assume that this problem is settled: Producers throughout the country have peacefully banded together in vocational groups and are satisfied with their line-up. Now the vocational organizations must provide a government. It is proposed that they elect a corporative parliament, and that this parliament appoint a government. The first question is: to how many deputies shall each vocational group be entitled? If we take the number of its adult members as the basis, we are back to the rules governing elections in democratic countries; yet, these rules were to be rejected. If, on the other hand, as is frequently suggested, the votes are to be "weighed" rather than "counted," we must seek the basis for such "weighing." Obviously, no solution is possible. One economic group will claim to be as indispensable as any other. In fact, the struggle for influence in such parliaments would be likely to cause the same contentions which occurred during the late Middle Ages when the various guilds were struggling for as great a share in the city government as possible.[2]

If the difficulties attending the formation of a vocational parliament had been solved, there would be the question of its functioning. Decisions could hardly be made dependent upon unanimity. Actually, majority rule is invariably proposed by the proponents of such institutions, no matter how incongruous it is from the point of view of their basic assumptions. Its application is, at the same time, certain to lead to incidents not likely to enhance the prestige of a vocational parliament. Thus there existed in Germany, during the period of the Weimar Republic, a Federal Economic Council[3] which, one day, found itself confronted with the hardiest perennial of Germany's economic problems: the conflict between the producers and the consumers of iron and steel. The owners of the big steel mills wanted high protective tariffs. Their customers manufactured products which might have to be exported under conditions of strong international competition, and would have preferred to have no tariff on steel at all. When a vote was taken the scales were turned by the representatives of the professional musicians! Similar incidents are certain to recur in such bodies. If the results are incongruous the basic reason is that no common denominator exists between the various interests.

Finally, there is the problem of the elite into whose hands the government of a country is to be placed. Both corporatists and syndicalists assert that all that political parties are able to produce is amateurs, whereas they can provide us with experts. The general aspects of this problem have been dealt with above. If we ask the specific question who the experts would be whom a vocational parliament could develop, the answer is simple. The milk dealers would delegate a milk dealer; the butchers a butcher; and the automobile manufacturers a magnate of the automobile industry. Obviously, the milk dealer has learned how to handle the problems of milk distribution, the butcher to kill a hog, and the automobile manufacturer to produce automobiles. But how can we expect them to take charge of the political affairs of the country, such as foreign policy, legislation on education or on the delimitation of federal and state functions and the like? In the summer of 1937, this writer, on the occasion of a visit to Vienna, discussed the "corporative" Constitution which Austria was then supposed to have with an economist, who had been appointed to Schuschnigg's parliament by the government as one of the representatives of the general public. He complained about the caliber of the Deputies delegated by economic organizations. "There is," he said, "somebody appointed by the dairy industry of Northern Tyrol. When any one of us talks about problems of general policy, he sleeps. When *he* speaks, *we* sleep, because all he talks about is the technical details of milk production and distribution in his district." My informant blamed such insufficiency upon the principles of democracy which, he thought, could not produce anything better. The parliaments of the large democratic countries give the answer: By adopting the right method of selection they achieve, on balance, the right results. We can only repeat our earlier conclusion, that the only "experts" in politics are the politicians. They have learned their trade by dealing with the subject matter of politics, namely, the affairs of the *polis,* the community as a whole, rather than with any specialized field.

CORPORATIVISM IN PRACTICE.

These theoretical considerations could be extended. Let us, instead, turn to practical experience and consider the claim, fairly popular for a time, that Mussolini's Italy proved the possibility of a "corporative state." For this view only second- and third-rate Fascist propaganda can be responsible, since both Fascist laws and Fascist leaders made it clear that Italy under Mussolini was a Fascist rather than a corporative state. Every "syndicate," "federation," and "confederation"—the agencies established on the basis of the law of April 7, 1926—had the word "Fascist" in its title (for example, "General Fascist Confederation of Italian Industry"). The active members of these organizations (who alone participated in their administration, whereas all employees or employers of the group concerned paid dues) had to be acceptable to the ruling party. Their officers had to provide "guarantees of ability and secure national faith." In order not to leave anyone under misapprehensions, qualified Fascists [4] have added that "secure national faith" meant support of fascism. When, in 1934, the final "corporations" were at last established, and the law stipulated that their presiding officer be appointed "by decree of the head of the government," a French cartoonist pictured a meeting of the 22 corporations with 22 Mussolinis sitting around the conference table. Certainly, the Fascist state did not abdicate when the various "syndicalist" and "corporative" institutions were set up. The party remained the party, its *Duce* "the Head of the Government," and its policies those of the nation. Some Fascists have openly said: "You cannot expect us to give autonomy to the newly established economic organizations. After all, we had first to establish them, and should we ever stop looking after them, the play of the divergent economic interests would lead to their collapse." Mussolini himself, who at one time called the corporative institutions "instruments of fascism," later listed as the first two conditions for a systematic and successful imitation of the Italian "corporative" institutions in other countries the following:

> [There must be] A single party, so that economic discipline may be accomplished by political discipline and so that rising above contrasting elements all may be bound together by a common faith.
>
> Nor is this enough. After the single party there must a totalitarian state, that is to say the state which absorbs all energies, all the interests, all the hopes of the people in order to transform and potentiate them.[5]

In other words, Mussolini did not replace the multiple-party system by a corporative state; he replaced it by a one-party system. He was frank enough to advise the world that any country desirous of introducing "corporative" institutions must do the same.

If the situation was different in the case of the Austria of Dollfuss and Schuschnigg and remains different in that of the Portugal of Salazar, the reason lies in the good intentions of these men rather than in their actual accomplishments. When in March, 1933, Dollfuss discarded a parliament no longer able to function, he did so in the sincere belief that without such action Hitler would take Austria over right then and there. But the government which he established was never one founded on "a corporative basis," as the preamble of the Constitution of May 1, 1934, proclaimed. Both Dollfuss and Schuschnigg did their best to give as much self-government as possible to the various "corporative" organizations which they established by government decree. But they were never able to permit free elections in these bodies. Few would deny that the central government in Vienna was a dictatorship, though it was as considerate (the Nazis called it *schlapp,* which may be freely translated as "sloppy") towards its opponents as it felt that it could afford to be—and as Mussolini (on whose orders the bloody conflict with the Socialist workers of February, 1934, was precipitated) permitted it to be. In later years there has been much criticism of Dollfuss and Schuschnigg on the part of writers who favor a "corporative state." Mistakes allegedly made by the two statesmen are held up as the reason for their admitted failure to establish a "genuine" (which means democratic) corporative state. Such criticism means blaming a person for not squaring the circle. Dollfuss and Schuschnigg were as sincere and courageous in their efforts as anyone has ever been before or is likely to be in the future; they just could not do the impossible.

Similar considerations apply to Salazar. Before he came to power, General Carmona and his fellow-officers had established a military dictatorship. It needed a brain, and the brilliant professor of economics at the ancient University of Coimbra was called upon to provide it. Salazar did much for his country; without him Portugal would hardly have been able to avoid being drawn into the Spanish civil war, not to mention the civil wars of her own which the conflicts between the different cliques of her "political class" might have precipitated. Still, of Salazar's much vaunted "corporative state" only the barest rudiments [6] exist. The test of genuine spontaneity, i.e., free elections, is nowhere applied. Salazar has modified the military dictatorship which existed before he came to power to such an extent that his country's government might be defined as absolutism moderated by both humanism and intelligence. He has not, however, changed the essential power structure. If the rule of the army should come to an end, Salazar and the institutions which he created would end with it.

As the example of Salazar's Portugal indicates, the very nature of the proposals to establish a true corporative *state* (rather than a mere corporative *order*) makes it difficult to submit the underlying theories to a practical test. Any reference to practical experience can be countered with the argument that a good idea has been perverted by an extraneous factor, such as a dictatorship. Under conditions of genuine freedom, we are told, the outcome would be different. We need not repeat that any attempt to institute a freely functioning corporative state would create a political vacuum. Since nature abhors a vacuum in politics as much as in physics, there would soon arise the opposite extreme, a dictatorship.

The basic political deficiency of corporative institutions may well be the reason why dictatorships are so hospitable to the corporative ideology, which provides them with a ready-made "political formula." This applies even to the Communist dictatorship in Russia. It wants to be referred to as "Soviet" Russia, and "Soviet" is the Russian word for "council." This is to create the impression that power lies in the hands of councils freely formed by workers, peasants and soldiers. This pretense was taken seriously even by as astute an observer as Guglielmo Ferrero, who considered the possibility that the "Soviet system" might develop into a "legitimate" form of government.[7] The true nature of this government was tragically illustrated during the Kronstadt sailors' revolt of 1921. Its slogan was: "The Soviets without the Communist party." These early fighters for freedom from Communist totalitarianism were right in proclaiming the difference between genuine "Soviet" rule and Communist party rule. Yet, they failed to realize that they were pitting a vacuum against a political reality; they had lost the battle of ideas even before they initiated the battle of the guns. At any rate, the reality of the one-party government as instituted by Lenin remained the same. The term "Soviet" is for this Russian reality what Walter Bagehot called the British monarchy: a "convenient disguise." The difference, of course, is that the British monarch does retain a measure of power, supplemented by what may be a not inconsiderable degree of influence, whereas the idea of government councils of workers, soldiers and peasants was never more than an illusion. It is, however, an appealing illusion, and even Lenin did not recognize its nature immediately. During the Russian revolution of 1905, the Menshevists and the Social-Revolutionaries —both sworn enemies of the Bolshevists—established a "Soviet of Workers' Deputies." In the words of David Shub: [8] "At first the novel revolutionary institution terrified him (Lenin) more than it did the Czar." The Bolshevist leader considered "this undisciplined organism as a dangerous rival to the Party, a spontaneous proletarian assembly which a small group of 'professional revolutionists' would not be able to control." Precisely because this, at that time indeed "spontaneous," organism was also "undisciplined," it did not constitute a danger to those for whom discipline was the beginning and the end of all political work. Its propagandistic usefulness was all the greater for that deficiency.

Brief reference must be made to the various attempts made since the end of World War I to set up economic councils. Their functions were more or less of a consultative nature. It might be argued that the practical experience with these bodies is, for that reason, not pertinent to the potentialities of a vocational parliament with real power. It must be recalled, however, that while the beginnings of political parliaments were modest, they exhibited enough vitality to attract more and more power to themselves. The vocational bodies instituted in recent years have failed to do this; if space permitted our going into details [9] it would not be difficult to show that all of them, instead of seizing the opportunity offered by their very existence and enlarging upon their functions, have failed to live up to even the most modest expectations of their founders. As was said in regard to the French "Economic Council": "Well received at the outset, it has rapidly disappointed, and some foretell its disappearance, or its fusion with another council." [10] To a limited extent this failure may be due to technical mistakes made in one respect or another; the main cause lies, however, in the deficiency of the principle involved.

It is significant that the corporative idea has never become popular in the Anglo-Saxon countries where a working democracy has existed; its popularity seems, in fact, to increase in direct proportion to the weakness of democracy. In fact, corporativism has an escapist function—people either cannot tackle the true source of the evil of a weak democracy, or they do not want to do so, and speculation in terms of a rebuilding of their country's institutions on a vocational basis offers a convenient way out. The only infatuation with this kind of ideology which has occurred in the Anglo-Saxon countries took, as mentioned above, the form of "guild socialism"; however, it is interesting to note that at least one of its supporters later became one of the most consistent proponents of more orthodox democratic constitutionalism, refuting, implicitly and explicitly, his earlier endorsement of the attempt to rebuild democracy on a "functional" basis.[11]

REPRESENTATION AND "PROPORTIONAL" REPRESENTATION.

If the corporative idea never became influential in the Anglo-Saxon countries, the same cannot be said of its logical twin, the advocacy of P.R. The Anglo-Saxon world, to be sure, has largely rejected systematic analysis, and in recent generations tended to be pragmatic to the extent of neglecting the intellectual examination of the institutional basis upon which the British and American experience with government rests. An intellectual vacuum developed and attempts to fill it with unsuitable contents have had a measure of success. The world movement for P.R., in fact, has for two generations now (ever since 1905, when the late John M. Humphreys became the secretary of the P.R. Society in London and devoted his great gifts to the propagation of its views) centered in Britain; the publications of the P.R. Society can be found in every major city in the world (and in many a minor one). If, in the United States, the P.R. League (operating, since 1932, as a department of the National Municipal League) has exceeded the peak of its influence, it still has exclusive control for the dissemination of information on P.R. in the columns of *The National Municipal Review*, which, for many, is the only regularly available source of information on the subject.

The principal objection to both proportional and vocational representation is that they separate the concept of representation from that of integration. Social groups of all types and kinds are to be entitled to a share in the seats available in a parliamentary body for no other reason than that they constitute a certain minimum—and at times minute—fraction of the electorate. No one asks these groups to get together with others and establish a common political denominator upon which all citizens could unite: It suffices that they remain what they are, without any thought of a function to be exercised on behalf of the community. The difference between vocational and proportional representation lies in the exclusive nature of the former, which is based on mere economic interests, whereas the latter opens the road for an infinite variety of minority elements to be "represented." Parties—or pseudo-parties [12]—reflecting an economic group are supplemented by others, expressing an ideology or a religious or racial difference. In measuring the strength of the rival groups the principle of "counting noses" is accepted, and the power of any of them increases in direct proportion to its support in the electorate, no matter from which social or ideological element this support is derived. This fact does make possible a degree of integration, of which mere "vocational representation" is not capable. On the other hand, no substitute is provided for that center of political gravitation which, even under the weakest types of majority voting, exists in the form of the undecided voter in the center of the political spectrum, imposing moderation, and some concern at least for national cohesion, upon Right and Left alike.

THE STATICS AND THE DYNAMICS OF P.R.

In dealing with the effects of P.R., we have to distinguish between their static and their dynamic aspects. The former imply that whatever divisions exist in a nation at a particular time are reflected in parliament in proportion to their strength. It is assumed that these divisions exist by themselves as objective quantities. The system of voting is passive—it merely measures what is. Actually, political divisions constantly form and reform themselves, and to some extent, they do this in response to a particular system of voting.

What has to be said about the static aspects of the problem was stated in the Italian Chamber of Deputies by the Deputy Alessio, just before this body, in 1919, took the fateful step of adopting Proportional Representation:

> What . . . . is the function of P.R.? It is to create (I use the words of a pamphleteer) an elected assembly in which the forces of the various parties exist in the same proportion in which they exist in the Nation.
>
> But that, Gentlemen, is absurd! Parliament is confused with the Nation.
>
> The Nation, Gentlemen, has continuity of existence, permanency. . . .
>
> Parliament has a duration of five years. In this short time it must carry out a program, strengthen a government, or replace it. Its action and its purpose cannot be realized without a majority.
>
> Now what is the effect of P.R.? To create, not a majority, but a union of minorities, often incompatible with one another, their ideas in mutual contradiction.[13]

Alessio meant to indicate that placing side by side the representatives of all the social and political divisions existing in a country at a particular time would not be enough. That process would reflect multiplicity, whereas the actual task of a representative body was to establish a basis on which unified action would be possible.

The situation is aggravated by the dynamic effects of P.R. As we have seen, it is a mistake to regard any substantial degree of political unity existing in any country at any particular time as a stable quantity; it is created, and recreated, in a constantly evolving dynamic process. Under P.R. no assistance is given to this process by the system of voting. In a second stage a tendency may develop to tear apart even what has been united before. Under the majority system, a great many differences have to be composed within a comparatively large party before anyone can enter the struggle for power with a reasonable chance of success. Under P.R. parties do not have to be so large, and the fact that more existing differences can be fully reflected means that they are aggravated.

In the first place, the dependence upon the undecided voter in the center of the political spectrum loses its strategic significance. Undecided voters are equally important, no matter which part of the political map they inhabit. The graph presented above (p. 168) to illustrate the integrating effects of even the weakest type of majority voting is modified below to represent conditions as they prevail under P.R. The rectangles represent the voters committed to a definite party, and the shaded areas between them represent the undecided voters:

Extreme Right	Moderate Right	Center	Moderate Left	Extreme Left

It will be seen that there is no longer merely one center of political gravity, as there was under the majority system; there are such centers between all parties. Nor can one small group turn the scales for the entire country. As mentioned before, in the British House of Commons elections of 1950, or in the New York gubernatorial elections of 1938 and 1954, the turnover of a fraction of one per cent of the votes could have reversed the result. The fact that these votes were to be found in the center anchored the entire process of political orientation at that point. Under a fullfledged system of P.R. a change in one per cent of the British vote would mean a change of six House of Commons seats, and this change could occur anywhere, not merely at the center. There would, therefore, be no reason to pay any more attention to centrist voters than to any of the others.

The effects of this change are immediately aggravated by the "organized interest of associations." Whoever, in countries with fully developed extremes, takes the trouble to interview ordinary voters will frequently be surprised to notice how insignificant the actual differences can be between the feelings of those who support a moderate and those who support an extremist party. It results again and again that the rank and file do not care for ideologies. Political differences at the bottom of the political pyramid tend to be skin deep. The party organization itself, of course, takes pride in its ideology; it may go to a considerable amount of trouble to develop an ideology not previously existing. In that way, it enhances its prestige; however, it also erects barriers between itself and others cooperation with whom for the formation of a common government P.R. tends to make imperative.

The ideological character of such parties is enhanced by the fact that they do not have what Maurice Duverger [14] calls "a majority bend." Parties contending for an overall majority are close not only to securing all power for themselves but also to shouldering the full burden of responsibility; they cannot shift part of it to a coalition partner. Of such parties Walter Bagehot has said that "They are involved with reality. An Opposition, on coming into power, is often like a speculative merchant whose bills become due." [15] Parties of this type will, in anticipation of such contingencies, limit themselves to taking a stand on a few concrete issues. In regard to these, they hope to satisfy the expectations of the voter. Inevitably, their whole character becomes practical and pragmatic. On the other hand, if under P.R. a party ever secures an overall majority, this is accidental. The party leaders do not anticipate such exceptions and feel that they can give the ideologists in their ranks a free rein. As a result, an ideological hardening of the arteries becomes part and parcel of a country's political system.

The effects of this tendency are aggravated by a trend which Helmut Unkelbach [16] has done much to elucidate: Parties with similar views will be likely to attack one another more than parties with tenets substantially different from their own. They know that they cannot expect to win many votes from competitors on the opposite end of the political scale. On the other hand, the differences between themselves and their friends are small enough to make a raid on each other's supporters appear profitable. Such tactics lead to a great deal of irritation. Thus, when, after the Dutch elections of 1956, it took close to four months to reëstablish the coalition of which the Party of Labor (the former Socialists) and the Catholics were the principal members, this particular aspect of the campaign certainly represented a part of the problem. Such developments can occur only to a limited extent where a multiple-party system is based on majority voting. As we have seen, even the weakest form of majority voting, the French, makes it necessary for related parties to form alliances *before* the election. Such alliances do not work unless differences between its partners are, from the outset, played down sufficiently to make the subsequent formation of a common government natural in the case of victory.

Thus, when the element of integration is separated from that of representation, as both the theory and the practice of P.R. do, a vital ingredient is lost. A good and sound principle is perverted; in the end, a mere caricature may remain. If this conclusion is not generally accepted one of the reasons lies in the general fact that social reality never confronts us with any one element in its purity; there are always other elements which counteract its effects.

TYPES OF P.R.

Furthermore, the different types of P.R. differ as much from one another as do the different types of majority voting. It is frequently assumed that the dividing line lies between the list system and the Hare system of P.R. Under the former, political parties present lists of candidates and obtain seats in proportion to the number of votes received. If 100 members of a parliamentary body are to be elected, and the entire country forms one constituency, a party with 25 per cent of the votes obtains 25 seats; in the case of the "rigid list" the first 25 candidates on the party's list will be declared elected.

The drawbacks of this system are obvious: The voter has no choice among the candidates. All he can do is to cast his ballot for the ticket as a whole, such as has been presented by the party's leaders. From the point of view of the logic of P.R., this is hardly a drawback. The "proportionality" of "proportional representation" is necessarily one between mathematical quantities, the goal being to approximate the percentage of the seats secured as closely as possible to that of the votes obtained. Nor is it an accident that virtually all of the inventors of the various systems of P.R. have been mathematicians. Authorities in the fields of public law and of political science have, at times, felt that this fact alone should make everyone think twice before accepting conclusions derived from premises not related to those of political life.[17]

Proponents of P.R. have felt, however, that inconsistency was not necessarily a weakness. As long as no major principle is involved—as in the choice between P.R. and the majority system—we need not quarrel with them. In the Anglo-Saxon countries, the official P.R. organizations have placed their efforts behind a system which is based on the person of the candidate rather than on that of any party. They advocate the Hare system, more correctly called the single-transferable system of P.R. It has found able exponents in both Britain and the United States, to whom reference must be made for the complicated details of its operation.[18] Candidates are nominated as individuals. Whoever has obtained the required fraction of the total vote—the quota—is elected. If, as is invariably the case, not enough candidates have obtained their quota through first preference votes, the candidate with the lowest number of such votes is eliminated and his second, third, etc., preferences are transferred to candidates still in the race. When only as many candidates remain as are to be elected, they are declared successful, whether all of them have reached the quota or not.

This is not the place to repeat [19] that, in itself, the Hare system does not weaken the disintegrating effects of P.R. The latter are the greater the smaller the percentage of the total vote required to elect a candidate. That percentage depends upon the number of seats to be filled. If this number is more than six hundred—the membership of the British House of Commons for which Hare's system was designed—a candidate would, if the entire country formed one constituency, need less than one-sixth of one per cent of the total number of votes. Nothing of the sort has ever been tried in a major country. Obviously, such a system would make it possible for a bewildering variety of cranks and faddists to enter the country's legislative halls.

Therefore, practically all systems of P.R. now in use provide for a more or less far-reaching restriction of proportionality. Comparatively small constituencies are established. If, for example, only nine seats are to be filled—which is the case in most of the American cities which adopted P.R. for their council elections—approximately one-tenth of the total vote is required [20] to ensure election. Candidates and parties whose followers constitute a lower percentage of the total will see their votes "wasted" as much as if the majority system were in force. In Ireland this restriction of P.R. has gone so far that some constituencies elect only three candidates. As a result, nearly one-third of the total is needed for success, and a party with one vote more than 50 per cent of the total takes two of the three seats. The splitting up of parties to be expected under "pure" P.R. is drastically reduced. A system results which constitutes a mixture of P.R. with elements of the majority system.

PROPORTIONAL VERSUS INTEGRATING REPRESENTATION IN
THE ANGLO-SAXON COUNTRIES.

The same result is accomplished if a country retains the majority system for its major elections and admits P.R. only for the minor ones. These have, as a rule, but a limited share in that molding of public opinion which is a vital aspect of the electoral process. Thus, while Australia uses a form of majority voting (the alternative vote) for its House of Representatives, which is the most important body, P.R. is used for the less significant Senate. Government majorities in the Senate may be cut down sufficiently to make it difficult for a government to carry out a coherent program, but as long as the party line-up is determined by what happens in the House elections, the "dynamic" effects of P.R.—the development of new parties with a consequent division of opinion—hardly develop.

Similarly, if an American city elects its councilmen by P.R. while all other elections, state as well as national, take place under the majority system, the political consciousness of the voters will continue to be guided into the molds provided by the two-party system. Inevitably, this fact will check the tendency which Thomas Hare, the inventor of the "Hare system," expressed in these words: "Many more candidates will be everywhere put in nomination . . . minorities . . . will far exceed the entire number of minorities now existing, by the operation of numberless affinities and compulsions, which, in a state of liberation, will dissolve the present majorities." [21]

Where American cities use Hare's system they, for the reasons mentioned, cannot fulfill his prediction. It does not follow, however, that none of the typical effects of P.R. have developed. That under the Hare system candidates are officially nominated and voted for as individuals may have the result that party lines (and, with them, the integrating effects of the two-party system) are ignored. Even when parties nominate candidates they may have to take men and women who are primarily representatives of minority blocs. In the first American city to adopt P.R., Ashtabula, Ohio, the influence of parties was small and that of minority blocs large. The results are reflected in an editorial published in the *Ashtabula Star-Beacon* on October 30, 1929, a few days before a popular vote abolished P.R.:

As election day approaches we are as firmly convinced as ever that in these amendments the people of Ashtabula have an opportunity to rid our governmental structure of some of its weaknesses. Should they fail to take advantage of the opportunity they will have only themselves to blame if the future sees a continuance of the boy-play, laugh provoking situations, lack of dignity, poor coordination and general inefficiency which, at times, have characterized the official acts and conduct of our public servants, acts made possible by the somewhat grotesque features of the charter as it now exists.

Are not all seven councilmen representatives of each citizen? Is there any sensible reason why a councilman should represent just a small group of people in his handling of city business? Is not the welfare of *all* the people in the hands of the individual council member? Does it make for the best kind of government to have Mr. A. represent the business men, Mr. B. the bankers, Mr. C. the Finnish, Mr. D. the Italians, Mr. E. the Liberals, Mr. F. the laboring man, etc? Who, out of this list is going to represent the public, the ordinary, average citizen, who, after all, pays the bills and gets the jolts, if any.

Unless there is someone in the list broad enough minded and sufficiently liberal in his conception of public duty, the average citizen gets mighty little representation. Your councilmen, under such a system, are kept too busy satisfying their own relatively small constituency to take much interest in the needs of the community as a whole. If you need proof of this, turn back the pages of your own councilmanic history.

What happened in Ashtabula was extreme. In other cities the integrating effects of the two-party system were stronger, although the typical effects of P.R. can be noticed everywhere. This includes Cincinnati, where bloc politics eventually caused the first manager to serve under the reform charter, Colonel C. O. Sherrill, to oppose P.R.[22] Furthermore, the council happened to be divided 4:4:1 three times, leaving it to one "independent" councilman to turn the scales. In Cincinnati there was, however, always another check in the background: On several occasions P.R. had been retained by a mere handful of votes. There was no doubt that any prolonged deadlock in the city council would provide the margin for its defeat in the next attempt to abolish it. In a popular vote on any issue, of course, majority rule applies, leaving little room for the obstructionist tactics of minority blocs. (P.R. was abolished in 1957.)

In New York City P.R. never succeeded in breaking the hold of the Democratic organization on the Council, although, on one occasion, this was due to accident.[23] On the other hand, two known Communists, and two candidates then generally regarded as fellow-travelers, were elected. When this happened, *The New York Post*[24] said about the council:

> . . . when it meets, there ought to be a banner stuck up in the room saying like in the movies, "Any resemblance between these representatives and the people they are supposed to represent is purely coincidental." . . .
>
> P.R. lends itself to any splinter group with enough drive to do a thorough job of canvassing and publicizing its candidate. It gives us a deliberative assembly that is as broken-up and splintered and bloc-y as the old French Chamber of Deputies.

This conclusion exaggerates, but it also expresses the exasperation of those who had expected much from P.R. They were all the more disappointed when it not only failed to produce a decisive change for the better, but exhibited some rather irritating drawbacks of its own. Clearly, these drawbacks could become a major factor if the system which permitted their development were extended all over the country.

The leading American proponents of P.R. do want to extend that system to state and national, as well as to local elections. In the United States racial and national divisions are added to the ones arising from the social structure and from religious differences. For that reason alone a break-up of the American two-party system could not easily be avoided if P.R. were adopted. A glance at the actual history of our party system shows that on more than one occasion it survived only on account of the plurality system. The authors of the American standard work on P.R., Clarence G. Hoag and George H. Hallett, explicitly discuss the possibility that under P.R. the American Congress might be as much divided (actually it would be more divided) as it was temporarily, in the 1920's, under the impact of the Progressive movement. They conclude:

> Under these circumstances we should have some questions decided by Republicans and Democrats against Progressives, some by Republicans and Progressives against Democrats, some by Democrats and Progressives against Republicans . . . The House of Representatives would become representative in fact as in name.[25]

The last sentence indicates that for the two authors, the House of Representatives would not be "representative in fact" unless it were divided into more than two parties. This, of course, is hardly representation as understood by the framers of our "representative republic."

Nor do we have to add that, whereas it was Madison's fondest hope that representative government would "refine and enlarge the public views," the proponents of P.R.—arguing consistently from the point of view of their premises—will excuse any and all shortcomings in a parliament as reflecting the weaknesses, and divisions, existing within the people. They imply, as Josiah Phillips Quincy [26] worded it, that "ours is a representative government, and not the government of the able men"—a thoroughly un-Madisonian view.

For Madison and his associates, at any rate, representation was not a dead and passive thing. The founders of the "representative republic" considered it a system apt to bring the best in their nation to the top and to equip them with the power they needed to "break and control the violence of faction," rather than merely to "represent" them.

~~~~~~

CONSTITUTIONALISM IN THE

CONCRETE

Chapter XI

PARLIAMENTARY GOVERNMENT IN BRITAIN

THE LOGIC OF SPECULATION AND THE LOGIC OF EXPERIENCE.

The living forces behind the more or less static forms of democratic constitutionalism do not exhaust its substance. The concrete way in which a constitution arranges "the magistracies in the state and in particular the highest of them all" has much to do with the reality of democratic government; its share in shaping political action goes so far that, as will be seen below, it even exerts a certain influence on the structure of the political parties. It is, therefore, important to discuss the more significant differences between the various types of democratic executive. Brief reference has been made to the principal characteristics of parliamentary and presidential government; there has to be added the Swiss type of executive—imitated in Uruguay with significant modifications and without giving substantial satisfaction. Switzerland and Uruguay are, however, countries with only about four million inhabitants. Either case is hardly comparable to that of large states. For the latter the effective choice does seem to lie between the parliamentary and the presidential systems. Since the parliamentary type is older, and has been used more frequently, we shall discuss it first.

A discussion of parliamentary government necessarily becomes a discussion of the British Constitution. One might say that its basic characteristic consists in the fact that it has developed the parliamentary type of government in "pure" form. It has often been said that the English are not logical, and that the British Constitution is less logical than the people themselves. By way of contrast, both the people and the constitutions of France (here we must use the plural as France has had 14 constitutions since 1789) are said to be logical. The English accept this characterization and take pride in it. Thus, when Sir Winston Churchill defended the decision of his war-time government to rebuild the House of Commons as it had been before being destroyed, he declared:

> Logic is a poor guide compared with custom. Logic which has created in so many countries semi-circular assemblies which have buildings which give to every Member, not only a seat to sit in but often a desk to write at, with a lid to bang, has proved fatal to Parliamentary Government as we know it here in its home and in the land of its birth.[1]

Sir Winston was referring to the fact that the shape of the House of Commons was due to accident: Henry VIII had assigned its members a chapel in which to meet. It was not large enough to hold all of its members (now more than 600), and Churchill pointed out that this both facilitated the conduct of debate in a conversational manner and prevented the House from looking empty on ordinary occasions when attendance was bound to be low. On the other hand, when the House is crowded, a sense of drama and urgency is imparted to the proceedings by the lack of space. Furthermore, the rectangular shape of the House, with a corridor separating its two sides, made it natural for the supporters of the government to gather on one side and the opposition on the other. This symbolic separation underlined the fact that business cannot be conducted with either efficiency or with a sense of responsibility unless there is a clearcut separation between majority and minority. The wish has often been expressed that the parliaments in Continental Europe in which, after the First World War, there was frequently an opposition consisting of extremists of the Right as well as of the Left, might adopt an arrangement like the one in the British House of Commons; in that case it would be brought home to extremists looking for a physical fight that they were the more logical sparring partners for one another than the moderates supporting the government.

Clearly however, when Sir Winston was pointing out the advantages of the traditional structure of the House of Commons, he was not opposing logic; he was endorsing it. His shafts were aimed not at reason, but at speculation—at the attempt, so characteristic of French political thinking, to "blue-print" in advance, on the basis of what was bound to be guesswork, the requirements of the political future. In this respect the English were not more clever than the French; they just did not try to be clever at all. Their Constitution is, indeed, "an accident of an accident"—but with the exception that when accidental developments led to satisfactory results, they were accepted; if they did not, they were modified. The British were as often tempted to make mistakes as any other nation. Thus, twice, in 1692 and 1700, measures were voted which excluded from the House of Commons all persons "holding an office or place of profit under the Crown." Had these measures been applied, they would have foreclosed the possibility of a development toward the parliamentary system which is based on the identity between the leaders of the majority and the members of the government. The first time King William refused his consent to the measure; the very fact that parliamentary government did not then exist made it possible for the King to keep the road open for its future development, although this was the last thing he either saw or wanted. On the second occasion, the particular provision of the Act of Settlement was repealed before it went into effect.

HOMOGENEITY, RESPONSIBILITY, SOLIDARITY.

Action in conformity with a clearly foreseen pattern was absent in the development of parliamentary government throughout. Its major features are said to be homogeneity, responsibility, and solidarity. Homogeneity means that all members of the cabinet belong to the same party. The first such cabinet was appointed in 1695; the Earl of Sunderland had advised the King that it would be easier for him to get along with his advisers, and easier for them to get along with parliament, if all were taken from the ranks of the majority party. This measure of practical accommodation was, of course, in the long run (the precedent was not to establish itself firmly for a long time) bound to hand all power over to the majority party and to its leader; if the King could no longer select his advisers freely, but instead had to accept a more or less ready-made team, that team would tend to act on its own rather than be guided by the King.

Responsibility of the cabinet to parliament was the second step in this development; otherwise, the identity between executive and the leaders of the parliamentary majority could not be obtained. This responsibility is of course, of a purely political type; it has nothing to do with the charge of a criminal offense as contained in either an impeachment or in a bill of attainder. Its nature was slow to be realized, however. Thus, when Sir Robert Walpole's cabinet, which had been in power since 1721, was, twenty years later, approaching its end, his opponents introduced, in the form of a motion, the following "prayer" to the King:

> That one person has grasped in his own hands every branch of government, that one person has attained the sole direction of affairs, monopolized all the favors of the Crown, composed the disposal of all places, pensions, titles, ribands, as well as all preferments, civil, mili-

tary, and ecclesiastical; that one person has made a blind submission
to his will, both in Elections and Parliament, the only terms of present
favor and future expectation. I therefore move that an humble address be presented to his Majesty, that he would be graciously pleased
to remove the R. H. Sir R. Walpole from his presence and counsels
for ever.[2]

Walpole, then, was to be made to appear like a criminal because he
was laying the foundations of cabinet government. His own understanding of the situation was no better than that of his enemies. His
defense was that, since no one had proven him guilty of a punishable
act, the request for his dismissal constituted an interference with the
royal prerogative. He survived on this occasion only to fall in 1742.

Solidarity [3] is only a shade less vital than homogeneity and responsibility. It means that ministers are to act as a team. While policy is
being made they may have a share in the processes involved, expressing their own views freely (if confidentially) to the Prime Minister
personally or in cabinet meetings. Once policy has been decided upon
it is to be accepted and defended by all. If a vote of censure is adopted
against any one minister, the entire government resigns unless the
House of Commons can be made to reconsider, or unless there is a
clearcut case of bad administration, or error of judgment on the part
of a minister for which the government does not always accept responsibility.[3a] Apart from such a—very unusual—case it is assumed that
the various aspects of government policy form an integrated whole
and that, if any part falls, the whole is in danger. At the same time,
in their public utterances all ministers are expected to defend the
government's decision. Bagehot [4] mentions an incident which, he
rightly adds, would be significant whether entirely true or not: "It is
said that at the end of the cabinet which agreed to propose a fixed
duty on corn, Lord Melbourne put his back to the door, and said,
'Now is it to lower the price of corn or isn't it? It is not much matter
which we say, but mind, we must all say the *same.*'" When such a
point is reached, the limit is approached beyond which teamwork
leads to hypocrisy. The principle, however, implies not only effective
cooperation but it also leads to a search for agreement whenever
there is an opportunity of finding it. This procedure is quite different
from that of coalition governments in Continental Europe where cabinet members may have no hesitation in stating views different from
those agreed upon by the cabinet; they will, in fact, always be inclined to place the responsibility for whatever is unpopular upon their
partners, claiming for themselves the authorship of whatever meets
with popular approval.

Coalitions lead to tendencies in this direction even on the rare occasions when they are resorted to in England. Thus, when, in 1932 the "National Government," under the pressure of its Conservative members, introduced a protective tariff, Mr. Snowden and other cabinet members voted against it in the House of Commons and, in an "agreement to disagree," they were allowed to state their reasons in public.[5] Incidents of this type constitute, on the one hand, the reason why Disraeli could say: "This country does not like coalitions." On the other hand, they prove that when the basic conditions under which the British Constitution has developed have changed even the most firmly established principles are disregarded. If Britain were to adopt a system of voting under which coalitions would be a permanent necessity, rather than an expedient resorted to for a limited time, the body of customs which now regulate political behavior would change radically.

TRADITIONS AND THEIR BASIS.

Traditions, in fact, which are so often quoted as the foundation of British government, have only a limited influence. They are comparable to an old house which has developed cracks; pieces of masonry, which would normally fall down, are kept in place by the strong vines which have grown around the house over the years. What the vines do is useful if the basic structural damage is repaired before everything collapses; if the restoration of the building's structural supports is delayed beyond that point, the vines—in our case the traditions—fall with the rest. Thus, what might have become a parting with the ways of old developed in 1924 when the newly elected House of Commons met. The Conservatives held 258 seats, the Liberals 159, and Labour 191. In virtually every other country such a situation would have led to a coalition which, had it been established, might easily have perpetuated the conditions giving rise to it through the adoption of a system of voting deviating from the plurality system. In England tradition was strong enough to prevail. It was expressed in these words by Asquith, the Liberal leader:

> I think, and I am sure I shall have with me the great majority of the House, that it is plain that when an admistration so situated [as the Conservative government in 1924] resigns, the party which naturally and properly succeeds to the task, if it is minded to undertake it, is the party that is numerically preponderant in the Opposition. . . . In the meantime, the present Administration are disqualified by the judgement of the country—a judgement which they themselves invited. . . . There is not, and cannot be, any question of coalition or of fusion.[6]

Had a coalition giving no party a majority become a permanent feature—rather than being one certain to pass with the next election—Asquith's arguments would have lost their force; a coalition would then have become as natural as one-party majority governments are now. If even the adoption of the single-transferable vote (in the general framework of the majority system) would have led to this result, it is easy to understand why the Royal Commission on Electoral Systems concluded, as early as 1910, that if P.R. were adopted:

> What arrangement might ultimately have to be made to induce any party to undertake the administration of the country in such circumstances . . . it is impossible to forecast: it is only clear that parliamentary government as now understood in England would become impossible.[7]

Serious modifications of the British political pattern would, in fact, be likely to result even from the alternative vote, which the House of Commons adopted in 1931. Apparently this was part of a bargain—hotly denied by the principals—arranged between the Liberals, who were willing to accept the alternative vote as an alternative (and perhaps also the first step) to P.R., and the Labour party which wanted support for Ramsay McDonald's second minority cabinet.[8] The bill failed to become law because the House of Lords modified it severely, and the 1931 elections took place before the change could be pushed through under the provisions of the Parliament Act.

Had the alternative vote been used, not only Liberals but also other small parties could have presented candidates all over the country; the fear that votes cast for them might be "thrown away," which constitutes the principal reason for the small vote cast for these parties, would have been removed. Even a casual glance at the results of elections of 1945, 1950, 1951, and 1955, shows that in every single case a small shift in the popular vote away from the major parties would have placed the minor ones in control and necessitated coalition governments as a permanent feature.[8a]

British proponents of either P.R. or the alternative vote, therefore, do not just make a demand for reforming the electoral system; the adoption of their plans would entail a change in the essential characteristics of the British government, a change which no tradition could stop. Some advocates of P.R. are aware of this fact even if they do not always state their conclusions with the clarity distinguishing the writings of Professor Ramsay Muir.[9]

A radical deviation from the plurality system would, in fact, not only destroy the structure of British government at the top; it would seriously affect that basis of consent which has developed in Britain since the Glorious Revolution. It is often overlooked that such symptoms of this consensus as the impartiality of the Speaker, and the characteristic phrase, "His Majesty's most loyal Opposition," date back little more than a century.[10] As late as in 1835 the Whigs, who had just won an election, ousted Speaker Manners Sutton and replaced him by a member of their own party. The new Speaker, however, was continued in office by the Conservatives when they returned to power. This custom has been followed ever since, although there have been several recent cases of the Speaker's seat being contested in an election. The official recognition of the part played by the opposition did not take place until 1937 when the Ministers of the Crown Act provided its leader with a salary of £2000. In all of these developments the plurality system acted as a "silent partner"; it encouraged all tendencies aiming at restraining not only extremists but all devotees of doctrinaire politics as well, and it forced both major parties into a mold in which moderation was the inescapable price of success.

This process has given rise to traditions of accommodation and toleration which are now important in their own right; but few will believe that the human animal in England is different from what he is in the rest of the world. When Lloyd George proceeded to the uncalled for dissolution of the House of Commons in 1918, precipitating the so-called "khaki elections," or when, in 1931, the government coalition took over the label "National Government," campaigns ensued in which passion manifested itself as strongly as in any other country. The same happened in 1951 when, during the last weeks of the campaign, Churchill and his Conservative party were charged with being the "war party"—posters were plastered all over the nation picturing the cemeteries, which were supposedly certain to be filled within a short period after Churchill's return to power.

Let it be added that manifestations of a not insignificant support for extremists could be noticed in the 1930's. Sir Oswald Mosley and his "British Union of Fascists" promoted a strange mixture of Fascist and Nazi policies. They organized provocative parades through East end streets filled with opponents, looking for, and frequently obtaining, those street fights which provide a party of this type with the kind of publicity it needs. For a time, Sir Oswald was able to fill Albert Hall, seating 8,000 persons, almost at volition—a feat which even a Prime Minister can accomplish only on rare occasions. The percentages of the votes obtained during those years by certain Fascist and Communist candidates [11] were high enough to indicate a strength which, under a radical system of P.R., would have made it possible for both parties to secure a handful of seats in the House of Commons. Once such a group has obtained a parliamentary foothold, its vote is likely to increase because people are then no longer afraid to "throw their votes away" by supporting it. Various measures in the field of "Militant Democracy" [12] can be taken, of course, to control such groups. While likely to be effective in countries such as England with a government strong enough to enforce them in a manner certain to attract wide public support, they can be quite ineffective under a coalition government, as they were, for example, in Czechoslovakia. [13] For all of these reasons one cannot but agree with what the Royal Commission on Electoral Systems stated as early as in 1910, when these specific developments could not be foreseen:

> This statement of the aims of Proportional Representation [i.e. it is to represent the parties in proportion to their strength at the polls] is in reality very incomplete. For the title conceals a root and branch attack on the single-member majority system and all its works—its effects upon the elector, upon the candidate, upon the member of the House of Commons, and upon politics, no less than upon the justice of representation. [14]

MONARCHY, MODERATION, AND DEMOCRACY.

These considerations affect the British monarchy as they affect every other part of British constitutional life. The reason, in fact, why the monarchy is so successful is that the political system is strong in itself. As mentioned previously, the legal fiction according to which "The Queen can do no wrong" makes sense only on the assumption that, in the main, she can do nothing. The minister who countersigns any particular act of the sovereign not only approves it; he and his colleagues can now safely be assumed to have initiated it. They are, therefore, responsible for it in fact as well as in name. This is, at the same time, the only way in which monarchy can be kept above the level of partisan controversy. The proper functioning of this process presupposes, of course, that there always are ministers strong enough to act on their own. Wherever there are prolonged cabinet crises, the active intervention of the head of the state may be required to overcome them, and his choice of men may also become a choice of policies. In such a case, even the most conscientious monarch may find it difficult to remain above the din of party battle.

This possibility, at the same time, indicates the general nature of the tasks accruing to the head of the state under a parliamentary system. He exercises a reserve function. Wherever a government based on an alternation of parties develops gaps, it is up to the head of the state to fill them. If, so far as the "effective" parts of the system are concerned, there are virtually no gaps, as happens under a two-party system, the "reserve power" need hardly to come into operation, and the sovereign will automatically remain above parties. If the gaps become real, the extent of the "reserve power" can become so great that, as happened in Belgium during the years prior to World War II, the government becomes a "royal" government almost as much in fact as in name, with the inevitable consequence of the monarch becoming the object of partisan controversy.[15]

Before we discuss the implications of this relationship for the British constitutional system it might briefly be mentioned that when the monarchy fills the gap which party government leaves in the field of symbolism, it is both the most useful and least controversial. This gap is so great as to be virtually a void, and this is a void which hardly any other agency of the government could fill. In England as in all other countries with a two-party system, government is based on direct popular support. Even if it does its work well, it is, however, as likely to encounter criticism as approval. Men such as Sir Winston Churchill, who came to symbolize the virtues of their nation, are rare; being active party leaders, they can perform this symbolic function only in times of national crisis, reverting to their status as party men with the inevitable "return to normalcy."

Parliaments may do better in regard to symbolism than governments. In Britain, the House of Lords, and in its own way, the House of Commons, do have a symbolic appeal, as do the counterparts of the latter in the Commonwealth countries. Even in England, however, a solemn opening of parliament by the Queen, preceded by a procession and followed by the reading of a "speech from the throne," all limited to one day, exceed in symbolic value what it takes parliament a year to accomplish.

If, then, the British monarchy occupies a near-monopoly in regard to the "dignified parts" of the Constitution, there do remain a few gaps for it to fill in its "efficient parts." The first case arises when a new Prime Minister has to be appointed. While his selection might be left to the House of Commons, appointment by a revered monarch, apart from its simplicity, lends dignity to the procedure even if it is a mere formality, as it is bound to be whenever one party has both an overall majority and a generally recognized leader. Conditions are different when, as it did happen not infrequently between the first and second electoral reform, there is no clear majority, or when the majority has no definite leader.

In such a case, it is the task of the sovereign to find the person most likely to secure majority support; [16] but even the most restricted freedom of choice implies the possibility that personal preferences might play their part. This is one of the reasons why the Labour party has formalized the selection of its leaders to such an extent that, whenever it has a majority, there is only one person to whom the Queen can turn. Yet, there has never been a time when a Labour Prime Minister has died or resigned while his party stayed in power. It must remain a matter of doubt whether, in such circumstances, the Labour party would immediately hold a meeting to elect a leader and advise the Queen to delay the appointment of the Prime Minister until after the election had been held. The Conservatives, at any rate, have so far been willing to allow the Queen to make the choice between the two or three men acceptable as Prime Minister; of course, there might be an even wider freedom of choice if a coalition were to be formed.

The first of the recent cases in which a sovereign exercised his right to select the Prime Minister under conditions where a real choice was involved concerns the elevation of Stanley Baldwin in 1923. There had been no particular problem in 1922 when Bonar Law was invited to become Prime Minister. At that time, Sir Austen Chamberlain, the official Conservative leader, had taken himself out of the race because he had been in favor of continuing Lloyd George's wartime coalition, a course of action against which the younger element in the party, led by Stanley Baldwin, had just successfully rebelled, and Bonar Law was acceptable to all. When Bonar Law retired in 1923, however, Lord Curzon expected the summons to Buckingham Palace and is said to have suffered a nervous breakdown when, instead, the invitation went to Stanley Baldwin. It has often been claimed that the reason was Lord Curzon's status as a member of the House of Lords which excluded him from access to the House of Commons where important decisions were made. L. S. Amery [16a] writes, however: "Lord Curzon's appointment was practically settled when two junior members of the cabinet, the late Lord Bridgeman and myself, intervened with Lord Stamfordham and urged reconsideration in favour of Mr. Baldwin as likely to be more acceptable to his colleagues and to the rank and file of the party." Lord Balfour whose advice was then sought did suggest that "Curzon's peerage was a sound reason for passing him over," [16b] but Amery insists that it would not have been, at that time, a decisive reason. At any rate, King George V, in weighing the evidence submitted to him (through his secretary) played the part of the impartial and objective arbiter which the Head of the State ought to play under a parliamentary system of government.[17] The same can be said for George VI who, in 1940, upon the resignation of Neville Chamberlain, selected Winston Churchill, although some had expected the choice to fall upon Lord Halifax, whom, apparently, Chamberlain preferred. In the decisive conversation which took place between the three men on May 10, Halifax himself stated the reasons against his appointment:

> He said that he felt that his position as a peer, out of the House of Commons, would make it very difficult for him to discharge the duties of Prime Minister in a war like this. He would be held responsible for everything, but would not have the power to guide the assembly upon whose confidence the life of every Government depended.[18]

Churchill adds that "by the time he had finished, it was clear that the duty would fall upon me—had in fact fallen upon me." [19] This means that there was, in reality, no choice by the King. Still, Churchill emphasized in his conversation with Chamberlain and Halifax that he would not communicate with either the Labour or the Liberal parties until he "had the King's commission to form a Government." He knew that such a formal act would squelch any opposition to him which there might be either among the government or the opposition.

A more real choice existed in January, 1957, when Sir Anthony Eden resigned and was commonly expected to be replaced by R. A. Butler. Interviews with Lord Salisbury and Sir Winston Churchill are said to have swayed the Queen towards Harold MacMillan, although it has also been asserted that they were part of a plan made weeks earlier. Butler, at any rate, had disagreed with the Anglo-French action in seizing the Suez Canal; a group of Conservatives in the House of Commons who had strongly backed this action would have resented Butler's appointment. Besides, if Sir Anthony resigned for health reasons, it must have been recalled that Mr. Butler had retired as Chancellor of the Exchequer for the same reasons. Sir Winston had, therefore, strong arguments on his side when he advised in favor of MacMillan. There were, on the other hand, arguments in favor of Butler; and it is interesting that *The Times* [20] should have deemed it necessary to state them even after the choice had been made. Butler, it said, represented the younger, and more progressive, element in the Conservative party:

> After the defeat of 1945 it was largely Mr. Butler and his young men who fashioned a new outlook and something of a new philosophy.

They not merely based their political faith on an acceptance of the responsibility "for ensuring a certain standard of living, of employment, and of security for all." They not only proclaimed their belief in "one nation." Conservatives also came to declare "Change is our Ally."

The editorial—written with restraint—added that no one would expect Mr. MacMillan to reverse this trend, but he might be less active in rebuffing "the old guard of the party." It was implied that the choice was the all but inevitable result of the procedure adopted; as long as only two "elder statesmen" were consulted, the voice of the younger men in the party—whose consultation would, of course, not have been easy—was bound to go unheard.

Under such circumstances it is natural that the candidate passed over, and his supporters, should have felt disappointed; in an interview published in the *Sunday Express*, Mr. Butler said so frankly, and some observers made charges [21] which went beyond those advanced by *The Times*. Still, the way the issue was decided proved again the value of the informal methods characteristic of the British system. There was no open contest to deepen the wounds which such a decision is likely to leave in the best of cases; the fact that the new appointee had the prestige of monarchy behind him helped to overcome the opposition within his party. At any rate, Butler stated immediately that he was giving his full support to MacMillan and gave every indication that he meant it.

The monarch, then, in the exercise of such powers as he still has, is expected to act as an impersonal force, aiming at keeping the wheels of party government moving with the least possible friction. Besides, during the last hundred years, custom has developed safeguards designed to make certain that the decisions in question are not made, as was previously the case,[22] on the advice of courtiers or personal friends. The designation of a new Prime Minister is not preceded by the lengthy discussions with political leaders characteristic of other countries, such as France. There is no need for this in a country where the choice of the Prime Minister (ever since the second electoral reform) has been comparatively simple, and where the practical advantages of a speedy decision are valued highly. The necessary contacts—in regard to this problem as well as all others on which the monarch may have to pass—are maintained on a permanent basis. Therefore, the King (or Queen) is always able to act without the need of spending days, or even weeks, in preliminary discussions, as the head of the state may have to do in Continental Europe. The task of maintaining these contacts lies largely in the hands of the Queen's private secretary. Baron Stockmar, who followed Prince Albert to

London, while sharply criticized by some,[23] is said by others to have
played a major part in the establishment of the pattern which is now
followed; the very precariousness of his own position, as well as that
of his master, forced him to act with the tact characteristic of all those
who have since performed the functions of the adviser "Behind the
Throne." [24] These men have tried to institutionalize, and thereby ob-
jectivize, what otherwise might, in spite of all the limitations surrounding it, still somewhat partake of the nature of "personal power."
Their existence also introduced the principle of selection on the basis
of personal ability as a supplement to that of monarchical heredity.

If the two-party system greatly simplifies the task of the Queen,
there still may arise the possibility, at least, of coalitions. In that case,
the discretionary power of the Head of the State increases, and with
it the danger of arousing public controversy. The formation of the
"National Government," in 1931, is a case in point. Ramsay Mac-
Donald's second government collapsed when the majority of its supporters failed to endorse its plans to deal with the economic crisis.
MacDonald might simply have resigned, and Stanley Baldwin, the
leader of the strongest opposition party, might have been called upon
to succeed him. Baldwin would have been free to form a Conservative government or a coalition with the Liberals; in the first case, a
dissolution would have been necessary almost immediately, since the
Conservatives did not command a majority, and in the second, it
might have been postponed. Both solutions would have prevented the
formation of a "National Government" which was never more than
the addition of the Liberal party, and of a few Labour leaders, to the
Conservative party. A frankly Conservative, or Conservative-Liberal
government, could not have campaigned against Labour under the
"National" label. Thus, some of the acrimony by which the campaign
came to be characterized would have been avoided. Also, Labour
might not have been beaten quite as disastrously as it was when its
membership in the House of Commons was reduced from 288 to 52,
less than one-tenth of the total membership of the House, and not
nearly enough to make possible the functioning of a forceful opposition at a time when the political system needed it badly. Lastly, a
less humiliating defeat would have caused less bitterness in Labour's
ranks; as it was, the radical wing of the party benefited from these
events, and a man like Harold Laski, who had been rather moderate
earlier in his career, began to assert [25] the possibility of a civil war in
terms almost advocating it.

Years after the event these reasons seem both obvious and convincing, but they could not be fully grasped during the hectic days

of 1931. The King and his advisers were above all impressed with the need of having a cabinet with as strong a backing as possible; it alone offered hope for heading off a type of depression which would have been more serious for a country in the throes of a deep moral crisis [26] than for a nation as young and vigorous as the United States. Events in the economic field have justified the hopes of King George V.[27] Britain not only avoided the worst of the world economic crisis but soon headed into a recovery which was better sustained than what the United States accomplished between 1933 and 1939.[28]

There were arguments, then, in favor of the decisions taken by George V in 1931. They gained weight by the fact that the appointment of MacDonald as the leader of a coalition, first suggested by the Liberal leader, Sir Herbert Samuel, was accepted both by Baldwin and, of course, by MacDonald himself. Thus, the leaders of all three major parties were in favor of a large coalition, even if, by that time, MacDonald had actually ceased to be the leader of the Labour party —a fact probably unknown to the King. In spite of all this, no act of a British monarch has, in recent generations, been criticized as severely as the appointment of MacDonald to head a "National" government. Definitely, the Labour leaders did not feel that "The King can do no wrong," even if their wrath was, in the main directed at MacDonald. The case was exceptional and has done no harm to the institution of monarchy. Still, it does show that if there were a multiple-party system requiring the formation of coalition governments as a matter of course, the impartiality of the Head of the State would be subjected to constant strain, even if a normal coalition would not meet with the type of objection raised against the "National" government.

At any rate, when the Queen appoints a Prime Minister she has "power," as she is exercising a right of her own which both the Constitution and the logic of the parliamentary system confer upon her. In regard to most other matters she only has "influence": she may do her best to persuade the Prime Minister, or a minister heading a particular department, of the wisdom of a certain course of action, but the advice must be offered in the full awareness of the fact that while it may be the right of the sovereign to *propose*, it is up to the responsible minister to *dispose*. Such influence is the natural result of the great prestige of the monarchy, considerably enhanced in recent decades; it may be supported by an awareness of the fact that the sovereign (or her advisers) are speaking with the background of an experience extending over many years. The Queen, at any rate, must always be informed, and in Bagehot's famous formulation, she has "the right to be consulted, the right to encourage, the right to warn." [29]

The royal influence resulting from this fact extends to all matters of government, including the appointment of cabinet members. Thus, it is said that when, in 1945, Clement Attlee presented his list of cabinet members to George V, the latter drew his attention to the great importance of having the best man available for the office of Foreign Secretary; he asked him who he thought was the best among his colleagues. Attlee is said to have answered that Ernest Bevin was, and to have changed his list, transferring Bevin from the position as Chancellor of the Exchequer to that of Foreign Secretary, and reversing the process so far as Hugh Dalton—an academic specialist in the field of public finance—was concerned, who would have preferred appointment as Foreign Secretary, although there is more than one explanation for his shift to the Exchequer.[29a] Within a few years Attlee probably lost any doubt which he might have entertained regarding the King's (implied) suggestion. Bevin made a good Foreign Secretary while his health held up, whereas Dalton proved rather erratic, and resigned from the cabinet as a result of an indiscretion.

THE ABDICATION CRISIS AND ITS LESSONS.

This is not the place to discuss additional details; suffice it to add that monarchy within the framework of parliamentary government can be safe as well as useful. Had proof been needed, the events connected with the abdication of Edward VIII would have provided it. In principle, under the parliamentary system, a cabinet with a stable majority can, if it is confident of popular support, force any Head of the State to resign at any time. All the cabinet has to do is to refuse to cooperate with him. In that case he can perform no valid act of government, as this requires the countersignature of a responsible minister. In theory the Head of the State might dismiss the cabinet and appoint a new one with the countersignature of the new Prime Minister. The latter, if defeated in parliament, could take a last, if desperate, step by requesting the dissolution of the existing parliament. A political leader acting in this fashion however, would not only have his regular partisan opponents to contend with but also those considering his actions contrary to the spirit of the Constitution. The chances for winning such an election would, therefore, be dubious.

The closest parallel to the case under consideration is the dissolution of the French Chamber of Deputies in 1877. The President of the Republic, Marshal MacMahon, whose constitutional position was analogous to that of a British monarch, forced a Republican government, which was supported by a majority, out of office for no other reason than that, as a monarchist, he disagreed with its policies. The President appointed the monarchist leader, the Duke of Broglie, as Prime Minister, and dissolved the Chamber of Deputies, having received the approval of the Senate as required by the Constitution. MacMahon was within his rights according to the letter of the Constitution, and entirely wrong according to the logic of the parliamentary system. Yet the spirit was to prevail over the letter. During the campaign, the Republican leader, Léon Gambetta, declared: "Listen well, M. Marshal, after the sovereign people will have made their voice heard you will either have to submit or to resign." Actually, MacMahon did both. The Republicans, in spite of all official pressure brought to bear against them, elected a majority of the new Chamber. The President first "submitted" by accepting a Republican cabinet, and, when this pursued a course which he felt his honor did not permit him to tolerate, he "resigned."

It is hard to imagine a British monarch conspiring against a cabinet supported by a parliamentary majority; yet, should this ever happen victory in the ensuing elections would be no less difficult to obtain than it proved to be in France. At any rate before Edward VIII was forced to make the choice of either abandoning his marriage plans or resigning, Prime Minister Baldwin had made certain that his course of action enjoyed the approval of the Liberal and Labour parties as well as that of his own; the Commonwealth governments were likewise in agreement. Against such formidable opposition the King's supporters could not have prevailed in an election even if a man of the stature of Winston Churchill was among them. All such an adventure could have accomplished would have been to compromise the future of the politicians involved in it, as well as the position of the monarchy.

No parliamentary majority will, of course, ever attempt to force the Head of the State into retirement unless it has a very strong case. Besides, when such a case exists, it may not be as readily intelligible to the public as it is to those immediately confronted with the facts. Thus, in regard to Edward VIII, there was a widespread popular feeling that he was as free to marry whom he wanted as was any one of his subjects. It was overlooked that a King's consort is an important part of the institution of monarchy. In the fulfillment of the symbolic functions the Queen is second only to the King. We are dealing here with the "dignified" parts of the Constitution—and one of the most responsible British papers touched on two sensitive spots when it wrote: "The King, as is now well known, is anxious to become the third husband of a lady of American birth." [30] Edward's willingness to accept a morganatic marriage—which would have made the then Mrs. Simpson his legal wife without making her Queen—only served to underline the awkwardness of the situation; a distinction of that type would have created the appearance of an official admission that his consort was not fit to be Queen.

If difficulties arose in regard to the "dignified" parts of the King's functions, his own views concerning his constitutional role conflicted with its "efficient" parts—a fact rightly deemed too delicate to be discussed much in public. Therefore, it was never fully appreciated by the people at large. Edward, apparently, was anxious "to *be* King"; to some extent, at least, he wished to *rule* as well as to *reign.* "Well considered inaction" which, according to Bagehot,[31] is the best course of action for a monarch under a parliamentary system, was not to his liking. This led him to attempts to substitute his own judgment for that of his responsible advisers. A few days after the abdication, Arthur Krock [32] quoted from a private memorandum which apparently had played a part in inducing the House of Commons to pass the abdication and succession acts "swiftly and overwhelmingly," and which

> relates at least five occasions since the accession of Edward, and one before, which led responsible British statesmen into the belief that the Duke of Windsor, impressed with the strength of personal government and forceful personalities throughout the world, intended to assert himself more than any of his predecessors had done since Queen Augusta whispered to her son, "George, be a King." These occasions include two speeches, only sketchily published abroad and hardly at all at home—one on military matters and one on humanitarian policies— as well as the address to the miners of South Wales which became so public a Cabinet annoyance.

It is interesting to note that, while such utterances in favor of the workers tended, in parts of the British as well as the American press, to earn Edward a reputation of being a social-minded monarch, enough of the leaders of the Labour party were trained in the principles of constitutional government to feel quite differently about the subject.[33]

Even less publicity has been given to Edward's attempts to strike out on a path of his own in the field of foreign policy. Both he and his future consort were reported to have fairly close social contacts with Hitler's ambassador, von Ribbentrop, and his British friends; the King lent credence to these reports when during his New Year's reception, he singled out Ribbentrop for special attention. Edward's indiscretions in this field have led to exaggerated charges; but when, after the abdication, he visited Hitler in Germany, he allowed his journey to be exploited extensively by Nazi propaganda.[34] This particular *faux pas* of the then Duke of Windsor, of course, could not be foreseen when, on December 8, the House of Commons met for the first time to receive a report on the issue, but contemporary accounts—which, as is so often the case, contain a flavor lost in the text books dealing with the subject—left no doubt that the majority of the members felt strongly that they were indeed confronted with the issue of "King versus parliament." [35]

Edward's case was, of course, highly exceptional; yet, the guardians of the British constitutional system are bound to be mindful of such events and of their implications for the future precisely because the public at large is, at present, even less inclined to view the institution of monarchy objectively than it was a generation ago. To a large extent, the popular press [36] is to blame; more sensational than ever since the end of World War II, it features royalty in a way suggesting adulation as well as admiration. Even serious publications seem to make concessions to the trend of the times; it is difficult to imagine any writer using, in these days, the language in which Bagehot discussed the English monarchy [37] although no one has emphasized the positive value of the institution more strongly. It is, at any rate, an accepted principle that all public and political acts of the sovereign must be controlled by his responsible advisers, and it is up to them to determine where matters of purely private concern end, and those of public interest begin. Inevitably, all members of the royal family are, to some extent, affected by this situation; the fact that they, and their descendants, occupy a more or less remote place in the line of succession is less significant than the active share they have in the fulfillment of royalty's symbolic functions. In that respect, they are part of the existing constitutional system and subject to its limitations; the marriage plans of the only sister of a reigning Queen, for example, are of considerable public importance.

PARTIES AND NATIONAL UNITY.

These brief remarks on the British monarchy must be concluded by a reminder of the close relationship existing between the "dignified" and the "efficient" parts of the British Constitution, a relationship in which the place of the "independent variable" is all but monopolized by the efficient parts. In this regard, as in others, Lord Balfour's brilliant Introduction to Bagehot's *English Constitution* has been a source of confusion. Balfour [38] was, of course, right in stressing the great, and in some respects growing, value of the British monarchy as "symbolic of . . . unity and continuity." Yet, no symbol has ever been able to symbolize something that did not exist. Balfour says that "partisan majorities do the nation's work and on the whole do it well; but is it not at the cost of deepening and hardening national divisions?" It need not be repeated that, actually, the very nature of partisan warfare brings both of the parties, and the nation, together. Reference has been made above not only to the "objective" but also to the "subjective" ingredients of the common will, meaning certain basic convictions held in common at any particular time by all those who have a significant part in the nation's political life. Thus, when in Britain the nineteenth century trend towards democracy began, the Conservative party had to convert itself to a belief in "Tory democracy"; similarly, when, during the twentieth century, first the Liberals and then the Labour party introduced a large measure of social reform, the Conservatives, once again, had to meet the new trend more than halfway. The existence of the monarchy certainly facilitated this tendency, but its basic cause was the simple fact that if the Conservatives wanted power, they had to pay the price.

These conditions not only created a "unity on fundamentals" which it was easy to symbolize, but also resulted, as a rule, in clearcut majorities. These not only make it simple for the monarchy to remain above parties but also can make it possible to overcome difficulties arising from within the monarchy without weakening the institution itself. Clearly, this is the way in which the abdication crisis of 1936 was solved; it left a bad taste in everyone's mouth, but it was certainly handled in a manner preferable to what happened in Belgium in the case of King Leopold III, who, after years of troubles, was forced out by riots, which followed a plebiscite he won with less than the overwhelming majority he needed from the psychological point of view. The Belgian monarch, since the first day of his reign, had been facing a multiple-party system which had much to do with not only creating the royal crisis, but also with the painful way in which it ended.[39]

THE PRIME MINISTER AND THE CABINET.

These considerations lead us back from the "dignified" to the "efficient" parts of the British Constitution. As mentioned above, the introduction of the plebiscitary element into British politics, caused by the rise of the popular party system, has strengthened the position of the executive in general and of the Prime Minister in particular. The latter, since that time, has not only enjoyed a type of popular sanction which none of his colleagues may claim, but he can also renew this sanction at any time of his own choosing by dissolving the House of Commons. Until 1918 he needed cabinet approval for a dissolution, but, in 1918, Lloyd George established the precedent according to which the Prime Minister can advise a dissolution on his own. Even so dissolution is, theoretically, an act of the Queen, except under very unusual circumstances, however, the Prime Minister is certain to have his advice accepted. This fact does much [40] to make the Prime Minister more than a *primus inter pares*.

The Prime Minister's eminence is evident, in the first place, in the choice of his colleagues. Some of the leaders of his party are so prominent that he cannot ignore them, but in most cases his freedom of choice is real;[41] insofar as the assignment of the various government departments is concerned, the Prime Minister's decision may prevail even over the wishes of his most prominent colleagues. As a result, the members of the cabinet, numbering about 20, know that their chances of future advancement depend, in the main, on their chief. This applies even more strongly to the additional approximately 50 junior members of the ministry. Their only reason for accepting what may be both a very modest and a very exacting assignment is the hope of using it as a stepping-stone to a more satisfactory position.

If all of this leads to an increase in the Prime Minister's power, it also has the effect of tending to make both cabinet and ministry into an effective team. It has been said that as soon as a French cabinet is appointed, some of its members start plotting against the Prime Minister, hoping that they will either succeed him themselves or have more power under his successor—or just wishing to be in the good graces of a successor bound to come sooner or later. If, in England, a member of the government is personally critical of the Prime Minister, as is not infrequently the case, he will do his best to keep his feelings not only from the public, but from all but intimate friends. Also, when a party elects a new leader who is, at the same time, a potential Prime Minister his rivals may, as R. A. Butler did in regard to Sir Anthony Eden in 1955, as well as in regard to Harold Macmillan in 1957, promise their loyalty in terms so strong as to exclude all possibility of intra-party factionalism being enhanced.

For all this power the British Prime Minister is not a dictator; he is, in fact, strikingly more dependent upon his official advisers than is the American President.[42] When the latter appoints a member of the cabinet (or the now equally important National Security Council) Senate approval is required; once it is granted, the appointee becomes the President's personal assistant whose tenure he can end at will. At the same time, since anyone who holds an executive office is barred from membership in Congress, some of a party's most prominent men are *ipso facto* excluded from cabinet service.[43] A member of Congress who accepts a proffered cabinet appointment surrenders much of the foundation upon which his influence rests. If leading Presidential advisers are so strongly opposed to a certain course of action that they resign, they have neither a dignified forum from which to express their reasons, nor do they retain a position in which they could continue to be an important part of their country's "political class." If they want to reënter Congress, they must wait for new elections and, if successful, they find themselves at the bottom of the ladder so far as committee assignments are concerned. This situation is well understood by most cabinet members; those who do not see matters clearly may find themselves enlightened in no uncertain terms as to their true situation, as happened to the "Primadonnas" in President Truman's cabinet.[44] A President may yet allow his cabinet members a greater or smaller measure of power, both within their departments and in regard to overall policy. Still, so far as the corporative operation of the cabinet is concerned there remains the precedent which Lincoln set in his usual humorous manner when, after having submitted a measure to a vote and having found that everyone was against it except himself, he announced: "Seven Nays, one Aye; the Ayes have it."

No English Prime Minister could even think of doing likewise, even if the fact that no formal vote is taken in cabinet meetings [45] allows him considerable leeway in interpreting the wishes of his colleagues. Nor can a Prime Minister ever supplant the official advice of his colleagues with that of unofficial ones, as more than one American President has done. Robert Sherwood reports Harry Hopkins to have commented as follows on the conference off Newfoundland, during which the Atlantic Charter was proclaimed: ". . . whereas Roosevelt was completely on his own, subject only to the advice of his immediate and self-selected entourage, which advice he could accept or reject, Churchill was constantly reporting to and consulting the War Cabinet in London, addressing his communications to the Lord Privy Seal, who was then Clement Attlee." [46] Churchill was perhaps, unusually meticulous in keeping in touch with his wartime colleagues; a Lloyd George might have acted differently. Still, the difference between the position of the American President and that of the British Prime Minister is too great to be ignored. If the cry of dictator is not raised in regard to actions of the former, neither should it be done in regard to the latter.

CABINET DICTATORSHIP.

The charge of dictatorship is certainly raised more frequently against the cabinet as a whole than against the Prime Minister. In one form or the other, it underlies all present-day criticism of the British political system. Since the rise of popular parties, Britain has no longer a *parliamentary* government in any literal sense; parliament has become an *intermediate* organ of government, the leading roles being played by the Prime Minister and the cabinet on the one hand, and the electorate on the other.

This fact dominates even the field of legislation which is usually considered the specific province of a parliamentary body. Most observers, would, of course, agree that parliaments are not fit to perform the tasks of government themselves. When they try to do so the result is what the French call "government by assembly," and French experience provides abundant illustrations for the confusion to which it leads.[47] Yet, as John Stuart Mill [48] wrote: ". . . it is equally true, though only of late and slowly beginning to be realized, that a large assembly is as little fitted for the direct business of legislation as for that of administration." Mill referred to this realization as a late development. It was, in fact, largely due to the rapid increase in the volume of legislation which began during the nineteenth century, as a result of social and economic changes, even if there is no lack of earlier incidents that could be quoted to support similar conclusions.[49]

The reasons why an unorganized parliament [50] has difficulty in legislating are not difficult to see. In the first place, the innovation which a law (properly so-called) will introduce should be closely related to the experience gained by those who executed the law which the new law is to replace. This purpose cannot be achieved unless the civil servants who are charged with the administering of the old regulations are given a share in the framing of the new ones.[51] In the second place, laws must be completely integrated, and they must fit into the general framework of a government's policies. Unorganized assemblies have proved themselves either incapable of providing for such consistent legislation or unable to do so with dispatch.[52] In the third place, no law is good unless it is properly drafted. Since litigation will develop it is necessary that the provisions of a new law be so clear that the courts will find it easy to make the new law work in the sense intended by its authors. Obviously, such a task involves many technicalities that are beyond the capabilities of a large assembly.

In England the existence of the two-party system makes it simple

for the government to fulfill these requirements. The permanent officials of the government departments do the spade work for new legislation; it is the task, first of the department's parliamentary head, and
then of the cabinet as a whole, to see to it that the typical drawbacks
of bureaucratic influence are eliminated before a bill is submitted
to parliament. In both Houses the executive now controls virtually all
the time set aside for legislation,[53] and it may take all when necessary.
Thus, there is a guarantee that, short of a defeat of a government
which would lead to new elections, government bills will, in the end,
be passed in the form either proposed or accepted by the government. As a matter of fact, if a serious situation arises a government
may deviate from any existing law, as it can, if necessary, secure a
bill of indemnity. The best illustration is provided by the government's authorizing the Bank of England to issue notes in excess of the
amount permitted under the Peel Act. This happened in 1847, 1857,
and 1866, and in every case a serious monetary panic was averted.[53a]

If this situation has led to the charge of cabinet dictatorship this
means, in the first place, overlooking the fact that the members of the
cabinet are none other than leaders of the parliamentary majority.
Not every one of them may describe himself as proudly and as properly as "a child of the House of Commons," as Sir Winston Churchill
did, but most of them could do so. They are, at any rate, familiar with
the customs of the House and the wishes of its members. In the second
place, the cabinet rarely resorts to coercion in its dealings with its
followers. Misunderstandings in this regard have often arisen from
the name given to the "Whips," [54] who are the intermediaries between
the cabinet and the rank and file of its supporters, the so-called "back-
benchers." About their methods of action Sir Ivor Jennings says: "The
mailed fist is seldom, if ever, employed. The efficient whip, to change
the metaphor, rides his horse with a free rein, and uses his whip only
to keep off the flies." [55] The whips stand, in fact, in the middle of a
two-way process of communication. They do transmit the wishes of
the cabinet to the back-benchers, but they also transmit the views of
the latter to the ministers. Britain being much smaller than the United
States, most members of parliament visit their constituencies every
weekend, and they are not slow in relaying to their leaders what they
have learned about the feelings of their electors. Lord Balfour said
rightly that the needs of Prime Minister, cabinet and majority are
"not unilateral; they are mutual." [56] Various institutional devices have
been adopted for the purpose of harmonizing the views of a party's
leaders with those of its followers; [57] they are, on the whole, rather
successful.

Therefore, if the government has means to influence the majority, the majority has means to influence the government. While the adoption of a motion of censure is hardly to be expected where one party has an overall majority, a government does have to take opposition within its own ranks seriously. If it wants to make a good impression in the country, it must also either know how to answer the objections of the opposition, or yield to them. Debate in the House, therefore, does influence policy. In the field of legislation, the government will not infrequently accept amendments. When it does not have to do so, the "rule of anticipated reactions" may be assumed to have been in operation. In the field of executive action, including foreign policy, the effects of debates within the House can be very noticeable. Thus, the debate following the British defeat in Norway in 1940 hastened, if it did not cause, the resignation of Neville Chamberlain. The parliamentary discussion of British policy toward Egypt in 1956 was one of the reasons for the British (and French) withdrawal from the Suez Canal. If, then, Britain does not have parliamentary government in the sense that parliament actually runs the government, yet parliament retains a substantial array of weapons with which to influence the government.

The control function is particularly effective when administrative details are involved. Sir Ivor Jennings writes, in regard to a case where it was charged that the police had used "third degree" methods: ". . . on such issues party divisions are forgotten, and the members give chase at the mere scent of an injustice like greyhounds after a hare." [58] The device most frequently used for such control purposes is the parliamentary question, which gives the rank and file of the House an opportunity to present their views on all matters of policy as well as on details of its administrative implementation. Naturally, its preventive function is more important than its use as a device of repression; as one British civil servant told this writer: "The mere thought of a question in the House of Commons is enough to send an icy chill down the spine of the bureaucracy."

PARLIAMENTARISM AND BICAMERALISM.

The British habit of relying on the logic of events rather than on the speculative approach which is characteristic of so much constitutional thought in Continental Europe (and Latin America) has also led to a solution for the problem of bicameralism. A great many writers have accepted the need for a second Chamber rather dogmatically. In that process they have been inclined to find rational reasons for historical accidents. The early parliaments did not represent one nation, but a multiplicity of estates—three in France, four in Sweden, and only two in England, because the "Lords Spiritual" merged with the "Lords Temporal." If we look at the matter systematically it would seem obvious that in a democratic system the coexistence of two chambers with equal rights can lead to friction, delay, mutual paralysis, and inconclusive compromises. In Federal countries such as the United States, we may want to accept these risks, all the more so since the two-party system has, in this country, proven strong enough to develop in the conference committee, an agency of integration between the House and Senate which, on the whole, works remarkably well.

In countries with a parliamentary system, however, the existence of two co-equal parliaments presents added problems. If the government is responsible to both—which it must be if they are to be truly equal—the danger of instability, always to be guarded against in a parliamentary system, would be enhanced; if two chambers rather than one can overthrow a government more governments will fall. Besides, if conflicts between government and parliament are to be decided by way of parliamentary dissolution, it may be necessary to dissolve both chambers simultaneously. This may interfere with the wish to have them differ in regard to terms of office and the methods of renovation.

The English did experience some of the drawbacks of bicameralism, but found a solution which has practically all the advantages of such a system and avoids the pitfalls. The House of Lords betrays the accidental nature of its origin by its composition, as its membership is hereditary.[59] This arrangement presented no particular problems before 1832, when the nobility controlled the House of Commons as well as the House of Lords and was about equally divided between the two major parties. Difficulties arose, however, after 1832; they were multiplied when, in 1886, many Liberal peers followed Joseph Chamberlain and his "Liberal Unionists" into the Conservative fold, providing the Conservatives with a permanent majority in the upper chamber. The life of Liberal governments became tenuous; it was due to the opposition of the House of Lords that, in 1893, the second bill providing for Irish Home Rule failed to become law. Had it reached the statute books, a long period of destructive conflict between the two countries—with all its repercussions in the international field—could have been avoided. Bicameralism then, on this occasion, served Britain badly. In 1909, the House of Lords rejected the progressive taxes proposed by the Liberal government, and the latter took steps to clip the wings of the upper House. In the Parliament Act of

ing of German cities. Within a few years after the end of hostilities most British, as well as most American, observers agreed that both measures had to be counted among "The Great Mistakes of the War," [63] but to say so when it mattered would not have been easy for members of the House of Commons.

A second Chamber, finally, provides an added reservoir of political leadership. If a prominent man who is not a member of the House would, in the opinion of the Prime Minister, be of great service in the government, he can be appointed to the House of Lords, as can any member of the House if defeated for reelection. Besides, older members of the House of Commons can retire to that body when they feel that they should leave their places to their juniors without giving up parliamentary work. There may be added reasons why they do not wish to remain in the House. Thus, when Clement Attlee abandoned the leadership of the Labour party, his continued presence in its factionally divided parliamentary group might have made matters more difficult for his successor. As a member of the House of Lords, he was the "elder statesman," far removed from the intra-party squabbles in which he had been forced to take part in the past. Lastly, there is the case of men who could significantly contribute to the political life of their country but would not, and perhaps on account of the nature of their work, could not submit themselves to the ardors of campaigning for a seat in the House of Commons. For them, too, the House of Lords is the logical place. England's "political class" is richer as a result.

The British constitutional system, then, has developed a solution for the problems of bicameralism which, instead of interfering with the popularly-elected body, supplements it. This does not mean that all is perfect; while the proposals emanating from the Conservative side for a "reform of the House of Lords" will, in general, be rejected because they aim at strengthening that body to such an extent that it can oppose the House of Commons more effectively, others are receiving serious consideration, such as the plan to make possible the appointment of life-time members. The hereditary principle does give the House of Lords a dignity which no other mode of constituting it could provide, but it could be supplemented by appointments for life.[64] Few countries other than England could even think of a parliamentary body with hereditary membership, and some of them have had fairly good experiences with the principle of appointment for life; thus constituted, the Senate of the Kingdom of Italy provided many useful services to the country, and the principle could be used elsewhere. (In England, the Life Peerages Bill, introduced in the fall of

1957, provided for life peerages as well as for the admission of women to the House of Lords.)

The principle of hereditary membership in the House of Lords, then, is the one major exception to the rule that parliamentary government, as it has developed in England, represents the "pure" version of this system.[65] This last contention is, however, of far-reaching importance; many would reject it. The issue can be decided only by examining the evidence. Therefore, the following chapters will be devoted to a discussion first of the general and then of the concrete aspects of parliamentary government in Continental Europe.

Chapter XII

DEMOCRACY IN CONTINENTAL EUROPE

A COMMON START IN CONSTITUTIONAL GOVERNMENT.

Most observers would agree that parliamentary government in England is highly successful, and at least satisfactory in the older Commonwealth countries, notably Canada, Australia, and New Zealand. In all of them the British pattern has been followed.[1] Conditions are different in Continental Europe, Latin America and the Far East where the parliamentary system has generally been regarded as synonymous with instability and inefficiency. There are two basic types of explanations for this difference. In the first place there applies to all of these countries what Bagehot said about France: their Constitutions are a "copy not of the whole effective part of the British Constitution, but only a part of it." [2] The deviations concern two major points: The plurality system of voting is not used and, in many cases, the right of parliamentary dissolution is either lacking or surrounded with so many conditions that its effective application is impossible. Either omission is serious. It could be argued that, where we have a combination of both, there is no need to look any farther for an explanation for the failure of parliamentary government.

The second possible reason for the failure of parliamentary government outside its area of success is identical with the reason why democracy may fail whatever constitutional form it assumes: A deficiency in social "matter." The general aspects of this case have been discussed above. In some countries of Continental Europe, however, no such general deficiency exists. In France and Germany, for example, modern economic and social conditions prevail, and they set these countries apart from the nations of Latin America, Asia and Africa, or, to stick to Europe, from Greece, Spain and Portugal. It has been held, however, that Britain constitutes a case of its own. The political action pattern which we call parliamentary government would not have worked, it is said, in a different political climate. Perhaps no other form of democracy would have been reasonably satisfactory either. In the countries in question, it is held, the historical basis for government by consent was lacking; there was, instead, an array of social forces making for social heterogeneity and political dissent. Therefore, such essential ingredients of "pure parliamentarism" as the plurality system of voting could not be adopted. Existing differences were too great to permit taking the risks associated with the most powerful device for integration. In this sense, even countries like France and Germany were not ready for democracy.

Arguments of this type are so sweeping that they are difficult to analyze. It may be useful, however, to break them down as much as possible into their concrete components. We shall first study the circumstances under which British political development broke away from the general European pattern, and, second, the lasting results engendered by the consequent divergence of social and political forces.

British constitutional history did start from the same foundations as that of the continental nations. For the sake of simplicity we may follow the customary view that the political institutions of all of these countries, including England, were established by Teutonic tribes.[3] Tacitus tells us that most of them, as they entered the period of recorded history, were republican. They did have their chiefs but these, apparently, were no more than the leaders in a modern democratic country: "About minor matters the chiefs deliberate, about the more important the whole tribe. Yet even when the final decision rests with the people the affair is always thoroughly discussed by the chiefs." Even so Tacitus adds that the authority of the chiefs is based more upon "influence to persuade" than upon "power to command." [4]

When the contacts between the Germanic tribes and the western world developed they were mostly of a warlike nature. Since wars promote a centralization of authority, more and more of these tribes became monarchies. The monarch, apparently, reached his position on the basis of military leadership. The institution itself continued to be rather democratic, and while, in the course of time, the non-democratic features gained over the democratic ones, no absolutism ever existed. In the case of the Western Franks, the King, in 614, had to give assurances concerning the liberty of his country's freemen in the form of the Edict of Paris. These assurances were remarkably similar to the Magna Charta, conceded by King John a full six centuries later. When, in the eighth century, the Merwings were replaced by the Carolingians, the elective principle regained a measure of strength. Pipin the Short had himself elected by an assembly of "the people" in 751. In the years that followed the "great of the realm" made every effort to interfere when the crown passed from one man to another. If, in most instances, this intervention had little significance, it was decisive in some.

Inasmuch as the history of British liberty is closely associated with the institution of parliament, it is important to bear in mind that the English parliament is not the oldest. Iceland has, perhaps, the best claim to priority, as its parliament first met in 830 and continues to do so to this day, with an interruption from 1800–1830. It was, at first, a rather aristocratic gathering, and it made more concessions to absolutism than its counterpart in Westminster. Still, its overall record is something in which the people of Iceland rightly take pride.

Italian writers will emphasize that the Normans in Sicily established what, in English parlance, would have been called a "full parliament" (representing all elements in the population) ten years before this was done in England. This parliament, furthermore, existed until the end of the eighteenth century. Its best known historian writes about its condition in the sixteenth century that "the complex physiognomy of the Sicilian parliament appears to be that not only of an important organ, but even of an organ fully invested and conscious of its functions as the representative of the island . . . One can, in fact, say that there exists from that time onwards a dyarchy of peers (King and parliament) with each equal to the other, or nearly so." [5] Meetings of this parliament are recorded for 1786, 1794 and 1798. The French occupation during the Napoleonic Wars made further gatherings impossible. Later the Bourbon rulers of the Kingdom of Naples and Sicily abrogated the Constitution of the latter and thereby abolished its parliament. This was said to have been done at the request of the Austrian Chancellor Metternich, who did not want a parliament, the mere existence of which presented a danger to the absolutist plans of the Holy Alliance.[6] If this is true, it was indeed a compliment to the moral force of this body. The former Italian Prime Minister, Vittorio Emmanuele Orlando, may be forgiven when he ascribes the general failure of historians to pay proper attention to the Sicilian parliament to the fact that "it is true that they (the developments in question) lacked the notoriety [7] and, consequently, the authority which a Constitution can derive from the importance of the state in which it is in force." [8]

It is clear that the reasons, at any rate, why parliaments were called in England were of a general nature. When, in 1295, King Edward I summoned the clergy to his "Great Parliament," he quoted the Canon Law to the effect that "What concerns all should be approved by all." The King needed the approval of all, or at any rate of all who mattered, for the decisions which he wanted taken; the obvious way in which to obtain the consent desired lay in calling a parliament. A similar need existed, however, in other countries. Nowhere could the revenue required by the slowly increasing scope of government activities [9] be raised from traditional sources. The remedy was the same in all cases; parliaments were the most expedient device for securing the approval of the leading men in the land for the raising of new taxes. The rulers in question did not copy from England any more than Edward I copied from the Sicilians (or for that matter, from the people of Iceland, or from the Iroquois Indians [10]); in all cases the same causes had the same effects. The situation was, to be sure, somewhat different centuries later when the period of absolutism ended; at that time the British example did exercise a certain influence.[11] Basically, however, the problem was again to meet a similar need with the help of similar institutions.[12]

MILITARISM AND ABSOLUTISM IN CONTINENTAL EUROPE.

Historians tend to be unaware of the way in which circumstances rather than the brain of man give rise to political institutions. They have been equally unaware of the fact that political developments in Continental Europe must be seen as a whole. The investigations which they make are, from the outset, "limited to a particular country, and thus some of the basic premises of the national state, as it has developed in modern times, are carried over into the investigation of medieval conditions, where no national state ever existed." [13] There has been, in fact, a tendency to assume that political institutions as they developed within a particular nation *must* be a product of that nation's peculiarities, while data supporting the opposite view have been disregarded.

The political history of France parallels, for a time, that of England, only to deviate from it decisively in the end. The first parliament representing all elements in the nation was summoned by Philip the Fair in 1302. This was only seven years after Edward I had called the first legal parliament, which included the knights from the shires and burgesses, thus representing the country as a whole.[14] Philip felt that he needed the largest possible amount of support in his struggle with Pope Boniface VIII. Therefore, he included the representatives of the "Third Estate" in his invitation.

The French Estates General met between 1302 and 1614. Their

members were elected (even if indirectly in the case of the "Third Estate") and the suffrage was comparatively democratic.[15] The powers of the Estates, to be sure, never did reach the extent of those attained by the British parliament which soon managed to add to its right to grant new taxes that of presenting wishes and grievances, and, in the end, that of approving new legislation.[16] French parliaments even failed to establish the principle of "grievances before supplies," although the grievances which they presented might lead to remedial action on the part of the King. The institution of the "imperative mandate" hampered the members of these parliaments in the attempt to widen their rights. In the fifteenth century the electoral assembly in each *baillage* began drawing up a "book of grievances," in which were listed the demands which the deputies were to make, and the concessions indicated which they might grant. The representative could be recalled if he deviated from his instructions. This circumstance naturally reduced the degree of authority with which he could confront the King.

There were, nonetheless, times when French political developments seemed to head toward the same goal as the British. The decisive deviation did not occur until the seventeenth century. The wars of the Fronde (1648–53), in which the nobles, and the citizens of Paris, rose against the King, coincide with the final phases of the British Civil War. The monarchy lost this struggle as decisively in England as it won it in France. This difference in the outcome of an otherwise quite similar [17] struggle is related, however, to a chain of events which sprang from circumstances outside the specific field of constitutional history. It arises from the realm of geography. Americans may justly take pride in the fact that the pertinent problems have never been set forth as clearly as in Nos. 5–8 of *The Federalist*, written by John Jay and Alexander Hamilton.

The two authors start from the possibility that the Constitution as drawn up in Philadelphia might not be ratified. The thirteen states, instead of forming an effective federal union, might either reassume their sovereignty individually or gather in three or four regional confederations. Both Jay and Madison warned that this would lead to never-ending friction, and finally to war and the loss of liberty. Contests would be most likely to develop among neighboring states. All of them would want something belonging to the other, and might nourish the memory of past grievances in those outbreaks of passion which often precede, and to some extent cause, the outbreak of a war. Hamilton quotes the Abbé de Mably, who said: "*Neighboring Nations* are naturally enemies of each other, unless their common weakness forces them to league in a *Confederative Republic,* and their constitution prevents the differences that neighborhood occasions, extinguishing that secret jealousy which disposes all states to aggrandize themselves at the expense of their neighbors." History indeed shows that unless there are balancing tendencies [18] of sufficient strength neighboring nations are indeed unlikely to pursue what we now call the policy of "the good neighbor." They are more likely to develop into "hereditary enemies," and to seek their allies among the countries bordering their neighbor on the other side.

From the danger of war there follows the need to guard against it. The means of doing so, in modern history, have been standing armies. Hamilton, in No. 8 of *The Federalist* [19] shows us with incomparable brevity how this institution may lead to militarism. In his words:

> The perpetual menacings of danger oblige the government to be always prepared to repel it; its armies must be numerous enough for instant defence. The continual necessity for their services enhances the importance of the soldier, and proportionately degrades the condition of the citizen. The military state becomes elevated above the civil. The inhabitants of territories, often the theatre of war, are unavoidably subjected to frequent infringements on their rights, which serve to weaken their sense of those rights; and by degrees the people are brought to consider the soldiery not only as their protectors, but as their superiors. The transition from this disposition to that of considering them masters, is neither remote nor difficult; but it is very difficult to prevail upon a people under such impressions, to make a bold or effectual resistance to usurpations supported by the military power.

Standing armies, then, will be established to repel attacks which may come at any time. They are of vital significance for the safety of their country. As *Montesquieu* saw so clearly,[20] their officers will feel that their work is more important than that of the civilian leaders whom they may come to call mere "talkers" in comparison to themselves as the "doers." The military, then, will cease to be an instrument for the attainment of certain, if vital, ends. What is logically but a means comes to be considered as an end, and it holds the power it needs to enforce its claims.

These tendencies can be counteracted in modern democracies, as they have been in smaller democracies in the past, notably Sweden and Switzerland.[21] They proved, however, decisive in the constitutional history of the major states of Continental Europe, beginning with France, the first country to have a standing army. In 1439, King Charles VII, toward the end of the Hundred Years' War with England, summoned the Estates General to Orléans, and persuaded them to vote him a permanent tax, with the help of which he could unite some of his mercenaries "in companies which would receive regular pay and be submitted to strong discipline." Thomas Basin, the Bishop of Lisieux, foretold the consequences in the following words:

> Our military organization will soon force the other nations to create permanent armies: at the first difficulty they will come to blows, and Europe will always be in trouble. Lastly, liberty is lost: Everybody is at the discretion of his armed force. It is the greatest flood which can envelop a nation.[22]

It did take some time before everybody was "at the discretion of this armed force." Besides, the officers of a standing army can no more form a government by themselves than a social class can govern as such. Somehow the principle of political form makes its entrance. In France the problem was solved when the standing army identified itself with its creator, the King. For the monarch and his advisers, the existence of this force was of decisive importance during the years preceding the formal establishment of "absolute" government. This occurred in 1614 when Catherine of Aragon had the doors of the hall in which the Estates intended to meet barred. The relationship between the existence of the standing army and the defense of absolutism is less clear during the wars of the Fronde as, at that time, the royal army was but a shadow of its former self. Still, after Cardinal Mazarin had succeeded in beating down the uprising, the newly reformed standing army was there to maintain order, and the fact that its higher officers were taken from the nobility helped to reconcile them to the loss of their political rights.

THE CASE OF PRUSSIA.

The relationship between geographical position, standing army and absolutism is clearer yet in the case of Brandenburg-Prussia. A standing army was established by Frederic William, "The Great Elector," at the end of the Thirty Years' War in 1648. During that war Germany had been the anvil rather than the hammer of Europe's power politics. From a nation of more than 18 million she was reduced to less than half that number (according to some figures, from 19 to 5 million). The country had to be repopulated by immigration from the outside to such an extent that of the racial stock of what was Germany in subsequent centuries more than half is due to such immigration. Little Brandenburg-Prussia suffered as much as any part of Germany, and Frederic William concluded that a standing army was vital for her protection. He retained some of the regiments which his father had hired during the war, and he ruled long enough to verify Bishop Basin's warning: He made his army so large that it could be used for aggressive warfare, and he began to suppress the Estates and establish absolutism. Under King Frederic William I (1713–40) Prussia's army was, for the first time, extended to a size altogether out of proportion with the country's extent, and it retained that size under Frederic II and his successors. Mirabeau, in one of his celebrated aphorisms, said: "Most states have an army; the Prussian army is the only one that has a state." In recent discussions this sentence has often been quoted. It might be well, however, to cite what Hamilton has said about the causes which lead to the establishment of a large (and therefore powerful) army in a comparatively small state. In his words:

> The weaker states and confederacies would first have recourse to them (standing armies) to put themselves upon an equality with their more potent neighbors. They would endeavor to supply the inferiority of population and resources by a more regular and effective system of defence, by disciplined troops, and by fortifications. They would, at the same time, be necessitated to strengthen the executive arm of government . . .[23]

In Brandenburg-Prussia absolutism grew in the same proportions as the size of the standing army. The Electors of Bradenburg had succeeded in curbing the independence of their cities somewhat in the fifteenth century. They also tried to limit the powers of the Estates in their various territories. During the two generations which preceded the Thirty Years War, however, including the first twenty years of that conflict, the power of the electors had been reduced sufficiently to make it comparable to that held by the English Kings of the same period. As soon, though, as the Great Elector (1640–88) had his new army in shape he strengthened the powers of the monarchy, making sure, in particular, that he could collect taxes more or less at his own discretion. The final struggle between the Kings (the royal title being acquired in 1701) and the Estates took place under King Frederic William I between 1713 and 1714. When the King ascended the throne he had confirmed the privileges of the Estates and, in fact, in 1713 he still permitted a Diet for the Western part of the monarchy on the lower Rhine. These Estates, however, did not grant the King as much money for his army as he wanted. He decided to collect the money anyway, and to discontinue the meetings of the Estates as they were "too expensive for the country to afford." The Diets for the other parts of the country had been discontinued earlier; that of Bradenburg met for the last time in 1653.

Frederic William I used rather strong words in his struggle against the Estates. Some of the noblemen attempted to reassert their rights by appealing to the courts of the Empire. The King instituted suits against them in the Prussian courts and said that they ought to be pushed around until the "itch" of those noblemen for their independence had been dissipated, and they would stop their "criminal and godless endeavors against the hereditary monarch." [24] The King also emphasized that he was going to establish his sovereignty like a *rocher de bronce*—"a rock of bronze."

From the constitutional point of view, there is no question that these monarchs were revolutionaries and that they broke the law of the land. One of the advisers of the Estates, the well-known economist, Moser, complained:

> To be sure, since 1713 and 1714 there has developed in certain countries a despotic, arbitrary and unlimited power, and one after the other would like to copy these originals. But their entire justification consists in the fact that they have 100,000 men on their legs and no justice above themselves, or else no reason to fear such a justice. [25]

In 1740, Frederick II, the so-called Frederick the Great, became King. He was expected to be liberal-minded, and to restore the privileges of the Estates, but he failed to do so. He soon embarked on a career of conquest against Austria in the three Silesian Wars during which constitutional limitations might not have been so practical. This King, at the same time, reconciled the Prussian noblemen by giving them the best positions in the army and in the bureaucracy. In that manner, he established what we now regard as the characteristic features of the Prussian state, a royal absolutism, supported by the nobility and a strong army.

In Brandenburg-Prussia then, the essential role of the standing army in beating down the Estates is obvious. Matters were similar in Austria. In the various Hapsburg territories absolutism could have neither arisen nor been maintained without the help of the armed forces. In the case of Russia, of course, the situation was different. The medieval period which, in the remainder of Europe, had witnessed the rise of a nobility in the country, and a bourgeoisie in the cities, both of which were keenly aware of their rights, was filled with the struggle for national independence which had to be waged against the Tartars. The old nobility was virtually exterminated in the process. No Estates parliaments on the model of Western Europe developed.

Russia, indeed, was destined to be a country without "Middle Ages," as it was a country without middle classes.

Standing armies, at any rate, were the court of last resort to which the monarchs of Continental Europe appealed, and appealed successfully, in their struggle against the nobility. The need for standing armies was caused by geography. Its effects could have been overcome by the political unification of Europe in the same way in which the political unification of the thirteen American states overcame them on this side of the Atlantic. Obviously, however, while the unification of countries such as Wales, England and Scotland was feasible at that time,[26] that of the comparatively vast lands of Continental Europe, inhabited by peoples of different languages and different nationalities, was not. In this area history had to take its course, and absolutism was the result.

The period of absolutism disrupted the continuity of constitutional development which had prevailed during the concluding phases of the Middle Ages. In England the forces of the new social and political world were never dammed up for long. After the one great explosion of the Civil War, they found a framework within which they could bring about a more or less gradual transition, their leaders assuming places of power and prominence almost as soon as they were ready for them. In Continental Europe, on the other hand, these forces found themselves outside the political system for generations. The consequences have been dealt with above: A slow constitutional transformation which would have allowed the "logic of development" to work itself out, was impossible. Change, when it occurred, was wholesale, allowing no chance for gradual adjustment. Besides, those excluded from political power and, therewith, from political responsibility became, if not radical, at least doctrinaire. When the time came for them to assay a new political order their approach was bookish and speculative rather than practical. They were, above all, carried away with emotional notions of liberty, apt to make them lose sight of the requirements of authority. The deviations from the pattern of "pure" parliamentary government noted above can easily be explained on this score alone.

THE SOCIAL LEGACY OF ABSOLUTISM: REACTIONARY CONSERVATISM.

The legacy of absolutism, however, extended to the whole of society as much as to the political order. As Walter Bagehot put it: "Great communities are like great mountains—they have in them the primary, secondary and tertiary strata of human progress; the characteristics of the lower regions resemble the life of old times rather than the present life of higher regions." [27] The nations which passed through an extended period of absolutism developed certain social elements which they have not entirely lost to this day. These elements were to play a large part in the events connected with those two catastrophes which we call World War I and World War II.

Thus there arose, in the first place, a "Conservative" element which degenerated into a rigid defense of social and political privilege instead of defending values of lasting validity. It was, indeed, reactionary rather than conservative.[28] The descendants of that nobility which had fought absolutism so fiercely became its pliant protagonists. Their continued social eminence owed much to the power and prestige which they had gained through their connection with the army and the bureaucracy. It owed, in some cases, no less to a sagacious use of political power for the improvement of their economic position. Thus, when Bismarck turned from free trade to protection this did much to strengthen the position of the large landowners. Most of them were noblemen, whose products were thus assured a privileged position in a domestic market which had expanded greatly as a result of industrialization. These elements defended their privileges to the bitter end; the Prussian Conservatives were, for example, entirely unwilling to abandon the *Dreiklassenwahlrecht* [29] to the Prussian Diet. They did this even during the First World War when the people's privilege of dying for their country was certainly not subjected to such limitations.

One of the results of the conservative element in the social structure of the countries was the existence of conservative political parties in Continental Europe even after the final establishment of democratic institutions. These parties—the survival of which was always fostered by systems of voting differing from the plurality system—by their very existence complicated the political pattern of their country, contributing to those deficiencies of democratic government which they denounced. To the extent that members of these groups dominated the civil service, the courts and the army, they might try to use this leverage to oppose democratic forces and, at times, to sabotage democratic processes. It will be seen, however, that the only cases in which they could do this to a significant extent occurred where "improper channels of government" caused democracy to be less strong than it should have been.

RATIONALISM AND RADICALISM AT THE LEFT.

The long delay in establishing democratic institutions where they were due had the further effect of promoting social and political radicalism in the ranks of those who opposed the existing political order. During the nineteenth century this radicalism assumed, in particular, the form of Socialist parties. Their protest was, ostensibly, directed against economic exploitation. Their programs frequently denounced "bourgeois democracy" and claimed that it differed little from reactionary autocracy. Yet, it is interesting to note that wherever "bourgeois democracy" was strong, Socialist radicalism was weak. The typical Marxist element was least popular in England—the country where *Das Kapital* was written and which, according to the views set forth so brilliantly by its author, should have been the first to give birth to socialism. Marx did not, however, reckon with the fact that the British constitutional system was not only open to the representatives of all social forces, but that it also possessed elements of strength which enabled it to absorb and even assimilate them. There did exist people in England who endeavored to create a Socialist movement of the Marxist persuasion. They were grouped in the "Social Democratic Federation." Its leader, Mr. Hyndman, complained to the Royal Committee on Electoral Reform about the fact that the majority system rendered the task of winning support for his movement doubly difficult. As to the existing electoral laws, he said that "They make the representation of an active and growing, but unpopular minority difficulty of attainment." He went on to say that although his party had been presenting candidates for 25 years and had obtained many thousands of votes, only once had it elected a member—and this only at the price of reluctant cooperation with a more moderate group. Referring to the general elections which had taken place shortly before he testified, and in which his party received more than 10,000 votes in two Lancashire districts alone, Mr. Hyndman said: "Such a poll cast in some other district would (with a P.R. system) have sufficed to secure the return of five or even more members to the House of Commons." He added that the votes obtained by the Social Democratic Federation would in later elections increase to an extent sufficient to secure the election of at least 20 candidates. In Mr. Hyndman's own words: "One reason for this change would be that with Proportional Representation voters would no longer be afraid of throwing their votes away by voting for a good candidate when they think he has no chance." [30]

Even the more moderate elements in the Labour movement had to learn the lesson of moderation the hard way. Thus in the elections of 1895 the "Independent Labour Party" decided to support none but real Socialists, refusing to cooperate even with moderate Labour men. The result was a complete failure. Even the seat of the party leader, Keir Hardie, was lost. Thereupon the party, in 1900, resumed cooperation with more moderate groups and was able to regain two seats.[31] Later, most of the Labour candidates cooperated not only with moderate Labour but with the Liberals as well. On this basis alone did the successes of 1906 (54 candidates elected) and 1910 (40 candidates elected) become possible. When the hour of opportunity struck after the First World War, Labour successively became the official opposition and provided "His Majesty's government."

French socialism occupied an intermediate position between radicalism and moderation. Jules Guesde and his followers, to be sure, accepted the gospel according to Karl Marx and preached it in the four corners of the land. Jean Jaurès and others were, however, more inspired by the humanist ideals of the French Revolution. This was the time when the prestige of German socialism outshone that of its rivals. During the International Socialist Congress of Amsterdam, held in 1904, August Bebel, the son of a German sergeant, laid down the law to the French: They must unite. When they did the result was a rather uneasy alliance. The Marxist element was strong enough to prevent, for a generation, the parliamentary group of the party from participating officially in any government, although the growth of the party after the First World War forced it to support some Left-wing cabinets. When, finally, in 1936, the Socialist party became the strongest group in the Chamber, Léon Blum did assume the prime ministership, forming a coalition with the so-called Radicals (practically a party slightly left of center) and similar Left-wing groups. When this happened, the integration of the Socialist party within the country's political system had been completed; evidently, no basic social heterogeneity stood in the way of that process.

The German Social-Democratic party acted and, even more, *argued* throughout the years before the First World War as the most thorough proponent of orthodox Marxism. To its economic demands it added the propagation of a substantial amount of tenets taken from the realm of enlightenment philosophy. Some of its agitators insisted on fighting the Christian churches as fiercely as capitalism, militarism, and autocracy. Such agitation, naturally, strengthened extremist tendencies on the other side. There was no lack of people in Germany who felt that everything possible must be done to ward off "the Red danger." The hold of reactionary elements on Germany society was strengthened as a result. "Revisionism," however, soon developed within the ranks of the Social Democratic party. The focal point of its attack was the contradiction between the conclusions reached by orthodox Marxism in the economic field and actual historical development. Still, "revisionism" always included a more favorable attitude towards democracy, extending to a willingness to compromise with the existing monarchies when these pursued a moderate policy. It caused quite a scandal within the party when some of its South German leaders attended court functions. Yet, that this should have happened was symbolic of a situation in which moderation on one side led to moderation on the other, just as the radicalism of one side strengthened that of the other. Certainly, the Social Democratic movement as a whole was as much a protest against a political system overburdened with carry-overs of absolutism and militarism as it was a protest against the existing economic order. This implies that the actual range of disagreement between the Socialist and the truly democratic "bourgeois" parties was not as great as it appeared to be. Within a democratic system the Social Democrats could have cooperated with the parties of the center before 1918 as they were to do beginning in 1919.

SOCIALISM AND CONSTITUTIONALISM.

In one respect, however, socialism as it developed in Continental Europe was to have far-reaching effects: its theory all but excluded an understanding of the constitutional forms in which democratic government must operate. Socialist "revisionism" might be strong in the economic field but, to this day, the Socialist parties of Continental Europe have experienced no adequate "revisionism" in the constitutional field.

Few observers are aware of the great difference existing, in this respect, between the British Labour party and the Socialist parties of Continental Europe. In the former, Ramsay MacDonald showed from the very outset a clear understanding of constitutional government and its needs. In his book, *Socialism and Government*,[32] he took a firm stand even on that part of the constitutional pattern on which Socialists are most sensitive: the system of voting. The economic interpretation of history is "materialistic" in the sense of attempting to reduce everything to the "matter" of social life. If considerations of political form are accorded substantial significance, an essential principle is abandoned. P.R. fits in with this attitude because its theory does not call for an element of political form to transcend social divisions. The majority system does so, and is anathema for that very reason.

Furthermore, the majority system is unpalatable for the orthodox Marxist in practice for the simple reason that it is hard on any type of orthodoxy. Cooperation with "bourgeois" groups becomes a vital requirement of success. Likewise, the behavior of governments which a Socialist party may have been able to form because the plurality system gave it an overall majority, or the behavior of coalition governments made possible by one of the weaker forms of majority voting, cannot be doctrinaire. Practical issues simply have to be met with practical solutions. This implies that Socialist hostility to majority voting does not so much stem from the party as a whole as from its doctrinaire wing. This wing senses that its own power position within the party is as clearly safeguarded by P.R. as it is threatened by any kind of majority voting, the plurality system in particular.

Ramsay MacDonald saw all these things. He was also aware of the fact that, at the time when he wrote, his party would have gained more seats under P.R. than under the plurality system. He felt, however, that the loss of a number of seats was immaterial while his party was in opposition, but could be fatal to it when it had a chance to exercise power. These views of MacDonald were never without opponents among Labour's leaders, but, in the end, men like Harold Laski,[33] Herman Finer,[34] and Ivor Jennings [35] helped to make this attitude so prevalent among the party's leaders that its reversal appears impossible.

Among the Socialists of Continental Europe there have always been a few who wanted "revisionism" in the field of political form as well as in that of economic policy. They remained, however, isolated and ineffective for generations. So far as P.R. is concerned, the German Social Democrats inserted it in their famous program of Erfurt, a step which almost automatically entailed endorsement by the Second International. Generally speaking, to the extent that, both after the First and Second World Wars, Socialist parties had a leading influence on constitution-making, it was negative: They insisted on minimizing authority, unmindful of the fact that they themselves would suffer, as governments headed by their leaders would be as much condemned to impotence as all others.

Yet, after the First World War, the adoption of P.R. in country after country did not reflect any objective differences of interest between the Socialist and the "bourgeois" proponents of democracy. It was indeed to be "a plague on both your houses." In at least one major country of Continental Europe, the Socialists have come to realize this. The French Socialists have, for some time, been turning their backs on P.R.; Léon Blum took the lead in a series of articles published in June 1949, in his party's daily, *Le Populaire;* [36] more recently, Guy Mollet endeavored to commit his party and his government [37] as strongly as possible to the cause of electoral and constitutional reform. His proposals, if adopted, would not only have meant great steps in the right direction; they certainly were based on the belief that a Socialist government, just like a "bourgeois" government, cannot act unless it is given the proper tools.

CHRISTIAN DEMOCRATS AND CONSTITUTIONALISM.

Conservative and Socialist parties do not constitute, however, the only type of party differing from the Anglo-Saxon variety. Christian Democratic groups likewise constitute a deviation from the pattern of purely "functional" parties. In the countries under review democracy was not religiously neutral. Its principal protagonists were hostile to either all Christian churches, or at least to the Catholic Church. Difficulties developed in a variety of fields, of which education was to prove the most persistent. In the beginning, in some countries, notably France,[38] Catholics were, with few exceptions, supporters of the monarchy. As a result, opponents of the monarchy felt constrained to be opponents of the Church, too. Christian Democratic movements not only defended the churches against discriminatory legislation, but also placed themselves clearly on the basis of democracy, demolishing by their very existence the claim that Christians must be reactionaries.

Just like their Socialist counterparts, however, Christian Democratic parties may overlook that the defense of democracy entails consequences in the field of constitutional government. For long periods, Christian Democratic parties tended to think of themselves as a minority, with both the interests and the outlook of a minority. At times, they were tempted to act like a pressure group rather than a political party, overlooking the fact that there must exist a government before it can be made to accept any demand, no matter how justified. The concern for the *bonum commune*—"the common good," which their social philosophy imposed upon them should have been their guide. It was, however, pushed aside when they joined with other minority groups in the introduction of P.R. They disregarded what the most respected of all Christian Democratic philosophers, Jacques Maritain,[39] stated in these words:

> In order to eliminate, in addition, every attempt to introduce the "Trojan horse" of proportional representation into the democratic structure, let us note that just as the common good is not a simple sum of individual goods, so the common will is not a simple sum of individual wills. Universal suffrage does not have the aim to represent simply atomic wills and opinions, but to give form and expression, according to their respective importance, to the *common currents* of opinion and of will which exist in the nation. The political line of a democracy must

frankly and decidedly be determined by the majority, while the parties composing the minority play the part, also fundamental, of the *critical* element, in an opposition which is not destructive, but as much as possible constructive and cooperative. Thus the majority and minority express the will of the people in opposite, but complementary and equally real, fashions.

The logic of Maritain's argument has been frequently ignored. Yet, in recent years, it has also made powerful friends. Thus, in Italy, where the Christian Democrats of the pre-Fascist era had been staunch defenders of P.R., their leader, Don Sturzo, came out in favor of a clear-cut return to the majority system [40] before his party made the mistake of proposing the ill-fated combination of P.R. with a premium for the majority under which they fought, and lost, the elections of 1953. As we shall see below,[41] Italy's post-war Christian Democratic leader, Alcide de Gasperi, came to favor the majority system during the last years of his life.

It must be added that Don Sturzo and De Gasperi advocated majority voting with run-off elections rather than a plurality system.[42] The only Christian Democratic party which has been committed to the plurality system since its foundation is Germany's Christian Democratic Union (CDU), called Christian Social Union (CSU) in Bavaria. As we shall see below, it had little opportunity to work for that system after the all-important first elections to be held after the war had been held under P.R. on the basis of arrangements made by the Allied Military Governments. Still, the mere fact that this party advocates the plurality system (as well as the fact that Don Sturzo and De Gasperi came to advocate run-off elections) is enough to show that Christian Democrats do not have to believe that they are separated from others by differences so deep that, instead of joining with them in the support of the same candidates, they must adopt P.R. as a device to let the basic disagreement stand. These Christian Democrats admit that, to speak in Maritain's terms, they must work as sincerely for the formation of a "common will" as they must work for the "common good," the one being, in a democracy, the only road which can lead to the other. They know that working with others in the search for a "common will" requires sacrifices. They are willing to make these sacrifices because they have learned from St. Thomas Aquinas [43] that, unless a government based upon "the rule of the many" adopts devices which, by their very nature, leads to the required "unity of peace," tyranny, with the most complete disregard of all that Christians stand for, is a likely result.

LIBERAL PARTIES AND CONSTITUTIONAL GOVERNMENT.

Social Democratic and Christian Democratic parties were new-comers to the field of democratic constitutionalism; it is not entirely surprising that they found it so difficult to arrive at an immediate understanding of its requirements. This is a field, however, in which Liberal parties should have felt at home. They had been the early leaders in the constitutional movement and had enough experience with political responsibility to learn that its discharge presupposes a certain amount of power. The latter part of the nineteenth century, nevertheless, saw their strength undermined by the rising tide of popu-lar parties. Some of the Liberal parties acquired the typical outlook of a political minority as soon as they lost their major party status. The guiding consideration no longer seemed to be how the goals, for which a Liberal party was bound to stand, were to be reached and among which the requirements of effective constitutional government oc-cupied such a high place. The question became, in the minds of party leaders and party organizers, at any rate, how the Liberal parties were to be saved. It did not matter how small and how ineffective a device for securing the ends of a Liberal movement they had become in the meantime. Once again, the "organized interest of associations" prevailed, turning mere means into ends.

The most typical change of the kind in question is that of the British Liberal party. The crucial point is, in this case as in most others, the system of voting; in Britain it rather clearly involves (for the reasons set forth in the preceding chapter, pp. 216–17) the political action pattern as a whole. Sir Austen Chamberlain was quite frank when he said:

> . . . the Liberal party in the long heyday of its power persistently opposed, with a few exceptions, this innovation (i.e. P.R.). It is only since it ceased to be a great party that the rump has professed to find salvation in it. Its adoption is more likely to destroy the constitu-tion than to strengthen parliament.[44]

On another occasion Sir Austen went into further detail:

> Mr. Gladstone bitterly opposed this change on a similar occasion. Mr. Bright, with the strong, bold, common sense which clung to him always, repeatedly and consistently condemned all freakish schemes of this kind throughout his long career. Now the party which claims them as two of its most illustrious leaders is, I am told, invited by its present leader to go into the Lobby in support of this amendment. If so, a profound change has been worked on their part. This scheme used to

be the monopoly of a few cranks, very distinguished men in some cases, but always unable to work in harness with other men, unable to make the concessions which are necessary, I do not care whether in politics, in business or in life, if men are to get on together and help one another. I protest against facilitating the entry into this House of that class of person. I protest against embarking on a scheme which sets sectional interests and little cliques above the broad genuine opinion of the nation . . .[45]

The Liberal leaders might have remembered that if, under the plurality system, the Liberal party was bound to disappear, the Liberal voters remained. They became an important part of the marginal vote, and their strategic position was better than ever. The result was obvious. As *The Economist* expressed it: "The very weakness of the Liberal party has induced both the other parties to become Liberal." [46] In the next issue it added, with regard to the program of the government: "*Prima facie,* this is a center party program." [47] The same journal could be quoted on virtually every subsequent election, commenting on the result in similar terms.

Among the Liberal parties which have taken a stand similar to that of their British counterpart are those of Belgium, Italy and Germany. In Italy the great representatives of Liberal political thought, such as Vittorio Emmanuele Orlando, Benedetto Croce and Luigi Einaudi, were forceful advocates of the majority system. The Liberal organization, however, since the end of the Second World War, has expressed itself the more vigorously in favor of unrestricted P.R. the fewer its followers became.

In Germany, Friedrich Naumann, the outstanding representative of Liberal thought during the twentieth century, warned against P.R. in terms perhaps more trenchant than those used by about any other political leader. His party, however, became a rather fervent advocate of P.R.[48] as did the Free Democratic party which took its place in the Bonn Republic. The two exceptions of Liberal parties having fought P.R. with arguments taken rather effectively from the arsenal of constitutional government are the so-called Radical party of Switzerland, and the so-called Radical Socialists in France.

Socialist parties, Christian Democratic parties, Liberal parties and Conservative parties do lend a variety to the party system of Continental Europe which is absent from the Anglo-Saxon scene, and they do reflect, in part, the historic difference in the development of democracy in England as compared with that of Continental Europe. Yet, their existence does not indicate any basic heterogeneity. The problems which they present derive, in the main, from the doctrinaire character of political thinking, from vested interests in the form of "the organized interests of associations," and from intellectual confusion, more than from any other source. This medley of attitudes is associated with an emotionalism which identifies authority—any kind of authority—with autocracy. To all of these countries there applies what André Siegfried,[49] speaking of France, expressed in these words:

> We pay dearly for the historical circumstance which has decided that we conquer democracy and liberty in a struggle against governments imbued with authoritarianism, which has had the result that authority, even legitimate, appears to many people of good faith as suspect. It is time that we free ourselves from these complexes which corrupt our political sanity.

The trouble with democracy in Continental Europe is, indeed, no longer a difficult historical heritage which, by this time, would have lost its disruptive potential had it been guided into the "proper channels of government." Nor did Conservative, Christian Democratic, Socialist and Liberal parties, when they rejected these channels, act from any inherent necessity, as is now being admitted by an increasing number of their leaders who endeavor to reverse the mistakes made along those lines in the past.

EXTREMIST PARTIES AND CONSTITUTIONAL GOVERNMENT.

There does exist, however, a type of party whose interests are deeply antagonistic to the requirements of constitutional government: extremist parties of the Fascist, National Socialist, and Communist type. This is not the place to deal with their principal characteristics in detail.[50] Their very starting point is a violent rejection of agreement between themselves and the democratic parties which they oppose. Fundamental heterogeneity, then, is for them a basic postulate. Their actions are governed by the motto: "We or They"; they want all power for themselves, and intend to use it for the destruction of everyone else.

Parties of this type are, indeed, separated from their moderate opponents by a wide gulf. Yet, the mere fact of their existence does not make an effective democracy impossible, not, at any rate, if the proponents of democratic constitutionalism are aware of their opportunities and make use of the institutions of the "representative republic" to "break and control the violence of faction." It may then result that democratic constitutionalism, instead of being the anvil on which extremist movements bring down their hammer, can be the hammer itself. In the first place, we only need to repeat what James Madison said about the representative republic's first line of defense against the violence of faction:

> If a faction consists of less than a majority, relief is supplied by the republican principle, which enables the majority to defeat its sinister views by regular vote. It may clog the administration, it may convulse the society; but it will be unable to execute and mask its violence under the forms of the Constitution.[51]

The extremists of our day have left no doubt that it is indeed their intention "to execute and mask" their "violence under the forms of the Constitution." Thus, the 1920 statutes of the Third International stated, in conformity with Lenin's views: "The Communist Party enters such institutions [as parliaments] not for the purpose of organization work, but in order to blow up the whole bourgeois machinery from within." Apparently in order not to allow the impression to gain ground that there might be any originality of the proponents of one totalitarian system as compared with that of another, Dr. Goebbels, Hitler's "Minister of Popular Enlightenment and Propaganda," took a few more words to say the same thing:

> We enter Parliament in order to supply ourselves, in the arsenal of democracy, with its own weapons. We become members of the *Reichstag* in order to paralyze the Weimar sentiment with its own assistance. If democracy is so stupid as to give us free tickets and salaries for this bear's work, that is its affair . . .[52]

If, thus, the spokesmen of contemporary extremism have left no doubt as to their intentions, they have also made it clear, on occasion, how big the hurdle is which the majority system erects between these intentions and their fulfillment. Thus the Italian Communist leader, Palmiro Togliatti, wrote, in the Moscow *Pravda* of March 7, 1956, under the heading: "On the Possibility of Using the Parliamentary Path for the Transition to Socialism":

> However, the achievement of universal suffrage in many countries has not yet given the opportunity to the popular masses to have in parliament the number of representatives which would correspond to the real number of the electorate voting for them. In order that this might occur it was necessary to achieve the establishment of a system of proportional representation. For, if a majority electoral system operates, the minority cannot be represented in accordance with its actual strength; its representatives splinter into small groups in Parliament and sometimes disappear altogether.

The proportional system, on the other hand, makes Parliament a kind of political "mirror" of the country, because each Party receives the number of seats in strict conformity to its actual strength. When in France and Italy, where communist and socialist parties enjoy great influence amongst the masses, parliamentary elections were conducted on the basis of the proportional system, then the political groups, which were orientated towards socialism, had in Parliament from one-third to one-half of the seats.

Togliatti, then, is not impressed by those calculations of certain observers within the Western countries who feel that when an extremist group has acquired the strength displayed by the Italian Communists and their Left-wing Socialist allies (one-third of the total in 1953) the majority system of voting, instead of hampering them, will only hasten their victory.[53] Togliatti knew that the political picture changes radically when the majority system is substituted for P.R. The two-thirds of the electorate opposed to an extremist group may be so badly divided in P.R. elections that if they voted the same way under a majority system they would, indeed, become an easy prey of their extremist opponents. As soon, however, as the majority system is adopted, the voters tend to unite on the strongest possible moderate candidate. As we shall see on the basis of practical examples to be discussed in Chaps. XIV, XVII Togliatti knew whereof he spoke when he said that under majority elections extremists would "splinter into small groups in Parliament and sometimes disappear altogether."

The results of such a victory for the moderates are not limited to the mechanics of representation; they are accompanied by a sociological process which tends as much to strengthen democracy as to undermine extremist influence. The rank and file of the extremist voters is less wedded to their party than are the leaders. Most of those who vote for Communist parties neither know nor care what communism is; they want to cast a protest vote. If these votes are "thrown away," as most of them will be under the majority system, the protest becomes an empty gesture. Experience shows that the extremists of the Right lose most of their followers rather quickly. Communist parties develop a following which is more immune to electoral failure. Still, if the majority system is used (and used for some time) in those elections which shape a country's political line-up,[54] a certain, and growing, number of these voters will cut loose from their Communist moorings.

If, after a return to the majority system, moderate parties stand to gain more rapidly in terms of seats than in terms of votes, this presents the immediate advantage of making it possible for the democratic system to function more satisfactorily than before. Thus an impression of strength and vitality will be created where it is badly needed. A properly functioning democracy will attract, rather than repel, voters. It will, in addition, be able to take measures to eliminate those social and economic evils which, in their turn, may have much to do with the strength of the extremist vote.

Extremist parties, then, are the only ones separated from their rivals by a true basic heterogeneity. To a significant extent, however, they are "the spontaneous shoots of an ill-constituted government." If the political forces of a country, which is at all ready for democracy, are guided into the proper channels, the extremists can be kept under control. Besides, many, and in the long run most, of their followers can be absorbed, and assimilated, by the moderate parties.

Chapter XIII

PARLIAMENTARY GOVERNMENT IN FRANCE: THE THIRD REPUBLIC

▄▄▄

CONSTITUTION-MAKING.

No country has experimented more with forms of government in general, and with parliamentary government in particular, than France. Success has been strikingly absent. The question arises whether this result is due to deviations from the "pure" form of this system, or to such aspects of social "matter" as a basic social heterogeneity or deeply rooted national characteristics.

The Constitution of the Third Republic (1870–1940) was not, in reality, a constitution but a series of constitutional laws. The monarchists who held a majority in the Constituent Assembly elected in 1871, had no intention of writing a republican constitution. They suffered, however, from dissension; as Adolphe Thiers, the temporary chief of state, told them: "There is only one throne and three men want to sit on it." The Bonapartists wanted the son of Napoleon III on the throne; the monarchists were divided between the Count of Chambord, the descendant of Charles X, who represented the more conservative tendency, and the Count of Paris, the descendant of Louis Philippe, who followed a more liberal line. Since the Count of Chambord had no heir, and the Count of Paris, or his descendants, were bound to succeed him anyway, both groups agreed in the end that the Count of Chambord was to ascend the throne. He wrecked his chances, however, by insisting that the old white lily banner become the French national flag, rather than the tricolor which, adopted during the Revolution, had become popular in the country.

While these quarrels continued, by-elections [1] reduced the monarchist majority substantially, and the long delay in reaching a decision as to the nation's future form of government caused dissatisfaction to become widespread. On January 30, 1875, the Assembly, in a somewhat confused parliamentary situation, voted the famous *"Amendement Wallon"* which, by implication, made France into a republic. The constitutional laws adopted were, however, designed to leave the door open for a restoration of the monarchy; the powers of the President, in particular, were patterned—or so the authors of these provisions thought—on the model of those of a constitutional monarch. Thus the Constitution bore a makeshift character. According to the historian Hanotaux,[2] the survivors of the National Assembly would say: "Don't search for the principles which have guided us; everything has been done without method, without design, in the dark, by the imperceptible balancing of undecided minorities; accident was our master." This procedure, of course, is totally un-French, and it may well explain why this Constitution lasted longer than any of its predecessors. The shortest "basic law" ever adopted in France, it did not tie up the country's political life into too many knots; enough room was left for custom to permit the "logic of developments" to operate within certain limits.

THE STRUCTURE OF GOVERNMENT.

The organs of government were to be a Chamber of Deputies, a Senate, a President of the Republic, and a Cabinet. The Chamber of Deputies was elected for four years on the basis of direct and universal manhood suffrage. Two hundred and twenty-five of the 300 members which the Senate had at that time were to be elected by special electoral colleges in the various *départements*, comprising, in the main, the representatives of the various units of local government. The Senators were elected for nine years, one-third being replaced every three years. Until the law was changed in 1884 there were also 75 Senators for life. The first of them had been elected by the National Assembly; as they died, they were to be replaced by the Senate itself. With their help the monarchist majority in the National Assembly hoped to make sure of a permanent majority in the upper House of the Republic.[3]

The President of the Republic was to be chosen for seven years by the Chamber of Deputies and the Senate, which was to meet for this purpose in a solemn joint session in Versailles. His functions were those customarily assigned to the head of the state under the parliamentary system: he was to appoint and dismiss the Prime Minister and the rest of the cabinet, to be the head of the armed forces, and to have the legislative initiative concurrently with the two chambers;

he was to promulgate the laws adopted, as well as to see to their execution with the help of administrative regulations. He could adjourn the chambers for one month and proclaim the end of a regular session if it had lasted at least five months; he could summon the chambers for a special session. Above all (or so it seemed), he had the power to dissolve the Chamber of Deputies after having received the approval of the Senate. In the wording of these rights the constitutional laws could have been more economical. As long as all acts of the President had to be countersigned by a responsible minister, virtually all executive and legislative powers could have been assigned to the President who, under the all-important condition that there existed a parliamentary majority which knew what it wanted, could still have done no more than perform the reserve functions assigned to him by the logic of the parliamentary system. In all matters of political significance he would have had to act on the advice of his cabinet, which in turn depended upon the parliamentary majority.

Inevitably, the situation was complicated by the existence of two chambers. Both had, in principle, the same rights, although financial laws had first to be presented to the Chamber of Deputies. Besides, the Senate had to pass judgment on a President of the Republic accused of treason by the Chamber of Deputies, and ministers accused (again by the Chamber) of crimes committed in the exercise of their functions; it could also, by decree of the President of the Republic, issued in the Council of Ministers, be constituted into a court of justice to judge any person accused of acts against the safety of the state. These rights were historical relics, dating from the time when parliaments had to resort to impeachment in order to make governments comply with their wishes; when the principle of ministerial responsibility was introduced it proved sufficient for all practical purposes.[4] As mentioned above, when the French parliament wanted to get rid of a Head of the State, it could, and did, do so simply by refusing any further cooperation. Such acts are of a purely political nature; no formal authorization is needed.

The existence of the Senate did, however, involve problems in regard to both legislation and executive stability. No measure became law until it had been passed by both chambers. In case of disagreement a bill could "make the shuttle" between the two houses indefinitely. In this process, quite apart from the time element involved, many an important measure was lost, there being nothing comparable to the American conference committee. Under a "pure" parliamentary system the government resigns as soon as it fails to secure parliamentary approval for any measure which it considers important. In

France, the original expectation was, apparently, that the government would resign in case of conflict with the Chamber, and not in case of conflict with the Senate. This was logical insofar as, theoretically at least, there existed the right to dissolve the Chamber and appeal to the electorate to settle a conflict between it and the government. There was no right to dissolve the Senate, and, on the other hand, not only was that body's approval needed for legislation, but the constitutional provision according to which the ministers were responsible "before the Chambers" implied responsibility to the Senate as well as to the Chamber of Deputies. The Senate did exercise these comprehensive powers with restraint; still, it always used its legislative powers and, beginning in the 1890's, it openly contributed to the overthrow of governments.

INSTABILITY AND PARTY STRUCTURE.

The lack of government stability was, in fact, the outstanding feature of the Third Republic; 106 cabinets held office between 1870 and 1940; their average duration was a little less than eight months. Since the Senate did make a contribution to this record of instability, some have laid the major share of the blame at its door; the best known among these critics was Pierre Cot, one of the young Radical leaders of the 1930's, and a fellow-traveller after 1944. Actually, only a few cabinets resigned on account of conflicts with the Senate and this fact should rule out such an explanation; besides, it will be seen later than if the Senate did contribute to executive instability, the ultimate reason did not lie in that body's existence, but in the fragile character of the majorities within the Chamber and the weakness of the governments resulting from this fact.

It seems more natural to do what most students of the subject [5] do, namely, to look to the nature of the party system as it manifested itself both in the Chamber of Deputies and in the Senate for an answer to the problem. As we have seen, the France of the Third Republic knew popular political parties [6] only in a rudimentary fashion. The first was the United Socialist party—"French Section of the Workers' International," usually referred to as S.F.I.O. It was founded in 1905 and proved fairly successful in holding together the Marxist and non-Marxist groups within the Socialist movement. Socialist leaders who found their party's prohibition against joining Left-wing governments too severe left it and joined the "Republican Socialists" or the "Independent Socialists," groups without any real basis in the country. Next, the Radicals,[7] officially founded in 1901, attempted to build up a popular organization at the grass-roots level; they decided, in

1911, that their members could not simultaneously belong to other parties. The main result was, however, a new nickname—they were called *Les Valoisiens,* after the *Rue de Valois* in which they established (and still maintain) their headquarters. Finally, there came, after the First World War, the Communists who stood, of course, outside the normal range of political decisions, and the "Popular Democrats," a small Christian Democratic group.

Before 1936, at any rate, the bulk of the Deputies were elected by groups with little popular organization. The parties of the Right and Center (including the Radicals) constituted "parties of notables," which means that, basically, they were not parties at all. The Deputies belonging to them would get themselves elected, in the main, by their own efforts assisted by a comparatively small number of friends in their constituencies; they did not feel that they owed much to whatever political group in the Chamber they might join. As a result they voted more or less as they pleased; if friction developed between them and the parliamentary group to which they belonged they would just leave it, in order either to form a new one—which feat, if nothing else, would earn them the coveted title *"Monsieur le Président"*—or remain independent; as such, they could, if they wanted to, join the parliamentary group of the "Independents" which included Deputies representing virtually all political tendencies.

This situation had its inevitable effects on government stability. A newly-appointed premier could not address himself to a few party leaders whose support would guarantee him a majority. He had to attach as many individual Deputies to himself as possible, appointing half-ministers (the so-called *"Sous-sécrétaires d'Etat"*) as well as ministers, up to 40 in all, in order to be reasonably sure of a majority. He might yet be overthrown on the very day he presented himself to the Chamber, but he would, as a rule, be given a chance to govern for a while. Dissent in his cabinet could be taken for granted, however, from the outset. In both the Chamber and Senate, the Prime Minister had to rely heavily on the power of persuasion which he and his colleagues were able to wield. Such a system placed a premium on the quality of individual, in particular oratorical, performance; for that reason it developed more brilliant men than any other political system has ever known. Rather than a harmonious ensemble these men constituted, on the contrary, a collection of primadonnas, jealous of one another. In the Chamber they fought each other incessantly. Frequently, after a session in the badly ventilated Palais Bourbon that had its beginnings during the early afternoon, had been prolonged into the early morning, the Deputies might wearily start to ballot at dawn and then discover that they had overthrown one more government.

Whatever name such a system deserved, it was not a democracy. It lacked the plebiscitary element, so strong in British politics since the second electoral reform. The system could, perhaps, be called *parliamentary* in the literal sense of the term, as the parliament was supreme in executive as well as in legislative matters; if this is the case, France provided, at the same time, the *reductio ad absurdum* of such a system. Parliament, of course, by its very nature, could not govern itself; all it could, and did, do was to prevent others from governing. There applies to the Third Republic's Chamber of Deputies what the Radical Deputy, M. J. P. David,[8] was to write about its successor, the National Assembly of the Fourth Republic: "The Assembly is sovereign, chaotic, and tyrannical, and by making everything its business, fails to keep a proper eye on anything."

Actually, the French Chamber and Senate failed even in the field of legislation. When a new law was introduced, it was first amended in the committees of the two houses, after which the same process started all over again on the floor. As Robert de Jouvenel[9] characterized the result: "A law is no longer a law. It consists of three hundred amendments, ten decrees, and three regulations of public order." If most of the laws passed suffered from such defects, it was equally detrimental that long overdue laws were never passed. For example, French civil, commercial and criminal legislation remained basically what Napoleon I had made it in the famous "codes" which bear his name; certain provisions in the field of administrative law went back to Louis XIV.

THE SIGNIFICANCE OF GOVERNMENTAL INSTABILITY.

Nor must we overlook the effects of governmental instability in the field of executive and administrative action, no matter how many attempts were made, during both the Third and Fourth Republics, to gloss over them with convenient, and witty, bromides. Thus it would be said that government instability did not matter; certain key positions, like that of the Minister of Foreign Affairs, might be held by the same person for years; besides, there was the permanent staff of the governmental departments which could carry on business "as usual." France, so it was said, "prospered in chaos while Britain decayed in order." Actually, the damage done by these conditions was cutting deep. As soon as a ministry resigned, no decisions would be made above the level of an "inspector"; this meant that nothing but the merest routine could proceed. Nor were conditions necessarily better when a new cabinet was in office. Its members did not know how long they would stay; they were, for that reason, inclined to resort to one makeshift arrangement after the other. The ministers did not always have enough time to acquaint themselves with their tasks, nor enough authority to prevail against their own bureaucracy. The permanent officials—often highly qualified—naturally did their best to fill the vacuum; instead of executing policy they tried to make it. The results, however, were what might be expected from the above (Chap. II) analysis of a bureaucracy's ways of action. In particular, the task of innovation suffered. Reference has already been made to the hidebound conservatism of French military policy during the two world wars, culminating as it did in the exclusive reliance upon the Maginot Line, which was outdated before it was even built, and yet it was a dictate of the military bureaucracy. General de Gaulle [10] was right when he said: "Such a conception of war suited the spirit of the regime. Condemned by governmental weakness and political cleavages to stagnation, it was bound to espouse a static system of this kind." Shortly, we shall see that these influences were similarly hostile to innovation in the field of foreign affairs.

A bureaucracy left to itself is not even efficient in detail. An American weekly recently printed the amusing story of a French prison run for years by its inmates [11]; the incident occurred during the Fourth Republic, but might have taken place during the Third just as well. Unless, in fact, a technical service is under constant control from the outside, it drifts in a vacuum, where anything may happen. This includes the possibility of corruption; however, it must be added that during the Third Republic some rather direct influences tending in this direction emanated from inside the Chamber and the Senate, the two bodies themselves, as the Panama scandal proved, not being immune to wholesale bribery. Besides, they always contained several hundred lawyers to whom anyone might turn who wanted either favors from the government or protection from justice. When a public prosecutor or a judge was confronted by a defense attorney prominent in the Chamber or Senate, or a former (or, for that matter, possibly future) Minister of Justice, he might not be so insistent on the full severity of the law. It was always easy to allow incriminating evidence to be disregarded, or the case to be adjourned. When, in 1934, for example, the case of the swindler, Stavisky,[12] at last reached the limelight of publicity, it was learned that, during the time when he perpetrated his most spectacular feats, he should have been under arrest for previous crimes; his "provisional freedom" had been extended nineteen times.

Contrary to a widespread opinion, the field of foreign affairs was not exempt from the effects of either constant parliamentary interference or bureaucratic conservatism. The former must be given priority in our considerations. It certainly did not constitute a problem before the outbreak of the First World War, when the average Frenchman did not preoccupy himself with foreign affairs except on the rare occasions when an enterprising foreign minister, rightly or wrongly, appeared adventurous. Ordinarily, that official made foreign policy as he deemed best, ably supported by the President of the Republic, whose moral influence very properly helped to assure stability in this field, and by a Foreign Service whose views, during that time, coincided more or less with what the situation required. The First World War, however, shook the French public out of its apathy; since that time Chamber and Senate have reflected, in numerous interpellations, the fears and wishes of their constituents.

When the war ended with complete victory, a number of outstanding political leaders realized that a new era had begun; the age-old rivalry with Germany had to be ended, cooperation being possible with such men as Wirth, Rathenau, Stresemann, and Bruening. The unruly Chamber of Deputies, however, blocked their way at every step. When, for example, Briand, during the Conference of Cannes in 1922, was on the point of making a few concessions to the Germans in the field of reparations, he had to go home suddenly to listen to a thunderous speech by a Deputy, Léon Daudet, who had the distinction of being the only man ever elected by the *Action Française*,[13] and who denounced Briand's plan as he denounced every other proposal of a republican leader. Undoubtedly, Daudet was boasting when he claimed that his speech was decisive in causing Briand to prefer resignation to a fight. There had been a telegram from the President of the Republic, Millerand, expressing reservations to Briand's negotiations. Yet, in this disorganized Chamber everything was possible, and Daudet's speech was no help to Briand. Poincaré, proponent of a "get tough with the Germans" policy became Prime Minister; the result was the occupation of the Ruhr Valley, which produced the runaway phase of the German inflation and Hitler's first rise to prominence. Parliamentary interference ceased briefly with the victory of the Left in 1924, only to be revived within a couple of years, and to hinder a forward-looking foreign policy, then again led by Briand, just as it seemed to have final success in its grasp.[14] It goes without saying that events in France and in Germany were interdependent during this period. There were forces at work east of the Rhine which were as much to blame for the failure of Franco-German reconciliation as were their counterparts in France. (The reasons why these forces became so destructive is discussed in Chapter XV.) Still, the chain of events which was to lead to disaster could have been broken on one side of the border as well as the other.

Men like Briand were hurt by bureaucratic feet-dragging as much as by parliamentary meddling. The members of the French Foreign Office—highly qualified and well-trained as they were—continued to see the ideal French foreign policy in the light of that initiated by Cardinal Richelieu, a balance of power policy calculated to keep Germany weak and divided.[15] Briand and others were convinced that France was no longer strong enough to pursue such a policy. They felt that, if comparatively minor concessions were not made to Wirth, Rathenau, Stresemann and Bruening, their reactionary—and later Nazi—enemies might soon acquire "positions of strength" within German political life [16] through which they would demand incomparably larger concessions. These considerations bore little weight with the rank and file of the French Foreign Office—although these conscientious officials should not be blamed for defects which, in the case of any civil servant, constitute but one side, the weak side, of a coin which displays solid virtues on its obverse. Wherever the men, whose task it is to give political directives, and to insist, above all, upon the necessity of innovation and integration, are strong enough to fulfill their tasks, the Civil Service will not fail to go along, just as in Britain the Civil Service fully cooperated with the complete shift of gears which the Labour government brought about in the field of colonial policy after 1945. The staff of the Foreign Office was called upon to preside over the liquidation of a colonial empire which it had taken pride in establishing and administering, but it did so without a murmur.

In France, the gap left by a weak executive was, then, not adequately filled by the bureaucracy, and the question of why this weakness developed forces itself upon the observer with added strength. Certainly, the individualistic character of the French party system had something to do with the country's difficulties; the mere existence of parties of the British type would have meant a considerable difference in end results. But were not French parties a natural product of the national environment? We should, of course, keep a safe distance from questionable terms and, in particular, remind ourselves that, according to Max Weber,[17] any reference to national character is "a mere confession of ignorance." Certainly, however, there existed in France an individualistic temperament which was favorable to the type of party prevalent in the country at that time. On the other hand, the fact that the development of a truly popular party organization continued ever since the foundation of the SFIO in 1905 would seem to demonstrate that matters in this regard were changing for the better.

IMPROPER CHANNELS OF GOVERNMENT.

The time has now come, however, to place these aspects of the social "matter" which characterized French politics side by side with those of the political "form" as it resulted from the Constitution of 1875 and from the election law. We might recall a remark made by Walter Bagehot in the preface to the second edition of *The English Constitution*,[18] written in 1872, but reflecting conditions which were to become permanent during the Third Republic:

> . . . the present polity of France is not a copy of the whole effective part of the British Constitution, but only of a part of it. By our Constitution nominally the Queen, but really the Prime Minister, has the power of dissolving the Assembly. But M. Thiers (the then French chief executive) has no such power; and therefore, under ordinary circumstances, I believe, the policy would soon become unmanageable. The result would be, as I have tried to explain, that the Assembly would be always changing its Ministry, that having no reason to fear the penalty which that change so often brings in England, they would be ready to make it once a month. Caprice is the characteristic vice of miscellaneous Assemblies, and without some check their selection would be unceasingly mutable.

Bagehot, then, saw no need to stop and consider the difference between the British and the French party systems, or the social "matter" behind that difference; for him the mere absence of an effective right of parliamentary dissolution was enough to create the conditions characteristic of the Third Republic. It could, in fact, be contended that with a party system like that which existed during the Third Republic the right of parliamentary dissolution might have been more effective than it was with well-organized parties. If there was anything that the individual French Deputy wanted more than to become a cabinet member, it was to remain a Deputy. If he had had to face new elections, to be fought, and financed, largely by himself—without a large party organization carrying the brunt of the burden—he would have thought twice before casting a vote which might lead to the dissolution of the Chamber. At the same time, if there was no disciplined party to tell him to support the government neither was there a party with enough power to make him oppose it and risk his job in the process. Such men, then, would have been inclined to give the government the benefit of the doubt.

The results of any dissolution would, of course, have been affected by the system of voting used during most of the Third Republic's life. As we have seen, it did what Woodrow Wilson said France could not afford to do: it "fostered factions." Under a plurality system the French Right and Left could not have afforded to splinter the way it did under the *"scrutin de ballotage."* Certain differences among what is rather picturesquely called "the French spiritual families" which were permitted to continue in existence through the medium of the second ballot (and, therefore, to harden) could not have survived as easily under the plurality system; the latter would have made it necessary to establish a common political denominator for all the groups of the Right and of the Left, and it might well have led to the development of a two-party system.[19] France is, however, a country where any proposal for a change is judged strictly according to its presumed effects upon the partisan balance of power. Indeed, in the long run the plurality system was likely to lead to a two-party system, but, in the short run—or so it seemed—it would have favored the Right over the Left. The Rightists were less divided among themselves than their opponents; they could, therefore, expect that the plurality system would favor them.

Paradoxically, on the occasion when a proposal to abolish the second ballot was made during the closing phase of the Third Republic, it was first introduced by a Radical Deputy. However, Georges Mandel, Clemenceau's well-known disciple, then President of the Chamber's Commission of Universal Suffrage, took the plan over on behalf of the Right. Partisan considerations caused it to be modified; the second ballot was suppressed only if the leading candidate had received at least 40 per cent of the votes and only if this amounted to at least 35 per cent of the registered voters. Election statistics, judiciously examined by the proponents of the change, had led to the conclusion that the Right would, indeed, be its beneficiary. Such calculations always overlook the fact that once new rules of the game have been established, everyone can adapt himself to them; in this case the Left could, wherever the Right was likely to elect a Deputy with more than 40 per cent and less than 50 per cent, have frustrated the game by presenting a common candidate from the start. Its partisan wrath was, however, aroused, and on February 26, 1932, the Senate, in which it had a majority, rejected the reform which had in the meanwhile been adopted by the Chamber.[20]

If this one serious move in the direction of the plurality system (and with it of the two-party system) was a failure, we must recall that the system of the second ballot did retain some of the beneficial effects of majority voting. A multiple-party system, when composed of parties closely related to each other by campaign alliances, and with the extremists "reduced to size" cannot be compared to the system of unrelated parties typical of P.R. Above all, we must repeat that under the *scrutin de ballotage* there was a clearcut division between the French Right and the French Left; this went far toward giving French election results a plebiscitary character in regard to both men and measures. Where such a condition is coupled with an effective right of parliamentary dissolution, there will be repercussions upon the party system itself. Walter Bagehot,[21] speaking of the situation in his own country, says: ". . . though the leaders of party no longer have the vast patronage of the last century with which to bribe, they can coerce by a threat far more potent than any allurement—they can dissolve. This is the secret which keeps parties together." If the right of parliamentary dissolution is "the secret which keeps British parties together," would it not also have promoted party cohesion in France?

A further step could, if this was deemed necessary, have been taken to promote political cohesion. The freedom of the individual Deputy was largely due to his election in the single-member constituency, the *arrondissement*. Some French republicans had, ever since Gambetta, demanded elections in multiple-member constituencies, with the *département* as the geographic unit. From the practical point of view it is correct to say that such a system was tried in the elections of 1919 and 1924. The law applied on those two occasions provided that, wherever one list of candidates secured the absolute majority, it took all the seats; in the other cases—limited to a few large urban and industrial areas—the seats were divided among the lists according to P.R.[22] Where an absolute majority of the votes appeared attainable, the various parties of the Right and of the Left did find it possible to forget their differences and present common lists. French individualism, then, and the variations among the various "spiritual families" into which France is at times assumed to be so hopelessly divided, did not stand in the way of unity when unity was called for by a system of voting which belongs to what Alexander Hamilton would have called "proper channels of government." The same tendency manifested itself when elections took place in single-member constituencies with a second ballot. The integrating effects of this system were weaker; related parties might combat one another in the first ballot whereas, when elections took place under the plurality system they had to unite from the start. Professor Goguel [23] has drawn attention to the fact that majorities arising from multiple-member constituencies combined with the plurality system tended to be more coherent than those issuing from elections in single-member constituencies which, under the Third Republic, were always combined with a second ballot.

The extent to which these majorities cooperated in supporting governments was always limited. In judging this fact we must remember that the parliamentary system is a "system" in the sense defined by a well-known French dictionary [24]: "*un ensemble de choses qui se tiennent*"—"an ensemble of things which hold one another in place." If one essential element is missing, none of the others will occupy its proper position. In our case the missing element is the right of parliamentary dissolution. A French Prime Minister might—such as Herriot in 1924, Poincaré in 1928, and Léon Blum in 1936—in the moment following an election, owe his position to a plebiscitary verdict comparable to (if not identical with) that of a British Prime Minister. However, he could not, like his British counterpart, always renew his contact with the people by dissolving parliament. By providing for a majority every time it was used, the majority system did—even in its weakened form—what it was supposed to do, but its effect on the Prime Minister and government was intermittant rather than permanent.

It must be added in passing that, if French elections did produce a clearcut decision between the Right and the Left, they did not do so at the price of either creating, or expressing, irreconcilable differences between the two "blocs." That this was the case was asserted by, among others, Charles Seignobos,[25] according to whom Right and Left were divided by "irreconcilable conceptions of social life and politics." Seignobos refuted himself, however, when he continued that the French Right, consisting originally of the defenders of the old order in State and Church, found itself compelled to absorb more and more republican elements. The prime ministers whom the Right provided after 1919 were all genuine republicans. The difference between Right and Left, therefore, became a difference between two types of republicans—the more conservative and the more progressive ones. Besides, the "law of moderation," [26] inseparable from the effects of the majority system, was clearly in evidence. When the Right ruled, the policies of the moderate Right were in the saddle, and when the Left ruled, those of the moderate Left were in the saddle in turn. From these facts, Professor Capitant rightly draws the conclusion:

> These are all undeniably British traits. English parliamentarism, therefore, after a fashion, underlies French parliamentarism. It is there in force, it attempts to assert itself, aided, in this effort, by the part of public opinion which aspires at a more efficient system of government which would enjoy more authority and more stability.[27]

DISSOLUTION AND CONSTITUTION.

If we ask ourselves why the British type of parliamentary government—the "pure" type as we have seen—asserted itself in France only under the surface, and "after a fashion," we must return to the more important of the two major ingredients of that system which were missing in France, the right of dissolution. Actually, the Constitution of 1875 gave the President of the Republic the right to dissolve the Chamber of Deputies *"sous l'avis conforme du Senat"*—"with the consent of the Senate." This restriction had found its way into the Constitution through one of those accidents which do, on occasion, make history. Marshal MacMahon, the Chief of State, felt that his personal authority might not be sufficient to pronounce a dissolution of the Chamber. He thought that the position of an elected President was, in this respect, not as strong as that of a monarch; he failed to grasp that the right of dissolution was not actually to be exercised by the President but by the Prime Minister, whose authority, then, was in question, rather than that of the Head of the State.

Making the right of parliamentary dissolution dependent upon the approval of another body was a serious step. Its purpose was preventive rather than repressive; it was to be "the big stick," always available in case the "bad boys" showed signs of wanting to "kick over the traces." Yet, it was to become effective, in the main, through its availability rather than through its actual use. A check on its application placed into the hands of the Head of the State does serve a purpose; a Prime Minister asking for a dissolution under conditions *obviously* contrary to the logic of the system ought to know that he might be refused. Apart from this—rather remote—possibility, however, the right should always be available to a Prime Minister, in particular in regard to a parliament as much inclined to rash action as was the French Chamber of Deputies. The need to secure the approval of another parliamentary body means that time will be lost; in the meantime, matters may have gone too far for the preventive potential of the institution to become effective.

Furthermore, the Senate's right to grant, or refuse, a request for the dissolution of the Chamber could not but influence the power of that body. In appearance, the possibility of dissolving the Chamber placed the latter in an inferior position with respect to the Senate. Actually, the use of that right would have led to a strengthening of the Chamber (and of the cabinet supported by it) in regard to the Senate. A newly-elected Chamber would have been able to point to a fresh popular mandate for the policies advocated by its majority; an upper Chamber, not subject to dissolution, and removed from the people by a nine-year term of office, as well as by indirect election, would hardly have been able to resist policies freshly approved by the people. Therefore, had the right of dissolution been freed from its psychological and constitutional fetters and had it become an accepted part of French political practice, the Senate would have had to accept the position of a supplementary rather than an (almost) coequal body. It would probably have become a very useful "chamber of reflection and of scrutiny," comparable to the British House of Lords. As we have seen, in 1911, the powers of the British upper house were curbed on the basis of a popular consultation. This consultation had been made possible by the dissolution of the House of Commons during the previous year. The Lords (threatened, of course, also with the possibility of the King's assenting to the creation of enough Liberal peers to give the government a majority) found it impossible to resist a lower house backed by the people even on this fundamental constitutional issue.

In France, the point of open conflict, under an effective right of dissolution, would hardly have been reached. The Senate did begin its career on a modest scale; it asserted itself only when, for two full decades, both the Chamber and the government proved to be so weak as to virtually invite the assumption of a larger role by the upper house. In fact, it is interesting to note that when, in 1890, the members of a cabinet for the first time reacted to a defeat in the Senate by leaving that chamber in order to manifest their will to resign, the result was "general stupefaction," and an attempt by several senators to cause the ministers to stay.[28] Six years later the Senate did want a cabinet to resign and used every means in its power in order to assert its right to overthrow a government.[29]

At any rate, the interpretation placed upon the right of dissolution after the unfortunate use made of it by Marshal MacMahon in 1877 served to destroy whatever usefulness it might still have had. Were French constitutional thought really governed by the logic so often claimed for it, it would have concluded that MacMahon's use of the right of dissolution for purposes not compatible with the requirements of the parliamentary system had led to a spectacular defeat for its author by which the institution itself was thoroughly vindicated. Instead, the impression prevailed that a dissolution was, in itself, an anti-republican measure; it was not attempted again. The road to a "government by assembly" was free. Its benefits accrued to the individual members of the two houses. Soon several hundred deputies and senators were able to claim the coveted title *Monsieur le Ministre* which courtesy was extended to them for the rest of their lives even if they had been ministers only for a day; a dozen or so were, as former prime ministers, addressed as *Monsieur le Président*. If a man himself did not place much value upon such honors, his wife might think otherwise. Those who had not yet been ministers were, of course, convinced that as long as the practice of frequent cabinet changes continued, lightning would strike sooner or later.[30] They were reluctant to help terminate a condition which gave them so many opportunities, and to become mere "backbenchers" on the British model. The confusionists and the alarmists stood ready, of course, to join forces with the vested interests in order to discredit any attempt at change. The right of parliamentary dissolution came to be accepted as being contrary to "the republican tradition"; its use, so it was said, would promote a dictatorship.

DOUMERGUE'S REFORM PLAN.

One serious effort at reform, however, was made. The Great Depression had reached France later than other countries. When it did so, it was severe and led to considerable political unrest accompanied by a greater than usual degree of government instability. There arose a number of "Leagues"—Rightist organizations, some of which deserved the name "Fascist" applied to them by their opponents, although the one among them which came to dominate them all in the end, the *Croix de Feu*, is not so easy to classify. Popular dissatisfaction increased sharply when the *Affaire Stavisky* reached the headlines; demonstrations of a clearly anti-parliamentary character took place before the Chamber of Deputies. During the night of February 6, 1934, an invasion of the Chamber by the angry crowd which had assembled just across the Seine River in the Place de la Concorde was prevented with difficulty.[31] The government, headed by Edouard Daladier, was forced to resign; calm was restored only when Gaston Doumergue, a former President of the Republic, was appointed Prime Minister. He assumed office with a program of constitutional reform, and for the first and only time during the Third Republic, there was a chance for a serious change in the political pattern. It did not come, however, and what happened in France between February 9 and November 8, 1934, the period covered by the cabinet Doumergue, is characteristic of the interplay of the factors which have made the road to reform all but impassable during the Fourth Republic as well as during the Third.

Intellectual confusion was as much in evidence as were the vested interests. It extended to the proponents of reform. They produced a substantial amount of writing, some of which was brilliant,[32] but they were inclined to lose themselves in details. Efforts should have been concentrated on an effective right of parliamentary dissolution. Once it was an accepted part of the French political pattern, the government could be expected to be strong enough to give a clear lead to the Chamber in the enactment of additional reforms. This applies, in the first place, to the rules of parliamentary procedure. As mentioned above, any parliament with a coherent majority will find a way to endow itself with a set of rules adequate to its tasks. Specifically, such a parliament will be able to limit, or exclude, the right of its members to initiate new expenses which, in England, has been done by a standing rule going back to 1707. Doumergue included a provision with his reform plans [33] which required that, before parliament could raise expenditures, it would have to provide for the necessary additional revenue. With this proposal he not only demanded something which would have been unnecessary had the government been strengthened by an adequate right of parliamentary dissolution, but he also lessened his chances of securing that right. Similarly, it was stipulated that government employees lost their Civil Service status once they went on strike. Where such strikes occurred they were a result of inflationary developments which a reasonably strong government could have prevented; on the other hand, for a weak government a constitutional right to dismiss striking civil servants would have meant little since parliamentary pressure would probably have led anyway to the reinstatement of the strikers.

If Doumergue tended to lose himself in details, he did not go far enough in regard to the right of dissolution. He had originally asked that such a right be granted to the President of the Republic, without Senate concurrence, after a new Chamber had been in existence for six months; later, he extended this period to a year. With such a delay the fundamental break with the old political habits which France needed might not have occurred; a Chamber able to play its usual cat-and-mouse game with a cabinet for a full year after its election would hardly have allowed the executive to reach its proper stature.

The vested interests opposing the reform took advantage, of course, of the intellectual confusion among its proponents; the apprehensions of the French people were stirred up as to the "Fascist" character of the proposed reform. Professor Gaston Jèze, who was later to become known the world over for his defense of Ethiopia against Fascist aggression in the League of Nations, commented:

> The struggle over the right of dissolution . . . is not a struggle of ideas. It is a bitter fight for the defense of sordid interests. The professional politicians who fight to defend their pecuniary interests menaced by the reform, constitute the bulk of the troops in the attack . . . It is not democracy that is in peril, it is the butter plate.[34]

The individual members of the Chamber and the Senate needed leadership in their resistance; this was, in the first stage, provided, not unnaturally, by the Senate. Its leading parliamentary group, the "Democratic Left" (more or less corresponding to the Radical group in the Chamber) whose chairman Doumergue himself had been, ironically enough, before he became President of the Republic, sent a delegation to him which opened the formal attack.

The most brilliant voice raised in the final phase of the assault on the reform [35] was that of the Socialist leader, Léon Blum. Paradoxically, his powerful effort at persuasion marshalled just about all the arguments against the change which should have clinched the case in its favor.[36] Blum stated that if the revised right of parliamentary dissolution went into effect the individual Deputy would no longer be able to vote "according to his conscience." He would be under pressure, a vote adverse to the government entailing the dissolution of the Chamber. According to Blum, the "sovereignty of the people" was, under a parliamentary system, "delegated" to parliament. With a dissolution, however, matters would be taken out of the hands of parliament; besides, there would be "only two categories of outgoing deputies, the partisans and the opponents" of the Prime Minister, between whom the people would have to choose.

Evidently, what Blum defended, was "parliamentary supremacy" in the literal sense of the term: sovereignty, according to him, had been delegated by the people to parliament, and parliament had to exercise it rather than the people themselves. Blum, then, opposed the coupling of the plebiscitary with the parliamentary principle which the electoral reforms of 1867 and 1884–85 had brought about in England; what he defended was an oligarchic, rather than democratic, conception of parliamentary government. His arguments are significant, however, on account of the sweeping nature of the effects which, in his opinion, an effective right of parliamentary dissolution was bound to produce; it would, according to him, create conditions in France comparable to those prevailing in England. Blum did not even pay attention to the fact that the watered-down version of the right of dissolution contained in Doumergue's final plan could not have had the results which he feared, and for which the logic of the parliamentary system so plainly called.

Blum was, above all, wrong in an assumption of a practical nature. In 1934 he felt that for the foreseeable future André Tardieu would be the leader of the Right and Edouard Herriot the leader of the Left; his own Socialists would, even in the case of a joint victory of the Left, have to play second fiddle to the Radicals. Within less than two years the parliamentary strength of the Socialists was to exceed that of the Radicals and, after the elections of 1936, the task of forming a government of the Left was to fall to Léon Blum. Had an effective right of dissolution been in force he, rather than either Tardieu or Herriot, would have become its beneficiary. As it was, Blum's first cabinet, relying on lightning-like reforms reminiscent of the early New Deal, did manage to stay in power for a year. It was, however, beset by all of the difficulties which Doumergue had intended to remove. When, on March 15, 1938, he formed his second cabinet he could not even rely on the *élan* which had carried him to power in 1936 and had to resign on April 8. In neither case could he ask the people to come to his rescue.

This experience contains a lesson of general significance. When parties consider problems of constitutional government from the point of view of their own advantage rather than from that of the general welfare, they tend to misjudge their interests. These are, in such cases, always viewed from the short-term point of view, and the "short-term" is often a great deal shorter than anticipated. If parties would try to think clearly, and objectively, in terms of the common good they might surprise themselves by discovering that this is also their own good.

It only remains to be added that men like Léon Blum are sincere when they claim that what is manifestly to the immediate interest of their party is also in the interest of the community. Political leaders find themselves in a whirlpool; they rarely have the time to think beyond the events of the day. It is up to less directly engaged observers to keep the record straight and to distinguish between the rationalizations of the partisans and the objective interests of the country. The difficulty is that even those who could afford complete detachment from the political scene, in particular, academic observers, frequently allow themselves to be engulfed by partisan emotions.

The history of French parliamentarism after the failure of Doumergue was disappointing. Efforts were made, to be sure, to strengthen the position of the Prime Minister. He was given an office of his own and, as a result, it was no longer necessary for him to head a specific department in order to have at least a pencil at his disposal, let alone a secretary and a few assistants. This helped a little, as did the repeated practice of parliament to vote the cabinet "plenary powers," allowing it to legislate by decree when the parliamentary process was manifestly inadequate to its tasks. Such a delegation applied only to limited periods. Besides, it had the result of eliminating parliament from the one function which it could and should exercise, that of examining laws in order to make sure that they would be free of the bureaucratic defects not easily avoided in projects emanating from the executive. A reasonably strong government would not have needed to walk on such crutches; it could have exerted enough parliamentary influence to have the necessary measures enacted in the regular process.

A FEW STRONG POINTS.

When we judge the overall picture of government under the Third Republic we must, however, take into account its virtues as well as its vices. Virtues did exist; the most important of them is characterized by the sentence: "The Republic governs badly but it defends itself well." The reason for this effective self-defense lay in the effects of the majority system; whenever the opponents of the Republic marshalled their strength for what they considered a final assault, be they Monarchists, Boulangists, or Fascists, they found it impossible to take the simple hurdle of the majority system in a sufficient number of constituencies. When the extreme Right was particularly active in an election, the result was unavoidably that the moderate Right lost some of the seats which it had held previously; this is illustrated, with particular clarity, by the elections of 1936.[37]

It must be added that if cabinet crises were frequent during the Third Republic, they could also be solved rapidly; they might last up to a week, but they never reached the marathon proportions characteristic of some of the crises which were to occur during the Fourth Republic. The very fact that the French political system suffered from a deficiency in regard to party organization entailed the advantage of flexibility. The host of undisciplined Deputies might be prone to overthrow a cabinet, but they did not form large obstructionist blocs either, and by a little shifting and shuffling new majorities could be assembled in short order.

Lastly, the Third Republic did experience governments which lasted long enough to carry out a substantial part of their program. Thus the cabinets headed by Waldeck-Rousseau, Combes, Clemenceau (both his pre-war and his war-time cabinets), and Poincaré [38] each lasted for more than two years. Also, when these cabinets came into existence in response to a particular crisis—as when Poincaré was recalled to cope with the runaway stage of the French inflation in 1926 —they managed to solve that crisis, although they could not alter the fundamental political pattern. The trouble with all "crisis cabinets" is, of course, that before they can come into existence there must be a crisis; a properly functioning government would prevent the crisis from occurring. Besides, in a country such as France, the individual Deputies and Senators resent the existence of any government capable of governing; their resentment keeps building up until, in the end, the government wielding more than usual power is overthrown and the "return to normalcy" takes place. Still, it was a help to have an occasional break in "normalcy" in favor of a cabinet able to act.

Therefore, if the Third Republic defended itself well it did not *always* govern as badly as it usually did, in particular during the period between the First and Second World Wars. When the Fourth Republic came into existence it soon proved both that it defended itself rather badly and that it governed, on the whole, a little worse than its predecessor. During the first dozen years of its existence only two cabinets (those headed by Queuille and Mollet) managed to live longer than a year; none established a record of accomplishment comparable to that of the leading performers during the Third Republic. It is not altogether surprising that, during the middle 1950's, the condemnation of the Third Republic, which had been universal at the end of the Second World War, began to be replaced by nostalgia. Actually, some writers seemed to feel that the Third Republic constituted the golden age of Republican France. That picture was, of course, far from portraying reality, even if it did contain a few small grains of truth. France did fare well before 1914 in regard to her internal economic development as well as in regard to her international position. During that period her citizens might well have felt that ineffective government should cause them little concern.

Chapter XIV

PARLIAMENTARY GOVERNMENT
IN FRANCE: THE FOURTH
REPUBLIC

~~~~~~

FROM THE THIRD REPUBLIC TO THE FOURTH.

The defects of the Third Republic were real enough to impair the country's moral and military readiness to resist the onslaught of Hitler's armies. Hitler, to be sure, got there "fastest and with the mostest men." In the long run, he would have won regardless of what the French could have done. Still, when French resistance collapsed so quickly, most qualified observers concluded that, had the Third Republic functioned better, the nation would have been stronger; the army might have been led and equipped according to more modern principles and the will to fight would have been enhanced. Similarly, when in July, 1940, parliament abdicated before the demands of Petain and Laval without offering any serious resistance, one of the reasons was its feeling of having long since been inadequate to its tasks.

That France had not failed for military reasons alone, and that political institutions occupied a key position in keeping her actual strength below her potential strength, was also the feeling of General de Gaulle. In March, 1941, he declared: "The abuses of the parliamentary regime which had become intolerable, had the result of a grave weakening of authority in the state and in the administration."[1] On a later occasion, he referred to certain fundamental "vices" in the functioning of the country's institutions, which resulted in "a kind of paralysis and seemed all of a sudden fatal in the extreme perils of 1940." He added that during the twenty-one years separating the First World War from the German invasion in 1940 twenty different men had been prime ministers. Some of them possessed high personal qualifications, but the forty-five cabinets which they headed were not strong enough to meet the problems of the time.[2]

The Resistance within France felt the same way about the situation; on this one point it was, in fact, more united than on any other (except, of course, the need to liberate the country). That the people at large shared this feeling was shown without a doubt when, in the referendum of October 21, 1945, no less than 96.4 per cent of those who voted opposed a return to the Constitution of 1875.

The wish for a fundamentally new pattern is, however, one thing, and its realization something else again. Whenever that task is entrusted to an assembly, as it was under the Constitution of 1875, everything depends on whether that body contains living forces within itself which have both the will and the strength to take the required action. During the Third Republic a simple majority, first of Chamber and Senate voting separately, then of the two meeting jointly, sufficed to amend the Constitution. So far as the written law was concerned, the process of revision could hardly have been simpler. Yet, the majorities needed to effect serious changes having a bearing on the basic aspects of the constitutional pattern could not be found. During the Second World War the question was whether the result would be different if the decision was left to another assembly dominated by vested interests and baffled by intellectual confusion. Americans will readily appreciate the difficulties connected with this problem. The framers of the Federal Constitution felt the same way about the vested interests in the parliamentary bodies of their time; they deemed it necessary to circumvent both the Congress of the Confederation and the (bicameral) legislatures of the states, through special ratifying conventions, which were, of course, unicameral, and decided by simple majority vote. Hamilton, Madison and Jay took the added precaution of setting forth their views in a manner which made it difficult to challenge them; *The Federalist* papers, both in form and content, were so superior to the pamphlets produced by the opposition that they were certain to dominate the argument.

Not a few Resistance leaders were apprehensive as to the implications of letting either the parliamentary bodies provided by the Constitution of 1875, or an unguided and omnipotent new assembly, make the necessary decisions. They felt that it was none too soon to bring about the required intellectual clarification, and to make certain that, when the time came, a unified effort at political renovation would be made. They suffered from the drawback of having to work underground; dissemination of ideas through the printed word was so dangerous that it could be attempted only on a very limited scale.

This was a tragic defect, as no solution could be adopted which was not supported by a substantial body of opinion.

At the same time, the desire for a thoroughgoing renovation was so strong that the easiest path to a solution was generally ruled out. As we have seen, the Constitution of the Third Republic was, on the whole, quite adequate. Professor Marcel Prélot [3] did not stand alone when he expressed the opinion that its real defect lay in the five words requiring Senate consent to a dissolution of the Chamber. If they were deleted, "the obstruction would be removed and the mechanism would be free and ready to function." It would have been quite possible to proceed to the election of a new Chamber of Deputies and a new Senate on the basis of the old election law, and to guard against the vested interests by asking the people for a vote on whether they wanted the required constitutional change to be made. If the vote was affirmative—as it was likely to be, had a positive answer been requested by General de Gaulle and the leading men of the Resistance,[4] the new Chamber and Senate would hardly have refused to make the necessary changes.

When, instead of recommending such a course, the Resistance leaders almost unanimously decided in favor of an entirely new Constitution, they acted from the natural feeling that considerations of morale made it advisable to discard the old and start afresh. Several plans were drawn up; outstanding among them was the one prepared on behalf of the "General Committee of Studies" (the French initials were C.G.E.) by young Michel Debré, later to become the Gaullist leader in the Council of the Republic.[5] Accepted, with minor changes, by most of the committee's members it was sent on to de Gaulle in Algiers. In the words of Professor Wright:

> The C.G.E.'s ambition was to secure such wide general acceptance that its draft would amount to a ready-made constitution by the time liberation came. The C.G.E. felt that if it could win the approval of the resistance movement as a whole, De Gaulle would then feel justified in accepting the document and putting it into operation as soon as Vichy fell. De Gaulle could decide whether to have it ratified eventually by the people or by a Chamber and Senate elected in the prewar manner.[6]

The draft itself rejected the idea of a presidential government for France; it proposed, instead, a rejuvenated parliamentary system with a greatly strengthened executive. In particular, there was to be a completely untrammeled right of parliamentary dissolution, assigned to the President of the Republic under the assumption that it was to be exercised upon the proposal of the Prime Minister. The system of voting was to be treated on the same plane as the Constitution, being regulated in a separate "organic law." [7] The plurality system was to be adopted; it was to be used in multiple-member constituencies, the *département* forming, as a rule, the constituency. Thus French political division was to be attacked with the strongest institutional weapons available. An unrestricted right of parliamentary dissolution would, in itself, have caused the Deputies to rally around a Prime Minister able to ask the President of the Republic at any time for a dissolution. To institute, simultaneously, the plurality system in multiple-member constituencies meant to increase the incentives to integration to a maximum.

Debré went, perhaps, a little too fast and too far. [8] Still, there is little doubt that his plan, even with minor modifications, would, if adopted, have helped France to use the *élan* of the Resistance for a thoroughgoing renovation. That was, however, not a purpose shared by all the political forces of the time. In the words of Professor Wright:

> The C.G.E.'s hopes were quickly wrecked on the hitherto submerged rock of Communist opposition. Until this moment, no one could say just where the Communists stood on the constitutional question. Before the war, the party had refused to waste its time in so un-Marxian a pastime as tinkering with democratic institutions. The Communists' long-run goal was fairly obvious, assuming that they could some day take power; but their program for the interim period of bourgeois democracy's survival had never been made clear.
>
> Early in 1944 the Communist Central Committee brusquely spoke. The verdict was handed down by the party's leading journalist, Georges Cogniot, in a clandestine issue of the revived party periodical *Les Cahiers du Communisme*. Cogniot's article, which furnished the first detailed exposé of French Communism's constitutional views, created a mild sensation in resistance circles. [9]

Cogniot, [10] it must be added, made his points both ably and suavely. He began with the admission—startling in a Communist publication in which constitutions are ordinarily treated as secondary in importance to the class struggle—that the events of 1940 had become possible "only on account of the more or less profound, more or less complete deficiency of the constitution in general, and the institutions and principles of our country" in particular. [11] Cogniot never referred to specific Communist tenets, but placed himself on the basis of "the republican tradition"—as interpreted to postulate the exercise of "popular sovereignty" by "the representatives of the people," in other words, a "government by assembly"—meaning, virtually no government at all. The Communists maximized the power of the executive in the countries behind the "Iron Curtain" where they controlled it; by the same token they endeavored to minimize it wherever others might, for the time being, have the major influence. In addition (and this leads us to the second ingredient of the Communist prescription for constitutional government on this side of the "Iron Curtain") Cogniot took it for granted that elections were to be held under P.R.; he was to endorse that system of voting with great force as the reporter of the "Commission for the Reform of the State and of Legislation" of the Consultative Assembly (which De Gaulle had summoned to Algiers) in August, 1945.[12] Once again he expressed himself in the terms used by leading Republicans rather than in those of his own party. Vincent Auriol, the Socialist leader who, as the first President of the Fourth Republic was to have ample time for regrets, was among those most strongly applauding Cogniot's demand for P.R.

A Constituent Assembly elected under P.R. was bound not only to perpetuate the weaknesses of the Third Republic, but to aggravate them. There is inherent in P.R. a tendency to "political pluralism." Pluralism,[13] to be sure, has its functions in the field of *social*—as distinguished from *political*—life; many of us favor as much autonomy for *social* groups as is practicably obtainable. The necessary characteristic of the *state*, however, being unity of action—the only alternative to anarchy—the highest organs of government must be established in such a way as to be conducive to unity.[14] When, instead, a parliament is elected under a fullfledged system of P.R.,[15] there is a tendency to ignore the need for unity.[16] If typical P.R. parties form a coalition each will bargain for as many important cabinet posts as possible (in particular those with a great deal of patronage) and run them according to its own wishes, without much attention to any overall government policies. Thus in France, during the period of "tripartism," when the major government parties were the Communists, the Socialists and the Christian Democratic MRP, this tendency was symbolized by the fact that in the offices of a ministry held by the Communists there would be a picture of Stalin on the wall; in one run by the Socialists a picture of Jean Jaurès or Léon Blum, and in one run by the Christian Democrats a picture of Georges Bidault. A Constituent Assembly dominated by parties of this type will not even try to write a constitution intended to do what constitutions ought to do—to channel the country's social forces towards the required unity of political action. It will, instead, devise a document which, in as many highsounding phrases as possible, preserves the *status quo* of a nearly anarchic political pluralism. This is exactly what the first French postwar Constituent Assembly did, and what its successor, elected after the people had turned down the first Constitution, repeated, with only slight modifications of the earlier model.

DE GAULLE'S POSITION.

De Gaulle's prestige among the Resistance leaders was so great that he might have been able to head off such developments. His personal preference was to work with the Resistance directly, rather than with the old political parties. Had he been able to act on this basis, a constitution along the lines suggested by Debré might have been adopted. When, in the summer of 1950, this writer asked one of his closest collaborators—an internationally known expert in the field of constitutional law—why the General failed to secure a constitution which would have at least *attempted* to harness France's social forces in channels likely to lead to true constitutional efficiency, the anguished answer was: *"Ah! Les Anglo-Saxons!—*"Oh, the Anglo-Saxons!" This was a reference to the fact that De Gaulle had been exposed to strong pressure from both Washington and London. Roosevelt and Churchill suspected him of undemocratic tendencies. There were points in his record, arising from his military background, and from his writings, which suggested that, while he expressed himself clearly in favor of democracy and criticized dictatorship most lucidly, he might not be aware of the concrete requirements of constitutional government. It will be seen presently that this fact could have caused De Gaulle to miss his opportunity to lead France to a thoroughgoing political renovation even if there had been no pressure on him from his country's allies. There was to be such pressure, however. Churchill and Roosevelt, of course, were not to blame when they wanted to make certain that France, liberated by the armies under their command, would be safely democratic. It was, however, one of the tragic shortcomings of this period that they had no concept of their own as to what democracy meant in terms of constitutional government. Otherwise, they might have hesitated before putting the kind of pressure on De Gaulle which weakened him in his struggle against the unholy alliance which was soon to be formed between the Communists and the vested interests left over from the Third Republic. So far as the share of the Communists in these events is concerned, their plans of disruption were ready—as all of their plans, for any kind of contingency, are always kept ready, years, and at times decades, ahead of the day when they will be needed.

Nothing comparable existed on the democratic side. The anti-intellectual bromide, "Let's win the war first," was always available to brush off those who suggested that it was none too soon to clarify, in its major outlines, the problems of constitutional reconstruction as they applied not only to the liberated countries, but to the Axis nations as well. All the English and Americans had to do was to preach a little of what, in the field of constitutional government, they had practiced for generations. The entire intellectual atmosphere in these nations was, however, deeply permeated with arguments indebted—even if, as a rule, rather vaguely—to the economic interpretation of history. Any reference to what observance, or non-observance, of the basic rules of democratic constitutionalism might mean for the success, or failure, of democratic government in the liberated and conquered countries, was likely to meet with little understanding. Some of us were told in so many words that, after all, political reality was ultimately determined by the class structure.

Roosevelt and Churchill added their—not necessarily decisive—contribution to the mistakes made in this field when they forced De Gaulle to contact the old political parties and offer them a partnership in his movement without any attempt being made to safeguard the political future of France from being mortgaged by the vested interests of the past. Professor Wright [17] describes these events as follows:

> De Gaulle, when he first began to negotiate with the underground through his agent Pierre Brossolette, favored the idea of replacing the old party system by a broad political *rassemblement*. A short time later, his views suddenly shifted. Jean Moulin brought instructions from London to encourage the revival of the prewar parties and to offer them a prominent place in the new National Resistance Council. Many "pure resistance" leaders balked at the idea, but they finally had to capitulate. So strong was the London pressure that certain Right-wing parties were resuscitated by a kind of artificial respiration.

When evaluating the effects of these events we must recall that, since the Communists had no difficulty adjusting themselves to the conditions of underground existence, they were then by far the best organized political group in France. Their influence was bound to be great wherever it was admitted; it became decisive where all they had to do was to lend political strength to the erroneous views of others. This, as we have seen, was the case in regard to the nature of the new constitutional pattern.

At this point the question arises whether De Gaulle played correctly the cards which he did retain in his hands. Characteristically, he approached the task of political reconstruction through a somewhat mystical concept of leadership which is not easily translated into the concrete terms of constitutional government. In his Memoirs—distinguished by a literary skill and indicative of a human greatness to which no one will fail to pay tribute—he was to write, speaking of the Consultative Assembly which he had summoned to Algiers:

> So far as I am concerned, seeing, through the opinions advanced by the groups, which outlined the future pretensions, and, at the same time, the impotence of the parties, I discerned what, to-morrow, the French constitutional drama would be. "To deliberate is within the province of a number. To act is within the province of a single person." For that very reason, one wanted only to deliberate.[18]

De Gaulle had good reasons to feel chagrined about the behavior of the party representatives in the Consultative Assembly. They did delight in fighting inconclusive battles of words. Besides, the more it became certain that the General would be the head of the government destined to enter Paris at the time of its Liberation, the more clearly they indicated their desire to make the new government as weak as possible. On the part of some of them, this represented a reversal of the attitude which they had taken earlier during the war. Writing during this period, Professor Simon was able to say:

> One of the striking characteristics of the new movement in favor of liberty is that it is not accompanied by that defiance of authority which haunted the old liberalism. This is a truly extraordinary fact, and one to provoke fruitful reflections . . .
> All of them [the Resistance fighters] want the France of tomorrow to have a strong government, a government capable of assuring the effective repression of crimes against the public weal, capable of assuring that unity of action without which there is no true social life, capable of impressing on all an effective direction towards the public good.[19]

Of this earlier attitude there was, among those playing a leading part in the old political parties, little to be noticed during the last year of the war, and the first year after the Liberation of Paris. The party leaders, once again, were unable to grasp the vital fact that the motives of those who set up the right kind of institution do not matter. Once established, such institutions have their own dynamics and, if the social "material" of the country is at all ready for democracy, they are likely to defeat any possible anti-democratic intentions of their founders. On the other hand, the above quotation from De Gaulle—to which others could be added—shows that the General's way of expressing himself could easily appear contrary to the spirit of constitutional government. "To act is within the province of a single person"—such a phrase can be interpreted as the advocacy of "personal power," all the more so since it is a quotation from Napoleon. Besides, De Gaulle's oft repeated scorn for political parties, while understandable in regard to the type of party with which he had to deal, was, in its terminology, frequently rather close to views expressed by contemporary autocrats. The institutions which his leading advisers in the constitutional field, René Capitant and Michel Debré, advocated—the plurality system of voting as well as the right of dissolution—were intended to create a type of party which would be a serviceable instrument of democratic government and there was a real hope that such parties would materialize. It should be added that both of these men rejected the presidential system. Debré did so in the introduction to his draft of a new Constitution, and Capitant in the thoughtful pamphlet which he contributed to the discussion of constitutional reform in 1934.[20] De Gaulle might have differed with them on this point; if he wanted a presidential system it would still have been necessary to have political parties, and it would still not have been prudent to speak in the terms of acting being the province "of a single person." [21]

In the the end, De Gaulle made tragic mistakes. On the one hand, we learn that he never gave any thought to the possibility of putting any ready-made Constitution into effect by decree; he felt that such an act was contrary to the requirements of democratic legitimacy.[22] On the other hand, he did take it upon himself to change, by decree, the old system of voting and put P.R. into its place. This step was to loom large in shaping the kind of political party which was to bedevil the life of his government after the election of the Constituent Assembly. Nor could it fail to anticipate much of the decision as to the nature of the new Constitution. Two years later, Debré was to treat the implications of P.R. in a forceful and brilliant, though bitter, book, entitled *The Death of the Republican State.*[23] In his words: "It (P.R.) is the system of voting which determines through which men or groups of men the will of the state is to be exercised . . . The system of voting makes the power, which means that it makes for the success of democracy, or kills it." [24]

Considerations of this kind were apparently impressed on De Gaulle by both Capitant and Debré[25] before P.R. was adopted. The General was, of course, under very strong pressure from the political parties to adopt that system of voting. However, when discussing these events in later years, De Gaulle did mention pressure, but defended the decision to adopt P.R. as correct. He stated that, at that time, both the plurality system and the second ballot would have played into the hands of the Communists.[26] Under the first system they would have benefited from the disunity of their opponents, and under the second, from alliances with other Leftists. Ever since the popular reaction against P.R. set in—which happened within a couple of years—this argument has been advanced by many who favored P.R. in 1945 and came to reject it later; it was, however, not a part of the discussion which took place in 1945.[27]

A study of political developments as they unfolded in 1945 would seem to indicate that the fear of great Communist successes under any form of the majority system was unfounded. Communist popular strength had increased substantially above the level reached in 1936. Still, the Socialists, France's strongest political party since 1932, maintained their lead. Besides, there was now a new political force in the center, the Christian Democratic "Popular Republican Movement" (M.R.P.).[28] Genuinely Republican, it was in a position to offer an alternative to left-of-center voters who found themselves confronted by a Communist candidate in the second ballot. (In the departmental elections of September, 1945, the political potentialities of this fact were to be demonstrated on a number of occasions.)

The M.R.P. offered the further advantage of extending the principle of popular party organization into the areas previously occupied by the more or less unorganized Right. In this connection, the fact that the two traditionally well organized parties of the Left, the Socialists and the Communists, encompassed (at that time) half of the electorate meant that the French political picture as a whole had changed for the better, as the principle of popular party organization now covered a good two-thirds of the electorate. Thus, the "matter" of French politics was continuing the process of maturation which had begun with the foundation of the SFIO in 1905. The question is how this solidified material would have reacted to the two types of majority voting.

So far as the plurality system is concerned, there are no definite figures on which to base our estimate. When, however, it was suggested during the Third Republic that the second ballot be abolished, the answer frequently given was: "What you want to suppress is not the second ballot, but the first." The first ballot presented the opportunity for the various political groups of the Right and Left to present their own candidates; for the second ballot the Right and Left presented, wherever possible, each a common candidate. It was taken for granted that if the second ballot were abolished, this concentration on two candidates would be attempted in the first ballot. Efforts in this direction would undoubtedly have been made had the plurality system been used in 1945, and, in this process, Communists were likely, on balance, to lose more than they could gain. As an extremist party, they could win added support only from one side; the Socialists could expect help both on their Right and their Left.

The concrete implications of this proposition become clearer if we bear in mind that, before the elections to the Constituent Assembly took place under P.R., France voted twice under the old type of majority voting with second ballot. In April and May municipal councils were elected, and in September departmental councils. Both elections were, to be sure, of a local nature. Yet, that voters should, in such elections, decide on the basis of local rather than national issues has long since, in most countries, become more the expression of a pious wish than of a political fact. In the France of 1945 local considerations did play their part, in particular in small communes. Yet, taking the country as a whole, everyone considered these two elections more an expression of opinion on national than on local issues. These were the first opportunities for the national political parties to flex their political muscles after the Liberation. Each of them did its level best to produce a good show of national party strength.

The results saw the Left advancing all over the country. The Radicals and the old Rightist parties lost most of their pre-war popular support; many of the former Rightists voted for the M.R.P. If, on the whole, the Left gained in these elections, it is interesting to note that the Socialists benefited much more than the Communists. The Socialists' lead in the popular vote was slight but the discrepancy was striking when it came to the distribution of the seats. It is difficult to summarize these results in a few figures as the size of the various municipalities differed greatly. Still, it might be mentioned that the Socialists obtained a majority of the seats in 4,115 municipal councils, and the Communists in 1,413, while Socialists and Communists together obtained the majority in 458 cases.[29]

The statistical picture is a little clearer in the departmental elections, since the size of the constituencies, the *cantons,* did not differ quite as much as that of the municipalities, although the differences were substantial, and operated to the disadvantage of the urban areas. The Socialists secured 811 seats, and the Communists 328. The statistics of the Ministry of the Interior gave the Communists 3,489,797 votes and the Socialists 3,615,855.[30] The Socialists, then, as the more moderate party, gained many more seats in proportion to their votes than the Communists—a clear indication that the law of moderation, characteristic of the majority system, was in effect. This becomes even more obvious if we bear in mind that the Radicals, with 2,127,180 votes secured 607 seats, although the Radicals, even more than the Socialists, owed a part of their advantage over the Communists to the fact that they were more likely to win in the relatively small rural areas, whereas the Communists carried most of the populous urban *cantons*.

All of this happened at a time when the Communists found it easy to form campaign alliances. As a typical extremist party they just never managed to do quite as well in placing their candidates as did their moderate allies. Where a Communist did carry the banner of such a combination he saw frequently moderate Leftists—including Socialists—turn away from himself to ensure the victory of a centrist candidate. The psychological effects of the relative failure of the Communists were strengthened by the fact that, of all the large parties, they alone did not secure an absolute majority of the seats in the council of any *département*. The Socialists, who had held such a majority in four cases before the war, jumped to fourteen.

The most significant aspect of the contemporary reaction to the elections is summarized by *L'Année Politique* in these words: "One expects the [Socialist] party to triumph in the general elections [to the Constituent Assembly]. 'We have the wind in our sails' said M. Blum in *Le Populaire*." A French journalist, writing in an American weekly,[31] was even more specific: "In the light of the result of recent cantonal elections, France seems likely to be the next big country in Europe where a conspicuous trend to democratic socialism will triumph." It seemed likely, indeed—until P.R. was used for the elections of the National Assembly, and the trend was reversed. The Communists then outscored the Socialists, the latter going into a tailspin in regard to both popular and parliamentary strength.

To an appreciable extent, this outcome could have been foreseen. To the Socialists, in particular, it should have been plain that, ever since 1936, they had gained from the majority system. Whatever else P.R. might do, it was certain to deprive them of their preëminent position in the leadership of the Left. Why did they fail to realize this? Unfortunately, when the political scientist of our day has to judge such matters, he is too much inclined to be guided by Hegel's dictum that "whatever is, is reasonable." He might do well to remember, on occasion, what the Swedish Chancellor, Oxenstierna, told his son (who was reluctant to take a position for which he did not feel qualified): "Don't you know, my dear son, with how little wisdom the world is governed?" The French Socialists, at that time, just did not have enough "wisdom" to take a good look at the election statistics. They had, for doctrinaire reasons, been battling for P.R. for generations. At the same time, they simply assumed that it would benefit them as, of course, it would have done when the party was smaller, and when they could not secure the adoption of P.R. When they acquired enough power to assist decisively in the adoption of P.R., it was to harm them just as the same step was to harm the German Socialists in 1919.

P.R. AND THE NEW POLITICAL FORCES.

If the Socialists failed to make a thorough analysis of electoral systems and their political impact they did not stand alone. It was then not easy to draw attention to the practical implications of the problem, as two of the men who did their best to stem the tide, René Capitant and Michel Debré, were to experience time and again. Their arguments did, however, impress General De Gaulle sufficiently to make him adopt a form of P.R. which, it was hoped, would avoid what appeared its most serious drawback: the rise of splinter parties. For this reason, "integral" P.R., which would have established a close proportionality between votes cast and seats obtained, was rejected. Comparatively small constituencies were instituted. The unit was, as a rule, the *département;* if it was entitled to nine seats, it was divided into several constituencies, bringing the total to 102 constituencies. No surplus votes could be transferred from one constituency to another. If, therefore, in the average constituency, electing six Deputies, a party failed to secure close to one-sixth of the total its votes were wasted.

This arrangement did prove remarkably successful so far as the elimination of "splinter parties" is concerned. Only, it was overlooked that parties are not suitable "instruments of democratic government" simply because they are large. They must also be moderate. In France the Communists were invariably the beneficiaries of the provisions intended to favor large parties but, instead of being an "instrument of democratic government" they soon demonstrated that, loyal to Lenin's injunctions,[32] they never intended to be anything but an instrument for the obstruction of democratic government. On the other hand, the Radicals, a centrist party, suffered severely from the effects of this system. In October, 1945, no less than 56.6 per cent of their votes remained unutilized—quite a contrast to the majority system in the departmental elections, which gave them several times as high a percentage of seats as of votes. Such as conditions were in France at that time, "integral" P.R. would have been preferable to the system adopted. De Gaulle, incidentally, insisted on P.R. in small constituencies against the protest of virtually all political parties, as well as of a number of political and semi-political organizations.

In its basic features the law decreed by De Gaulle tended to perpetuate itself, thanks to the vested interests which it had created. It governed the elections to the second as well as to the first Constituent Assembly and to the first National Assembly under the new Constitution as well. Some of its features were submerged by the new provisions of the election law adopted in 1951, only to reassert themselves in 1956.

At any rate, the three large parties dominated the Constituent Assembly; they were determined to dominate the government as well. The following table lists the percentages of the total valid vote obtained by the parties between 1945 and 1956:

Party shares in the popular vote, 1945–56.[*]

	Oct. 1945	June 1946	Nov. 1946	June 1951	Jan. 1956 [***]
Communists and Progressives	26	26.2	28.6	25.9	25.6
Socialists	23.8	21.1	17.9	14.9	15.
Various Leftists	—	—	—	0.1	1.6
Radicals and Resistance group	11.1	11.5	12.4	11.2	13.6
M.R.P.	24.9	28.1	26.4	12.8	10.6
Moderate Right	13.3	12.8	12.8	12.3	14.1
Gaullists [**]	—	—	1.6	20.4	4.2
Poujadists	—	—	—	—	12.1
Various	0.9	0.3	0.3	—	1.5

[*] *Le Monde,* January 5, 1956.
[**] The figure for November, 1946, refers to an unofficial Gaullist group, that for 1951 to the R.P.F., and that for 1956 to the so-called "Social Republicans," the unofficial successors to the R.P.F.
[***] Figures for 1956 do not include results for the *Département Moselle.*

An attempt had been made to provide the executive with a measure of independence. When the voters elected the new Assembly, they not only decided to declare the Constitution of the Third Republic defunct, but they also adopted De Gaulle's proposals—watered down considerably at the insistence of the political parties—to limit the powers of the Constituent Assembly. The provisions in question were, in some respects, similar to those aiming at government stability in the Constitution of the Fourth Republic. The Assembly was, by an absolute majority of its members, to elect the President of the provisional government, who was then to form his government. The rejection of a measure sponsored by a government was not to suffice in order to overthrow it. A formal vote of censure was needed; it had to be moved two days before being voted upon and was adopted only if the absolute majority of the Assembly's members supported it.

This attempt to secure a measure of executive stability was so weak as to be all but meaningless. That the President of the provisional government, once elected by the Assembly, was to be free in the choice of his ministers, was a fiction. De Gaulle, to whom this task fell, had to negotiate for seventeen days with the parties on the distribution of the ministries and to submit to most of their requests; it is, however, one of his historic merits that he managed to keep the Communists out of the key positions (Interior, Foreign Affairs, Army) which they wanted. Nor did the rules designed to limit cabinet crises amount to a real check. To require a "cooling off period" between moving a vote of censure and balloting on it was one thing during the Third Republic, when individual Deputies made their own decisions, so often in an atmosphere of confusion. It was something else again after elections had been held under P.R. Party organization became for a time, at least,[33] as rigid as it had been previously loose; the party bosses decided which way the Deputies were to vote, and the element of surprise had vanished from the French political scene. That this should have happened—even if, in its extreme form, only for a couple of years—is one more testimony to the fact that the effects of political institutions may transcend all differences of nationality. During the debates of the first Constituent Assembly René Capitant quoted what Leopold Boissier, the Secretary General of the Interparliamentary Union, had told him after having watched a meeting of this body: "I thought I was present at a meeting of the German *Reichstag*, a few months before Hitler's rise to power."[34] French parties were, at that time, indeed as rigid as those of the Weimar Republic.

Another part of the limitations upon the Constituent Assembly adopted on October 21, 1945, provided that a government was to resign only after the adoption of a formal vote of censure. This provision, too, was meaningless. No government operating under the parliamentary system can forego threatening its resignation—in other words, asking the question of confidence—when vital parts of its policy are at stake. No political leader worthy of his salt will want to stay in power if measures which he deems essential are rejected. If a government has the right of parliamentary dissolution it is in a relatively strong position; if it has no such right it can only hope that parliament will not relish the task of having to replace it. Nor will it make a difference whether the motion of confidence has been rejected by a simple majority of those present, or by an overall majority. The government's ability to pursue a policy for which it can assume responsibility is destroyed in either case.

The logic of this situation was to force itself upon General

De Gaulle during the final days of the year 1945, not much more than a month after the formation of his new government. The Communist-Socialist majority wanted to reduce military appropriations below the level which he deemed safe; its spokesman, the Socialist leader, André Philip, declared that the government should stay in office even if the cut were adopted. The implications of this theory were that the Assembly should have the right to give the government directions on all matters of policy; the cabinet was to be no more than an "executive" [35] with the duty to "execute" what the Assembly had decided. De Gaulle rejected this interpretation—which, of course, amounted to "government by assembly" in its purest form—and left no doubt that he would resign unless the appropriation was left intact.[36] He won on this particular occasion, but the incident brought the fact home to him that he could confront the Assembly with no more than his personal prestige, and that this was wearing thin.

Indeed, De Gaulle could not fail to recognize the futility of the checks supposedly imposed upon the Assembly. On January 20, 1946, he suddenly resigned. There had been no hostile vote against him; he just "had enough." At the very moment when the Constituent Assembly elected under P.R. met, there had taken place what Rudolf Smend,[37] a generation earlier, had termed a "shift in the constitutional order," control passing from parliament as a body—which might yet have heeded De Gaulle's appeal for support—to the political parties, then no longer democratic in their structure; [38] the Socialist-Communist majority was definitely opposed to De Gaulle.

The primary task of the Assembly was the writing of a Constitution. We need not repeat that France's "living Constitution" had taken shape as soon as the election law of 1945 had been put into effect. France's political material had been cast into the mold of a multiplicity of unrelated parties, limited, to be sure, in number by the small size of the constituencies. None was large enough to govern itself, but several strong enough to prevent anyone else from governing. Nor need we repeat that, when these parties formed coalitions they had, like the feudal barons of the past, little interest in a common government. They preferred to carve out small realms for themselves, little ministerial kingdoms in which they endeavored to exercise their own sovereignty, willing to leave their partners the government departments which had been entrusted to them, for similar exploitation.

However, a Constitution had to be written. It was part of the popular decision made on October 21 that this was to be done within seven months; the result had to be submitted to the people. Socialists and Communists combined to draft a document which went as far as it could in establishing (or, rather confirming) a government by a unicameral assembly, to be exercised, of course, by the parties. The MRP tried hard to reach a compromise with its coalition partners but balked, in the end, at the demands of the Socialist-Communist majority.

The people rejected the draft on May 5. The new Constituent Assembly was, however, elected in the same way as its predecessor, and it was inclined to follow the same path. The MRP secured a number of concessions intended to lead away from "government by assembly" and from unicameralism; they were not important enough to affect the basic political pattern. On October 13, 1946, the new Constitution received 9,257,000 positive as against 8,126,000 negative votes, out of a total of 25.8 million registered voters. The number of affirmative votes was about 200,000 less than those cast for the first draft which had been opposed, however, by 10.5 million negative votes. Clearly, the result achieved in October was unimpressive. The people felt uneasy about the new Constitution but, limited to a simple "yes" or "no," a bare majority considered a resigned "yes" the lesser evil.

THE STRUCTURE OF GOVERNMENT.

While little has to be said about the structure of the new government, it is important to bear in mind that not all of the criticism directed against it is to the point. Some critics hold that the French government came to be so weak because not enough power had been given to the President of the Republic, or because there was too much emphasis on unicameralism. Under the parliamentary system the cabinet in general and the Prime Minister in particular are the principal agents of government. Whatever strengthens their authority (within the limits of democracy) strengthens the government. Overemphasis on either the Head of the State, or the powers of a second chamber, would detract from this goal.

The Constitution of 1946, like its predecessor, provided for the election of the President in a joint meeting of the two chambers. (The first of them was now given the name "National Assembly" in order to underline its claim to be the depository of popular sovereignty. The second was, with appropriate modesty, named "Council of the Republic." [39]) This mode of selection must be defended against the widespread criticism which it has encountered. Some, in particular the Gaullists, proposed an enlarged electoral college; others would have preferred direct popular election, which would be natural if the presidential system were to be established. As long as the basic rules of parliamentary government are to be followed, the present method has two advantages: it avoids the impression of presidential authority being set up in competition to cabinet authority, and it deëmphasizes the partisan background of the President. The narrower the body electing the President, the likelier it is that the partisan career of the man chosen to represent the nation as a whole, and to set the wheels of government by party in motion when they are stalled (as in the case of a government resignation), will recede into the background. For similar reasons it is logical that a majority of those voting should be required in the joint session of the National Assembly and the Council of the Republic. This requirement did lead to prolonged wrangling in December, 1953, when the second President of the Fourth Republic had to be chosen. During the Third Republic when both Deputies and Senators were elected under the majority system, there never was any difficulty in choosing a President by an absolute majority of the votes cast; if matters turned out differently under the Fourth Republic, the reason lies in a system of voting which led to the election of too many Deputies not animated by a spirit of compromise.

Even under such conditions there is everything to be said for requiring the election of a President by an absolute majority. If a mere plurality sufficed, a fairly large group of the Right or of the Left could place its candidate into the President's chair without coming to terms with the center. For example, a candidate of the major Rightist groups not even acceptable to the center would hardly enjoy the confidence of the Left. On the other hand, there should be no objection if the search for a man able to secure an absolute majority eliminates all "strong" candidates. The presidency is not intended for outstanding political leaders, who should, instead, aim for the premiership. All the President ought to do is to promote the smooth functioning of the political mechanism. When Georges Clemenceau said, on the occasion of a presidential election, "I vote for the most stupid one," he indicated that, so far as his knowledge of parliamentary government was concerned, he was a little "stupid" himself. Men of his type are little suited to the President's task of impartial moderator. In 1953 it developed that while Joseph Laniel, a definite partisan, could not secure an absolute majority, René Coty, who not only had many friends and few enemies, but was also an expert of some note in the field of constitutional government, was able to vault this hurdle. The Republic was well served by the result.

The criticism directed against the Constitution of the Fourth Republic is equally unwarranted when it is directed against the type of bicameralism which finally emerged. It should be obvious that a weak government would become weaker if confronted with two power-ful parliaments rather than one. The compromise adopted by the second Constituent Assembly is basically sound: The Council of the Republic is not to have the right to overthrow a government; it is to have a share in legislation, but no absolute veto. Originally, a hostile vote of the Council of the Republic could be overridden only by the affirmative vote of an absolute majority in the National Assembly. Such majorities were difficult to obtain in a body so badly divided, and the Council of the Republic soon became more important than it had been anticipated. On the other hand, the Council of the Republic did not have the right to initiate legislation; during the first weeks of a new session its members might have to cool their heels as no measures on which they could act had as yet been sent to them by the National Assembly.

The modification of the Constitution embodied in the Constitu-tional Law of December 7, 1954, changed this situation. The Council was given the right to initiate legislation, with the exception of bills intended to authorize the ratification of treaties, or budgetary and financial bills. Since that time the "shuttle" is again in operation be-tween the two chambers, as bills can be sent back and forth repeatedly until agreement is reached. In the case of ordinary laws the Assembly may now override a veto by the Council of the Republic with a simple majority one hundred days from the day on which a bill was submitted to the Council for the second reading; the time interval is reduced for emergency bills. This new arrangement has, by and large, proven satisfactory. The Council (whose members reassumed, in December, 1948, officially the title "Senator," which courtesy had bestowed on them all along) is now, in the main, the "Chamber of Scrutiny and of Reflection" which a second chamber ought to be.

However, one, so far minor, development should be noted in pass-ing. First, the constitutional rule to the contrary, ministers have begun to state before the Council that, if a certain measure were rejected, they would resign. This, of course, means putting up the question of confidence. No serious difficulties have as yet arisen out of this situa-tion, and none are anticipated. Still, the situation is quite different from what it was intended to be.

It is interesting to note that the rise in the prestige of the Council of the Republic dates from the election law of September 23, 1948. The first elections had taken place under a complicated, indirect sys-tem of P.R. It gave the larger parties an even greater advantage over the small ones than the law for the election of the National Assembly. Apart from this fact the Council constituted, in its composition, a duplicate of the National Assembly. Since 1948 the Senators have been elected by special electoral colleges which meet in each *département*. Its members are the *département's* Deputies to the National Assembly, the members of the departmental councils, and the representatives of the municipalities, who constitute the largest number by far. In cities of more than 9,000 inhabitants which elect their councils under P.R., the councillors themselves are members of the electoral college; in all others the councillors, themselves elected under the majority system, elect delegates by majority vote. In these cases the majority principle is applied twice in succession, and its moderating effects are cumulative. So far as the electoral colleges are concerned, the 79 *départements* with three Senators or less decide by majority vote with a second ballot. In these *départements* Communists are, as a rule, not elected. In the 11 largest *départements* elections take place under P.R., and extremists have an opportunity. In the first Council of the Republic elected under indirect P.R. the Communists constituted, with 88 members, the strongest group. Its successor, elected under the new system, saw Communists and fellow-travellers reduced to 24 Senators, the fifth strongest group. The Radicals, as typical centrists, naturally again became, with 85 members, the leading group, as they had been in the old Senate.

The new method of election had its drawbacks as it strongly favored the rural over the urban areas. Still, it produced a body free from the confusion characteristic of the National Assembly. The Council's procedure was dignified, and it could always reach decisions. Thus, it was able to make the most of its limited constitutional opportunities. Somehow it seemed to represent the French nation better than its more powerful rival, the National Assembly, which continued to be elected by *proportional* representation.

THE CONSTITUTION AND EXECUTIVE STABILITY.

The most important provisions of the Constitution of 1946 are those relating to the appointment, and functions, of the executive. According to the original Constitution, the Prime Minister was to be "designated" by the President of the Republic. He was then to present himself to the National Assembly, where he had to be confirmed by an absolute majority of that body's members. This requirement might have worked well enough in a parliament elected under the majority system where, as a rule, adequate majorities could be expected. It was bound to lead to considerable difficulties in a parliament elected under P.R. Some of the crises of the Fourth Republic were aggravated by this circumstance. Thus, during the interval between May 21, 1953, when René Mayer resigned, and June 26, when Joseph Laniel was confirmed by the Assembly, Mendès-France failed because he had only obtained 301 votes instead of the required 314, and Bidault failed with 313 votes, one less than the absolute majority; both had obtained a simple majority.

The requirement of an absolute majority for the confirmation of a Premier is among those abolished in the Constitutional Law of December 7, 1954. According to the new version of Article 45, the Premier designate is to choose his ministers first and then [40] to appear before the Assembly where he can now receive his "investiture" by a simple majority. The fear has been expressed that, while crises are now easier to solve, they might occur more frequently; the Deputies, realizing that it is now easier to replace a cabinet, might hesitate less before overthrowing it. So far this fear has not been confirmed.

The law of December 7, 1954, also slightly modified Articles 49 and 50 which deal with votes of confidence and votes of censure. The requirement that votes of confidence cannot be requested except by the Prime Minister, and after deliberation by the cabinet, is continued. It had been circumvented in the past and will be circumvented in the future, as nothing prevents a Prime Minister from stating in the course of debate that he will resign if a certain measure is not passed. Originally, however, the balloting on a formal request for a vote of confidence, or a vote of censure, could not take place until "one full day after the request has been made to the Assembly." This meant that, if the request was made at noon on Monday, the balloting could not start until the following Wednesday, beginning, of course, immediately after midnight—when such votes were indeed taken repeatedly. The "cooling-off period" is now limited to 24 hours; in the above case, voting could begin at noon on Tuesday. Thus, the time interval remains long enough to rule out the element of surprise. While this is no longer as important as it would have been during the Third Republic, the provision can, in its present form, do no harm as it avoids the delays and the irritations connected with the old one. Since a French Prime Minister may have to request votes of confidence "by the dozen," this saving of time and nerves is significant. Besides, the splintering of groups and the loosening of discipline which have occurred in recent years do make a "cooling-off period" desirable.

No change was made in the provision that a vote of confidence can be refused only by an absolute majority (Article 49), or in the companion rule that a vote of censure can be adopted only in the same manner (Article 50). Both rules constitute an attempt to solve a problem by looking away from it. No government will be able to perform its duties if it has received a negative reply to the question of confidence, whether its opponents constitute a majority of a parliament's total membership or not. Thus, when in February 1952 a request for a vote of confidence by the first cabinet of Edgar Faure was denied with 309 to 283 votes (the absolute majority being 314), Faure resigned immediately. On the other hand, Premier Joseph Laniel who, on June 12, 1954, had been defeated by a vote of 306 to 293, would have liked to stay in office. Instead of simply notifying the President of the Republic that he was resigning, he merely "offered" to resign, hoping that a way might be found for him to remain. Several of his ministers declared, however, that they were definitely resigning. President Coty did not relish the prospect of having to find a new Prime Minister during the height of the Indochina crisis, but soon discovered that he could not avoid it, and he accepted Laniel's "offer." Certainly, the usefulness of any cabinet has come to an end with the announcement of a negative vote by the Assembly on a question of confidence (or a postive vote on a motion of censure), whether an absolute majority has been reached or not. A government trying to take advantage of legal technicalities in order to stay in office would deprive itself of that degree of moral credit without which even the weakest French cabinet cannot carry on.

Actually, the attempt to protect a cabinet made in Articles 49 and 50 of the Constitution created the appearance that something was being done to promote stability where there was no intention to pay the price. The same applies to the right of dissolution as it is regulated in the original version at least of Articles 51 and 52 of the Constitution. The entanglements surrounding it were typical of what Professor Mirkine-Guetzévitch [41] has called "rationalized parliamentarism"— detailed written constitutions calculated to spell out every possibility in detail, and to guard against every conceivable danger of abuse on the part of the government. Nothing serious was ever done to prevent abuses of parliament or the parties composing it.

In France, under the Constitution of 1946, there was to be no dissolution during the first eighteen months of a new National Assembly. The purpose was to prevent arbitrary dissolutions of the type carried out in Germany in 1932, which will be discussed below. Afterwards, if during an eighteen-month period two cabinets had been overthrown with an absolute majority of the votes, the cabinet could decide to dissolve the Assembly. The President of the Republic was then, as a matter of duty, to promulgate the official decree. Thereupon the Prime Minister was to be replaced by the President of the Assembly who, in turn, had to appoint a new Minister of the Interior "with the approval of the Bureau of the Assembly." Members of the political parties not represented in the cabinet would have to be appointed as ministers without portfolio. These tortuous provisions were to prevent a government which had dissolved the Assembly from using its power over the administration, and the police, to influence the elections. In this respect, the constitution-makers were haunted by the ghost of Napoleon III, as they were haunted by the ghost of the Weimar Republic in others.

If these rules were intended to make the weapon of dissolution into "a wooden sword," as it was called by Pierre Cot, the architect of the first (and, therefore, also more or less the second) Constitution, they were excellent; otherwise they constituted an exercise in stultification. A Prime Minister requesting his cabinet to vote the dissolution of the Assembly would, at the same time, have asked them to put him, and his Minister of the Interior, out of office. That parties not represented in the cabinet before the dissolution were afterwards to provide ministers without portfolio meant that whatever remained of the government's homogeneity was to be jeopardized. Alongside with other opposition parties the Communists would, of course, have had the right to be included in the cabinet.

These specific requirements were scrapped in the law of December 7, 1954. Henceforth, the entire cabinet was to remain in office after dissolution. Only if a motion of censure had been adopted by an absolute majority, the Speaker of the National Assembly was to become Prime Minister and Minister of the Interior. Such a possibility was, however, unlikely to materialize. If French cabinets fall because of a vote in the National Assembly (instead of resigning before a vote is taken), the occasion is virtually always provided by a request for a vote of confidence.

Thus the sillier restrictions surrounding the right of parliamentary dissolution were eliminated, but the more serious ones remained intact. An Assembly, able to overthrow a cabinet during the first eighteen months of its term without having to fear a dissolution, was bound to develop habits of irresponsibility certain to be carried over into the balance of its life. Furthermore, there were ways of avoiding a dissolution even in the ensuing period. One of them was to defeat a government with less than an absolute majority, enough Deputies voting against it to place it into a minority, but not enough to produce an absolute majority. This maneuver was executed on June 12, 1954, when Laniel was overthrown. Two days earlier, under conditions not deemed decisive, 324 Deputies had voted against him, ten more than the "constitutional" majority. Some Gaullist Deputies included in that number were, however, persuaded not to vote on June 12,[42] and the result was the above-mentioned vote of 306 to 293.

Just to complicate matters, if it is possible to maneuver in such a way as to subvert the constitutional provisions granting the right of dissolution, there is also room for counter-maneuvers. Thus, on November 29, 1955, a vote of confidence requested by the second cabinet of Edgar Faure resulted in 318 votes cast against, four more than an absolute majority, and 218 in favor. Faure's opponents were flabbergasted; they had wanted to force him out, but with less than "the constitutional majority." A glance at the low number of votes cast *for* the cabinet (218) while as late as on November 12, 285 Deputies had voted for it, and only 247 against, suggests the answer: some of Faure's supporters had voted against him in order to give his cabinet a chance to dissolve the Assembly.

This does not end the list of possible maneuvers. Whenever a cabinet—such as the one headed by Mendès-France—takes office within eighteen months of the time that another cabinet was overthrown with an absolute majority, the Assembly may, if the eighteen-month period is expiring within a relatively short time, simply wait before it puts its knife in the cabinet's back. Or it may find it possible to resort to the device described by Dorothy Pickles: [43] ". . . it has been alleged that at least one Prime Minister took office only on an unofficial understanding that he would *not* dissolve, if constitutionally empowered to do so." The dependence of a French Prime Minister upon the Assembly is so great that the temptation to yield to the request for a "gentleman's agreement" of this type may be overpowering.

Therefore, the manner in which the French Constitution grants the right of dissolution constitutes a standing invitation to political dishonesty. It can be said (and it has been said frequently) that all that is needed is political leaders with a strong enough conscience to make the Constitution work as intended. A theologian would say that such advice comes under the heading of "counsels of perfection." There are many things which people should not do but which, human nature being as it is, are likely to be done just the same. Where institutions of the type described exist, the facts of political life make action in conformity with moral standards difficult. Keen competition for power is a major characteristic of political life; he who hesitates in this game may find that his place has been taken by someone else. Again, we must recall Professor Goetz Briefs' "law of marginal morality": in political, as well as in economic competition, there is a tendency for the people with the lowest morality to force their standards on the others. This happens all the more easily because political leaders find themselves in the midst of a whirlpool; decisions have to be taken with little time to reflect.[44]

There is a solution to this problem and, as Americans, we can, once again, take pride in those responsible for our Constitution. On August 14, 1787, Roger Sherman said, in the course of the debates in the Constitutional Convention: "The Constitution should lay as few temptations as possible in the way of those in power." [45] Alexander Hamilton stated: "We must take man as we find him; and if we expect him to serve the public, must interest his passions in doing so. A reliance on pure patriotism had been the source of many of our errors." [46] This remark has often been interpreted as evidence of Machiavellianism; it was merely intended to warn against perfectionism. What Alexander Hamilton and his associates meant to do was to "put human nature to work." They wanted institutions which would make it possible for people to work for the general welfare without sacrificing their own legitimate interests. The need for such institutions was denied in the America of the 1780's as much as in the France of the 1940's and 1950's. Those advocating a new Constitution were told that, if only the states would do their duty under the Articles all would be well. Hamilton and his associates knew that the "law of marginal morality" made such action unlikely; as long as, for example, one state did not make its contribution to the common treasury, most of the others saw no reason why *they* should pay. The result was perennial bankruptcy for the Congress of the Confederation. The situation changed when the new Constitution went into effect; the Federal Government itself was given power to impose, and collect, revenues (in particular in the painless way of import duties); the beggar became a prince, and was able to pay the debts of the states as well as his own.

If, then, the French want to eliminate political trickery in regard to the right of parliamentary dissolution, they should deprive potential tricksters of their opportunities. As we have seen, in the "pure" form of parliamentary government the Prime Minister can ask the Head of the State for a dissolution in the reasonable expectation that he will get it. No politician can interfere. The ones who bear the burden of responsibility make the decision, after which everything depends upon the vote of the people.

THE ELECTORAL SYSTEM.

In France, the people cannot decide the issue between government and opposition even if there is a dissolution. They can do no more than vote for one of a number of unrelated political parties, none of which is ever strong enough to form a government of its own. France is, in the words of William Henry Chamberlin,[47] "A Nation in Fragments."

Ultimately, of course, any nation consists of "fragments." Unless the proper "channels of government" are available to direct the different and divergent currents of social life into one major political stream, and keep it there, fragments are all that exist. Countries as large, and beset with as many problems in the fields of both domestic and foreign policy, as France, are particularly exposed to the dangers of fragmentation. The Anglo-Saxon countries have enjoyed the benefits of the "proper channels of government," in particular the plurality system of voting, for so long that they are not even aware of their operation. Republican France has not been that fortunate. A decade before the vote of January 2, 1956, which *The Economist* termed "A Vote Against Government," [48] Michel Debré [49] wrote:

> The division of society into particularist fragments is encouraged (by P.R.) and the mental equilibrium of a nation is definitely affected. Politics is no longer an appeal to the civic sense of the citizens. It becomes the appeal to their interests, and a dramatic tendency is encouraged: the one which causes politics to be dominated by professional, religious, and social rivalries, and, at the same time, feeds these rivalries on poison incessantly renovated by politics.

That France should have voted as a "nation of fragments" is, therefore, hardly surprising. There can, of course, always be compensating factors. In this case, *The Economist* predicted: "The parties which support the Republic will find themselves thrust together by common weakness more compulsively than before . . ." [50] The threats from the Algerian rebels and from Colonel Nasser did the rest. If, however, Guy Mollet was enabled to outlast his predecessors, he himself was well aware of the precariousness of the situation, just as he himself had gone far in the direction of pointing to the remedy.[51]

It is, then, the tragedy of France that while, under the Third Republic, she had a type of majority voting which, in spite of its weaknesses,[52] did offer the people a clear choice between positive alternatives, she lacked an effective right of parliamentary dissolution; under the Fourth Republic there was to be a case of parliamentary dissolution, but without the majority system. The two belong together; neither can have adequate results without the other.

While, however, constitution-makers may be inclined to provide for a right of dissolution (even if, as in France, a right of sorts), they will insist on ignoring the majority system of voting. Yet, without the majority system a dissolution may be inconclusive, as it was in France in 1956, or dangerous, as it proved to be in Germany during the final years of the Weimar Republic. Debré, as mentioned above, had wanted to treat the system of voting as a special "organic law"; Capitant insisted during the debates of the first Constituent Assembly that the system of voting would determine basic aspects of the Constitution. Therefore, it could not be regulated by the Assembly as an ordinary law; the people themselves should be given an opportunity to decide between the major types of electoral systems.[53] He found the support of a few Deputies, such as René Pleven, the Resistance leader, and of Edouard Herriot, but not of a majority.[54]

A few words on the effects of P.R. Its immediate results, as the German sociologist, Max Weber,[55] put it, may be a relative stability in the strength of the major parties, whose "representatives sit peacefully side by side and, sharing the jobs, conduct affairs by compromise." Weber continues that this is "a most peaceful state of affairs for *normal* times," implying that matters may change in abnormal times. In France they changed on account of the feeling of revolt caused by some of the aspects of "tripartism." In the words of Professor Wright: [56] "The 1946 experiment in government left an offensive odor in the nostrils of many truly democratic Frenchmen."

One of the results of this popular reaction was the reappearance of General De Gaulle on the political scene. According to official statistics, his "Rally of the French People" secured, in the municipal elections of 1947, in cities with more than 9,000 inhabitants, 28.1 per cent of the votes for its own lists, while 10.6 per cent of the votes were cast for coalition lists in which the RPF participated. This marked the beginning of that revolution in the party system which may follow upon the "pluralistic stagnation" [57] characteristic of the first phase of P.R. The French Republicans had the good fortune that no new elections to the National Assembly were due at this time. Jules Moch, the Socialist leader, reminded his friends several years later of what they could have expected had they been forced to face the voters:

> We forget quickly. Let us recall the year 1947. The Communist party saw its effectives grow and increased its pressure on the state . . . At the same time Gaullism, like a straw fire, seemed to encompass all of public opinion. A dissolution of parliament was demanded everywhere. New elections would have yielded a Chamber absolutely incapable of governing, consisting, a third each, of Communists, Republicans, and Gaullists. No designated Prime Minister could have obtained the 310 votes needed, according to the Constitution, in order to obtain the "investiture." [57a]

The situation, then, would have been similar to the one which arose in Germany in 1932, when Nazis and Communists combined had a majority, and the formation of a Republican cabinet was impossible. De Gaulle was, of course, no Hitler, and there is at least a possibility that, had elections taken place at that time, a constructive compromise between the RPF and some of the Republicans could have been reached.

Still, it was realized that the moderate parties—Léon Blum coined for them the term "Third Force"—could not confront the people again with the old system of voting. It did not escape public notice that in the departmental elections, where the old version of the majority system was still in use, the results were quite different from those obtained in P.R. elections. Thus, in March, 1949, when one-half of the *cantons* elected their councillors, 1,508 in all, the Communists gained only 37 seats, a little more than two per cent of the total, although, as in 1945, most of these seats were won in large urban constituencies. The Communist percentage in the popular vote had declined to 23.5 per cent as against 28.6 per cent in the elections to the National Assembly.[58] The RPF saw its percentage of the total vote decline to 25.3 per cent; it did secure 380 seats, some of which were also situated in populous urban constituencies. If we disregard this modification we may say that the RPF received about the same percentage of seats as of votes. It did not, therefore, obtain any of the benefits of the majority system. The moderate parties between them secured more than 70 per cent of the seats. Obviously, while they were certain of a disastrous defeat in elections held under P.R., they were able to face any majority elections with confidence, even if an apportionment favorable to rural areas played into their hands in the provincial elections.

Consequently, when, in the fall of 1950, the current Prime Minister, René Pleven, outlined his program of government, he said: "When I am asked about the political future of France, I am often tempted to answer: 'We need a majority.' For that reason . . . I made it a part of my declaration of 'investiture' that my government should engage its existence on a reform of the election law." [59] Pleven overestimated his strength. He could not govern without the MRP, which had, on previous occasions, teamed up with the Communists to save P.R. and was ready to do so again. Still, in 1950 and 1951, the MRP leaders realized that a measure of electoral reform was imperative, and a rather ambiguous law was adopted. Its most important feature [60] was the "linking" of lists, the so-called *apparentement*. Wherever a single list, or a group of linked lists, secured a majority of the votes cast, it took all of the seats; a group of lists would distribute them among its affiliates in proportion to their strength.

THE 1951 ELECTIONS.

This is not the place to discuss the numerous and fundamental objections which can be raised against this system. At this juncture, suffice it to say that its immediate purpose was accomplished. It has been calculated that, under the old system (assuming, of course, that the distribution of the votes had been the same) the RPF and Communists with a little less than 49 per cent of the votes would have secured a clear majority of the seats.[61] The reason is that the distribution of the seats under the old law favored large parties, not only on account of the small size of the constituencies, but also on account of the system governing the distribution of the seats among the lists. Actually, the parties of the moderate Right and center secured 402 of the 625 seats which form the basis for this comparison.[62] The Communists had secured only 103 seats instead of the 180 the old law would have given them, and the RPF 120 instead of 144.

Thus the parties of the center and the moderate Right had secured a breathing spell. The Right divided into the new "Independents" and the "Peasants" parties and experienced a political revival. The moderate parties as a whole secured the further advantage of room for a little maneuvering when first a part of the RPF Deputies became willing to support a cabinet, and later most of the remainder as well. This meant that it was no longer necessary for all moderate parties to vote for a government; some could afford to oppose it without placing it in a minority. French parliamentarism, for the time being, regained that "safety valve"[63] which is so vital for the health of democratic government.

It was no less important that the government of Antoine Pinay (March 8 to December 22, 1952) managed to slow down the inflationary process. The French economy was given a fairly stable monetary basis. With its help it entered a phase of vigorous expansion. The Pinay government was also remarkable for the popularity of its chief, whose personality strongly appealed to the "average Frenchman." This helped his policies, but also led to resentment within the Assembly, as the Deputies see in every Premier with a genuine popular appeal a threat to their own position. In the end, Pinay found it necessary to resign without risking a final vote by the Assembly. Subsequently, a characteristic incident occurred during the crisis which extended from May 21, the day when René Mayer resigned, to July 26, 1953, when Joseph Laniel secured an absolute majority. Pinay was one of those upon whom President Auriol called to form a new cabinet. The Deputies, however, reacted negatively to him from the start. They left little doubt that they did not want a man who had a definite appeal with the people.[64]

Laniel was succeeded by Mendès-France, who deliberately sought the popular appeal which had come to Pinay spontaneously. Lightning-like actions in the field of foreign affairs (including the agreement on Indochina and the granting of autonomy to Tunisia) caught the eye of the public. They gave the Premier a reputation which, again, could not but lead to resentment in the Assembly. The manner of Mendès-France was certainly at times so brusque as to appear undemocratic. Besides, by bringing about the defeat of the European Defense Community (EDC)[65] with the help of Communist votes, he understandably incurred the enmity of the "Europeans" in the Assembly, in particular the MRP. When he lost his final request for a vote of confidence, he made the unprecedented attempt to address the Assembly after the announcement of the vote; he was hooted off the tribune with charges that he was a "Fascist."

THE 1956 ELECTIONS.

A serious improvement in the institutional framework of French government seemed, however, to be in the making during the final weeks preceding Edgar Faure's defeat on November 30, 1955. The cabinet Mendès-France had proposed a return to the old single-member constituency with second ballot, and the bill had the signature of every minister. No serious debate on the subject took place before October 30, 1955.[66] At that time it was intertwined with Faure's demand for early elections, which could be arranged by a special law. A most confused situation developed. The National Assembly tended toward the retention of P.R., and the Council of the Republic insisted on the majority system. Finally, on November 9, the National Assembly voted against the majority system 298 to 293. There followed several "rectifications of the vote," which changed the figures to 301 votes for the majority system and 294 against it. Legally, the result stood as first announced, but the moral pressure in favor of the old system became stronger than ever. Mendès-France and his friends emphasized that, according to the latest investigations by the French Institute for Public Opinion Research, 52 per cent of the voters favored the majority system (with second ballot) and only 25 per cent opposed it,[67] the rest having no opinion.

These discussions became irrelevant when the debate which began on the afternoon of November 29 ended, in the early hours of

November 30, with the rejection of the vote of confidence demanded by Faure, and the Assembly was dissolved. This dissolution has led to a great deal of controversy, mostly along partisan lines. Faure's supporters argued that if nobody ever used the right of dissolution, the old taboo, dating from the misinterpretation of the results produced by MacMahon's dissolution, would never be lifted. Faure's opponents were on safe ground, however, when they argued that a dissolution without a return to the majority system would only aggravate the divisions in the Assembly. On this occasion, they predicted that the *apparentements*, with the help of which the moderate parties had saved themselves in 1951, would not be concluded this time in a manner guaranteeing enough moderate victories.

The *apparentements*, indeed, did not accomplish much on this occasion. The moderate parties were divided into two major groups, the followers of Faure and those of Mendès-France. The latter established the "Republican Front," consisting of the Socialists, most of the Radicals, and certain minor elements. *Apparentements* straddling this "great divide" were impossible. The effectiveness of Right and center combinations was further reduced by the strong showing of Pierre Poujade's "Union for the Defense of Merchants and Artisans" (U.D.A.C.); this newcomer on the political scene secured 12.1 per cent of the votes instead of the 5 per cent conceded it at the start of the campaign.[68]

This development was the final factor which deprived the parties of the moderate Right and center of a chance to secure a parliamentary majority.[69] Fifty-two of Poujade's followers entered the National Assembly. At the extreme Left, there were 150 Communists (including the fellow-travelling "Progressives"). The total number of Deputies elected was 596, since elections for the 30 Algerian seats could not be held. The Communists and Poujadists thus constituted a third of the new Assembly's members. As a result, the moderate parties had lost the freedom of maneuver which they had enjoyed in the old Assembly; henceforth, most of those who, in 1955, had lined up behind either Edgar Faure or Mendès-France had to join in supporting a cabinet in order to provide it with a majority.[70]

This element of weakness was, at the same time, an element of strength. It encouraged the moderate parties to "cooperate with the inevitable." Premier Mollet decided to form a relatively homogeneous government of the "Republican Front," and this proved to be an added advantage. The moderate Right and center supported him on account of his willingness to use force against the Algerian rebels; in this respect it was said that the men of the Left were in power, but the policies were those of the Right. When he fell, it was inevitable that more or less the same majority should be constituted; yet, it was more brittle than ever, and *The Economist* [70a] called the cabinet of Bourgès-Maumaury "the weakest cabinet France has had since the war."

CONSTITUTIONAL REFORM PROPOSALS.

Nobody saw a prospect of stability in this situation. Advocates of a fundamental reform remained numerous; their plans, however, were different to the point of mutually excluding, and defeating, one another. It may be well to summarize the major proposals. We begin with those aiming at changes within the framework of the parliamentary system.

So far as the right of parliamentary dissolution is concerned, there are first the advocates of "discretionary dissolution." They would give the right to the President of the Republic, expecting it to be exercised on the proposal of either the Prime Minister or of the cabinet. Some would grant this right without any restrictions; others would stipulate that certain conditions must be met, for example, that the Assembly must have been in existence for a certain period of time. As we have seen, such restrictions can have the result of jeopardizing the purpose of the reform; there will be no fundamental break with the bad habits of the past unless the Assembly is, from the very outset, put on notice that any serious move against a cabinet is as dangerous to itself as to the intended victim.

Others, such as former Premier Paul Reynaud, are of the opinion that "dissolution will be automatic or it will not be." They are afraid that a Premier or a cabinet might not make use of the right of dissolution for fear of being ostracized by their colleagues. Reynaud's latest plan [71] provides that, if a cabinet is, within two years of its installation, placed into a minority as a result of the denial of a motion of confidence, or the adoption of a vote of censure, the Prime Minister can demand that the Assembly take a new vote within three days. If it is again negative, the Assembly is automatically dissolved. Reynaud expects that adoption of this plan would assure each cabinet a duration of at least two years.

However, the first question is to what extent a Prime Minister would make use of his new right. He might prefer to resign upon learning that enough of his supporters have left him to place him in a minority. Nor would it increase his authority if he had to confront the Assembly again after having lost a formal vote before that body. Lastly, one wonders why, if there is to be a reform at all, it should not set its sights higher. As long as the aim is the introduction of the plebiscitary element into French politics, this goal should be pursued consistently. There ought to be a clear understanding that governments are to rest upon a popular decision; changes in the nature of a government (barring exceptional cases, such as war), could be made only after a new popular consultation.[72] Such results cannot be anticipated unless a clear alternative is presented to the people in an election; this requires the use of the majority system, as well as an effective, and *always* available, right of dissolution.

As long as there is no clear awareness of the goal to be reached, any reform (of the right of dissolution in particular) risks bogging down in half-measures. Certainly, there is a measure of progress as a result of the dissolution of November, 1955. Regrettable as its consequences were in other respects, it seems to have cleared the air of some of the complexes which surrounded this institution since its misuse by MacMahon. It is characteristic of the good sense of Guy Mollet that when, on January 31, 1956, he outlined his program to the National Assembly, he should have specifically endorsed the principle of further facilitating the right of dissolution.

Half-measures remain, however, popular. Thus it is proposed that the Assembly elect a Prime Minister for the full extent of its term. If nothing else were done,[73] instability would probably be the same as now. French cabinets ask the question of confidence for the simple reason that there is no other way for them to make a majority stay together, and in order to have it pass badly needed measures. A cabinet unable either to resign or to dissolve would soon be unable to do anything at all.

Other proposals aim at imitating the so-called "positive vote of censure" contained in the Bonn Constitution. The Assembly is not to have the right to overthrow a cabinet unless its majority approves at the same time either a new Prime Minister, as required under the West German Constitution, or a new program, or both. Again it is overlooked that the real threat to the life of a French government does not arise from the threat of assassination from without, but from that of the coalition cancer within. Once enough of its supporters break away to destroy its majority, its usefulness has come to an end.

We may omit a discussion of a number of minor reform proposals. Brief reference must be made, however, to the proposed reform of the amending procedure. At present, Article 90 of the Constitution provides that the National Assembly, with an absolute majority of its members, has first to vote that there is to be a revision. The change is then made in the form of an ordinary law. Unless it is adopted by a two-thirds vote of the Assembly, or a three-fifths vote of both the

Assembly and the Council of the Republic, it is submitted to a referendum. Paul Reynaud and his friends propose that henceforth the
Assembly and the Council are to adopt a reform separately; afterwards, they make the final decision in a joint session by majority vote.
On the whole, these were the rules of the Third Republic.

Such proposals have, however, the drawback of antagonizing the
Socialists who know that, as long as a two-thirds or a three-fifths majority is required, no reform can be adopted without them. They conclude that the very purpose of the proposal is to promote changes
which they could not accept. The Socialists of our day are, it seems,
inclined to repeat the mistake made by Léon Blum when he opposed
Doumergue's reform plans. They overlook that any increase in executive authority would be as likely to benefit them as anybody else. Still,
one wonders why Socialist approval should not be sought from the
start for the reforms to be made. It would be a great advantage to
have their cooperation. There can be no amending of the amending
procedure without them anyway; thus, it would be simpler to agree
with them first on the required changes in the constitutional structure.
In the end, there is always the safety valve of passing reforms with a
simple majority and submitting them to the people in a referendum.
Public opinion polls have long since shown that popular majorities
for the necessary measures exist. Or are French political leaders so
fearful of the people that they do not want to invoke their verdict even
in the case of constitutional reforms prepared by themselves?

A PRESIDENTIAL SYSTEM FOR FRANCE?

The fact that the proponents of a reform of the parliamentary
system have been so half-hearted in their proposals goes far toward
explaining why there has been a revival of plans providing for a presidential system. In appearance, at least, they go to the heart of the
matter. If the aim is to give the executive a plebiscitary character, it
seems natural to suggest that this not be done in the roundabout way
provided by the type of parliamentary system existing in England and
in the older Commonwealth countries, but directly, by having the
people elect the executive for a definite period.

The current discussion of the presidential system was initiated
by Professor Georges Vedel, whose most stimulating report to "The
Committee of Studies for the Republic" has been mentioned before.[74]
According to him the "chief of the executive power" is to be elected
by the people directly. In view of the French multiple-party system
two or three ballots, possibly telescoped into one by the alternative
vote,[75] might have to be held in order to secure an absolute majority.

Vedel admits that it might be desirable to have, in addition to the head of the government, a Head of the State patterned on the model of the President of the Republic. This modification was one of those suggested by Professor Duverger. Vedel insists that the members of the cabinet be appointed by the head of the executive, and be responsible to him alone; Deputies and Senators would have to resign before accepting ministerial office.

Such a system introduces a dualism between the executive and the legislature. Naturally, in the ensuing debate, the question was asked whether this dualism had been overcome to a sufficient extent even in the United States, or whether, on certain occasions, American executive leadership had not been less effective than desirable. It was added that in this respect matters would be more difficult in France than in the United States. In the words of André Philip:

> Under the American system, the President's impotence is compensated for by the fact that the President is more often than not the leader of a party which holds the majority in Congress, and especially by the spoils system, which gives the President, at least at the beginning of his term of office, the possibility of exerting pressure on the members of the Assembly by refusing to appoint their candidates to important official positions.

The multiple-party system, as it exists in France, would, indeed, make the task of the chief executive more difficult. The American President does have to deal with individual members of Congress who are at times difficult to handle. All of them, however, have been elected under the plurality system. Thus, all true extremists have been kept outside the halls of Congress, and the majority of its members have always been fairly close to the political center. In France, this would be vastly different under P.R., and still different under a majority system with second ballot. Executive leadership would, for this reason alone, prove harder to achieve than in the United States.

The more detailed discussions of the subject have shown the possibility of compromises. Both Vedel and Duverger would accept the possibility of resolving a deadlock between executive and Assembly by a dissolution, which could be brought about by either the executive or the Assembly, and which would lead to a new election for both. Under such conditions, a presidential system might have a fair chance to accomplish what the proponents of a genuine reform of the parliamentary system want: the combination of the parliamentary and the plebiscitary principle. The good points of the two systems could be combined even more easily if ministers taken from the ranks of parliament could retain their seats; it is, however, interesting to note that Professor Goguel,[76] in one of the most stimulating contributions made to this discussion, insists not only on excluding this possibility, but also on making members of Assembly and Senate ineligible for cabinet membership even if they are willing to resign their seats.

The reception of these proposals has been disappointing to their authors. Rejection has been almost uniform on the part of the leading political groups, as well as of the non-political organizations. The proponents of the presidential system feel, however, that the deficiencies of the French political system might, some day, become so glaring as to necessitate a rapid and radical solution; if this should happen their plans would be available.

Furthermore, we must take exception to the claim advanced by Vedel that the combination of an effective right of parliamentary dissolution and of the old type of majority voting would not suffice to overcome the social heterogeneity underlying French politics. As mentioned above, much of this heterogeneity is fictitious. Most Communist voters, for example, are anything but convinced Communists, just as most Poujadists are not convinced opponents of parliamentary government. The people attracted by these two groups present, in their great majority, nothing but a protest vote. Vedel and his friends do not deny that the majority system would, even in its weakest form, trim down the parliamentary strength of the Communist party by at least two-thirds; it would take away virtually all of the Poujadist seats. The results, we need not repeat, would not be limited to parliamentary bodies. Many of those who want to cast a protest vote tire of it in the long run when all they accomplish is to throw their votes away. Therefore, under a majority system, there would be a chance to reintegrate many Communist, and virtually all Poujadist, or other Right-wing extremist, voters, into the moderate parties.

The disappearance of most of the Communists and nearly all of the extremists of the Right from the National Assembly would, in addition, make a difference in the functioning of the French political system. As Vedel himself has put it: "If the Communist problem weakens our institutions, reciprocally the weakness of our institutions strengthens the Communist party." [77] By the same token, a better working political system (brought about by the elimination of most Communist and nearly all Rightist extremists from the Assembly) would leave fewer voters with an incentive to support extremists.

Nor should we overlook the overall difference between a multiple system of related parties, as produced by a majority system with second ballot, and a multiple system of unrelated parties, as produced by P.R. In recent years, French writers rarely recall what they, and their predecessors, wrote during the 1930's on the semi-plebiscitary nature of elections then held for the Chamber of Deputies. When, in the P.R. elections of November, 1946, the Communists secured, with 30 per cent of the total, the largest number of seats, and thereupon claimed the right to form the government, Léon Blum [78] commented:

> If one party has an absolute majority, the situation presents no difficulties. It is naturally the right of that party to form a government and to designate the premier. If a coalition of parties has presented itself to the voters with a common program . . . . the solution is just as simple: this coalition then has the right to form the government. . . . In either case, there is a right to power. This right exists because a majority exists. The authority which confers power, be it the President of the Republic or the Assembly, could not disregard this right without weakening one of the principles of democracy.

Blum, then, placed the victory of "a coalition of parties" which had "presented itself to the voters with a common program" on a par with the victory of one party. Obviously, he thought of the elections of 1936 with the clearcut victory of the Popular Front. Under the same system of voting a similarly clear decision could be expected at the present time. Thus, January, 1956, would have seen a battle between the Republican Front, headed by Guy Mollet and Pierre Mendès-France on the one hand, and its opponents, as led by Edgar Faure, on the other. One of these two groups was likely to win a parliamentary majority. Everything points to the further conclusion that within this majority those closest to the center would have had the same moderating influence that they had before 1940. The nearer a group is to the center, the nearer it is to the "marginal voter" upon whom victory depends. Social heterogeneity would not stand in the way of this process in the 1950's or 1960's any more than it did in the 1930's.

If proof for this fact was needed, it was provided in the by-election which took place in the first sector of the *Département Seine,* comprising the part of Paris which is situated on the left bank of the Seine River. Under the law of 1951, such by-elections take place under the majority system with second ballot. This particular election was the first one to test the Communist vote after the Hungarian uprisings in October, 1956. The Communist share in the total vote cast in the first ballot amounted to 20.5 per cent as compared with 26.3 per cent in the P.R. elections of January, 1956. There was no Poujadist candidate in the first ballot, but Pierre Poujade, who had not been a candidate for the elections of 1956, presented himself for the second ballot. In the Assembly elections the local Poujadist ticket, led by a young law student, had secured 7.8 per cent of the votes. Poujade himself expected to do much better, in particular since the candidate presented by the extreme Right for the first ballot, who had secured 2.1 per cent of the votes, withdrew in his favor. When Poujade received only 6.4 per cent of the vote, and the candidate of the moderate Right, Julien Tardieu, raised his percentage from 33.1 in the first ballot to 54.9 in the second, the result was a defeat for both extremes which, in its psychological reactions, went far beyond the limited decline in the voting percentages suffered by either. Speaking of Poujade's candidacy, *Le Figaro* commented:

> Paris has comprehended the danger of this candidacy of division. It has replied as it should to the noisy propaganda of the chief of the movement of Saint-Céré [the town where Poujade's headquarters are located]. Paris has, once again, voted "reasonable" and has, with discipline, presented a common front against communism.[79]

To "vote reasonable," and "with discipline" in a "common front against communism"—this is about all the French voter would have to do as the first step to place his political system back on the road to sanity. It need hardly be added that extremist groups at the Right can be as dangerous as those at the Left, and would require—and, under the majority system, be certain to elicit—the same response. The mere defeat, or disintegration, of any one group at the extreme Right, such as the Gaullists after the elections of 1951 and the Poujadists after those of 1956, does not constitute a true solution; as soon as one such group collapses others are ready to step into its shoes. A true solution requires political institutions which will always not only be strong enough to ward off an attack from the extreme Right or the extreme Left, as was done during the Third Republic, but which will also function well enough to make possible that absorption of the Republic's opponents of which the Third Republic proved incapable.

Nationwide elections under the majority system would, at any rate, produce results all over the country comparable to those achieved in the first sector of the *Département Seine*. That should suffice to reduce the present emphasis on social heterogeneity as the major source of France's political ills. Naturally, the French political pattern would derive the full benefits of such a change only if it were accompanied by a workable right of parliamentary dissolution; only in that way could the contact between a relatively homogeneous parliamentary majority, and the people, which even the "second ballot" permits, become a permanent feature. If both of these conditions were granted for some time, the parties might find it easier to take the last step needed to create a "genuine" parliamentary system: adopt the plurality system of voting.

THE PROSPECTS FOR REFORM.

There is, therefore, no lack of opportunities for fruitful reforms. The practical chances are something else again. The "vested interests" remain in evidence; André Siegfried [80] noted in 1953 that there were no less than 350 men and women in France who had been members of post-war cabinets. Not all Deputies (and Senators) are willing to relinquish the prospects enshrined in this figure; to be able to have one's name followed by *Ancien Ministre* may, in addition to everything else, be useful in an election campaign. Then, of course, there is the opposition of the Communists to any and all serious reforms, and that of the MRP to a change of the voting system.

Intellectual confusion and, in particular, lack of unity among the sincere proponents of reform is, however, an equally great obstacle. When the framers of the American Constitution prepared for their battle against the vested interests in 1787, they united in advocating those reforms which a majority of their number favored. Alexander Hamilton, for example, deemed the Constitution inadequate, but there was to be no more powerful advocate of its adoption than he.[81] So far, the French proponents of reform have shown no similar readiness to unite. Their disagreements tend to give the average Frenchman the impression of "confusion worse confounded." The need for constitutional reform has been drummed into people's ears for a full generation; the similarity of the discussion in the days of Doumergue and in our day is striking. One possible solution after another has been talked up by some and talked down by others; by this time, they have, for the average person, all been talked to death. What *The New York Times* on one occasion called "the corroding effect of Gallic wit" has done its part. What elsewhere would be accepted as a logical conclusion from established facts can, in France, always be countered with a witty remark; the listener will appear convinced as well as delighted.

It is, however, one of the most heartening aspects of the French political situation that attempts at reform never cease. Thus, the cabinet of Premier Félix Gaillard made special efforts in this direction in 1957 and in 1958. One of its members, Robert Lecourt, undertook the arduous task of bringing about agreement among the parties represented in the government. The "round table" which he organized did manage to produce a reform program. It was rather technical, and potentially ineffectual, in some of its aspects, but insofar as it attempted to make the right of parliamentary dissolution easier it aimed in the right direction.

As was pointed out immediately, however, a reform of the election law was needed even more urgently than changes in the Constitution. Both the Radicals and the Socialists took this view, and so did many Independents. The great difficulty which the cabinets formed after the 1956 elections had to face was their utter lack of homogeneity, as Socialists and Conservatives had to vote for the same men and the same measures. It is not surprising that these cabinets collapsed eventually; it is surprising that they lasted as long as they did. New elections might bring a measure of improvement even under the law of 1951, provided that enough *apparentements* were made to exclude the extremists in a sufficient number of constituencies, and that the Poujadist vote declined without being absorbed by another radical group. Still, that law had long since lost whatever moral credit it might have possessed. A more definite step toward the majority system seemed necessary even if the Assembly elected in 1956 should not be willing to adopt the majority system outright. Various compromise proposals were made; the adoption of some of them might pave the road for a more consistent reform at a later date.

ARE THE PEOPLE TO BLAME?

Whatever the result of the discussion, it makes no more sense to condemn *the* French for the deficiency of their political system, than it did to condemn *the* Germans for the crimes of Nazism. Peoples are more than a sum of individuals. What an individual may do depends on his character, but the type of "formation" which we call "character" in an individual is represented by "political form" in a nation. We have seen that John Locke rightly spoke of "the variety of views and the contrariety of interests which unavoidably happen in all collections of men." We have also seen that the establishment of the necessary unity of action as well as of the necessary degree of unity of thought to make a viable *state* depends upon those institutions which represent the country's "living Constitution." When a nation has found what Hamilton would have called "the proper channel of government," it can make full use of its potentialities. If ever a country finds itself afflicted with the type of pseudo-form with which France was saddled during the Third Republic, and even more so during the Fourth, it is constantly threatened with disruption, and to find a way out is difficult indeed.

In this respect, the people in the Anglo-Saxon countries have been a great deal more fortunate, but not through any merit of the present generation, which, in fact, is hardly aware of the blessings which the men of the past conferred upon it in this regard. During the Second World War, American and British authorities might have assisted the French with a type of guidance towards that truly democratic, and truly effective, type of political form for which the Resistance worked and suffered. Our failure to do so was complete.

We might also bear in mind what the people of France have accomplished in those fields where they were able to act without, or in spite of, their deficient political form. When, during the war, Michel Debré wrote the above-mentioned memorandum in which he set forth the motivations guiding him in drawing up the new Constitution, he emphasized that France needed renovation in three respects: an increase in the birth rate, which would renovate the country biologically, a renewed dynamism in the economic field, and political renovation. The people of France have, by this time, exceeded even the keenest hopes which Debré might have entertained in regard to the first two points. The French birth rate has increased substantially, and the country is well on its way toward biological health.[82] The French economy has maintained the upward development which began under Pinay in 1952; at the time of this writing, its rate of growth is greater than that of the United States.

We can only conclude with the words in which Robert du Jouvenel ended his classic work, *La République des Camarades* [83] on the eve of the First World War: *"La France, dont les forces sont intactes, cherche des institutions"*—"France, whose forces are intact searches for institutions." With the proper type of political institutions France would, indeed, have every reason to expect that she could not only solve her own problems but also contribute effectively to a solution of the problems from which the world around her is suffering.[84]

Chapter x v

PARLIAMENTARY GOVERNMENT
IN GERMANY: THE WEIMAR
REPUBLIC

PARLIAMENTARY MONARCHY?

In no country had the major social elements of the old feudal, bureaucratic monarchy entered into such a viable combination with the forces of the new economic and social world as in Germany. Democratic institutions were bound to come, but it would have been a gain if the substance of the new could have been allowed to take hold by saving as much as possible of the outer forms of the old. This is what happened in England, where the monarchy was the most essential ingredient of this process. Winston Churchill favored a similar solution for Germany. In his words:

> Wise policy would have crowned and fortified the Weimar Republic with a constitutional sovereign in the person of an infant grandson of the Kaiser, under a council of regency. Instead, a gaping void was opened in the national life of the German people. All the strong elements, military and feudal, which might have rallied to a constitutional monarchy and for its sake respected and sustained the new democratic and parliamentary processes, were for the time being unhinged.[1]

Mr. Churchill apparently felt that the responsibility for these developments lay exclusively with "the prejudice of the Americans against monarchy, which Mr. Lloyd George made no attempt to counteract."[2] This is, however, a misreading of history. What Churchill wanted had been done in October, 1918, when the parliamentary system of government was introduced. At first this was done on a pragmatic and inadequate basis. On September 28, 1918, Field Marshal von Hindenburg and General Ludendorff had advised the Emperor that a government must be formed immediately which could request an armistice within 24 hours; it was to be based upon the parties commanding a majority in the Reichstag. Prince Max of Baden did form a cabinet corresponding to these criteria; for the time being, it was necessary to circumvent the provisions of Bismarck's Constitution which stood in the way of parliamentary government.[3] During the night of October 3, Prince Max dispatched a note to President Wilson requesting the conclusion of an armistice, and the initiation of peace negotiations on the basis of the Fourteen Points and the subsequent addresses.

In principle, then, the road was free for parliamentary monarchy which, in the expression of a French observer, is "the best republic." [4] Besides, in Germany, the formal assumption of responsibility for the armistice and the peace by the monarchy, and the military and aristocratic elements supporting it, had all of the advantages stated by Sir Winston.

Several factors combined to frustrate what had begun not inauspiciously. Popular sentiment in the Allied countries strongly favored not only deposing the Emperor but trying him as a war criminal. The slogan "unconditional surrender" had developed a powerful appeal. Woodrow Wilson took his political life into his hands when he reached the conclusion that he was duty-bound to accept the German offer of negotiations; more than one observer felt that his willingness to do so cost his party the control of Congress in the November elections. This popular pressure was one of the reasons why Wilson, in his note to the German government of October 23, used rather vigorous language:

> Feeling that the whole peace of the world depends now on plain speaking and straightforward action, the President deems it his duty to say, without any attempt to soften what may seem harsh words, that the nations of the world do not, and cannot trust the word of those who have hitherto been the masters of German policy, and to point out once more that in concluding peace and attempting to undo the infinite injuries and injustices of this war, the Government of the United States cannot deal with any but veritable representatives of the German people, who have been assured of a genuine constitutional standing as the real rulers of Germany. If it must deal with the military masters and the monarchical autocrats of Germany now, or if it is likely to have to deal with them later in regard to the international obligations of the German Empire, it must demand, not peace negotiations but surrender. Nothing can be gained by leaving this essential thing unsaid.[5]

Wilson did accept the final changes in the German Constitution as adequate. On November 5, Secretary of State Lansing dispatched the note in which the American government, in cooperation with its Allies, undertook to bring about both an armistice and peace negotiations on the basis of the Fourteen Points and the subsequent addresses, with modifications concerning the freedom of the seas and reparations for war damage done in the occupied territories.[6] This note had been addressed to the "Imperial Government" as it then existed. Yet, it was obvious that if the monarchy was to be saved, both the Emperor and the Crown Prince [7] would have to abdicate. There was a strong revolutionary current in Germany, a part of which was not only republican, but *Spartakist*—Karl Liebknecht, Rosa Luxemburg, and others· were inspired by the example of the Russian revolution, and there was danger that the more moderate Social Democrats would lose control. If this was to be prevented, it was vital that the Emperor abdicate immediately either in favor of his grandson, or of a regent, leaving in that case the decision concerning Germany's future to a freely-elected National Assembly. William II blocked this last possibility to save the monarchy. His attitude oscillated between morose defeatism and belligerent defiance, and ended in ignominious flight. The Republic was proclaimed on November 9. A "Council of People's Commissars," consisting of three representatives of the moderate Social Democrats, and three of the Left-wing "Independents," assumed power, promising the early election of a National Assembly.

ALLIED MISTAKES.

As a result of these events the principle of monarchy became a matter of nostalgic regrets rather than of serious action. A powerful wave of negation, directed against the old order and all of its manifestations, thundered across Germany. The past seemed dead and buried. When a year or so later, a reaction against the Republic developed, it was characterized more by nationalism than by conservatism. Even as the monarchy had become unpopular on account of what had happened under William II, the republic became unpopular because it was identified with defeat and disaster. The leaders of the victorious republics in the West did nothing to forestall this development. The German republicans were naive when they expected that all would be forgotten after the change of government in their country. Still, the leaders of the great democracies in the West would have done well to concede to their fledgling German counterparts that small measure of face-saving which they craved. The German government, having been refused the right to oral negotiations, made detailed counter-proposals to the terms of peace as handed down by the Allies. Professor James T. Shotwell [8] was to comment perceptively:

No fair-minded reader of these few paragraphs can fail to ask how much of Germany's grievance against the Treaty of Versailles lay in the substance of its exactions and how much in the manner in which they were imposed. The German people, bewildered by defeat that had belied their military expectations and exhausted physically and spiritually by hardship and disaster, were now called upon to face a humiliation which struck fully as deep into their moral life as the material losses seemed to threaten their chance of economic recovery.

To be sure, the Allied leaders did not act as they did on account of their personal preferences. They yielded to that "sudden breeze of passion" to which even a well ordered "representative republic" may become prey in times of war.

NO CONSTITUTIONAL ATTEMPT TO "BREAK AND CONTROL THE VIOLENCE OF FACTION."

Whatever the reasons for the Allied attitude, it provided the opponents of the German Republic with a battle cry more potent than a call for the return to the discredited old order. The German republicans should have been all the more anxious to provide themselves with institutional bulwarks strong enough to help them "break and control the violence of faction." They were not even aware of the existence of that task. The Social Democrats, who held absolute power between November 9 and the elections of the National Assembly on January 19, were the prisoners of their ideological past. Since the economic interpretation of history continued to be the official party creed, it caused them to regard the devices of constitutional government as irrelevant. Characteristically, the party leader, Friedrich Ebert, as chairman of the revolutionary government, entrusted Professor Hugo Preuss, a Left-wing Liberal, rather than a Socialist, with the preparation of the new Constitution. Germany's "bourgeois" parties, however, were unable to compensate for the lack of constitutional knowledge on the part of the Social Democrats. Their leaders had become accustomed to the authoritarianism of the Empire, and did not know what to do with power when it fell into their hands. As a result, with much democratic, and some socialistic, rhetoric, the Weimar National Assembly erected a political structure which not only permitted, but invited, any and all of its opponents to attack it from within.

There were exceptions to this general rule of ignorance in constitutional matters. The well-known sociologist, Max Weber, and the chairman of the (Left-wing Liberal) Democratic party, Friedrich Naumann, were aware of the nature of the task to be solved. Weber had been trying to hammer the point into his countrymen that while constitutional problems were of a "technical" nature, they were important. The mistakes made by the civil servants, who had been running German affairs for some time, constituted so much proof for this fact that "Those for whom all of these experiences are not enough are not amenable to any kind of proof." [9] Weber knew that the principal weakness of his countrymen was devotion to a *Politik der Unpolitischen* —"a politics of the unpolitical." They believed that the truly political functions were not really important. Most of the work could be done by experts, or a combination of businessmen and labor leaders. Weber vigorously emphasized not only the vital implications of political decisions but also the need to have political institutions provide for the proper channels of political selection, as well as the proper instruments of action for those selected. For him the mistakes made in Germany before and during the war were not just mistakes of individuals. They were defects of "the system as such." [10] When told that certain political institutions developed in the Western countries were not adaptable to German conditions, he sarcastically referred to the "vanity of the literati," for whom Germany just *had* to differ from other nations, even if these were of Germanic origin.[11]

Weber was amazingly clear and farsighted in his methodological views; but he failed in his attempt to apply them to constitutional reality. He realized that lack of executive stability was the principal characteristic of parliamentary government as it had developed in France and Italy. He hoped to overcome it by combining the principles of the parliamentary and of the presidential systems. The President was to be elected by popular vote, and he was to be given important powers of his own. As the man endowed "by the confidence of millions," he would be superior to the parliamentary majority of the day even if he were bound to it in the selection of his ministers.[12] The Weimar Constitution followed this advice in part. The President was elected directly by the people, for a term of seven years. He could be reëlected, and was ostensibly given many powers of his own. At the same time the responsibility of the cabinet before the *Reichstag* was stipulated (Art. 54), and the countersignature of a responsible minister for every political act of the President was required (Art. 50). Under such conditions the Reichstag was bound to prevail as long as there existed in that body anything even faintly resembling a positive majority. Matters might have been different had the presidential system been adopted consistently, without parliamentary responsibility of the cabinet. In that case, the fact that the President was elected by majority vote might have secured, in the face of a Reichstag divided by P.R., a measure of stability not otherwise obtainable, provided that constant deadlocks between legislature and executive could have been avoided. Max Weber also overlooked that, while he hoped to mitigate the effects of P.R. by the plebiscitary nature of the presidency, the plebiscitary element might, to some extent, be offset by the effects of P.R. in the party structure. In the words of Professor Brecht:

> Presidential election by popular vote, while satisfactory under a two-party system, is bound to be a most dangerous method wherever there are numerous and disintegrating parties. If no party is able to get its own candidate elected, the natural result is the nomination of popular outsiders who are political laymen lacking strong affiliations with any parliamentary party. Had the election of the President been left to a joint meeting of the two houses, as in France, Hindenburg would not have been even a candidate after Ebert's death, and the election of a genuinely democratic parliamentarian would have been secured.[13]

In Germany the presidential election law made the further mistake of adopting the weak French type of majority voting. If no candidate obtained an absolute majority in the first ballot, anyone could be a candidate in the second ballot even if he had not run in the first. In Germany, a system of run-off elections had prevailed before P.R. was adopted; the second ballot was limited to the two candidates leading in the first. Apparently, the parties which adopted the presidential election law were aware of the ever-increasing degree of disunity among themselves; they wanted a maximum leeway for maneuvering in the second ballot. Yet the Rightist opponents of the republic were to be the beneficiaries of that arrangement. After the first ballot of the 1925 presidential elections had demonstrated that the Rightists could not win with any of their own leaders, they put great pressure on Field Marshal von Hindenburg, who lived contentedly in retirement. It would have been impossible to make him enter the partisan free-for-all of a first ballot, and this meant that, under a system of run-off elections, he would not have been in the race.

Max Weber, then, was unable to translate his sound methodological views into meaningful constitutional action. Friedrich Naumann concentrated his fire on P.R., although the illness which was to take his life left him little physical strength. In the Constitutional Committee of the National Assembly [14] he declared: "The consequence of P.R. is the impossibility of forming parliamentary governments; the parliamentary system and P.R. mutually exclude one another." He probed even more deeply when he declared, in a letter to a follower: [15]

I do not believe that we shall get to a satisfactory solution of the problem of forming a majority, but I fear that we are creating a condition, which can be remedied only by a later *coup d'état*. However, I know well that I am alone in my far-reaching pessimism on this question. Since one does not want to endow the President with strong governmental rights of his own, one ought to take care that there is a natural majority in Parliament. This is what is not being done and what, so far as I am able to see, is not accomplished by the method chosen. Therefore, the new Constitution lacks a state-forming organ.

What Naumann said was similar to what the Deputy, Alessio, predicted, at about the same time, in the Italian Chamber of Deputies, namely, that P.R. would paralyze the formation of a country's political will, and no force from within the democratic system might prove strong enough to overcome the resulting paralysis. As Naumann's disciple, Professor Theodor Heuss,[16] reported, only a few of the Deputies within Naumann's own Democratic party shared his view. They felt that political minorities (evidently, they thought of themselves) would not fare as badly under P.R. as under a majority system. They overlooked the fact that others, particularly the representatives of the Right, and of interest groups, would preëmpt the areas which they hoped to cultivate under P.R. The time was to come when their electoral strength was to evaporate in spite of (or because of) P.R. In the elections of July, 1932, the parliamentary group of the State party dropped to four members; they were reminded that they could go to the *Reichstag* in a taxicab!

Naturally, Naumann was aware of the difficulties which his party would have to face under a majority system. But, in the words of Professor Heuss: "He believed that the dynamics of such an electoral system which aimed not at 'justice' but at the gaining of power would dynamite [17] the German party tradition and transform it—its fate appeared to him as being absolutely of second rank." Naumann, then, was utterly free of any considerations dictated by the "organized interest of associations." He foresaw clearly that the majority system would tend to abolish Germany's ideological parties and to replace them with functional parties of the Anglo-Saxon type, and he welcomed the prospect. On the other hand, he knew that P.R. would have dynamic effects of its own. To quote Professor Heuss again:

> It need not be demonstrated how clearly he [Naumann] foresaw future developments; the searching for a majority was bound to shift the power of decision, and the responsibility, to the small groups which, formed on an economic, denominational or geographic basis, were still just "needed" and therewith, if one wants to accept a political "mar-

ginal utility" or "marginal cost" theory, determined the parliamentary "price formation." [18]

Clearly, this meant that Germany was to be governed by an oligarchy of political parties rather than by any decision taken by the people themselves.

Naumann's warnings had no effect. The Social Democratic "Council of People's Commissars" had decreed P.R. as the basis of the elections to the Constituent Assembly.[19] It is difficult to find a rational explanation for this fact. It should have become clear to the Social Democrats since the elections of 1912 that they would benefit from the plurality system if it were coupled with a fair reapportionment of electoral districts; in 1919, they would have made the reapportionment themselves. There had been, however, no systematic analysis of the issue by those, or on behalf of those, who made the party's decisions in such matters. In the words of Dr. Ziegler: "The Erfurt party congress in 1891 had decreed P.R., as the electoral arrangement most beneficial to the party. Critical analysis of the system by Socialists thereafter ceased." [20]

P.R. AND THE NATIONAL ASSEMBLY.

Subsequent German developments were to demonstrate the truth of what Montesquieu [21] expressed in these words:

> In a democracy the people are in some respects the sovereign and in others the subject.
>
> There can be no exercise of sovereignty but by their suffrages, which are their own will; now the sovereign's will is the sovereign himself. The laws, therefore, which establish the right of suffrage are fundamental to this government.

Montesquieu continues that election laws are as important for a democracy as the law governing the succession is for a monarchy. The comparison is apt. As we have seen, hereditary monarchy, in the historical periods to which it was adapted, has assured a maximum of stability. Elective monarchy, as practiced in the Kingdom of Poland and in the German Empire, has led to instability and disintegration.

If, in a democracy, the plurality system is comparable to hereditary monarchy, the Weimar Republic has demonstrated that a radical system of P.R. is comparable to an elective monarchy of the Polish type. The National Assembly approached the subject with typical German thoroughness. It not only accepted the principle of P.R., as practically every assembly elected under that system will do, but it made it a part of the Constitution (Art. 22) prescribing it, for good measure, for the parliaments of the states (*Laender*) and of the municipalities (Art. 17) as well. Thereafter, a change of the election law required a two-thirds majority, and the fact that this was unattainable placed a damper not only on practical plans of reform, but also on all theoretical discussions of the subject. Three stages can be distinguished in the subsequent operation of P.R.:

First, in the elections to the National Assembly, P.R., in all probability, deprived the Social Democrats of an overall majority.

Second, between the elections to the first *Reichstag* under the new Constitution in 1920, and the first elections held under the impact of the world economic crisis in September, 1930, Germany witnessed a period of "pluralistic stagnation." While a measure of economic stability led to a degree of political stability, the parliamentary situation was confused.

Third, with the elections of September 14, 1930, there began that totalitarian revolution which periods of economic crisis will produce as a natural reaction to a period of pluralistic stagnation.

Let us consider these periods one by one. In the elections to the National Assembly, the moderate wing of the Social Democratic party secured 37.9 per cent of the popular vote, and the Left-wing "Independent Socialists" 7.6 per cent. As competent a statistical analyst of election results as Dr. Johannes Schauff [22] takes it for granted that the Socialists would have won an overall majority had the majority system of voting been used. The reasons for this assumption are primarily of a statistical nature. At that time only the Social Democrats and the Christian Democrats (then calling themselves "Christian People's party" but soon to resume the old name "Center party") had a substantial number of local strongholds in which they could not easily have been defeated, and the Social Democrats with 37.9 per cent of the total vote clearly led the Christian Democrats, who polled 19.7 per cent.[23]

On the other hand, a Social Democratic victory would hardly have entailed that prospect of violent conflict which many observers connect with it. At the same time, it would have been a victory of the moderates within the party. A good many of the constituencies which the Socialists had a good chance to carry could have been carried only by definitely moderate Socialists, and these would have occupied a key position within the parliamentary group of the party. The natural leader of a Socialist government was Friedrich Ebert, then in his prime. Under his guidance the party would have likely developed into something not too remote from the pattern of the British Labour party. Besides, a Socialist government would have been confronted, in 1919, with formidable tasks in the field of foreign policy. For this reason alone it would have had every reason to steer a course based upon as wide a measure of popular consent as it could possibly obtain. Ebert himself would not have wanted to pursue a different policy in the first place.

PLURALISTIC STAGNATION.

There was little, then, in the prospect of a Social Democratic majority in the Weimar National Assembly to scare anyone aware of the facts of political life. On the other hand, the assumption of complete responsibility by the Social Democrats might have led to a quick reaction against them, as the difficulties confronting the country were enormous. But it would have been all to the good to have an alternation of Socialist and non-Socialist governments rather than coalitions in which neither a Socialist nor a non-Socialist program could be carried out and in which both parties were to be worn down for the benefit of irresponsible extremists.

Before the German Republicans delivered themselves to the period of pluralistic stagnation they insisted, however, on making things a little more difficult for themselves. For the elections of the National Assembly, the territory of the Reich had been divided into medium-sized districts which elected between six and seventeen Deputies each. The distribution of the seats took place according to the so-called d'Hondt system. No surpluses could be transferred from one district to another. Inevitably, parties which were large in a given constituency were favored over small ones. This meant that there was no chance for those "splinter parties" which were to bedevil the later history of the Weimar Republic. Of the small parties, only the Guelphs and the Bavarian Peasants party secured seats, and they owed this fact to their local strongholds. On the other hand, the (Left-wing) "Independent Socialists" obtained only 22 seats in comparison with the 32 which complete proportionality would have given them.[24]

One should think that the republican leaders would have recognized a good thing when they saw it. Instead, all they were able to see was that the figures showed a discrepancy between the actual distribution of the seats and the "just" distribution provided by "integral" P.R. So, "integral" P.R. it had to be.[25] The "automatic" system, previously applied in the state of Baden, was instituted. Each party list won a seat for every 60,000 votes obtained in a constituency. Two or three such constituencies were combined to form a *Wahlkreisverband* —an "association of constituencies," to which all surpluses were transferred, and where there was to be another seat for every 60,000 votes. The surpluses still remaining went to the *Reichsliste*, a "national list" where the same procedure was repeated, with the modification that a final remnant of 30,000 votes would entitle a party to a seat.

There came to be a slight modification and "thereby hangs a story." While the new law was under consideration the Minister of the Interior, Dr. Erich Koch-Weser, was visited by a delegation of midwives. The visiting ladies were angry and threatened that, unless their demands were met, they would found a party of their own and send several Deputies to the *Reichstag*. Koch-Weser made a quick calculation. As a result, he had the draft of the law changed so that no party was to obtain more seats from the *Reichsliste* than the number obtained by it in the *Wahlkreise* and the *Wahlkreisverbaende*. A party with no seats from either a *Wahlkreis* or a *Wahlkreisverband*, then, secured no seats at all. That was not much of a limitation on splinter parties, but it sufficed to take the wind out of the midwives' sails. Generally speaking, it crushed the hopes of all freak parties, such as stamp collectors, anti-vivisectionists, anti-inoculation enthusiasts, and the like.

The effectiveness of even such limited control measures serves to emphasize what might have been accomplished by the retention of the d'Hondt system in medium-sized constituencies as applied in 1919. The ghost of half a dozen splinter parties would have been laid; it is just conceivable that the effects of this system might have gone far enough to administer a fatal blow to the Nazi party. Unfortunately, throughout the entire period of the Weimar Republic, the number of those who took a serious interest in election statistics could have been counted on the fingers of one hand.[26] There was, at that time, only one writer who pointed out the implications of the new election law. It was, not accidentally, an associate of Naumann's, the Democratic Deputy, Anton Erkelenz, who published an article under the significant title, "An Impossible Election Law"[27] in Naumann's periodical, *Die Hilfe*.

It took some years, however, before a statistical analysis of the actual effects of the "automatic system," as compared with the probable effects of the d'Hondt system, was made.[28] The government interested itself in the subject after the formation of the (first) cabinet of Dr. Bruening in 1930, in which Dr. Joseph Wirth was Minister of the Interior. The sole question considered was a modification of P.R. which might lead to a measure of political concentration;[29] no return to the majority system was contemplated because there was no chance to secure the two-thirds majority for amending the Constitution which such a step required. After the elections of 1930 even these minor reform plans became academic. The Nazi party had resurged from its nadir, reached in the elections of 1928, and could no more have been contained by a combination of P.R. and small constituencies than could the Communists. By that time the situation had become analogous to what it was to be in the France of the Fourth Republic.

If P.R. in smaller constituencies could have done certain things for political cohesion in Germany, the majority system could have done even more. It would not only have barred the door to typical "splinter parties" but, in addition, it would have placed all extremists under severe pressure, thus keeping the Communists within narrow bounds, and it would have rarefied the political air for the Nazi party sufficiently to make likely its demise in the middle 1920's. Furthermore, the majority system would have forced the remaining parties to form campaign alliances which would have substituted a system of multiple, but related, parties for one of multiple and unrelated parties.

So far as the principal beneficiaries of P.R., the Nazi and Communist parties, are concerned, we may relate what the leading proponents of P.R. in the United States, Messrs. Hoag and Hallett, had to say on the matter. They state that they "do not doubt that the rise of new parties, extreme as well as moderate, is often facilitated by P.R.," and add that, in Germany, in May 1924, the "New Freedom Party" (the name under which the Nazi party appeared on the ballot) which secured 32 seats, "could scarcely have made a creditable showing under a majority system." They place the Communist party, which elected 62 deputies, more or less in the same category.[30]

The elections of May 1924 represent in Germany the high water mark of pre-depression radicalism. Messrs. Hoag and Hallett, to be sure, concede a little too much. Some Communist Deputies were likely to have been elected, as that party had local strongholds. Conceivably, a couple of Nazis might have made the grade in May, 1924, but certainly none in December of that year, when new elections took place after economic conditions had improved.[31] When a party as devoid of friends as the Nazi party—which vigorously, and at times venomously, attacked all others—and as devoid of a solid financial foundation,[32] loses election after election it ceases to be a going concern. Hitler might have found it more profitable to return to his trade as a house painter than to try to "awaken" a nation which gave no signs of desiring to be "awakened." Contrary to the assumptions of Hoag and Hallett, he was quite unlikely to answer electoral failure with a revolution. He had pursued that path in the beer hall *putsch* of November, 1923, and it had landed him in jail. During the ensuing years he did all he could to stress compliance with the outer forms of legality—a course of action which P.R. made easy for him.

It did not hurt either Hitler or the Communists that the general pattern of government, as it developed after 1920, did not allow the republic to become either vigorous or popular. Between February 2, 1919, when the cabinet of the Social Democratic leader, Scheidemann, was appointed, and January 30, 1933, when Hitler was installed as Chancellor, there were 20 different cabinets. Eleven of them were minority cabinets. They were in power for a total of eight years, two-thirds of the time between 1920 and 1930.[33] The majority cabinets formed for four and a half years [34] were rather heterogeneous, extending either from the militant republicans contained in the Democratic (later State) party to the monarchist Nationalists, or from the Socialists to Stresemann's Populists (the party of big business).

These cabinets contained some excellent men, and they did perform a measure of constructive work which history has not always properly recorded. Yet, they all bore marks of instability and paralysis. Only three fell as a result of a vote taken in the *Reichstag;* the remainder just resigned because either one of the coalition partners, or one of the parties in the *Reichstag* on whose toleration a cabinet had to rely, had turned against it. As to the overall results, something is to be said for what Count Westarp, a moderate monarchist, expressed in these words:

> Blockade and the urgencies of war had made the German people thoroughly accustomed to substitutes for food. But in 1920 for the first time the practice indulged in by the various parliamentary groups introduced them to a substitute for governmental authority in parliament. Instead of there having been expressed, or at least not withheld, the confidence of the majority, which according to Section I of Article 54 of the Constitution the Chancellor and his ministers must have, the people were offered as a substitute the unexpressed "non-confidence" of an opposition majority, which for one reason or another . . . refrained from passing the resolution provided for in Section 2, whereby "the *Reichstag* withdraws its confidence from the government." And what is it that enables this minority government to continue? Not the homogeneity of a parliamentary majority, but the heterogeneity of the opposition. Not their joining of forces for the purpose of discharging a clear responsibility, but their craven shrinking from any parliamentary responsibility whatsoever. Not the fact that they enjoy the firmly established confidence of their fellows in parliament, but the fact that the lack of confidence is so feebly expressed.[35]

Germany, then, had *Ersatzdemokratie* even during the period of pluralistic stagnation when all went comparatively well. It might be mentioned in passing that during this time the presence of Field Marshal von Hindenburg in the President's palace proved to be a help rather than a hindrance. The old man took his oath of office so seriously that, within a few months after his inauguration, his photograph vanished from the mantelpiece of many a conservative household. When a cabinet crisis occurred, von Hindenburg indefatigably searched for the candidate to the Chancellor's chair most likely to gather a parliamentary majority. After, in the elections of 1928, the Social Democrats secured 153 out of 491 seats,[36] giving them a plurality in that (by then badly divided) body, Hindenburg, without hesitation, entrusted their leader, Hermann Mueller, with the chancellorship. Mueller's cabinet, comprising five parties and extending to Stresemann's "Populists," was hampered, however, by more internal divisions than any of its predecessors. It collapsed in 1930 for reasons quite similar to those which, little more than a year later, were to bring about the end of Ramsay MacDonald's second cabinet: The Social Democrats in the *Reichstag* were unwilling to support the measures for ending the deficit in the unemployment fund which the cabinet deemed necessary.

THE TOTALITARIAN REVOLUTION.

By this time von Hindenburg had grown tired of patching up one coalition after the other. Instead of embarking on a new round of negotiations with party leaders he asked the young Centrist leader, Dr. Bruening, to form a cabinet of a different kind, based as much on the President as on the *Reichstag*. If Bruening could not induce the *Reichstag* to accept vital measures, the President stood ready to sign an emergency decree under Article 48 of the Constitution, enacting the government's proposals into law. They had then to be submitted to the *Reichstag*, and became invalid if this body voted them down. In that case, von Hindenburg was prepared to sign a decree dissolving the *Reichstag*.

Dr. Bruening hoped that, armed with such weapons, he would induce enough Nationalist Deputies to vote for his measures—or, at any rate, against their invalidation—to secure a majority. Luck was with him for a time. Eventually a majority of those elected as Nationalist Deputies in 1928 left that party and supported him. They included Count Westarp, the long-time chairman of the Nationalist parliamentary group. On July 18, however, the *Reichstag* rejected Bruening's first decree laws by a vote of 236 to 221, and Bruening dissolved the *Reichstag*. On this fateful occasion, then, the margin was narrow; few would deny that, under a majority system, the number of Nazis and Communists, all of whom voted against the government, would have been sufficiently reduced to reverse the result.

The new elections took place on September 14. They were not, as in England where elections took place a year later for similar reasons, a straight fight between government and opposition, both of which, if victorious, could carry on the burden of "His Majesty's government." In Germany the elections were a free for all. Some 30 different parties were listed on the ballots and a dozen of them were likely to secure seats. None of them had entered any pre-election relationship with any other, and two of them, the Nazis and the Communists, were bent on destroying everyone else. Soon the effects of the depression became the dominant theme of the elections. The German economy had begun its downturn early in 1928; thus, the burdens of large-scale unemployment had been upon the country for a good two years when the elections took place. The Nazis and the Communists, rather than the Social Democrats, were the principal beneficiaries.

This is not the place to discuss the results of these elections in any detail.[37] Suffice it to mention one basic fact. If the territory of the *Reich* is divided into 400 constituencies of approximately equal size, the result is that the Nazis did not get as much as 40 per cent of the vote in a single one of them. On the other hand, the Social Democrats with 186 pluralities, and the Christian Democrats (the Center party) with 87 pluralities, remained strong. Under any form of the majority system they would have attracted votes both at their Right and their Left, and would have been certain of a joint majority of the seats. As long as that was the case, the republic was safe.

Actually, the Nazis obtained 107 and the Communists 77 of the 577 seats. They voted automatically against any measure proposed by the government. Under the circumstances, a dictatorship could be avoided only if all moderate groups combined, both those which had supported Bruening before the dissolution of the *Reichstag* and those who fought him in the elections, in particular the Social Democrats. The latter, after some soul-searching, decided to give indirect support to the Chancellor: the government would issue its decree laws and, when these were challenged in the *Reichstag*, the Social Democrats would vote against the motion to invalidate them. This very responsible attitude naturally was grist in Communist propaganda mills. It was easy to say that the Social-Democrats had "sold out to the bourgeoisie." Similarly, the Deputies of the moderate Right, by their equally responsible attitude, made it easier for the Nazis and Nationalist propagandists to claim that they had "sold out to the Black-Red coalition." Since the world economic crisis was getting worse [38] the position of the moderate parties was bound to deteriorate.

In the two elections held in 1932, the Nazis and Communists together held a majority of the seats in the *Reichstag*, thus excluding the possibility of a democratic government. During this year, when elections held under P.R. led to paralysis (in the *Laender* as well as in the *Reich*), one major decision took place under the majority system: the presidential elections, in which von Hindenburg, supported by all the moderate parties, barely missed the absolute majority in the first ballot, which he secured easily in the second. On this occasion Hitler, who was Hindenburg's principal opponent, suffered a disastrous defeat from which, however, he recovered immediately in the P.R. elections to the *Reichstag*.

A few remarks remain to be added concerning certain systematic aspects of these developments. The first question concerns the use of Article 48 for the purpose of ordinary legislation. Clearly, this provision was not intended to be used in that manner; it was meant to serve during times of insurrection and disorder. On the other hand, Weimar Germany does not represent the only case in which a legislative vacuum was filled by the executive. There are parallel cases, in particular in Italy and in France, although in France the government always acted on the basis of a parliamentary enabling act. It is interesting to note that while the Constitution of the Fourth Republic explicitly excluded such a possibility, it developed again in practice.

In Germany, Bruening might have argued that all he tried to do was to adapt British practice to German conditions. In England, the cabinet exercises uncontested leadership in drafting legislative measures and guiding them through parliament. As we have seen, in the case of obvious emergencies, it may authorize a deviation from a law, certain to secure a bill of indemnity from parliament. The British cabinet remains always dependent, however, upon the confidence of a parliamentary majority, and parliamentary criticism plays a more vital part in the process of legislation than it did in Bruening's emergency decrees. Still, Bruening was not the first German Chancellor to have resorted to such decrees. Dr. Wirth, supported by President Ebert, did so in 1922 in order to curb currency speculation. Subsequently, the cabinets of Stresemann and Marx had the measures needed to end their country's runaway inflation enacted either on the basis of an enabling act or, in some cases, with the help of Article 48.[39] When President Ebert was criticized for this, he answered in terms not dissimilar to Rousseau's remark that "The people's first intention is that the State shall not perish," which Professor Rossiter aptly takes as a motto for his analysis of "Constitutional Dictatorship." [40]

Naturally, Bruening's use of Article 48 differed from all precedents in the intended range of its application. All of the government's activities, including the budget, were involved, and this was revolution. Bruening's backing came primarily from the President. For the first time in the history of that office, von Hindenburg tried to use its plebiscitary foundation in the manner contemplated by Max Weber: As he had found it impossible to get along with the parties—or, rather, to induce enough parties to get along with each other—he set out to get along without them. The best that can be expected from such a course of action is that it will help to overcome an emergency, and then yield to other, and more truly institutional, procedures. Both Hindenburg and Bruening did see matters in this light; they were looking forward to a time when legislation could again proceed in the manner provided by the Constitution.

From the point of view of hindsight there is something to be said for the Social Democratic charges that the chances involved in governing with a combination of Article 48 and the threat of parliamentary dissolution should not have been taken. Yet as matters stood in Germany in 1930, there were at least equally powerful arguments in favor of the course chosen by Bruening and Hindenburg. The two men did succeed in causing the true conservatives to break away from Hugenberg's sterile leadership in the Nationalist party. For the time being it seemed as if that reconciliation of the old and the new which a parliamentary monarchy might have brought about could yet be achieved. Matters went so far that, in the summer of 1930, the term "Tory democracy" was used. Given a little more time, it might have become a reality. The true conservatives had tired of sterile opposition. Besides, there were the "loaves and fishes"—less the fruits of patronage than those of assistance to economic groups in distress, particularly agriculture. Dr. Bruening was prepared to give such assistance, and even the powerful *Reichslandbund* (a Rightist organization of farmers, dominated by the owners of large estates) favored cooperation with him.

Dr. Bruening has always felt that if only the Social Democrats had given him, during the early weeks of his government, a part of the help which they accorded him so freely after the elections held in September, 1930, both the political and the economic crisis might have been overcome. The Social Democrats, instead of moving that the decree laws be invalidated, might have "tolerated" them from the outset. During the summer of 1930 it would have sufficed had they abstained when proposals of invalidation made by other opposition parties came to a vote. However, had the Social Democrats been accustomed to argue in the terms of the theologian—which they were not—they might have answered that what Bruening wanted them to do was to perform a "work of supererogation": they were called upon to act with more foresight, and a greater sense of responsibility, than is to be expected from a party operating under the kind of condition which they had to face. The system of voting had its part in their predicament. In the words of George N. Shuster and Arnold Bergstraesser:

> Meanwhile proportional representation of course provided the voter with an opportunity to choose any of what at one time were two dozen political parties (during 1930 there were actually twenty-seven), ranging from the fantastically leftist to the curiously rightist groups of three or four hundred followers. This plain political fact could not be ignored by the major partisan organizations. The social democrats, for instance, were permanently handicapped by reason of communist rivalry. If they acceded to a compromise solution of some problem affecting the interests of the workers, the communists, being a purely opposition party at the beck and call of the Comintern, could pose as the sole untarnished defenders of the laboring class. Therefore the social democrats were sometimes compelled to oppose the government even when their own leaders least desired to do so.[41]

DEFLATION, DEPRESSION, AND THE NAZI VICTORY.

In addition, it is well to take up a point on which the case of the Social Democrats is stronger than on the others. They would have preferred to fight the "cumulative downward trend" of prices with which Germany was then so badly afflicted by a policy entailing the risk of an early devaluation of the mark; they might, in fact, have sought a devaluation deliberately. What such a fall in price levels means can best be illustrated by an example based upon American developments. Suppose a farmer bought a $10,000 farm in 1929 with $4,000 of his own and a $6,000 loan. Between 1929 and 1933 American wholesale prices fell by 40 per cent, while prices of farm products as paid to the farmer fell by more than 60 per cent. Our farmer was bound to encounter great difficulty in taking care of his interest and amortization quota as well as his operating expenses. The prices for the industrial products which he had to buy had not fallen nearly as much as the prices for his own products. If he could not cope with the situation, and the bank decided to foreclose, chances are that the sale would have netted not much more than a third of the original price.

Thus, the farmer would have lost his entire investment, and the banker would still have felt that his debtor had defaulted.

Few human beings can be expected to resign themselves to such a fate, and matters were not much better when the farmer managed to hold on to his farm. So far as the political repercussions are concerned, the natural tendency is to vote "agin." Hundreds of thousands of American farmers did so in the presidential elections of 1932, as did industrial workers. Under the plurality system no one could make his protest count unless he voted for the Democratic party—the Socialists were keenly disappointed in their failure to derive large-scale benefits from the depression. Dr. Gosnell, speaking specifically of Pennsylvania, has ascertained that "the areas hardest hit shifted the most to Roosevelt." [42]

German farmers, and German middleclass voters in general, voted under the impact of the same forces, but with entirely different results. Thanks to P.R. there existed an extremist party, the Nazis, to whom they went over in ever increasing numbers. Other middleclass groups did the same, and the workers, threatened by unemployment, turned to the Communists. Naturally, the "cumulative downward trend of prices" had affected industry and commerce as well as farming, and so far as employment was concerned, the effects were worse. Konrad Heiden [43] was right when, speaking of the 1930 elections, he wrote: "Speakers busied themselves with Conservatism, Liberalism and Parliamentarism in the belief that the electorate was opposed to democracy. In reality it was only opposed to unemployment and taxation."

The chain of causation which led from the economic into the political field could have been broken. Thus, when the pound was devalued the pressure under which the British economy had labored as much as that of Germany or the United States was lifted as if by magic. The price level first became stationary, and then began a slow rise.[44] A rather conservative financial management, soon to be guided by Neville Chamberlain, presided over the transition from a severe depression to a sustained recovery. A similar policy could have been pursued in Germany; had this been done, there is every reason to assume that the trough of the depression would have been reached immediately, rather than in the summer of 1932, as it actually happened.

If the type of situation which confronted Germany in 1930 should develop again, there is little doubt that effective steps to stop a further fall in the price level would be taken without delay. Three considerations cooperated, however, to keep Dr. Bruening from taking that step. In the first place, unilateral action would have been a violation of

Germany's obligations under the terms of the Young Plan.[45] A release from these obligations was not obtainable since the French would not have agreed. In the second place, in Germany, as in all countries which had gone through a severe inflationary period after the First World War, there was the strongest reluctance to contemplate any step which appeared to jeopardize monetary stability. In the third place, Dr. Bruening had good reasons to expect that his own policy would succeed in spite of all the sacrifices that it entailed. It was not a policy of "deflation" in the sense that it aimed at a fall in the price level. That fall was worldwide; it had been brought about by factors over which the German government had no control. It was so disastrous because while the prices received by producers fell rapidly, their costs fell slowly or not at all. All the measures taken by Dr. Bruening's government had no goal other than to promote the adjustment of "sticky" costs to reduced prices.[46] Insofar as a reduction of wages and salaries was involved, it never reached the extent to which the cost of living had fallen, let alone wholesale prices. Insofar as the reduction of civil servants' salaries was concerned, it was comparable to what the Economy Act of 1933 did in the United States: the "cut" was less than the increase in purchasing power brought about by the reduction in the cost of living. These facts were obvious enough for anyone to see who wanted to see. As John Maynard Keynes had emphasized, however, since the days when he wrote his *Tract on Monetary Reform*,[47] people have great difficulty in realizing the difference between money incomes and real incomes, particularly when that realization might entail immediate disadvantage for themselves.

The misunderstandings surrounding Bruening's policy were one of their great drawbacks so far as the course of German politics is concerned. The German word for "emergency decrees" is *Notverordnungen*, the word *Not* meaning "misery" as well as "emergency." Nazi and Communist agitators made every effort to make it appear that Bruening's very intention was to "decree misery." Still, from the economic point of view that policy did bear fruit; during the summer of 1932 the symptoms of improvement were clearly discernible. The authoritative *Institut fuer Konjunkturforschung* ("Institute for Business Cycle Research") repeatedly drew attention to this fact.[48] By the time Bruening was forced out of office, the foundations for a future recovery had been laid.

These considerations of economic policy refer to issues of "policy" rather than to issues of "form." So far as the final collapse of the Weimar Republic is concerned, the implication is clear: While a defective form did lead to the development of an unimpressive "pluralistic parties state," the latter could have continued to exist had effective measures been taken to stop the "cumulative downward trend of prices" and thereby end the depression. The close relationship between the rise of the extremist vote and the increase in unemployment is too obvious to overlook,[49] and it seems clear that a decline in unemployment would have been followed by a decline in the Nazi vote. Actually, the mere stabilization of unemployment which occurred in 1932 did bring about a fall in the percentage of the Nazi vote from 37.3 per cent achieved in July, 1932, to 33.1 per cent in November. Subsequent municipal elections brought reductions in the Nazi vote ranging up to 50 per cent. It is sufficient to read Goebbels' diaries for the following weeks and months in order to realize that the impact of these events was almost catastrophic.[50]

ALLIED HESITATIONS.

Other developments coming under the general heading of "policy" could have forestalled Hitler's rise to power. Dr. Bruening was Chancellor until May 30, 1932. He tried desperately to secure a few concessions in the field of foreign affairs which would have induced Hindenburg to continue his support for him. A final solution in the field of reparations—the Allies were soon to grant more to von Papen than Bruening requested—would have been helpful, and so would a satisfactory compromise in the field of rearmament. Bruening's goal was expansion of the *Reichswehr* from 100,000 to 300,000 men, a far cry from the army of millions which the Allies were soon to allow Hitler to raise. On May 30, the American Ambassador called upon Bruening with the urgent message that Hugh Gibson had met Edouard Herriot, the leader of the French Left which had just won an electoral victory, and persuaded him that the German proposals presented "a sound and honest basis for negotiation." [51] The American Ambassador realized what this meant for Germany's domestic situation, and he lost no time in relaying the message to Bruening. However, this happened on May 30, and Bruening's audience with von Hindenburg which led to his resignation had taken place the day before. W. John Wheeler-Bennett [52] comments:

> Here is one of the great "ifs" of history. Had Mr. Gibson's news arrived but twenty-four hours earlier, the destiny of Europe, and of Germany, might well have been changed, and the name of Brüning might have been numbered amongst those great ones who succeeded, instead of among those who went down fighting. Now, however, he could only thank the Ambassador for his swift action and communicate the news to the permanent head of the Foreign Office.

SOCIAL FORCES.

Various types of action in the field of "policy" might, then, have saved the Weimar Republic in spite of its inherent weakness. In addition to political form and to decisions in the field of policy, there were the influences resulting from hostile social forces.

So far as the businessmen, whose financial assistance to the Nazi party is frequently blamed for Hitler's success, are concerned, reference has already been made to the detailed refutation of this charge by Louis P. Lochner. German industrialists gave much more money to Hitler's opponents than to him, particularly on the occasion of the presidential elections of 1932. To the extent that some of them did give financial assistance to the Nazi party, Konrad Heiden has rightly observed: "Actually the funds were attracted by success, rather than the other way round." [53] Even so, between November, 1932, and January, 1933, when Hitler was appointed Chancellor, his party's treasurers had to do some fancy stepping to dodge the creditors who besieged them.[54] Had it been possible to keep Hitler out of power for just another six months, the burden of debt and the impact of defeat would have forced his party to the ground.

The social forces associated with Germany's past did play, however, a crucial part in bringing Hitler to power. When the first step was taken and Bruening overthrown, the *Reichswehr* and the large estate owners of Eastern Germany, the *Junkers*, worked hand in hand. The second step, Hitler's appointment in January, 1933, was actively opposed by the *Reichswehr*, and the man who then personified it, General von Schleicher. Some of the *Junkers* persisted in their intrigues, however, and, together with the cooperation of others, they succeeded in bringing Hitler to power. These *Junkers* were deathly afraid of the prospect of seeing more and more of their estates parcelled out to small farmers. Part of their troubles arose from the effects of the depression, which affected them as much as the American farmer mentioned above. By this time, incidentally, von Hindenburg had been made to share in the economic fate of the *Junkers*. For his eightieth birthday, in 1927, he had been presented with his ancestral estate, Neudeck, and thanks to the extravagance of his son, Oskar, there were enough debts, as the depression struck, to require part of the presidential salary (most reluctantly given) to cover the annual deficit. Thus, Hindenburg knew part of the plight of his neighbors from firsthand experience. The large estate owners finally became alarmed when, toward the end of 1932, a committee of the *Reichstag* investigated the *Osthilfe*, the government action with the help of which those estates which could be made to pay their way were to be saved. Scandals developed, and the *Junkers* hoped that Hitler's appointment as Chancellor, with their own Nationalist party as his ally (and presumed guide), there would be no more publicity about them.

A discussion of the part played by the *Reichswehr* and the *Junkers* in Hitler's rise to power must avoid the danger, however, of oversimplification. Neither constituted a serious problem as long as matters remained half-way normal, and as long as the republican government could function in accord with the provisions of the Constitution. Between 1924 and 1930, the period of republican consolidation, the government interfered more with the army (and properly so) than the army with the government. The incident characteristic of this period is the dismissal of General von Seeckt, the creator of the *Reichswehr*, in 1926. He had permitted the eldest son of the former Crown Prince to participate in maneuvers with the temporary rank of an officer. The Minister of Defense, Dr. Gessler, managed to secure Hindenburg's consent to his dismissal. This did not mean that the superiority of the civilian element over the military went as far as it should have gone, but it constituted a milestone on the road to that goal. On the other hand, as soon as the authority of the republican government disintegrated, the army, under von Schleicher, regained its political influence.

Similar considerations apply to the large estate owners. A republican government with any degree of authority could have put them in their places. Furthermore, they secured their later importance through von Hindenburg, which again brings into play the provisions of the Constitution and of the presidential election law which allowed von Hindenburg to become President. Still, the old Field Marshal was not just a puppet of economic interests. It weighed heavily on his conscience that he had to sign one decree law after the other. Before he agreed to be a candidate for reëlection in 1932 he complained, with a sigh, about *"Die ganze Verantwortung mit diesen Notverordnungen"* —"The whole responsibility with these emergency decrees." [55] The clinching argument in favor of appointing Hitler as Chancellor was that this step would relieve von Hindenburg of the need to govern with decree laws; Hitler would secure a parliamentary majority for his coalition in the new election. Konrad Heiden, who has gone into the details of these events as much as anyone, concludes: "Hitler came to power because he seemed to be the only man who could restore to Germany a parliamentary government such as Hindenburg had demanded in August and even more in November." [56] In August and November, Hitler had demanded that he be appointed Chancellor as a matter of right, because he led the strongest party in the *Reichstag*. Hindenburg's answer, given in letters signed by State Secretary Meissner, was that no one had the *right* to be appointed Chancellor unless he could command a parliamentary majority.[57] Hindenburg's personal comments on Hitler's claims had culminated in the remark: "That man for a Chancellor? I'll make him a postmaster, and he can lick the stamps with my head on them." [58] In January, 1933, Hitler appeared as the nominee of a coalition which included the Nationalists. His claim that he would secure a majority for his government in new elections had a better foundation than before, although this was actually accomplished with the help of wholesale terror.

At any rate, when German republicans characterize Hitler's appointment as merely the result of a reactionary conspiracy they present an alibi rather than an explanation. The conspiracy existed and played its part, but the republic failed to play *its* part. It was simply not devised to be strong enough to be able to "break and control the violence of faction"; instead, its own weakness created a vacuum which was a constant invitation for factions to develop and to take it over from within. Professor Brecht, speaking specifically of the popular election of the President and of P.R., said:

> The dangerous implications of these "few lines of mistakes" that had slipped into a long and otherwise exemplary democratic constitution were simply "overlooked" during the formative period, in the absence of advanced theory and in the presence of a genuinely republican president. Thirteen years later, the arms and hands of their democratic leaders fettered by such institutional monstrosities, the people drifted like a helmless ship into the catastrophes of 1932 and 1933. The whole tragedy of this concatenation is still far from being understood in our age, where the prevailing interest in psychology in all its scientific and popular brands has led to neglect, if not ignorance, of institutional problems.[59]

Chapter XVI

PARLIAMENTARY GOVERNMENT IN GERMANY: THE BONN REPUBLIC

∿∿∿∿∿∿∿∿∿∿∿∿∿∿∿∿∿∿∿∿∿∿∿∿∿∿∿∿∿∿

There was to be a substantial difference between the Weimar Republic and its successor. Instability had been the characteristic of the Weimar Republic from the outset, but the "Federal Republic of Germany" began its career with three cabinets headed by the same Chancellor, each lasting, or promising to last, for a full four-year period. There were changes in these cabinets, but they were comparatively unimportant, in particular in view of the dominating position of the Chancellor. Not a few observers, German as well as foreign, concluded that the ghost of political instability had been laid. The Bonn Republic, they felt, had developed constitutional principles which sufficed to safeguard it against the dangers which came to engulf its predecessor.

ELECTING THE PRESIDENT.

A closer examination of the facts may lead to less optimistic conclusions. The "Fundamental Law," as the Constitution of the Federal Republic is called,[1] does represent an improvement over the Weimar model. It follows, however, the general pattern of "rationalized parliamentarism." Professor Mirkine-Guetzévitch, who, as we have seen, not only coined this term after the First World War, but also came to be rather critical of what it stands for, has emphasized repeatedly that basic aspects of a constitutional order, in particular executive stability, depend on political facts rather than upon legal provisions. The basic political fact is the presence or absence of a majority which is both stable and moderate. Where such majorities exist even the worst Constitution is likely to work;[2] where they are absent, the best Constitution may avail but little. Still, the authors of the Bonn Republic can claim that, if the—inevitably tortuous—path of "rationalized parliamentarism" is to be entered at all, they have managed to smooth it over as much as possible.

The improvements in the Bonn model, as compared with the Weimar model, begin with the election of the Head of the State, called the *Bundespraesident,* "Federal President." Popular election has been discarded. Instead, there is a special electoral college, called the *Bundesversammlung,* "Federal Assembly" (Art. 54). It consists of the members of the Federal Diet, plus an equal number of members elected by the Diets of the *Laender* on the basis of P.R. This latter provision means no more than that the relation of forces inside the various Diets is reflected in the composition of the contingent which they send to the *Bundesversammlung.* If the Diets were elected under a majority system, large and moderate parties would hold virtually all of the seats. As long as P.R. elections prevail in the Diet of the Federation as well as in those of the *Laender,* the members of the Federal Assembly are bound to be scattered over a number of parties, not all of which may be moderate.

The Constitution provides that a candidate must have the support of a majority of the Assembly's members in order to be elected on either the first or the second ballot. On the third ballot, a plurality suffices. The requirement of the first two ballots is higher than those governing the election of the French President, who needs only a majority of those voting. As long as the higher requirement can be complied with it is advantageous, as the prospects with which a President begins his work are the better the more generally he has been accepted. French experience suggests, however, that electoral bodies constituted according to P.R. may encounter considerable difficulties when called upon to produce anything exceeding a mere plurality. To require a majority of those voting for the election of a President makes sense, but anything going beyond this may lead to difficulties.

On the other hand, the provisions of the *Grundgesetz* fall below what can be considered safe in the long run when they permit election by a mere plurality on the third ballot. Any group stronger than any likely alternative combination, but short of an absolute majority, can simply wait for the third ballot in order to secure the election of its candidate. Such a group does not have to make any effort to reach an understanding with anyone else. In the French presidential elections of 1953, a provision of this type would have meant the election of Joseph Laniel rather than of René Coty, in other words, the election of a definite partisan rather than of a man suited to the role of the symbol of national unity and of the conciliator of partisan differences.

In Germany, the possible pitfalls of Article 54 of the Basic Law have been obscured by the conditions which prevailed in the first Federal Assemblies, in which the Christian Democrats and their allies had an absolute majority, and the election of their candidate, Professor Theodor Heuss, a member of the Free Democratic party, took place on the first ballot. He has made a very good President. His political convictions placed him in the center of the German political spectrum, and his personality made it easy for him to fill his office with the quiet dignity for which it calls. That a man of his type might not have been a strong candidate in a popular election is obvious.

The decisive question is, however, what would happen if German party life were to return to the confusion which characterized it during the concluding years of the Weimar Republic. Thus in the 1932 elections to the Prussian Diet, the Nazis were by far the strongest single party, but had no chance of securing enough allies to obtain an overall majority. The original rules of the Prussian Diet provided for the election of the Prime Minister by a mere plurality. Had they not been changed, the Nazis would have elected Hermann Goering Prime Minister, who, together with a cabinet composed of loyal followers, would have taken over the Prussian administration, including the police, and turned it upside down. The Diet would have passed a motion of censure against him but, as long as it could not replace him, he would have stayed in power as a "caretaker," in full control of the state's administration and police.

Clearly, it is possible that at some future date a party considerably to the right of center, even if not as radical as the Nazi, might be able to elect a Federal President with a mere plurality of the votes in the third ballot. Such a President would have difficulty in fulfilling both his symbolic and his political functions. On the other hand, the range of the President's political functions is now carefully limited, and he could not act contrary to the rules of the democratic game the way von Hindenburg did in 1932 and 1933. Under the Bonn Constitution the President does not appoint the Chancellor; he does not have an unrestricted [3] right of parliamentary dissolution, nor can he issue emergency decrees on the model of the old Article 48. While it was thoughtless to permit the election of the President by a mere plurality, the potential effects of this mistake are limited.

SELECTING THE CHANCELLOR.

The modes of thinking characteristic of "rationalized parliamentarism" are most clearly discernible in the provisions governing the election of the Federal Chancellor, and the powers of the executive.

On the model of the French Constitution of 1946, the Federal President designates a candidate. Deviating from the French model in this particular, the Federal Diet votes on the nominee without discussion (Art. 64). Election requires a majority of all the members of the Federal Diet. If the candidate fails to secure the required number, the Diet has two weeks to elect a Chancellor on its own initiative; again a majority of its members is needed. If this result is not achieved, a new vote takes place, and the candidate who obtains the largest number of votes is elected. If the plurality also constitutes a majority of the Diet's members, the President must appoint the victorious candidate. If fewer votes are obtained, the President may either appoint the victor Chancellor within seven days or dissolve the Diet.

The purpose of these elaborate provisions is obvious: Every safeguard is to be applied to prevent the President from appointing unsuitable Chancellors as von Hindenburg did when he appointed von Papen, von Schleicher, and Hitler. These men could not have passed the gauntlet of the new provisions. However, we need not repeat that von Hindenburg would not even have thought of appointing these Chancellors had not the German political picture been so confused; he *could* not have appointed them had he wanted to do so if a positive majority had existed in the *Reichstag*, as was likely to be the case with elections under the majority system. The authors of the Bonn Constitution might, therefore, have saved themselves the trouble of devising the complicated provisions intended to guard against any possible emergency. All they had to do was to call for a system of voting which would have left it to the people themselves to provide for positive majorities, certain to punish anyone who would have acted contrary to their wishes. By 1948–49, however, the facts of political life, as they did follow from the P.R. elections decreed by the occupation powers after the war, went far toward precluding the adoption of the majority system. As long as that was the case it was, indeed, logical to adopt provisions intended to avoid as many consequences of this fact as possible. French experience would seem to indicate, however, that election of the Chancellor by simple majority of those voting would have been preferable to an absolute majority of the Diet's members. On the federal level Germany has so far not experienced extensive difficulties in the formation of a new cabinet, but this does not mean that no such difficulties will arise in the future, when absolute majorities may be hard to secure.

Dangers may also arise from the fact that the *Bundestag* can, eventually, elect a Chancellor by a mere plurality vote, even if more voted against him. If this is the case, the President may either appoint the victor or dissolve the *Bundestag*. The second possibility would hardly arise unless the political picture were already confused. If it is, new elections, presumably to be held again under P.R., might improve the situation no more than did the French elections of January, 1956. In regard to the appointment of the Chancellor, then, the Basic Law has done less well than it might have done. The provisions of the French Constitution (as amended by the constitutional law of December 7, 1954) are simpler and more satisfactory, as a majority now suffices for a designated candidate to be elected; the President may nominate new candidates if his first choice fails to make the grade. On the other hand, no party can ever hope to have a Prime Minister approved by a mere plurality.

THE "POSITIVE VOTE OF CENSURE."

The pleasure and pride of the framers of the Basic Law is, however, Article 67, which governs the conditions for a vote of censure. A motion of censure is adopted only if a majority of the total membership of the Diet votes for a new Chancellor. If that is the case, the Federal President must appoint the choice of the Diet. The purpose of this provision is to prevent the overthrow of cabinets by "negative" majorities, which may combine to overthrow a cabinet but could not cooperate to replace it. During the Weimar Republic, Nazis, Nationalists, Communists, and others frequently combined to vote down a government, without any thought of replacing it. Article 67 of the Basic Law intends to make it clear that there cannot be an unlimited right to overthrow a cabinet, and that the positive aspects of such a step are inseparable from the negative ones. This is all to the good, but it does not follow, as not a few observers assume, that the longevity of the Adenauer cabinets is due to this provision. As mentioned above, only three of the cabinets of the Weimar period fell because of a hostile vote in the *Reichstag;* the vast majority resigned because the combination supporting them or tolerating them, had collapsed. Article 67, then, can protect a cabinet against assassination from without, but not from the coalition cancer within. The fact that Adenauer has held on as long as he has is simply due to the fact that he has had the support of a majority.

If the "positive vote of censure" does not have the virtues attributed to it, it can, at the same time, do no harm, and may tip the scales in favor of stability in marginal cases. An interesting situation developed in February, 1956, in the *Land* of North Rhine-Westphalia which, in Article 61 of its Constitution, had a provision similar to the "positive vote of censure" contained in Article 67 of the Federal Republic's Basic Law. The *Land* government, led by Prime Minister Arnold, was supported by the Christian Democrats (90 Diet members), the Free Democrats (25), and the small Center party (9). The Free Democrats decided to leave the coalition, and to ally themselves with the Social Democrats, who commanded 76 votes. These two parties, then, had a total of 101 votes, out of a total Diet membership of 200, as against 99 for the remaining coalition parties.

Under the circumstances it would have sufficed for one member of the FDP or SPD not to vote for the motion of censure to deprive the opposition to Arnold of the required constitutional majority, provided that all of the members of the two remaining coalition parties voted against censure. Had these conditions been granted, Arnold was prepared to stay in power. The case was unusual. The Free Democrats had left the coalition not on account of any dissatisfaction with the Prime Minister and his government but on account of an attempt by the Christian Democrats in the Bonn *Bundestag* to introduce elements of the majority system into the Federal election law.[4] This attempt had been defeated by the time the vote in Duesseldorf took place, and Prime Minister Arnold had been among those who contributed to that result. Besides, some of the Free Democratic leaders in North Rhine-Westphalia who were instrumental in causing their party to leave the coalition belonged to its right wing;[5] their alliance with the Social Democrats was criticized for that reason. This combination of factors created a psychological atmosphere favorable to Arnold which would have made it easier for him to stay in power even if one more vote had been cast against him than for him. In addition, *Land* politics is more concerned with administration than with policy making; Arnold could have gotten along well enough even if he could not count on a safe majority for new legislation.

There might have been, therefore, a real test for the "positive vote of censure." However, 102 Deputies voted for the motion of censure and only 96 against it.[6] One Free Democrat had abstained but, evidently, two members of the remaining coalition parties (presumably of the Center party) had voted against the government. The vote was secret, and while the Center party opposed the motion of censure it had not made a vote against it compulsory. In the one case, then, where all conditions were favorable for the provisions concerning the "positive vote of censure" to assume real significance, this did not happen after all, and one wonders whether similar conditions will ever develop again.

DISSOLUTION AND EMERGENCY LEGISLATION.

If the actual significance of the "positive vote of censure" is small, the authors of the Bonn Basic Law have been more successful in framing provisions intended to deal with attempts by a heterogeneous opposition to frustrate the work of a government which they cannot force to resign. The most significant part of this effort is Article 68, which empowers the Federal President, if asked to do so by the Chancellor, to dissolve the Diet if a request by the Chancellor for a vote of confidence is not accepted by a majority of that body's total membership. There must be an interval of 48 hours between the introduction of the motion and the vote. This provision means that, as long as Chancellor and President are in agreement,[7] there can be a dissolution whenever there is a real conflict between government and Diet. It is interesting to note that the right to make a request for a vote of confidence as well as a request for a dissolution is given to the Chancellor alone. He does not have to consult the cabinet as the French Prime Minister must do in both cases. Furthermore, the Chancellor can invoke this right at any time when an essential part of his program is in danger; he does not have to wait until the Diet has been in session for a certain period, or until one or two other Chancellors have been overthrown. An English Prime Minister, of course, can dissolve the House of Commons for any reason at all, such as a desire to have an election at a time when his party's chances seem best, or to terminate the existence of a particular House which is too close to the end of its term to keep its mind on its work. On the other hand, a French Prime Minister has every reason to envy a German Chancellor the comparatively far-reaching rights conferred upon him by the Basic Law. In this respect, as in others, the Federal Republic's venture into the field of "rationalized parliamentarism" has been fairly fortunate.

The same conclusion holds for the provisions governing emergency legislation. There exists nothing comparable to the old Article 48 which gave the President of the *Reich* rights to issue decree laws which he and his Chancellor could interpret rather liberally. Instead, Article 81 of the Basic Law specifies a procedure which may be followed if the *Bundestag* has failed to accord the Chancellor a vote of confidence as requested according to Article 68 and if the *Bundestag* has not been dissolved as a result. The Federal Government—in this case the government is mentioned rather than the Chancellor—may then, with the approval of the *Bundesrat* declare a state of legislative emergency in regard to a bill which the government has declared urgent and which the *Bundestag* has nonetheless rejected. The same rule applies if a bill has failed to pass although the Chancellor had coupled it with a request for a vote of confidence according to Article 68. Such a bill, if rejected again by the *Bundestag*, becomes law.

Once this procedure has been invoked any other bill may be passed in the same way during a period of six months, provided that the same Chancellor remains in office. After this period has expired no further state of legislative emergency may be declared while the same Chancellor is in power.

For a period of six months, then, the passage of all vital laws is assured. The *Bundestag* can end this situation only by electing a new Chancellor with a majority of its members. Will half a year suffice to terminate the conditions which have led to the emergency? Both in 1923–24 and in 1930–33 economic conditions (an inflation in the first and a "deflation" in the second case) provided the background for the emergency. The former might have been brought under control in a period of six months, but the second would have required more time. The Bonn Republic has not witnessed any similar economic disturbance. If the prosperity which it has known since its inception continues, a protracted emergency is unlikely to develop, and the safeguards provided for in Article 81 of the Basic Law are likely to prove adequate—if, in that case, they are ever needed!

THE BUNDESRAT.

This conclusion, however, is subject to qualifications, the first of which arises from the need to secure the approval of the *Bundesrat* for emergency legislation. The *Bundesrat* [8] consists of members of the governments of the various *Laender*, or of delegates appointed by these governments. Each *Land* has at least three votes; *Laender* with more than two million inhabitants have four, and *Laender* with more than six million have five. For some classes of legislation the positive consent of the *Bundesrat* is needed. This applies to the invocation of a legislative emergency, to changes of the Constitution (which require a two-thirds majority of the *Bundesrat* as well as the *Bundestag*), and to all laws which the Constitution declares to be of particular interest to the *Laender*. So far as other laws are concerned, the *Bundesrat*— to which all laws originating with the government have to be sent before they go to the *Bundestag*—has a suspensive veto. If this veto power is exercised with the support of a majority of the *Bundesrat's* members, it can be overridden only by a similar majority of the *Bundestag*. If two-thirds of the *Bundesrat* votes are cast against a bill, the *Bundestag* can override the veto by two thirds of those voting, which must equal at least a majority of its members.

When the *Bundesrat* was instituted it was assumed that it would express primarily the objective interests of the *Laender* and protect them against encroachments by the Federation. Besides, it was hoped that the governments of the *Laender*, themselves aware of the difficulty of carrying on responsible government, would sustain the Federal Government wherever possible. The experience with the comparable body of the Weimar Republic, the *Reichsrat*, seemed to warrant this assumption. The Weimar period, however, lacked the systematic opposition between Social Democrats and Christian Democrats which came to be characteristic of the Bonn Republic. The Center party was a part of all Federal Governments until 1932. It was also part of a coalition with the Social Democrats in Prussia, the *Land* which controlled two-fifths of the total votes in the *Reichsrat*, even if one half of these votes was controlled by the executive committees of the Prussian provinces which, in their partisan composition, did not differ too much from the *Land* government. Under these conditions, a majority in the *Reichsrat* systematically opposed to the Reich Government was impossible.

The Bonn Republic started out with Social Democrats and Christian Democrats opposing each other vigorously on the federal level. At times the Social Democrats controlled the governments of several *Laender* (Schleswig-Holstein, Hesse and Hamburg) with one-party majority governments,[9] and they had a decisive influence in the coalitions governing others. Whether a *Bundesrat* majority systematically opposed to the Adenauer government developed depended upon the coalitions formed in various *Laender*. It could be taken for granted that there would always be a tendency to consider the *Bundesrat* a potential tool of the coalitions formed in the *Laender* against the coalition governing the Federation. Chancellor Adenauer was keenly aware of this situation, and he brought great pressure to bear upon the parties represented in his government, including his own, in the *Laender* to make them enter into coalitions friendly to his policies. It remains to be seen whether, in this respect as in others, his successors will be able to duplicate what his friends call his leadership and his enemies his domination.

JUDICIAL REVIEW.

The powers of the *Bundesrat*, then, create problems for the Federal Government which may yet become serious. Similar considerations apply to the Federal Constitutional Court. The Basic Law confers upon it the task of judicial review of legislative acts as well as certain other duties. The institution itself was highly recommended by

American advisers not all of whom were guided by the proper diagnosis of the problem to be solved. The government of Germany during the Third *Reich* was, to be sure, characterized by too much concentration of power, but the question was whether this did not constitute the swing of the pendulum from the extreme weakness characteristic of the Weimar Republic to the opposite extreme. Wise policy would have proposed an arrangement likely to arrest the swing of the pendulum at the center; it would have aimed at the proper combination of democratic authority and civic liberties.

The Germans who drew up the Basic Law might have benefited, however, from the actual record of judicial review in the United States and might have tried to delineate the function of the Court accordingly. In that case, their guiding consideration would have been caution. Instead, a rather doctrinaire solution was adopted—another demonstration of German "thoroughness." The result was, in the words of Professor Loewenstein, "an effort to commit possibly all political conflicts to a judicial decision as if they were merely legal disputes. This effort may be called the 'judicialization of political dynamics.' " [10] The difference between what the French call "acts of government" and "acts of administration" was overlooked; while the latter may safely be subjected to judicial review, the former, by their very nature, never can be handled satisfactorily that way.

At any rate, Article 93 of the Basic Law says that the Constitutional Court rules, among other cases, on "the interpretation of the Basic Law on the occasion of controversies concerning the extent of the rights and duties of a higher organ of Federal Government or others who are accorded rights of their own through the Basic Law or the rules of one of the highest organs of the Federal Government." This, then, is a wide range of competence, and it is extended by the subsequent provisions of Article 93, as well as by other articles. The implications are aggravated by the fact that cases do not have to come to the Constitutional Court by way of ordinary litigation. A *Land* government, a third of the members of the *Bundestag*, or any group accorded rights by the basis of the Basic Law, or claiming such rights, may institute a suit. Ordinarily, the opposition does control a third of the votes in the *Bundestag* and is then always able to question the validity of any act of the Federal Government. During the first *Bundestag*, the Social Democratic opposition, which had in its ranks a very able exponent of its claims, kept the Constitutional Court busy from the day it began its work.

The law setting up the Court added to the problems connected with it.[11] Thus, in the United States a Supreme Court of nine members handles constitutional as well as ordinary litigation. In Germany, the Basic Law established a Supreme Federal Court for ordinary legislation (*Oberstes Bundesgericht,* Article 95), in addition to the Constitutional Court, which the law then regulating details concerning this body at first endowed with no less than 24 judges who were to decide in two separate Senates of 12 members each. Commonsense would have indicated that a body of 24 members was less likely to work expeditiously than a body of nine, and that even 12 judges may take longer to reach a decision than nine. The reason for the large number of judges, however, is not far to seek. According to Article 94 of the Basic Law, half of the members of the Constitutional Court are to be chosen by the *Bundestag* and half by the *Bundesrat.* Practically speaking, this meant election by the political parties constituting the *Bundestag* and the governments of the *Laender.* If all, or nearly all, political parties were to be accommodated it was imperative to make the cake large enough to go around. In the end, the criticism directed at the Court caused certain changes to be made,[12] one of which was the gradual reduction of the members of each Senate from twelve to eight, this figure to be reached on September 1, 1959.

Actually, the members of the Constitutional Court are able men. They are expected, however, to have the same general political orientation as the parties by which they were nominated. Partisan controversy, therefore, has its echo in Karlsruhe (where both the Constitutional Court and the Federal Supreme Court meet) although the rule that deliberations are strictly confidential, and that no dissenting opinions are published, has helped to establish a certain *esprit de corps.* In a general way, the division between the Adenauer coalition in Bonn and its opponents was reflected in Karlsruhe, and Adenauer soon found it necessary to anticipate substantial difficulties from the Constitutional Court as well as from the *Bundesrat.* The situation became serious when legislation which was intended to lay the basis for rearmament and for European integration became necessary. The SPD claimed that neither step could be taken on the basis of the Constitution as it stood. While this was by no means the opinion of all qualified observers, Adenauer found it advisable to be guided by it. It was therefore decided to amend the Constitution, and this meant that in the *Bundestag* as well as in the *Bundesrat* the Chancellor needed a two-thirds majority in order to carry out his foreign policy. The coalition formed in 1953 lasted just long enough to provide for this majority, although, in the case of rearmament, agreement on the necessary constitutional changes was eventually reached with the SPD.

THE "MATTER" OF GERMAN POLITICS AND THE
MAJOR PARTIES.

The Constitutional Court, then, as well as the *Bundesrat*, are to
be numbered among those institutions which confronted Dr. Adenauer
with unexpected difficulties. He managed to overcome them as he
managed to overcome others. The question arises, however, whether
a successor would be able to accomplish as much. An examination of
the reasons why Adenauer could achieve his dominating position leads
to a variety of factors, enough of which are of a temporary nature to
threaten the future stability of the entire edifice.

The first factor to be mentioned is that the "matter" of German
politics was more favorable to the functioning of democratic institutions at the end of the Second than at the end of the First World War.
This circumstance is a gift bestowed upon German democracy by its
most ardent opponents. Thus, Russian policy under Stalin severely
limited the chances of the German Communist party. The looting and
raping of the Russian-occupied part of Germany, the retention of
German prisoners of war for slave labor, the knowledge acquired by
German soldiers of the primitive living conditions in Russia, the expulsion of fifteen million Germans from the territory east of the Oder-
Neisse Line, the Sudetenland and other areas, and last but not least,
the conditions in the Russian-occupied zone of Germany with its totalitarian terror, made the task of the German Communist party
(KPD) all but hopeless. In 1932 it had been one of the largest parties
in Germany, polling 16.9 per cent in the elections of November of
that year. In 1945 when the American occupation authorities licensed
newspapers, radio stations and news agencies in Germany they considered it natural to treat the Communists as if they represented a
major political party.[12a] Actually, total Communist strength in Western Germany dropped from a high of 9.2 per cent in the earliest
elections,[13] held in 1946, to 5.7 per cent in the *Bundestag* elections of
1949, reaching a low of 2.2 per cent in September, 1953.

What the Communists lost went to the Social Democrats. The
SPD, therefore, never had as formidable a competitor at its Left as it
had to contend with during the Weimar Republic. This accession of
votes from the Left, of course, added to the stresses and strains within
the party. Those favoring the orthodox Marxist line were strengthened
both among the rank and file of the party's followers and among its
leaders. Under a majority system these elements could easily have
been neutralized as, in that case, the strategic position of the inde-

pendent voters in the center would have been so obvious that attracting it to the party's ranks would have been given priority over all
other considerations. Under P.R. there always was the possibility that
the Communist vote might increase again, be it because the Social
Democratic party assumed heavy political responsibilities or because
of a turn in Russian policies. For this reason the SPD stayed farther
to the Left of center than otherwise would have been the case. Also,
it might be mentioned that the attempt of those who, in 1945 and
1946, wanted to jettison the name and the tradition of the party entirely, and establish a labor party on the British model, was handicapped by the accession of the votes from the Left, which was not
compensated by that strengthening of the party's Right wing which
the majority system would have entailed.

On the opposite end of the political spectrum, the Christian
Democrats benefited from the results of Hitler's actions. The Nazis,
instead of pursuing a policy of "divide and rule" in regard to the
major Christian denominations, had persecuted Protestants as well as
Catholics. As a result, the relation between the two leading Christian
denominations became rather friendly in the very land of the Reformation. After the war, it appeared natural to most of the Protestant and
Catholic leaders to cooperate in the political sphere as their churches
had cooperated in the religious sphere during the war. The result was
the foundation of the Christian Democratic Union (CDU), called
Christian Social Union (CSU) in Bavaria. The establishment of this
new party meant that the bulk of the German Protestant vote no longer
went to the anti-republican opposition, as it had done during the
Weimar Republic, when it favored the Nationalists and, subsequently,
the Nazis.[14] The Protestant contingent to the CDU included a great
many judges, civil servants and university professors. If all of them
could be reconciled to the new state, the serious cleavages with which
the history of the Weimar Republic had begun could be avoided. In
this respect the foundation of the CDU could confer upon German
political life some of the advantages which a parliamentary monarchy
might have yielded in 1919.

Inevitably, this accrual of votes from the Right meant difficulties
for the Christian Democrats comparable to those faced by the Social
Democrats on account of their gains from the radical Left. The CDU
leaders endeavored to eliminate from prominent positions in both
party and government all those who had occupied a significant post
under the Nazis, but the line was hard to draw. Again, the difficulties
were greater under P.R. than they would have been under a majority
system. Had everything depended upon the undecided vote in the

center, the pressure on former Rightists inside the CDU (former Nationalists as well as former Nazis) would have been much stronger than it turned out to be. In the long run, all depended on who would assimilate whom, and this is one of the points where the preëminent position of Dr. Adenauer became decisive. His guidance was exercised firmly in the direction of democracy at home and of peace abroad; his great prestige neutralized many an opponent of such policies who might have been harder to handle under a less effective leader.

THE MINOR PARTIES.

Both the SPD and the CDU, then, did have their internal problems. By way of compensation, they were towering giants when compared with the minor parties. Reference has been made to the troubles of the Communist party, and the question arose to what extent parties of the extreme Right would manage to establish themselves. A number of groups and grouplets were founded, particularly after the licensing of a new party by the Allies was no longer required. Eventually, the Socialist Reich's party (SRP) became the leading contender for the new Nazi vote, polling a sensational 11 per cent in the elections to the Diet of Lower Saxony, held in May, 1951. As sober an observer of the German political scene as Professor Ludwig Bergstraesser reached the conclusion that the SRP was there to stay.[15] In this case, a remedy was provided by action on the basis of Article 21 of the Basic Law, which stipulates that parties which "according to their goal or according to the actions of their members aim at interfering with the free democratic order or to eliminate it or to endanger the existence of the Federal Republic of Germany are contrary to the Constitution." The Constitutional Court has to decide whether a particular party fulfills the requirements of this provision, and this was done in a decision announced on October 23, 1952. The party was deemed a revival of the Nazi party and declared dissolved. After this decision its membership dispersed, and it has not presented a political problem since.

There were other attempts to set up parties of the Right, and the most successful one assumed the name of *Deutsche Rechtspartei* (German Right party—DRP). It did win five seats to the *Bundestag* in 1949 and achieved smaller successes on other occasions. Theoretically anti-Nazi, it yet strongly appealed to former Nazi elements. So far, neither it, nor its latter-day version, the *Deutsche Reichspartei* (German Reich party—also abbreviated as DRP) have, to any extent, managed to cope with certain limitations on proportionality in the German election laws which will be discussed presently; in the elections to the Diet of Lower Saxony of April, 1955, for which there were no such restrictions on minor parties, the *Deutsche Reichspartei* secured six out of a total of 159 seats.

The most important of Germany's smaller parties was the Free Democratic party (FDP) which was intended primarily as a successor of the Left-wing Liberal Democratic party (later "State" party) of the Weimar Republic. Many of the leaders of that party had, however, joined the CDU and some have since gone over to the SPD. Both groups preferred, as Friedrich Naumann seemed to demand, a two-party system to the existence of a separate party of their own. On the other hand, when the FDP was established it appealed to the liberalism of the Right, as well as to that of the Left, and finally to elements of a nationalist persuasion, some of which had a Nazi background. Two elements, then, fundamentally different from each other, have constituted both the party's following as well as its leadership. The FDP elected 52 deputies to the first *Bundestag*, 48 to the second and 41 to the third; meanwhile, the membership of that body had been increased from 402 to 497. The party had lost some of its Deputies [16] in 1956 when its leaders decided on a definite break with Dr. Adenauer, but held on to most of its popular following. It remains the strongest of the minor German parties.

The German party (DP) started from a nucleus formed by the former Guelphs who had protested the absorption of the Kingdom of Hanover by Prussia after the war of 1866. The Guelphs cooperated rather closely with the Center party during the Empire and less closely during the Weimar Republic. In 1947 an attempt was made to broaden the party's basis all over Germany. There seemed to be a "gap" in the German party system as long as there was no specific party of the Right. The DP elected 17 Deputies in 1949, 15 in 1953 and 17 in 1957, when it was combined with the "Free People's party," the pro-Adenauer Free Democrats. It cooperated rather closely with the Adenauer cabinet in Bonn, but lost part of its popular following as a result.

The Refugee party, whose original German name gave it the initials BHE, and later called itself *Gesamtdeutscher Block* (GB), seemed to be able to count on a large readymade following on account of the fact that close to 10 of the 50 million people living in the Federal Republic are expellees or refugees. For the election of 1949 it had not been licensed, but in the Diet election in Schleswig-Holstein, held in 1950, it managed to secure 23.4 per cent of the total number of votes, becoming the second strongest party in that *Land*. In the *Bundestag* elections of 1953, it secured 5.9 per cent of the total number of votes and 27 seats; thereupon, it joined the second Adenauer cabinet. As in the case of the FDP the rank and file of the party, both in the *Bundestag* and in the country, chafed under the inhibitions resulting from this coalition, and the bulk of the BHE Deputies seceded from it, leaving the rest, including some former leaders, to join the CDU. In 1957, the party failed to secure five per cent of the total vote, and obtained no seats.

The remaining parties have either proven ephemeral, as the so-called Economic Reconstruction party of Mr. Loritz, or they are typical splinter parties. A possible exception is the Bavarian party. As its name indicates it is to emphasize the demands for Bavarian autonomy within the Federal Republic, but its followers, who first supported the CSU, are at times also tinged by a measure of anti-clericalism. With 4.2 per cent of the total vote the party obtained 17 seats in the first Bonn Diet, whereas with 1.7 per cent in the second Diet election (9.2 per cent of the votes cast in Bavaria) it secured no seats at all. In 1953, a party not electing at least one Deputy in a single-member district had to poll five per cent of the votes cast in the entire country rather than in a particular *Land*. Reference has already been made to the Center party, a small Christian Democratic group which objects to the Adenauer leadership, and places itself to the Left of the CDU. Its electorate is almost exclusively Catholic, and its following has shown a tendency to decline. Still, it was able to play a crucial part in the politics of North Rhine-Westphalia, the *Land* where it has the largest following. It had nine Deputies in the first *Bundestag*, and two in the second. For the elections of 1957 the Bavarian party and the Center party had combined to form the "Federalist Union." The combination obtained, however, only one per cent of the vote cast in the Federal Republic. In Bavaria, it did secure four per cent, but in North Rhine-Westphalia, the stronghold of the Center party, only 0.8 per cent. The provisions of the election law deviated sufficiently from "pure" P.R. to prevent either party from securing a seat.

THE ELECTORAL SYSTEM.

The list of smaller parties is, then, rather long; in addition to those mentioned there have been several dozen others. Still, in 1946, the preponderance of the CDU and the SPD was overwhelming, and it was to become so again for elections to the third *Bundestag* in 1957. Under a plurality system, and perhaps under any other form of majority voting, a two-party system would have established itself from the outset in the same sense in which it exists in England: one party would, as a rule, have obtained an overall majority of the seats, enabling it to form a homogeneous cabinet, certain of ruling for the duration of the parliament in question.

Germans belonging to all democratic persuasions had demanded the majority system during the Nazi reign. After the war, there developed at the University of Heidelberg an intellectual center which provided for coordination among those demanding a plurality system.[17] Everything depended on the first elections to be held. Had they taken place under a plurality system, this would have become a permanent feature of German politics, and the two-party system with it. On the other hand, the use of P.R. was bound to mean two things: The rise of minor parties which, even with a small percentage of the total popular vote, might be able to turn the scales in favor of P.R., and a shift of the balance of power within each major party towards the party bureaucracy, and the permanent and organized party members. These elements found P.R. more to their liking than an electoral system which makes everything dependent upon the undecided voters whom the party organizers despise as "driftwood."

Two major groups of factors cooperated to bring about the readoption of P.R. First, among the occupying powers the Russians were in favor of P.R. as a matter of principle. Molotov underlined this fact when he demanded, during the Moscow Conference of 1947, that the peace treaty make P.R. compulsory for all German elections, including those in municipalities; and the Russian demand for P.R. was repeated during the Berlin Conference of January, 1954. On the other hand, the American military government represented a nation deeply wedded to the plurality system. At the same time, the intellectual centers in favor of that system of voting were located in the American zone, Heidelberg and Frankfurt. This is not the place to discuss in detail the decisions of the American military government, as those responsible for them acted with the best of intentions. Yet much is to be said for what the then Congressman (now Senator) Francis Case (who had been in Germany in the summer of 1947 as the head of a subcommittee of the Herter Committee), expressed in these words:

> The War Department sets up military government. Military government acquiesced in the decision, if it did not encourage it—and I am inclined to think that they encouraged it—that they should use proportional representation in electing members of the *Landtag* and setting up the ministries in the various *Laender* . . .[18]

General Clay and those of his advisers at whose suggestion the procedure leading to P.R. was adopted have always emphasized that the decision was made by Germans. As in the British zone, committees were appointed representing the various licensed political parties in proportion to what the occupying powers considered their strength in the electorate. This meant that the principle of P.R. was embodied in the very composition of these committees, in which the minor parties turned the scales between the major ones. It should have surprised no one that these bodies decided in favor of P.R., and that the Diets elected under that system continued it. The only way to make possible a genuine German decision on the electoral system would have been a plebiscite. Opponents of P.R. demanded it only to be turned down by the occupation authorities.

The final adoption of P.R. would nonetheless not have taken place except for the SPD's decision in its favor. During the closing years of the Weimar Republic and during the Third *Reich,* there had been no lack of Social Democrats who demanded the majority system. The so-called "Prague Manifesto," issued in January, 1934, by the party's executive committee, then in exile in Prague, demanded for the time after Hitler's defeat a "popular representation elected according to a universal, equal, direct and secret franchise, in single-member constituencies." [19] The reference to "single-member constituencies" does not necessarily entail the advocacy of majority voting but was, apparently, meant to do so.

Two factors were responsible for the party's changing its stand in 1945 and 1946. In the first place, the SPD's traditional strongholds were situated in what became the Russian zone of occupation. This meant that the SPD could not hope to benefit from the majority system in the same way as the CDU. In the second place, the fiery Dr. Kurt Schumacher became the party's leader. Before 1933, he had been only one of several prominent men in what was then the younger generation in the party's leadership. Dr. Karl Mierendorff and Julius Leber were better known to the general public, and would, under normal conditions, have had at least as good a chance to become party leaders as Dr. Schumacher. Mierendorff, however, after having been released from a Nazi concentration camp, was killed in an Allied air-raid, and Leber was executed by the Nazis for his participation in the attempt to assassinate Hitler. Both had been vigorous opponents of P.R. There remained eloquent proponents of majority voting in the party, such as Herman Lüdemann, the first Social Democratic Prime Minister of Schleswig-Holstein, Gustav Dahrendorff in Hamburg, Emil Peter Walk in Darmstadt, and of the younger party members, Fritz Piefke in Berlin. Schumacher's decision in favor of P.R., however, although contested step by step, particularly by Lüdemann, tilted the scales inside the party in favor both of the party bureaucracy and the elements of the party's Left which used their influence against the majority system in all subsequent discussions.

THE NEW ELECTION LAWS.

The first elections on a *Land*-wide scale were held in the American zone. They were organized, rather unimaginatively, on the basis of the system of rigid lists as it had existed during the Weimar Republic. English influence brought modifications for the British zone which eventually were adopted for federal as well as for most of the *Land* elections. A *Land* would be divided into a certain number of constituencies, within which the candidate with the plurality of the votes would be declared elected. In addition, there was a so-called reserve list, which was intended to produce the overall effects of P.R. On this list a number of seats was made available to the parties, which was later to range up to 50 per cent of the total. The overall strength of a party would be determined on the basis of P.R. for the *Land* as a whole. The seats obtained in single-member constituencies were deducted from the total attributed to it.

In *Land* after *Land*, the CDU and the SPD would take almost all of the seats won by pluralities, whereas the minor party would secure all, or nearly all, of their seats through the reserve list. Also, whichever of the two major parties was comparatively weak in a given *Land* was able to make up for that deficiency in part by securing a number of seats from the reserve list, thereby helping to prevent its leading competitor from securing an overall majority.

This type of election law does have its advantages when compared with the system of rigid lists which prevailed during the Weimar period. As we have seen, the rigid lists meant that various groups within a large party would force it to place their representatives on the list regardless of the qualifications for political leadership which these candidates might have. Besides, nobody was specifically responsible for a particular local area, and the relationship between the voters and their representatives was rather tenuous. Under the new dispensation, the candidates presented in single-member constituencies must be more than representatives of just one economic interest. They must appeal to the general type of voter upon whom the party in question relies. He need not be the undecided voter in the center whom the majority system makes the uncrowned king of democracy; he may, in fact, have his political domicile close to the extremes. Still, he appreciates, and is likely to get, a more rounded personality than the voters of the Weimar period could expect. The visitor to the

Bundestag, in particular, soon notices that there is no lack of men with a general ability; the material for political leadership is distinctly better than it was in the *Reichstag*. The beneficial effects of the new system of selection extend to the Deputies elected from the reserve lists; many of them were, at the same time, candidates in single-member constituencies. Besides, assignment to a particular district makes the Deputies a little less dependent upon the party bosses (and the party bureaucrats) who, under the system of rigid lists, could decide whether a Deputy was to have a chance to be reelected or not. When, for example, the executive committee of the SPD in Schleswig-Holstein decided that their own former Prime Minister, Herman Lüdemann, was to be dropped for the Diet elections of 1954, the local committee in Lübeck presented him again, making it possible for him to return to the Diet.

This independence, however, has its limits. The voter, invariably confronted with at least half a dozen candidates and parties thinks more in terms of parties than in terms of candidates. The power of the party bosses remains great, as most Deputies appreciate a place on the reserve list as a form of insurance against defeat. The minor parties, beginning with the FDP, elect virtually everybody from the reserve list. This gives their leaders almost as absolute a power over the political life of their party's Deputies as Hugenberg wielded over the Nationalist party during the Weimar Republic.[20]

LIMITS ON PROPORTIONALITY.

The reason why Germany's new election laws have contributed to political stability is to be found, however, mainly in limitations on proportionality, which may operate indirectly as well as directly. Thus, as long as the occupation authorities reserved the right to license political parties, they kept various minor groups off the ballot. Their leaders might appear as candidates in the single-member constituencies, where their chances were small anyway, but they could not participate in the distribution of the seats from the reserve lists. These Allied restrictions had a definite effect on the outcome of the *Bundestag* elections of 1949 which (by a very small margin) were to allow Dr. Adenauer to set the political pattern of the Federal Republic.

Indirect limitations upon the proportionality of P.R. in the current German election laws arise further from decisions of the Constitutional Court which, under Article 21 of the Basic Law can—upon the request of the government—declare parties unconstitutional. Thus the Socialist Reichs party (SRP) was declared unconstitutional in 1953 and the Communist party (KPD) in 1956. Such parties are disbanded; they cannot participate in elections. Insofar as this prohibition is not circumvented—which has not been done to date—the splitting up of parties characteristic of P.R. is limited.

Political splintering is restricted even more effectively by the so-called *Sperrklauseln*, the provisions according to which a party, in order to share in the distribution of seats from the reserve list, must poll a certain fraction of the total vote, usually five per cent. Most laws permit an exception to this rule for parties which elect at least one candidate in a local constituency, although for the Federal elections of 1957 this number had been raised to three. Typical splinter parties find either hurdle too high. A larger party may assist them by not presenting a candidate of its own in certain constituencies, but this will be done only in favor of parties which are expected to cooperate in the furtherance of certain common policies, and it is not necessarily effective.

The practical significance of these provisions is difficult to overestimate. They placed the minor parties, from the outset, under heavy pressure, and this pressure was even more effective in preventing voters—who were afraid to "throw their votes away"—from supporting them than it was in keeping votes actually cast for these parties from being turned into seats. When, in both 1953 and 1957, the choice between parties that mattered narrowed down to the Christian Democrats and the Social Democrats this decreased the incentive to support one of the minor parties.

German observers have not always realized that the *Sperrklauseln*, have been fairly efficient for a particular reason: The extremist parties were small enough to be affected by a five per cent clause, and the two minor parties of democratic persuasion, the FDP and the DP, which may be said to represent "principle" rather than mere "interest" and which, at the same time, are not mere splinter parties, have, so far, been able to take these handicaps. In France neither the Communists nor the Gaullists nor the Poujadists would have been hurt by such limitations. Conditions are similar in Italy, where Communists and Left-wing Socialists are certain, and neo-Fascists and Monarchists likely, to overcome such limitations, but where Republicans and Liberals could not have survived them, with the Social Democrats never entirely certain whether they could accomplish such a feat. The reason, then, why these clauses have, in Germany, more or less served the purpose which they were intended to serve is, again, to be found in the particular shape of the "matter" of the country's politics, which need not be of a permanent nature.

The effects of the limitations on proportionality were clearly discernible as early as in the Federal elections of 1949. Adenauer's first coalition consisted of Christian Democrats, Free Democrats and the German party. The CDU, with complete proportionality between votes cast and seats received, would have obtained 125 instead of 139 seats; the FDP would have secured 48 instead of 52, and the DP 16 instead of 17. The three parties actually had a total of 208 out of 402 seats; complete P.R. would have given them 189. That most of the gains were made by the CDU is particularly important because several Rightist Deputies elected by the DP and the FDP did not vote for Adenauer in the crucial ballot where he needed 202 votes to become Chancellor and received exactly that number.[21] The 14 CDU votes due to deviation from complete proportionality could not have been replaced from any other source.

There were, at that time, enough politicians in Germany who wanted coalitions of the weak, and necessarily unstable, Weimar type. These men were willing to resort to almost any device to get rid of a man with as much personal authority as Dr. Adenauer. They did not succeed, although one experienced Western official felt that Germany's new government was "off to a shaky start," [22] even after Dr. Adenauer had been elected. The new Chancellor had been forced, in fact, to make all kinds of concessions, including the appointment of ministers to non-existent ministries. New ministerial departments were created in order to accommodate all parties; the head of one of them soon found himself called "the most superfluous Federal Minister of all times"—"*Uebaz*" [23] for short. Eventually, Dr. Adenauer was to take the measure of his opponents, but this is one of the cases where it is *not* possible to say that "all's well that ends well" simply because not all is over yet. Adenauer and his party experienced serious difficulties before riding to the unexpected triumphs scored in the *Bundestag* elections of 1953 and 1957. These difficulties may recur and change the pattern of German politics completely.

THE THREAT TO THE MAJOR PARTIES.

For a time it seemed, indeed, that the ascendency of the two major parties was in jeopardy. In the earliest elections, held in various *Laender* in 1946, the SPD and CDU together had obtained more than 90 per cent of the total number of votes. The *Bundestag* elections of 1949 saw their percentage decline to 70.2. Professor Alfred Weber of the University of Heidelberg [24] was not alone in fearing that Germany might have entered what one of the country's best known parliamentary correspondents, on a later occasion, called "the Weimar express." [25] The Lower Saxon elections of May, 1951, seemed to more than justify such apprehensions. On that occasion the CDU had presented a joint ticket with the German party which, in the Federal elections of 1949, had secured 17.8 per cent of the total vote cast in Lower Saxony. This combination of CDU and DP, and the SPD, together obtained 67.4 per cent of the total vote, whereas the three parties had obtained 87.1 per cent of the vote in the state election of April 20, 1947. During this period the strength of the SPD had declined from 43.3 to 33.7, and that of the CDU and DP combined from 47.8 to 23.7 per cent.

In some of the *Land* elections the decline of the CDU went so far as to constitute a collapse. Thus, in Hesse, where it had reached 38.1 per cent in the county elections of April 28, 1946, it went down to 17.8 in the local elections of May 4, 1952. In Bremen the CDU declined from a high of 22.0 per cent in the elections of October 12, 1947, to 9.1 in the elections of October 7, 1951.

Hesse and Bremen demonstrated that the following of the CDU is by no means as consolidated as that of the SPD. Generally speaking, the Catholic vote which had followed the old Center party stayed with the CDU, whereas the Protestant vote, which previously had mostly gone to parties farther to the Right, left it in large and overwhelming numbers, to return whenever the party took a definite upswing, as in the Federal elections of 1953 and 1957.

THE SOCIAL MARKET POLICY.

Two main factors, not easily separated, are responsible for the fact that the trend toward a catastrophic decline in the vote cast for the CDU was reversed in the *Bundestag* elections of 1953 and 1957: Konrad Adenauer's leadership and the success of the "social market policy" pursued by his government. The theoretical outline for this policy had been developed by a group of academic economists informally headed by Professor Walter Eucken of the University of Freiburg during the final years of the Third *Reich*. It is typical that a professor of economics, Ludwig Erhard, should have become the leading economic expert of the CDU and successively the Director of the Bizonal Department of Economic Affairs and the economics minister of the Adenauer cabinet.[26] By 1957 the success of the social market policy was so obvious that it was being taken for granted. During the early years it was beset, however, by a most formidable opposition, and even certain members of the coalition, particularly those belonging to the left wing of the CDU, were inclined to believe that it constituted the high road to catastrophe. When Erhard resisted all attempts to introduce a substantial measure of centralized economic planning, he had to fight almost as strongly against a trend as Secretary of Agriculture Ezra S. Benson did in the United States when he opposed rigid parities for farm products.

Erhard's policy had its drawbacks. Thus, a number of new millionaires appeared who, even though their fortune was measured in D-marks rather than in dollars, were conspicuous enough in a country in which misery and destitution continued to appear among the expellees and those who had lost their homes through bombing. On the other hand, this policy succeeded in paving the way for the employment of millions of people who had come from the outside and whose economic integration at first appeared utterly impossible. After provision had been made for the most primitive needs, the German standard of living began to improve. With a top group of industrial workers, the improvement soon went far enough to bring about a perceptible lessening of class tensions. These workers no longer considered themselves "proletarians" in the traditional Marxist sense of the term. In addition, there was the increasing number of white-collar employees, who rejected any Marxist ideology outright. The overall benefits of the social market policy—which was, of course, assisted by the Marshall Plan—were more clearly discernible in 1953 and 1957 than they had been in 1949, and German specialists in the field of public opinion research are inclined to attribute the great electoral victory obtained by the CDU on both occasions more to the success of the coalition's economic policy than to any other single factor.

THE ADENAUER LEADERSHIP.

Dr. Adenauer's leadership must, however, be said to be part and parcel of the success of the social market policy.[27] His personal interests have always been concentrated on foreign affairs, and his share in the formulation and execution of the social market policy is generally considered minor. Yet, it was he who formed the coalition which carried out this policy, and held it together; it is difficult to see how the social market policy could have succeeded without him. Besides, both in 1953 and in 1957, Adenauer's foreign policy made its contribution to the success of the CDU. By 1953 Germany had been promised recognition as an equal. European integration, as evidenced by the Schuman Plan and the EDC, was at the height of its popularity, and the Chancellor's reception during his first trip to the United States, made at Easter in 1953, was regarded as a triumph. By 1957 the work for European integration had recovered from its earlier setbacks. The treaties providing for a Common Market of six European nations had been ratified, and Adenauer managed to demonstrate that his firm alliance with Washington was based on equality of rights for his country.

All of these specific points are overshadowed by Adenauer's general characteristics. It is difficult to discuss them in terms likely to meet with complete acceptance, as his opponents will attach a negative valuation to anything which his proponents praise. The basic features stand out, however, rather strongly. Adenauer undoubtedly is the first German political leader since Bismarck who had both a genuine political vision and who was, at the same time, fortunate enough to encounter conditions making it possible for him to govern in accordance with that vision. The average German politician is overawed by the *Fachmann*, the expert who had such a large share in the government and the glories of the Empire; to this day, few Germans pay attention to Max Weber's warning that the ultimate collapse of the Empire was due precisely to a system which entrusted to experts tasks which they were not equipped to perform. Bismarck put these experts into the saddle, but he never allowed them to hold the reins. When, for example, he wanted the draft of a new law on a particular topic, he would call in the *Geheimrat*, the "Privy Councillor" in charge of that particular subject, whose title added so heavily to this official's feeling of importance. When the expert had completed his assignment, Bismarck would not let him come to his office to present him with a long speech, emphasizing that everything just had to be the way the *Fachmänner* deemed best. The "Iron Chancellor" might invite him to go horsebackriding with him in the *Tiergarten*, the park adjoining the *Wilhelmstrasse*, and in the ensuing conversation, the political leader would hold the initiative, asking the expert the pertinent questions rather than allow himself to be overwhelmed by a mass of technicalities.

Adenauer did not take his experts for horseback rides, but in all other respects he treated them in the same way Bismarck did. When, for example, he called in his economic advisers to get their opinions on the proposed common market for iron and steel, the so-called Schuman Plan, he told them from the outset that what he wanted to know from them was not whether the plan was to be carried out but merely *how* it was to be carried out. The Chancellor had made up his mind that a new split between Germany and the Western world must be prevented at all costs, and that as close a measure of integration with France as possible had to be sought. The Iron and Steel Community did have its drawbacks from the German point of view; Germany had to export coke and coal to France and Belgium at a low price, and reimport coal from the United States at a much higher price. For Adenauer this was a regrettable, but minor, matter. He did not want a repetition of the events following World War I when for years there were men at the helm both in France and Germany who sincerely wanted cooperation between their two countries, but who were again and again thrown off the track by disagreements on comparatively minor issues, which partisan agitation could manage to magnify out of all proportions. Adenauer persisted in this attitude when it became difficult, as it did in the case of the EDC, and in particular in the case of the Saar agreement. In its original form the latter entailed sacrifices to which Germans, particularly nationalistic Germans, were highly sensitive, as the Saar was to remain separated from Germany. The French wanted this arrangement to be ratified by a plebiscite, and this plebiscite unexpectedly yielded an overwhelming majority against the agreement, indicating a strong wish for a return to Germany. New negotiations had to be initiated, and the French agreed to the Saar becoming a *Land* in the Federal Republic. It was fortunate that while these matters were being dealt with there were men in power, both in France and in Germany, who were determined that there should be no nationalistic agitation of the kind which had undermined incipient friendly relationships between the two countries repeatedly during the Weimar period. In France Guy Mollet lasted just long enough to carry through the French part of the bargain. As it happened, this display of courage on both sides of the Rhine did not inflict any serious political damage on either of the two principals involved, although Adenauer and the CDU were taunted during the 1957 election campaign with their apparent willingness to "sacrifice" the Saar. Men of lesser stature would never have assumed such risks.

All of these decisions had aspects which were bound to lead to resentment on the part of Adenauer's coalition partners, in particular since there were strongly nationalistic elements in the Free German and, to a lesser extent, in the German party. Besides, the Social Democratic party had, under Dr. Schumacher, taken a turn which always brought it close to nationalistic demands in the field of foreign affairs. The way coalitions normally function, all important steps would have been taken up not only in cabinet meetings, but also in protracted negotiations between party authorities outside of the government. Such conditions rarely permit true leadership. At times the tail is allowed to wag the dog; the power of the smaller coalition partners can be great enough to give them a clearcut veto on all decisions. Adenauer was determined never to allow matters to reach such a point. He would take the initiative and press it for whatever it was worth, always ready, however, to back down, and apparently even to capitulate, when it seemed that he had reached the limit of what was possible. Patience, in fact, is as much one of his attributes as is political vision and determination. On various occasions during his tenure, it appeared that he was not only "down" but "out" (at any rate during his first term), but "the old one" knew that there would be another day and that time might allow him to recuperate his political as well as his physical strength.

Yet, it is natural that Adenauer's attitude, with all its obvious advantages, should have been resented by his coalition partners. They had not been consulted beforehand on decisions for which they would have to bear the responsibility as much as the Chancellor or his party, the CDU—which he, incidentally, might not consult any more seriously than the coalition partners. Besides, while sharing in the risks of the coalition the minor parties never fully shared in its results. The German *Wahlwunder* [28]—"Election Miracle"—of September, 1953, saw the FDP's percentage of the total vote decline from 11.9 to 9.5, and that of the DP from 4.0 to 3.2 at the same time that the leading coalition party, the CDU, increased its share from 31.0 to 45.2. Actually, the limitations on the proportionality of the election law had made it possible for the CDU to obtain a—bare—absolute majority of the total number of seats, 244 out of 487. The FDP leaders, in particular, considered this outcome highly unfair. They felt, so far as the social market policy was concerned, that they had made a decisive contribution to its initiation and continuation; during the Korean crisis not a few of the members of the CDU would have been willing to resort to a substantial measure of centralized economic planning, which the resistance of the FDP prevented. Yet, all the advantages of that policy went to the CDU.

This being the case, the FDP and the DP were determined to secure an authoritative share in the new coalition, and so was the Refugee party which Adenauer had decided to take into his government in order to secure a two-thirds majority in both *Bundestag* and *Bundesrat*. The immediate result was prolonged and somewhat unseemly bargaining about seats in the new cabinet. Adenauer had been compelled to create additional cabinet posts in 1949 in order to satisfy the demands of his coalition partners, and he had to go even farther on this occasion, enlarging the cabinet to 19 members. The FDP with 14.4 per cent of the total coalition strength secured four of these seats, equal to 22 per cent of the total number of cabinet members, and the DP with 4.5 per cent of the coalition's Diet seats two cabinet positions, equal to 7.1 per cent of the cabinet's membership. In appearance, then, some of the typical features of coalition government developed, although in reality the figures told only a part of the story because the minor parties did not obtain any of the key positions in the cabinet, nor did their influence on government policy increase.

At any rate, Adenauer soon managed to exceed the limitations which his partners believed they had imposed upon him. Complaints were again made that the Chancellor had decided important issues without consulting his allies. Relations became more strained as time went on. In 1955 the BHE left the coalition and in 1956 the FDP, although some of the Deputies of both parties decided to stay with the government. The official leaders of the two groups stated that their objections were not to any genuine coalition with the CDU, but to the chancellorship of Dr. Adenauer who, they charged, wanted to dominate rather than to lead. It might be added in passing that Adenauer never had any experience in cabinet government before he became Chancellor. His personal habits had been shaped by his long and successful tenure as Lord Mayor of Cologne. The administrative system under which he served during that period gave him virtually unlimited control over the city executive. The men with whom he worked were qualified, to be sure, but they played a purely technical part, looking to their chief for guidance in regard to policy. Adenauer simply transferred this system to his tenure as Chancellor, and managed to make it yield results in spite of the furore he created not only among his coalition partners but, at times, within the ranks of his own supporters.

Objections to the way in which Adenauer managed the coalition, therefore, were not unnatural. Those who raise them have not always been aware, however, of the implications of their charges. It is easy to talk of a "true partnership" between coalition parties, but the experience of not a few countries, including that of Weimar Germany, show the results of attempts to govern in that manner. Inevitably, there develops a tendency toward mutual paralysis. A strong personality may assuage it for a time, but in the long run it will leave its mark on everything such a coalition does or does not do. Also, we must repeat that, not infrequently in a "coalition among equals" the small parties are, like some of the animals in George Orwell's *Animal Farm,* "more equal than others." It will be useful to quote, once again, what Professor Heuss had to say about the consequences resulting from the rejection of Friedrich Naumann's criticism of P.R.:

> How clearly he [Naumann] foresaw coming developments it is not necessary to demonstrate; the searching for a majority was bound to shift the power of decision and the responsibility to the small groups

which, formed on an economic, denominational, or geographic basis and kept alive only by P.R., were still just "needed," and therefore determined, if one wants to accept a kind of political "marginal utility" —or "marginal cost"—theory, the parliamentary "price formation." [29]

If then, the Adenauer leadership meant too much power for the coalition's leader and for his party, the leaders of the minor coalition partners were perhaps not unaware of the disproportionate influence which would have accrued to them under the type of coalition practice typical of P.R.

If those who were looking forward to the end of the "Adenauer era" were inclined to forget what the Weimar experience had taught them about the facts of life characterizing coalition governments, one of the reasons is that as long as men like Dr. Adenauer are active in political affairs they cast a shadow over everything else, including the action patterns of their opponents. A comparable case is that of Prime Minister De Valera in Ireland, who remained the recognized leader of Fianna Fail, the strongest party in the country, when he had to relinquish the premiership in 1948 and 1954. That party and its leader, as everyone knew, stood ready to reassume control as soon as the coalition formed against them should slip. De Valera's leading opponent, the Fine Gael leader, John Costello, had been obliged to form his "inter-party governments" on the principle of "ring around the rosie": He united all parties against Fianna Fail, those at its Left as well as those at its Right, just as it was done in Bavaria in 1954 against the CSU and in North Rhine-Westphalia in 1956 against the CDU. Except for the overpowering wish to check the strongest party, the coalitions formed against it would have been too heterogeneous even to have come into existence, let alone to last. They could be expected to last, however, only as long as the strongest party retained its strength. An eclipse of that party would mean the end of such a coalition. [30]

In a post-Adenauer Germany, then, coalitions formed against the CDU-CSU would be one thing as long as that party could maintain its strength as Fianna Fail did after 1948 and 1954; they would lose their *raison d'être* with a decline of the common enemy. It remains to be seen whether the CDU would hold together in defeat the way Fine Gael did. The CDU-CSU does contain elements differing strongly from each other; there is the conflict between Protestants, Catholics, and Liberals; between those favoring Dr. Adenauer's Western orientation and those lukewarm toward it; between those strongly in favor of free enterprise and those willing to meet the Social Democrats half-way on the road to centralized economic planning. There is tension also around other issues and, therefore, the disintegration of a post-Adenauer CDU-CSU remains a distinct possibility. It is often said that not a few Social Democratic leaders look forward to it as it would leave them in the field as Germany's only major political force. The fulfillment of their wish might lead, however, to a weakening of their own party. After 1953 many voters turned to the SPD because they felt that this was the only way to check Dr. Adenauer and the CDU. Should the CDU ever be deprived of its status as a political power always able to bid for the control of the government, that incentive would vanish. Voters might again disperse in all directions, with a separate party for every interest and for every ideology.

It is difficult to see how, in such a case, a return to the coalition practice of old, with its haggling among the parties (the Germans call it *Kuhhandel*—"cow bargaining") could be avoided. The minor parties would again attempt to impose the law of action—or inaction— upon the major ones. It is not necessary to delve into past history in order to find illustrations for such procedures. While coalition practice in Bonn was characterized by the leadership (or "domination") of the CDU, matters were quite different in some of the *Laender*, with parties large and small cheerfully imitating the principals of an oriental bargain bazaar in settling points of policy and patronage. The ten-week crisis which took place in the Saar, the youngest of the Federal Republic's *Laender*, in the spring and early summer of 1957 is a case in point, but there is no lack of parallels elsewhere, particularly in Lower Saxony.

Should such conditions ever develop on the Federal as well as on the *Land* level, the relative consolidation of democratic institutions which has taken place in Germany would be in danger. While one cannot say that there has been any widespread enthusiasm for democracy in the Federal Republic, there yet has been a growing willingness to accept the democratic order as at least relatively satisfactory— certainly preferable to a totalitarianism of either the Right or the Left. The German voter is not "sold" on democracy; like the man from Missouri, he "wants to be shown." If political conditions begin to be less satisfactory than they have been under Adenauer, the criticism of democracy, always influential on the literary level,[31] will again affect the people at large and express itself in votes cast against the SPD as well as the CDU. Certainly, those who have always felt that the absence of a major party to the Right of the CDU constituted a "gap" in the German party system will, when treated again to years of ineffectual coalition government, be likely to have enough others agree with them to bring about the rebirth of something similar to the old Nationalist party. The mere existence of such a group would not only complicate the functioning of the parliamentary game but also provide a background for intensified intellectual criticism of democracy.

MILITANT DEMOCRACY.

In theory, the turning away from the SPD and the CDU could not be extended to the founding of new totalitarian parties of the Right and Left. Article 21 of the Basic Law remains in existence, and so does the ban of the neo-Nazi SRP and of the KPD. Legal rules providing for "militant democracy" [32] have not, however, always given satisfaction. They have achieved their purposes easily in countries such as England where the plurality system of voting keeps all extremists under such popular pressure that the only measures needed are of a marginal nature, consisting, for example, of a ban on private armies and on provocative party parades. Wherever the political system through the use of P.R. has encouraged (rather than repressed) the growth of totalitarian parties, it has found itself brought up against its own inconsistencies in its attempts to provide for legal controls. It has found it particularly difficult to cope with the possibility of camouflage. Thus, in Czechoslovakia, the official Nazi party was banned under legislation providing for "militant democracy," but the supposedly non-Nazi "Sudeten German Heimat" party of Konrad Henlein proved to be a more than adequate substitute. Similar legislation may be circumvented in similar ways in other countries, in particular, since under a political system governed by P.R. a small party may force the hand of the larger ones to bring about inaction in regard to a totalitarian group.

Measures of "militant democracy" have other disadvantages if they must resort to a ban on a political party. Thus, in Germany, the outlawing of the Communist party constituted a serious propagandistic setback for the Federal Republic in its efforts to secure the country's reunification. Russian and satellite propagandists lost no time in broadcasting the claim that the ban on the KPD constituted a serious interference with the freedom for political parties which Western Germany demanded for the Russian-occupied zone. It goes without saying that the outlawing of a political party constituted in such a way as to threaten the existence of all other parties is one thing, and the suppression of all political freedom something else again. Yet, Communist propagandists found it easy to win sympathy for their claims among the uncritical. Admittedly, at the time the ban was issued, the German Communists would have been unable, under a majority system, to have elected a single candidate anywhere, a fact which would have deprived them even more securely of the possibility of sabotaging parliamentary institutions from within than did the hurdle of the five per cent clause (which the Communists might have been able to vault at some future date). Communist failure in elections would not eliminate, of course, the need for close surveillance of the underground apparatus which, in the case of more than one Communist party, is more important than the visible organization. However, such problems are in no way lessened by a legal ban.[33] The dangers of treason, espionage, sabotage and subversion (by infiltrating either the government or private organizations, including political parties) remains; to engage in such conspirational activities may appear even more glamorous after a party has been officially outlawed.

There is the further problem of punishing those who take part in the activities of an outlawed party. One of the judges concerned with these matters, in referring to the consequences of the ban of the Communist party, spoke of a "flood of potential prosecutions,"[34] and rather conservative writers[35] argued that a political amnesty was imperative. All of these difficulties resulted from the fact that the judicial process was burdened with a task primarily political in nature. That task the German voter himself, if armed with the simple instrument of majority voting, would have handled to the satisfaction of everyone except the Communists themselves.[36]

There is also the problem of other parties which might develop. At the Left a party on the model of the Independent Socialists of 1917 might succeed. Tickets under this and similar designations have been presented repeatedly. So far they have not been successful, partly because of the five per cent clause. Matters would change materially if the SPD had to assume the burden of government in difficult times, or in coalition with "bourgeois" parties of a type which the Leftists in its ranks would resent more strongly than the parties with which the SPD has cooperated to date.

Minor parties could also arise on the basis of economic interest. So far the constant pressure for the foundation of a new Farmers' party has been resisted; most farmers support the CDU. Farming is, however, in as difficult a situation in Germany as in the United States. Farm prices show a tendency to decline in relation to industrial prices, and costs, particularly labor costs, mount sharply. The prosperity in German industry causes deep inroads on the market of farm labor, and even small German farmers may now find it necessary to rely on foreign, especially Italian labor, which also requires a higher outlay than many a farmer's budget can stand. The Adenauer government, led by the very competent Minister of Agriculture Luebke, is trying its best to give the farmers both temporary relief of a type the consumer can tolerate, and assistance in adapting themselves to change by reducing their costs, particularly by the consolidation of the widely separated plots of land which many German farmers now cultivate. The latter measure involves new sets of both farm and residential buildings and is, therefore, both slow and costly. It will at any rate, be a long time before the German farm problem is solved and, in the meantime, the rise of a Farmers' party is always a possibility.

So is the development of a new Middle Class party. At present, its prospects are impeded even more drastically by the five per cent clause than are those of a Farmers' party. All of these limitations on proportionality may be eliminated, however, under the pressure of the small parties now represented in the various Diets.

ELEMENTS OF DEMOCRATIC STRENGTH.

The danger of new political splintering in the Bonn Republic is, for all of these reasons, real enough, but it is definitely of a long-run rather than of a short-run variety. It is vital to warn against overconfidence so far as the prospects of democratic stability in Germany are concerned; on the other hand, there are impressive elements of strength, which no one should disregard. Some of the accomplishments of the Adenauer period do promise to be lasting. This applies particularly to the "social market policy" and to the "economic miracle" which it has produced. The Federal Republic has not only avoided a serious depression; its economy has been dynamic to such an extent that it can be compared only to the boom conditions existing in the United States between 1924 and 1929. Much depends on whether this kind of dynamism can be maintained. Professor Erhard and his associates are inclined to answer this question with an unqualified "yes," provided that no basic elements of this policy are changed. The number of professional economists who agree with Erhard is not inconsiderable. If these optimists are right, the economic disturbances which had an essential share in the downfall of the Weimar Republic will not recur. If they are wrong, Germany's political prospects are, of course, of an entirely different nature.

It is interesting to note in passing that the prospects for a continuation of an economic policy geared (primarily) to the market as the organizer of production and distribution were immeasurably enhanced by the results of the 1953 and the 1957 elections. On both occasions the limitations on proportionality,[37] combined with the appeal of Dr. Adenauer's policies and personality, had managed to introduce some of the characteristics of majority voting into the German political system. Adenauer's victory had some of the plebiscitary features which we take for granted in countries with a two-party system, as well as elements of a majority decision. At the same time it was demonstrated that clearcut majority decisions, instead of implying a violation of a minority's rights and feelings, constitute "a struggle with the tendency to integrate." [38] When the debate following the presentation of Dr. Adenauer's second cabinet took place, his Social Democratic opponent, Erich Ollenhauer,[39] caused considerable surprise by stating that his party, too, was in favor of a market economy. Ollenhauer was able to add with a smile that all he had been doing was to quote from a policy statement of his party which was several years old. That statement had crept into the "Action Program" of the SPD virtually unnoticed; its authors were Professor Alfred Weber of Heidelberg University and the then Hamburg Economics Minister (called Senator) Schilling. When Ollenhauer underlined this statement as representing the actual policy of this party, his change in emphasis was equivalent to a change of policy. It remained to be seen how these changes would affect the SPD when confronted with the responsibility of government; among the party's left wing, there is no lack of keen believers in the advantages of centralized economic planning. Still, Ollenhauer's speech indicated a long step on the road to agreement on basic issues, and it was followed by others. Those leaders of the SPD who wanted to make it into a true "people's party" made substantial headway. When the 1957 elections approached, every effort was made to attract every possible element to the party and to antagonize no one if it could be avoided. Evidently, that deliberate "public relations" approach which had been characteristic of the CDU campaign in 1953 was to be taken over, and it could not fail to modify some of the SPD's former attitudes and policies in the sense of greater moderation. The defeat which the SPD suffered on that occasion, however, led to recrimination within the party, and its left wing claimed that Ollenhauer's moderation had made his campaign ineffective. All available indications point in the opposite direction; demands made by some of the Left-wingers for a nationalization of certain industries, for example, were heavily exploited against the Social Democrats. The SPD did manage, however, to secure a third of the total number of seats (169 out of 497), which had not been the case in 1953. Thus, they were able to prevent any revision of the Constitution, and to challenge the constitutionality of any law before the Constitutional Court.

The most significant result of the 1957 elections, at any rate, was to give the Christian Democrats, with 270 seats (54.3 per cent of the total) a working majority by themselves which was backed up by a majority of 50.2 per cent of the valid votes cast. This placed them in a stronger position than they had held in 1953; they were no longer dependent upon allies the way they had been when, in addition, there was a need to think in terms of the two-thirds majority required for a revision of the Constitution.

Under these conditions, the opinion that the two-party system was "coming by itself" [40] was expressed more strongly than ever. The two leading parties together had gathered more than four-fifths of the popular vote. The German Party had operated as a virtual appendix of the CDU, and the only other party to be represented in the third *Bundestag*, the FDP, continued to be badly divided. We must recall, however, that political definitions are not a matter of mathematics. That two parties share four-fifths of the total vote does not change the country's political system if, ordinarily, neither is strong enough to form a government of the one-party majority type. In 1957 the Christian Democrats, quite unexpectedly, were given a chance to do so, but, for good reasons, decided not to use it. Evidently, the Social Democrats were far removed from any such possibility. The best they might have done would have been to become the strongest party, and to form a cabinet together with one or two minor parties. As long as only one of the two major parties has a chance to form a one-party majority government, the prevailing pattern of political action will be that of coalition government.[41]

Besides, what the Christian Democrats were able to accomplish in 1953 and 1957 was less due to their attractiveness as a party than to the appeal of their leader, Konrad Adenauer. It is interesting to note both that in all *Land* and municipal elections since 1953 the Christian Democrats found it necessary to campaign on the basis of the Chancellor's personal popularity, and that the appeal failed. Thus, in 1952, the Christian Democrats suffered a resounding defeat in the municipal elections of North Rhine-Westphalia, being outdistanced by the Social Democrats on the Chancellor's own political home grounds. Then came the *Wahlwunder* of 1953. Immediately afterwards in the Hamburg elections the Christian Democrats did much less well; a coalition which they had formed with the FDP and the DP barely secured a majority in the *Land* parliament, the *Buergerschaft*. In the *Land* elections held in North Rhine-Westphalia in 1954, the Christian Democrats, who had swept the *Land* in the federal elections of 1953, found themselves with only 90 out of 202 seats; as we have seen, the time was to come when their opponents united against them and drove them from power. The situation was the same in the Bavarian elections of the same year with the difference that a coalition government under Social Democratic leadership was formed immediately.

A low point in the fortunes of the CDU was reached in the local elections held, in October, 1956, in North Rhine-Westphalia, Lower Saxony and Hesse.[42] In North Rhine-Westphalia the SPD secured 44.1 per cent of the votes as against 38.2 per cent for the CDU. The latter had gained more votes than in the municipal elections of 1952, when it polled 35.6 per cent, but it saw the control of one city council after the other fall into the hands of the SPD; this included Chancellor Adenauer's own city of Cologne where he had been Lord Mayor for so many years. In Hesse, the SPD outdistanced the CDU with 47.1 per cent as against 21.2 per cent, and in Lower Saxony with 38.5 per cent to 20.5 per cent.

The upswing in Christian Democratic strength was so great in the Federal elections of 1957 that it appeared irreversible to many. Yet, within less than two months elections took place in Hamburg. In that city-state, to be sure, the Social Democrats, led by the highly success-ful former Lord Mayor Max Brauer, had been able to resist the Chris-tian Democratic tide even in the Federal elections, outpolling their opponents with 45.8 per cent as against 37.4 per cent of the total popular vote. On November 10, however, they decisively improved upon this result, taking 53.9 per cent of the total popular vote as against 32.3 per cent for the CDU. It might be noted in passing that this great Social Democratic victory was achieved by the local organi-zation in pointed disregard of the (Left of Center) party bureaucracy in Bonn. The two prominent party members invited from the outside were Herbert Wehner and Professor Carlo Schmid, both of whom had long since been prominent among those who wanted to make the SPD into a German counterpart of the British Labour party.

The CDU, at any rate, has invariably done less well when the Adenauer leadership was not involved than when it was a factor. Federal elections, of course, differ from *Land* and municipal ones in more than one respect. Economic and foreign policy, in particular, are crucial in Federal elections and mean little, if anything, in *Land* and local elections. Yet, the conclusion seems inescapable that there are two CDU electorates—the one that responds to the magic name of Adenauer, and the other that comes forth when the party campaigns by itself, in spite of all the assistance which the Chancellor may give it. Some day, the CDU will have to campaign without Adenauer be-ing present (directly at the federal level and by proxy at the *Land* and local levels), and, in that case, it is not only certain to lose the po-litically non-attached voters whom Adenauer attracted to its colors in

1953 and 1957, but it may also be again exposed to the internal stresses and strains which had so much to do with its catastrophic losses in the *Land* elections held in Lower Saxony, Hesse, and Bremen in 1951.

Meanwhile, it is interesting to note that German politics move on different tracks in the *Bund* and in the *Laender*. In Bonn, the Adenauer leadership has managed to lead the country beyond many (not all) of the woes normally associated with coalition government, even if the Chancellor's methods have stirred up a good deal of resentment on the part of his coalition partners. On the *Land* level, the pattern of government by coalition is now firmly entrenched, with the small parties invariably exacting a more than proportionate share of the cabinet posts, of political power, and of patronage. The question is which pattern will prevail in a post-Adenauer Germany. If the CDU, on a federal level, loses as much as 15 per cent of the votes which it obtained in 1957 (which would cause its share of the total vote to decline from 50.2 per cent to 44 per cent), it is, even with the present election law, certain to lose the majority of the seats, and will have to cooperate with minor parties if it is to stay in power (unless a coalition with the Social Democrats is formed). If ever the CDU wants again to cooperate with the FDP it will have to pay, however, a stiff price; coalitions with the CDU in a position of "hegemony" will be "out."

The weakening of the CDU, and of the two major parties as a whole, will be accentuated if the minor parties should succeed in whittling away the limitations on proportionality which German postwar legislation developed. Here again we are confronted with a double track system in the German political pattern: On the Federal level these restrictions have been tightened from election to election, and on the *Land* level they have been loosened. Schleswig-Holstein, Hesse and Hamburg have abandoned their systems with majority elements; Bavaria changed the law for the elections of 1954 in order to make sure that no party obtained more seats than corresponded to its percentage of the total as determined by the d'Hondt system,[43] even if candidates who had secured a plurality in their constituencies had to be declared defeated. This was a move of the minor parties, and of the SPD, against the leading one, the CSU. In Lower Saxony the SPD's dependence on the smaller parties caused it to consent to the abolition of all restrictions on minor parties, with the result that this *Land* makes it now as easy for splinter parties to succeed as did the system used for the *Reichstag* elections of the Weimar Republic.

The pressure for a relaxation of the provisions against splinter parties is noticeable on the Federal as well as on the *Land* level. So far, it has been offset by attempts of the CDU to introduce elements of the majority system. These attempts, made in 1953 and in the winter of 1955–56, failed, but they placed the initiative into the hands of those who favored political concentration. Thus, in 1956, both the SPD and the FDP agreed to a law limiting the distribution of seats from the "reserve lists" (called *Landeslisten*) to parties which had either secured five per cent of the total vote in the entire country, or won three seats in direct elections. Unexpectedly, however, in January, 1957, the SPD demanded that the law be changed, and a party be given seats from the *Landeliste* of any *Land* in which it had obtained five per cent of the total, rather than having to poll that percentage in the country at large.[44] The reason soon became apparent: The SPD needed the continued support of the Bavarian Party for the government which it headed in Munich, and the proposed changes were part of the price to be paid. The Christian Democratic majority in the *Bundestag* rejected the plan, and as long as such a majority exists there will, presumably, be no relaxation of the provisions aimed at splinter parties. Whenever there is no such one-party majority in the *Bundestag* the situation may change radically, however; it may then be difficult to resist the pressure of the smaller parties for a Weimar-type election law,[45] with Weimar-type results.

On the other hand, the adoption of the plurality system—or even the majority system with run-off elections—would forestall such developments once and for all. Germany does not now have a two-party system, but she can have one for the asking. Yet, in 1957, even steps in that direction were unlikely. The CDU had, on two occasions, suffered a defeat when advocating such steps, and it would not easily create a situation which might again deprive it of the support of the minor parties in the *Laender*. A change could come about only if informed public opinion would demand it; in that case, there might be enough pressure on the minor parties and perhaps even a modified attitude on the part of the SPD.

Several points would have to be made clear. In the first place, any assumption that since the CDU, by virtue of having taken 193 of the 246 single-member districts, would have taken a similar percentage of all the seats under a plurality system, represents, once again, a case of "milkmaid's arithmetic." The CDU-CSU was able to do this with 51.2 per cent of the popular vote only because the people did not cast their ballots as they do under a majority system. The voters knew that the overall result did not depend on what happened in the single-member constituencies, but on the distribution of the seats according to the d'Hondt system for the country as a whole. What the CDU, or any other party, won in the local constituencies would be deducted from the total which it won in the nation. On the other hand, under a straight plurality system, the desire not to "throw one's vote away" would have led to the concentrated support, on the part of the CDU's opponents, for whichever candidate was most likely to beat the Christian Democrat. The CDU, therefore, could not have taken nearly as many seats with a mere plurality of the vote as it actually did.

On the other hand, whenever there are such fears, no matter how unreasonable, prudence compels laying them to rest. The election law could provide that when a party secures 45 per cent of the votes it obtains no more than 55 per cent of the seats; when it obtains 50 per cent of the votes, no more than 60 per cent of the seats, and so on. This would leave an adequate margin for the majority, but also enough seats for the minority.[46] It goes without saying that the minority seats would all go to the leading party of the opposition (in this case the SPD), not to a number of parties. Such an arrangement, at any rate, would dispel the fear that one party might come to dominate the *Bundestag* the way in Turkey the Democrats dominated the Grand National Assembly as a result of the elections of 1950 and 1954.

The availability of a rational solution does not mean that it is going to be used. To the vested interests which P.R. has created in the form of the minor parties, as well as in the form of certain elements within the major ones (including the CDU) we must now add a good measure of intellectual confusion. Political conditions, on the whole, have been surprisingly good in the Federal Republic, so why not leave well enough alone? It is overlooked that institutional stability is one thing, and stability largely based upon the work of a man who won his third electoral victory as he was approaching 82, is something else again. The Germans have made a similar mistake before. The institutions of the Empire contained radical defects. As long as Bismarck was at the helm, these defects could not produce any serious results, at any rate not in the vital field of foreign policy. With Bismarck gone, the artful arrangements upon which the peace of the world was based began to crumble overnight. Konrad Adenauer has done much to overcome the institutional defects of the Bonn Republic, but it is more than likely that they will become all too apparent once he leaves his post.

Chapter XVII
PARLIAMENTARY GOVERNMENT
IN ITALY

‸‸

PARLIAMENTARY MONARCHY AND PARLIAMENTARY STABILITY.

Parliamentary government in Italy has developed several significant variations from the general pattern of the relationship between political form, as represented by the parliamentary system, and the concrete conditions of a country, all of which, however, fit in well with the general theory of that system.

Italian experience is interesting, in the first place, because it demonstrates that parliamentary monarchy, while very useful under conditions where the political system is sound in itself, becomes a subject of controversy and an element of division where the mechanism of parliamentary government develops serious gaps. The strength of the Italian monarchy, of course, cannot be compared to that of other countries. When Italy was united under the leadership of the House of Savoy, the other reigning houses were displaced. While there was no persistent loyalty to any of these dynasties, except perhaps to the Bourbons in Naples and Sicily, the new royal house could not look back upon the centuries of tradition which, for example, shield the monarchy of Britain. Besides, the conquest of Rome placed the state in conflict with the Church to which a majority of the people belonged, at least in name.

On the other hand, the very backwardness of economic and social conditions—in particular in the South and in the Islands—served to enhance the appeal as well as the value of monarchy. The humble peasant at the foot of the Italian boot might have no understanding at all of the complex constitutional system by which he was governed in Rome, but he could easily grasp the idea of a government exercised by a King. His wife and children were interested in the royal family in the same way in which this was the case in England when Bagehot wrote his book, *The English Constitution*—before there developed that vast degree of popularization, not untainted with adulation, which was brought about by the modern media of mass communication since the end of the First World War.

If, then, the symbolic appeal of monarchy could not be as strong in Italy as in England, it was quite real, and it might have grown as basic political conditions became stabilized. There did exist a trend toward stabilization, especially after Giovanni Giolitti became the boss of the Italian parliament at the turn of the century.[1] Giolitti was, to be sure, a rather unscrupulous boss, but, clearly, under his guidance parliamentary government was becoming more stable in Italy than it was in France. The availability of an untrammelled right of parliamentary dissolution compensated, to some extent, for the deficiencies of social "matter" in Italy. It may also have helped that Italy had bicameralism in a moderate and rather serviceable form. The Senate, apart from the princes of royal blood, consisted of members appointed by the government for life. Thus the Senate lacked the authority which popular elections might have conferred upon it. This was one reason why it developed into a genuine "chamber of scrutiny and reflection" without imitating its French equivalent by becoming an added source of executive instability. The other reason was the ever present possibility that a government might "pack" the Senate with its own supporters, as the King could appoint an unlimited number of new members. Cavour used this threat as early as 1855,[2] and in later years, the Senate gave little cause for complaint. Its work, if inconspicuous at times, was always dignified and useful. Men of high distinction belonged to it and many of them could not have been brought into active association with the country's political life in any other way.

The position of the monarchy was, in general, as useful, and as free from controversy, as that of the Senate. It soon became a tradition for the King to limit his role to the attempt of being that impartial moderator for whom the spirit of the parliamentary system calls. Certainly, the Italian political system left fairly large political gaps which the King was able to fill at his own discretion; at the beginning, court intrigues played their part in this process. There was no serious criticism, however, between the time when Victor Emmanuel III ascended the throne in 1900 and his appointment of Mussolini as Prime Minister in October, 1922. This appointment has been the center of extensive (and intensive!) controversy, and since it was indeed crucial for all subsequent developments, it is not surprising that it should have led to substantial and continued charges against the King. Once Mussolini was in power, the King had little choice except to sign the laws and decrees submitted to him by the Fascist government, including the declaration of war on the Allies, thereby compromising his personal reputation as well as the institution of monarchy. Besides, Mussolini tried to involve as many members of the royal house as possible in the responsibility for his own actions. Thus, Crown Prince Umberto was placed in charge of the armies which attacked the French in June, 1940.

The most diligent search of the literature would not yield, however, any serious complaint against King Victor Emmanuel III for the years immediately preceding Mussolini's appointment, although a most confused situation developed in the period following the First World War. In the words of Hamilton Fish Armstrong: "In Italy, the four years from the end of the war to the day Mussolini seized power from the feeble hands of Premier Facta saw no less than ten cabinets under five prime ministers."[3] In analyzing these events, the most authoritative of Italy's anti-Fascist writers, Professor Gaetano Salvemini, distinguishes between two different periods, the one of "post-war neurasthenia," and the one of "parliamentary paralysis." The post-war neurasthenia was caused by the inevitable difficulties of effecting the transition from an unpopular and highly costly war to peace. Hundreds of thousands of deserters had to be dealt with (in the end by the only available means, that of amnesty); the disappointment resulting from the Allied failure to fulfill some of Italy's territorial demands had to be overcome; and, above all, the problem of inflation had to be solved. It led to serious social unrest which culminated in a wave of strikes, and in the occupation of the factories by the workers. In due course, however, the most important steps needed were taken, and by the end of 1920 the post-war neurasthenia was dying down. In the words of Professor Salvemini: "At the beginning of 1921, the moment was ripe for the government to resume its proper functions— to maintain public peace and respect for the law as opposed to any form of disorder."[4] Salvemini continues that, in that case, the major problems remaining would have solved themselves. Actually, there developed a period of parliamentary paralysis. To quote Professor Salvemini in some detail:

> While the forces which were to destroy democratic institutions in Italy were being massed and organized, the Chamber of Deputies was discrediting itself with inconclusive battles of words and trivial acts of violence. It finally reached a point where it was unable to create a cabinet that was worthy of anything but contempt.

Decidedly, a disease was undermining the Italian political constitution—a parliamentary paralysis. And outside Parliament there was another disease at work—civil war. Either Parliament must recover its powers and put an end to the civil war, or parliamentary institutions would break down in Italy.[5]

Paralysis, however, is exactly what Professor Alessio had predicted in the memorable warning which he uttered in the Italian Chamber of Deputies before P.R. was adopted in 1919. In his words:

. . . . the nature of the minorities of which we obtain expression with the system of P.R., excludes that possibility of coalition within Parliament, whereas the passion for power for power's sake, which is so strong in the Latin peoples, leads to paralysis and destruction.
. . . . The application of this system under present conditions would provoke a very bad functioning of the Chamber, would make it impossible to form a lasting cabinet, and would in the long run bring about the paralysis of public life.[6]

What happened in 1921, then, was clearly foreseen, and its cause identified, in 1919. Specifically, the effects of P.R. expressed themselves in two major directions. First and foremost, that degree of integration was prevented which the majority system, even in its weaker forms, forces upon political parties. There had been a remarkable demonstration for the effects of majority voting in the elections of 1913, the last ones to be held under the majority system (with runoff elections), and the first ones under which a virtually universal manhood suffrage had existed. These elections were complicated by the fact that whereas in past elections the Catholics had, on account of the Church-state conflict, for the most part abstained from voting, in 1913 they officially voted in most constituencies. In 48 cases they presented their own candidates; in the main, however, their participation in the elections was confined to the support of candidates who agreed to the conditions of the "Catholic Electoral Union" and signed the so-called *Patto Gentiloni*. These candidates were numerous, and more than 200 of them were elected. No government could be formed without the support of at least a good number of these Deputies.

The significance of the *Patto Gentiloni* lies in the agreement on "men" as well as on "measures," which it entailed. Its principal planks were the defense of the Constitution, particularly of the liberty of conscience and of association, free scope for the development of denominational schools, clarification of the right of heads of families to demand religious instruction for their children in public schools, opposition to divorce, and the like. Such demands Italian non-Catholics as well as Catholics could accept. Agreement before the elections meant that there was a definite settlement, and that this was endorsed by the voters themselves. There was, for that reason, little room for the type of bickering in regard to such questions that was to develop after the adoption of P.R. in 1919, when each party entered the contest on its own, without any pre-campaign alliances and understandings.

The majority system demonstrated its integrating effects not only by forcing early agreements on the moderate parties, but also by putting a damper on extremists. At that time, Socialists and Republicans found themselves in that position although they were not "extremists" in the sense of the Fascists and Communists of a later period. Still, it is interesting to note that both in 1909 and in 1913 Republicans and Socialists secured a much smaller percentage of the seats than they had obtained of the votes.[7]

The twofold effect of the majority system was, then, to make certain that although Italy had a multiple-party system, it was a system within which the moderate parties were related by pre-campaign agreements on men and measures, and in which the parties of a more "extreme" variety were kept under control. This control is, of course, not absolute in the sense that it prevents the rise of such parties. It does mean that, if such groups want to obtain a decisive share in power, they must earn it by progressive moderation. Furthermore, the necessary adjustments are made by candidates in single-member constituencies who, as a rule, are inclined to go very much farther along those lines than the "militant" members of the official party organization, particularly those who participate in directing the party's affairs on a national level.

These effects of the majority system vanished with the adoption of P.R. Italy, all of a sudden, found itself confronted with a multiple system of unrelated parties, with ample scope for expansion, and it had to pay the price. There were, of course, basic changes in the electorate itself. There now was a Christian Democratic party, called the Italian Popular party, which obtained 20.6 per cent of the total number of votes, and 100 out of the Chamber's 508 seats.[8] At the Left 32.3 per cent of the votes were cast for the official Socialists, who took 156 seats.

The Italian version of socialism was dominated by a Left wing which exhibited a radicalism otherwise unknown among parties of the Second International. On the other hand, there were enough non-Socialist Deputies to make possible the formation of an effective government, but a tug of war arose between the followers of Giolitti and those of Don Sturzo. In spite of a temporary eclipse brought about by his opposition to the war, Giolitti was still the strongest force among the non-Catholic elements of the center and the moderate Right. He looked upon the Christian Democrats and their leader, the young and energetic priest, Don Sturzo, as upstarts. Sturzo, in his turn, was repelled by the unsavory political methods which Giolitti had never hesitated to use. Yet, the cooperation of the political forces represented by these two leaders was necessary if Italy was to have an effective government. The majority system would have forced this cooperation upon the two men and their parties no matter how distasteful this might have been to them. While Giolitti's followers were strong enough in Central and Southern Italy to contest most constituencies under their own power, the Christian Democrats were strong in the populous northern parts and in some of the central parts of the country, and had a significant following everywhere. Under such conditions, the alternative to campaign alliances would have been the offering of a large number of seats to the Socialists as a gift. The rank and file of the voters would not have stood for such a policy even if their leaders had been inclined to adopt it. In other words, there would have been, under a majority system, enough campaign alliances between the Popular party and the Democratic and Liberal elements to defeat the more radical among the Socialist candidates, and to tie the partners of the alliance together with sufficient strength to make the prospects for effective parliamentary government quite different from what they turned out to be under P.R.

This is not the place to deal with subsequent developments in any detail, particularly not with the elections of 1921 and their consequences, part of which was the election of a number of Communists and Fascists which would be difficult to imagine under a majority system.[9] As it was, the Popular Democrats remained strong enough to force Giolitti, under whose premiership these elections had been held, to resign, but the rivalry between the two groups made effective government impossible. In the end, in February, 1922, Facta became Prime Minister, and his name has since been synonymous with weak government. Facta was but a stopgap, and he knew it, but the party leaders found it impossible to replace him. Mussolini declared rather contemptuously: "With this parliament 30 crises could only result in 30 Factas." [10] An American writer was no less explicit: "Meanwhile the press and public opinion were becoming daily more exasperated, until by fall Parliament had hardly a single friend in the country. The members themselves were disgusted with each other and the King was weary of selecting impossible Prime Ministers." [11]

In early October, 1922, the Fascists, whose numbers had grown by leaps and bounds in the meantime, decided that the time had come to seize power. As a military force they still meant little. As the then General, later Marshal, Bagdolio put it, "five minutes of gunfire" would suffice to put an end to any Fascist uprising. Such gunfire the Fascists were careful to avoid; indeed, they decided to "play it safe." In the words of Don Sturzo:

> . . . on October 26 Facta was challenged by certain Fascisti to hand in his resignation at once; and that very evening, in an emergency cabinet meeting summoned in the hope of finding a middle course that would save appearances, all the Ministers decided to place their portfolios at the Premier's disposal. But on October 27 the Fascisti, in the name of their leader, declared themselves still unsatisfied and, with threats of risings, insisted that Facta should agree to their demand; whereupon that excellent man that very evening tendered to the King the resignations of the entire cabinet.[12]

Thus, when the Fascists began their "March on Rome," they were confronted by a cabinet which had submitted its resignation to the King, although the resignation had not yet then been accepted. During the night of October 27–28, this cabinet decided to request the King's signature for a declaration of martial law. However, when Prime Minister Facta saw the King at eight o'clock the next morning, he told him he was still negotiating with the Fascists, hoping to avoid bloodshed. Professor Salvemini described these events in the following words:

> The King clutched at these negotiations as a drowning man clutches at at a straw: since there was hope of a peaceful understanding, why should he proclaim martial law? The cabinet would do well to reconsider the question. Facta therefore returned to the cabinet.
>
> The Ministers stuck to their first decision. When Facta, at ten in the morning, brought the decree back, the King refused to sign it. In the interval, a group of Nationalists had spoken with him and had assured him that the army would refuse to fight the Fascists. The news that the Duke of Aosta was among the Fascists, ready to take up his cousin's crown as soon as the King should let it fall, gave the final push.[13]

When the King's refusal to sign the decree establishing martial law became public, matters got out of control. All resistance ceased, as it was understood that force was not to be used against the Fascists, whose armed bands soon filled the streets of Rome, terrorizing all opponents. The Nationalists had meant to establish a cabinet of their own, headed by the veteran Salandra, giving Mussolini only a minor post. Mussolini, however, held out for the premiership for himself as

Hitler was to do in January, 1933, and, after matters had gone that far, the King felt that he had to entrust it to him. After this, Fascist terror took care of the rest, although the utter disunity among the opponents of fascism, fostered by P.R., had something to do with the final defeat which they were to suffer in 1924 after the assassination of Matteotti. Then the prestige of fascism was first dealt what, for a time, appeared a fatal blow. On that occasion the King would have been willing to dismiss Mussolini and appoint a new Prime Minister, but no one with any authority was willing to take his place.

These facts were known, and they should have made it plain to the opponents of fascism that in October, 1922, the King was as much a victim of circumstances as they were themselves. By 1946 they needed a scapegoat, however, and the King was the most available candidate. Nevertheless, he had managed to perform a final great service to his country. Mussolini submitted to him his resignation after the "Grand Council of Fascism" turned against him, but *Il Duce* was very much surprised when the King accepted that resignation and had him arrested as he left the palace. Thus, the totalitarian government of Italy, unlike that of Germany, was terminated before the bitter end was reached, and this was possible only on account of the existence of monarchy. Had the Allies immediately accepted the new Italian government, headed by Marshal Badoglio, as an ally, rather than to lose weeks forcing upon her a humiliating armistice,[14] it might have been possible to consolidate the power of the anti-Fascist government over most of the country before the Germans had an opportunity to move in in force.

The other factor connected with the demise of the monarchy was the utter lack of wisdom shown by Victor Emmanuel. He should have resigned at once, not in favor of his son who had been compromised by his activities under Fascist rule, but in favor of his grandson for whom a council of regency could have been instituted. This was pointed out by the spokesmen of the democratic parties, and one of the King's most devoted servants, Marshal Badoglio, who agreed with them, took it upon himself to transmit their message to the King. Victor Emmanuel, however, reacted abruptly, accusing Badoglio of disloyalty and "of seeking to advance his own interests at the expense of the Crown."[15] The King, then, acted with as much unwisdom as William II had done in Germany. All he was willing to do was to retire from formal participation in the government by conferring his powers upon the Crown Prince, whose title became Lieutenant General of the Realm. Victor Emmanuel finally did resign in May, 1946, just three weeks before the plebiscite on the issue of monarchy versus republic was held on June 2 of that year. Umberto was to be King for 35 days. Had he been made King in his own right when he was made Lieutenant General of the Realm, even that fact would have improved the prospects of the monarchy. The officially declared vote was 12.7 million for the republic and 10.7 million for the monarchy— 54.3 as against 45.7 per cent. Italian monarchists have always claimed that some "deft counting" on the part of the then Minister of the Interior, Romita, had something to do with the Republican majority; the visitor to Rome may find the same opinion conveyed to him by impartial observers not subject to any preferences for the monarchy. The question arises, however, whether a monarchist victory obtained by a small margin would have been a solution. The value of parliamentary monarchy depends upon its general acceptance. The opposition of any substantial part of the people makes it a matter of partisan controversy to such an extent that it will be difficult for the King to fulfill either his symbolic or his political functions properly. On the other hand, had the monarchy won a strong majority many of its opponents might have rallied to it. At any rate, within a decade of the proclamation of the Republic, Italians were made to realize that an elected President can present problems unlikely to be raised by a monarch.

The most serious effect of the contest over the monarchy was that it obscured the need for a more thoroughgoing discussion of the reasons why the Fascist victory became possible. To blame everything on the monarchy meant to advance an argument which was simple enough to make it popular. Few troubled to look deeper and to analyze the reasons why the moderate parties were so badly divided among themselves that they created a power vacuum which the Fascists were only too happy to fill. The old leaders of Italy's great liberal tradition were, of course, aware of the basic facts involved. Reference has already been made to the brilliant speech against P.R. made in the Consultative Assembly by Luigi Einaudi,[16] who was to become the country's first President after the Republican Constitution had gone into effect. His warnings were echoed by others, including Benedetto Croce. These opponents of P.R., however, knew that the "big battalions" were on the other side. The "mass parties" (the Communists, the Socialists, and the Christian Democrats) were determined on P.R. just as were their counterparts in France. There was, surprisingly enough, some hesitation among the Socialists, including Pietro Nenni. The Christian Democrats, however, in whose ranks a remarkable change of opinion was to occur within a few years, were at that time strongly in favor of P.R. On the part of the Communists such a stand was a foregone conclusion.

PURE P.R. AND THE CONSTITUENT ASSEMBLY.

The elections to the Constituent Assembly took place on June 2, 1946, together with the plebiscite on the issue of monarchy versus republic. They were held under a system of "pure" P.R. Thirty-one constituencies were formed, not including the single-member constituency of the autonomous region of the Valle d'Aosta. As a total of 556 Deputies was to be elected the constituencies averaged about 18 Deputies, three times as many as the French average. This fact alone made possible a much higher degree of proportionality, but small parties were also favored by the rules governing the distribution of the seats. Each list received as many seats as it had "quotas," which were computed by dividing the total number of votes cast into the number of seats plus one if less than 20 Deputies were to be elected, and plus two in the others. This system is much more favorable to small parties than the d'Hondt system used in France. Finally, seats not distributed regionally were transferred to a National List where they were assigned in accordance with the number of surplus votes which had also been transferred from the regional constituencies; this feature again benefited small parties more than large ones.[17]

On this basis even typical splinter parties managed to do well. The Christian Social Party with 0.2 per cent of the votes obtained one seat—0.2 per cent, and the Democratic Republican Concentration, with 0.4 per cent of the votes obtained 2 seats—0.4 per cent. Minor deviations from proportionality followed from the fact that sixty lists, totalling 1.8 per cent of the votes, represented altogether too small a following to reach a quota; their votes resulted in seats for the other parties.

So far as the overall results of these elections are concerned, the controlling fact was the strength of the three "mass parties": The Christian Democrats obtained 35.2 per cent of the votes, the Socialists 20.7, and the Communists 19.0. Between them these three parties, then, accounted for three-fourths of the votes, as well as three-fourths of the seats. Until the spring of 1947 all three (including the Communists) participated in the government. Therefore, the actual distribution of party strength mattered little during this period. The coalition partners shared the power and the spoils in the same way as was done in France during the era of "tripartism." In regard to physical reconstruction much was accomplished, but basic decisions, in particular in the fields of foreign and of economic policy, could not be made because of the condition of semi-paralysis prevailing inside the government. In the words of an Italian journalist: "The Communists were in the government as a chain, and in the opposition as a whip." [18]

Even during this difficult period one factor served as a stabilizer. Whereas Don Sturzo's Italian Popular Party had never exceeded 20.9 per cent of the total popular vote,[19] its successor, Alcide De Gasperi's *Democrazia Cristiana* was, as we have seen, to start its electoral career with 35.2 per cent, and it was to increase this percentage perceptibly later. There was no Liberal-Democratic combination, led by another Giolitti, which could have engaged in a tug of war with the Christian Democrats. Furthermore, there not only was but one large moderate party, but it also had a leader whose prestige extended far beyond its ranks. De Gasperi was a man of honest convictions (which, incidentally, placed him somewhat to the left of center, opposing him to the Monarchists as well as the neo-Fascists), but he also knew how to assess the realities of Italian politics. He was particularly anxious to avoid even a semblance of "clericalism," and his devotion to democracy had been tested well enough to spare him the reproach of "Fascist" tendencies which was—quite wrongly, but with a tinge of plausibility —made against his successor in the leadership of his party, Amintore Fanfani. Under De Gasperi's guidance, Italy's young democracy overcame crises which might have been fatal under a man of lesser stature.

The strength of his party provided De Gasperi with at least some of the tools without which no leader can lead. Like the strength of the CDU in Germany, that of the *Democrazia Cristiana* developed from outside the political sphere. There was, in the first place, the enfranchisement of women. While the present-day strength of all the Christian Democratic parties in Western Europe is largely due to this fact, Italian public opinion polls—the only available source of information on the subject—indicate that, in 1953, of the total of 10.9 million votes cast for the *Democrazia Cristiana* 7.5 million, more than two-thirds, came from women.[20] In that particular election, according to the same source, close to 54 per cent of all the votes cast by Italian women went to the Christian Democrats. The latter's gains were, for the most part, made at the expense of the extreme Left and the extreme Right. It is, then, obvious that women are a major, and apparently decisive, reason why Italian democracy as a whole was so much stronger after the Second World War than it had been after the First; their concentration on the center helped greatly to offset the more serious effects of P.R.

The second factor responsible for the strength of the *Democrazia Cristiana* is the wholehearted Church support from which it benefited. Don Sturzo's Popular party had never enjoyed more than benevolent neutrality on the part of the Vatican and the Bishops, but the support given to De Gasperi's *Democrazia Cristiana* was both open and vigorous. The Vatican had had one experience with totalitarianism and it did not want a second one, particularly if it threatened to come from the Communist side. Since the old Church-State conflict had been eliminated by the Lateran Treaty and the Concordat, the Church felt freer to give such support which, at the same time, meant more than it did before the war. Pope Pius XII has been more popular among the Italians than any pope in living memory; his actions, both during the war and after the end of hostilities are gratefully remembered even among the large number of Italians who tend to be skeptical in religious matters.

It goes without saying that the wholehearted Church support given to the Christian Democrats was particularly effective among the women; the two factors which caused the *Democrazia Cristiana* —and with it Italian democracy as a whole—to be as strong as it was are, therefore, interrelated. Still, with all this strong influence emanating from the realm of "social forces" tending to correct the effects of P.R., Italy passed through a period of grave uncertainty before the elections of 1948 inaugurated five years of unprecedented, if uneasy, stability. At times it seemed like the very anchor of Italian post-war democracy, the *Democrazia Cristiana*, was about to fall apart. The electorate was attracted towards opposite political poles—the Communist and their Socialist allies at the Left and the Qualunquists at the Right. The latter, led by the playwright, Giannini, did not quite deserve the name "neo-Fascist" applied to them in large sections of the press, but they did appeal to the Fascist vote. There was, at that time in Italy, what one observer characterized in conversation with the author as "a nostalgia for Mussolini," and the Qualunquists exploited it. The high-water mark of the success of this group, and of the temporary eclipse of the *Democrazia Cristiana*, was the municipal elections held in the city of Rome in November, 1946. The "Peoples Bloc," consisting of Communists, Socialists and some smaller Leftist groups, came at the top with 190,038 votes, followed by the Qualunquists with 106,780, and the Christian Democrats with 104,627. At that time Pietro Nenni coined the slogan, *"In mezzo non si sta"*—"One does not stand in the middle." In other words, Italy's political future seemed again to lie with the extremists, the only question being whether the extremists of the Right or of the Left were to prevail. As usual, such conditions are complicated by a process of splintering; the 80 seats in the Municipal Council in Rome were shared by a total of 11 parties. It was impossible to form a majority; in the end a government commissar had to be appointed.

Meanwhile, De Gasperi had a hard time carrying on the government. At that time, in Italy as well as in France, Belgium and Holland, the Communists participated in the coalition. They were carrying water on both shoulders, however, attempting to grab as large a share in power as possible and endeavoring to shift responsibility for unpopular decisions onto their partners. Their presence paralyzed the government. Certain vital issues in the field of economic policy could not be resolved. Finally, the Communists' subservience to Moscow caused their ouster in the spring of 1947. Between that period and the elections of April, 1948, De Gasperi had to work with a minority cabinet. The 207 Christian Democrats in the Constituent Assembly found themselves opposed by 115 Socialists and 104 Communists at the Left. They needed 72 additional votes in order to have a majority, and they could never rely on more than a part of these, depending for the remainder on either the support, or the abstention, of a number of Deputies either of the Right or of the moderate Left. Even before the Communists were ousted and these numerical difficulties developed, Anne O'Hare McCormick, in her column in *The New York Times*,[21] compared the Italian situation unfavorably with the French and went on to say that in Italy: "Anything may happen at any time, but holding it (the political structure) together is a job for a contortionist or a conjurer."

THE NEW CONSTITUTION.

De Gasperi did manage to steer the ship of state through these turbulent waters. In the meantime, the Constituent Assembly, no matter how badly divided, succeeded in drawing up a Constitution which kept a relatively safe distance from the type of "rationalized parliamentarism" which was then dictating political fashions in Paris and other capitals. The appointment of a government follows the simple and sensible patterns of the past. Article 92 provides that: "The President of the Republic appoints the President of the Council of Ministers, and on his proposal appoints the Ministers." The government does need the confidence of both the Chamber and the Senate, to which it presents itself within 10 days of its formation (Article 94) but this confidence is accorded with a simple majority of the votes cast.

In the second place, the President of the Republic, acting, presumably, on the advice of the Prime Minister [22] and, as the Constitution (Article 88) says, "having heard their respective Presidents may dissolve both Chambers or only one of them." He cannot do this during the last six months of his term. This limitation is hardly significant; from the practical point of view an Italian government can dissolve parliament as freely as the British Prime Minister. In this regard, then, the Italian Prime Minister is better off than even the German Chancellor, and, of course, a great deal better off than the French Premier.

Such flaws as there are in the Constitution result from provisions which were regarded as minor at the time. In the first place, the position of the President of the Republic is not defined as clearly as it might have been. The method of his election certainly follows sound precedent. The Chamber and Senate (Article 83) meet in joint session, and to their number there are added three delegates from each of the country's 18 major regions, with the minor region of the Valle d'Aosta having one single delegate. On the first three ballots, a two-thirds majority is required for the election of the President. This rule is not very practical but not very important either, as an absolute majority suffices afterwards. This, as we have seen, is the requirement best suited to combine the practical possibilities existing in a parliament divided by P.R. with proper regard for the duties of the office. The President's term is seven years, and he may be reëlected.

A mistake that cannot be considered unimportant, was made, however, when the Constitution required a secret ballot in the election of the President. Similar possibilities are admitted in the rules of both the Chamber of Deputies and of the Senate, where they have caused difficulties of their own. They owe their origin to a predemocratic period when it seemed necessary to protect members of parliament against royal reprisals; they do not at all agree with the requirements of a democracy.[23] The individual member of parliament should, of course, be able to vote against his party whenever he feels that his conscience leaves him no other choice, but he should do so openly. Otherwise, responsible government is not obtainable. The antiquated provisions making secret ballots possible became important after the elections of 1953 in which the center parties failed to secure the absolute majority of the votes cast; much bickering developed among them as well as within the ranks of the factionally divided *Democrazia Cristiana*.

When, in 1955, new presidential elections became due, the leaders of the *Democrazia Cristiana* proposed Cesare Merzagora, the President of the Senate. He was ideally suited for the post; also, the circumstance that he was not a Christian Democrat offset the fact that the Prime Minister belonged to that party. De Gasperi had insisted on such an arrangement, both when De Nicola was elected for the period covered by the transition from monarchy to republic, and when Luigi Einaudi, a Liberal, was chosen as the first President under the new Constitution. The Christian Democrats had, after all, never secured an absolute majority of the popular vote, and it seemed only fair to make it plain that they had no intention of monopolizing the highest offices in the state.

The *Democrazia Cristiana* was, however, by that time badly split. Amintore Fanfani, the leader of their moderate Left, had secured control of the party in its National Congress of 1954, but resentment against him developed both at his Right and at his Left. At the Left there was, among others, Giovanni Gronchi, the President of the Chamber of Deputies. The Communists saw their chance to cause trouble by promoting the presidential candidacy of Gronchi as against that of Merzagora. When Fanfani realized that, covered by the secrecy of the ballot, enough members of his own party had voted for Gronchi on the earlier ballots to make his success likely, he threw his own support to him, and Gronchi was elected by a large majority.

Gronchi's views on the nature of the presidency differed radically from those of his predecessor. Luigi Einaudi [24] took the traditional view of the President as the impartial moderator among the parties, who might try to use his "influence" where he deemed it necessary, but who could claim few "powers" of his own. Most of the constitutional provisions clearly point in this direction. The acts of the President have to be countersigned by either a responsible minister alone, or by a responsible minister and the Prime Minister (Article 89). The President is not responsible for what he does in the fulfillment of his functions (Article 90). If democratic government is responsible government, it would seem to follow that those who are responsible—the Prime Minister and the cabinet—should make all major political decisions. The Constitution itself seems to lay down that rule in Article 95: "The President of the Council of Ministers directs the general policy of the Government and is responsible for it. He maintains the unity of political and administrative orientation by promoting and coordinating the activity of the ministers."

Naturally, as in all similar cases, the Italian President has the "reserve powers" connected with the appointment of a new cabinet and the dissolution of parliament, apart from the "influence" which he may acquire in other matters. The Italian Constitution, however —again, as most other Constitutions—lists a number of specific presidential functions, some of which expert opinion now does tend to consider powers to be exercised by the President personally. This applies, for example, to the appointment of the five Senators to serve for life and of the five members of the Constitutional Court whose appointment the Constitution assigns to the President. It is also held that while, in such cases, the countersignature [25] of a responsible minister is required, it may not be refused.

Prevalent opinion—or opinion tending to become prevalent—is, therefore, inclined to allow the President certain, not unimportant, powers of his own. Yet, there is a difference between powers such as those mentioned above which, if exercised with the intention of making the constitutional system as a whole work as planned, can be well enough reconciled with the requirements of parliamentary government, and the right claimed by President Gronchi to influence the general policy of the country to such an extent that the result is to set up a presidential power different from, and easily in opposition to, the power of the cabinet. Clearly, his inaugural address [26] pointed to a political course which did not seem to be that of the government. He was favorable to an "opening to the Left," in other words, to a policy aiming at enlarging the coalition by including the Left-wing Socialists. He also discussed Italy's alliances, particularly her membership in NATO, by insisting on greater Italian "independence" in such a way that his words could be interpreted as a demand for a revision of the policy pursued since De Gasperi ousted the Communists from his cabinet in 1947.

President Gronchi is a man of ability, and he could not have fulfilled his functions as President of the Chamber of Deputies had he not also been a man of tact and discretion. Besides, there is always the possibility of a President stretching the range of his "influence" to the advantage of his country, particularly in the field of foreign policy. Thus, Gronchi's visit to the United States, made in March, 1956, was a success both from the political and personal point of view. The relations between him and his cabinet, then headed by Antonio Segni, became strained, however, when the President, in March, 1957, attempted to answer a communication from President Eisenhower in a manner indicating his preference for a modified foreign policy. As *The New York Times* [27] reported: "It appears that President Gronchi wrote a highly polemical reply, touching on several foreign policy issues . . . Foreign Ministry officials were said to have noted that President Gronchi had taken a position diametrically opposed to that of the Italian Government on almost every question." Under the circumstances it is not surprising that Premier Antonio Segni, Vice

Premier Giuseppe Saragat, and Foreign Minister Gaetano Martino should have returned the President's communication to him and told him that, in the opinion of the government, it should not be forwarded. As this incident shows, any attempt to enlarge the President's powers [28] creates risks. It implies the recreation of the dualism between the Head of the State and the government which it was the very purpose of the parliamentary system to avoid. On the other hand, as we have seen in the case of President von Hindenburg, any political system which lacks clear majorities—not accidentally but more or less permanently—invites political action by the Head of the State. When such action occurs and is ill-advised, parliament is too much divided against itself to permit it to apply the remedy which the French Chamber of Deputies under the Third Republic applied against Marshal MacMahon and Alexandre Millerand. Other considerations apart, the parties composing such a parliament are unpopular. In Italy one section of the press has taken the view that "an energetic presidency is necessary and gives trust to the country." [29] That sounds remarkably like certain German reactions to von Hindenburg's charting a political course of his own with "presidential" cabinets. President Gronchi certainly is no von Hindenburg; there is no army which could become his personal tool, and there is, at the moment, no strong extremist party at the Right which could muddy the political waters. Still, it is difficult to see how Gronchi's actions could have had the stabilizing effect at which they undoubtedly aimed; they may have contributed, even if only slightly, toward making the crisis which followed upon Premier Segni's resignation in May, 1957, more serious than it was expected to be.[30]

THE SENATE.

Italian political life is further and unexpectedly complicated by a type of bicameralism for which recent constitution-making has no equal. Whereas in all other cases the powers of second chambers were limited, the Italian Senate was placed on the same plane as the Chamber of Deputies. As the Senate is elected by direct popular vote, it shares with the Chamber of Deputies the prestige of a popular mandate. The differences are slight. The Senate is elected for six years, and the Chamber of Deputies for five. Eligibility for the Chamber begins at 25 years, and at 40 for the Senate, while the minimum age for the senatorial elector is 25 and that for the Chamber 21. Former Presidents of the Republic are Senators for life, and the President of the Republic may confer the same distinction upon up to five distinguished citizens.

The equality between Chamber and Senate is emphasized by the fact that the Constitution (Article 94) explicitly requires that "the government must have the confidence of both Chambers" and that laws have to be approved by the Senate as well as by the Chamber of Deputies (Article 70). A new government must go through the procedure of securing a vote of confidence from both the Chamber and the Senate, and a law which has passed the gauntlet of one house must also pass that of the other. Governments with strong and reliable majorities might be able to face such requirements without losing more than time, but governments as tenuous as those characteristic of Italy during most of its recent parliamentary history were bound to be seriously embarrassed by these requirements. The wear and tear which they place on the members of the government was dramatically illustrated when the Minister of the Treasury, Ezio Vanoni, one of the country's leading economic and financial experts, died after a heart attack suffered while addressing the Senate.

THE CONSTITUTIONAL COURT.

In the opinion of some, another unexpected complication of the work of the executive arose from the Constitutional Court.[31] Although the issues involved are by no means as serious as those which developed in Germany, Articles 134–137 of the Italian Constitution do sketch a rather far-reaching range of competence for the Court which, in addition, takes care of impeachments of the President of the Republic and of ministers. The Court is primarily concerned with the constitutionality of laws, and with disputes relative to the respective jurisdiction of the three powers of the state—executive, legislative and judiciary—or of the state and one or more of the regions.

The composition of the Court resembles that of its German counterpart insofar as the number of justices is high. There are 15 who, as in Germany, decide only constitutional matters, whereas the American Supreme Court, with 9 members, rules on ordinary legal issues as well. Five of the justices are to be appointed by the President of the Republic, five are to be elected by parliament, meeting in joint session and deciding by a three-fifths majority, and five selected by the highest judiciary organs of the country. Agreement on the five justices to be elected by parliament was difficult to reach because the Communists insisted on nominating at least one. Finally, in November, 1955, the Christian Democrats accepted a candidate who had been a member of the Communist party in the past, but left it without engaging in anti-Communist activities, and thus remained acceptable to his former party.[32]

When the Court met early in 1956 it found a full docket. It had first to decide whether it had jurisdiction over laws promulgated before the 1948 Constitution went into effect, and whether it was competent to decide whether a particular provision of the Constitution was immediately valid or of only a "programmatic" nature. The Court affirmed its jurisdiction in both respects. This means that a substantial body of law inherited from the Fascist period came under its scrutiny, and the first casualty was part of the Consolidated Law of Public Safety, dated June 18, 1931. One of its provisions enabled a commission established by the provincial prefect to sentence a person to special surveillance, which required that he return to the place of his birth and be at home every night at a certain time. This the Court declared to be "in glaring conflict" with the constitutional guarantee of a person's freedom of movement, which was to be interfered with only by a court of law. The Minister of the Interior bitterly complained to parliament that, under this interpretation of the Constitution, the police were deprived of powers essential to combat crime. There had been another of the many sporadic outbreaks of banditry in Sicily, with dozens of people being killed, without there being any definite evidence on the basis of which suspects could have been brought to court. Informed opinion, however, generally rallied to the view that the long-run problem of firmly establishing civil liberties was more important than the short-run task of dealing with an outbreak of banditry in a part of the country.

The real difficulty for the government arose from the problems which it had to face in securing the adoption of adequate laws to fill the gap caused by the Court's decision. That difficulty is, of course, of a general nature when a parliament is as badly divided as were the Italian Chamber and Senate after the elections of 1953. There is, therefore, as much reason to sympathize with a government which has to fight hard to keep alive and which then finds itself confronted with added tasks, as there is reason to sympathize with a Constitutional Court which does no more than what it feels that the plain language of the Constitution compels it to do. It might be added that, apparently, the members of the Court have no intention of allowing themselves to be drawn into political questions to the extent that their German colleagues did. The Court's first President, De Nicola, who had been President of the Republic between the plebiscite and the inauguration of the new Constitution, declared in his report on the Court's first year: "It is very significant that no issue so far has been raised involving any clash affecting the powers of the state." [33] The fact that De Nicola emphasized this point would seem to indicate that he would not have welcomed such a development and was aware of the need to allow the government to govern. De Nicola subsequently resigned and it remains to be seen how the Court will operate in the future.

A PERIOD OF RELATIVE STABILITY.

The problems arising for Italian government from the Constitutional Court were not to become acute until 1956, and the difficulties presented by the existence of a Senate duplicating the work of the Chamber were at first alleviated by the great electoral victory achieved by the Christian Democrats in 1948. Between 1948 and 1953 in fact, Italy experienced a period of unprecedented—if relative—political stability and economic progress.

Yet, the elections of 1948 had been preceded by a year filled with anxiety. The alliance of Communists and Left-wing Socialists proved strong. Under the guise of a "People's Bloc," it attempted, with a measure of success, to attract voters who were neither Communists nor Left-wing Socialists. Economically, the country was in a bad position. The burdens of the policy of monetary stabilization then being pursued were evident, and its future fruits were not yet discernible. As events were to show, however, a great many voters who were not Christian Democrats were willing to rally to that party as long as there appeared to be a serious Communist threat. The nature of that threat was highlighted by the Communist seizure of power in Czechoslovakia and the subsequent suicide of Jan Masaryk. Besides, there were municipal elections in the city of Pescara, in which the Socialist-Communist bloc increased its strength to such an extent that as serious an observer as Armaldo Cortesi reported to *The New York Times:* "The election result . . . . confirms the opinion that the left-wing parties have a good chance of winning the election scheduled for April." [34] This was all that was needed to galvanize the proponents of democracy into doubling their efforts.

The most effective anti-Communist force was organized in the form of the "civic committees" of Catholic Action; its members carried the battle, with skill and enthusiasm, into areas where the professional politician, at any rate those of the moderate parties, had never set foot. Besides, De Gasperi had the satisfaction of knowing that Marshall Plan assistance had just become effective and promised to become a substantial factor in promoting the country's recovery.

The result was that the Christian Democrats secured 48.5 per cent of the votes and 53.5 per cent of the seats in the Chamber.[35] This constituted such a resounding defeat for the Leftists not because the latter lost many votes, since their combined percentage actually declined by no more than one percentage point if we take into account that the Right-wing Socialists presented lists of their own, but because what mattered was that the anti-extremist majority was not as hopelessly splintered as it had been before the election. To the negative element of defeating the opposition there had been added the positive factor of uniting the moderates. Italy seemed a different country after these elections. The defeatism rampant previously disappeared overnight, and the people began to face the future with confidence. A great period of sustained economic progress began, which would hardly have been possible except for the degree of stability brought about by the Christian Democratic victory.

This victory had, incidentally, been secured under a slightly modified election law. The quota which a party had to obtain in order to secure a seat in a constituency was lower, since the number of valid votes was divided by the number of seats plus three. Thus, more seats were distributed in the constituencies themselves and fewer on the national list. Small parties found it somewhat easier to secure a seat in a constituency, but they lost by reason of the fact that fewer seats were available on the national list. Besides, tables were turned on them by stipulating that no party could secure a seat on the national list unless it had secured at least one seat in a constituency. Thus, the Christian Social party which, as we have seen, in 1946 secured a seat with 0.2 per cent of the vote, in 1948 secured none with 0.3 per cent.

Few would regret the elimination of such typical splinters, but it was of more serious import that the so-called "lay" center parties, meaning the Liberals, the Republicans and the Social Democrats, with a total of 13.4 per cent of the vote, secured only 10.7 per cent of the seats. This fact indicated that any modification of the election law directed against splinter parties would, among the moderates, benefit only the Christian Democrats and discriminate against their smaller allies. As was to happen in Germany after the 1953 elections, the advantage secured by the Christian Democrats made their allies harder to deal with than they had been before; they were more anxious than ever to demonstrate their independence. De Gasperi was determined to continue the alliance with them, regardless of all difficulties. He was not only aware of the temporary character of the Christian Democratic majority, but he also wanted to emphasize the lay character of the state. Many of his political friends were somewhat less anxious to do so, but he was able to remind them of the fact that the Christian Democrats had no majority in the Senate. According to the transitional provisions of the Constitution (Clause III), the first Senate

of the Republic contained, in addition to the 237 elected members
(with Christian Democrats in the majority), 106 members of the
Constituent Assembly who fulfilled certain requirements. Many of
them were Leftists, and their presence placed the Christian Democrats
in a minority.

Apart from this special factor, when P.R. elections result in victories such as those obtained by De Gasperi in 1948 or Adenauer in
1957, a reaction in the opposite direction is likely to follow. With the
immediate threat of a Communist victory overcome, many people relaxed and began to look forward to a "return to normalcy." That meant
a lessened inclination to concentrate their votes on the Christian
Democrats, although events were soon to demonstrate that the "lay"
center parties were not to be the beneficiaries of that trend. The
extreme Left began to regain a little of the ground it had lost, and
more was lost to the Right, where the Monarchists made considerable
gains, and the MSI succeeded in getting a neo-Fascist movement of
some significance under way. The Sardinian elections of May 8, 1949 [36]
left little doubt about these trends.

The elections of 1948, then, presented for Italian democracy in
general and Italian Christian democracy in particular, the appearance
of having won in a lottery. Pleasant as such a contingency is, it can
hardly be expected to occur again. A firmer basis, then, had to be
found for the country's political life, and attention was concentrated
on a reform of the electoral system.

The criticism of P.R. which, in the past, had been expressed
mainly by the leading representatives of Liberal and Democratic
thought began to find an echo among the Christian Democrats. The
veteran Don Sturzo, who had been faithful to the cause of P.R. until
that time, came out in favor of a return to the old Italian version of
the majority system, which provided for run-off elections in cases
where no candidate secured an absolute majority of the vote on the
first ballot. He emphasized that, after the Fascist and Communist
parties had developed, the effects of P.R. were bound to be entirely
different from the ones expected, and that, as a result, a return to the
majority system was the only possible solution.[37]

De Gasperi did not express such views at that time, but, on the
occasion of the 1954 Congress of the *Democrazia Cristiana* in Naples,
he had this to say in his report as secretary of the party: "More logical
[than the law which was finally adopted for the Chamber elections]
would have been a return to the single-member constituency with
run-off elections, or the alternative ballot, but since we had to take
other forces of democracy into account we thought of an electoral

alliance between the democratic parties (with majority premium)." [38] De Gasperi here refers to the fact that the minor parties would have been unwilling to consider majority elections. He preferred to act in agreement with them; besides, they had to support the new law in order to give it a majority in the Senate.

Changes in the electoral system were first made for municipal elections. At that time the majority system was used for the smallest municipality which elected less than five councillors. In the next group of cities up to 30,000 inhabitants (providing that they were not simultaneously provincial capitals), the limited vote existed. Voters could vote for only four-fifths of the local councillors, but had the right to add the names of some other lists to those of their own. Practically, however, four-fifths of the seats went to the strongest party, and one-fifth to the next strongest. All other communities had P.R.

The Christian Democrats would have liked to extend the limited vote to the larger cities, a move which the small democratic parties, naturally enough, opposed, because it tended to make elections a contest between the Christian Democrats and the Socialist-Communist bloc. That would have been anything but fostering a desirable concentration. Contrary to what has often been said, Italy does not have even a tendency toward a two-party system. In the first place, no one party ever expects to get a majority on a national level and is, therefore, not what Duverger called "a party with a majority bend." In the second place, whereas the one of the two large political groups, the *Democrazia Cristiana*, is moderate, and able to fulfill the functions of a political party, the other, the combination of Communists and Left-wing Socialists, is not. The Communists are definitely an extremist party, and, until the summer of 1957, the Left-wing Socialists had not managed to adopt any truly independent policy in regard to the Communists. As a result, one of the two major political forces was totally unable to fulfill the integrating functions which are the *raison d'être* of a political party.

The leaders of the minor democratic parties were, therefore, right when they opposed the extension of limited voting to all Italian communities; that system would indeed have tended to stabilize a party system of which an essential element was entirely unable to fulfill the true function of a political party. It was something else again, however, when Liberals, Republicans, and Social Democrats advocated the extension of P.R. to all communities. As the Deputy Carignani said, referring to the town of Viareggio, where two parties had 19 seats each, and two independents turned the scales between them: "No one can ignore the precarious character of such a city administration where the two independents make rain or sunshine and make fun first of one side and then of the other." [39]

The municipal election law finally adopted admitted limited voting only for communities up to 10,000 inhabitants. In all larger communities two-thirds of the seats would go to the list with the largest number of votes, which might also be a combination of allied lists. The minority seats were divided among all other groups according to the principles of P.R.; if a plurality had been won by a combination of allied lists, the seats would also be divided among the allies according to P.R. The municipal elections of 1951 and 1952 took place according to this system. From a mechanical point of view it served its purpose, as all municipal councils obtained clearcut majorities. The difficulty was that the change was rather mechanical. The result was changed at the top, but nothing was done to promote a regrouping of the voters at the bottom of the political pyramid in conformity with the requirements of democracy. In this respect a clearcut majority system would have acted differently. In the German *Bundestag* the Deputy Scharnberg [40] remarked on one occasion that the majority system was, in fact, a majority *forming* system—a *mehrheitsbildendes System;* it did not simply reflect a majority when there was one, but also tended to create one when there was none. This implies that more is accomplished than to invite the voters to group themselves into a majority and a minority. For the reasons set forth above, this process is also one of integration; it promotes the formation of a civic consensus as well as the formation of numerical majorities, the reason being that the final power of decision is handed over to the undecided voter in the center, to whom the two major parties have to adjust their opinions as well as their tactics. In Italy, a clearcut majority system (even if combined with run-off elections [41]) could be expected to produce adequate majorities in the country's parliamentary bodies from the outset and to make a beginning, at least, with the formation of a true political consensus, even if that process would have required time.

Nor was there any reason to expect that the minor parties of the center would have fared less well under such a majority system than they did under P.R., which reduced them to fragments anyway. As President Einaudi pointed out, while the plurality system would have set up a tendency to the two-party system, an arrangement providing for the possibility of run-off elections was unlikely to do so. When used before the First World War it had led to unsavory bargaining among the parties after the first ballot but, as Einaudi was to show later, any possibility along such lines could have been forestalled by substituting the alternative vote for the run-off elections; in this case,

whatever instructions parties and candidates might give their supporters had to be given beforehand, without there being any chance
of later bargaining.[42]

Majority elections would, however, have turned the entire Italian
party system upside down, and it is not certain that all elements
of the *Democrazia Cristiana* looked upon such a contingency with much
more kindness than did the bureaucracy of the small "lay" parties.
Therefore, the discussion of the law under which the Chamber elections of 1953 were to be held was once again dominated by that type
of compromise thinking which attempts to reconcile irreconcilables
and leads to inorganic results. In the minds of the government leaders,
the primary need was to get away from a condition in which the actual
majority of the Chamber, supported by a majority of the people, would
not be allowed to govern. The opposition, even though it was a heterogeneous opposition, would be hard at the heels of the government,
and the rules of both the Chamber and the Senate placed so many
weapons of obstruction into the hands of the minority that it could
all but paralyze the actual majority at almost any time of its own
choosing. This is what De Gasperi emphasized in his above-mentioned
report to the Naples Congress of his party,[43] and what Minister of the
Interior Scelba had in mind when, presenting the government draft
of a new election law, he spoke earnestly of the "functionality of parliament with which [the possibility of a workable] government is
closely connected."[44] The new plan provided that a party or group
of allied parties which obtained more than 50 per cent of the vote
was to receive 385 of a total of 590 seats in the Chamber. The majority
seats were to be divided among the allies in proportion to their
strength. Thus, there was to be a premium for the majority, but the
small center parties were to share in it fully.

Such electoral systems have been repeatedly proposed in the
course of history, particularly by people who insisted on combining
what they considered the advantages of both electoral systems. When
the Commission of the Chamber of Deputies reported on this subject,
its majority was able to quote a statement of Nenni made in 1945 to
the effect "That electoral system is most democratic which gives the
majority the right to govern. Pure P.R., without majority premium,
has the disadvantage not to allow anybody to govern, neither the Left
nor the Right . . ."[45] In Italy, however, the government plan soon
ran into heavy fire, particularly on account of a certain similarity with
the law which was adopted under Fascist pressure on November 18,
1923. That law guaranteed the strongest party two-thirds of the seats
if it secured at least 25 per cent of the ballots. It was clear at that time

that the Fascists were the only party which could secure that plurality. De Gasperi and Scelba, of course, were planning truly free elections, with every opportunity for the opposition—if there was terror during the 1953 elections, more of it came from the extreme Left, where the Communists practiced it wherever possible, than from the Center. In addition, it makes a difference whether a law is to confer a premium upon an actual majority of the electorate or just upon the strongest party, even if that party should poll only 25 per cent of the popular vote. Still, the very idea of a majority premium on a national scale had become the symbol of Fascist oppression. Symbols have their significance, and De Gasperi and Scelba would have done well to stay away from a system which could be so easily tainted with the Fascist brush.

The law was finally adopted by both Chamber and Senate, although this meant that neither house could do much other business during the entire winter of 1952–53. Professor Ferri has characterized its inconsistency in telling terms: To propose both P.R. and the premium for the majority meant two things were being coupled, one of which was the negation of the other. It certainly did not help matters that the privileges customarily associated with the majority system were to be accorded to a group of parties differing fundamentally from each other and constituting a collection of minorities rather than a true majority. Besides, some of these parties were so small that their combination with others should have been encouraged. Nor were the voters given an opportunity to indicate a clearcut preference for a particular government. This scathing commentary, it is interesting to note, appeared in the official weekly of the Liberal party,[46] although by that time the Liberal party organization had come to insist on P.R. as vigorously as the leaders of the great Liberal tradition had rejected it.

When the law was finally adopted it provided that the majority would secure 380 rather than 385 seats. The proposal of the Liberals to make the majority premium effective if the allied parties should secure at least 45 per cent (instead of more than 50 per cent) of the votes was rejected.

The new elections took place on June 7. They had the surprising result that the allied parties of the center were officially credited with only 49.7 per cent of the total vote.[47] Thus, the premium for the majority did not materialize, although the provisions of the 1948 law, which were to be applied in case the absolute majority was not reached, still accrued to the center's advantage by giving the four parties 51.3 per cent of the seats.

Actually, the official results—declared to be "provisional" but ultimately accepted as final—were published only on June 10. The members of the cabinet were aghast when the results were reported to Rome, and it soon developed that some rather deft counting on the part of those who represented the opposition parties in the scrutiny of the ballots had something to do with the outcome. In that process the representatives of the neo-Fascists and Monarchists cooperated with those of the Left, as well as those of the splinter groups which had been formed with the encouragement of the Leftist parties. Whenever a ballot which was evidently intended for one of the centrist parties could be challenged under some pretext or other, this was done. Altogether, 1,289,082 votes were declared invalid.[48] 427,109 ballots had no markings at all, and were, therefore, plainly invalid, but there is little doubt that a large part of the remaining 850,000 votes were intended, and should have been counted, for the moderate parties, particularly the Christian Democrats. The centrist alliance needed an additional 110,076 votes in order to secure an absolute majority; apparently, impartial counting would have credited it with more. Specifically, 335,100 votes had been declared invalid because more than one list had been marked. In many cases, this had been done because voters felt that, in order to express their approval of the centrist alliance, they had to mark the lists of the allied parties.

There were, in addition, 402,482 cases in which it was supposedly impossible to ascertain which list the voter favored. The reason lay, for the most part, with the institution of preferential votes. In Italy, voting for the Chamber of Deputies is according to lists, but these are not "rigid." After it has been ascertained how many seats a party has won, those candidates of that particular list are declared elected who have obtained the largest number of preferential votes, the voter having three such votes when up to 15 Deputies are to be elected and four if the number is larger. In earlier elections the names of the candidates favored had to be written down, but in 1953 it sufficed to list the number under which they appeared on the list. Unless, in such a case, the list itself was marked, there might be confusion as to which list the voter favored. During the counting the representatives of the opposition parties questioned any ballot which justified as much as a semblance of doubt. It is very democratic in theory to permit the voter himself (meaning that minority which could be expected to make use of that right, in Italy somewhat less than one-third of the possible preferences being expressed in 1953) to pick the candidates on his list who are to fill the seats attributed to it, but it may also confuse the voter sufficiently to cause him to make his ballot invalid.

Furthermore, the preferential vote causes candidates appearing on the same list to fight one another. This tendency was particularly strong among the Christian Democrats. Any party of this type tends to include a considerable variety of elements, and the preferential vote makes it possible for the factions which represent these elements to assert themselves. Christian Democratic candidates, or campaign speakers supporting a certain faction within the party, would, at times, concentrate all their efforts on hammering into the voters' minds the numbers under which they or their friends appeared on the ballot, even if the party itself was literally forgotten in the process. This is one reason why De Gasperi could say: "We have lost on account of the struggle for the preferential votes." [49]

Last but not least, this struggle did not just represent the various factions in proportion to their strength; it made factional rivalry inside the party so easy that it aggravated it. Many of the difficulties experienced by Christian Democratic premiers in the years to follow had their origin in this fact.

Let us return, however, for a moment to the question of the ballots declared invalid. There was a group in the cabinet, headed by Minister of the Interior Scelba, which advocated remedial action. Under the provisions of the Constitution (Article 66), each Chamber was the judge of the qualifications of its own members. Such a provision works well enough when exception is taken only to individual members, and there is no doubt concerning overall party strength. On this occasion the question at issue was whether the center was going to have a two-thirds majority or the barest majority of the Chamber's membership. In the latter case, the obstruction to be anticipated on the part of opposition members was certain to be persistent enough to eliminate any possibility of serious action. Scelba favored the closing of what was an evident gap in the country's legislative system by a decree law. The government has the power to issue decree laws "in extraordinary cases of urgent necessity." It must submit such a decree to the Chamber which has to be summoned within five days (Article 77, 2nd par.). The government might have utilized this provision to establish an impartial agency charged with the task of reexamining the doctoral ballot, although the question then was to what kind of Chamber the decree was to be submitted. Amintore Fanfani, however, led a group within the government which opposed such action; referring to the fact that the center parties, after all, did have a majority in both the Chamber and the Senate, even if a very small one, he advocated letting matters stand as they were. He prevailed, and the "provisional" election results became final.

RETURN TO "PURE" P.R.

The immediate effect of these elections was bickering among the center parties. The Socialist-Democrats, Republicans and Liberals felt that they had been hurt more strongly by the unpopularity of the election law than the Christian Democrats. Besides, whereas the latter with 40.1 per cent of the votes obtained 44.3 per cent of the seats, the three small moderate parties, with 9.1 per cent of the votes, received only 6.5 per cent of the seats. Giuseppe Romita made himself the spokesman of the smaller parties in their demand for a return to "pure" P.R. The Christian Democrats countered that pure P.R. would encourage the rise of new splinter parties and that, in addition, it would prove a boon to the neo-Fascists. The latter, with 5.9 per cent of the votes, had obtained 4.9 per cent of the seats, and since they were in the throes of an internal crisis, "corrected" P.R., as used in 1948 and 1953, particularly if the conditions for smaller parties should be strengthened rather than weakened, might soon reduce that party to insignificance. Besides, the center parties together had, after all, secured 51.3 per cent of the seats with 49.7 per cent of the votes, which means that whereas they could not even have attempted to govern under pure P.R. they had a chance to do so under corrected P.R. They were, in fact, to manage not too badly for three years before something like an impasse developed among them.

The minor parties were determined, however, to have an electoral system under which they felt that they could maximize their appeal to their potential followers. They expected, in particular, to regain the votes of several splinter parties which developed in 1953 on account of their opposition to the election law of 1953.

There were, then, arguments on both sides. The way the issue was resolved is characteristic, however, of what happens when the normal rules of P.R. are in force. Vital decisions are not made as a result of free discussion by the supposedly sovereign parliament, but they are resolved in a process of backstage bargaining between party leaders. According to Don Sturzo, the minor parties simply confronted Fanfani, when he was trying to establish a new government in 1954, with the "classical" alternative: "The money (P.R.), or the life (of the government)." [50] When Fanfani refused to accede to Romita's imperative demand for "pure" P.R., he was overthrown.

Ultimately, a compromise was reached which lies somewhat between the "pure" system adopted in 1946, and the "corrected" system designed for the elections of 1948 and also used in 1953.[51] At first an attempt was made to adopt a provision against splinter parties but exempt from it parties already represented in the Chamber. Eventually, this evident departure from the principle of "equality before the law" was discarded. Article 36 of the new election law provides that a party, in order to secure seats in the distribution on a national level, must have secured at least 300,000 votes. It is hoped that this will be an adequate barrier against typical splinter parties.

The wish of the smaller parties to secure pure proportional representation extended to other elections, including those to the Senate in which the lack of proportionality was even greater than in the Chamber elections. For the Senate elections the country is divided into as many single-member constituencies as there are senators to be elected. Any candidate who obtains 65 per cent of the total number of votes cast is declared elected outright; in this case (it is rare but benefits virtually only the Christian Democrats), the votes cast in the respective constituency are not taken into account in further proceedings. Otherwise, the votes of the senatorial candidates are added up for a particular region, and each party is assigned a number of seats proportional to the number of votes cast for it. These seats are then given to the candidates who obtained the highest number of votes in their respective constituencies. This system has its drawbacks, one of them being that no candidate is declared elected from certain constituencies and more than one from others. The great advantage of the arrangement is, however, that the person of the candidate is much more of an issue in the campaign than it is in that for the Chamber of Deputies. In 1953, when elections to both the Chamber and the Senate took place on the same day, there was a striking contrast between the posters for the Chamber election which concentrated on parties and symbols, and the Senate election which emphasized the name of the particular candidate, usually with the accompaniment of his picture. The natural result is a stronger emphasis on the candidate and his personal qualifications. At the same time, that strengthening of factional battles inside a party which results from the preferential votes cast in the Chamber of Deputies elections, is avoided. If a country is to have P.R. this personalized type is certainly preferable to either a "rigid list" or a list system with preferential votes. It is also preferable to elections under the Hare system which, wherever they have been used on a large scale, such as in New York City, have led to a large number of invalid and "exhausted" ballots.[52]

These solid virtues of the election system for the Senate may be the reason for the failure of the minor parties to have it altered. The same applies to the provincial elections, which are held under a system similar to that used for the Bonn *Bundestag*.[53] Each province is divided into a number of single-member districts corresponding to two-thirds of the seats to be filled, and in each district the candidate with the highest vote is declared elected. The remaining third has the same function as the German *Reserveliste*. It serves the purpose of establishing overall proportionality between votes cast and seats obtained. There is, however, no separate list for the province as a whole. The seats assigned to a party [54] go to those of its candidates who, while they failed to secure a plurality, had the highest percentage of the votes cast in their respective districts. This system is appreciably less favorable to small parties than "pure" P.R.; in fact, some of the features characteristic of the majority system make their appearance, as small parties will present no candidates in some districts, and common candidates in others.

If the smaller centrist parties did not succeed in having the senatorial and provincial election laws changed they had their way in regard to the election of municipal councils,[55] where P.R. was adopted for all cities with more than 10,000 inhabitants. This law was to be applied shortly after its passage, as new municipal (as well as provincial) elections took place on May 27, 1956. At that time, most American correspondents reported an overall success of the center parties. This success was limited, however, to the communities of up to 10,000 inhabitants, where either the majority system or the limited vote applied, and in the provincial elections. In the cities where elections took place under P.R. the center parties taken together lost a little ground, although there is a slight gain if "mixed groups of the center" are taken into account.[56] The Christian Democrats were mostly responsible for this loss whereas gains by the Social Democrats more than compensated for losses by the Liberals and Republicans. In the provincial elections the percentage of the votes obtained by the "lay" center parties increased from 9.2 per cent in 1953 to 12.8 per cent, although the Republicans saw their total decline to 267,000, which raises the question whether they will survive the minimum clause of the new law for Chamber elections. In terms of seats, however, not only the Republicans but also the Social Democrats and Liberals fared less well than they had done in the provincial elections of 1951.[57] Still, what mattered for the small moderate parties was their reaffirmation in the electorate. In this respect, paradoxically, they did best where "pure" P.R. did not apply.

The most significant result of the new municipal election law is the confusion which followed its application. The number of provincial capitals without definite majorities in their local councils increased from 0 to 38. Altogether there was no definite majority in 199 of the 539 communities with more than 10,000 inhabitants, including provincial capitals. In all of these cities conditions returned to what they had been before the municipal election law of 1951 was adopted. In some cases coalitions could be formed without too much difficulty, but in others government became very unsatisfactory, requiring, at times, intervention by the national government. The case for the strengthening of local government promised by the Constitution was greatly weakened by this development.

POLITICAL PLURALISM VERSUS DEMOCRATIC
PARLIAMENTARISM.

The most important aspect of the change which took place in Italy after the elections of 1953 is the radical departure from the plebiscitary element in the country's parliamentary system which the elections of 1948 had produced. The "return to normalcy" which immediately afterwards developed in regional and local elections took place with a vengeance on a national plane on June 7, 1953. Not everyone was unhappy about this development. A few days after the election the author discussed the matter in Rome with a veteran American correspondent, whose comment was: "The politicians just love it." In 1948 a direct verdict by the people had settled every outstanding issue, and there was little for the politicians to do, even though they certainly made the best of their opportunities.

After June 7, 1953, the sky became the limit, although it took some time before matters became serious. De Gasperi was still in office and would have liked to govern with the support of the small parties. When these deserted him, he had to form a government solely of his own party. He was defeated and succeeded by Giuseppe Pella, whose Christian Democratic cabinet, supplemented by certain non-party "technicians," lasted until early January, 1954.[58] Pella had the support of the Monarchists. This fact created much uneasiness among a great many Christian Democrats whose official leader, Fanfani, made a statement sufficiently critical of Pella to cause the latter to resign. Fanfani's own cabinet, limited again to Christian Democrats, lasted only 12 days, but then Mario Scelba, De Gasperi's Minister of the Interior, succeeded in forming a coalition with Liberals and Social Democrats which lasted until June, 1955. When he fell, Antonio Segni became Prime Minister, governing again with the same allies. Surprisingly, Segni lasted 22 months, having to resign in May, 1957, because the Social Democrats decided to withdraw from the government. The crisis which then followed proved to be the most serious the country had known since before the elections of 1948. Finally, Senator Adone Zoli formed a government consisting of Christian Democrats alone, which found itself opposed by his party's former allies, and, contrary to its own wishes, received neo-Fascist as well as Monarchist support. In the Senate Zoli secured a majority without counting the neo-Fascist votes; at first it seemed that he had just managed to do the same in the Chamber. However, a recount brought out the fact that this was not the case, and that without the support of the neo-Fascists Zoli would have been defeated by one vote. He submitted his resignation to President Gronchi who, unable to secure a new cabinet, in the end simply decided to request the Premier to remain in office. This development led to much scorn and ridicule; the consolidation of democracy which had taken place in Italy since 1948 appeared to be in serious jeopardy. A fresh breeze seemed to swell the sails of the Communists whose strength had shown the first signs of a serious weakening as a result of the downgrading of Stalin and of the Hungarian uprising. Thus, in the Senate session of June 27, the Communist Terracini leveled his sarcasm at the "majority" of Zoli's cabinet, claiming that its essential feature was to have reintroduced fascism into the Italian government. The result, Terracini added, would be the rise of anti-Fascist sentiment, and the Communist party would become its leader.[59] These Communist hopes were far from being fulfilled, but there can be no doubt about the general uneasiness in regard to democracy which had developed in the country.

ECONOMIC AND POLITICAL DEVELOPMENTS.

What has happened in Italy since 1948 is particularly interesting on account of the widespread view that economic conditions determine political action. The great victory achieved by the center in April, 1948, occurred during a period of economic stress and its defeat of June, 1953, at a time of obvious economic progress. In September, 1947, the fourth cabinet of De Gasperi, having gotten rid of the Communists, took the measures needed to bring the country's inflation under control and laid the basis for future economic recovery. This was done under the guidance of the then Minister of Finance, and subsequent President of the Republic, Luigi Einaudi. The immediate result was a decline in the price level and in the volume of production. Business started to improve, however, between March and September, 1948. Toward the end of 1948 there began that rapid expansion which, in the main, has continued to this day. De Gaspari was frequently pressed to resort to measures promising a more direct attack on Italy's chronic unemployment and underemployment problem than seemed possible on the basis of Einaudi's policies, but he stuck to his guns and the result more than justified his expectations.

Italian industry, in fact, resumed the upward trend which had been interrupted by Mussolini's deflationary currency stabilization in 1926, and progress has continued year after year. The Index of Industrial Production (1938 = 100) stood 156 in May, 1953, and at 214 in December, 1956. Expansion slowed down a little in 1956, to be sure, but still, the increase of 7.1 per cent in the course of 1956 was substantial, exceeding that of the United States. The country remained overpopulated, of course, but when the Vanoni Plan [60] was published in 1955 it showed, for the first time, that given certain conditions Italy might be able to solve her unemployment problem. That would mean a profound change, even if two decades should be needed rather than one, as Vanoni hoped.

Even a brief visit to Italy suffices to demonstrate what the figures of increased industrial production mean for the people's living standards. There is now a large number of automobiles and an even larger number of motor scooters. Most industrial workers can now afford the latter—quite a change from the day when they had to make their way from the factories on foot or on bicycle. A new aristocracy of skilled workers has developed. In the industrial regions of Northern Italy improvement progresses so far that the country's social structure, hitherto so very rigid, began to be flexible.[61] These workers, as well as the new group of white-collar workers, have begun to be fairly prosperous and to develop both an economic condition and a mental outlook entirely different from the "proletarians" of the past.

Progress was not limited to the field of industry. Agriculture had been the sore spot of Italian political and social life all along. Developments detrimental to social stability in that field have a history of two thousand years, beginning with the origin of the *latifundia* in Republican Rome. Subsequently, almost incredible complications developed in Italian agriculture, resulting particularly in the divergence between ownership and operation. Statistics might show that a large number of acres was owned by one family, but this area would be farmed in a multitude of small, and sometimes very small, lots by tenants or sharecroppers, some of whom might live a considerable distance from the land.[62]

Under such conditions any reform is difficult. Measures make sense only if reclamation and irrigation are combined with changes in ownership; the widespread notion that there are uncultivated lands in Italy, which could be brought under cultivation at will and without substantial improvement, is due to sheer illusion which is carefully nourished by Communist propaganda. Still, something had to be done. As one British observer put it: "Italy cannot afford agrarian reform, and she cannot afford not to have agrarian reform."

Under such conditions only compromise solutions are possible, and this is the route which De Gasperi entered. For the first time in Italian history agricultural reform measures were taken, the characteristic of which was so unlike what happened under Mussolini: performance outshone propaganda. A substantial acreage was transferred into the hands of new peasant owners, and a great deal was done, and continues to be done, in the field of land reclamation, irrigation and the improvement of agricultural methods. It lies in the nature of the situation that the results are not perfect. More might yet be done in one field or the other, but ultimately the important fact to remember is that in Italy as well as in other modern countries industry has long since begun to outshine agriculture. Agricultural income now constitutes a little more than one-fifth of the total national income and it continues to decline. Clearly, the solution for Italy lies in the field of industry, and a little more perfection in the field of agriculture does not matter.

General economic prospects are good, then, and developments which occurred during the 1950's might have made them better yet. Substantial oil deposits were discovered. Had they been exploited efficiently, they would, for the first time, have enabled the country to cover a good part of its raw material requirements from domestic production. However, politics were soon to block much of what economics might have accomplished. There existed a state agency (ENI) with a monopoly for the development or distribution of oil. A relic of Fascist days, it was administered by a man who became an influential Christian Democrat. This fact helped the leaders of that party to overlook that the development of new oil wells is one of the most dynamic parts of the modern economy. Government enterprise can do certain things, but it has never given satisfactory performance in the prospecting and development of oil. Reason required Italy to permit the development of her oil resources by private enterprise, both foreign and domestic. Foreign capital should have been particularly welcome, because if the Vanoni Plan demonstrated anything, it was that the goal of eliminating the country's chronic unemployment could be achieved in a short period only if Italian capital resources were supplemented from abroad.

Naturally, the Communists denounced any and all concessions to foreign enterprise as a new form of "colonialism." The Socialists, both

Right- and Left-wing, felt bound to take a similar line on account of their commitments to centralized economic planning. Nor was there any lack of men among the Christian Democrats who favored government ownership and operation in this case. It has often been said that the patronage available through a government-operated enterprise played its part in this preference. At any rate, the restrictions finally placed upon private industry in the law governing the development of oil resources went so far that no major foreign oil company retained any interest in the subject. Matters are somewhat different in Sicily where the government of the Autonomous Region had a law of its own enacted which makes possible the cooperation of foreign and domestic capital on a basis acceptable to both.

It is interesting to note that American companies were not the only ones to point out to the Italian government that it was following the wrong path. Thus, *The New York Times* reported:

> Pressure of a more material nature was brought to bear this month by West Germany, France and other European nations which Italy is to join in a common market and an atomic pool.
>
> When Premier Antonio Segni was in Paris last week putting final touches on the treaties that are to bring these two international organisms into being, he pleaded eloquently for a maximum freedom of movement for Italian workers within the area covered. France and West Germany were in the forefront of countries replying that Italy could not expect others to remove their bars to Italian workers while Italy maintained intact her bars against foreign capital.
>
> They pointed to oil concessions as a concrete example of Italy's forbidding attitude toward foreign capital. Signor Segni was finally obliged to say he would ameliorate the conditions on his return to Italy.[63]

The development of oil resources constitutes one of the cases where the close interrelationship of politics and economics becomes obvious. Post-war Italy has known only one comparatively stable type of government: a coalition between the Christian Democrats and some or all of the small "lay" parties of the center. The trouble with such combinations is that they include all the differences in their ranks which, in a normal party system, fill the entire political spectrum. There are the proponents of socialism at the Left and those of economic liberalism at the Right, plus Republicans and Monarchists, "clericalists" and "anti-clericalists." If we limit ourselves to the economic field we may say that in Germany the social market policy became possible only because the Christian Democrats, the Free Democrats, and the German Party could form a majority government without being dependent upon the votes of the Social Democrats.

Thus, the groups of the center and moderate Right were able to develop a coherent policy of their own, leaving the Social Democrats an opportunity to develop an alternative policy. In Italy a similar coalition would include the Christian Democrats and the Liberals. In fact, as we have seen, in 1947 and 1948, when Einaudi was Minister of Finance, the two parties combined to lay the basis for Italy's subsequent economic development. They never had a majority except in the Chamber elected in 1948. Therefore, the votes of Social Democrats were indispensable unless the Monarchists were to be taken into the coalition. To do that seemed impossible because it led to complications not only in regard to the form of government but also in regard to agrarian reform, foreign policy and other matters, although, as some of the major issues in these fields are being resolved, cooperation may be easier in the future. Meanwhile, governments including irreconcilable elements had to be formed. Cynics said that they constituted a case of cohabitation rather than of coalition.

Italian government, then, has had to follow the model of what the Prussian Prime Minister, Otto Braun, called "a government of all reasonable men." As it was mentioned above, such a government constitutes the opposite of reason, as it implies punishment of men of reason: they must serve on the same team regardless of all differences among them. They should be able to oppose one another as the democratic government and the democratic opposition, and this they cannot do. Thus, life is made difficult for them even during a time of prosperity. During a period of economic crisis enforced cooperation may become fatal, as in that case the voters' desire for "a change" may drive a majority into the arms of the extremists. Even in normal times the wear and tear is great on any team which has been in power for a long time. Indeed, a political system cannot be sound unless there exists that "safety valve" which Luigi Einaudi emphasized so strongly in his warnings against the adoption of P.R. in 1946.

Ultimately, it is difficult to see how Italy's politics can be placed on a sound basis without a general breakthrough which would open the "safety valve" again. When conditions became as difficult as they did after the fall of Segni in May, 1957, there developed a tendency in parts of the American press to blame it all on the capricious tactics of Giuseppe Saragat, who precipitated the crisis. It has been said that he wanted "to run with the hare and to hunt with the hounds." Saragat was, however, simply in the situation of the man who is "damned if he does and damned if he doesn't." If he participated in governments including men with Rightist convictions, he risked losing his moral authority among his own followers. If he did not participate, he risked defeating the country's only hope for a safe Republican government. He did, indeed, seem to tend in opposite directions, but the trouble was that there were powerful forces pulling him constantly toward one and the other.

Similar considerations apply to the complaint which Cyrus L. Sulzberger [64] rightly expressed in his column to the effect that "any cabinet to obtain legislative approval must depend upon the support of small center parties which are sometimes outrageously greedy in naming a price for cooperating." As in the case of Germany this greed of the small parties simply follows from a sense of inferiority. Because they are so small they are constantly waging a fight for survival, and if they ask a disproportionately large share in political power, they do so because it seems to be the only way in which they can demonstrate to their supporters that they still count.

Basically, then, the trouble is one of institutions rather than of persons or parties. There will be no solution until definite institutional changes are made; their nature results from what has been said above. As in France, the vested interests stand in their way, but so does ignorance. Everywhere, knowledge must precede action. The vested interests, certainly, go so far as to oppose even the development and the spread of the proper type of knowledge, but, then, that condition hampers all types of social research, and it need not be fatal. As we have seen, Germany's social market policy was planned by academic economists years before it was put into practice. Recently, Professor Erwin von Beckerath of the University of Bonn, the chairman of the Advisory Council of the Ministry of Economics, delivered a highly stimulating paper [65] on the relationship between economic analysis and economic policy which mentions the same type of pressure against economics in his own country. Those pressures, then, were overcome to a sufficient extent to make action possible on the basis of scientific knowledge, and this can be done in the political field as well.

Inasmuch as Italy's system of voting constitutes the major weakness in the political system, it is interesting to note that shortly before his untimely death, De Gasperi was ready to undertake the task of gathering the pertinent facts necessary to elucidate this problem, and to place them before the public. As we have seen, he expressed a preference for the majority system during the Naples Congress of his party. Somewhat earlier, in opposing certain rather sensational English and American interpretations of the prospects of a Communist victory in Italy, he had asked the significant question: "What would have happened, for example, in England and in the United States [during the depression] if those countries had had P.R.?" [66] Behind this rhetorical question there was, as this writer was assured by one of the former Prime Minister's friends, a full realization of the implications of P.R. De Gassperi's death ended a great opportunity to bring about a truly "great debate" on what Arnold Zurcher has called "Democracy's Declining Capacity to Govern," [67] and it may be a long time before a similar opportunity recurs.

Chapter XVIII

PRESIDENTIAL GOVERNMENT
IN THE UNITED STATES*

▼▲▼▲▼▲▼▲▼▲▼▲▼▲▼▲▼▲▼▲▼▲▼▲▼▲▼▲▼▲▼▲▼▲▼▲▼

PARLIAMENTARY AND PRESIDENTIAL SYSTEMS.

The difficulties connected with the practice of parliamentary government in recent decades have strengthened the interest in the independent executive as developed in the United States. Indeed, parliamentary government has not infrequently proven what Charles A. Beard called a "hair-trigger government." [1] Henry Hazlitt [2] and others have pointed out that wherever parliamentary government was unstable there was a deviation from essential aspects of its institutional pattern. Their evidence was too abstract in nature, however, to prevail against the overwhelming psychological impact of the repeated failure of parliamentary government in country after country.

If parliamentary government has left a sad record in altogether too many cases, a development in the opposite direction took place in the United States. Woodrow Wilson, in his *Congressional Government*,[3] had described a political action pattern hardly distinguishable from what the French call "government by assembly," although French practice places the emphasis on parliament as a whole whereas the American Congress, since the days of George Washington, has acted through the medium of committees.[4] In its basic elements, the Wilsonian criticism followed the lines laid down in Walter Bagehot's *The English Constitution*.[5] To Wilson it seemed at the time that inefficiency was an all but inevitable feature of the American system of government, even if he was never explicit in proposals for a change.[6]

* This chapter deals with a topic to which only a full-length book could do justice. The author hopes that the required brevity will not lead to misunderstandings. It seemed, however, that the argument developed in the preceding pages would not be complete without some reference to the structural peculiarities of the separation of powers.

By this time we have come to realize that Wilson was writing under the impact of the events following the Civil War. President Johnson was, indeed, the football of a congressional majority which found it difficult to unite in anything but negation. Grant and his successors did a little better, but it was not until the presidency of Grover Cleveland that a change began, and not until that of Theodore Roosevelt that it became definite. Woodrow Wilson himself was to help greatly in carrying this process forward. Still, during the final half of his second term there developed one of the worst manifestations of "Congressional Government" ever to be encountered in American history. Likewise, the period from 1920 to 1932 was characterized by a lack of presidential power and provided more ammunition for those willing to talk in terms of "Congressional Government."

With the advent of Franklin Delano Roosevelt, however, there began a significant change which has only in part been reversed since his death. Precedents for presidential leadership were established which did not permit any simple "return to normalcy"; the tools for such leadership accumulated to an extent undreamt of in the past. The rapid growth of the Executive Office of the President, established in 1939, tells the tale. Besides, the new agencies set up to deal with the depression added to the President's power and patronage. So did the change toward an active foreign policy which was enough in itself to make the President the crucial factor in the country's overall policies. Finally, the Second World War inflated the "Commander-in-Chief" clause of the Constitution to a magnitude unthought of even by Lincoln, and the "Cold War" which followed prevented a thorough deflation. References to the "aggregate powers of the President" might be hazardous in the field of constitutional law, but they came to represent a political reality which no one could ignore.

These changes in political practice were soon to be followed by changes in political analysis. Woodrow Wilson's impact on the academic world had been powerful. There was a widespread tendency to assume that the defeat which not only he but also the cause of an active American foreign policy suffered in 1919 was a confirmation of the worst fears expressed by the author of *Congressional Government*. Under Franklin D. Roosevelt, however, the presidency appeared again in a totally different light.[7]

THE SEPARATION OF POWERS.

The question is to what extent the changes in practice and in theory invalidate the basic criticism advanced by Bagehot, Wilson, and Hazlitt—the latter's *A New Constitution Now* representing the critical view of the American system in its most modern form. In the framework of this chapter the subject can be dealt with but briefly. It will help, however, to clarify matters if we do not immediately speak of a "presidential system." The use of that term would imply that, to some extent, we take for granted what we have to prove, since the existence of a "presidential system" as a continuous and coherent force is denied to this day. What the framers of the Constitution meant to establish was neither "presidential," nor "congressional" government; their aim was a system based upon the separation of powers. They accepted that system in theory, and worked it out in detail so far as the practice of the new "instrument of government" was concerned.

Thus, there is a clearcut separation between the executive and the legislature. The President, to whom the executive is entrusted, is elected in one process, and the two Houses of Congress are chosen each in a process of its own. The President cannot be held responsible by Congress (the possibility of impeachment representing a—rather anachronistic—sideline problem) and he cannot dissolve either House. Furthermore, "no person holding any office under the United States shall be a member of either House during his continuance in office." Finally, both President and Congress are flanked and, at times, frankly rivaled, by the Supreme Court, as the judicial review of legislative acts casts a large shadow over much of what the President and Congress do. It goes without saying that the rivalry between the Federal Government and the states adds to the general effects of the separation of powers, although few of those who want the Federal Government organized along different lines would want to interfere with the rights of the states.

The various powers have been separated systematically, then, and an evaluation of the implications cannot proceed either in a piecemeal or in a pragmatic fashion. A basic issue is involved and, when all is said and done, we cannot escape the conclusion that it was formulated by Montesquieu in such a manner that its critical examination has to return to the interpretation presented by that writer.[8] This does not mean that factors other than political theory did not enter into the making of the Constitution. On the floor of the Convention, John Dickinson said: "Experience must be our only guide; reason may mislead us." [9] The experience to which he referred was largely that of colonial government, characterized by the dualism of a governor appointed by the King and a legislature elected by the people. The transfer of such colonial practice to one of free government would seem to have called for a study of the difference between the two, but this analysis was not made. The general atmosphere of distrust directed against all power which the long struggle against royal power was bound to engender was one of the reasons. Nor can sheer accident be disregarded in the framing of the Constitution. On the basic issue, for example, of whether the President was to be elected by the Congress or by the people, the Convention reversed itself repeatedly; it voted five times for election by the Congress before abandoning that solution in favor not of direct election by the people but by an electoral college which was not expected to be as insignificant as it turned out to be. Nine of the state constitutions in force at that time provided that the executive be elected by the legislature, and both the Randolph plan (largely the work of Madison) and the Paterson plan suggested the same solution for the federal executive.

MONTESQUIEU AND THE DANGERS OF DEADLOCK.

Neither historical precedent nor accident, however, work entirely in the dark. John Dickinson had a good point in warning against relying on speculative reason and pleading for experience, but experience must be analyzed, and reason is the only power capable of doing so. Thus, we must return to Montesquieu's highly appealing theory according to which political liberty can be guaranteed only by a "moderate" government, based on the separation between executive, legislative, and judiciary powers.[10] Montesquieu's theory, evidently, was the great catalyzer, establishing a common denominator for precedent, accident and the emotional distrust of power. It was so appealing because it claimed not to be speculative theory at all, but to have been abstracted from reality, the reality of British government as observed by the French nobleman in the 1740's. Blackstone's *Commentaries*,[11] more widely read by Americans than *The Spirit of the Laws,* implicitly endorsed the views expressed in that volume. As Professor Prescott [12] has said, the Convention did not even debate the principle of the separation of powers because its validity was taken for granted. Certainly, during the Convention nothing was accepted as authoritatively as a reference to Montesquieu. Subsequently, when, in No. 47 of *The Federalist,* Madison defended the Constitution against the charge of not providing for an adequate separation of powers, he said:

> No political truth is certainly of greater intrinsic value, or is stamped with the authority of more enlightened patrons of liberty, than that on which the objection is founded. The accumulation of all powers, legislative, executive, and judiciary, in the same hands, whether of

one, a few, or many, and whether hereditary, self-appointed, or elective, may justly be pronounced the very definition of tyranny. . . .

The oracle who is always consulted and cited on this subject is the celebrated Montesquieu. If he be not the author of this invaluable precept in the science of politics, he has the merit at least of displaying and recommending it most effectually to the attention of mankind.[13]

It seems, then, permissible to analyze the system's logic on the basis of its defense by Montesquieu.[14] The basic question is that, when three powers of government must cooperate in order to secure a positive result, one of them might refuse its cooperation, in which case a deadlock would result. Montesquieu himself was aware of this possibility but he dealt with it rather off-handedly: "The three powers should naturally form a state of repose or inaction. But as there is a necessity for movement in the course of human affairs, they are forced to move, but still in concert." [15]

Montesquieu's mistake was to assume that there can be only one outcome where, in fact, three are possible. Movement in concert is one of them. Then, there may develop a definite deadlock, and finally, a deadlock, or near-deadlock, may be broken by a process of domination: Either Congress may, as the younger Wilson considered normal, overpower the President or the President may overpower Congress, with the Supreme Court, in the end, likely to "follow the election returns."

It is natural to think of the possibility of voluntary cooperation first. There never has been a lack of patriotic men on both sides of the line dividing the executive and the legislature who have realized that the general welfare was bound to suffer unless effective cooperation took place. They have made every effort to bring about such cooperation, and Ernest Griffith [16] has demonstrated in detail how Congress has developed a number of methods which enable it to work in that direction. In recent history the potentialities of such cooperation were demonstrated during the Eightieth Congress, elected in 1946, and the Eighty-fourth and Eighty-fifth Congresses, elected in 1954 and 1956, respectively. When President Truman found himself confronted with a Republican majority, some of the best observers of the American political scene feared a repetition of what had happened after the mid-term elections of 1918 and 1930; two of them went so far as to suggest that the President resign and arrange for a Republican to succeed himself. There was, to be sure, no lack of conflicts between the President and the Eightieth Congress, which Mr. Truman called a "do-nothing Congress." Still, there was also a substantial measure of cooperation, which included aid to Greece and Turkey and the Marshall Plan. Similarly, while the Democratic majority issuing from the elections of 1954 and 1956 presented President Eisenhower with difficulties, these were by no means overwhelming.

The question arises whether a period of—comparatively—harmonious cooperation constitutes a precedent likely to be followed in the future or merely an exception likely to prove the rule. Certainly, the two periods of deadlock which followed the midterm elections of 1918 and 1930 are a historic reality. So far as the former is concerned, the result was the rejection of the Treaty of Versailles, and it need not be repeated that the consequences of that step were serious.

Nor is the second period of deadlock without significance. In the course of the hearings of the Joint Committee on the Organization of Congress, Senator Fulbright said:

> I think in Hoover's later years, the severity of the depression was vastly accentuated by the 2 years between 1930 and 1932 in that Congress would not go along with him. We could not do much. We just sat there and things got much worse in that period. You had a 2-year period in which perhaps something should have been done to prevent or lessen the severity of that situation.

When Representative Cox asked: "Is that a criticism of Mr. Hoover or of the Congress?" Senator Fulbright answered: "I think it is a criticism of the system. There was no way out of the situation." [17] What Senator Fulbright meant to say hardly was that there was absolutely no way out of the situation, but rather that to find such a way went "against the grain." Our leaders were confronted with what the medieval theologian would have designated as a call for "works of supererogation." Conceivably, such works might be performed, but in the ordinary course of events this will not, or at least not always, be done by ordinary men. On such ordinary men we must, however, rely.

The deadlock which occurred after 1930 was, at any rate, not much less serious than the one that developed after 1918. In such cases it is not numbers that matter; it is the importance of the event, and the importance of the direct and indirect consequences that spring from it. Therefore, the fact that only two such deadlocks occurred in living memory does not necessarily make the system acceptable which made them possible; the world has suffered too much from these events, particularly the first. Besides, if deadlocks rarely develop in such classical form, it does not follow that their essential ingredients are ever absent from the political scene. In fact, the tendency to oppose the executive exists, to a substantial extent, within the President's own party. As far as the Congress is concerned, the President and the members of his cabinet are outsiders. Under a parliamentary system, the Prime Minister and the members of his cabinet are members of parliament. They have not only rubbed shoulders with their fellow-members for years, but they continue to do so. In the United States it is a rare occurrence that a former member of Congress becomes President. The men most likely to be nominated and elected are the governors of large pivotal states, or men who, like Wendell Willkie or Dwight D. Eisenhower, had gained a reputation outside the political scene. Exceptions confirm the rule. Thus, Harding was nominated as a result of a deadlock, and Truman first became President as a result of the death of the President; his nomination as Vice-President had been due to the simple desire to "balance the ticket." [18] It soon became clear that neither Harding nor Truman got along with Congress any better because they had belonged to it; they, too, became outsiders and were treated as such. There is a similar tendency in regard to members of Congress who leave that body in order to join the cabinet, although they will often benefit more from their old contacts in Congress than a President. Cordell Hull, at any rate, enjoyed rather good relations with both the House and the Senate after he became Secretary of State.

When considering the cases of certain other cabinet members, both past and present, one is, however, immediately reminded of the terms in which Walter Bagehot [19] discusses the difficulties which arise when such outsiders have to confront a body of men highly conscious of their constitutional functions and responsibilities:

> A great popular assembly has a corporate character; it has its own privileges, prejudices, and notions. And one of these notions is that its own members—the persons it sees every day—whose qualities it knows, whose minds it can test, are those whom it can most trust. A clerk speaking from without would be an unfamiliar object. He would be an outsider. He would speak under suspicion; he would speak without dignity. Very often he would speak as a victim.

When a situation arises which recalls this characterization, we must resist the temptation to think in terms of personalities. The point is that members of both Congress and the administration, equally public-spirited as a rule, are placed into a position where conflict is easy and cooperation difficult. Bitter contests date back to the administration of George Washington, during whose second term a violent struggle [20] arose between the majority of Congress and the Secretary of the Treasury, Alexander Hamilton, as a result of which the latter retired from public life.

What Bagehot had to say about the difficulty of having a government department defended by a parliamentary outsider is important in more than one respect. We risk stating our terms improperly when we say that the separation of powers exists in the United States and does not exist in England. This is correct so far as the *structure* of government is concerned, but the opposite relationship exists in regard to its functions. The Indian political scientist, A. Appadorai,[21] quoting W. F. Willoughby [22] in his first paragraph says:

> "A close study of the English Government in its practical working shows that, organically, the principle of the separation of powers has been carried out with a rigidity that is found in few or no other governments."
>
> The exercise of legislative power is vested in the Legislature, which is a department of government distinct from the Executive. The executive power is vested in the Crown, and Parliament never attempts to deprive it of any of its executive powers, nor takes to itself the function of administration.

Certainly, the British or Canadian House of Commons would not dare deal with details of the administration in the way the American Congress, and in particular congressional committees, often try to do. Whenever a member of the British House of Commons as much as refers to a government official by name, he is liable to be called to order. Any and all criticisms are supposed to be addressed to the responsible minister who, a member of parliament himself, has an opportunity to make an immediate and effective reply, provided that he has a good case. If he does not have a good case, both he and the cabinet as a whole suffer. The Prime Minister is quite likely to disavow, or even drop, a member of his cabinet who proves to be a burden. Therefore, every minister knows that he has to be ready with a good and persuasive answer to any question; he also knows that his policies must never be allowed to conflict with the general sense of the House.

For this reason, when we discuss the lack of responsible government in the United States, we must be careful not to place the blame exclusively on Congress. Both the Senate and the House of Representatives contain a number of members whose ability and devotion to duty would do honor to any parliament in the world. It is only natural that they should resent the fact that, for long periods, policy may be made by government officials whose views they do not share and whose ability they doubt. In case of conflict, these members of Congress may have as many good arguments on their side as the members of the administration. Under a parliamentary system the conflict would simply not arise. Members of Congress would be in charge of administrative policy-making, and their colleagues would have every opportunity to bring pressure to bear upon them to make them correct what they consider mistakes. The executive of the parliamentary system, then, constitutes a type quite different from the one we have in the United States, as it is both a part of, and responsible to, the legislature. This makes it safe to entrust it with a wide degree of autonomy and discretion in matters pertaining to its realm. On the other hand, we cannot simply apply maxims gleaned from this type of political practice to the American Congress, and tell it to leave the executive alone in what we may consider the latter's proper functions.

THE DANGERS OF DOMINATION.

A variety of factors produces the result, then, that even when there is a reasonable degree of cooperation between our legislature and our executive, the relationship is never without a sting. The members of Congress do not feel happy about the concessions which they make to an administration of outsiders. They show their feelings in a great many ways, both large and small; this the policy-making members of the administration, who may also be very competent men, resent in their turn. Furthermore, the "pure" type of voluntary cooperation has never existed. No President in history has ever been able to effect a reasonable measure of coordination between himself and Congress without resorting to some of the devices which come under the heading of "domination." Whenever a President attempts to rely upon persuasion alone, as Dwight D. Eisenhower did in the early months of 1957, great difficulties develop. What looks like a supremacy of Congress will immediately produce some of the serious drawbacks which John Stuart Mill [23] noted when he distinguished the "Proper Functions of Representative Bodies" from the improper ones.

Certain Presidents have, of course, been able to rely more upon persuasion than others. Both Thomas Jefferson and Woodrow Wilson were ideally placed for the use of such methods: Many of the congressional members of the party which they had led to victory were newcomers to the Washington scene and willing to accept leadership from the outside. This leadership was offered by men of undoubted intellectual superiority.[24] These circumstances were exceptional, and in both cases fierce storms raged around the President during the final years of his tenure.

Virtually every President, then, who amounted to anything, has had to dip more or less deeply into the arsenal of weapons which was first assembled by Andrew Jackson.[25] From that source there comes the appeal to the people over the heads of Congress which was, more recently, made so much easier by radio and television, but which "Old Hickory" knew how to make effective even without such devices; there comes that reliance upon patronage which no President has ever resorted to quite as blatantly, but not a few quite as thoroughly, as Jackson. There are other weapons, such as the use of the veto. Congress may submit to the policies forced upon it with such weapons, but its members will not like it and, on occasion, will not hesitate to show their feelings by frustrating the President.

As a result, presidential "leadership" is always a cross borne rather than a gift welcomed, and the congressional horse never shows much reluctance in throwing its rider for a spill. Even a "strong" President may have to take such spills, whereas under the others the congressional horse, lacking any positive direction of its own, may wander about aimlessly. There is, then, something to be said for the assumption that, at best, we may look forward to "a government of fits and starts." [26] The experience of the period following upon the Second World War might cause us to express ourselves more guardedly, but we should not close our eyes to the "ups and downs" in our political system; we should conclude, with Walter Lippmann, "that it is not a stable balance, that the tendency of the system is to become unbalanced—and especially after wars when Congress is, for a time, predominant." [27] When this happens there is little sense in just blaming either Congress or the President; it is fairer to conclude with Professor Kerwin that "The Constitution Is at Fault." [28]

Even if we draw such conclusions, it does not automatically follow that we either could or should abolish our political system. There is always the preliminary question whether the parliamentary system would work in this country; we shall discuss this later. For the time being, let us broaden the basis of our criticism, particularly in regard to the theory of checks and balances as developed by Montesquieu. We do not always bear in mind that the two elements in this formula are not identical: "Checks" are one thing and "balances" are something else again. Clearly, the term "balance" is derived from an analogy to the field of physics. Students of logic tell us that the attempt to draw conclusions by way of analogy constitutes the easiest path to a fallacy. In physics, the term "balance" is used most frequently in connection with a pair of scales. When scales are "in balance," there exists complete equality of forces on both sides. This means the absence of movement. In the language proper to the political field this can mean only one thing: a "deadlock." Therefore, when a stalemate actually develops under a system of checks and balances, it is no more than a logical result of our premises, and we must add that with the potentiality of a stalemate there goes the temptation to resort to domination.

A certain view of the nature of man is implied in both the premise and its results. When Montesquieu feared that "every man invested with power is apt to abuse it," [29] he clearly foreshadowed Lord Acton's famous warning against the corrupting influence of power. Interpreted with moderation, both Montesquieu and Acton are right, but matters go a little far if we hold with Elbridge Gerry that "Confidence is the road to tyranny." [30] If that is the case, man, particularly political man, is presumed to be thoroughly bad, and the only way of checking one bad man is to pit another bad man against him. Madison came close to demanding just that when he wrote that "Ambition must be made to counteract ambition." [31] It could be shown in detail that there is a middle road between utter pessimism in regard to the nature of man (which, incidentally, befits an advocate of dictatorship more than one of constitutional government), and the blithe optimism of Rousseau, which is the logical corrollary of anarchism. At this juncture let us confine ourselves to just one point: If we assume that there can be no trust in politics—which was not at all the view of the framers of the Constitution [32]—there is only one conclusion to be drawn so far as the operation of a political system based upon a structural separation of powers is concerned. This conclusion is that voluntary cooperation is neither to be expected nor to be desired. Its existence would border on collusion: Congress and the executive ought, indeed, to confront one another constantly as rival rows of gladiators; in that way alone could our freedom be secured.

If we reject that extreme pessimism which cannot conceive of any safeguards for political liberty except by chaining someone with power to someone else with enough power to stop him, there is yet room for a sound realism which accepts power but insists on surrounding it with effective safeguards. At this point the distinction between checks and balances enters the picture. Significantly, the French speak of *freins et contrepoids*—"reins and counterweights." The term "counterweights" is the exact equivalent of "balances," but the reference to "reins" suggests an analogy more germane to the political field. Any horse needs a rein, but not because he is necessarily a bad horse; a natural tendency to develop speed is, in fact, one of the reasons for his usefulness. The reins serve a double purpose: they reduce speed to a safe limit, and they give the horse the direction he needs if he is to serve his master's ends.

A tendency to ambition in a political leader is no more bad in itself than a tendency to speed in a horse, and the political power which ambition may abuse is a necessary instrument for holding communities together. Clearly, both ambition and power need to be confined within their proper limits; for this purpose there are checks. In the chapter on constitutional government we have said that checks serve a threefold purpose: they force our leaders to explain themselves to others before they act and thus bring about the benefits of free and frank discussion; they make it possible for these actions to be undertaken democratically, as the people, or at least their representatives, must be kept informed; finally, they protect the rights of the people. As we have also seen, the more such checks are made part of the procedure into which we channel political power, the less will the flow of power be impeded where it is essential, and the more effective are the restraints likely to be where they are needed.

We now must add that the dangers inherent in a system based on a rigid separation of powers result not only from the fact that "balances" may lead to deadlocks, but that, when there is any danger at all that such deadlocks might develop, the demand for action will become so strong that any response to it will be accepted even if it sweeps organic checks aside together with the balances. Since the need for action is now greater than it has ever been, there are more opportunities for a type of domination which dispenses with checks as well as with balances.

It is interesting to note that the existence of such a possibility did not escape the attention of Madison. For him the immediate danger to guard against were encroachments by the legislature. Yet, he was aware of the fact that the frustrations brought about by long periods of such "congressional government" might push the pendulum in the opposite direction. In his words:

> It might, however, sometimes happen, that appeals would be made under circumstances less adverse to the executive and judiciary departments. The usurpations of the legislature might be so flagrant and so sudden, as to admit of no specious coloring. A strong party among themselves might take side with the other branches. The executive power might be in the hands of a peculiar favorite of the people. In such a posture of things, the public decision might be less swayed by prepossessions in favor of the legislative party.[33]

Examples to illustrate Madison's forecast could be chosen from the record of more than one President; if we discuss only the case of Franklin Delano Roosevelt, the reason is that he was the most recent of our "strong" Presidents and that the decisions taken during his tenure had a far-reaching influence on the course of world events. In his first inaugural President Roosevelt expressed himself, with his customary frankness, on the subject of constitutional balances, saying that "it is to be hoped that the normal balance of executive and legislative authority may be wholly adequate to meet the unprecedented task before us. But it may be that an unprecedented demand and need for undelayed action may call for temporary departure from that normal balance of public procedure." [34] Thomas K. Finletter follows this quotation with the sentence: "It was an understatement." [35] In fact, during the first hundred days of the new administration bill after bill was pushed through Congress without the benefit of adequate debate. The Emergency Banking Bill, for example, was pushed through Congress in eight hours, and since only one copy was available, "The House proceeded to consider the measure, pretending that a folded newspaper was the copy which it did not possess." [36] In this particular case no harm was done as the bill was properly conceived. Yet, it would certainly have been preferable had the nation's government been sufficiently capable of functioning during the preceding two years to make it unnecessary to take such shortcuts with constitutional procedures. Congress, to be sure, has its weaknesses, but it also constitutes, in the words of Robert A. Taft, "a good sound jury" [37] which should not be bypassed.

Actually, however, Congress was bypassed during the Second World War to an extent that was not required by objective circumstances. As Walter Lippmann commented in January, 1943:

> The separation of powers under our system of government has always tended to produce ignorance, and then suspicion, and then jealousy, and finally antagonism between the Congress and the Executive. . . .
> When Mr. Churchill goes to Moscow or to Washington, one of the first things he does on his return is to pay his respects to the House of Commons by telling them as much as he can tell publicly, and a lot more besides off the record. But when Mr. Hopkins or Mr. Harriman goes to London or Moscow, Congress never gets a chance to see what they are like and to hear what they sound like.[38]

Mr. Churchill's speeches on inter-Allied conferences were, indeed, for many Americans the source to which they, too, looked for information; they knew that there might be less to learn from President Roosevelt's radio addresses, or from his addresses to Congress.

LACK OF RESPONSIBLE ADVICE TO PRESIDENTS.

More than *congressional* checks are, in fact, eliminated when executive action can follow the patterns set by "strong" Presidents to the extent that President Roosevelt did during part of his tenure. The *internal* checks within the administration itself (demanded by regard for sound principles of administration) may equally be swept away. The proper focus for such checks is the cabinet; if, under modern conditions, the National Security Council should take its place, the change would not affect the principle involved. The only important considerations are that the checks be exercised by men who are thoroughly familiar with the concrete aspects of the work being done by the government (and this means that the heads of the major departments must be included), that they are equally conversant with the overall problems of policy-making and, finally, that they be in sympathy with the aims of the administration.

President Roosevelt had enough sense of humor to be able to joke about the way in which he was handling cabinet meetings. When his then Secretary of War, Henry L. Stimson, related this incident, he added: "The Roosevelt Cabinets are really a solo performance by the President interspersed with some questions and very few debates." [39] Yet, this was a time of momentous decisions, some of which had to be taken rapidly, but all of which would have benefited from a discussion with men who, after all, were handling important aspects of the work which the administration had to shoulder and who certainly wanted it to be a success. Looking back on the matter in 1947, Stimson felt that the President would have done well to surround himself with a war cabinet of the type that Churchill had to work with. What bothered Stimson was not that his own advice was so infrequently taken, which he knew to be inevitable, but "it was rather that Mr. Roosevelt's policy was so often either unknown or not clear to those who had to execute it, and worse yet, in some cases it seemed self-contradictory." [40] Stimson concludes these remarks with the words: "Franklin Roosevelt as a wartime international leader proved himself as good as one man could be—but one man was not enough to keep track of so vast an undertaking." [41]

One man, in fact, could not make all the essential decisions on his own. If he failed to take the advice of his responsible collaborators, he was likely to act on the advice of men who lacked the proper background. An early case, which influenced the subsequent shape of world events more than the general public ever came to realize, occurred in 1933. The London World Economic Conference had been called to consider the situation which had arisen as a result of the devaluation of the dollar, which had a deflationary effect on many other nations and particularly on those which attempted to keep the gold value of their currencies stable, such as France. The devaluation of the dollar was as severely criticized within the United States as without. Yet, while there was a constructive alternative,[42] a devaluation did create better conditions for an early "reflation"—an attempt to raise the level of prices again to something closer to the pre-depression level—than any other policy. When the World Economic Conference was summoned, the British and the French were merely interested in having limits set to the devaluation of the dollar. From the President's point of view this could not be done if the limits were too narrow, but there should have been no objection at all if the limits were adequate. Actually, by the time the conference met, the gold value of the dollar had declined even more than Roosevelt had originally hoped for; [43] the pound reached a high of $4.43 on June 28, the day when the President's special emissary, Raymond Moley, arrived in London. On June 17, Roosevelt had told Moley that he was willing to keep the dollar at $4.25 to the pound, and he was prepared to accept stabilization even at a low of $4.05.[44] The road, then, seemed prepared for a general currency stabilization. Roosevelt could eat his cake and have it, too—he could have a dollar sufficiently reduced in gold value to make possible a substantial degree of "reflation," and, in addition, a stable monetary parity with the leading countries of the world.

Moley knew about Roosevelt's intentions, and he was as sympathetic to "reflation" as to stabilization. He reached agreement with the official delegation, headed by Secretary of State Cordell Hull, on a course of action which followed the President's instructions. A rather mild declaration was then drawn up which the European powers accepted and which the American delegation was to transmit to the President. Both Neville Chamberlain, then the British Chancellor of the Exchequer, and Prime Minister Ramsay MacDonald, stressed to Moley the great importance which such a declaration would have for the gold standard countries—France, Switzerland, and Holland, in particular.[45] Moley comments that "knowing what F.D.R.'s state of mind had been when I left I had not the slightest doubt that he would approve it." [46] The President, however, was, at that time, aboard the cruiser "Indianapolis," with the journalist, Louis Howe, and Henry Morgenthau, Jr., then a junior member of the administration, the only men with whom he could consult. He did not wait to get home and discuss the matter with his official advisers, including Secretary of the Treasury Woodin. Instead, he dispatched a message to London which became known as "The Bombshell" [47]; he not only rejected the declaration but did so in terms none too favorable to the self-respect of the members of the Conference. By doing so, he placed himself in conflict with the advice not only of the two competent cabinet members, the Secretary of State and the Secretary of the Treasury, but also with all qualified unofficial advisers, such as his own emissary, Raymond Moley, and Bernard Baruch.[48]

The consequences of this step might have been disregarded by an isolationist, but they should have been alarming for a man as much in favor of international cooperation as Roosevelt. France, until then barely touched by the world economic crisis, was to find herself in the throes of a serious deflationary crisis for another three years. This weakened her internally, as well as externally, and facilitated Hitler's advances. Had Roosevelt lived to write his memoirs, he could only have pleaded that he was but one man and that any man can make mistakes; but, then, in such matters, the decision should never lie with one man. Had Secretary of State Hull and Secretary of the Treasury Woodin still been members of Congress, they could have talked to the President from "a position of strength" and they would have attempted to force upon him the decisions reached by their two departments; instead, they had no alternative except to submit or to resign. Resignation would have returned them to the status of private citizens with no official forum to address and no power of their own to wield.

Inasmuch as the cabinet officer most directly affected was the Secretary of State, it is interesting to note that Cordell Hull was kept from any knowledge of the essential aspects of the preparatory work for the conference "by F.D.R.'s express orders." [49] The British Ambassador, Sir Ronald Lindsay, one of the principals of these negotiations, was not aware of this situation, and he considered it necessary to discuss the conclusions reached with the Secretary of State. Moley reports that when the interview took place, "Hull cut the talk short. He suggested that the British Ambassador communicate with the President. It took Sir Ronald two days to recover from the shock of this conversation. I don't know that Secretary Hull ever did." [50]

The British Ambassador, apparently, thought in terms of British experience. Ordinarily, a British Prime Minister will take some pains to work through his Foreign Secretary in matters pertaining to the latter's field. There are exceptions, as occurred under Lloyd George and Neville Chamberlain, but in such cases the Prime Minister runs a serious risk: a Foreign Secretary who resigns has a parliamentary forum from which to express his views and he will remain a thorn in the Prime Minister's side. An American cabinet member who leaves his office becomes a mere private citizen; he may call a press conference and make public speeches, but these lack the weight of what a leading member of a parliamentary body is able to tell colleagues on whose continued confidence the existence of a cabinet depends. When Cordell Hull joined the Roosevelt cabinet he lost not only his seat in the Senate, but also the added strength which the chairmanship of the Committee on Foreign Relations would have given him. Had he later resigned from his position as Secretary of State he would have had to wait some time for an opportunity to reenter Congress, which practically could have been done only from the State of Tennessee. In case of reelection he would have started at the bottom of the seniority ladder. He was well enough versed in the ways of practical politics to be aware of these handicaps, and he knew from the start that the weight which he could throw against what he considered ill-advised actions of the President was limited. Such matters would not be so serious if they did not mean that when the Secretary of State is shortcircuited all the expert knowledge accumulated in his Department is shortcircuited as well.[50a]

The full drawbacks of such procedures were to manifest themselves during the Second World War. Before we take them up let us, however, emphasize that Roosevelt would have every reason to plead "not guilty" to the charges of having been a "warmonger," the accusation which the latest wave of "revisionist" literature has been leveling against him. One thing Roosevelt did want to do: He wanted to use the great power of the United States to prevent the aggressors of his day from becoming a law unto themselves, and reaching a degree of strength which would have made them a direct danger to the United States. No American statesman could have wanted to act otherwise.

Still, it is interesting to note at least two instances in which Roosevelt demonstrated that, in order to preserve the peace, he was willing to come to terms even with Hitler. The first is an interview with Mr. Joseph E. Davies, whom he had just then decided to send on his "Mission to Moscow." Davies had lunch with the President in late August, 1936. Roosevelt declared that, while he was not "overly optimistic that peace could be preserved," yet he wanted to do all in his power to that end. Everything depended upon Hitler. Should he be motivated by a "will to peace" rather than a "will to conquest," he "should have the cooperation of all peace-loving nations in an effort to compose any economic or other situations which bred war. Access to raw materials, political security and disarmament were all necessary, if the world was not to be deluged with the horror of war . . ."[51]

If this was merely a part of a confidential discussion, there was definite action along such lines during the Munich Conference. A little more than a month after it broke up, and before the hope for "Peace in our time" had faded, Arthur Krock, in one of his columns in *The New York Times*,[52] referred to a detailed "time-table" of the Conference. It was circulated by friends of the administration to show that American intervention had saved the day for peace. Certainly, it was not long before no one was claiming credit for Munich, but the fact that the Roosevelt administration was doing so for a short time goes a long way to show that it was not planning for war.

The situation changed when Hitler demonstrated that he did not know how to stop, and war broke out in Europe, aggravated by the continued Japanese aggression against China. Roosevelt did want effective opposition to both Hitler and the Japanese War Lords, even at the risk of war. Various measures were taken before Pearl Harbor which may have contributed to American involvement in the conflict, although it is doubtful whether they were a major factor. On this occasion, suffice it to refer to their constitutional background. As Thomas K. Finletter has reminded us, there are many things which the President can do in the field of foreign affairs, fortified by his powers as "Commander-in-Chief," but:

> This peculiar authority of the Executive gives it the power to create the conditions which make war inevitable, or, contrariwise, to avoid war by yielding to the pretensions of other nations. But it does not give the President the power to stop war by affirmative collaboration with other nations, and to impose our own plans and principles on those nations who believe in war as an instrument of national policy. That can be done only by teamwork between Congress and the President—by treaties, by appropriations, by the support of armaments and by many other similar steps, all part of a coherent and consistently applied plan to reach the far distant goal of removing the causes of war.[53]

Such teamwork with Congress for the purpose of preventing the war proved impossible; the reaction to Roosevelt's Chicago speech of 1937, in which he had used the memorable phrase of "quarantining the aggressors," left no doubt that the measure of congressional cooperation required for preventive steps was not available. This was the time when the findings of a congressional committee, whose counsel was Alger Hiss, according to which our "munitions makers" had a large share in involving us in the First World War, dominated the thinking of large groups.

Reasons for doubt do remain in regard to this or that of Roosevelt's measures during the months preceding Pearl Harbor. Thus, in retrospect, something can be said in favor of the advice given from

Tokyo by both the American and British Ambassadors in favor of a meeting between the President and Prince Konoye. Hindsight is of little help, however, and a fairly strong case can be made for Roosevelt's overall policies during this period. Essential aspects of his policy during the conflict are a different matter. Some of the "Great Mistakes of the War" not only *should* have been avoided; they apparently *would* have been avoided had policy-making in the United States been less personal, and had the advice tendered so strongly by the departments involved been given the attention required by orderly government procedures.

There is, first, the policy of "unconditional surrender." During, as well as after, the war its defenders told us that the alternative would have been a negotiated peace with the Axis leaders. That, of course, was not the case. The alternative advocated by responsible critics was a policy of stated war aims, as it had been pursued under Wilson's leadership during the First World War. The peoples of the Axis nations could have been advised of the principal purposes for which the Allies fought the war; the demands of the Atlantic Charter, supposedly adopted by all the Allies, could have been made more specific. As soon as, in any of the nations concerned, governments arose which had eliminated Fascist, Nazi, or War Lord control, they could have been given an opportunity to negotiate concerning the way in which the demands proclaimed by the Allies were to be carried out. Such a policy had its drawbacks, as has any policy. It provided, however, two great advantages: The Allied leaders could have fixed their own aims with a measure of finality before war-time opinion —that "sudden breeze of passion" which may engulf even the large territory of a "representative republic" in times of stress—swept them off their feet and into an ocean of irrationality. In the second place there was the well-founded hope that such a policy might shorten the war. This, in turn, would have meant more than the saving of Allied lives, important as that was to all who had not taken leave of their senses (which some of our propagandists, including certain radio commentators, had obviously done). It would have meant ending the war, both in Europe and in the Far East, before our Russian ally had penetrated to positions from which no paper promises would be able to dislodge him, and which would enable him to place the fruits of victory in jeopardy. Thus, when the German oppositionists attempted to assassinate Hitler in July, 1944, Stalin's armies had not yet taken Warsaw. Support of these German anti-Nazis, as was urged by such men as Allen W. Dulles,[54] might have rallied enough waverers to the cause of anti-Nazi rebellion to make the difference between success and failure. In the case of Japan matters are simpler; there now exists ample evidence that, had we been willing to make the concessions which, in this case, were actually made in the end (the assurances contained in the Potsdam declaration on Japan, plus our willingness, expressed subsequently, to let the Japanese themselves decide on the retention of the Emperor), there might have been peace before the atom bombs were dropped and before Russia had a chance to enter the war.

The antecedents of the decision in favor of "unconditional surrender" have not yet had the exploration they deserve. However, the demand did not just occur to the President during the Casablanca news conference of January 24, 1943, when he made it public. There had been discussions of the subject, centering in the State Department Subcommittee on Security Problems, headed by former Ambassador Norman Davis.[55] "Unconditional surrender" was one of the recommendations of this group although there is reason to assume that the phrase was meant in a military sense. There was to be no armistice, but the question whether the Axis nations as a whole, rather than merely their armies, should be surrendered without any kind of either negotiations or more detailed Allied assurances, apparently remained open. At any rate, Cordell Hull was to express himself as follows in his Memoirs:

> The principle of unconditional surrender overshadowed our policy toward the Axis and their satellites and our planning for their future.
>
> Originally this principle had not formed part of the State Department's thinking. We were as much surprised as Mr. Churchill when, for the first time, the President, in the Prime Minister's presence, stated it suddenly to a press conference during the Casablanca Conference in January, 1943. I was told that the Prime Minister was dumbfounded.[56]

Hull, and many of his associates, were opposed to "unconditional surrender," even if Hull was misinformed about Mr. Churchill's role in the matter. The State Department, the British Foreign Office, and (for reasons of their own) the Russians, made attempt after attempt to have this policy changed.[57] So far as the President's military advisers are concerned, General Eisenhower, it is reported, opposed the "unconditional surrender" policy strongly, and, in April, 1944, when he could see what it meant in reality, asked the then Secretary of State Stettinius to transmit his views to the President.[58] There is some reason to assume, then, that if the decision to ask for "unconditional surrender" had passed through the channels established for major policy matters it would at least have been modified in such a manner as to deprive it of its rigidity.

The President's official advisers were even more disregarded when the Morgenthau Plan was adopted by Roosevelt and Churchill during the second Quebec Conference, in September, 1944.[59] A State Department publication has this to say on the matter:

> No policy official of the Department accompanied the President to Quebec.
>
> Certain political matters were discussed at Quebec, however, and one important decision with far-reaching postwar implications was taken, namely, acceptance by the President and the Prime Minister of the plan for the treatment of Germany after surrender presented by Secretary Morgenthau, who had accompanied the President to Quebec. This plan was in fundamental conflict with the recommendations on this matter made earlier that month by the Secretary of State and with the views of the War Department. While this decision was later modified, it was to have an important bearing on the Government's subsequent position on this problem.

Cordell Hull said this about the Morgenthau Plan, as initialled in Quebec by Roosevelt and Churchill: "Essentially, this was a plan of blind vengeance." [60] He added:

> This whole development at Quebec, I believe, angered me as much as anything that had happened during my career as Secretary of State. If the Morgenthau plan leaked out, as it inevitably would—and shortly did—it might well mean a bitter-end German resistance that could cause the loss of thousands of American lives.[61]

If the Secretary of State was not consulted about the Morgenthau Plan, neither was the cabinet officer next concerned, the Secretary of War. Henry L. Stimson later commented that, when Morgenthau told him the story of the Quebec Conference, he did so "modestly and without rubbing it in, but it was the narration of a pretty heavy defeat for everything that we had fought for." [62]

Stimson objected primarily on economic grounds, but the Morgenthau Plan, as made available to us later by the man whose name it bears,[63] had military implications. Germany was to be totally disarmed, and its policing was to be entrusted to "the military forces of Germany's continental neighbors." Among those neighbors the military power of Russia outstripped that of all others. Drew Middleton, one of the few who favored the Morgenthau Plan at the time and who had the courage to admit it later, aptly commented: "Who would run Germany today if, as Mr. Morgenthau suggested, its occupation had been left up to Germany's continental neighbors led by the Soviet Union and including Poland, Czechoslovakia and Yugoslavia?" [64] The Morgenthau Plan, then, if fully implemented, might have handed all of Germany over to Russia, and jeopardized Western Europe.

Thus, on two vital occasions American foreign policy was made in complete disregard of not only the two responsible cabinet officers but of all the expert opinion at their command—just as had been done when "The Bombshell" was dropped on the London Economic Conference. The separation of powers, to be sure, did not compel President Roosevelt to act as he did; he might have acted differently. We need not repeat, however, that whenever the "balances" contained in our system are swept away by a "strong President," there are no effective "checks" either which could *force* the process of presidential policy-making into rational channels, and no government is truly institutional unless this is the case. Reference has been made above (p. 232) to Harry Hopkins' astonishment over the situation which he encountered during the Conference off Newfoundland: "Roosevelt was completely on his own, subject only to the advice of his immediate and self-selected entourage which advice he could accept or reject," whereas "Churchill was constantly reporting to and consulting the War Cabinet in London." The personal preferences of Roosevelt and Churchill explain this difference only in part. Given the constitutional arrangements under which he had to operate Roosevelt found it as natural to work the way he did as Churchill found his entirely different way germane to a system in which his fellow cabinet members were political powers of their own rather than merely his assistants.

If we summarize the discussion up to this point it would seem to follow that voluntary cooperation among the powers separated by the Constitution is difficult, that plain deadlocks have occurred on important matters, with partial deadlock never entirely absent from the scene, and that, finally, domination of either the executive by the legislature, or of the legislature by the executive, is one of the tendencies inherent in the system.

Before we consider whether this political structure can be reformed, let us hasten to stress certain virtues which may place the situation into a different light. The structure of government with which we deal is, after all, still that of the "representative republic," whose authors were so keenly concerned with the need to "break and control the violence of faction." In this respect, their measure of success is greater than is often assumed. We do have the majority system of voting—for Madison, as we have seen, the first line of defense in the battle against faction—and its results are clearly discernible in our political history. This country has had its share of people willing to make others happy by using a little political violence. We have, on the whole, managed to control them rather well. Every now and then there was a major flare-up, as in the cases of the Anti-Masonic party, the "Know-Nothings," and the Ku Klux Klan. These movements might affect the situation in parts of the country quite strongly but they never conquered the nation as a whole. There always remained enough undecided voters to turn the scales between the two major parties. Whatever else undecided voters are, they are no believers in the claims of any one party that it has a right to impose its own prescription for happiness upon the rest by violent methods.

All of this means that while our system has its defects it is, contrary to a widespread opinion, not open to the inroads of dictatorship. Periods of deadlock or near-deadlock do develop, with a power vacuum which, seemingly, clamors to be filled. Yet, even when there was such a near-vacuum, our liberty was safe—for the simple reason that majority elections never allowed a rival political force to muster enough strength for a concentrated assault on the citadel of freedom. Recent decades have witnessed, on our shores, a few movements inspired by the success of fascism, communism, and national socialism. A few isolated members of Congress made more concessions to such movements than any friend of freedom could have liked. Not one of them, however, stayed in Congress for long after he had manifested such tendencies; there always were enough undecided voters in his state or district to secure his eventual defeat.

If, then, there is hardly an opportunity for a political movement to arise in this country which could make a serious attempt to set up a dictatorship from within Congress, there is no more opportunity for such an event to occur from within the executive. We do now have a tendency toward "strong" Presidents, and these do resort to political domination. Yet, we should not lose our sense of historical perspective. Many of the extreme critics of President Roosevelt, for example, would have done well to read the charges made against Andrew Jackson: Virtually everything that was said about Roosevelt had been said about "King Andrew The First." That type of opposition had no result other than to strengthen the man against whom it was directed. President Roosevelt thoroughly enjoyed it, and one of its results was to cement the alliance between a man whose own tendencies were conservative with political groups clearly "to the Left of center."

In this connection the important fact is, however, that Roosevelt, too, operated within the framework of our political system. His first step on the road to national power was nomination by one of our major political parties, and no one secures such a nomination unless he fulfills certain minimum requirements so far as democratic reliability is concerned. The need for election and reelection had the same result. Roosevelt knew that a majority of the voters would allow him to do certain things, but he also knew that there were certain things which he could not do. When he came to them he could go as far as to give the appearance of surrender; certainly, before September, 1939, he did not always oppose isolationism in as persistent and forthright a manner as a Theodore Roosevelt would have done. In addition, we can only agree with Professor Rossiter that some of the checks imposed upon a President by explicit provisions of the Constitution [65] were as real in regard to F.D.R. as they would be in regard to anyone else. Laws, including the budget, do require congressional consent, and key presidential appointments do have to be ratified by the Senate. When Roosevelt overreached himself, as he did in the attempt to "pack" the Supreme Court in 1937, he did suffer his setbacks at the hands of Congress, as he suffered setbacks at the hands of the people when he tried to "purge" some of his Democratic opponents in the 1938 primaries. The power of our Presidents, then, may, at times, be larger than it should be, but it has never deserved, and is unlikely to ever deserve, terms such as "dictatorship." The freedom with which such words are bandied about is, perhaps, but a tribute to the safety of our institutions. Had we ever lived under a real dictatorship we would know what the word means. A visit to a Latin American country ruled by a dictator might be a useful corrective; none of these dictatorships has ever been comparable in severity to those run by the totalitarian rulers of Europe and Asia, but even the mildest leads to a disregard of human life and human liberty which this country has never witnessed.

It must be added that the "built-in" safeguards of our political system also cause the prospects of harmonious cooperation between the President and Congress to be a little better than they might appear on the basis of the above analysis. No true extremist has ever been elected to the presidency, and very few have ever sat in Congress. Even they had to represent a watered down type of extremism. While they have been, on occasions, a nuisance, they have never been a danger—sensational outcries to the contrary notwithstanding. Most members of Congress have always been of a type willing to "live and let live." Cooperation with the President, even with a President of their own party, might "go against the grain" so far as they were concerned, but a great many of them have done their best, time and again, to bring it about.

A PARLIAMENTARY SYSTEM FOR THE UNITED STATES?

These considerations are bound to temper any tendency to conclude that our political system must be fundamentally revised, and the same conclusion will result from asking the question whether the parliamentary system would work in this country. That this could not be taken for granted is a point which, as noted at the beginning of this chapter, has been made by scholars of note.[66] Reference is made to the fact that this country is a continent rather than a nation in the European sense of the term, and that the range of diversity which our political system has to integrate is much greater than that of a country like Great Britain. We achieve integration, so the argument runs, in spite of allowing for a great deal of freedom, not only in the states but also within our "national" parties in Congress. We compensate for this diversity by providing for overall unification through the presidency. Here the very one-man nature of the office comes to the rescue. It makes it imperative that the President be elected, in one great decision, by the people at large, the possible distortions of the electoral college notwithstanding. Use of the plurality system of voting does the rest. The greatest office in the land, then, is national, rather than sectional, in nature, and its function is to unite what other factors separate.

These arguments are not necessarily the final word on the subject. Thus, when it is said that this country is a continent rather than a nation, and that our country is federal rather than unitary, a thoroughgoing supporter of a parliamentary system, such as Henry Hazlitt, can refer to the example of Canada.[67] There, geographic dimensions are also of a continental nature; a federal system exists which, in spite of all legal differences, is comparable to ours. Above all, the basic heterogeneity of a country with a large French-speaking element is hardly less pronounced than is our own. Yet, the parliamentary system exists and, on the whole, it works well. There might be an election in which no one party secures an overall majority of the seats, as happened in 1957, but, as long as that is accepted as a temporary phenomenon it need not threaten the existence of one-party majority governments in the long run any more than similar occurrences did in Britain.

So far as the workability of a parliamentary system in the United States is concerned, much depends upon the structure of the party system. Our major parties are, indeed, in many respects, loose federations of sectional groups. Could they unite sufficiently to make a smooth functioning of the parliamentary system possible? Perhaps the looseness of our party structure is, to some extent, the result of our political institutions. Our parties do unite when they have to unite—in presidential elections. In Congress they appear "all dressed up with no place to go." There, under our system, parties as such have no direct and compelling function. Under a parliamentary system, the entire task of government would be dumped into their laps; they would have to swim or sink with it, and they might well learn how to swim. The formation of a cabinet with room for the leaders of all major factions within a party would by itself tend to promote harmony. Working side by side, they might overcome some of their differences. The emergence of a national party leader would assist this process. In England the development of a popular party organization had the result of providing the party leader of the day, the Prime Minister, with a plebiscitary basis. The same might happen in this country which has had, after all, a popular party organization since the days of Jackson. The factions which such a Prime Minister would have to unite do not differ nearly as much from one another as do the political parties of a typical P.R. country. In the United States, all members of Congress elected by a political party have been designated by a common electorate—a "modern Republican," for example, could not often succeed without the help of "un-modern" Republicans, and vice versa. Besides, as Professor Kerwin has reminded us,[68] there is no rigidity among our factions. Their members line up differently on different issues, and there never exists among them the systematic hostility characteristic of a multiple-party system. The task of pulling them together, then, is not as difficult as it has often been made out to be, although a realignment of the present parties might take place.

Where disagreement, under a parliamentary system, persists there is, finally, the weapon of dissolution to control it. Let us, once again, quote what Walter Bagehot, speaking of England, had to say on the power of dissolution as a unifying force: ". . . though the leaders of party no longer have the vast patronage of the last century with which to bribe, they can coerce by a threat far more potent than any allurement—they can dissolve. This is the secret which keeps parties together." [69] There is little reason to assume that what is so effective in England would be of no avail in this country, particularly since the threat of dissolution would not be made against Congress by a group of outsiders; it would be done by men who reached their positions because they were the leaders of the congressional majority. The possibility of dissolution, then, might operate as much as a catalyzer of agreement as a threat would to those who prefer to disagree.

The case for a parliamentary system is, then, stronger than it appears. Yet, the arguments in its favor have one great defect: They are of a hypothetical nature. Abstract reasoning forms the link between that which is and that which is expected to emerge from what is advocated to replace it. Such reasoning certainly is no more than the procedure followed by the framers of the Constitution themselves, but the situation is not what it was in 1787. The alternative proposed has, rightly or wrongly, suffered by its use (or abuse) abroad and, on the other hand, enough adjustments have been made in our own system during the last two generations to make it more serviceable.

This does not mean that we should be "stick-in-the-muds" so far as reform is concerned. It could be said, for example, that the case for a parliamentary system is very much stronger on the state than on the federal level. State government is, indeed, so ineffective as to contribute to the assumption of state functions by the national government, and it often seems that the Canadian provinces, with all their inferior legal status, show more vitality than our states, part of which may be attributed to the parliamentary system. Besides, the task of integration is more manageable on the state than on the federal level. The State of New York, for example, may be large but it is not a continent, and it is difficult to see how a parliamentary system could fail to bring its executive and its legislature closer together. Certainly, the relations between the two during the 1957 session of the legislature were not a model of harmony; the Democratic governor and the Republican majority seemed, at times, to spend as much effort on sparring for a position of partisan advantage as on getting ahead with the business at hand. Under a parliamentary system, no such chances to evade responsibility would exist.

MAKING THE PRESENT SYSTEM WORK THROUGH
REFORMING IT.

If, then, systematic reform, at any rate on the federal level, is not the path to follow, at least for the time being, this does not mean that the above analysis was idle. It is always useful to know the nature of things, even those which we cannot change. This knowledge helps us to anticipate events which follow from the dynamics of, in this case, the institution involved. It might, in fact, be rather useful to present, at the beginning of every session of Congress, the President, the members of Congress, and all interested observers with a little manual mapping out some of the pitfalls with which their path is studded. The members of both the executive and of the Congress might be warned that disagreements, and even conflicts, between them tend to follow from the position into which they have been placed. Perhaps the admonition, "Bear ye one another's burden" will be heeded a little more when the existence of that burden is known.

The public (and the press!) could make a contribution of their own. At present, a member of Congress who lashes out at the administration is certain to reap a rich crop of the headlines; if he persists, and is reasonably popular, he may soon be able to wind the coveted laurels of the "Independent" around his head. He will be credited with "courage"; it will be said that, at least, he is no "yes-man" and no "rubber-stamp." On the other hand, those members of Congress who work hard to build bridges may get little publicity and no acclaim. Both the public and the press might change their attitude on this matter. Similar considerations, of course, apply to the executive. Our historians tend to reserve the coveted characterization of "strong President" for those who were more likely to inveigh against Congress than to seek ways of cooperating with it. Awareness of this temptation on the part of historians—and political scientists—might help to avoid succumbing to it.

Encouragement for those who endeavor to make the system work in spite of its inherent difficulties should be accompanied by efforts to secure those reforms which would not interfere with the strong parts of our present political structure. Some of the provisions in the Constitution, and some of our political practices, go beyond what is essential to the separation of powers; they should be changed. Take the following examples:

First, there is the provision according to which treaties must be ratified "with the advice and consent of two-thirds of the Senate." The significance of this provision should not be minimized because comparatively few of the treaties submitted have been defeated. In the words of Henry Hazlitt: "Treatises go by importance, not by number." [70] As long as the Treaty of Versailles, and the companion treaty guaranteeing France's borders against Germany, were among the victims the vital nature of the subject is obvious. [71] Nor are executive agreements the solution. If they deal with major matters they flout the obvious intent of the Constitution, and they add to those powers of the President which can be exercised without a reasonable check. [72] The solution would be a constitutional amendment requiring a simple majority of both House and Senate for the ratification of treaties.

Certainly, the present provision, as James Wilson pointed out during the debates of the Constitutional Convention, "Puts it into the power of a minority to control the will of a majority," [73] and if simple majorities in both House and Senate were required, constructive checks would be as much in evidence as destructive balances would be excluded.

Another possibility of reform concerns the electoral college. The members of the Constitutional Convention assumed in their majority that electors would be chosen in the same way as members of Congress: two at large and the remainder in congressional districts. When, however, the Federalists saw their hold on power slipping they attempted to retain the presidency by having the votes of the states in which they expected a majority cast as a unit, depriving their opponent of the minority votes which they would normally have garnered. The Republican-Democrats frustrated the maneuver by adopting the same tactics, and the choice of presidential electors at large soon became general practice.

Individual states can do nothing to remedy the situation; something neither required by the Constitution—nor wanted by most of its framers—became so much a part of its operation that only a formal amendment could do away with it. The most logical reform would be a return to the district system (with two electors chosen at large), as proposed by the Mundt-Coudert Amendment. Other considerations apart, it might help a little to bring President and Congress together. The basis for their choice, at any rate, would be the same; they would face the same constituency.

Besides, the unit vote as it now operates creates a definite tendency to pull Congress and the President apart. The decision in presidential contests lies with the large and doubtful states—New York, Pennsylvania, Ohio, California, etc. Within these states all may depend upon a comparatively small number of votes. Organized minority groups have, particularly during the last generation, claimed that they controlled enough of these votes to turn the tide. Such claims can never be checked accurately, but their basis is real enough to cause them to be taken seriously by both campaign managers and White House advisers. It has been claimed, for example, that this is the reason why the center of political gravity in the Roosevelt and Truman administrations lay to the Left of the Democrats in Congress. That fact was, in part, also due to an apportionment which favored the rural areas, and set up a tendency in the opposite direction. The remedy, therefore, should be applied both ways: Fair apportionment to the House,[74] and the district system for choosing presidential electors—or determining the decision on presidential votes, as there is something to be said for doing away with the electors.[75] Certainly, there is little to commend a system which means that first Congress is pulled to the Right by an unfair apportionment and then the executive to the Left by the artificial leverage given to organized minorities.[76]

It would be logical to supplement a reform of the electoral college with the extension of the term to four years for which members of the House of Representatives are elected, the elections to coincide with those for President. This step would eliminate the danger of the House turning against the President in mid-term elections, and it would fit in well with the thought guiding the framers of the Constitution, as these men wanted political leaders who would be able to lead rather than having to bow to every "sudden breeze of passion." When they decided on a two-year term for the House, they had to face an opposition which claimed that tyranny began where annual elections ended. By this time we should have outgrown such pseudo-democratic notions! We might also bear in mind that the institution of the popular primary has aggravated the problem. Many members of the House must now spend one of their two years campaigning. A four-year term would improve this situation immeasurably.

The reforms discussed so far would in no way interfere with the essentials of the separation of powers system, and they might help to make it more workable. More serious questions arise when tendencies inherent in the operation of our political structure are tackled.

The first possibility arises in connection with efforts as commendable as were those which aimed at the reform of the organization and the working methods of Congress, which were brought about by the Legislative Reorganization Act of 1946. In that case there exists the danger that we might deal with mere symptoms, and that these, if we eliminate them in one form, would crop up again in another. Still, this is a field where only actual experience will tell. It is, therefore, imperative to work on such minor reforms in the hope that they will accomplish at least *some* positive results.

The efforts which found their culmination in the Legislative Reorganization Act of 1946 are a case in point. There existed, at the time of its passage, 81 full standing committees in House and Senate, altogether too many to permit either Senators or Representatives to fulfill their duties in attending them. Besides, members of the administration found themselves wasting their time by having to give testimony on a particular subject before the committee of one house and having to repeat it before that of the other. The act of 1946 cut down the number of full standing committees to 34 and encouraged the formation of joint committees. It provided for adequate committee staffing and placed, at last, the means at the disposal of the Legislative Reference Service, without which it could not function as it has functioned since that time under the leadership of Dr. Ernest Griffith and his successor.

Still, when Dr. George B. Galloway, without whose patient efforts the reform would never have come to pass, "revisited" congressional reorganization,[77] after a lapse of nearly ten years, he had to note that there were then 185 standing subcommittees on Capitol Hill, 87 in each house, and 11 joint subcommittees. He concluded:

> All told, in 1955 there are 235 congressional committees of all types (exclusive of special subcommittees) compared with a total of 230 in 1945. Thus, the total number of these "little legislatures" has risen to its former pre-reform level.[78]

This experience would seem to demonstrate that it is difficult, indeed, to provide for the proper internal leadership within Congress. From the beginning, such leadership has taken, and has had to take, the form of specialized committees. It was but natural that the process of fission, thus initiated, should grow rather than abate. Leadership by committees is natural to a parliament lacking an organic connection with the executive. Its members are ever jealous of their equality, resembling in this respect the aristocratic parliaments of the past. Thus, they tend to minimize the prerogatives of any overall leadership. Committees and subcommittees, on the other hand, multiply opportunities to participate in leadership—even if they do so to such an extent that, in the end, little real leadership remains.

It is all to the good that the history of the Legislative Reorganization Act should have demonstrated the existence of this tendency; the result should encourage farther-reaching reforms. This, to repeat it, does not mean that the Act has been entirely without positive results. The more adequate committee staffing is and remains a fact; so is the strengthened position of the Legislative Reference Service, which has now become a model for the world. Also, the encouragement of joint committees has been all to the good. Other points could be mentioned, and additional improvements could be made if the necessary legislative sanction could be secured.

The probing of ways to more effective reforms was the purpose of the report made in 1950 by the Committee on Political Parties of the American Political Science Association, fittingly entitled *Toward a More Responsible Two-Party System*.[79] This is not the place for a detailed evaluation.[80] One general criticism has to be made, however: The entire notion of responsibility as used by the authors of the report is taken from the vocabulary of the parliamentary system which the authors reject. What they mean by responsibility is effective coordination between the majority party and the executive. This coordination is natural when there is the "fusion" between the two which Bagehot described, but it is not easily accomplished under any other arrangement. Certainly the national conventions of our political parties and their platforms are no such means. The convention disbands once it has nominated the candidates, and if it met biennially, as proposed, it would have little more to do than talk. The platform's major function is to make all groups within the party happy. Afterwards, it is forgotten as soon as possible. This is not just the result of opportunism and insincerity. It need not be repeated that the belief that politics could be governed by preconceived ideas is erroneous; political life consists too much of the unforeseen and the unexpected. Nor could the National Committee of each party, under the present set-up, do more than it is actually doing, and the proposed "Party Council" would be an experiment in futility, as all experiments tending in that direction have been.

The report remains a highly stimulating piece of work, but all we can do on this occasion is to end upon one more note of criticism: The cooperation which it wants to be established between the legislative and the executive branches of government is, in spite of protestations to the contrary, conceived as a one-way street. Congress is regarded as the wayward child; it must neither pull itself together or be pulled together by someone else. The product of some outside body, called the platform, interpreted by another outside body, must be shoved down its throat. It goes without saying that Congress does have its defects, but whenever something is advocated which, if it could be translated into reality, would diminish the position of Congress, it would push us away from the path of democracy. The overall powers of the government certainly need to be strengthened, but this should be done by allowing both the Congress and the administration to make their proper contributions.

MAJOR REFORM PROPOSALS.

Definite machinery is required to bring about the needed cooperation. To this end, Thomas K. Finletter has proposed "a joint executive-legislative cabinet." [81] Congress should first centralize power within itself. Its standing committees might be reduced to a manageable number, perhaps nine for each house. These could then combine into nine joint committees with common chairmen. The chairmen would constitute "the complete Joint Cabinet of Congress." [82] This legislative cabinet would then, Finletter assumes, more or less naturally combine "with the corresponding body on the executive side into a Joint Executive-Legislative Cabinet which would be the meeting ground for the two branches of government." Finletter continues: "Here would be the forum where policies could be worked out by discussion and compromise instead of at arm's length and by antagonism. The Joint Executive-Legislative Cabinet would be the bridge which could link the two branches together into harmonious action in the national interest." [83] The constitution of such a body would not need a constitutional amendment. A joint resolution of House and Senate, plus an executive order of the President, would be all that is needed.

This plan does go to the heart of the problem, which is to associate Congress and the executive as much as possible in the formulation of a common policy. The difficulty lies in the strong and persistent forces which drive the executive and the legislature apart and, at the same time, cause Congress to break up into committees. These forces are deeply imbedded in the theory as well as in the practice of the separation of powers. As we have seen, the executive and the legislature are *supposed* not only to be different from one another, but to *oppose* one another; that alone is deemed capable of guaranteeing our freedom. The two branches of our government have different origins and different functions; none of the vital forces connected with their constitution or operation tends to pull them together.

Besides, it seems unrealistic to expect Congress to unite behind nine joint committees, with the seniority rule abandoned.[84] Practically every member of Congress has a measure of seniority which he treasures and would not want to jeopardize. For that reason alone the concentration of congressional powers would not come about. Nor would the legislative lions ever lie down (and work) peacefully beside the executive lamb—or should the metaphor be reversed?

Difficulties would be particularly great when the President and the majority of Congress belong to different parties, a contingency which Finletter regards as incompatible with either effective or responsible government.[85] He, therefore, proposes to amend the Constitution in two respects: The President would have the right to dissolve simultaneously both houses of Congress and the presidency. The terms of all three, the President, the Senate and the House, should be fixed at the same number of years, perhaps six, which would maximize the opportunities for harmony among them. Finletter adds that "The right to call a dissolution would . . . . in practice be-

long to the Congress as well as the President." [86] All Congress would
have to do in order to invoke that right is to offer systematic opposition to the President who, in that case, would have no alternative to
ordering a dissolution.

To state these final ingredients of the reform plan is to indicate
that fundamental changes are to be made in the constitutional structure. These would hardly be less significant than the open introduction of the parliamentary system, and most of the objections raised
against the latter apply to Finletter's plan, by comparison with which
the parliamentary system would have the additional advantage of
greater logical consistency. Thus, Finletter takes it for granted that
a simultaneous choice of President, Senate, and House would guarantee majorities from the same party in all three cases. The elections
of 1956, when a Republican President was elected, but a Democratic
House and a Democratic Senate, shows that this need not be the case.
Finletter's argument would find itself strengthened, however, by recent experience insofar as the division in the partisan composition of
administration and Congress which occurred in 1946, 1954 and 1956
did not lead to the systematic deadlocks which followed upon the
elections of 1918 and 1930.

A proposal similar to that of Finletter has been made by Professor Corwin,[87] according to whom "the President shall construct his
Cabinet from a joint Legislative Council to be created by the two
Houses of Congress and to contain its leading members." At times
such heads of departments are to be added as are indicated by the
business to be transacted. There would be no constitutional obstacle
to such a plan, and the unifying force of the presidency would not be
impaired, as the members of the new cabinet would still be no more
than advisers, even if advisers with a difference:

> But there are advisers *and* advisers. The proposed Cabinet would
> comprise men whose daily political salt did not come from the presi-
> dential table, whose political fortunes were not identical with his,
> who could bring presidential whim under an independent scrutiny
> which today is lacking, and yet who, by putting the stamp of their
> approval upon his proposals, would be able to facilitate their enact-
> ment into law.[88]

Professor Corwin aims to strike at the principal weakness of the
presidential office, namely, its highly personal character. The President is to be surrounded by a core of men who will force him into
a truly free and frank discussion, if not quite among equals, at least
with people who have enough *standing* of their own to have, and express, *opinions* of their own.

The basic problems which arise in this connection are the same as those applying to the Finletter proposal: It would be difficult to make Congress unite behind a legislative council, and there would remain the divergence between the outlook engendered by membership in Congress, and that engendered by work in administrative departments.

CABINET MEMBERS WITH SEATS IN CONGRESS.

Under the circumstances, one wonders whether the first step to be considered should not, after all, be removal of the constitutional barrier against simultaneous membership in Congress and the holding of administrative office below the level of the presidency. It might well be made permissible—not obligatory!—for members of Congress appointed as heads of an executive department (or agency) to retain their seats. It would still depend entirely upon the President whether, and to what extent, he would want to make use of his opportunity. Constitutionally, the members of the cabinet, whether they had a seat in Congress or not, would remain his assistants. It suffices, however, to consider the case of Cordell Hull and to ask oneself whether, if, as Secretary of State, he had continued to sit in the Senate, his advice could have been disregarded the way it was during the London World Economic Conference as well as in regard to the policy of "unconditional surrender" and to the Morgenthau Plan.

The advantages of the suggested change would be limited, but they might well prove to be real, particularly in the field of foreign affairs, as it would be logical to apply the new rule to the Secretary of State if it is applied at all. Action in this area is more urgent than most of the American people as yet realize. In the words of Secretary of State Dulles: [89] "Already large nuclear weapons are so plentiful that their use in general war could threaten life anywhere on the globe. And as matters are going the time will come when the pettiest and most irresponsible dictator could get hold of weapons with which to threaten immense harm." The world in which even a small state can threaten the rest of the world with destruction is totally different from the one which we have known, yet it may not be too far off in the future. It is imperative that an attempt be made to organize an effective international control, and to do so is most difficult when there are (in addition to democratic nations with which all problems can be resolved in the end) countries in the "twilight zone" of constitutional government where irresponsible actions of irresponsible rulers are always possible, and where outright tyrannies exist which are difficult to restrain internally or externally. Under such conditions, no type of international control is free from serious objections. Yet, the absence of control means courting catastrophe. Action, then, is as imperative as some of its conditions are bound to be unpalatable. There has been a natural tendency in Congress to concentrate on objectionable features of the plans outlined to date. If this attitude persists, no solution is conceivable, although one cannot but sympathize with the unwillingness of Congress to write what would amount to new blank checks for the executive.

Congress and the administration must, then, pull much closer together than they have heretofore done, at least in the field of foreign policy. Would it not, indeed, be a step in the right direction if at least the Secretary of State were simultaneously a member of Congress—familiar with that body's mind and mood and also able to transmit his department's anxieties to them? That task, incidentally, requires full command of, and responsibility for, the administrative machinery of the State (or any other) Department; occasional contacts will not do. Reference is frequently made to the desirability of having people in the administration whose minds would not be too clogged up with details to keep them from thinking in terms of overall policies. For the kind of contribution which can be made that way there are such institutions as the State Department's Policy Planning Board. It occupies a useful part in the government machinery, a part on which more frequent reliance might well have been placed. This kind of body can, however, never be the final answer to the problems involved. Political thinking must remain intimately linked to political action, and this is possible only if, in the last resort, the two functions are united in the same person, or the same set of persons. Such action must extend to both the legislative and the executive field. For that reason it seems difficult to expect much from a dual system in which there would be both a legislative and an administrative head for a particular field of government activity.

The road to reform within our political system is, for all of these reasons, beset with difficulties. The modest beginning suggested in the preceding lines serves, in the main, the purpose of opening a path for further steps. If it is permissible for members of the cabinet and the heads of administrative agencies to belong to Congress, the possibilities of a more systematic coordination of the two branches could be explored by experiment. The President would continue to be elected for a four-year term, and thereby remain in a position to guarantee stability in the same (at times awkward) way in which he now does. To the extent that members of the administration taken from the ranks of Congress should prove a success, their number could be increased, and further steps toward a linking of the two branches of government could be considered.

A word remains to be added on another aspect of the personalization of power which we have in the highest office in this country, in other words, the burden which it places on the President. He is, as Professor Rossiter, in his little book on "The American Presidency" [90] has emphasized, Pooh-Bah in triplicate. That "particularly haughty and exclusive person" held, in the Gilbert and Sullivan operetta, *The Mikado,* an imposing array of highsounding titles. Our President is more; Professor Rossiter lists ten functions, each of which could claim any man's energy in full. They come under the general categories of Head of the State and Head of the Government, the President combining the functions of the British Queen and Prime Minister, and absorbing, in his second capacity, the constitutional powers of the entire British cabinet. That is, indeed, a backbreaking job, and there has been much concern about reducing the load. Some have suggested that the work devolving upon the President as Head of the State be delegated to someone else, but the answer [91] has rightly been that much of the prestige—and the publicity!—gained by the President in that trivia-studded field is translated into badly needed power when it comes to his tasks as the chief executive. Others have expressed a wish for an executive Vice-President, overlooking that the President's office is so highly personal that no such sharing is possible. The delegation of subordinate and, at times, petty tasks is something else again, but ample authority for it exists.

Even to mention other reform proposals—such as those relating to presidential inability—is equivalent to making it even clearer that the nature of the highest office in our land is of unprecedented complexity. It is easy to point to the complications of the task, but objections arise immediately if these are to be reduced by reforms which move within the general framework of the existing system.

There is still good reason to hold that this system is here to stay. The case for it is better than it seemed to be even a generation ago, and the case for the alternative is weaker, at least from a psychological point of view. Still, it seems also fair to conclude that our presidency is *sui generis*—that it represents a case of its own, based on long and difficult historical adjustments, which it would be impossible to transfer to other countries.

Chapter XIX

FORM, MATTER, AND THE FUTURE

The preceding chapters have dealt with countries which, in spite of all differences, have the one feature in common that, generally speaking, the social matter is favorable to the political forms of democracy. To the extent that this material is not guided into "improper channels of government"—which in some cases has been done rather extensively—democratic constitutionalism can be expected to work. No other large country has such favorable "material" conditions although a number of smaller ones do. In fact, the decision in the contest between the out and out totalitarian countries of the Communist bloc and the free countries of what we call the "Western World" will be made in the general area of the "twilight zone" of government, in which the social and economic conditions conducive to the maintenance of stable monarchies and aristocracies have long since ceased to exist, but where the "material" foundations of democratic constitutionalism are far from having been laid. This area comprises all of the nations of Asia and Africa, in most of which independence and self-government are recent developments, as well as those of Latin America which have enjoyed independence, and experimented with various forms of constitutional government, for a century and a half.

The complex problems presented by these countries could be handled adequately only if each were treated extensively. Since this is impossible, the remarks which follow are bound to be fragmentary, and some of the conclusions reached are tentative.

INDIA: THE BACKGROUND.

India is by far the most important of the countries in question. Her population, soon to reach 400 million, is exceeded only by that of Communist China. Her prestige in world affairs has been considerable. The direction in which that prestige will be used cannot remain unaffected by political form as it develops domestically, be it the freedom—even if relative freedom—of democratic constitutionalism or the tyranny of Communist totalitarianism.

At first sight, everything in India seems to predispose that country for the type of near-anarchy which has so often preceded the rise of dictatorship. No other nation in the world contains all the elements making for heterogeneity in such completeness, and in such intensity. Illiteracy extending to a good 80 per cent of the people leaves ample room for superstition, and for demagogic exploitation. The religious differences between the Hindus and the 40 million remaining Moslems, as well as the ten million Christians of all denominations, not to mention minor religious groups, are great. The Hindus are divided into castes, all of which are opposed by some 80 million untouchables. Social conflicts arise from the fact that a country with more or less feudal conditions was cut loose from its ancient moorings with the result that an old order was destroyed without a new one taking its place. A tendency to overpopulation is aggravated by a backlog of 30 million unemployed. Differences of nationality and language exceed everything known in any other democratic state; in both respects the people inhabiting the southern part of the sub-continent have nothing in common with the remainder of their fellow-citizens. There is, then, plenty of material on which radical agitation of both the Left and the Right can feed.

These disadvantages are countered by definite assets, some of which are due to British rule to a larger extent than some Indians are willing to admit. What the British left to the Indians was, in addition to such economic achievements as a good railroad system, a combination of three factors: a political ideal, a political elite, and a workable set of political institutions.

The political ideal results from the fact that while there might have been strong opposition to colonial rule there has always been rather open admiration of the combination of liberty and order characteristic of British government. The nationalist leaders of India, like those of other British colonies, might oppose their overlords with vigor but, at the same time, they admired them. It helped matters considerably that young people from colonial countries who went to study in England discovered that the Labour party shared with them a general agreement not only on basic political ideals but also on the procedures for their realization. People like Nehru and Krishna Menon could hardly have been expected to favor the Conservative party, but the ties of friendship which sprung up between them and the Labour leaders could not but imbue them with the knowledge of, and admiration for, constitutional government as it worked in Britain.[1]

As a result, Indian nationalists, like the leaders of all other territories emancipated from British rule, acquired one great advantage which is definitely lacking, for example, among the former Spanish possessions in the Western Hemisphere. Some of the best minds in Latin America are desperate because they cannot see an ideal for which to strive, but the existence of such an ideal and the need to approximate it has been as dogmatic in India as it has, to take a totally different environment, in theory ever been in Ghana.[2]

The existence of an elite not only imbued with the ideals of British government but, to some extent, also trained in the efforts to translate them into reality, is equally important. Under British rule, to be sure, more Indians might have been employed in the government, the civil service, and the judiciary than were actually given such jobs. Still, the doors were open to a considerable number of Indians in all of these fields. Valuable political experience was gained. Besides, the ideals of an incorruptible civil service and an incorruptible judiciary were firmly established, even if the Indian Civil Service properly speaking is, like its British counterpart, limited to the upper brackets of the administration. While in England the lower levels of the bureaucracy share in the ideals and the standards of their superiors this is to a much lesser extent the case in India, where a pitifully inadequate pay makes the temptations of corruption often too great to resist.

The best political elite will fail unless it can operate within the framework of institutions which provide it with the tools of action it needs, and which also constitute a channel of selection that makes it possible for it to rejuvenate itself. When British India obtained self-government on the provincial level the dynamics of the new political pattern were in all essentials those of the parliamentary system—the "genuine" variety rather than the perversion developed in France and scored by Robert Redslob and others. The Constitution adopted by independent India struck out along the same path. There is a Head of the State, with the title of President. He is elected for a five-year term (with reëligibility) by a special electoral college, which consists of the members of the Union's central parliament, plus the members of the lower house (or only house, whatever the case may be) of the state legislatures.[3] The members of this body vote by single transferable vote—which hardly affects the outcome as long as they themselves are elected under the plurality system. The President appoints and dismisses the Prime Minister and, at the latter's proposal, the ministers, without any of the fuss and the fetters characteristic of "rationalized" parliamentarism. The President has an untrammelled right to dissolve the lower branch of parliament, the House of the People, with the understanding, of course, that this is done upon the advice of the Prime Minister. Parliament is bicameral, but the House of the People predominates, and the Council of States (with the seats distributed among the states roughly in proportion to their population) is, in the main, a "Chamber of scrutiny and reflection." [4]

THE SYSTEM OF VOTING.

These provisions form a coherent pattern, all the more since they are completed by the plurality system of voting.[5] Its adoption was preceded by a debate in which popular attention was largely absorbed by the question whether the various religious and national communities of the country ought to vote separately ("communal voting") or jointly. Still, there was an extensive discussion of the merits of P.R. and, in some cases (in particular in newspaper editorials) it reached as high a level as such a debate has reached anywhere. In a country with so many divisions the *prima facie* case for P.R. appeared overwhelming. The leaders of the Congress party, however, knew that precisely on account of these divisions only one course of action was open if the country was ever to function as one nation: the adoption of the majority system in its most consistent form, the plurality system, which would invite the voters themselves to look for a common denominator on a strictly political basis, capable of transcending social, religious and national differences. The minor parties, including the Communists and the Socialists, demanded P.R.[6] It is interesting to note that Dr. Ambedkar, the leader of the untouchables, should have stated at an early date:

> We are a group of warring camps and I may go even to the extent of confessing that I am probably one of the leaders of such a camp. But, Sir, with all this I am quite convinced that given time and circumstances nothing in the world will prevent this country from becoming one. With all our castes and creeds, I have not the slightest hesitation that we shall in some form be a united people. . . . Our difficulty is not about the ultimate future. Our difficulty is how to make the heterogeneous mass that we have today take a decision in common and march on the way which leads us to unity.[7]

Later, when the Constituent Assembly took up the system of voting, Dr. Ambedkar, by that time Minister of Law and in charge of framing the constitution, led the fight for majority voting, together with Shri M. A. Ayyangar of Madras. Dr. Ambedkar gave as one of his reasons: "I have not the least doubt in my mind whether the future government provides relief to the people or not. Our future government must do one thing—they must maintain a stable government, and maintain law and order." [8] What Dr. Ambedkar had in mind was formulated by Ortega y Gassett [9] to the effect that "The State is the orthopedic agency which society develops in order to cure itself of its manifold and inevitable evils"—which meant for India that, since the evils of society were particularly grave, they could not possibly be cured unless there was a government strong enough and stable enough to marshall what was healthy in the body politic against all that was diseased.

The crucial test for the electoral system resulting from this analysis came in the 1951–52 elections to the House of the People.[10] There was a multitude of political parties,[11] reflecting every possible shade of political opinion as well as every one of the different social and national elements in the vast sub-continent, plus a host of independent candidates. Had there been P.R., chances are that enough of these differences would have each been rewarded by an appreciable number of seats (and, thereby intensified!) to blow the country's political system to the skies. The plurality system, on the other hand, allowed the Congress party to present itself effectively as the one nationwide and coherent political force. With 45 per cent of the votes it secured 74 per cent of the seats, and fared equally well in most of the state legislatures. It was opposed, at its Right, in the main by a couple of Hindu groups, the Hindu Mahasabha (whose symbol was a man on horseback!) and the Jana Sangh.[12] The former elected four candidates and the latter three—which means that what is usually called communalism suffered a resounding defeat from which there could hardly be a recovery. At the Left there were the Kisan-Mazdoor-Praja party (a reformist offshoot of the Congress party, later to merge with the Socialists) with nine seats, the Socialists with 12 and the Communist party with 23 (including certain fellow-travellers). The Communists had obtained this relatively large number of seats with fewer votes than the Socialists; they had concentrated, with their customary organizing ability, on constituencies where they stood a chance, whereas the Socialists had presented candidates rather indiscriminatingly.

ECONOMIC PROGRESS AND SOCIAL REFORM.

An election result which failed to develop a large and moderate opposition party had its drawbacks. For the time being, however, it was vital that in a country where both cohesion and action were so badly needed, one moderate party had emerged with a majority which gave it a chance to work effectively for the general welfare. The Congress party and its leader, Prime Minister Jawaharlal Nehru, whatever their defects, were aware of the nature of the domestic task awaiting them: They had to demonstrate that democratic procedures were adequate to the gigantic task of pulling several hundred million of their countrymen out of their utter backwardness. Communist China was tackling a similar task with means not hampered by any moral inhibitions, which appeared to many as more forthright and more effective.

Nehru yielded enough to the temper of the times to engage in this competition with the help of five-year plans,[13] the first of which was to extend from April, 1951, to the end of March, 1956, and was realistically conceived. Tasks of more or less immediate significance were tackled which could be brought to early fruition, and would not require extensive foreign assistance. In "under-developed" countries such as India there is, as a rule, a fairly wide scope for successful work along those lines. In some respects they are what the Latin American countries have been called: "Beggars on Golden Stools." [14] Considerable resources exist, and it is only necessary to apply to their development methods tested in other countries for generations, even if tremendous psychological obstacles may have to be overcome in the process.

This is particularly true of rural areas. Indian farm yields could be improved in large parts of the country. The major obstacle is not lack of capital—which government assistance could provide at relatively small cost—but inertia, often fortified by religious beliefs. Thus, Sir Winston Churchill has said that India's threat of famine could be removed immediately if only the holy cows—which destroy more food than they eat—would be killed. The members of one religious sect even hold that their religion prohibits the war on mosquitoes, the carriers of malaria. In dealing with such superstitions totalitarian methods are, indeed, superior to those of democracy; the necessary measures are taken, and the reason for them becomes obvious fairly soon. A democracy must resign itself to "the inevitability of gradualness," and rely on patient persuasion rather than on authoritative command.

In India this task has been tackled through the Community Development Program.[15] Qualified workers are established in a village, and they attempt to make the farmer use crop rotation, better seeds, build such irrigation and drainage ditches as he (or a cooperative) can undertake, and the like. At times, the psychological difficulties encountered have been tremendous. Yet, there are also spectacular achievements, such as the case in which the overall production of wheat per acre could be doubled in three years; in some of the fields concerned it was even tripled and quadrupled.

The most important result was the changed mental outlook of the people. They no longer accepted poverty fatalistically; they realized that something could be done, and their minds began to respond to the challenge by which they were confronted. Such programs can, indeed, lead to a chain reaction, the people beginning to do on their own initiative, and cause many others to do, what government workers have had, at first, to teach them in a very slow process. The slowness of that process inevitably leads to disappointments and, in a report made by the Indian government's Program Evaluation Board [16] criticism outweighs praise. The criticism underlines the fact that wherever physical change, such as construction for irrigation and other purposes, and also the modernization of agricultural techniques, are concerned, progress was comparatively satisfactory whereas the change in popular attitudes has not been as deep and as lasting as had been hoped. That, however, could hardly have been expected: attitudes developed in centuries do not change in five years.

Actually, the greatest drawback of the Community Development Program is the lack of emphasis which it has received. It is not spectacular. The press finds little material for headlines in it, which may be one reason why the government does less in this field than it might. So far, only a small percentage of the Indian villages has benefited from the program.

Still, during the first five-year plan, about one-sixth of the government's total outlay covered agriculture and community development, and many other outlays benefited agriculture. The immediate task was to prevent a decline in living standards; this was not so easy to achieve where every year brings a population increase of five million. There is such a thing as the law of declining returns which, as long as production techniques remain static, would lead, in case of an increase in the labor force, to diminishing yields and declining living standards. Under such conditions it takes a considerable effort just to hold one's own. In India progress was disappointing at the start of the first five-year plan, but during its final years enough was accomplished to cause an average annual rise of per capita income by one per cent. This was possible only because total production increased more than twice that fast. When former U. S. Ambassador Chester Bowles [17] revisited India in 1955 he reported "spectacular progress." Robert Trumbull,[18] surveying conditions during the following year, could report that it had been possible to raise average food consumption by several hundred calories a day, and to increase the life expectancy of the population from 27 to 32 years.

Conditions in India being what they are, this degree of progress was no more than a beginning, but it was an impressive beginning. A prudent policy would have congratulated itself on what had been accomplished, realizing that, once the start had been made and momentum gained, a more rapid rate of improvement was to be expected. Instead, official criticism fastened on other facts—that, for example, industrial employment remained stationary while the index of industrial production increased by 50 per cent. It was decided to seek a more rapid degree of industrialization and a large increase in industrial employment.

This is not the place to discuss the controversy preceding the second five-year plan. Theoreticians—"Some of them from the Iron Curtain countries" [19]—fascinated by Stalin's accomplishments, played their part in them, and at first the plan figures were entirely utopian. Expert criticism brought about revisions. Still, the plan remained of such a nature that *The Economist* discussed its first effects under the heading of "India's Crisis of Ambition." [20] Too much was to be accomplished in too short a time. To the extent that the capital outlay required was financed by means tending to be inflationary, it operated to suck in goods from abroad which had to be paid for, in part, by depleting the country's currency reserves, even if stringent import restrictions attempted to limit additional imports to the capital goods required for industrial expansion. In addition, taxation was increased to such a degree as to call for the comment: "The taxpayer is being squeezed to the pip, and if he gasps rather than groans, it is only because the government has successfully persuaded him that all this, and more next time, and the time after that, is necessary if the five-year plan is to succeed." [21]

India, then, was almost called upon to pass through something similar to what William Henry Chamberlain, speaking of Stalin's first five-year plan, had called "Russia's Iron Age." [22] Democratic methods, of course, did not permit the country to go even remotely as far as Stalin had done; yet unnecessary pressures and hardships did develop. The Indian leaders might have eased their task by taking a leaf, if not from Germany's "Social Market Policy," at least from Lenin's "New Economic Policy": [23] Where a rapid economic expansion was desired, the incentives should have been multiplied. This, however, India, together with so many other "under-developed" countries, was reluctant to do. Prime Minister Nehru's personal preferences go in the direction of the traditional type of socialism with centralized economic planning.[24] In the words of *The Economist:* "A mixed pattern of socialism and private enterprise in the Indian economy has been proclaimed; but it is heavily loaded toward the public sector." [25] Public pressure, and professional advice, did cause the Minister of Finance to eliminate some of the bitterest grievances of the business community, but the country's economic and financial system remained far from being favorable to the development of that native managerial class which a country like India needs so badly, and toward which a good start had been made. Besides, the attraction of foreign capital was made more difficult, although Nehru carefully abstained from anything resembling Egyptian President Nasser's wholesale irrationality in that field.

Some of the burdens of the second five-year plan inevitably came to rest on the weak shoulders of average people, including the workers. The government had always felt it necessary to insist on a degree of discipline on the part of trade unions which Western countries would not easily accept. When Victor Riesel dealt with the subject in one of his columns, *The South Bend Tribune* [26] published it under the heading, "Discrimination and Oppression Flourish in Nehru's India." The situation was aggravated when, in the late summer of 1957, under the impact of the rise in the cost of living stimulated by the new plan, the "Confederation of Central Government Workers" called a strike. The government reacted by introducing a bill which outlawed strikes in "essential services," subjecting violators to fine, imprisonment, or both.[27] Eventually, the strike was avoided, but at first the Union responded by calling a mass demonstration which, inevitably, led to anti-Congress propaganda, a good deal of which was bound to benefit the Communists, whether they originated it or not. Under such conditions it is, indeed, natural that the question be asked: "Can heavily populated India, operating at the margin, carry out industrialization democratically—without resorting to the authoritarian methods of Communist China?" [28]

Nehru might, indeed, have lightened the burden for himself and his country by permitting a more organic economic development— one based primarily upon providing the necessary incentives for private business to do the job. To show how much can be accomplished by such methods even under the most adverse conditions would require retracing much of the history of modern industrialism. It is impossible to go into the matter on this occasion, helpful as it might be at least to attempt to demonstrate the possibilities existing in this field in a language which would appeal to men strongly affected by Socialist theory, and dazzled by the example set by the

Communist countries. Nehru, of course, felt that he must meet the latter on their own ground; in a nation with a crying need for additional employment he felt that spectacular investments in establishments as much appealing to the imagination as steel mills were needed. Even those who disagree with his logic may sympathize with him, however, if all the psychological and political factors are taken into account with which he had to reckon.

Still, the shift in economic policy contained in the second five-year plan, with all the sacrifices which it entailed, was bound to aggravate the dangers which threaten Indian democracy. The crucial aspect of these dangers lies in the country's basic political shortcoming: India is—as yet—a "democracy without a safety valve." There is one large and moderate party which has shown that it can shoulder the burdens of government. It does have its weaknesses, however. In particular, the Congress leaders do not always seem to realize the difference between, on the one hand, the somewhat mystical independence movement of the past with its emphasis on such things as spinning and, on the other hand, the task of carrying on the country's government and of organizing the electorate. There is, at any rate, no large and moderate opposition party which could assume the burden of government should its present bearers succumb under an admittedly heavy load. At the Right of Congress there has, so far, been little except what is widely regarded as shortsighted Hindu communalism. At the Left, the Socialists have done less well than expected whereas the Communists did achieve a measure of success. It has often been held that the Congress party could have assisted the process of developing a democratic alternative to itself by making common cause with the Socialists in certain constituencies. By and large Nehru has rejected such requests. His opponents [29] hold that he is too autocratic to want a real opposition but, as far as the Socialists are concerned, he may also be influenced by the fact that, basically, he is a Socialist himself. Besides, it is not easy for one political party to aid another where there is not a strictly reciprocal interest. Party leaders—including those who carry the banner of the Congress party in a particular district—want to win; tactics aiming at helping someone else might, in addition, appear to the voter in the same light as an attempt of one athletic team to "throw" a contest to another one.

Be that as it may, as long as present conditions last, the people lack a real choice between governments. Inevitably, a party with a persistent hold on power attracts opportunists, not all of whom are impervious to graft. This fact strengthens the tendency on the part of the voters to support some opposition party regardless of its nature, and in India the Communists have benefited from this fact. The elections of 1957 have made this clear. The Communists managed to increase their share of the total popular vote from 4.3 per cent to 8.87 per cent, although this was not quite as alarming as it seems, as they had presented a much larger number of candidates than they had done in the preceding elections. (Under P.R. they would have presented candidates everywhere, of course, and therefore would have obtained even more votes.) Still, there were Communist, and occasional Rightist advances, although for the country as a whole the Congress party has been credited with an increase of its share in the total popular vote to 48 per cent.[30] This is, in part, due to the fact that it entered nearly all races, which had not been the case in the earlier elections. It again obtained an overwhelming majority in the House of the People and was able to organize 12 of the 14 state legislatures. The plurality system had, once again, produced a clear and positive decision in the Congress party's favor. Yet, at a time when Nehru and his associates court unpopularity with their economic policy even limited local losses in votes are significant and they are, in fact, accepted as such by the party's high command. The Congress may regain the ground it lost, and its ascendancy is a long way from being threatened on a national scale, but India would be better off if a democratic alternative were available.

At any rate, the election results in the State of Kerala [31] have made it clear that where no other party presents an effective alternative to the Congress, the Communists are willing to rush into the vacuum. Together with their allies they secured 38.6 per cent of the votes and 65 of the 126 seats in the state legislature. The territory of Kerala consists, in the main, of the former state of Travancore-Cochin, augmented by a part of Madras in which Communists were strong. Travancore-Cochin had been considered a "problem state," and "Serious economic strain arising out of overpopulation, underemployment, food shortages and unsatisfactory land tenure conditions had harassed a shaky Congress government." [32] There were, in addition, grave linguistic difficulties as the people of this area insisted on their own native language and preferred English to the artificial Hindi as the country's *lingua franca.* Dissatisfaction extended to the Christians. Among the Catholics, for example, about a third of whom claim to descend from the converts made by the Apostle Thomas, opposition to certain discriminatory tendencies was so great that,

in spite of all the efforts made by their Bishops, some viewed the
Communist party with favor.[33] The latter, of course, put its best foot
forward, acting as a party aiming at no more than the fulfillment of
those parts of the Congress program which the Congress itself had
neglected,[34] even if, after its conquest of power, it soon alienated all
Christian support by measures calculated to place all schools under
state control.

Whatever the reasons for this development, Kerala presents a
case in which a Communist government was made possible by the
plurality system.[34a] The results are neither as insignificant as Prime
Minister Nehru holds [35] nor as serious as sensational writers want
us to believe. Nehru is right in insisting that Kerala is, after all, but
one state in a large Union. He could have quoted Madison to the
effect that the large size of a "representative republic" will help to
control the effects of a "factional" majority developing in any part of
it. The central government—whose victory was, once again, due entirely to the plurality system—has extensive powers in regard to the
states. In the extreme case in which it is held that state government
cannot be carried on in accordance with the Constitution, "the President's rule" may be proclaimed (with the approval of the Federal
legislature) and the powers of the state be transferred to Federal
organs, which may delegate it. If, at some later time, the Federal
government decides that constitutional government is again a possibility, it may order new elections. That the Kerala Communists did
not command the allegiance of a popular majority in the elections
means that they risk being deprived of their parliamentary control
in such new elections. This presupposes, of course, in the first case,
that the Communists do not win additional popular support. In the
second place, their opponents have to forget past rivalries and unite,
as they did in the 1955 elections in the State of Andhra, where a united
front of the major moderate parties, led by the Congress, administered
the Communists a stinging defeat,[36] from which they have not recovered to date. Lastly, a considerable restraint upon the Communist
government will result from the fact that its parliamentary supporters
were elected in single-member constituencies where they depend
upon margins for their political survival which were quite tenuous in
a number of cases.

India's moderates in general, and the Congress party in particular, retain, then, most of the trumps in their hands so far as their
struggle with the Communists is concerned. It is up to them to play
these cards right—to do what they can to permit the success of a

democratic alternative, to pursue an economic policy which does not impose unnecessary strains on either the country's living standards or on her economic expansion, and to make effective the concern for linguistic and religious minorities which men like Nehru can claim with full sincerity, but which is not always translated into practice. It goes without saying that the economic assistance given by more fortunate nations, such as the United States, can play a significant part in this great attempt to make democracy work under conditions where few critical observers expected such an outcome when independence was granted. Some of this foreign assistance may well take the form of "a business deal, not a philanthropy" as *The New York Times* [37] called the sale of $400 million worth of American surplus wheat, flour, rice and cotton, to be shipped over a three-year period and to provide for "famine insurance." Also, when, as happened in the fall of 1957, as conservative, and as competent, an official as Finance Minister T. T. Krishnamachari canvassed the possibility of loans from abroad which, in the case of the United States, did not imply a substantial new cash outlay, there was much to be said in favor of offering the help desired, regardless of what one might think of the details of the second five-year plan.

In conclusion it must be said that for any overall evaluation of India's history since independence the positive factors outweigh the others. India's leaders may not always have made the best of their opportunities (those in the field of foreign policy are outside the scope of this discussion), but the country still represents a much closer approximation to democratic constitutionalism than any serious critic could have expected in 1947, when independence was accompanied by partition and large-scale bloodshed. The potentialities of political form were realized to the full, and thanks to this fact, those who have made mistakes in the field of policy have time to correct them. This is what matters.

In order to evaluate properly what has been accomplished, it may be well to recall what J. N. Joshi,[38] wrote shortly after the adoption of the Indian Constitution: "Unlike other Constitutions, the Indian Constitution is intended not merely to serve as an instrument for the governance of the country. . . . It is an instrument for making the Indian nation and the Indian States. . . . It is an instrument of governmental power and energy to be used to achieve definite ends."

Political form in India, then, was called upon to "form" a rather heterogeneous collection of groups into a state, and to do this with respect for human rights. The result has been far from perfect, and no one can say what the final outcome will be. Yet, what has been accomplished is a great deal better than what anyone aware of the difficulties of such an undertaking had reason to anticipate.

INDONESIA.

If there should be any tendency to minimize India's accomplishments in the way of providing for democratic government, a comparison with Indonesia [39] would suffice to restore the balance. Indonesia, of course, started on the road to democracy with comparative liabilities as well as with comparative assets. The latter are obvious, however, and might well have become decisive: In the first place, heterogeneity never reached the dimensions which it assumed in India. Most of the population is, at least nominally, Moslem. Thus, there is no opening for the type of communal conflict which in India separates Hindus and Moslems (not to mention minor religious groups), but also opposes the members of the various castes within Hindu society against each other, and all of them against the untouchables. Besides, Indonesia had national resources, in particular in regard to oil deposits, which India lacks. Properly administered these could have provided the key to a type of economic development which, in an India devoid of such assets, could be initiated only with great difficulty.

The list of Indonesia's liabilities begins with her recent history. The country was occupied during the war, and independence was preceded by a military conflict. These developments aggravated the natural difficulties which arise out of the country's geography, since Indonesia consists of a number of islands, some widely separated from the others. Then, too, literacy was limited, some estimating it at 10 per cent of the population, as compared with 17 per cent in India. Besides, Dutch rule in Indonesia was, in major features, not comparable to the English rule in India. The Dutch believed in orderly, but more or less paternal, government. They did not develop an elite of political leaders, civil servants and judges on nearly the same scale as the English did in India.[40] Furthermore, the democratic ideal was shining with less splendor in The Hague than in London; suffice it to recall some of the marathon cabinet crises which The Netherlands witnessed in the 1930's, a time during which both communism and national socialism had secured a foothold in The Netherlands.[41] One of the reasons is that the Dutch had adopted P.R. (in 1917). Also, this system of voting replaced the system of multiple, but related, parties which they had previously used with a multiple system of unrelated parties. Thus the people were deprived of an opportunity to pass a direct verdict on rival party coalitions during the elections. Whichever coalition was formed later—often after prolonged delays—had only a parliamentary, rather than a plebiscitary, basis. It was, for that reason, always weaker than even a coalition government ought to be.

The Dutch failure to train an adequate Indonesian elite and to develop political institutions capable of serving as an effective guide for their former colony was not entirely unrelated to the new country's party system, although the major responsibility for its actual shape must be borne by other factors. At any rate, an Indonesian observer felt compelled to express himself as follows:

> The divided and chaotic party system in Indonesia is at present one of the great weaknesses of the nation. One can even say that what is happening in Indonesia at present is a failure of leadership. At the moment when the country needs them most, the leaders are squabbling with one another. There is no longer that unity of purpose and spirit which fused them during the revolutionary years. Instead there is confusion, suspicion, and weakness, and even more dangerous, there is also corruption.[42]

Such divisions are, to some extent, natural in a country where democratic institutions are new. Still, rivalries among the elite have played a disproportionate part.[43] Where such rivalries exist, systems of voting do make a difference. The majority system requires a large measure of agreement as a condition of success. Experience shows that this factor serves to play down most elements of division, in particular artificial ones. The Indonesian leaders decided, however, on a system of P.R. which was sufficiently "pure" to provide opportunities not only for all political parties but also for all kinds of social groups. In the words of Professor Bone:

> However praiseworthy the intent, the result has been to compound confusion. In addition to numerous independent candidates and those of some twenty-odd political parties, the voter is now also confronted with weighing the merits of those sponsored by such varied groups as the Humanist Society, the Indonesian Younger Generation Association, the Organization of Prosperous Peasants, the Union in Defense of Indonesian Independence, the Executive Council for Minangkabau Customary Law (Adat), the Retired Pensioners' Association, and many others. The result is that in virtually ever election there are between 40 and 50 political parties, private individuals, and other organizations which have qualified for a place on the ballot.[44]

To make matters more complicated yet, separate elections were held for a parliament (beginning on September 29, 1955), and for a

Constituent Assembly (beginning on December 1 of the same year).[45] For all of Indonesia, the total number of parties and groups competing was 190.[46] Nearly 85 per cent of the votes were nonetheless cast for the four major parties: The two Moslem parties (Masjumi and Moslem Teachers party), the Nationalist party, and the Communist party. Still, close to 20 splinter groups shared in the seats not taken by the "Big Four." As Professor Bone [47] commented when the first results became known: "So evenly balanced are the two leading parties that neither can form a cabinet without the other unless prepared to pay a high price for splinter group support." Finally, Mr. Ali Sastramidjojo formed a cabinet consisting of three major and five minor parties. There had been no need for these groups to effect a measure of unity on men and measures during the campaign, which then the people could have endorsed. Each of them had appealed to the voters on the basis of its own favorite tenets, no matter how little the variations between them were appreciated by the largely illiterate electorate and, naturally, each of them played its own little game in the government. The government did not last because it could not last.

When, five months after this cabinet took office, Robert Alden [48] reviewed its record, he concluded that it appeared "to be on a treadmill." There had been high hopes in the country that a cabinet based on a parliament resulting from free elections would, at last, enable the country to make headway in the solution of its problems, and to "get cracking" in exploiting the nation's vast natural resources. The Ali government, however, never seriously faced up to its responsibilities; its record confirmed what had been predicted when the results of the elections became known: "Indonesian political life seems destined to continue in an atmosphere of embittered and atomized partisanship offering little basis for sober and constructive action." [49]

When President Sukarno evaluated these developments he reached the conclusion that they constituted proof for the failure of "Western democracy." To the extent that the system of voting played a part in these events it should have been obvious that what did fail was, rather, a clearcut deviation from any logical pattern of democracy, which failed wherever tried, in the West as well as in the East. In Indonesia, none of the splinter parties which did so much to bedevil the country's political life could have accomplished much without P.R., nor is it easy to see how the two Moslem parties, which were united until 1952 and polled 24 and 21 per cent of the votes, respectively, could have afforded to stay disunited under a majority system. Had they combined, they would have formed a combination which it would have been difficult to beat, whereas, under P.R., with their almost equal strength, they all but offset one another.

Instead of paying attention to these problems, President Sukarno set up a "National Council" which was to contain "the cream of society." Its major result was to reintroduce Communists into the government, although parties were not officially represented. The cabinet of Dr. Djuanda was to be "non-partisan" (as cabinets have had to be frequently in P.R. countries), but it included Communist sympathizers, and it gave (in spite of the recognized technical ability of its chief) little promise of being capable of the kind of action required.

When President Sukarno spoke of the need for "guided democracy," he overlooked the fact that democracy must guide itself. He laid himself open to even more severe criticism when he paid tribute to Communist totalitarianism in China. Subconsciously, he seemed to realize that if "Western democracy" fails there is no safe refuge in reviving the political forms of the past. In the long run, a "guided democracy" can only be an intermediate solution. The only alternative to Western democracy is dictatorship—of which the West has developed some rather well remembered examples of its own.

THE MALAY FEDERATION.

The spirit with which the problem of government was tackled in the Malay peninsula was quite different from that of Indonesia. Once again, political reorientation took place against the background of British rule and British training. As in India, a highly intelligent adaptation of the British model to local conditions was due to native leadership. The "material" difficulties encountered were certainly not smaller than in India or in Indonesia. The country's population consisted of 2,808,400 Malays, 2,155,700 Chinese, 651,000 Indians and Pakistanis, and 83,000 members of other communities.[50] The Malays, then, had reason to fear that they were in the process of being overrun in their own country. It would have been logical for them to attempt to safeguard their hold on power by all means, at least as long as the fact that many Chinese and Indians were not yet citizens enabled them to do so. Besides, the differences between the two major racial communities were aggravated by the bitter civil war, conducted, in the main, by Communists of Chinese extraction. Many Chinese might not agree with the guerillas and their terroristic tactics, but large numbers were forced into acquiescence, and all had to suffer from the actions inspired by a few.

Under such conditions the case for either P.R. or at least communal representation—with a number of seats reserved to the minority groups—appeared overwhelming. In Malaya, however, the fundamental issues involved were tackled perhaps even more thoroughly than they had been in India, where a special form of reserved seats was adopted as a temporary expedient. Indian experience had demonstrated that separate electorates are likely to provide for "minority representation with little minority power." [51] Those elected by a particular community are inclined to think in terms of that community's welfare exclusively. The majority comes to take such an attitude for granted and tends to disregard the minority representatives in parliament. The situation is different where both a common electorate and the plurality system exist. The plurality system channels developments toward a two-party system; as soon as the latter arises, even comparatively small minorities may be able to turn the scales between the major parties. Those in charge of devising an electoral system for the Malay Federation started from a realization of these facts and reached the conclusion that "the only way to overcome communal tensions . . . is to ignore them." [52] The country was divided into 52 single-member constituencies. Registration was voluntary and, due to the civil war atmosphere, only 143,000 of the about 600,000 eligible Chinese registered. As a result, there was a clear Malay majority in 50 constituencies and a Chinese majority in two. In the ordinary course of events this would have meant the election of 50 Malays and two Chinese, the latter being reduced to expressing impotent protests against the decision of an implacable majority.

The actual result was different, due to the fact that the positive potentialities of the plurality system were fully exploited by an intelligent and courageous leadership, exercised by Tengku Abdul Rahman, a prominent and progressive Malay leader.

The Tengku (Prince), as he is called, took considerable chances among his own fellow Malays when he brought about an electoral alliance with the Chinese and the Indians. For the elections of July 27, 1955, the Alliance presented 35 Malay, 15 Chinese, and two Indian candidates. Most of the Chinese and all of the Indian candidates stood for constituencies where their fellow nationals formed only a small part of the electorate. Still, the Alliance won 51 of the 52 seats; in the one case where it lost, a Malay was defeated by a candidate of the Pan-Malayan Islamic party by only 450 votes. Altogether the Alliance scored four times as many votes as its opponents. The result was a clear vindication of those who had claimed that the electorate was prepared to vote on an inter-communal basis, and a resounding refutation of the claim that to expect such a result was utopian.

The Constituent Assembly was able to write a Constitution which all of its members accepted, and, on August 31, 1957, the Federation of Malaya became a sovereign member of the Commonwealth. It goes without saying that the new country's troubles are not over; Tengku Abdul Rahman is being constantly challenged by more nationalistic leaders, who accuse him of "selling the Malays down the drain." [53] There are difficult problems of citizenship, and the Constitution as finally adopted contains provisions in favor of the Malays which will lead to Chinese and Indian opposition in the future. More important, perhaps, there is as yet no effective and constructive parliamentary opposition. As in India, its absence represents even more serious problems in the long run than it does in the short run. What the government of Prime Minister Tengku Abdul Rahman has to do in the formative years of the new country will not always be popular, quite apart from the normal wear and tear of democratic government. If the Alliance should lose its majority before a constructive alternative becomes possible much of what has been gained would be lost. Yet, the new country has managed to take the first, and by all odds the most difficult, hurdle in its struggle for a state in which all racial communities can cooperate. The intrinsic merits of the principles which inspired this achievement are such that they may yet prove acceptable to the more intelligent members of whatever opposition the future may bring.

JAPAN.

The problems of Japan differ vastly from those of Southeast Asia. Japan is the only Far Eastern country which has managed to modernize itself by its own efforts. After 1867, it established a modern economy, a modern army and a high degree of literacy but, like Imperial Germany, whose Constitution it followed in essential aspects, no modern solution was found for the problem of political form. The old feudal elements had insisted on a type of Constitution which made it possible for executive power to keep comparatively free from parliamentary control, and which gave the armed forces a veto power over the appointment of the ministers in charge of the service departments. In the 1930's this right operated as a veto on governments attempting to pursue a reasonable course in both domestic and foreign affairs. As in Germany, the true representatives of the old feudalism dug their own graves in the process; the younger officers whose terroristic societies were to bring a Tojo to power had little respect for the ideals of the past and little connection with the old families. They represented a mixture of nationalist intellectuals and young military professionals.

The Japanese defeat in the Second World War was bound to mean moral discredit for this group as well as for the constitutional provisions which allowed it to become so powerful. Prudent Allied policy would have recognized this fact, and been mindful of the nation's great positive possibilities. Japan should have been allowed to recover her economic strength immediately, permitting her to take care not only of the needs of her fast-growing population, but also to help in rebuilding what her armies had destroyed. Since this required strong and reliable democratic institutions the aim might well have been to make Japan into a model of democratic constitutionalism, capable of serving as an inspiration to her neighbors.

Allied, in this case American, policy utilized some of these opportunities, but neglected others. Such men as Henry L. Stimson and Joseph Grew managed to win out over an artificially inflamed public opinion and to give Japan a chance to retain her age-old monarchy; this concession, at the same time, greatly facilitated the country's peaceful surrender. The American military authorities in Japan did much to help modernize the country; an agrarian reform which eliminated much social friction without interfering with productivity is a case in point. The overall result of all of these changes was a "New Japan." [54] Yet, what the Japanese saved in regard to the political order was, beginning with the retention of the Emperor as a symbol, due to their own efforts. The pitfalls of rationalized parliamentarism were avoided. While the Prime Minister had to be elected by the Diet, a simple majority decided, and he was given the right of parliamentary dissolution.

A major deficiency in the Japanese political pattern concerns the system of voting. Since 1900 the country has, with interruptions, experimented with the single, non-transferable vote in multiple-member constituencies. Under this system, as embodied in the law of 1925 and again in the law of 1947, the members of the House of Representatives are chosen in constituencies electing from three to five Deputies each.[55] The voter can cast his ballot for only one of them, and there is no way of designating other candidates to whom, as is the case under the Hare system, his vote could be transferred when a number sufficient to elect the first choice has been reached. In Japan, the candidates with the largest number of votes are declared elected, regardless of the difference in the number of votes obtained. The

overall results of this system are those of an "awkward kind of proportional representation favoring small groups." [56] Groups cannot be
too small, of course, if they want to benefit from this system; there
are few constituencies where it is possible to be elected with much
less than 15 per cent of the votes.

The effects of this arrangement are obvious. Comparatively small
parties do secure opportunities which the plurality system would deny
them, although the percentage of the seats which they win tends to
be appreciably smaller than their percentage of votes.[57] The extent
to which this is the case depends upon the size of the constituencies.
The 1946 elections were held with constituencies electing from four
to fourteen representatives. T. A. Bisson, of whom the dustjacket on
his book, *Prospects for Democracy in Japan*,[58] says that "during
1946–47 he was an important member of the Government Section of
General MacArthur's Headquarters in Tokyo," speaks of post-war
developments in this field:

> The Election Law discarded the large-constituency, plural-ballot system
> that had governed the election of April 10, 1946. Fifteen months earlier,
> liberal Japanese sentiment had cordially welcomed SCAP's initiative
> on behalf of this system, which was regarded as a preliminary step
> toward full proportional representation. Now the Liberal-Democratic
> majority in the Diet reversed the process by returning to the small-
> constituency, single-ballot system of the old regime.

This paragraph constitutes an unqualified admission that a part of
SCAP at least regarded P.R. as the ideal election law for Japan.

The smaller constituencies could be restored, in 1947, only after
a bitter parliamentary battle under the leadership of Prime Minister
Yoshida. The elections of 1947 were still inconclusive, but those of
1949 gave Yoshida's "Democratic-Liberals," with 43.8 per cent of the
votes, 56.7 per cent of the seats. The result was a period of comparative political stability (which continued with modifications, after the
elections of 1952, 1953, and 1955) [59] and of substantial economic
progress. To some observers the country seemed definitely on the
road toward a two-party system when, in October, 1955, the two Socialist factions reunited "after four stormy years of conflict and
separate existence," [60] and in May, 1956, the Liberal party, led by
Prime Minister Yoshida, and the Japan Democratic party, led by
Hatoyama, united in their turn.

This optimism, however, is premature and will remain so as long
as the present electoral system is retained. If any sizable group within
either of the two major parties is dissatisfied—and there are con-

tinuous rumblings of dissatisfaction—it can break away, being certain that it will do fairly well in the elections. The mere existence of this possibility encourages that factionalism which is the curse of Japanese politics. In Japan, as in Italy, the candidates of the major parties run not only against those of the opposition but also against each other. Thus the groups within a party do not have to unite on a common candidate; each of them presents its own and asks its followers to vote for them. This is the reason why Professor Yanaga [61] was able to write: ". . . no visible change in the substance and method of politics followed in the wake of mergers that had been greeted with enthusiasm by all." The factions within the major parties continued to "do business at the same old stand," and they will continue to do so as long as the present voting system exists.[62] As long as that is the case, "Political stability . . . . is still very much in the distant future." [63]

Still, where a country is so close to an important goal the question arises why the final step is not taken. The adoption of the plurality system has been advocated by many Japanese political leaders as well as by scholars. However, when the author asked a Japanese diplomat about the prospects of a change the answer was: "The Deputies who have been elected under the present system do not want a different one under which they might not be reelected." The vested interests, then, stand in the way of a change, and the American occupation authorities missed a golden opportunity to break their hold. It goes without saying that, as in all other countries, the vested interests find a powerful friend in the lack of intellectual clarity.[64]

GREECE

While the problems of Greece differ substantially from those of the countries mentioned in the preceding pages, similarities arise from the far-reaching absence of economic and social conditions making for the success of democratic government. Much illiteracy remains in Greece, which is indicative of a general state of affairs, ill-suited in assisting a government based upon the active consent of the governed to send its roots deep into the soil. There is, in addition, the great and disturbing problem of the expellees, dating from the end of the First World War. Writers dealing with the subject speak euphemistically of a "population exchange" between Greece and Turkey. Actually, what happened was the expulsion of the Greeks from Turkey to which Greece retaliated by the counter-expulsion of the smaller number of Turks residing within her borders. Greece has never been able to absorb these expellees. Her economy cannot compare with the dynamism shown by that of Western Germany since 1948 which made it possible to find employment for virtually all of the German expellees.[65] The Greek expellees continue to form a center of both social and political unrest; during the civil war which followed the Second World War they provided not only the leaders but most of the followers of the Communist insurrection.

Under such conditions even the proper "channels of government" cannot as easily lead to satisfactory results as they do in more developed democratic countries. Still, when *improper* ones are combined with a social material so deficient the result is explosive. C. M. Woodhouse had this to say about developments in Greece before the Second World War:

> Because too, Greece usually elects its Parliament (when it has one) by proportional representation, there is a chance for any number of splinter-parties to obtain representation. Because there is little danger of these having to form a Government by themselves, they need not bother with a social programme; or with any sort of programme beyond the slogan, "Down with everyone else!" Even absolute power never corrupted so absolutely as absolute irresponsibility.[66]

Woodhouse had in mind, in particular, the elections of January, 1936, which gave the parties of the Right 143 out of 300 seats, to those of the Moderate Left 141 seats, and to the Communists 15 seats, and therewith the power to turn the scales. On the results Woodhouse expressed himself as follows:

> The election of January 1936 finally exposed the bankruptcy of democracy as conducted by these men, by leaving the balance of power in the House in the hands of fifteen Communist members. In April the House prorogued itself, and was replaced by a Committee which reproduced its proportions and defects; in the same month Metaxas became Prime Minister through a process of elimination by death. The deadlock precipitated his *coup d'état*, and left in the hearts of many Greeks the feeling that it was about time too.[67]

The dictatorship of Metaxas was no more a final solution for Greece than any dictatorship has ever been for any country, although, after the near-anarchy which reigned for years, the people at large were more than willing to accept it. Liberation after the Second World War meant a new chance for democracy, and the question arose which electoral system was to be used. Prominent Greek leaders strongly advocated the majority system. They included Sophocles Venizelos, whose father, Eleutherios Venizelos, had reintroduced the majority system by decree in 1928 and, on that basis, given the country the only respite from instability which it knew between the two world wars. The Allies favored P.R. however; Ernest Bevin, the British Foreign Secretary, felt that if elections were held under that system of voting there would be fewer complaints that they had been conducted unfairly. In spite of P.R. the prevailing civil war mentality produced, in 1946, the result that the Populists (Monarchists) obtained an absolute majority but they were a party without a genuinely popular organization and, therefore, without cohesion.

The next elections, held in 1950, showed the typical results of P.R., three major parties and a number of minor ones being represented in the Chamber. The formation of governments became difficult, and there was an agreement that something had to be done about the electoral system. The result was "reinforced P.R." meaning an electoral system which reduced the proportionality between votes cast and seats obtained in order to favor the large parties. That mathematical result was obtained but, as in France, none of the comparatively large parties had a majority. Nor had the large size of the major parties led either to moderation, or to the establishment of those ties between parties of similar tendencies which distinguish a multiple-party system of related parties from the one of unrelated parties characteristic of P.R.

Under the circumstances, it was natural that the advocates of a return to majority voting found their hands strengthened. Many came to agree with the elder Venizelos, who had said that he reintroduced the majority system because "proportional representation with a people of such pronounced individualism was bound to lead to political anarchy." [68] In 1952, however, last-minute hesitation developed. The government was led by the ailing Prime Minister, General Nicholas Plastiras; the Deputy Prime Minister was Venizelos. The latter, as we have seen, had been in favor of majority voting in 1946, but, after some hesitation, he changed his mind in 1952. There had developed, in the meantime, the Rally of the Greek People, led by Field Marshal Alexander Papagos, the hero of the defense against the Italians in 1940 and of the civil war.[69] Venizelos was afraid that the majority system might enable Papagos to secure control of the government.

These discussions led to the one known case of an American representative taking steps in favor of the majority system of voting. When Ambassador John E. Peurifoy was officially notified that General Plastiras, who had suffered a stroke, was feeling better, he added to his congratulations a commendation of the Prime Minister for his stand in favor of the majority system. In certain Greek circles there were immediate outcries about American intervention, which were seconded in the American press. The point was frequently made that the Greek people themselves had to decide such an issue. It was overlooked that, under the conditions created by P.R., the Greek people had no chance to express their views. The parties with seats in the Chamber represented more the vested interests connected with P.R. than the views of the people. There was the additional fact that the readoption of P.R. in 1946 was, to some extent, due to Allied advice. Greece had to get off dead center, and the majority system, which was finally adopted, was the only device which could make this possible.

Actually, for the election held on November 16, 1952, a plurality system was used in multiple-member districts, 300 deputies being elected in 99 constituencies. This system made it possible for the Rally of the Greek People to obtain 241 seats with 49.2 per cent of the votes, leaving but 59 for the opposition. Evidently the new majority would have been much better off with, let us say, 60 per cent of the seats than with 80 per cent. In that case it would have been forced to pay more attention to the opposition, and the tendency to factionalism in its own ranks, which became important within a year, would have been mitigated by the necessity of closing ranks against a formidable enemy.

Still, there remained the fact that, for the first time since 1928, free elections had yielded a clear majority. Overnight, Greece seemed to have become a different country. As a French observer put it:

> First of all, it is undeniable that something has changed in the country. On the parliamentary plane there are no longer the sterile and tedious oratorical contests. Important economic and social measures have been adopted by parliament after debates held in an excellent manner. Dignity from now on reigns in the House. It is the same in the ministries and the administration. Public life has perhaps lost in color and originality, but the anti-chamber of a minister is no longer the subsidiary of a cafe of Syndagma Square. And yet the ministers have never been more accessible.[70]

The same author came to review the scene several years later when the Cyprus dispute had begun to obscure everything else, and to cause even some Greek patriots to cast longing glances in the direction of Russia. He said:

> Those who have known martyred Greece in the aftermath of the Liberation are astonished by her prodigious recovery. In that country advances achieved are not translated into mysterious graphs, into percentages which it would be difficult to interpret. The science of statistics remains unknown in Greece, but the testimony of the eyes is better than that of too subtle calculation. A net of highways leading to rapid

communications, modernized ports, a more rational, better-equipped and more active agriculture, an industry which no longer recoils before the construction of a large petroleum refinery . . . numerous hydroelectric dams, a tourism in full development: all of this constitutes a rather encouraging balance sheet . . .[71]

A. C. Sedgwick,[72] reporting for *The New York Times,* wrote in more restrained terms, but also had noticeable improvements to relate. Clearly, the increase in Greek production had begun to outstrip the increase in population, and while considerable difficulties remained before social stability could be attained, a start had been made.[73]

The psychological effects which this improvement might have produced were, however, completely lost with the outbreak of the Cyprus crisis. Its destructive effects upon the Western alliance are well known, but it was equally detrimental to the prospects of Greek domestic stability. This is not the place to go into details on this issue, but one must wonder whether events might not have taken a different turn had all concerned been aware of the relationship between domestic and foreign policy.

There are, in the first place, the effects of the substantial rise in price level which took place in both Greece and Turkey. Such developments always tend to unsettle established social relationships and to create political unrest. In Turkey they had much to do with the fact that when demonstrations against the Greek claims on Cyprus occurred they took a violent turn. Greek shopkeepers were the main target of the rioters but, then, their nationality was but a part of the picture. Shopkeepers are always unpopular in times of inflation as they will be blamed for the rise in prices. The inflation in Turkey was largely due to an over-ambitious program of economic expansion against which American experts had been advising for some time. In Greece the increase in price levels—the cost of living rose from 100 in 1952 to 125.9 in 1955—was largely the result of the 50 per cent devaluation of the drachma undertaken in April, 1953, which, in itself, was long overdue. One way to control the effects of this measure would have been adequate American economic aid (in addition to which there was substantial military aid), which had amounted to $181 million in 1951–52, and declined to $80.6 million in 1952–53, and to $21.3 million in 1953–54. This decline was not the result of deliberate American policy. The work of the Papagos government was definitely looked upon with favor. Within the limitations of a policy aiming at reducing the overall amount of foreign aid, as much as possible was done to favor Greek plans for economic development.[74]

Payments occasioned by such projects were, however, bound to be slow in materializing. They increased to $41.9 million in 1954–55 and $66.7 million in 1955–56. An attempt to cushion the effects which the devaluation of the drachma produced upon the price level would have had to concentrate payments upon the time immediately following upon that step. The amount required would hardly have been large, since the Greek government established, and maintained, a balanced budget, thereby stopping what normally is the primary source of inflation. This was one of the cases in which the timing of financial aid was as important as its amount; keeping down the increase in the Greek price level would have paid off in terms of a calmer political atmosphere as well as in terms of long-term economic gains.

That there was something new in Greece might also have been taken more strongly into account by the British government. The British, of course, did have their obligations for the military security of the Near East, in particular after the evacuation of Suez. They also had to consider the justice of the Turkish claims in regard to Cyprus, some of which were, and are, well-founded. Still, when, at the time of the first manifestations of the crisis, British spokesmen declared that Cyprus could not be allowed to join Greece because that country was threatened by Communist subversion, it might well have been borne in mind that the possibilities of such an eventuality had been reduced by the advent to power of the Papagos government. They would be further reduced if the new departure in Greek politics could be assisted sufficiently to bring about a permanent change for the better. Certainly, this was only one of a number of considerations to be borne in mind, but one wonders whether the outcome of the negotiations might not have been different had it been given its proper weight.

The Cyprus crisis, then, presents an important variation of the interplay between political form, social forces, and free policy decision. In Greece social forces made the working of democratic government difficult, but, when they were tackled with the right kind of political form, constructive results were achieved which could not have been reached in any other way. This does not mean that the adoption of majority voting was followed by that change in the party structure which was needed for it to produce its full benefits. Greek political life has always been characterized by a kind of individualism which is, in many ways, reminiscent of France. Political parties largely constitute the personal following of a political leader. Papagos dominated the Greek scene sufficiently to cause a number of these leaders to fall in line behind him. He did accommodate them within limits, but the mere fact that these accommodations were decided before the elections, and sanctioned by the voters, did much to facilitate further co-operation. What was gained under Papagos was not entirely lost when death removed him from the Greek political scene in 1955, but the great task of a final consolidation of Greek political parties remained. Such tasks can never be solved in less than a generation. As long as their nature is realized, however, and as long as an electoral system is retained which maximizes the incentive to consolidation, enough may be achieved to make the political system fairly workable in the short run, and to promise improvement in the long run.

It might be added that Greece also demonstrates the relation between monarchy and national unity. The dynasty had never found it easy to keep above the level of partisan differences. Integration by parties left important gaps which the King attempted to fill at the cost of partisan involvement. The foundation of the Rally of the Greek People had been preceded by the resignation of Marshal Papagos from his military functions in May, 1951, reportedly on account of differences of opinion with the Royal household, if not the King himself. It is, however, interesting to note that the actions of Papagos after the elections of November, 1952, show a remarkable understanding of the nature of parliamentary government. The Marshal proclaimed his complete respect for the prerogatives of the Head of the State; he knew that what mattered was a stable executive and that this was perfectly attainable under the parliamentary system—something which may never have been clear to General de Gaulle, whose example inspired the foundation of the Rally of the Greek People. Papagos, then, managed to preserve the integrating value of the Greek monarchy by making it possible for the King to be more truly above parties than either he or his predecessors had ever been. King Paul, ably assisted by Queen Frederika, played his part in making this development possible.

However, as mentioned above, the Cyprus crisis came close to writing *finis* to the remarkable effort of both political and economic reconstruction initiated by Field Marshal Papagos. His government certainly had factional difficulties, encouraged by its overlarge parliamentary majority; it suffered a considerable blow when Mr. Spyros Markezinis, who had been the author of what some have called "the Greek economic miracle," resigned from the cabinet and went over to the opposition without, however, uniting with his former enemies. The latter lost no time in exploiting the rise in prices and the disappointment over Cyprus.

The government was soon to be handicapped further by the illness of the Prime Minister who had never recovered from the hardships suffered during his wartime internment by the Nazi government. After his death he was replaced by Konstantin Karamanlis who, while a competent and conscientious administrator, lacked the popular prestige of his predecessor. The Rally of the Greek People was officially declared disbanded, but most of its followers joined Karamanlis' National Radical Union. This group was opposed by what was called the Democratic Union; it consisted of a very loose coalition of virtually all anti-government parties, including one with scarcely veiled Communist tendencies, the E.D.A.

Karamanlis fought the election under a new law, dated December 19, 1955, which established 41 multiple-member constituencies, and provided for an unusual mixture of electoral systems. According to the government it combined the advantages of the majority system with those of P.R., and guided, at the same time, Greek political developments into the channels of the two-party system. According to the opposition, it represented no more than a combination of three electoral systems calculated to allow the government to win a majority of the seats with a minority of the votes. In the smallest constituencies, electing three Deputies or less, the plurality system obtained; in the next group the limited vote; in the one electing eleven Deputies or more the seats were divided among the two strongest lists in proportion to the votes obtained by them. The second strongest list had to secure, however, at least 15 per cent of the votes or, if it represented a coalition, 25 per cent.

At first sight the results of the election held on February 19, 1956, confirmed the opposition's view of the electoral system; the National Radical Union won 161 seats (out of 300) with 45.8 per cent of the votes, and the Democratic Union 139 seats with 49.8 per cent of the votes. The rural areas of the country in which the government was strong had voted either under the plurality system or under a system of limited voting favorable to the majority; in the urban areas, where the opposition was strong, a system had been used which assured the government of a substantial share of the seats. The government could emphasize, however, that the opposition did not represent a coalition which was ready and able to govern. It was an opportunistic medley of a variety of parties which owed its numerical ascendancy to the Communists. The latter had been willing to give their support with the prospect of gaining only 20 seats in the Chamber and their moderate allies felt confident that after victory was won they, rather than the Communists, would be able to call the tune. The Communists, however, had another trump up their sleeve. In the words of C. L. Sulzberger: [75] "Their only basic condition was a pledge that new elections should be held under a system of proportional representation. This was accepted by their partners." New elections under P.R. bade well to return the country to the political frustration of the past.

Karamanlis could claim, then, that he was contending with a rather opportunistic amalgam of forces whose leaders could hardly have weighed the long-run consequences of their actions. By comparison, his "National Radical Union" did represent a fairly homogeneous political force, for which he felt he could claim the right to a majority of the seats with as much moral justification as, let us say, the British Conservative government of 1924. Actually, his appeal to the people to close ranks behind his government, made after the election results became known, met with a fair measure of success. Greece, in fact, demonstrated enough internal stability to develop a potential for leadership in Mid-Eastern affairs which the West may not always have utilized to the full [76]—a far cry from the country's condition before Field Marshal Papagos took over, and from what it would have been had Karamanlis not won the elections. Yet, Greece has not found a final solution for that important ingredient of her political form which is represented by the electoral system. On that issue, agreement between the major moderate groups of the country is needed. It could be facilitated by Allied action making the position of the government a little easier in both the economic and diplomatic fields whereas, as late as in February, 1956, C. L. Sulzberger was able to say about Prime Minister Karamanlis: "He has not been aided by the Western Powers, whose diplomacy has been lamentable." [77] He resigned in 1958.

TURKEY.

What has been said about Greece must be coupled with a few remarks about Turkey. In that country the elections of 1950 presented the Western world with an agreeable surprise. The government, supported by the Popular Republican party, had permitted the formation of an opposition, the Democratic party, but few expected that the latter would be given a serious chance. Yet, it was credited with 52 per cent of the popular vote and won 408 out of 487 seats. The Popular Republican party accepted its defeat with good grace and permitted the opposition to take over. The new government had one feature in common with the Papagos government in Greece: an overlarge parliamentary majority due to the use of the plurality system in multiple-member constituencies. The top-heavy majority encouraged the new government to go a little far in promoting its own policies and made it liable to factional dissension. Still, in the elections of 1954 the Democrats managed to increase their share of the vote to 55 per cent; they took 503 out of 541 seats.[78] They had the fullest support of the farmers for whom the government had done much. As we have seen, the government was, at the same time, in favor of industrialization.[79]

The uneasiness caused by the above-mentioned inflationary pressures is related to the fact that the government of Prime Minister Menderes has "beaten a steady retreat toward authoritarianism." [80] Measures were taken to restrict the rights of the opposition, to deprive it of financial resources (some of them were, as the Democrats charged, derived from its former control of the government, but some of them were properly its own), to restrict the freedom of the press, and even to threaten the independence of the judiciary. When there were defections from the ranks of the majority, and all opposition groups agreed to combine forces for the elections, the election law was changed in such a manner as to exclude the possibility of presenting coalition tickets. The government declared that opportunistic combinations would lead to weak and incoherent cabinets which the country could ill afford. The result of the 1957 elections (as announced officially, but challenged by the opposition) was that the Democrats obtained 424 Assembly seats, the Republicans 178, and the Freedom and Nation parties four seats each. Turkish press reports claimed that the total opposition vote was substantially larger than that of the government; one newspaper placed the Democrats' percentage at 42 per cent of the total and that of their opponents at 58 per cent.

Clearly, such results are unsatisfactory. Yet, none of the troubles which beset Turkish democracy after 1950 need to be any more than growing pains. To quote *The Economist:* "Turkey's democracy is like a precocious child who is not fulfilling his early promise; if he had not done so well so early, his later lapses would not arouse nearly so much comment or disapproval." The free election of 1950 looked so good to Western observers that too many of them assumed that all difficulties would disappear immediately, overlooking the fact that a couple of decades might be needed for Turkish democracy to find its bearings.

Meanwhile, not all looks black for Turkish democracy. There remain limits to government authority; when the government exceeds them its own followers will rebel and force a change. Where that happens, matters may yet improve. The prospects of future stability would be enhanced if a system of voting acceptable to government and opposition alike were adopted, and if an economic policy which burdens the country with a serious inflation were modified.

LATIN AMERICA BETWEEN DICTATORSHIP AND DEMOCRACY.

The pattern of the problems involved and the relationship of political form, social matter, and free political decisions changes again when we turn to Latin America. Of the twenty republics involved two-thirds or more are usually anything but democracies. Their governments have not, however, always been evaluated properly. The typical Latin American dictatorship is of the "authoritarian" variety, even if Perón in Argentina, and Arbenz in Guatemala, did try hard to develop certain forms of totalitarianism. Wherever a dictatorship is primarily authoritarian, it represents a problem of limited gravity. As a rule, it will not be "dynamic" (meaning aggressive) in the sense of totalitarian dictatorship, although some Latin American dictators have interfered with the governments of neighboring countries. Nor is the authoritarian dictatorship likely to be aggressive in the ideological sense. Its spokesmen frequently protest democratic intentions, and these protestations are not of the type familiar to us in totalitarian rulers. If they are not sincere, they represent an illustration of what Voltaire had in mind when he said that "Hypocrisy is the last tribute paid by vice to virtue." Latin dictators do usually find it necessary to recognize the basic democratic aspirations of their people through a great many acts of omission and commission.

Under such conditions, the opinion will be expressed that the countries in question are, after all, different from our own, and that dictatorship may well be the answer to their problems. Actually, as we have seen, no dictatorship is ever the final answer to any country's problems; it is essentially unstable and connected with serious drawbacks, including the failure to provide the people with that practical training in democratic methods without which no true institutional stability can be attained. It is a further drawback that such dictatorships may fail to provide for badly needed reforms in the social structure, and finally, dictatorship always means a disregard of vital human values.

There is, however, another extreme in the evaluation of such governments. It consists in assuming that all that has to be done is to denounce them as if their existence were due exclusively to their rulers' lust for power and self-enrichment. Actually some of these men began their careers as fighters for freedom and reform; conditions, they felt, rightly or wrongly, could not be mastered with the devices of constitutional government.

Among those who oppose Latin American dictatorships there is, on the other hand, invariably a hard core of genuine idealists. They find it difficult to accept the argument that the authoritarian dictatorship differs substantially from its totalitarian counterpart. They have seen, and at times experienced, so many violations of human rights that their minds have reached a saturation point; that there is much more along such lines under totalitarian rule will not impress them. Their patriotic pride makes them rebel against the assumption that while other countries should be able to have orderly representative government their own could not. They have a point if they feel that if India, with less than 20 per cent literacy, can achieve a fair degree of success with constitutional government there is no reason why their own country, with a literacy rate at times exceeding 50 per cent, should not do as well. Besides, it is barely conceivable that there has, by now, been enough of an improvement in the social "matter" of Latin American countries that a decisive step toward a more stable democratic order has become possible. Thus, there has been a slow, but definite, rise in literacy. The middle classes are stronger than they have ever been. The press is, under certain conditions, a more powerful factor than it was in the past, although it must not be overlooked that its freedom can be subverted by favors as well as curtailed by censorship and ended by open suppression. Finally, in Argentina, Colombia and Venezuela the Catholic Church, to which most Latin Americans give at least nominal allegiance, has taken a stand against dictatorship; this attitude may spread to other countries.

Still, the lessons of what has been a long and tragic history should keep us from being as optimistic in these matters as we should like to be. In our day there is the special factor that opposition to dictatorships is usually combined with far-reaching programs of social and economic reform for which there is, more often than not, a genuine need. Unless, however, the necessary plans are well conceived, and unless conditions permit their being carried out rationally, the result will be the kind of chaos which provides the best breeding ground for a new dictatorship. Nor should we forget that, after the Second World War, there arose the added danger that revolutionary leaders with ambitious reform plans which they were too weak to carry out might accept the help which, in such cases, the Communists are not slow to offer. This is what Arevalo and Arbenz did in Guatemala, without realizing that they were becoming the prisoners of their allies; it could happen to others.

At any rate, sooner or later every authoritarian dictatorship will come to an end, and as long as the totalitarian version does not take

its place, there will be new experimentation with democratic constitutionalism. When that time comes something depends, again, on
whether the social material of the country in question will be cast into
the proper channels of government. Political thinking in Latin America
is largely conditioned by the categories of Continental Europe, particularly France, rather than by those of the Anglo-Saxon nations. In
this connection, this means that there is a tendency to reason that
since the essence of dictatorship is too much power, the only safeguard of democracy consists in minimizing power. In some cases the
result has been an attempt to introduce certain features of the parliamentary system which were devoid of the elements of strength which
that system of government can command. Thus, in Cuba, the Constitution of 1940 created a Prime Minister along with the President;
some of the cabinet members may belong to parliament, and all have
to resign if a vote of censure is adopted. The logical counterpart of
such provisions, the right of parliamentary dissolution, was lacking.
As a result, there developed what one of the best observers of the
Cuban political scene had called "semi-parliamentarism," [81] and what
might even be termed pseudo-parliamentarism. Some say that one of
the motives behind the adoption of such institutions is the wish of
certain individual members of parliament to have cabinet crises so
that they, too, might become ministers, if only for a day. In practice,
when constitutional provisions of this kind are effective,[82] they minimize the power of legitimate government to such an extent that they
augment what many will consider the need for a "strong man."

Among the "improper channels of government" threatening attempts at democratic reconstruction in Latin America there is also,
and to an increasing extent, P.R. Argentina elected its Constituent Assembly of 1957 that way, with 35 parties participating in the race and
enough of them winning seats to cause extensive speculations as to
who actually "won" the elections. Cuba has had her share of the
trouble, having elected her House of Representatives by P.R. since
independence was won. The President, to be sure, is elected under the
majority system—there is hardly any other possibility if only one person is to be elected by popular vote.[83] But, then, a multiplicity of
parties in a parliamentary body presents problems of its own even
under the presidential system. Thus, in 1944, Dr. Grau San Martin
was elected to the Cuban presidency in the country's freest election
to date. The majority of the members of Congress belonged to various
opposition parties. When asked what he intended to do he is said to
have answered: "If I don't have a majority I'll buy myself one." He
is also said to have done just that, with the direct and indirect help of

the national lottery. Corruption, thus let in through the back door at the beginning of Cuba's first genuine experiment with constitutional government, soon entered through the front door and the windows as well. Under Grau's successor, Prio Socarras, conditions turned from bad to worse, and inefficiency was added to large-scale corruption, with the police not always able to guarantee the safety of the country's highways.

Such devices as P.R. may have but a limited effect [84] in this connection but they do no more good in a Latin American than in any other setting. A country with much inherent strength may do well enough in spite of P.R.; Switzerland and Sweden [85] are cases in point, but a country where democracy goes into the battle with two strikes against it is likely to find her major organs of government grievously weakened. Nor is there much of a *prima facie* justification of P.R. on the basis of the claim that it is needed to assure "fair representation." The differences of opinion which that system of voting is supposed to represent may be treasured by a handful of intellectuals at the top, and a few thousand of their followers in the country. For the rank and file of the people they are non-existent; the average person's views would be much better represented, and certainly his interests better served, by a system of voting encouraging parties which seek to establish a common political denominator for members of all social groups.

CONCLUSIONS

^^

The discussion of developments in Latin America underlines the need of being aware of the dynamics of political form even where it is not a primary factor. It is not always possible to hope for immediate results from the proper "channels of government," but it is important to bear in mind what these channels are and what they are not. Otherwise, all of the mistakes made in such abundance in France and other countries after the Second World War may be repeated again and again. Latin America, in fact, represents almost a vacuum so far as the proper type of constitutional thinking [1] is concerned; this does not bode well for the political future of the vast and increasingly important sub-continent.

The countries emancipated from British colonial rule after the Second World War have done better so far than could have been expected in the field of democratic constitutionalism. Certainly, none of them has as yet reached a condition of stable democratic government; decades will be required to attain this goal even if no major setbacks occur, and, in the meantime, the new elite governs more autocratically than it is willing to admit. Yet, as King George III had to do in England when he tried to assert his own power, this autocracy has to be exercised through the outward forms of constitutional government. Given enough time, these forms may yet create their own content as they have done in England.

At any rate, the leaders of these countries have been proven right when they rejected the suggestion that they ought to develop "more indigenous" forms of government. In a few cases it may be possible to use the ancient forms of tribal organization for certain practical purposes; the Westernized elite in the nations in question is, perhaps, a little too much inclined to destroy—or disregard—what it cannot yet replace. It is equally possible, and often imperative, to think in terms of a true federalism on the Swiss model when differences are as great inside a country as they are in India, Indonesia, or even in Ghana.

500

Most certainly, everything possible should be done to develop viable forms of local government.

Still, it is incurable romanticism to ask, for example, the Indians to "create their own, specifically Asian, forms of democracy." [2] Such admonitions take us back—not just to Burke, who is easily misquoted —but to such masterminds of confusionism and reaction as Adam Mueller and his fellow romanticists in Germany. In the case of these writers, the ancient "estates" were the object of idealization. In their original form—the division into clergy, nobility and bourgeoisie—these estates meant nothing for the reality of the nineteenth century. When an attempt was made to substitute vocational groups for them, all those problems arose which have been taken up above in the discussion of the demand for "vocational representation." Yet, this incongruous ideology—handed down from one generation to the next —helped drive Conservative Germans into the arms of Hitler, just as it conditioned some of the best minds of the Western world to accept first Mussolini, and then Hitler.[3] Similarly in Russia, the idealization of a distant past by the *Narodniki* assisted no one in coming to grips with the problems of the nineteenth and twentieth centuries. Someone should write a comprehensive history of ideas of this ideological "War against the West"; if this were done on the basis of international comparison, it would be seen that what the people of one nation considered typical of their own national history was no more than a repetition of what those of another one considered typical of their own.

In all of these discussions it would be well to bear in mind two basic facts: first, that human beings in Asia (or Africa) are the same as human beings in what we call the Western world; second, that the social changes now operating in Asia, Africa, and Latin America are all related, directly or indirectly, to the same cause, the rise of modern industrialism, and are likely to lead to the same results. These results are not always desirable. Thus, at a recent international conference of criminologists, the Burmese representative said that, his country being rather backward, he had nothing to report on such items as sex crimes. He added, however, that matters were changing in his country and, in a not too distant future, he expected to have some figures to relate. To speak of the specifically political level, there is now hardly any other choice for the new ties between the increasingly free individual and the demands of society, except that between the forms of constitutional democracy, at first inevitably weak, and of dictatorship. Dictatorship has, in the past, more often than not assumed the authoritarian version in which it has, at times, been not too intolerable. Yet, many signs point to the conclusion that the prospects for totalitarian dictatorships are improving whereas those of authoritarian dictatorships are deteriorating.

This does not mean that matters should be rushed. Anti-colonialism [4] can be overdone; countries can be pushed into independence long before they are even half-way ready for it. An interesting incident occurred when a Liberian compared the comparatively far advanced development of the Gold Coast, then about to become the sovereign state of Ghana, with the backward condition of his own country; he ascribed the difference to the fact that while the Gold Coast had the advantages of colonial rule his people had been neglected by all.[5]

However, one point can be made in favor of combining the forms of the old with the realities of the day. It concerns the institution of monarchy. Reference has been made above to what Germany lost when the attempt to reconcile the old and the new on the basis of parliamentary monarchy failed, even if it failed, as in the case of Italy, as much through the fault of the then reigning sovereign as of anyone else. Monarchies still do exist in some of the countries of the "twilight zone of government," such as in the Near East and North Africa; at least in Iran and Jordan they did prove to be elements of stability, constituting an effective barrier against governments yielding so much to the totalitarians of the Left that they might soon have reached the "point of no return." The King of Morocco, to take a different case, can render his country great services in assisting it to become a viable modern state, a goal from which it was rather remote when it became independent; the attitude of the Emperor of Ethiopia does seem to have been constructive, although anything but democratic, all along.[6] The Constitution of the Federation of Malays made an original contribution to the problem when it arranged for a Head of the State who is to be surrounded by all the attributes of monarchy (including the title, "His Majesty"), to be elected for five years by, and from among, the country's ruling princes.

Monarchy could also be of assistance in effecting the transition from dictatorship to constitutional government on the Iberian peninsula. Franco has long since proclaimed Spain to be a monarchy; Salazar has, more recently, sent up a trial balloon in that direction. It is, however, important to remember that the principal value of monarchy is that of a symbol. Except (perhaps) in Africa and Asia, it can no longer solve the problem of government itself. In both Spain and Portugal it might become the façade for a dictatorship as it was in Mussolini's Italy, to its own ultimate detriment. If that blind alley is to be avoided, there can only be a more or less immediate transition to a parliamentary monarchy of the British type in which the King merely "reigns," and the shoulders of others carry the burdens of "ruling." On the other hand, it is not easy to see how monarchy could be reestablished where it has been discarded, such as in France and Germany. Yet, if in those countries the proponents of monarchy would realize that they cannot possibly be opponents of democracy—that all they could sensibly do is to advocate a monarchical head of the state under a parliamentary system—they would at least avoid the danger of becoming the pacemakers of dictators, as some of them have been in recent history.

To return to the "under-developed" countries: if none of them has anything to gain from a romantic devotion to the political forms of the past, neither do they stand to benefit by rejecting the West's pattern of action in the economic field. There is, to be sure, every reason to avoid the drawbacks of "*laissez-faire*," just as the "Neo-Liberals" [7] responsible for Germany's "social market policy" have avoided them. In the modern economy, there is room for intelligent government efforts to make certain that vital social goals are reached. If governments want to take over certain fields, such as public utilities, for their own operation, there are ways of doing so efficiently, even if in that case corporations jointly owned by private and public interests have proven superior. On the other hand, what *The Economist* called "Labor Fundamentalism" [8] is no more helpful in India or Indonesia than it is in England. Besides, in those countries devotion to the nineteenth century type of socialism is accompanied by an equally strong, and equally dogmatic, devotion to nineteenth century nationalism. Economic nationalism makes little sense anywhere, but least of all in a country badly in need of foreign capital, and a country perhaps also so small that it can never develop a complete industry of its own. Cuba, for example, is one of the more populous Latin American countries. Yet, with six million inhabitants—not more than half of them with enough purchasing power to form an effective part of a modern economy—it should never have attempted any kind of economic planning except in the confines of a wide area—or on the basis of free trade.

In most of these countries there has been a measure of economic progress in recent years, even if economic expansion has been so very much faster in the leading industrial nations that it has left the "under-developed countries" farther behind than ever. [9] The first step in economic modernization is bound to be the hardest; if it is taken successfully, more rapid progress will come automatically, provided that its path is not blocked by artificial barriers.[10]

Important as these economic problems are, it is one of the effects of the economic interpretation of history on the subconscious mind of our generation that they are frequently emphasized—both by proponents of socialism and by proponents of free enterprise—as if they were the only ones. The problems of political form are, however, quite real, and they have their way of taking their revenge when they are ignored. On the other hand, there are opportunities to exploit the positive potentialities of a "representative republic" now as they were exploited in the eighteenth century. Unless this is done the world will not reach political stability.

FOOTNOTES

‍

FOOTNOTES TO CHAPTER I

1. Immanuel Kant, *Perpetual Peace* (New York, 1939), p. 17.
2. On this subject see John Fiske, *The Critical Period in American History* (Boston, 1888)
3. *The Federalist*, Modern Library edn. (New York, n.d.), p. 326.
4. Charles A. Beard, *An Economic Interpretation of the Constitution of the United States* (2nd ed.; New York, 1935).
5. On this point see Walter Lippmann's column entitled "On the Debunking of History," *The Cleveland Plain Dealer*, October 3, 1940.
6. Oscar Handlin, *Chance or Destiny: Turning Points in American History* (Boston, 1955).
7. Aristotle, *Metaphysics*, Bk. VII, Chap. 8, Par. 1933b, quoted from Richard McKeon, ed., *The Basic Works of Aristotle* (New York, 1941), p. 794.
8. *Parliamentary Debates: Official Report, House of Commons*, Vol. 253 (1930–31), June 2, 1931, Col. 101.
9. This is rightly emphasized by Heinrich Rommen, *The State in Catholic Thought* (St. Louis, 1945), pp. 274–5.
10. John Locke, *Of Civil Government*, Everyman's Library edn. (New York, 1924), Bk. II, Chap. VIII, Par. 98.
11. St. Thomas Aquinas, *On Kingship: To the King of Cyprus*, trans. Gerald B. Phelan, ed. I. Th. Echmann (rev. ed.; Toronto, 1949), Bk. I, Chap. 1, pp. 5–6. Quoted by permission of the Pontifical Institute of Medieval Studies.
12. It was, however, to be an elective monarchy, and all officials were to be elected as expressed in the *Summa:* "The best arrangement of rulers in any city or kingdom is had when one man is, according to merit, set at the head to preside over all, and under him are others ruling according to merit; yet such a regime is the concern of all because the rulers are not only elected from all but also elected by all."—St. Thomas Aquinas, *Summa Theologica, Prima Secundae*, Quaestio 105, A. 1. Quoted from John A. Ryan and Francis J. Boland, *Catholic Principles of Politics* (New York, 1940).
13. *Madison's Journal*, quoted from Arthur Taylor Prescott, *Drafting the Federal Constitution* (Baton Rouge, 1941), p. 750.
14. Crane Brinton, *The Anatomy of Revolution* (2nd ed.; New York, 1952), p. 29.
15. Professor Robert E. Brown in *Charles A. Beard and the Constitution* (Princeton, 1956), has drawn our attention to an episode which is characteristic of this intellectual atmosphere. When Charles A. Beard published the first edition of his *Economic Interpretation*, he said in his preface that his conclusions were "frankly fragmentary." They were designed to suggest new lines of historical research rather than to treat the subject in an exhaustive

fashion. (Beard, *Economic Interpretation*, p. xix.) This warning was disregarded by those who agreed with Beard as well as by those who opposed him—so often on emotional rather than on rational grounds. The result was a type of success which, to be sure, had in itself elements of what the French call *succès de scandale*—success achieved by scandalizing people—but which was nonetheless real. Beard allowed himself to be carried away by it. In the second edition the doubts expressed in the first have disappeared: Beard accepted as proven what, judging more soberly, he had set forth merely as tentative.

Beard was, to be sure, always more reserved in his conclusions than some of his followers and expressed himself repeatedly in such terms as to restrain the more enthusiastic ones among them, but to no avail. See, for example, his *The American Party Battle* (New York, 1929), pp. 41–2. He could not even check the trend which he had started when, apparently, he wanted to do so; in his book, *The Republic* (New York, 1943), there are passages which can be interpreted only as intending to make clear that political form did, after all, have a dynamism of its own, enabling it to mold social matter. In an age of dictatorships Beard had, evidently, come to realize the value of constitutional government (See Richard Hofstadter, "Beard and the Constitution: The History of an Idea," *The American Quarterly*, Fall, 1950, pp. 210–11) but his students wanted none of it. One of the best of them (an outstanding scholar by any standard) wrote a book on "American Political Parties" whose subtitle "Their Natural History"—Wilfred E. Binkley, *American Political Parties: Their Natural History* (New York, 1943)—makes it clear once again, that all concern for form and function had been discarded, and social forces could be treated as if they were on their own. Beard, apparently, fully endorsed it. (See *Economic Interpretation*, p. ix.) The student had won over the master, and the spirit of the times over the scholar who was willing to yield to the facts when these were in obvious conflict with his theories.

Lately, it has been shown that Beard's empirical data were as inadequate (Brown, *Charles A. Beard . . . ,*) as his basic conception had been questionable from the start; it remains to be seen what the impact of this demonstration on political (and historical) writing will be.

16. Friedrich Engels, *The Origin of the Family, Private Property, and the State*, quoted from, Karl Marx and Friedrich Engels, *Selected Works* (Moscow, 1955), II, 170 ff. The following is the key passage:
   "The state, then, has not existed from all eternity. There have been societies that did without it, that had no conception of the state and state power. At a certain stage of economic development, which was necessarily bound up with the cleavage of society into classes, the state became a necessity owing to this cleavage. We are now rapidly approaching a stage in the development of production at which the existence of these classes not only will have ceased to be a necessity, but will become a positive hindrance to production. They will fall as inevitably as they arose at an earlier stage. Along with them the state will fall. The society that will organize production on the basis of a free and equal association of the producers will put the whole machinery of the state where it will then belong: into the Museum of Antiquities, by the side of the spinning wheel and the bronze axe." *Ibid.*, p. 321.

17. *Commonsense*, quoted from the *Basic Writings of Thomas Paine* (New York, 1942), p. 1.

18. For a comprehensive discussion of these matters, see Yves R. Simon, *The Nature and Functions of Authority* (Milwaukee, 1940), as reviewed by Jacques Maritain, *The Review of Politics*, April, 1941, pp. 250 ff. For Simon's final

conclusions, see his *The Philosophy of Democratic Government* (Chicago, 1951), pp. 25–6.

19. St. Thomas Aquinas, *Summa Theologica, Prima Secundae, Prima Pars*, Quaestio 96, A. 4.

20. As defined by Simon, *The Philosophy of Democratic Government*, pp. 83–4.

20a. Goetz Briefs, "The Ethics Problem in the Present Pluralistic Society," *Review of Social Economy*, March, 1957. In this article Briefs speaks of "marginal ethics" rather than of "marginal morality." For the purposes of this discussion "marginal morality" seemed preferable.

21. "Political theology" makes sense only insofar as our answers to political problems depend upon our assumptions as to the nature of man; even then it is, as Heinrich Rommen emphasizes, *rational* theology. Rommen, *The State*, pp. 57 ff. and 91 ff.

22. Karl Marx and Friedrich Engels, *The Communist Manifesto*, ed. Samuel Beer (New York, 1955), p. 9.

23. Lewis H. Morgan, *Ancient Society* (New York, 1877).

24. Engels, *The Origin of the Family, Selected Works*, p. 185.

25. Morgan, in tune with the times, was given to evolutionist generalizations. His most effective challenger is Robert H. Lowie, *Primitive Society* (New York, 1925), although Lowie somewhat overstates his case, coming close to rejecting any generalization on principle. Sylvester A. Sieber and Franz H. Mueller, *The Social Life of Primitive Man* (St. Louis, 1941), have summarized the views of the Viennese school of anthropologists headed by Schmidt and Koppers. This writer would be inclined to agree with Alexander Ruestow— *Ursprung der Herrschaft*, Vol. I of *Ortsbestimmung der Gegenwart* (Zurich, 1950), pp. 27 ff.—that the Viennese school represents the proper mixture of factual knowledge and systematic analysis. For the particular problems with which we are concerned, reference might be made to their extensive treatment in Richard Thurnwald, *Werden, Wandel und Gestaltung von Staat und Kultur*, Vol. IV of *Die Menschliche Gesellschaft im Rahmen ihrer ethnosoziologischen Grundlagen* (Berlin, 1935).

26. Joseph Schumpeter, "Social Classes," *Imperialism, Social Classes*, trans. Bert Hoselitz (New York, 1955), pp. 101 ff.

27. Ruestow, *Ortsbestimmung der Gegenwart*, pp. 21 ff.

28. The norm for the most primitive groups which secure their livelihood through hunting and collecting is the monogamous, bilateral family. Where horticulture is the next step forward, the women, who develop it, tend to become the dominant element in social life, and we have the kind of matriarchy characteristic of the Iroquois. If, as is equally possible, the next step is agriculture or cattle-breeding, both of which are men's primary preserve, man's social position is sufficiently enhanced over that of the woman to make polygamy possible. For the details see Sieber and Mueller, *The Social Life*, pp. 107 ff.

29. Morgan, *Ancient Society*, pp. 72–3.

30. *Ibid.*, p. 85.

31. *Ibid.*, pp. 88 ff.

32. *Ibid.*, p. 117.

33. Critical versions of the Indian tradition concerning the foundation of the Iroquois Confederacy have been presented by, among others, J. N. B. Hewitt, "A Constitutional League of Peace in the Stone Age of America," *Annual Report* of the Smithsonian Institute (1918), and Paul A. W. Wallace, *The White Roots of Peace* (Philadelphia, 1946). For a bibliographical note, see Wallace, pp. vii–ix.

34. Morgan, *Ancient Society*, p. 85.

35. *Ibid.*, p. 117.

36. The significant parts in Morgan read as follows:
    "It may be here premised that all forms of government are reducible to two general plans, using the word plan in its scientific sense. In their bases the two are fundamentally distinct. The first, in the order of time, is founded upon persons, and upon relations purely personal, and may be distinguished as a society (*societas*). The gens is the unit of this organization; giving as the successive stages of integration, in the archaic period, the gens, the phratry, the tribe, and the confederacy of tribes, which constituted a people or nation (*populus*). At a later period a coalescence of tribes in the same area into a nation took the place of a confederacy of tribes occupying independent areas. Such, through prolonged ages, after the gens appeared, was the substantially universal organization of ancient society; and it remained among the Greeks and Romans after civilization supervened. The second is founded upon territory and upon property, and may be distinguished as a state—*civitas*. The township or ward, circumscribed by metes and bounds, with the property it contains, is the basis or unit of the latter, and political society is the result. Political society is organized upon territorial areas, and deals with property as well as with persons through territorial relations." *Ibid.*, pp. 6–7.
37. Morgan himself is not averse to drawing analogies with modern institutions. To give one more illustration: "A council of Indian chiefs is of little importance by itself; but as the germ of the modern parliament, congress, and legislature, it has an important bearing in the history of mankind." *Ibid.*, p. 119.
38. For a thoroughgoing discussion of the nature of, and the essential need for, political form, see Luigi Sturzo, *The Inner Laws of Society: A New Sociology* (New York, 1944), pp. 50 ff.
39. Engels, *The Origin of the Family*, Selected Works, p. 254.
40. Karl Marx, *Das Kapital: Kritik der politischen Oekonomie*, ed. Karl Kautsky (Stuttgart, 1919), I, 648 ff.
41. Carl J. Friedrich, *Constitutional Government and Democracy* (rev. ed.; Boston, 1950), pp. 22 ff. and pp. 583 ff. of the separately printed chapter entitled "A Sketch of the Scope and Method of Political Science," emphasizes the mutuality in the relationship between ruler and ruled.
42. Such a "class-monopoly" is, however, never comparable to a monopoly held by an individual or a closely knit group; the competition among the members of the ruling class of the British type eventually nullifies its value from the point of view of class advantage.
43. This point was made by Max Eastman in his article, "Russia and the Socialist Idea," *Harper's Magazine*, March, 1938.
44. Vernon V. Aspaturian, "The Contemporary Doctrine of the Soviet State and Its Philosophical Foundations," *The American Political Science Review*, December, 1954.

Footnotes to Chapter II

1. Carl Schmitt, *Verfassungslehre* (Munich, 1928), quoted from reprint (Berlin, 1955), p. 223.
2. Rousseau, *Social Contract*, Bk. III, Chap. 15, quoted from J. J. Rousseau, *Contrat Social, Ou Principes du Droit Politique*, Classiques Garnier edn. (Paris, n.d.), pp. 301–2.

3. *Ibid.*, Bk. III, Chap. 4, pp. 280–1.
4. This description does not in all points follow the views of Rousseau; the purpose is to present "the ideal type" of a certain interpretation of democracy, parts of which were developed in antiquity, and which are also traceable among the "levelers" of seventeenth century England.
5. J. A. Schumpeter, *Deutscher Volkswirt*, IV, Issue 12–13.
6. The term *standortsbedingt* was used by Karl Mannheim, *Ideologie und Utopie* (Berlin, 1929). Mannheim assumes that all attempts at objective knowledge in the social sciences are vitiated by the *Standort* of those who make them. His views have been aptly criticized by Charles Frankel, *The Case for Modern Man* (New York, 1956), pp. 117 ff.
7. *Gesammelte Politische Schriften* (Munich, 1921), p. 300.
8. Plato, *The Statesman*, in *The Dialogues of Plato* (New York, n.d.), III, Par. 289, 575.
9. Rudolf Smend, *Verfassung und Verfassungsrecht* (Munich, 1928), pp. 127 ff.
10. Baron de Montesquieu, *The Spirit of the Laws*, Hafner Library of Classics edn., trans. Thomas Nugent (New York, 1949), Bk. I, Chap. 1.
11. Aristotle, *Politics*, trans. Benjamin Jowett, Modern Library edn. (New York, 1943), Bk. III, Chap. 11.
12. Harold Laski, *The Limitations of the Expert* (London, 1931).
13. Walter Bagehot, *The English Constitution*, The World's Classics edn. (New York, 1928), p. 172.
14. Winston S. Churchill, *Their Finest Hour*, Vol. II of *The Second World War* (Boston, 1949), pp. 381 ff.
15. Thucydides, *The Peloponnesian War*, Everyman's Library edn. (London, 1910), p. 90.
16. A joke comes close to putting the difference between the expert and the political leader in a nutshell: The expert is a man who knows more and more about less and less, until in the end, he knows everything about nothing. The political leader is a man who knows less and less about more and more, until, in the end he knows nothing about everything.
17. Bagehot, *op. cit.*, p. 172.
18. For the details see Sir Alfred Zimmern, *The Greek Commonwealth* (New York, 1922), pp. 174 ff.
19. Maurice Croiset, *Aristophanes and the Political Parties at Athens* (London, 1909), p. 102.
20. Wilhelm Hasbach, *Die Moderne Demokratie* (Jena, 1912), pp. 136 ff.
21. Robert Michels, *Political Parties: A Sociological Study of the Oligarchic Tendencies of Modern Democracy* (London, 1915), cited from: *Zur Soziologie des Parteiwesens in der modernen Demokratie, Untersuchungen ueber die oligarchischen Tendenzen des Gruppenlebens* (2nd ed.; Leipsig, 1925).
22. *Ibid.*, p. xvii.
23. Quoted from Max Eastman, "Russia and the Socialist Ideal," *Harper's Magazine*, March, 1938, p. 379.
24. See, for example, Eben Mumford, *The Origins of Leadership* (Chicago, 1909).
25. V. I. Lenin, *State and Revolution* (New York, 1922), p. 38.
26. For illustrations see Max Eastman, *The End of Socialism in Russia* (Boston, 1937), pp. 29 ff.
27. F. A. Hermens, *Demokratie und Kapitalismus: Ein Versuch zur Soziologie der Staatsformen* (Munich, 1931). The review by Robert Michels in *Jahrbuecher fuer Nationaloekonomie und Statistik*, Vol. 83, 1933, contains these sentences: "Trotz der hier vorgebrachten Bedenken stehen wir nicht an, das Werk von Hermens, wenn auch mit Abstand, fuer eins der wertvollsten und bedeutendsten zu halten, welche seit Tocqueville und Lecky ueber diesen Gegenstand geschrieben wurden. Der Verfasser ist weit ueber das uebliche Mass belesen und kenntnisreich und besitzt Gedanken in Huelle und Fuelle.

Seine Untersuchungen ueber Herrschaftsstaat und konstitutionelle Monarchie, ueber die Axiomatik des Kapitalismusbegriffes und die . . . folgenden Kapitel verraten viel Scharfsinn." Pp. 288–9.

28. The discussion ended with a plan for a friendly controversy on the subject in a German periodical; the plan could not be carried out because, while, after the stabilization of Hitler's power in Germany, Michels could have presented his point of view, this could not have been done by those opposing it.

29. Ferdinand Toennies, *Kritik der Oeffentlichen Meinung* (Berlin, 1922).

30. Edmund Burke, *The Works of the Right Honorable Edmund Burke* (5th ed.; Boston, 1877), II, 89 ff.

31. John F. Kennedy, *Profiles in Courage: Decisive Moments in the Lives of Celebrated Americans* (New York, 1956).

32. Walter Lippmann, *Essays in The Public Philosophy* (Boston, 1955), pp. 16 ff.

33. Benito Mussolini, *Camera dei Deputati, Discussioni*, Legislatura XXVI, p. 10670.

34. Machiavelli, *The Prince and the Discourses by Niccolò Machiavelli*, Modern Library edn. (New York, 1940), p. 264.

35. Vilfredo Pareto, *The Mind and Society* (New York, 1935), Par. 2251.

36. Mussolini, *op. cit.*, p. 10671.

37. Carl J. Friedrich, *Constitutional Government and Democracy* (rev. ed.; Boston, 1950), pp. 589 ff. of the separately printed chapter entitled "A Sketch of the Scope and Method of Political Science."

38. Aristotle, *Politics*, Bk. V, Chap. 11, Par. 1314.

39. For a summary of plebiscites as organized by the dictatorships of Napoleon I, Napoleon III, and Hitler, see Friedrich, *Constitutional Government*, pp. 548–50, 564–67.

40. *Napoléon Le Petit*, translated from *Oeuvres Complètes de Victor Hugo* (Paris, n.d.), p. 162. Hugo ascribed the qualities listed in connection with the plebiscite to the officials who performed the operations in question. If he was a little rhetorical, he did give a good analysis of conditions under which a plebiscite makes sense, *ibid.*, pp. 154–62.

41. Charles E. Merriam, *The New Democracy and the New Despotism* (New York, 1939), p. 109.

Footnotes to Chapter III

1. One of the earliest writers in the field of political science to draw attention to this fact, and to realize its implications was Professor W. A. Bonger. See his *Problemen der Demokratie: Ein sociologische en Psychologische Studie* (Groningen, 1934), pp. 46–52.

2. Lewis H. Morgan, *Ancient Society* (New York, 1877).

3. Robert H. Lowie, *Primitive Society* (New York, 1925). Quoted by permission of Liveright Publisher Corporation.

4. Sylvester A. Sieber and Franz H. Mueller, *The Social Life of Primitive Man* (St. Louis, 1941).

5. Richard Thurnwald, *Werden, Wandel und Gestaltung von Staat und Kultur*, Vol. IV of *Die Menschliche Gesellschaft im Rahmen ihrer ethno-soziologischen Grundlagen* (Berlin, 1935).

6. Julius E. Lips, *The Origin of Things* (New York, 1947), p. 353. Quoted by permission of A. A. Wyn, Inc.

7. Lowie, *op. cit.*, p. 385.

8. Lowie mentions this in connection with the passage quoted above, and adds: "This is illustrated by the Plains Indian police organizations at the time of a communal buffalo hunt, when a single false step might have scared off the entire herd and jeopardized the food supply of the entire camp. Hence the utmost rigor temporarily supplanted the extreme individualism of normal times. Women were not allowed to chop trees, men were not permitted to go hunting by themselves lest their premature efforts imperil the success of the cooperative enterprise. The police not only confiscated an offender's game, but severely beat him, broke up his weapons, and destroyed his tent. If he offered resistance, he was likely to be killed on the spot. The constabulary had other functions, though less conspicuous ones. They would restrain war parties from setting out at an inopportune moment, and it was their duty to effect a reconciliation between tribesmen whose personal hostility might lead to a feud." *Ibid.*, pp. 385–6.

9. Lips, *op. cit.*, p. 326.

10. John Locke, *Of Civil Government,* Everyman's Library edn. (London, 1924), Bk. I, Chap. 5, Par. 26.

11. Joseph Schumpeter, "Social Classes," *Imperialism, Social Classes,* trans. Bert Hoselitz (New York, 1955).

12. They are discussed in Lowie, *op. cit.*

13. Alexander Ruestow, *Ursprung der Herrschaft,* Vol. I of *Ortsbestimmung der Gegenwart* (Zurich, 1950), pp. 58 ff.

14. F. E. Adcock, "The Reform of the Athenian State," *Cambridge Ancient History* (Cambridge, 1926), IV, 26 ff., takes the more traditional view of the subject, which emphasizes the grievances of the poorer population groups.

15. For the details see C. Hignett, *A History of the Athenian Constitution to the End of the Fifth Century, B. C.* (Oxford, 1952), pp. 86 ff.

16. All of these figures follow Sir Alfred Zimmern, *The Greek Commonwealth* (New York, 1922), pp. 171 ff. See also A. H. M. Jones, "The Economic Basis of Athenian Democracy," *Past and Present: A Journal of Scientific History,* February, 1952, pp. 13 ff. Inasmuch as the weight of German classical learning has, traditionally, been brought to bear on the side of those who are critical of Athenian democracy, it is interesting to note two recent publications which, in a highly stimulating manner, follow a different line: Friedrich Warncke, *Die Demokratische Staatsidee in der Verfassung von Athen* (Bonn, 1951), and Hans Erich Stier, *Die klassische Demokratie,* pub. *Arbeitsgemeinschaft fuer Forschung des Landes Nordrhein-Westfalen* (Cologne, 1954), III, 7 ff. Professor Stier, in particular, it would seem, has destroyed the foundations of both the argument that the Athenian Constitution was not democratic, and that this democracy lacked the merits which we associate with that form of government at present. He emphasizes the need to distinguish between the democracy of the fifth and fourth centuries, many of the charges made against Athenian democracy in general being valid for the later period, but not for the former.

17. Lionel Pearson, "Party Politics and Free Speech in Democratic Athens," *Greece and Rome,* October, 1937, pp. 41 ff.

18. Thucydides, *The Peloponnesian War,* Everyman's Library edn. (New York, 1910), p. 122.

19. Plato, *The Republic,* trans. Benjamin Jowett, Modern Library edn. (New York, n.d.), Bk. VIII, Par. 562, pp. 318–19.

20. The Constitution of Athens, by "The Old Oligarch," quoted from *The Greek Historians* (New York, 1942), II, 635.

21. Thucydides, *op. cit.*, p. 142.

22. *The Federalist,* Modern Library edn. (New York, n.d.), No. 10, p. 58.

23. Herodotus, *The Persian Wars,* trans. George Rawlinson, Modern Library edn. (New York, 1942), Bk. III, Par. 81, p. 253.

24. Gustave LeBon, *The Crowd* (London, 1896).
25. For the details see Fustel de Coulanges, *The Ancient City* (Boston, 1874), pp. 441 ff.
26. Xenophon, *Hellenica*, Bk. I, Chaps. 6 and 7, quoted from *The Works of Xenophon*, trans. H. G. Dakins (New York, 1890), I, 28 ff., in particular p. 32.
27. Plato, *Apology*, quoted from *The Dialogues of Plato*, trans. Benjamin Jowett (New York, 1892), II, 125.
28. Polybius, *The Histories of Polybius*, trans. Evelyn S. Schuckburgh (New York, 1889), I, 468 ff.
29. M. V. Clarke, *The Medieval City State* (London, 1926), p. 145.

The historical experience which led to such drastic steps was well known to the founders of the "representative republic." We have quoted above what Madison said on the subject in No. 10 of *The Federalist,* and we might add what Alexander Hamilton—not without exaggeration—had to say upon the subject in the New York Ratifying Convention:

"The ancient democracies, in which the people themselves deliberated, never possessed one feature of good government. Their very character was tyranny; their figure, deformity. When they assembled, the field of debate presented an ungovernable mob, not only incapable of deliberation, but prepared for every enormity. In these assemblies, the enemies of the people brought forward their plans of ambition systematically. They were opposed by their enemies of another party; and it became a matter of contingency, whether the people subjected themselves to be led blindly by one tyrant or by another."—Jonathan Elliot, *The Debates of the Several State Conventions on the Adoption of the Federal Constitution* (Philadelphia, 1863), II, 253–4.
30. Henri Pirenne, *Belgian Democracy: Its Early Origin* (Manchester, 1915), pp. 175–6.

Footnotes to Chapter IV

1. It was first developed in Plato's *Statesman*, rather than in Aristotle's *Politics* as is often assumed. See *The Dialogues of Plato* (New York, n.d.), III, 577 ff.
2. Baron de Montesquieu, *The Spirit of the Laws,* Hafner Library of Classics edn., trans. Thomas Nugent (New York, 1949), Bk. II, Chap. 4, pp. 15–16.
3. Gaetano Mosca, *Teorica dei Governi e Governo Parlamentare* (Rome, 1884). His views were later amplified in his "Elements of Political Science," translated into English under the title, *The Ruling Class,* ed. Arthur Livingston (New York, 1939). Quoted by permission of McGraw-Hill Book Co.
4. *Ibid.,* p. 51.
5. Walter Scott, *Life of Napoleon,* quoted from A. D. Lindsay, *The Modern Democratic State* (New York, 1947), I, 233. Quoted by permission of Oxford University Press.
6. Walter Bagehot, *The English Constitution,* The World's Classics edn. (New York, 1928), pp. 30 ff. For a modern discussion of the subject, see Karl Loewenstein, "The Influence of Symbols of Politics," in Roy V. Peel and Joseph F. Roucek, *Introduction to Politics* (New York, 1941), pp. 62 ff.
7. Bagehot, *op. cit.,* p. 30.
8. *Ibid.,* p. 34.
9. For some vivid personal glimpses into these preparations, see a little book written by the wife of a man who, for a generation, was in charge of the

technical aspects of these events: Phyl Hopkins, *Village Royal* (London, 1955).

10. Bagehot, *op. cit.,* p. 48.
11. Aristotle, *Politics,* trans. Benjamin Jowett, Modern Library edn. (New York, 1943), Bk. III, Chap. 14, Par. 1285.
12. Carl J. Friedrich, *Constitutional Government and Democracy* (Boston, 1941), p. 23. Quoted by permission of Ginn and Co.
13. Karl A. Wittfogel, *Oriental Despotism* (New Haven, 1957).
13a. Margaret Landon, *Anna and the King of Siam* (New York, 1951).
14. Personal incompetence does not matter if compensated for by the appointment of a capable deputy. For Montesquieu, "The creation of a vizier [to whom absolute power is entrusted] is a fundamental law of this government." Montesquieu, *op. cit.,* Bk. II, Chap. 5, p. 18.
15. *Ibid.,* Bk. IV, Chap. 14, p. 57.
16. Against these the apparatus of repression is held in constant readiness. See Montesquieu, *ibid.,* Bk. III, Chap. 9, p. 26.
17. Prince von Bülow, *Memoirs of Prince von Bülow: The World War and Germany's Collapse, 1909–1919* (Boston, 1932), pp. 156–7.
18. See his works: *The Reconstruction of Europe: Talleyrand and the Congress of Vienna, 1814–15* (New York, 1915), and *The Principles of Power: The Great Political Crises of History* (New York, 1942).
19. Plato, in his *Statesman,* lists three criteria to distinguish genuine forms of government from perversions. In his words, "There is a criterion of voluntary and involuntary, poverty and riches, law and the absense of law . . ."— Plato, *The Statesman,* in *The Dialogues of Plato* (New York, n.d.), III, 577. This distinction, when applied to aristocracy and democracy, invites the charge made by Hobbes against any distinction between genuine forms of government and perversions: that the latter were simply "forms of government misliked." The situation is different in the case of monarchy and tyranny, provided that we eliminate the weak link in Plato's list of criteria which ever since Aristotle's *Politics,* has, unfortunately, been the mainstay of those trying to make the distinction: "poverty and riches." Its meaning is interpreted by Aristotle (*Politics,* Bk. III, Chap. 7.) to read: "The true forms of government, therefore, are those in which the one, or the few, or the many, govern with a view to the common interest; but governments which rule with a view to the private interest, whether of the one, or of the few, or of the many, are perversions." Whether a ruler rules for his own good or for that of the people is difficult to judge with any degree of objectivity; Hitler and Stalin were probably sincerely convinced that they did rule for the benefit of their nations, and yet they can lay claim to the title of tyrants if anyone can. With the twin criteria of "voluntary and involuntary" and "law and the absence of law" we are on firmer ground. If terror (to be discussed in some detail later) is "an instrument of policy" this fact, by definition, excludes the rule of law, and it also makes a government "involuntary."
20. Herodotus, *The Persian Wars,* trans. George Rawlinson, Modern Library edn. (New York, 1942), Bk. III, Par. 80, p. 252.
21. Lord Acton, *Essays on Freedom and Power,* ed. Gertrude Himmelfarb (New York, 1955), p. 335.
22. *The Federalist,* Modern Library edn. (New York, n.d.), No. 58, p. 361.
23. Machiavelli saw clearly the difference between legitimate monarchy and what he calls a monarchy "of recent foundation," meaning one of the dictatorships of Renaissance Italy:
". . . the difficulty of maintaining hereditary states accustomed to a reigning family is far less than in new monarchies; for it is sufficient not to transgress ancestral usages, and to adapt one's self to unforeseen circumstances; in this

way such a prince, if one of ordinary assiduity, will always be able to maintain his position, unless some very exceptional and excessive force deprives him of it; and even if he be thus deprived, on the slightest mischance happening to the new occupier, he will be able to regain it. . . .

"In as much as the legitimate prince has less cause and less necessity to give offence, it is only natural that he should be more loved; and, if no extraordinary vices make him hated, it is only reasonable for his subjects to be naturally attached to him, . . ."—Machiavelli, *The Prince and the Discourses by Niccolò Machiavelli,* Modern Library edn. (New York, 1940), pp. 5–6.

24. Attilio Tamaro, *Twenty Years History, 1922–43,* quoted from the weekly, *Der Volksbote,* Innsbruck, March 14, 1954.

25. See the description of these events by H. R. Trevor-Roper, *The Last Days of Hitler* (New York, 1947), pp. 106 ff. After the war, some of the shorthand notes were retrieved which had been taken during Hitler's conferences with his military leaders. In the *Times Literary Supplement,* "Hitler In Conference" (April 13, 1951) the reviewer of *Hitler Directs His War*—ed. Felix Gilbert (New York, 1951)—summarizes a part of the comments on these notes in these words: "As matters went from bad to worse he [Hitler] lost touch with realities and the conferences became more and more a world of make-believe."

26. "The Anti-Stalin Campaign and International Communism," *A Selection of Documents,* ed. Russian Institute, Columbia University (New York, 1956), pp. 43–5.

27. Khrushchev speaks of some of Stalin's proposals in the field of agriculture as "the fantastic ideas of a person divorced from reality." *Ibid.,* p. 79.

28. *Ibid.,* p. 44.

29. See Isaac Deutscher, *Stalin: A Political Biography* (New York, 1949), p. 495.

30. "The Anti-Stalin Campaign . . . ," p. 50.

31. *Ibid.*

32. *Ibid.,* p. 52.

33. The execution of so many senior officers had, however, the compensating effect of promoting younger men who were often better attuned to the technical requirements of modern war than were their elders.

34. "The Anti-Stalin Campaign . . . ," pp. 84–5.

35. Harrison Salisbury, *American in Russia* (New York, 1955), p. 157.

36. In theory the Emperor exercised his powers only as the leader of the German princes who were his "allies" rather than his "subjects," and who were represented in the *Bundesrat.* In some fields the influence of this body was considerable, but it did not affect the decisions with which we are concerned.

37. Emil Ludwig, *William Hohenzollern, The Last of the Kaisers* (New York, 1926), p. 68. Quoted by permission of G. P. Putnam's Sons.

38. *Ibid.,* p. 69.

39. *The Letters of Queen Victoria,* ed. A. C. Benson and Viscount Esler, popular edition, first series (London, 1911), second series (London, 1926–28), third series (London, 1930–32).

40. Frank Hardie, *The Political Influence of Queen Victoria, 1861–1901* (London, 1935).

41. Carl Schurz, *The Reminiscences of Carl Schurz* (New York, 1908), pp. 268 ff.

42. Bismarck, *Gedanken und Erinnerungen. Die drei Baende in einen Band,* edn. Deutsche Buch-Gemeinschaft (Stuttgart, 1928), p. 607.

43. *Ibid.,* p. 625.

44. They included well-known American figures. See, for example, the letter by Nicholas Murray Butler in the special issue published by *The New York Times,* June 8, 1913, in celebration of the 25th anniversary of William's accession.

45. Ludwig, *op. cit.*, p. 459.
46. *Ibid.*, p. 459.
47. Even in this respect what George N. Shuster and Arnold Bergsträsser, *Germany: A Short History* (New York, 1944), p. 120, called the "Ludendorff dictatorship" was to have its effects, but it took a William to make it possible.
48. Franz von Papen, *Der Wahrheit eine Gasse* (Munich, 1952), p. 82.
49. Machiavelli, *The Prince . . .* , pp. 87–89.
50. Machiavelli holds that the man in question might usurp the throne for himself—a danger still real during the Renaissance, but no longer so in a country such as the Germany of William II.
51. Ludwig Quidde, *Caligula: Eine Studie ueber den roemischen Caesaren-wahn*, quoted from the 32nd edn. (Berlin, 1927). The booklet was first published in 1894.
52. Graf Ernst Reventlow, *Kaiser Wilhelm II und die Byzantiner* (Munich, 1906).
53. The difference is, of course, that Stalin could take liberties with the lives of his subjects that were beyond the reach of William II.
54. St. Thomas Aquinas, *On Kingship: To the King of Cyprus*, trans. Gerald B. Phelan (rev. ed.; Toronto, 1949), Bk. I, Chap. 9, p. 41.
55. "The Anti-Stalin Campaign . . . ," pp. 1 ff.
56. Thomas Paine, *The Rights of Man*, constituted an answer to Burke's attack on the French Revolution. See *Basic Writings of Thomas Paine* (New York, 1942), p. 140.
57. *Daily Telegraph*, October 27, 1908.
58. Bismarck, *Gedanken . . .* , p. 628.
59. Camillo Cavour, quoted from J. Barthélemy, *La Crise de la démocratie contemporaine* (Paris, 1931), p. 221.

FOOTNOTES TO CHAPTER V

1. We disregard despotism because it does not lie on the path of the historical pattern in the Western world, and even in those areas where it still enjoys a lease on life its days are clearly numbered.
2. "Germany and Its Tribes," quoted from *The Complete Works of Tacitus*, Modern Library edn. (New York, 1942), pp. 709 ff., in particular pp. 712–14.
3. Werner Sombart, *Der moderne Kapitalismus* (6th ed.; Munich, 1924), II, Part 1, p. 10.
4. There were exceptions to this rule; see Fritz Hartung, *Deutsche Verfassungsgeschichte vom 15. Jahrhundert bis zur Gegenwart* (Leipzig, 1914), pp. 50 ff.
5. The social and political history of these problems is rarely treated in scientific literature. For exceptions, see Joseph Schumpeter, "Social Classes in an Ethnically Homogeneous Environment," *Imperialism, Social Classes*, trans. Bert Hoselitz (New York, 1955), pp. 101 ff.; Georg von Below, "Adel," *Handwoerterbuch der Staatswissenschaften* (3rd ed.); Carl Brinkmann, "Die Aristokratie im Kapitalistischen Zeitalter," *Grundriss der Sozialoekonomik*, IX, Part 1.
6. See the article published under this title by *The Economist*, July 28, 1956.
7. For some details see Lotz, *Geschichte des deutschen Beamtentums* (Berlin, 1909), pp. 345 ff., and 636 ff.

8. Such developments were not new. Bismarck complained that his representatives in Paris were unwilling to associate with republican leaders, including members of the French cabinet, preferring the company of their fellow-noblemen, who were mostly monarchists without political influence.

9. For some significant details, see F. C. Endres, "Soziologische Struktur und ihr entsprechende Ideologie des deutschen Offizierkorps vor dem Weltkriege," *Archiv fuer Sozialwissenschaft und Sozialpolitik,* Vol. 58.

10. Walter Bagehot, *The English Constitution,* The World's Classics edn. (New York, 1928), p. 152.

11. For the details see J. Gouault, *Comment la France est devenue Républicaine; les élections générales et partielles à l'Assemblée Nationale, 1870–75* (Paris, 1954).

12. F. A. Hermens, "Die antiparlamentarische Bewegung in Frankreich," *Zeitschrift fuer Politik,* March, 1933.

13. Wilhelm Hasbach, *Die Parlamentarische Kabinettsregierung* (Jena, 1919), p. 113.

14. It might be mentioned in passing that while the principle of the separation of powers, as embodied in the American Constitution, does present similar problems, there is the difference that, both executive and legislature are democratic in origin; in this fact the American President, for example, can find a source of strength which, if he knows how to use it, places him in a position quite different from that of the constitutional monarch.

15. Sigmund Neumann, *Die deutschen Parteien: Wesen und Wandel nach dem Kriege* (Berlin, 1932), pp. 20–1.

16. Quoted from Carl Schmitt, *Politische Romantik* (2nd ed.; Munich, 1925), p. 137.

17. Significantly, the chapter of his memoirs which deals with this subject is entitled "Breach with Conservatives." Bismarck, *op. cit.,* pp. 446 ff.

18. A great many details could be added. For some of them, see F. A. Hermens, *Demokratie und Kapitalismus: Ein Versuch zur Soziologie der Staatsformen* (Munich, 1931), pp. 167–209.

19. Alexis de Tocqueville, *Democracy in America,* Vintage Books edn. (New York, 1955), p. 6.

20. Fernando D. Urdanivia, *La Situación de Mexico y la Successiòn Presidencial* (Mexico City, 1940), pp. 32–3.

21. "Viva" means literally "that you may live," but the English equivalent is "hurrah."

22. See the chapter entitled "El Partido Nacional Revolucionario," in his book, *Quinze Años de Politica Mexicana* (Mexico City, 1941), pp. 197 ff.

23. *Reflections on the Revolution in France,* quoted from the Library of Liberal Arts edn., ed. Thomas H. D. Mahony, with an analysis by Oscar Piest (New York, 1955).

24. *Ibid.,* p. 66.

25. *Ibid.,* p. 46.

26. Karl Loewenstein, *Brazil under Vargas* (New York, 1942), p. 8.

27. For details see Harold M. Vinacke, *A History of the Far East in Modern Times* (5th ed.; New York, 1950), pp. 243–6.

FOOTNOTES TO CHAPTER VI

1. F. M. Watkins, "The Problem of Constitutional Dictatorship," *Public Policy*, eds. C. J. Friedrich and E. Mason (Cambridge, 1940), pp. 324 ff.
2. Carl Schmitt, *Die Diktatur: Von den Anfaengen des modernen Souveraenitaetsgedankens bis zum proletarischen Klassenkampf* (2nd ed.; Munich, 1928).
3. Herbert Agar, *A Time for Greatness* (Boston, 1940), p. 90.
4. Plato, *The Republic*, trans. Benjamin Jowett, Modern Library edn. (New York, n.d.); Aristotle, *Politics*, trans. Benjamin Jowett, Modern Library edn. (New York, 1943). There are further references to tyranny in Plato's *Statesman* and *The Laws;* they conform to the pattern developed in *The Republic.*
5. St. Thomas Aquinas, *On Kingship to the King of Cyprus*, trans. Gerald B. Phelan, ed. I. Th. Eschmann (Toronto, 1949).
6. For medieval literature on the matter, see W. Parsons, "The Medieval Theory of the Tyrant," *The Review of Politics*, April, 1942.
7. For an approximation see E. E. Kellett, *The Story of Dictatorship* (New York, 1937). A brief discussion of the earlier dictators has been given by A. Cobban, *Dictatorship: Its History and Theory* (London, 1939), pp. 307–33. Most books dealing with the subject suffer from the lack of a proper definition of dictatorship. Thus, J. Bainville, *Les Dictateurs* (Paris, 1935), includes democratic leaders like Solon and Pericles; A. Carr, *Juggernaut: The Path of Dictatorship* (New York, 1939), starts out with Richelieu, Louis XIV, Frederick the Great, and Bismarck, none of whom can be regarded as a dictator in the proper sense of the word. G. Ferrero's, *The Reconstruction of Europe: Talleyrand and the Congress of Vienna, 1814–15* (New York, 1915), and *The Principles of Power: The Great Political Crises of History* (New York, 1942), deal with Napoleon I and the Rightist dictatorships of the present time, and therefore cover only part of the ground, but are characterized throughout by a correct analysis of the essence of dictatorship. Two highly stimulating books on the subject are: Hannah Arendt, *The Origin of Totalitarianism* (New York, 1951), and W. F. Hallgarten, *Why Dictators? The Causes and Forms of Tyrannical Rule since 600 B.C.* (New York, 1934). Miss Arendt limits her concept of totalitarian rule too much—she excludes Italian fascism although it not only gave rise to the term "totalitarian" but it also provided Hitler with a systematic and, at that time, vital knowledge of its techniques, which stood him in such good stead when he seized and consolidated his power, a knowledge which Mussolini had to acquire in a slow process of trial and error. Professor Hallgarten, on the other hand, takes in too much territory, including among others, Savonarola, who not only attempted, but succeeded in establishing a constitutional system which survived him; it might have lasted indefinitely had it not been overthrown by what, in the main, was force from the outside, supplemented only at the last moment by an uprising from inside the city.—The book by Carl J. Friedrich and Z. K. Brzezinski, *Totalitarian Dictatorship and Autocracy* (Cambridge, Mass., 1956) became available after the completion of this study. The same applies to Norman L. Stamps, *Why Democracies Fail: A Critical Evaluation of the Causes of Modern Dictatorships* (Notre Dame, 1957), which contains a useful summary of the explanations given for the rise of modern dictatorships.

8. Charles L. Sherman, "A Latter-Day Tyranny in the Light of Aristotelian Prognosis," *American Political Science Review*, XXXVIII (1934), 434.

9. Plato, *The Republic*, Par. 562, p. 318. All page references to Modern Library edn.

10. *Ibid.*, Par. 565, p. 323.

11. *Ibid.*, Par. 564, pp. 320–1.

12. *Ibid.*, Par. 562, p. 318.

13. *Ibid.*, Par. 564, p. 321.

14. Plato assumes that this weakness is inevitable; from the experience of modern democracy we know that this is not the case.

15. *Ibid.*, Pars. 556–7, p. 310.

16. Aristotle, *Politics*, Bk. V, pp. 209 ff. All page references to Modern Library edn.

17. We limit ourselves, of course, to those cases which did constitute tyranny in the proper sense of the term—something which many, if not most, of the writers dealing with the subject fail to do.

18. Ferrero, *The Reconstruction of Europe* . . . , p. 56.

19. M. V. Clarke, *The Medieval City State* (London, 1926), p. 113.

20. The best comprehensive treatment of these events remains J. C. Sismondi, *A History of the Italian Republics*, Everyman's Library edn. (London, 1907). See also the article, "Signorie e Principati," *Enciclopedia Italiana*, XXI (1936), 754 ff. The most detailed presentation of the material is, of course, to be found in the histories of individual cities, such as Machiavelli's or Davidson's *History of Florence*.

21. Sismondi, *A History of the Italian Republics*, p. 54.

22. Kellett, *The Story of Dictatorship*, p. 7.

23. Waldemar Gurian, *Bolshevism: Theory and Practice* (New York, 1937), pp. 61–2. Quoted by permission of Sheed and Word.

24. I. Balbo, *Diario 1922* (Milan, 1932).

25. Emil Ludwig, *Hindenburg* (Amsterdam, 1935), p. 320.

26. C. M. Woodhouse, *Apple of Discord* (London, 1949), pp. 12–13.

27. Plato, *op. cit.*, Par. 566, p. 324.

28. Th. Aquinas, *On Kingship* . . . , pp. 48–9.

29. Plato, *op. cit.*, Par. 571, pp. 329–30.

30. *Ibid.*, Par. 567, p. 326.

31. *Ibid.*, Par. 575, p. 334.

32. Sismondi, *op. cit.*, p. 239.

33. Quoted from Leslie C. Stevens, "The Future of Communism: Some Uses of Power," *The New Leader*, September 17, 1956. Stevens, in an otherwise excellent article still finds it necessary to state that "a good dictator is certainly conceivable"—a contradiction in terms.

34. Friedrich Nietzsche, *The Will to Power*, Aphorism 859. The translation is the author's, as the version given in Friedrich Nietzsche, *The Will to Power*, trans. Anthony M. Ludovici (London, 1910), II, 296, does not seem to render the text correctly.

35. *Ibid.*, Aphorism 1026, Ludovici translation, pp. 404–5; here again translated from the German original by the author.

36. Winston Churchill, *Step by Step* (New York, 1939).

37. Hitler had revealed many of his designs in *Mein Kampf*, but few of those who read it credited the author with any serious attempt to carry out his declared intentions.

38. Plato, *op. cit.*, Par. 566, p. 325.

39. *Ibid.*, Par. 565, pp. 323–4.

40. Th. Aquinas, *On Kingship* . . . , p. 16.

41. Sismondi, *op cit.*, p. 240.

42. Plato, *op. cit.*, Par. 567, pp. 325–6.

43. "These negative characteristics of his developed steadily, and during the last

years acquired an absolutely insufferable character." Quoted from, "The Anti-Stalin Campaign and International Communism," *A Selection of Documents,* Pub. Russian Institute, Columbia University (New York, 1956), p. 9.
44. Aristotle, *op. cit.,* Bk. V, Chap. 11, pp. 246–7.
45. *Ibid.,* pp. 246–7. See also p. 154.
46. Th. Aquinas, *op. cit.,* pp. 16–17.
47. Aristotle, *op. cit.,* Bk. V, Chap. 11, p. 247.
48. Sismondi, *op. cit.,* p. 249.
49. Plato, *op. cit.,* Par. 566–7, p. 325.
50. "Human Character and World Order," one of the Merrick Lectures for 1943 on *Christian Bases of World Order* (New York, 1943), p. 232.
51. Sismondi, *op. cit.,* p. 151.
52. Benjamin Constant, *On Conquest and Usurpation,* ed. and trans. by Helen Byrne Lippmann, under the title *Prophecy from the Past* (New York, 1941), p. 51.
53. For an example see Sismondi, *op. cit.,* p. 150.
54. *Ibid.,* p. 151.
55. *Ibid.,* p. 157.
56. Ferrero, *The Reconstruction of Europe* . . .
57. Plato, *op. cit.,* Par. 578, p. 339.
58. Th. Aquinas, *On Kingship* . . . , p. 17.
59. Sismondi, *op. cit.,* p. 237.
60. Joseph E. Davies, *Mission to Moscow,* Pocketbook edn. (New York, 1943), p. 355. Quoted by permission of Simon and Schuster, Inc.
61. George F. Kennan, "America and the Russian Future," *Foreign Affairs,* XXIX, No. 3 (April, 1951).
62. E. de la Boëtie, *Discours sur la servitude volontaire,* trans. H. Kurz, under title, *Anti-Dictator* (New York, 1942).
63. Sinclair Lewis' *It Can't Happen Here* (New York, 1935), is an excellent antidote, as is also Lewis Browne's, *See What I Mean?* (New York, 1943). See also the discerning remarks by George F. Kennan, *op. cit.,* pp. 364–5.
64. Plato, *op. cit.,* Par. 577, p. 339.
65. Sismondi, *op. cit.,* pp. 185–6.
66. *Ibid.,* p. 238.
67. *Ibid.,* p. 238.
68. Rousseau, *Social Contract,* Bk. I, Chap. 2.
69. Constant, *On Conquest and Usurpation,* pp. 113–14.
70. *Ibid.,* pp. 56–7.
71. *Ibid.,* p. 57.
72. "The Anti-Stalin Campaign . . . ," p. 31.
73. See the brilliant analysis of his case in George N. Shuster, *In Silence I Speak* (New York, 1956), and the review of this book by Stephen D. Kertesz, *Books on Trial,* October, 1956, p. 64.
74. "The Anti-Stalin Campaign . . . ," pp. 22 ff.
75. Sismondi, *A History of the Italian Republics,* p. 240.
76. Plato, *The Republic,* Par. 569, p. 329.
77. Aristotle, *Politics,* Bk. V. Chap. 11, Par. 1314, p. 249.
78. Th. Aquinas, *On Kingship* . . . , Bk. I, Chap. VI, p. 24.
79. *Ibid.,* pp. 24–5.
80. "Foes Fear Chaos if Perón Topples; Radical Leaders Believe His Fall Would Not Necessarily Mean Democratic Rule," *The New York Times,* September 11, 1955.
81. Th. Aquinas, *On Kingship* . . . , Bk. I, Chap. VI, p. 25.
82. Aristotle, *Politics,* Bk. V, Chap. 10, p. 243.
83. They are not dissimilar, in their more sensible aspects, to those which it has been necessary to develop to protect the President of the United States. For

some details, see Don Wharton, "How the Secret Service Protects the President," *The Reader's Digest*, August, 1956. The American President has to be defended, in the main from cranks, rather than from political opponents.

84. J. Burckhardt, *Die Kultur der Renaissance in Italien*, ed. W. Götz (Leipzig, 1925), p. 37.

85. Evidently the situation is no different at the present time. Mr. Joseph E. Davies reports, under the heading, "Mistrust among Leaders Themselves": "The philosophy of communism justifies all acts if done in its name. There are no considerations of honor or loyalty which control against duty to the party. The result is that there can be no confidence between these men, in leadership. No man can trust another." Mr. Davies continues: "It is a serious and basic weakness and a constant threat to existing government." Actually it is, of course, the opposite; it is the only form of security which a dictator can obtain.—Joseph E. Davies, *Mission to Moscow*, p. 352.

86. Sismondi, *op. cit.*, pp. 244–50.

87. *Ibid.*, pp. 242–4.

88. *Ibid.*, p. 157.

89. *Ibid.*, p. 159.

90. Kennan, "America and the Russian Future," pp. 364–5.

91. Yves R. Simon, *The Philosophy of Democratic Government* (Chicago, 1951).

92. The party with the lowest official membership is the Bolshevist party, whose membership figures for November 1917 have been placed, by various writers, as low as 25,000 and as high as 75,000. Lenin did keep the number of officially enrolled members down deliberately in the belief that a small number of full-time revolutionaries was preferable to a large number of more or less inactive members. Besides, the party was illegal most of the time. It did, however, have a vast popular following, scoring in the (more or less free) elections to the Russian Constituent Assembly with 9.8 million out of a total of 41.7 million. For the details, see Oliver Henry Radkey, *The Election of the Russian Constituent Assembly of 1917* (Cambridge, 1950), pp. 16–17.

93. This remark, first used by Mussolini in his famous speech in the Scala in Milan, was repeated, and amplified, by him on various occasions, such as in a speech he made in the Chamber of Deputies on May 26, 1927. Here quoted from Benito Mussolini, *La Dottrina del Fascismo: Con una Storia del Movimento Fascista di Gioachino Volpe* (Rome, 1933), p. 34.

94. See, for example, the article by Francesco Ercole, "La funzione del partito nell' ordinamento corporativo," *Archivio di studi corporativi*, II (1931–1932), pp. 41–71. It must be borne in mind that the "doctrine" of Fascism owes its formulation to former Nationalists, such as Giovanni Gentile and Alfredo Rocco, who were more literate than the original Fascists, and who preferred to express themselves in terms of Hegelian glorification of the state, even if they were unable to overcome the reality of the Fascist one-party state with such semantic devices.

95. It is well to recall what Mosca said about formulas: ". . . political formulas are not mere quackeries aptly invented to trick the masses into obedience. Anyone who would view them in that light would fall into grave error. The truth is that they answer a real need in man's social nature; and this need, so universally felt, of governing and knowing that one is governed not on the basis of more material or intellectual force, but on the basis of a moral principle, has beyond any doubt a practical and a real importance."—Gaetano Mosca, *The Ruling Class*, ed. Arthur Livingston (New York, 1939), p. 71. Quoted by permission of McGraw-Hill Book Co.

96. See Noel Barber, "Personal . . . From Budapest," *The Saturday Evening Post*, December 15, 1956.

97. The reason was, on the one hand, simple "empire building" on the part of their commander, the former army captain Roehm, and, on the other, the

desire to bring as many young men as possible into a kind of organization where they would be sufficiently under Nazi control to keep them away from other activities.

98. Their opponents, however, will not be inclined to give them credit for this and say that their apparent moderation is simply a result of the limitations placed upon them by circumstances.

99. F. A. Hermens, *Democracy or Anarchy? A Study of Proportional Representation* (Notre Dame, 1941), pp. 294–300.

100. This is rightly, and with more reasons than can be given here, pointed out by Robert M. MacIver, *The Web of Government* (New York, 1947), pp. 147 ff.

101. When Perón attacked the Catholic Church openly this was a step difficult to explain rationally. While the activities of the younger priests in regard to the development of Catholic Action, and of younger laymen aiming at the establishment of a Christian democratic movement did conflict with his attempts to imitate totalitarian rulers, he clearly could have handled the situation with means less extreme than the open declaration of war to which he resorted.

102. Walter Bagehot, *The English Constitution,* The World's Classics edn. (New York, 1928), p. 181.

103. "Behind the Blood Bath," in the Column entitled "Matter of Fact," *The Washington Post and Times Herald,* November 5, 1956.

FOOTNOTES TO CHAPTER VII

1. Karl A. Wittfogel, *Oriental Despotism* (New Haven, 1957), p. 101.

2. This is, however, not necessarily the original meaning of the term. Cicero did use it in the modern sense, but "In the Roman Empire the word in its Latin form became the technical term for acts of legislation by the emperor . . ."— Charles Howard McIlwain, *Constitutionalism: Ancient and Modern* (Ithaca, 1940), pp. 25–28. On the concept of constitution in both ancient Greece and Rome, see E. Crosa, "L'Idée de la Constitution dans l'Antiquité classique," *Revue Internationale d'Histoire Politique et Constitutionnelle,* July–December, 1951.

3. Oswald Spengler, *The Decline of the West* (New York, 1928).

4. "Practically everything that has been achieved in world history . . . has been the product of living unities that found themselves 'in form.' " *Ibid.,* II, 330.

5. *Ibid.,* p. 431.

6. Carl Schurz, *The Reminiscences of Carl Schurz* (New York, 1908), p. 276.

7. Wittfogel, *op. cit.,* p. 103.

8. This is also what John Locke implies in his criticism of absolute rule as defended by Thomas Hobbes. See John Locke, *Of Civil Government* (London, 1924), II, 123–4.

9. The superiority of the institutional over the personal element is also a characteristic of aristocratic government. Its extent is, however, lessened by the fact that where a comparatively small number of families rule, considerations of a more personal nature invariably influence such processes as the election, or the appointment, to a particular office.

10. Aristotle, *Aristotle's Politics,* trans. Benjamin Jowett, Modern Library edn. (New York, 1943), Bk. III, Chap. 6. Aristotle gives two other definitions of

constitution. The first is contained in this sentence: "And the legislator or statesman is concerned entirely with the state; a constitution or government being an arrangement of the inhabitants of the state."—*Ibid.*, Bk. III, Chap. 1. The second: "A constitution is the arrangement of offices in a state, and determines what is to be the governing body, and what is the end of the community."—*Ibid.*, Bk. IV, Chap. 2.

11. Thus, the Greek term *politeia* means "above all the state as it actually is." McIlwain, *Constitutionalism . . .* , p. 28.

12. "Die Objektivitaet sozialwissenschaftlicher und sozialpolitischer Erkenntnis," *Archiv fuer Sozialwissenschaft und Sozialpolitik, 1904,* republished in *Gesammelte Aufsaetze zur Wissenschaftslehre* (2nd ed.; Tuebingen, 1951), pp. 146 ff.

13. *Letters and Other Writings of James Madison* (New York, 1884), I, 427.

14. *The Writings of Thomas Jefferson*, ed. H. A. Washington (Washington, D.C., 1853), VII, 31.

15. "Speech in the New York Assembly, January 19, 1787." Quoted from Lynton K. Caldwell, *The Administrative Theories of Hamilton and Jefferson* (Chicago, 1944), p. 19.

16. *Ibid.*, p. 20.

17. On the use of the term "bourgeois," see Rudolf Smend, *Buerger und Bourgeois im deutschen Staatsrecht* (Berlin, 1933), quoted from *Staatsrechtliche Abhandlungen* (Berlin, 1955), pp. 309 ff.

18. "1944 Christmas Message of His Holiness Pope Pius XII," Pub. National Catholic Welfare Conference (Washington, 1945). The following two paragraphs might be quoted in full:

    "The people lives and moves by its own life energy; the masses are inert of themselves and can only be moved from outside. The people lives by the fullness of life in the men that compose it, each of whom—at his proper place and in his own way—is a person conscious of his own responsibility and of his own views.

    "The masses, on the contrary, wait for the impulse from the outside, an easy plaything in the hands of anyone who exploits their instincts and impressions; ready to follow in turn, today this flag, tomorrow another."—Pars. 23, 24; pp. 4–5.

    For a commentary which is stimulating even if one might call for dissent in detail, see Sister Thomas Albert Corbett, *People or Masses: A Comparative Study in Political Theory* (Washington, D.C., 1950).

19. See the paper on this subject delivered by the Rev. Stanley Parry on "A Thomistic Conception of Human Nature and its Influence on Political Theory," during the symposium on "Ethics and Politics" held under the auspices of the Department of Political Science of the University of Notre Dame in April, 1956.

20. Smend, *Verfassung und Verfassungsrecht*, quoted from *Staatsrechtliche Abhandlungen*, p. 125.

21. This is the reason why C. J. Friedrich was able to change the title of his book dealing with the presentation of a modern analysis of constitutional government from "Constitutional Government and Politics" to "Constitutional Government and Democracy," without the need of revising the book's contents.

22. Smend, *Verfassung und Verfassungsrecht.*

23. This is also the thought of Aristotle, who wrote:

    "For, since the state is a partnership, and is a partnership of citizens in a constitution, when the form of government changes, and becomes different, then it may be supposed that the state is no longer the same, just as a tragic differs from a comic chorus, although the members of both may be identical. And in this manner we speak of every union or composition of elements as different when the form of their composition alters; for example, a scale containing the same sounds is said to be different, accordingly as the Dorian or the Phygian mode is employed. And if this is true it is evident that the sameness of the state consists chiefly in the sameness of the constitution, and it may be called or not called by the same name, whether the inhabitants are the same or entirely different."—*Politics*, Bk. III, Chap. 4, p. 130.

24. Alexander Hamilton to Gouverneur Morris, May 10, 1777, *Works of Alexander Hamilton*, ed. Henry Cabot Lodge, IX, 71–2. Quoted from Caldwell, *op. cit.*, p. 20.

25. *Basic Writings of Thomas Paine* (New York, 1942), pp. 171–2.

26. If we resort for a criterion to the different principles on which different forms of government are established, we may define a republic to be, or at least may bestow that name on, a government which derives all its powers directly or indirectly from the great body of the people, and is administered by persons holding their offices during pleasure, for a limited period, or during good behavior. It is *essential* to such a government that it be derived from the great body of the society, not from an inconsiderable proportion, or a favored class of it; otherwise a handful of tyrannical nobles, exercising their oppressions by a delegation of their powers, might aspire to the rank of republicans, and claim for their government that the persons administering it be appointed, either directly or indirectly, by the people; and that they hold their appointments by either of the tenures just specified . . ."—*The Federalist*, Modern Library edn. (New York, n.d.), pp. 243–4.

27. The pertinent passage reads as follows:
"But so different was the style of society then [at the time of Aristotle] . . . from what it is now and with us, that I think little edification can be obtained from their writings on the subject of government. They had just ideas of the value of personal liberty, but none at all of the structure of government best calculated to preserve it. They knew no medium between a democracy (the only pure republic, but impracticable beyond the limits of a town) and an abandonment of themselves to an aristocracy, or a tyranny independent of the peoples. It seems not to have occurred that where the citizens cannot meet to transact their business in person, they alone have the right to choose the agents who shall transact it; and that in this way a republican, or popular government, of the second grade of purity, may be exercised over any extent of country . . . The introduction of this new principle of representative democracy has rendered useless almost everything written before on the structure of government; and, in a great measure, relieves our regret, if the political writings of Aristotle, or of any other ancient, have been lost, or are unfaithfully rendered or explained to us."—Jefferson, *The Writings of* . . . , pp. 31–2.

28. Herodotus, *The Persian Wars*, trans. George Rawlinson, Modern Library edn. (New York, 1942), Bk. III, Par. 80, p. 252.

29. For details see Ferdinand A. Hermens, *The Tyrants' War and the Peoples' Peace* (Chicago, 1944), pp. 4 ff.

30. *The Works of John C. Calhoun* (New York, 1883), p. 112.

31. William Howard Taft, *Popular Government* (New Haven, 1913), p. 24.

32. *The Federalist*, No. 10, p. 55.

33. *Ibid.*, p. 57.

34. Arnold Zurcher, "Democracy's Declining Capacity to Govern," *Western Political Quarterly*, December, 1955.

35. *The Federalist*, No. 55, p. 361.

36. *Ibid.*, No. 39, p. 244.

37. *Ibid.*, No. 39, p. 243.

38. *Ibid.*, No. 10, p. 61.

Footnotes to Chapter VIII

1. See the article published under this title by Samuel Blythe, *The Saturday Evening Post*, March 25, 1922.
2. M. Ostrogorski, *Democracy and the Organization of Political Parties* (New York, 1922), II, 55 ff., and *Democracy and the Party System in the United States: A Study in Extra-Constitutional Government* (New York, 1910), pp. 440–42. As Ostrogorski puts it: "As soon as a party, even if created for the noblest object, perpetuates itself, it tends to degeneration." So far as the proper solution is concerned, Ostrogorski suggests: "Party, as a wholesale contractor for the numerous and varied problems, present and to come, should give place to special organizations, limited to particular objects and forming and reforming spontaneously, so to speak, according to the changing problems of life and the play of opinion brought about thereby. Citizens who part company on one question would join forces on another."—*Democracy and the Party System . . .* , p. 441.
3. There has, however, been substantial improvement since the writer dealt with the subject in his article, "The 1938 Elections and the American Party System," *The Review of Politics*, April, 1938. See, in particular, the forceful book by E. E. Schattschneider, *Party Government* (New York, 1942), and the discussion which followed the publication of the report of the Committee on Political Parties of the American Political Science Association ("Toward a More Responsible Two-Party System," Supplement to *The American Political Science Review*, September, 1950). Its high points are summarized in: Austin Ranney, *The Doctrine of Responsible Party Government* (Urbana, 1954). Maurice Duverger's *Political Parties*—English edn., foreword by D. W. Brogan (New York, 1954)—has greatly enriched the discussion of the subject, but the book suffers, in some parts, from an uncritical empiricism, which is responsible for the pessimistic assumption that a final theory of political parties is impossible until many more "facts" have been accumulated. A systematic comparison of existing party systems has been initiated by Sigmund Neumann, ed., *Modern Political Parties* (Chicago, 1956). A history of party theory has been given by F. G. Wilson, *The Elements of Modern Politics* (New York, 1936), pp. 116 ff., and in particular in the book by Austin Ranney and Willmoore Kendall, *Democracy and the American Party System* (New York, 1956), pp. 116 ff. For a summary of the leading German theories of political parties, see Otto Koellreutter, *Die Politischen Parteien in modernen Staat* (Breslau, 1926), pp. 18 ff.
4. Weber's complete definition was: "Parties shall be called associations based on (formally) free recruiting with the purpose of providing for their leaders power within a community and, thereby, for their active participants chances (be they ideal or material) for the attainment of objective ends or of personal advantages, or both." Weber continues that parties may be either "temporary associations or associations intended to be permanent." This is, of course, a mistake, as the permanent nature of political parties (permanent, at any rate so far as the intent is concerned) is one of their characteristic features. See Max Weber, *Wirtschaft und Gesellschaft* (Tuebingen, 1925), I, 167.
5. C. J. Friedrich, *Constitutional Government and Democracy* (rev. ed.; Boston, 1950), pp. 420–21.

6. Schattschneider, *Party Government*, p. 4.
7. Of purely verbal intolerance there never has been a lack, in particular during election campaigns, when it still seems expedient to "satanize" the opposition. Most of this, however, has come to be looked upon as just "campaign oratory," deemed necessary for the deception of simple souls, but recognized for what it is by everyone else.
8. See the paper published under that title in Saul K. Padover, *The Complete Jefferson* (New York, 1943), pp. 278 ff.
9. Charles Maurras, *Enquete sur la Monarchie* (Paris, 1925), p. 119.
10. On the peculiarities of American political parties, see pp. 452 ff.
11. For the most systematic discussion of this subject yet to appear, see Helmut Unkelbach, *Grundlagen der Wahlsystematik: Stabilitaetsbedingungen der parlamentarischen Demokratie* (Goettingen, 1956), pp. 68 ff.
12. Victor Considérant—next to John St. Mill the most original theoretical proponent of P.R.—wrote: "Generally speaking, change the conditions in which people find themselves with regard to each other, and you will change the character of the relations between them."—"La Représentation nationale est un mensonge," *La Phalange*, June 17, 1842. This article is not signed, but obviously written by Considérant. Its reasoning agrees closely with that of Considérant's pamphlet: *De la sincérité du gouvernement représentatif, ou exposition de l'élection véridique*, which was originally published in 1846 and reprinted in Zurich in 1896.
13. Georges Vedel, *L'Instabilité Gouvernmentale*, Comité d'Etudes pour la République. Rapport presenté par Georges Vedel (Paris, 1956).
14. Duverger, *Political Parties*.
15. Woodrow Wilson, *The State* (Boston, 1902), pp. 221–2.
16. Duverger, *op. cit.*, pp. 241–2.
17. This point is rightly made by Jerome Kerwin, "The Presidential Elections," *The Review of Politics*, April, 1948, p. 148.
18. Benjamin Disraeli, *Coningsby* (Berlin, 1923), Bk. V, Chap. 4.
19. F. A. Hermens, *Democracy or Anarchy? A Study of Proportional Representation* (Notre Dame, 1941), pp. 129–30.
20. Woodrow Wilson, *Congressional Government* (Boston, 1890), p. 215.
21. Quoted from Sir Alfred Zimmern, *The Greek Commonwealth* (Oxford, 1922), p. 204.
22. Quoted from G. Horwill, *Proportional Representation: Its Dangers and Defects* (London, 1925), p. 113.
23. Disraeli, *op. cit.*, Bk. II, Chap. 2.
24. If a change were to be made it should be remembered that the shortest distance between two points is a straight line. The safest way to secure both an adequate majority and minority would be to provide explicitly for such a result. Thus, it could be stipulated that when one party secures more than 60 per cent of the seats the total number of the members of the parliamentary body in question be augmented for one term, the opposition being assigned the additional number, to be chosen from those defeated candidates whose popular strength was the greatest. By the same token it could be provided that when a party has a majority, but an inadequate one (as did Labour in 1950), that a certain additional number of its defeated candidates be given seats for one term. The difficulty with any such arrangement would be its somewhat mechanical character: Candidates would be declared elected who were actually defeated, and elections could become a statistical race with each party presenting candidates in every constituency because the number of popular votes might govern the number of seats won. It is, therefore, not unnatural that no such arrangement should have been adopted, but its possibility should be kept in mind, as situations of the kind mentioned frequently lead to reform plans which would constitute a *reformatio in pejus*. In large cities, normally

dominated by one party, a somewhat similar system might, however, be tried. See Hermens, *Democracy or Anarchy?*, pp. 361–3.

25. Disraeli, *op. cit.*, Bk. VIII, Chap. 3.
26. By comparison with conditions in France and most other countries which adopted the parliamentary system, British conditions were, of course, ideal even during this period.
27. For the details see A. L. Lowell, *Government of England* (New York, 1919), II, 76–8.
28. *Ibid.*, I, 516.
29. Sigmund Neumann, *Modern Political Parties* (Chicago, 1956), p. 410.
30. Walter Bagehot, *The English Constitution*, The World's Classics edn. (New York, 1928), p. xxiv.
31. It is interesting to note what Montesquieu had to say about seventeenth century England: "A very droll spectacle it was in the last century to behold the impotent efforts of the English towards the establishment of democracy. As they who had a share in the direction of public affairs were void of virtue; as their ambition was inflamed by the success of the most daring of their members; as the prevailing parties were successively animated by the spirit of faction, the government was continually changing: the people, amazed at so many revolutions, in vain attempted to erect a commonwealth. At length, when the country had undergone the most violent shocks, they were obliged to have recourse to the very government which they had so wantonly proscribed —*The Spirit of the Laws*, Bk. III, Chap. 3, The Hafner Library of Classics edn. (New York, 1949), p. 20.
32. André Siegfried, *Tableau Politique de la France de l'Ouest sous la Troisième République* (Paris, 1913), pp. ix and 497.
33. Basically, our "functional" theory has, of course, been implied all along in some of the major works of political science, beginning with Walter Bagehot's *English Constitution*. Burke and others anticipated some of the points to be made more fully generations later. The views contained in this chapter were first developed in my article, "The 1938 Elections and the American Party System." (See citation, footnote 3.) A similar view has been set forth brilliantly by Schattschneider, *Party Government*. (See citation footnote 3.)
34. G. De Ruggiero, *The History of European Liberalism* (Oxford, 1928), p. 283.
35. Charles A. Beard, *The Republic* (New York, 1943), pp. 261 ff.
36. *Works of Thomas Jefferson*, ed. Paul Leicester Ford (New York, 1904/5), Vol. VIII, p. 252.
37. In this regard, as brilliant a scholar as W. I. Binkley is entirely on the wrong track; see his book—interesting and stimulating in detail, but beside the point in principle—*American Political Parties: Their Natural History* (New York, 1943).

FOOTNOTES TO CHAPTER IX

1. Aristotle, *Aristotle's Politics*, trans. Benjamin Jowett, Modern Library edn. (New York, 1943), Bk. III, Chap. 4.
2. *Ibid.*, Chap. 6.
3. P. H. Douglas, *Real Wages in the United States, 1890–1926* (New York, 1930), pp. 572 ff.

4. Rudolf Smend, *Verfassung und Verfassungsrecht,* quoted from *Staatsrechtliche Abhandlungen* (Berlin, 1955), pp. 35–6.
5. *Notes on the State of Virginia;* quoted from Saul K. Padover, *The Complete Jefferson* (New York, 1943), p. 648.
6. A. Allan Nevins, *The American States during and after the Revolution* (New York, 1924), p. 335.
7. A Baltimore newspaper had opposed the war with England. A crowd gathered, smashed the printing plant and attacked the editors in their homes. To save them from the violence of the mob, they were taken into custody. The mob, during the night, forced the prison; one of the editors was killed on the spot, the others left for dead. The jury acquited the guilty parties when they were brought to trial.—Alexis de Tocqueville, *Democracy in America,* ed. Phillips Bradley, Vintage Books edn. (New York, 1955), I, 271–2.
8. The following passages may be taken to present de Tocqueville's case in his own language:

   "A majority taken collectively may be regarded as a being whose opinions, and, most frequently, whose interests, are opposed to those of another being, which is styled a minority. If it be admitted that a man possessing of absolute power may misuse that power by wrongdoing his adversaries, why should not a majority be liable to the same reproach? Men are not apt to change their characters by agglomeration; nor does their patience in the presence of obstacles increase with the consciousness of their strength . . ."

   "No one will assert that a people cannot forcibly wrong another people; but parties may be looked upon as lesser nations within a greater one, and they are aliens to each other: if, therefore, it be admitted that a nation can act tyrannically towards another nation, it cannot be denied that a party may do the same towards another party." (*Ibid.,* p. 269.)

   The arguments later presented by Calhoun are strikingly similar to those of de Tocqueville, as the following sentences will indicate:

   "One portion of the community may be crushed, and another elevated, by systematically perverting the power of taxation and disbursement, for the purpose of aggrandizing and building up one portion of the community at the expense of the other. That it *will* be so used, unless prevented, is, from the constitution of man, just as certain as that it *can* be so used; and that, if not prevented, it must give rise to two parties, and to violent conflicts and struggles between them . . ."—*The Works of John C. Calhoun* (New York, 1883), p. 22.

   "Neither religion nor education can counteract the strong tendency of the numerical majority to corrupt and debase the peoples." *Ibid.,* p. 51.
   Calhoun does not reject majority rule outright, but wants decisions by "concurrent majorities." Practically, this means that federal issues pertaining to the interests of the South are not to be decided without the South's consent. Within each of the "concurrent majorities" majority rule is in order.
9. Saul K. Padover, *op. cit.,* p. 385.
10. Since this was realized by Alfieri in the eighteenth century, we may quote in full what was quoted in part in the preceding chapter:

   "If in some things the English republic seems more firmly based than the Roman, this is because there is in England a permanent and vitalizing disagreement, not, as in Rome, between the nobles and the people, but between the people and the people: that is, between the ministry and the opposition. Thus, because this disagreement is generated not by disparity of hereditary interests, but by disparity of changing opinion, it does perhaps more good than harm; for no one so completely belongs to one party that he might not often pass over to the opposite; neither of the two parties having interests permanently opposed to and incompatible with the good of the whole." G. de Ruggiero, *The History of European Liberalism* (Oxford, 1928), p. 283.

11. Josiah Phillips Quincy, *The Protection of Majorities* (Boston, 1876), p. 6.
12. William Henry Chamberlain, "The Sources of Russia's Strength, *Harpers' Magazine*, March, 1943, p. 402.
13. Quincy, *op. cit.*, p. 66.

FOOTNOTES TO CHAPTER X

1. G. Salemi, "Il nuovo diritto pubblico e le sue caratteristiche fondamentali," *Revista di Diritto Pubblico*, Anno XIII, 1921, pp. 37 ff.
2. See above, pp. 55 ff.
3. See Lindsay Rogers and W. R. Dittmar, "The Reichswirtschaftsrat: De Mortuis," *The Political Science Quarterly*, L (1935), pp. 481–501. Rogers and Dittmar share the rather skeptical view of the value of the institution which is implied in the above remarks. Friedrich Glum, *Der deutsche und der franzoesische Reichswirtschaftsrat* (Berlin, 1929), is more optimistic, as is the best known of the authors writing on the subject from the point of view of inside knowledge, Professor Ludwig Heyde. See, in particular, his essay "Prinzipien- und Gestaltungsfragen eines Reichswirtschaftsrats," published in *Festschrift fuer Max Pappenheim, Veroeffentlichungen der Schleswig-Holsteinischen Universitaetsgesellschaft* (Breslau, 1931), pp. 484 ff.

   E. Pendleton Herring, "The Czechoslovak Advisory Board for Economic Questions," *The American Political Science Review*, XXIV (1930), deals persuasively with the general problem. On the overall aspects of the matter see also Carl J. Friedrich, *Constitutional Government and Democracy* (rev. ed.; Boston, 1950), pp. 460 ff. and 649 ff.
4. For a frank and revealing treatment of the relation between the "corporative" organizations and the Fascist party, see Francesco Ercole, "La Funzione del Partito nell' Ordinamento Corporativo," *Archivio di studi corporativi*, II (1931–1932). Much material on the matter is also to be found in the bimonthly *Critica Fascista*, ed. Giuseppe Bottai, who had more to do with the details of the "corporative" system than any other man.
5. Benito Mussolini, *Fascism: Doctrine and Institutions* (Rome, 1935), p. 60. See also pp. 40–41, Notes 15 and 16.
6. It is interesting to note that the books praising Salazar's "corporative state" have the feature in common that when they reach the point where they should give concrete descriptions of practical developments, they quote excerpts from Salazar's speeches, which at best are promises, and add analyses of his "doctrine." The word "doctrine" is, in these cases, used in the sense of Maurras, from whose ideas, incidentally, Salazar has borrowed freely. This is evident from the collection of his early speeches, edited by M. Maeterlinck, under the title, *Une Révolution dans la Paix* (Paris, n.d.).
7. Guglielmo Ferrero, *The Principles of Power: The Great Political Crises of History* (New York, 1942).
8. David Shub, *Lenin*, Signet Book edn. (New York, 1950), p. 50.
9. For the most important of the vocational parliaments now existing, the French "Economic Council," see my contribution on "Functional Autonomy" in Arnold Zurcher ed., *Constitutions and Constitutional Trends since World War II* (New York, 1951), pp. 116 ff., and the literature quoted there. For more recent developments see Maurice Aubry, *Le Conseil Economique* (Paris,

1953) and Edward G. Lewis, "The Operation of the French Economic Council," *The American Political Science Review*, March, 1955.

10. This sentence is taken from the editorial introduction to a series of articles on the "Conseil Economique" published by the periodical *Politique* of July–August, 1948.

11. See Herman Finer, *Representative Government and a Parliament of Industry: a Study of the German Federal Economic Council* (London, 1949), and, for his later views, *The Theory and Practice of Modern Government* (rev. ed.; New York, 1949), pp. 543 ff.

12. We call them "pseudo-parties" because they are not basically intended to function as parts of the whole. Thus the program of the "French Agrarian and Peasants' Party" which existed during the final decades of the Third Republic, contained these sentences:

"The mass of the peasants is becoming, little by little, aware of its class interests, and of the enormous advantages which it could derive from an organization into a compact and disciplined bloc. The peasant class has in the economic field no interest in common with the other classes of producers."
—Fernand Corcos, *Catéchisme des partis politiques* (Paris, 1932), p. 36.

13. *Camera dei Deputati, Discussioni*, Legislatura XXV, p. 19737.

14. Maurice Duverger, *Political Parties*, English edn., foreword by D. W. Brogan (New York, 1954), pp. 284 ff.

15. Walter Bagehot, *The English Constitution*, The World's Classics edn. (New York, 1928), p. 127.

16. Helmut Unkelbach, *Grundlagen der Wahlsystematik: Stabilitaetsbedingungen der parlamentarischen Demokratie* (Goettingen, 1956), pp. 59 ff.

17. Thus Esmein, the noted French jurist wrote:

"Ingenious people have set themselves to the task of giving to it (P.R.) an exact and practical expression. They were not at all always jurists and political philosophers; more often indeed they were mathematicians, because it was above all necessary to solve a mathematical problem. This fact, I admit, would be sufficient to put me on my guard against this system, for I believe that the juridical spirit is quite different from the mathematical spirit."—A. Esmein and H. Nézard, *Eléments de Droit Constitutionel Français et Comparé* (Paris, 1927), I, 348.

18. See in particular, C. G. Hoag and G. H. Hallett, Jr., *Proportional Representation* (New York, 1926), and G. H. Hallett, Jr., *P.R.—The Key To Democracy* 2nd ed.; New York, 1940).

19. F. A. Hermens, *Democracy or Anarchy? A Study of Proportional Representation* (Notre Dame, 1941), pp. 43–50.

20. The "quota" is usually computed by taking the lowest possible number of votes which only as many candidates can reach as are to be elected. This means for a city council of nine that the total number of valid votes must be divided by ten and one added to the result. If, for example, 100,000 valid votes are cast, the quota would be 10,001. If a quota were computed by dividing the number of votes into the number of seats, in this case nine, candidates might be elected who poll a smaller percentage of the total vote than others who have been defeated. See Hoag and Hallett, *Proportional Representation*, pp. 378 ff.

21. Thomas Hare, *The Election of Representatives, Parliamentary and Municipal* (4th ed.; London, 1873), pp. xv and 26–7.

22. Colonel Sherrill stated:

"For a long time, the bad effects of the P.R. system have been apparent to the thinking people of this community. We have seen how this method of election accentuates racial, religious and other differences emphasizing the importance of minority groups rather than the welfare of the entire citizenship.

"The P.R. system lends itself to block or group voting rather than consideration of the individual candidate's character and ability."—*The Cincinnati Times-Star*, January 16, 1951.

23. One newly-elected member had decided to go to Ireland for his honeymoon and did not return in time to be present for the meeting in which the new council was organized. See Hermens, *Democracy or Anarchy?*, pp. 395 ff.; on subsequent events see Hermens, *P.R., Democracy, and Good Government* (Notre Dame, 1943), pp. 41 ff.

24. See the editorial entitled "The Great What Is It?," *The New York Post*, November 15, 1943.

25. Hoag and Hallett, *Proportional Representation*, p. 117.

26. Josiah Phillips Quincy, *The Protection of Majorities* (Boston, 1876), p. 22.

FOOTNOTES TO CHAPTER XI

1. *Parliamentary Debates: Official Report, House of Commons*, Vol. 393 (1943), 28, October 1943, col. 406.

2. Lord Mahon, *History of England*, II, 304. Here quoted from W. Hasbach, *Die Parlamentarische Kabinettsregierung* (Berlin, 1919), p. 51.

3. It is defended with particular acumen in Bagehot's *The English Constitution*, The World's Classics edn. (New York, 1928), pp. 156 ff.

3a. Sir Ivor Jennings, *Cabinet Government* (2nd ed.; Cambridge, 1951), pp. 461–3.

4. Bagehot, *op. cit.*, p. 13.

5. Philip Viscount Snowden, *An Autobiography* (London, 1934), VI, 1010 ff.

6. *Ibid.*, II, 601–03.

7. *Report of the Royal Commission appointed to Inquire into Electoral Systems* (London, 1910), p. 29.

8. For the details, see D. E. Butler, *The Electoral System in Britain* (Oxford, 1953), pp. 58 ff.

8a. See the figures as given in the Nuffield series on these elections in: R. B. McCallum and Alison Readman, *The British General Election of 1945* (London, 1947); H. G. Nicholas, *The British General Election of 1950* (London, 1951); D. E. Butler, *The British General Election of 1951* (London, 1952), and D. E. Butler, *The British General Election of 1955* (London, 1955).

9. See Ramsey Muir's book, *How Britain Is Governed* (London, 1930), Chapters IV and V, and, for a criticism of Muir's views, Harold J. Laski, *Parliamentary Government in England* (New York, 1938), pp. 57–60.

10. In the words of Sir Ivor Jennings: "In truth, the rights of minorities depend not only upon expressed rules but upon the customs of the House. It is not a custom which goes back to immemorial antiquity. The impartiality of the Speaker, for instance, has lasted little more than a century—a short time in the history of Parliament. In the days when any minister was liable to impeachment after his fall, ministers in the full glory of their power were not tender of their opponents' rights. So long as the House was ruled by bribery and corruption, the conventional rules implicit in a democratic system could not be developed."—I. Jennings, *Parliament* (London, 1940), p. 52.

11. For all details, see F. A. Hermens, *Democracy or Anarchy? A Study of Proportional Representation* (Notre Dame, 1941), pp. 110–14.

12. Karl Loewenstein, "Militant Democracy and Fundamental Rights," *The American Political Science Review*, August, 1937.

13. F. A. Hermens, *Europe Between* . . . , pp. 88–93.
14. *Report of the Royal Commission* . . . , p. 29.
15. F. A. Hermens, *Democracy or Anarchy?*, pp. 309 ff.; *Europe Between* . . . , pp. 102 ff.
16. For the details see Jennings, *Cabinet Government*, pp. 20 ff.
16a. L. S. Amery, *Thoughts on the Constitution* (London, 1947), pp. 21–2.
16b. *Ibid.*, pp. 21–2.
17. For the theory of this system see, in addition to Bagehot's *English Constitution*, Robert Redslob, *Die Parlamentarische Regierung in Ihrer Wahren und in Ihrer Unechten Form* (Tuebingen, 1918), and *Le Régime Parlementaire* (Paris, 1924). For a more recent discussion, see Friedrich Glum, *Das Parlamentarische Regierungssystem in Deutschland, Grossbrittannien und Frankreich* (Munich, 1950).
18. Winston Churchill, *The Gathering Storm*, Vol. I of *The Second World War* (Boston, 1948), p. 663. Quoted by permission of Houghton Mifflin Co.
19. *Ibid.*, p. 663.
20. See the editorial entitled "The Road Forward," *The Times*, January 11, 1957.
21. See, for details, the report by Jean Wetz published in *Le Monde* of January 12, 1957, under the title "En formant le nouveau cabinet M. Macmillan devra ménager les diverses tendances du parti conservateur." It is held that maneuvers in favor of Macmillan antedated Eden's decision to resign, and that they were facilitated by the aristocratic background of those who influenced the Queen's choice, including the Queen's private secretary, Sir Michael Addane, as well as Lord Salisbury and Sir Winston Churchill. The British press was much more restrained in its comments. Thus *The Manchester Guardian* began its comments (article entitled "Courage and Personality—Traits Needed in New Leader," January 17, 1956) with the sentence: "It was a mercy that doubts about the succession were so quickly put to rest." Similarly, an article by Roger Fulford, appearing in the same issue (dealing with the general topic of "The Queen's Prerogative: The Choice of Premier") concludes: ". . . the country . . . can be deeply grateful that the Sovereign made a swift and clear decision which gave scant opportunity for the rather discreditable intrigues which have too often marred these occasions in our past history."
    So far as the choice between Butler and Macmillan is concerned, attention might also be paid to what *The Atlantic Magazine* expressed as follows: "Lord Salisbury, Sir Winston, Sir Anthony, and Mr. Macmillan have one striking thing in common. They all refused to vote for the Munich agreement in 1938. But R. A. Butler, Macmillan's rival for the post, had voted for Munich as Foreign Under Secretary. The issue of appeasement perhaps had come up once again. The views of Tory members of Parliament were also brought to the Queen. The feeling against Butler, in spite of his pre-eminence as the Tory tactician and philosopher, was stronger among right wingers than the feeling against Macmillan was among moderates."—"The Atlantic Report on London," March, 1957, p. 8.
22. For some of the results see Bagehot, *op. cit.*, pp. 60, 64.
23. Such as Jennings, *Cabinet Government*, p. 319.
24. Paul Emden, *Behind the Throne* (London, 1934).
25. From the time of his book, *Democracy in Crisis* (Chapel Hill, 1934).
26. This mood is reflected in André Siegfried's book, *La Crise Britannique au Vingtième Siècle* (Paris, 1931), according to which Britain had entered a period of apparently unstoppable decline.
27. There is a great deal of literature on the subject, but the few pages on it in Herbert Morrison's *Government and Parliament: A Survey from the Inside* (London, 1954), pp. 77–80, while critical of the formation of the National Government, probably present as fair a summary of the situation as can be obtained. Jennings, *Cabinet Government*, pp. 40–42, is less critical.

28. F. A. Hermens, *Der Staat und die Weltwirtschaftskrise* (Vienna, 1936), pp. 178 ff.
29. Bagehot, *op. cit.*, p. 67.
29a. For Hugh Dalton's own version, see his memoirs, *The Fateful Years* (London, 1956), pp. 468–9. Dalton makes no reference to any advice by the King.
30. "Clearing the Issue," *The Manchester Guardian Weekly*, December 11, 1936.
31. Bagehot, *op. cit.*, p. 63.
32. See his column entitled "Political Background of Abdication Now Emerging," *The New York Times*, December 15, 1936.
33. Thus Herbert Morrison writes: "It was a Conservative Government and the words in themselves were acceptable to the Labour Party. But I did not think well of it, for it was a case of the Sovereign publically expressing views on matters which were the subject of political controversy."—*op cit.*, p. 82.
34. See, in particular, his internationally broadcast tour of a German factory made under the guidance of the "Leader of the Worker's Front," Dr. Ley. *The New York Times* of October 12, 1937, reported the incident under the heading: "Windsor Received Warmly by Nazis; Sees Model Plant. He Is Taken to Machine Works by Ley; Hears Concert and Shares Workers' Fare."
35. Thus F. Kuhn Jr., reports in *The New York Times* of December 8, 1936: "The history of far-off days leaped back to life in the House of Commons to-day as Parliament men and King's men clashed again for the first time in almost 300 years.

"There was an echo of long ago in the roar of cheers that swept the Chamber as Prime Minister Stanley Baldwin entered and strode to his place. The ovation rolled and reverberated from all parts of the House long after he had taken his place on the front bench.

"It was not a tribute to Mr. Baldwin alone, although the members could see from his face that he had been going through a terrific struggle in the past few days. The cheers had a deep-throated and defiant ring about them, as if to show that the House of Commons was still master and could even prevent a King's marriage, if necessary." Mr. Churchill, then outstanding among the King's supporters, took the view that the issue of "King versus Parliament" was not involved; see his contribution to the House of Commons debate of December 10, 1956, in *Parliamentary Debates: Official Report, House of Commons*, vol. 318 (1936–37), col. 2175 ff. Brief declarations were made by Mr. Attlee for the Labour party, Sir Archibald Sinclair for the Liberals, followed by personal statements by Mr. Churchill and Col. Wedgwood. The equally brief remarks by Mr. Maxton, speaking for the Independent Labour party, and Mr. Gallagher, the lone Communist member of the House, are more interesting. According to both, the events connected with the abdication crisis showed that the institution of monarchy allowed the country to be drawn into difficulties which, they felt, a republic could avoid. Mr. Gallagher, in addition, drew attention to "The fact that Mrs. Simpson has a social set, and every Member of the Cabinet knows that the social set of Mrs. Simpson is closely identified with a certain foreign government and the Ambassador of that foreign government"—*Ibid.*, pp. 2194–5.

The answer to the republican conclusions drawn from these premises was given by Col. Wedgwood: The King (Edward VIII) himself, by the act of abdication, had made sure of undivided loyalty being accorded to his successor. *Ibid.*, p. 2194.

The entire discussion lasted only from 3:47 P.M. to 6:53 P.M. and was conducted with the decorum characteristic of the House at its best. There is no other parliament in the world which could have debated such an issue with an equal lack of acrimony. Personal feelings ran deep, but they were controlled. Few observers stopped long enough to ask themselves whether any of the various reforms of the British political system recommended, in particular those pertaining to the system of voting, would not have jeopardized the basic homogeneity on constitutional issues, and the ability to make rapid decisions, which allowed the House (and the Cabinet which it supported) to settle the issue in a manner which, contrary to the expectations of Mr. Maxton and Mr. Gallagher, not only did not expose any weakness of the institution of parliamentary monarchy, but heightened its value.

Sir Winston Churchill, incidentally, commented on the crisis briefly in *The Gathering Storm*, pp. 217–19. For the Duke of Windsor's version of these events, see *A King's Story: The Memoirs of the Duke of Windsor* (New York, 1951).

36. It has not escaped serious criticism in Britain even if it may be difficult to find a remedy for its excesses which would be compatible with the freedom of the press. See "The Press of Our Time," *The Economist*, July 21, 1956.

37. Bagehot, *op. cit.;* see, in particular, pp. 52, 63–4; 76–7.

38. *Ibid.,* p. xx.

39. For details, see Hermens, *Democracy or Anarchy?* pp. 309–11; *Europe Between Democracy and Anarchy*, pp. 101–06.

40. Such circumstances might, of course, arise, and they were difficult to define in any constitutional document. It is, therefore, useful both to have a potential restraint on a Prime Minister and to have it flexible. The very existence of the restraint should make it unnecessary to use it; a Prime Minister who has to ask a King for a dissolution will want to have good arguments available in favor of his decision should he be called upon to produce them.

41. Basically, the situation has not altered since Bagehot wrote: "The position of most men in parliament forbids their being invited to the cabinet; the position of a few men ensures their being invited. Between the compulsory list whom he must take, and the impossible list whom he cannot take, a Prime Minister's independent choice in the formation of a cabinet is not very large; it extends rather to the division of the cabinet offices than to the choice of cabinet ministers. Parliament and the nation have pretty well settled who shall have the first places; but they have not discriminated with the same accuracy which man shall have which place."—Bagehot, *op. cit.,* p. 11.

42. For an apt comparison of cabinet members in England with those in the United States, see Harold J. Laski, *The American Presidency* (New York, 1940), pp. 70 ff.

43. Unless there is to be a purely Congressional cabinet, whose members would not hold any executive office. See Edward S. Corwin, *The President, Office, and Powers* (3rd ed.; New York, 1948), pp. 361–2.

44. Harry S. Truman, *Year of Decisions*, Vol. I of *Memoirs* (Garden City, 1955), 327–30; 550–60.

45. For the details see Morrison, *op. cit.,* pp. 5–6.

46. Robert E. Sherwood, *Roosevelt and Hopkins; An Intimate History* (New York, 1948), p. 31. Quoted by permission of Harper Bros.

47. As Walter Bagehot puts it: ". . . the principle of parliament is obedience to leaders. Change your leader, if you will, take another if you will, but obey No. 1 while you serve No. 1, and obey No. 2 when you have gone over to No. 2. The penalty of not doing so is the penalty of impotence. It is not that you will not be able to do any good, but you will not be able to do anything at all." *Op. cit.,* p. 125.

48. John Stuart Mill, *Considerations on Representative Government* (New York, 1862), p. 109.

49. So far as the United States is concerned, suffice it to mention an incident which occurred during the first Congress of Madison's administration. The House was endeavoring to reduce military expenditures, and a resolution to this effect was adopted by a vote of 60 to 31. Resolutions were then offered to carry out the details, "but no sooner did the House go into committee (of

the Whole) than the members astonished themselves by striking out each section in succession. Gunboats, frigates, navy yards, and marines each managed to obtain a majority against reduction."—Henry Adams, *History of the United States*, V, 204. Quoted from W. E. Binkley, *The Powers of the President* (New York, 1937), p. 55.

50. In the United States, organization is provided by the standing committees; in addition, executive leadership has become a vital part of the legislative process. For a brief comparison between British and American experience, see George B. Galloway, *Congress and Parliament: Their Organization and Operation in the U.S. and the U.K.* (Washington D.C., 1955).

51. As John Stuart Mill put it: "It is true that a great statesman is he who knows when to depart from traditions, as well as to adhere to them; but it is a great mistake to suppose that he will do this better for being ignorant of the traditions."—*Op. cit.*, p. 104.

52. Walter Bagehot compares the workings of an unorganized parliamentary assembly with those of the "quarter sessions" in English counties to which the government entrusted the duty of combating the cattle plague: ". . . the scene in most 'shire halls' was unsatisfactory. There was the greatest difficulty in getting, not only a right decision, but *any* decision. I saw one myself which went thus. The Chairman proposed a very complex resolution, in which there was much everyone liked, and much which everyone disliked, though, of course, the favourite parts of some were the objectionable parts to others. This resolution got, so to speak, wedged in the meeting; everyone suggested amendments; one amendment was carried which none were satisfied with, and so the matter stood over."—*Op. cit.*, p. 123.

53. Concerning "private members' bills," see Jennings, *Parliament* (London, 1940), pp. 348 ff. and A. P. Herbert, *The Ayes Have It* (New York, 1938), pp. 68 ff.

53a. For the monetary situation as it prevailed on these occasions, and the results of the government's action, see H. D. MacLeod, *The Theory and Practice of Banking* (London, 1866), II, 139, 153, 158–9.

54. Herbert Morrison, rightly says: "The word sounds aggressive, tyrannical, and even physically painful. Doubtless this adds to the feeling that the Whips are more terrible people than they are."—*Op. cit.*, p. 100.

55. Jennings, *Parliament*, p. 79.

56. See his Introduction to Bagehot's *English Constitution*, p. x.

57. On the relation between party leader and party in the two major parties, see R. T. McKenzie, *British Political Parties* (London, 1954), pp. 297 ff.; on party committees, see Galloway, *op. cit.*, pp. 47–51.

58. Jennings, *Parliament*, pp. 95–6.

59. The exceptions are the 9 "Law Lords," the 2 Archbishops and 24 Bishops, and the 16 representatives of the Scottish peerage elected for each parliament. There remain a few survivors of the Irish peers elected for life before the passing of the Free State Act in 1922.

60. On the entire incident, as well as on the House of Lords in general, see Charlotte and Denis Plimmer, "Britain's Ermine-Trimmed Encyclopedia," *The Diplomat*, quoted from *Reader's Digest*, January 1957, pp. 97 ff., 99–100.

61. "The Future of the House of Lords," special issue of *Parliamentary Affairs*, edited by Sydney D. Bailey, Winter 1953–54, pp. 154 ff.

62. See, for example, the essay by Walter Elliot, in *The Future of the House of Lords* (London, 1954), pp. 121 ff., and Herbert Morrison, *op. cit.*, pp. 171 ff.

63. See the book published under that title by Hanson W. Baldwin (New York, 1950).

64. On "Life Peerages," see the essay contributed under this title by Sydney D. Bailey, *op. cit.*, pp. 109 ff., and the "Agreed Statement on Conclusion of Conference of Party Leaders in the Parliament Bill," 1948, Bailey, pp. 170 ff.

65. Not all important aspects of British parliamentary government could be treated; the Civil Service is one of them. Its existence, however, is closely related to the modern two-party system which, instead of having been made acceptable by the Civil Service, as Lord Balfour suggests, has created and respected this Civil Service.

Similarly, many observers attribute the success of British parliamentary government to the rules of the House of Commons. These rules are, again, the creatures of the two-party system; wherever clear majorities exist, rules will be adopted which exclude obstruction; at the same time, wherever the influence exerted by the undecided voter in the center in favor of moderation is as great as it is in Britain, it will be logical for the rights of the parliamentary minority to be protected by parliamentary rules and customs, all the more since each party knows that it will be the minority at times.

FOOTNOTES TO CHAPTER XII

1. The exception is the use of the alternative vote for the Australian House of Representatives and of proportional representation for the Senate. Both deviations from the "pure" pattern of parliamentary government have had their effects, of which the rise of the Country party has been most notable; it has given to cabinets under Liberal leadership some of the aspects of coalition government.
2. Walter Bagehot, *The English Constitution*, The World's Classics edn. (New York, 1928), p. 297.
3. A more detailed investigation would have to take into account that the political institutions of the non-Teutonic, in particular Celtic population elements were not too different from those of their Teutonic rivals.
4. "Germany and Its Tribes," *The Complete Works of Tacitus*, Modern Library edn. (New York, 1942), p. 714.
5. Marongiu, *L'Institution Parlementaire en Italie des origines à 1500* (Rome, 1949), pp. 144 ff.; quoted from V. E. Orlando, "La Forme de Gouvernement en vigueur en Italie aux terms de la Constitution de 1948," *Revue Internationale d'Histoire Politique et Constitutionnelle*, July–December, 1951, p. 171.
6. V. E. Orlando, "La Forme de Gouvernement. . . ."
7. "Publicity" would, perhaps, be a better English word for the French *"notoriété."*
8. Orlando, *op. cit.*
9. Wars provided, as a rule, the immediate cause for summoning parliaments. The overall expenditures of the King had, however, begun to rise. This long-term trend, continuing in our time, was more important than any war.
10. On the representative institutions of the Iroquois see above, pp. 13 ff.
11. To this "transfer" of institutions from one country to another there applies what Robert von Keller has said in regard to the medieval guarantees of individual and corporate rights:

"In the field of law, as in other fields of culture there develop in a given time certain *basic forms* which from there on are available to those who form new institutions again and again as at least a possibility of formation and formulation. Where new tasks of political formation must be solved there develop spontaneously out of the cooperation of foreign thought and domestic thought new legal norms, which will prove themselves as weapons in the struggle for spiritual and material goals."—*Freiheitsgarantien für Person und Eigentum im Mittelalter* (Heidelberg, 1933), p. 261.

12. The prestige enjoyed by England in recent centuries is the principal reason why advocates of parliamentary institutions would refer to the British example; otherwise, some attention might have been paid to the case of Sweden. See Robert Redslob, *Le Régime Parlementaire* (Paris, 1924), pp. 136 ff.

13. Robert von Keller, *op. cit.*, p. 262.

14. Simon of Montfort had convoked such a parliament in 1265, but since he was a revolutionary leader, only his partisans attended.

15. For a brief summary see Duverger, *Les Constitutions de la France* (Paris, 1946), pp. 27–8; for the details, see Jacques Cadart, *Le régime électoral des états généraux de 1789 et ses origines, 1302–1614* (Paris, 1952).

16. Even in England the power of parliament did not move upwards in a straight line. It was great through much of the fourteenth century, but receded during the fifteenth, reaching a low point under Henry VIII and Elizabeth.

17. A colonel of the English revolutionary army came to Bordeaux and proposed that the French adopt a Constitution translated from the act which the army had imposed upon the British parliament in 1648. It contained a long preamble on the natural rights of man, about which Charles Seignobos says: "That is the oldest declaration of rights in French, and it is the work of an Englishman."—*L'Histoire Sincère de la Nation Française* (Paris, 1933), pp. 290–1.

18. Such tendencies may arise from the excessive weakness of a state; Luxembourg or Liechtenstein, for example, are not likely to build up large standing armies. Also, once a modern democracy has fully established itself its political processes will, contrary to the records of the "republics" mentioned by Hamilton in No. 6 of *The Federalist*, operate to restrain warlike tendencies. See F. A. Hermens, "Peace and Democracy," *America*, June 16, 1945.

19. *The Federalist*, Modern Library edn. (New York, n.d.), p. 45.

20. Baron de Montesquieu, *The Spirit of the Laws*, Hafner Library of Classics edn., trans. Thomas Nugent (New York, 1949), Bk. XI, Chap. 6, p. 161.

21. Adolf Gasser, *Geschichte der Volksfreiheit und der Demokratie* (Aarau, 1949), pp. 76 ff. and 104 ff.

22. E. de Laveleye, *Le gouvernement dans la démocratie* (Paris, 1891), II, 435.

23. *The Federalist*, No. 8, p. 43.

24. No English translation can give the full flavor of the rather ungrammatical German original. See E. Hubrich, *Deutsches Fürstentum und Deutsches Verfassungswesen* (Leipzig, 1905), p. 48.

25. *Ibid.*, p. 49.

26. Force was not absent from this unification, and it could be used successfully again on account of reasons arising out of the field of geography; no foreign country could easily take advantage of the conflict between England and Scotland to invade the island. In this regard matters were different when, for example, the Hapsburgs had all but succeeded, in the Treaty of Prague concluded in 1635, in uniting Germany on their own terms, and Cardinal Richelieu sent the armies of France to help the German Protestants against the (Catholic) Emperor. The Treaty of Westphalia, which was the result, sealed the disintegration of Germany. At the same time, it created that power vacuum in the northern part of that nation which Brandenburg-Prussia lost little time in filling.

27. Bagehot, *op. cit.*, p. 6.

28. This process, in all of the countries concerned, was fostered by the fact that the nobility passed on titles of nobility to all of the children rather than to the eldest son. It has been stated that, had no titles of nobility been granted in England since 1789, the English nobility would have become extinct, whereas that of France would be strong even without the addition to the ranks of

noble families made by the monarchy after the Restoration and by the two empires.—"Peers from the People," *The Economist,* July 21, 1956.

29. Members of the Prussian Diet were elected by an electoral college. The first third of the electors were chosen by those paying the first third of the taxes, the second third by those paying the next third, with the bulk of the people (who payed enough indirect, but hardly any direct taxes) limited to the last third.

30. "Minutes of Evidence," *Report of the Royal Commission appointed to inquire into Electoral Systems* (London, 1910), pp. 129–150.

31. A. L. Lowell, *The Government of England* (New York, 1912), I, 31 ff.

32. Ramsay MacDonald, *Socialism and Government* (London, 1909).

33. See Harold Laski, *The Grammar of Politics* (3rd ed.; London, 1934), pp. 315–18, and *Parliamentary Government in England* (New York, 1938), pp. 58–60.

34. Herman Finer, "The Case against Proportional Representation," Fabian Tract #211 (London, 1935).

35. Sir Ivor Jennings, *Parliament* (London, 1940), pp. 120; 128.

36. For the details see F. A. Hermens, *Europe Between Democracy and Anarchy* (Notre Dame, 1951), pp. 150–1.

37. See Guy Mollet's speech to the National Assembly of January 31, 1956.

38. Waldemar Gurian, *Die Politischen und Socialen Ideen des Franzoesischen Katholizismus, 1789–1914* (Muenchen, 1929), a classic in the field which should be translated into English in spite of the time which has passed since its publication.

39. Jacques Maritain, *La République Française,* December 1943. The best of Maritain's work on political philosophy has been gathered in a convenient volume by Joseph Evans and Leo R. Ward, *The Philosophy of Jacques Maritain* (New York, 1955).

40. See Don Sturzo's letter to the editor, *Il Giornale d'Italia,* issue of June 11, 1952, and, for a more comprehensive statement of his views, his articles "Proporzionale e Governo," *l'Avvenire d'Italia,* January 24, 1954, and "Proporzionale, pura, corretta, mista," *Il Giornale d'Italia,* February 9, 1954.

41. See pp. 410; 426–7.

42. In this regard they followed their country's pre-Fascist tradition.

43. St. Thomas Aquinas, *On Kingship to the King of Cyprus,* trans. Gerald B. Phelan, ed. I. Th. Eschmann (Toronto, 1949), Bk. I, Chaps. 2 and 5.

44. Sir Austen Chamberlain, "How Democracy Was Extinguished in Spain," *The Daily Telegraph,* October 13, 1936.

45. G. Horwill, *Proportional Representation* (London, 1925), p. 132.

46. "A Quiet Election," *The Economist* (London, 1925), p. 132.

47. "Mr. Baldwin's Victory," *The Economist,* November 23, 1935.

48. There were always exceptions. Thus a prominent Liberal, Erich Koch-Weser, for some time Minister of the Interior during the Weimar Republic—and, as such, in charge of constitutional and electoral legislation—expressed himself critically of P.R. Speaking of conditions prevailing during the Weimar Republic, he wrote:
"The system of proportional representation only increased the evils of the situation. It had been claimed that proportional representation in the Reichstag would afford a mirror of public opinion. But actually it shattered that mirror into splinters that could not be used for government purposes."— *Hitler and Beyond* (New York, 1945), p. 39. Quoted by permission of Alfred A. Knopf, Inc.

49. See André Siegfried's article entitled "Remettre la Montre à l'Heure," *Le Figaro,* December 16, 1955.

50. For an outline of a theory of these parties see my article "Die Antiparlamentarische Bewegung in Frankreich," *Zeitschrift fuer Politik,* March, 1933.

51. *The Federalist,* No. 10, p. 57.

52. Quoted from *National Socialism: Basic Principles: Their Application by the Nazi Party's Foreign Organization and the Use of Germans Abroad for Nazi Aims,* prepared in the special unit of the Division of European Affairs, U. S. Department of State, by R. E. Murphy and Associates (Washington, D.C., 1943), p. 63.

53. On this claim in regard to Germany, see F. A. Hermens, *Democracy or Anarchy? A Study of Proportional Representation* (Notre Dame, 1941), pp. 288–9.

54. The controlling factor is the electoral system used for a country's major parliament—in France the National Assembly, in Italy the Chamber of Deputies, etc. If, in France, the elections to the departmental councils are held under the old type of majority voting, while the Assembly elections are held under P.R., this does not perceptibly influence a country's political line-up.

Footnotes to Chapter XIII

1. For the details see J. Gouault, *Comment la France est devenue Républicaine: Les élections générales et partielles à l'Assemblée Nationale 1870–75* (Paris, 1954).

2. Quoted from Joseph Barthélemy and Paul Duez, *Traité de Droit Constitutionnel* (Paris, 1933), p. 28.

3. Badly divided, the Monarchists failed to take advantage of their opportunity, and there were 50 moderate Republicans among the 75 elected.

4. In the words of Sir Ivor Jennings: "Impeachment in the seventeenth and early eighteenth centuries was a means for 'liquidating' opponents. The ballot boxes are now available for political opponents and the criminal courts for criminals." —*Parliament* (London, 1940), p. 381.

5. For a comprehensive discussion of the various explanations given for the political instability of the Third Republic, see A. Soulier, *L'Instabilité Ministérielle sous la Troisième République, 1871–1938* (Paris, 1939).

6. For a discussion of French political parties during the Third Republic, see André Siegfried, *France: A Study in Nationality* (New Haven, 1930).

7. The full name is "Republican, Radical, and Radical Socialist party." The three parts represent three different layers in the party's historical development. It grew out of the Republicans who opposed the dictatorship of Napoleon III. When, subsequently, "Radicals" developed at the party's Left, this name was added, true to the slogan, "No enemies at the Left"; in the same manner the designation "Socialist" was acquired.

8. Quoted from Dorothy Pickles, "The Reform of French Political Institutions, *Parliamentary Affairs,* Winter 1956–7, 101.

9. Robert de Jouvenel, *La République des Camarades* (Paris, 1914), p. 89.

10. Charles de Gaulle, *War Memoirs: The Call to Honour, 1940–42* (New York, 1955), p. 8. Quoted by permission of The Viking Press, Inc.

11. Toni Howard, "The Case of the Jolly Jailbirds," *The Saturday Evening Post,* February 25, 1956. See also the series of articles entitled "Il faut réformer notre justice," by Pierre Seize, published in *Le Figaro,* from February 19 to March 12, 1955.

12. Alexander Werth, *France in Ferment* (London, 1934), pp. 79–99.

13. On the political nature of the *Action Française* see my article, "Die Anti-

parlamentarische Bewegung in Frankreich," *Zeitschrift fuer Politik*, March, 1933. It is interesting to note that Daudet was elected thanks to P.R. which, at that time, was in operation in those departments where a party, or combination of parties, failed to secure a majority of the votes cast.—See F. A. Hermens, *Democracy or Anarchy? A Study in Proportional Representation* (Notre Dame, 1941), pp. 125–6; 132.

14. For details see F. A. Hermens, "Parlament und Aussenpolitik in Frankreich," *Hochland*, December 1931.

15. In this respect, matters were to be the same during the Fourth Republic as they had been during the Third. C. L. Sulzberger commented as follows on the efforts to bring about the ratification of the European Defense Community: "Premier Laniel's Cabinet is not only harassed by powerful opposition in the National Assembly but also by civil servants in key positions who are determined to do everything within their power to sabotage E.D.C.'s chances."—"Franco-German Crisis Shaping Up over E.D.C.," *The New York Times*, March 28, 1954.

16. It must, of course, always be borne in mind that the weaknesses in the internal political structure of Germany affected Franco-German relations as much as those in the French political structure; this subject will be discussed below.

17. *The Protestant Ethic and the Spirit of Capitalism* (New York, 1930), p. 88.

18. Walter Bagehot, *The English Constitution*, The World's Classics edn. (New York, 1928), pp. 297–8.

19. René Capitant, "La Crise et la Réforme du Parlementarisme en France," *Jahrbuch des Oeffentlichen Rechts* (Tuebingen, 1936), Vol. 23, p. 68.

20. For the details see *ibid.*

21. Bagehot, *op. cit.*, pp. 125–6.

22. For the details see Hermens, *Democracy or Anarchy?* pp. 125–9, and the literature quoted there.

23. Francois Goguel, "L'Influence des Systèmes Électoraux sur la Vie Politique d'après l'expérience Française," ed. Maurice Duverger, *L'Influence des Systèmes Électoraux sur la Politique* (Paris, 1950), pp. 71–4.

24. The "Littré"—see Jean Mazé, *Le Système* (Paris, 1951), p. 1.

25. "La signification historique des élections françaises de 1928," in *L'Année Politique Française et Etrangère*, July, 1929, p. 259.

26. Capitant, *op. cit.*, p. 27.

27. *Ibid.*

28. Soulier, *op. cit.*, p. 177.

29. *Ibid.*, pp. 177–9.

30. Sheer accident did, at times, play its part in the selection of cabinet members; see Joseph Barthélemy, *Valeur de la Liberté et Adaption de la République* (Paris, 1935), pp. 157 ff.

31. For an account of these events, as well as an analysis of their background, see Laurent Bonnevay, *Les journées sanglantes de février 1934* (Paris, 1935).

32. André Tardieu had published a series of articles in the periodical, *L'Illustration*, beginning in 1931; they appeared later in book form: *L'Heure de la Décision* (Paris, 1934). A booklet by Maurice Ordinaire, entitled *Le Vice Constitutionnel et la Révision* (Paris, 1932), carried a preface by Gaston Doumergue. René Capitant, *La Réforme du Parlementarisme*, contributed a pamphlet to the discussion which was as soundly reasoned as it was unpretentious. For a survey of the extensive literature on the subject, see Karl Braunias, "Die franzoesische Staatsreform im Schrifttum," *Zeitschrift fuer Auslaendisches Oeffentliches Recht und Volkerrecht*, VII (1937), 644 ff.

33. For their final text see *Le Temps*, November 4, 1934.

34. Gaston Jèze, "La Crise Politique," *Journal des Finances*, October 26, 1934.

35. The movement for reform was, as is always the case in France, enmeshed in a great deal of partisan maneuvering. The Left which, after all, had won the

elections of 1932 and been driven from power by the riots of February 6, not unnaturally wanted to take over again. Doumergue (himself a Radical) came to rely more and more on Rightist supporters, including some whose loyalty to the Republic was dubious. The actual effects of institutional reforms bear no relationship, of course, to the motives of those who undertake them, but that was something which the politicians of the Third Republic grasped no more than their successors during the Fourth were to grasp it.

36. See, in particular, Blum's two articles, "Plus de République," *Le Populaire,* October 22, 1934, and "Le Coup d'Etat Légalisé," *Le Populaire,* October 23, 1934.
37. For the details, see Hermens, *Democracy or Anarchy?* pp. 135 ff.
38. The fourth cabinet of Poincaré (July 23, 1926 to November 6, 1928) and the fifth (November 11, 1928 to July 27, 1929) may, in this connection, be regarded as one, as there was continuity of policy as well as of leadership.

FOOTNOTES TO CHAPTER XIV

1. *La France SERA LA FRANCE, Ce que Veut Charles De Gaulle,* pub. by the Rassemblement du Peuple Français (R.P.F.) (Paris, 1951), pp. 18–19.
2. *Ibid.,* pp. 19–20.
3. Marcel Prélot, "Sur le Soixantennaire de Notre Constitution," *Politique,* July–August, 1935, p. 591.
4. The Communists and the Socialists, who polled a majority of the votes cast in the elections of October, 1945, were opposed to a simplified right of parliamentary dissolution. They were, however, unable to cause a majority of the people to ratify the Constitution which they drafted. The same combination of forces which defeated them on that occasion should have been able to win a plebiscite of the kind suggested.
5. For all details see Gordon Wright, *The Reshaping of French Democracy* (New York), 1948, pp. 36 ff. For the text of the draft see "Le Projet de Constitution du Comité Général d'Etudes," *Les Cahiers Politiques,* October, 1945. The basic thought guiding Debré is contained in a memorandum of his written in 1943, published originally in *Les Cahiers Politiques* for April, 1944, and republished as a pamphlet under the title, "Le Problème Constitutionnel Français" (Angers, 1945).
6. Wright, *op. cit.,* p. 38. Quoted by permission of Harcourt, Brace and Co., Inc.
7. For the text see *Les Cahiers Politiques,* October, 1945, pp. 15–17.
8. So far as the system of voting is concerned, he himself later expressed a willingness to accept, temporarily, elections in single-member constituencies with second ballot. See the Council of the Republic's debate on the electoral law in November, 1955, *Journal Officiel de la République Française, Débats Parlementaires,* Conseil de la République, November 9, 1955, pp. 2509 ff.
9. Wright, *op. cit.,* p. 38.
10. For the text of the article, see *Les Cahiers du Communisme,* Organe Théorique du Parti Communiste Français, 20 (1944), pp. 42–51.
11. *Ibid.,* p. 42.
12. See *Le Journal Officiel, Débats Parlementaires,* August 3, 1945.
13. Even in this field the term is burdened with so many psychological connotations that it is well to replace it. The Rev. Stanley Parry has proposed to

speak of it as "The Multicentered Society." See his mimeographed outline on this subject, made available to the author.

14. Political decentralization, leaving as much power as possible to lower units of government, is perfectly compatible with the required unity at the center. Paradoxically, where a national government is reasonably strong, as in the United States, Canada, or Britain, there is a tendency to leave a great deal more autonomy to the lower organs of government than is the case in countries where the central government is weak. The fate of the promises of local autonomy made in the constitutions of France and Italy is a case in point. See F. A. Hermens, "Local Autonomy in France and Italy," *Constitutions and Constitutional Trends since World War II,* ed. Arnold Zurcher (2d ed.; New York, 1955), pp. 95 ff.

15. It must be recalled that few P.R. systems are consistent enough to permit the tendencies inherent in that system of voting to manifest themselves fully. Either the proportionality between votes cast and seats obtained is limited (as by the small constituencies used in Ireland) or the effects of P.R. are, to an appreciable extent, offset by electing the executive directly, under the rules of the majority system. Thus in Cuba the Chamber of Representatives is elected by P.R. but the President under a majority system.

16. F. A. Hermens, *Democracy or Anarchy? A Study of Proportional Representation* (Notre Dame, 1941), pp. 75 ff.

17. Wright, *op. cit.,* p. 35. Apparently, Wright was not aware of the fact that De Gaulle acted under pressure from his allies.

18. Charles De Gaulle, *L'Unité, 1942–44,* Vol. II of *Mémoires de Guerre* (Paris, 1956).

19. Yves Simon, *The March to Liberation* (Milwaukee, 1942), pp. 88, 90–1.

20. Capitant, on that occasion, qualified any change which would cause the country to come back to a dualist system (meaning a dualism between independent presidency and parliament) as "a grave error."—*La Réforme du Parlamentarisme,* pp. 20–21.

21. This particular expression was, of course, used long after the events discussed here, but it clearly characterized his thought at that time.

22. René Capitant, *Pour Une Constitution Fédérale* (Paris, 1946), pp. 15–16.

23. Michel Debré, *La Mort de l'Etat Républicain* (Paris, 1947), pp. 165 ff.

24. *Ibid.,* p. 168.

25. Gordon Wright, *op. cit.,* p. 90.

26. De Gaulle, *La France SERA LA FRANCE,* pp. 63–4.

27. François Goguel, *France under the Fourth Republic* (Ithaca, 1952), p. 52.

28. François Goguel, "Christian Democracy in France," in Mario Einaudi and François Goguel, *Christian Democracy in Italy and France* (Notre Dame, 1952), pp. 109 ff. What the emergence of this movement meant for French politics is best seen against its historical background as described masterfully in Waldemar Gurian, *Die Politischen und sozialen Ideen des franzoesischen Katholizismus, 1789–1914* (Muenchen Gladbach, 1929).

29. For the table see *L'Année Politique, 1944–45,* Preface d'André Siegfried (Paris, 1946), p. 491; for other details, see pp. 200–04.

30. For the table see *ibid.,* p. 492; for details, *ibid.,* pp. 292–4. I am aware that some of the best French experts in the field do not share my interpretation of the chances for effective Communist-Socialist alliances in national elections held under a majority system in 1945. It has been pointed out to me that, in the first place, the French electorate tends to vote more moderately in local and provincial than in national elections. In the second place, many of the *militants* in the French Socialist party (the active party members who are in control of the local and provincial organization) were, in 1945, more favorable to alliances with the Communists than were their national leaders. All of this is correct, and it is also true that, if an attempt were made to make

allowance for the different size of the *cantons* the prospects of the Communists under a majority system in national elections would appear better even if they had had "to go it alone."

If I nevertheless adhere to the interpretation given in the text the reason is that, so far as the inequality of the *cantons* is concerned, the disparity between the percentages of seats won and votes obtained is so great that the adjustments which would attempt to take the inequality of these constituencies into account would hardly affect the order of magnitude.

The same applies to the tendency of the voters to support more moderate candidates in local and provincial than in national elections; it is not sufficiently pronounced to reverse the qualitative element in the results discussed. The pressure of the Socialist *militants* in favor of campaign alliances with the Communists in national elections held under the majority system would have been a serious factor. Yet, the national party leaders, in their reluctance to enter into a new Popular Front type agreement with the Communists could refer to the fact that elections in doubtful constituencies are decided not by *militants* but by undecided voters, who might have defeated candidates presented by a Socialist-Communist coalition in national elections as they did defeat them, in some cases, in the cantonal elections. It is interesting to note that between the two world wars the parliamentary group of the S.F.I.O. in the Chamber was always more moderate than was the majority of the *militants*. As long as the majority system was used, the *militants* simply could not prevail.

31. A. Leduc, "Gallic Trends: Will France Swing Towards Democratic Socialism?" *The New Leader*, October 20, 1945.

32. Lenin wrote on Communist participation in parliaments: "Communism rejects parliamentarianism as a form of future society . . . It rejects the possibility of a protracted conquest of parliaments. It has as its objective the *destruction* of parliamentarianism. Therefore, the point in question can only be the utilization of bourgeois state institutions in order to destroy them. In this sense, and this sense *only*, can the question be raised . . . Communist parties are entering these institutions not to carry out there any regular parliamentary work but in order through their actions to help the masses, via parliament, to destroy the state machinery of the bourgeoisie and parliament itself from within."—Lenin, *Sobrannye sochineniya—Collected Works* (3rd ed., Moscow), XXIII, 581–2. Here quoted from A. Avtorkhanov, "Current Soviet Political Problems," *Bulletin of Institute for the Study of the USSR*, January, 1957, p. 5.

33. Matters were to change when, during the life of the first National Assembly elected under the new constitution, political wear and tear began to take its toll, leading to a splintering process within the Chamber, as well as to a loosening of discipline, in particular within the parties of the Right and Center. Subsequently the loosening of party ties was accentuated as more and more Deputies were the only candidates on their list to be elected. Whoever could manage to do so with a reasonable chance of success tried to be the head of a list of his own since the French electoral system is, to all practical intents and purposes, one of "rigid" lists and the candidates at the top of a list are the ones to be declared elected. In 1951, 209 lists elected only one candidate, and in 1956 the number had increased to 285, a clear majority in the National Assembly. See François Goguel, "Géographie des Élections du 2 Janvier," in *Association Française de Science Politique, Les Élections du 2 Janvier 1956*, Sous la direction de Maurice Duverger, François Goguel and Jean Touchard (Paris, 1957), pp. 504–5. Professor Goguel emphasizes that, since P.R. is advocated in France largely for the purpose of strengthening party organization through the list system the fact that more than half of the Assembly's members were elected as the only members of their list destroys

the supposed advantage and constitutes one more reason for being critical of P.R.

34. See the report on the meeting of the Constituent Assembly of April 1, 1946, pp. 1337 ff. Capitant's speech is reprinted in René Capitant, *Premiers Combats pour la Constitution* (Strasbourg, 1945), pp. 25 ff.

35. It is interesting to note that English terminology uses the term "government" rather than "executive." "Government" is derived from the Latin word *gubernare*, which means "to steer," and a British government fully intends to "steer" rather than merely to "execute" parliamentary directives. "Steering" means, in politics as well as in navigation, choosing a definite course rather than to submit to the zigzagging inevitably resulting from orders of a parliamentary assembly.

36. One of those who took De Gaulle's side was René Capitant; See *Premiers Combats . . .* , pp. 5–6.

37. *Die Verschiebung der konstitutionellen Ordnung durch die Verhaeltniswahl,* first published 1919; here quoted from *Staatsrechtliche Abhandlungen* (Berlin, 1955), pp. 60 ff.

38. See Hermens, *Democracy or Anarchy?* pp. 51 ff.

39. Of course, there are also the "Economic Council" and the "Assembly of the French Union," but neither affects the basic structure of the government.

40. In a few cases, however, the cabinet, even before the reform of the Constitution, had been formed before the Premier-designate presented himself to the National Assembly.

41. *La Quatrième République* (New York, 1946), p. 72. See also his article, "L'échec du parlementarisme 'rationalisé,'" *Revue Internationale d'Histoire Politique et Constitutionnelle,* April–June, 1954.

42. For the background of these events see "Sturz der Regierung Laniel: Erfolgreiches Maneuver der Gaullisten zur Verhinderung einer Aufloesung der Nationalversammlung," *Neue Zurcher Zeitung,* June 14, 1954.

43. "The Reform of French Political Institutions," *Parliamentary Affairs,* Winter (1956–57), p. 98.

44. Professor Romano Guardini drew the author's attention to this circumstance in a conversation dealing with certain aspects of the relationship between politics and ethics.

45. Arthur Taylor Prescott, *Drafting the Federal Constitution* (Baton Rouge, 1941), p. 761.

46. *Ibid.,* p. 750.

47. See William H. Chamberlin, "A Nation in Fragments," *The New Leader* of July 6, 1953.

48. *The Economist,* January 7, 1956.

49. Debré, *La Mort de L'Etat Républicain,* pp. 194–5.

50. *The Economist,* January 7, 1956.

51. See the references on the need for both constitutional and electoral reform in his speech of January 31 to the National Assembly.

52. One of the earliest writers to emphasize that the *scrutin de ballotage* had something in common with P.R. was Yves R. Simon; see his *La Grande Crise de la République Française* (Montréal, 1941), p. 138.

53. See Capitant's speech in the session of the Constituent Assembly of April 2, 1946; here quoted from Capitant, *Premier Combats . . .* , pp. 25 ff.

54. On other attempts to submit the question of the system of voting to the people see Hermens, "Die Wahlrechtsentwicklung der Nachkriegszeit in Frankreich, Italien und Griechenland," *Jahrbuch des Oeffentlichen Rechts,* 1956, pp. 259–61.

55. Max Weber, *Gesammelte Schriften zur Politik* (Munich, 1921), p. 367.

56. Wright, *op. cit.,* pp. 222–3.

57. See Hermens, *Democracy or Anarchy?* pp. 76–7.

57a. Jules Moch, "La Defense de la République," *Le Populaire,* June 13, 1950.

58. The two percentage figures do not refer, however, to the same territory, only half of the country voting on this occasion, and no vote taking place in Paris, where the Communists' strength was above their national average.

59. "A St. Brieuc, M. Pleven a dit," *Le Figaro,* September 11, 1950.

60. For a convenient summary of the various (and at times contradictory) provisions of this law, as well as of the laws preceding it, see *La Documentation Française, Les Elections Legislatives du 17 Juin 1951* (Paris, 1953), pp. 9 ff. This excellent volume also contains the official election statistics. For the author's comments see his articles "The Fourth Republic in Transition," *The Review of Politics,* January, 1952, and "Die Wahlrechtsentwicklung der Nachkriegszeit . . . ," pp. 267 ff. and the literature quoted in both.

61. Peter Campbell, "Remarques sur la loi électorale française du 9 Mai 1951," *Revue Française de Science Politique,* October–December 1951, pp. 489–99.

62. The total membership of the second National Assembly was 627; two seats were not filled at the time for which this calculation was made.

63. Luigi Einaudi, later to become the first President of the Italian Republic after the new Constitution went into effect, emphasized the need for a safety valve strongly in a speech given before his country's Consultative Assembly, in which he opposed the readoption of P.R. See the reprint "Contro La Proporzionale," *Discorso Pronunciato Alla Consulta Nazionale Nella Seduta dell' 11 Febbraio, 1946* (Rome, 1946).

64. For a comment on these events see Jean Farran, "5e Episode: Le Tour de Monsieur Pinay," *Paris-Match,* June 27–July 4, 1953.

65. Formally, the cabinet took no position on the matter. This might in itself have been enough to defeat the treaty, since it hardly ever happens in France that the Assembly makes up its mind on such a subject without government leadership. In addition, Mendès-France's lack of sympathies for the EDC were well known.

66. *Journal Officiel* . . . Assemblée Nationale, issue of October 31, 1955, pp. 538 ff., and the following issues, terminating with the one of November 30, pp. 6038 ff.

67. For the details of the poll see the daily, *L'Express,* of November 3, 1955.

68. See the election results in *Le Monde* of January 4, 1956, and Stuart Schram, "Tableau de la France 1956," published in the Belgian periodical *Socialisme,* January 1956. Since the above was written, the analysis of the elections published by the Association Française de Science Politique (see above Footnote 33) has become available. See, in particular, the contributions by Jacques Fauvet (pp. 14 ff.) and François Goguel (pp. 467 ff).

69. François Goguel, "Les Elections Françaises du 2 Janvier 1956," *Revue Française de Science Politique,* January–March, 1956, p. 6. See also the study by the same author entitled "Partis . . . et Tendances dans Notre Pays," *Recherches,* March, 1956.

70. The *apparentements* were not entirely ineffective. The absolute majority was achieved in 11 cases, compared with 39 in 1951. Besides, allied lists were treated as a unit in the first distribution of the seats; this meant that the advantages accruing to large parties from the small size of the constituencies, and from the method of distributing the seats (the so-called d'Hondt system) were secured by the allied groups. For a comparison between the percentage of the votes and the percentage of the seats, see Schram, *op. cit.,* p. 7.

70a. "The Art of the Impossible," *The Economist,* July 27, 1957.

71. "Pour Assurer la Stabilité Ministérielle M. Reynaud Propose Une Profonde Reforme de la Constitution," *Le Figaro,* Sélection Hebdomadaire, March 19, 1956.

72. The nature of a government does not change when, as in England in January 1957, a new Prime Minister is appointed from the same political party.

73. André Fontaine, "Can the French Save Their Republic," *The Reporter*, November 1, 1956, p. 30, mentions a plan which would give the Premier the right of dissolution, as well as have him elected for the full term of the Assembly. The former feature would, of course, make a difference, and be all that is needed if combined with a return to the majority system.

74. Georges Vedel, "L'Instabilité Gouvernementale," Vedel's report was discussed by Maurice Duverger in articles published in *Le Monde*, issues of April 12 and 13 and May 18, 1956, on which Vedel commented in an article published in the weekly, *Demain*, issue of April 19–25, 1956. The articles by Duverger and Vedel were made available in English by the *Service de Presse et d'Information* of the French Embassy, as Numbers 6–02, 6–03 and 6–04 of its series, "Articles of Opinion." See also Numbers 6–05 and 6–06 in this series, the first containing an article by the prominent Socialist, André Philip, published in *Le Monde* of May 30, and the second an interview with Paul Coste-Floret, one of the MRP leaders, published in *Le Monde* of July 4, 1956. In the following discussion these articles will not be cited in detail.

75. This would make it possible for the voter to indicate a second choice on his ballot.

76. "Vers Une Nouvelle Orientation de la Révision Constitutionelle? *Revue Française de Science Politique*, July–September, 1956.

77. Vedel, *op. cit.*, p. 9.

78. See Léon Blum; in an article in *Le Populaire*; here quoted from "News from France," published by the *Service de Presse et d'Information*, December 5, 1946, p. 9.

79. "Victoire du Bon Sens," *Le Figaro*, weekly edition, February 1, 1957. The term "vote reasonable" is no more grammatical than its equivalent "vote useful," but it serves well to describe the feelings of the French voter who does not want to "throw his vote away." Such considerations are typical of majority voting.—For further details see the report in the weekly edition of *Le Monde*, issue of January 24–30, 1956.
The reduction of both the Communist and the Poujadist vote was, to an appreciable extent, caused by factors not related to the system of voting. Still, one only needs to read the comments on the result in the Parisian press (the sentences quoted from *Le Figaro* are typical) in order to see that the psychological situation is radically different under majority voting from what it is under P.R. Under that system people are not reminded of any social heterogeneity which might make it impossible for them to sink their differences and unite on candidates with a chance of success. They are, in the name of "good sense" (the headline in *Le Figaro*) told what they are expected to do, and enough of them do it to produce an acceptable result.

80. "350 Ministres!" *Le Figaro*, July 3, 1953.

81. In the Constitutional Convention Hamilton said, as summarized by Madison: "No man's ideas were more remote from the plan than his own were known to be; but is it possible to deliberate between anarchy and convulsion on one side, and the chance of good to be expected from the other?"—Prescott, *Drafting the Federal Constitution*, p. 787.

82. The following figures, comparing the years 1935–39 with the years 1948–52 ("Population and Welfare in France," Ambassade de France, Service de Presse et d'Information, No. 43, March, 1957), demonstrate the striking nature of the change which took place:

	Before World War II	After World War II
Average yearly number of births	620,000	850,000
Average yearly number of deaths	640,000	540,000
Net yearly gain or loss	−20,000	310,000

France is, in this respect, much better off than is Western Germany. By

1965 the number of Frenchmen coming of military age will be greater than the number of Germans, although the population of France is 43 million and that of the Federal Republic close to 50 million; see "How France and the U.S. Compare: Populations Growing Rapidly," *France Actuelle*, May 15, 1954. On the overall aspects of the changes for the better which have taken place in France in recent years, see André Maurois, *La France Change de Visage* (Paris, 1956).

83. Robert de Jourenel, *La République des Camarades* (Paris, 1914).

84. In recent years the world has had some reason to complain about French deficiencies. On this matter see the excellent study of F. Furniss, Jr., "Weaknesses in French Foreign Policy Making," published as Memo. No. 5 of the Center of International Studies of Princeton University, February 5, 1954.

FOOTNOTES TO CHAPTER XV

1. Winston S. Churchill, *The Gathering Storm*, Vol. I of *The Second World War* (Boston, 1948), p. 11.
2. *Ibid.*, p. 10.
3. For the details see Friedrich Glum, *Das parlamentarische Regierungssystem in Deutschland, Grossbrittannien, und Frankreich* (Munich, 1950), pp. 62–4, and *The Memoirs of Prince Max of Baden* (New York, 1928), II, 167 ff.
4. The French expression is: "La monarchie constitutionnelle est la meilleure des républiques." The term "constitutional monarchy" is, of course, at best ambiguous; in the above discussion we have limited it to the cases in which the monarch retains the control of the executive.
5. *The Memoirs of Prince Max . . .* , pp. 187–8.
6. For the text of the note see *ibid.*, pp. 305–6.
7. "The Crown Prince was so well-hated by the masses as to be now impossible." —*Ibid.*, p. 303.
8. James T. Shotwell, *At the Paris Conference* (New York, 1937), p. 119. Quoted by permission of The Macmillan Co.
9. See Max Weber, "Parlament und Regierung im Neugeordneten Deutschland," quoted from *Gesammelte Politische Schriften* (Munich, 1921), pp. 126 ff.
10. *Ibid.*, p. 196.
11. *Ibid.*, pp. 256–7.
12. Max Weber, "Deutschlands Kuenftige Staatsform," quoted from *Gesammelte Politische Schriften*, pp. 341 ff.; the quotation itself will be found on p. 363.
13. Arnold Brecht, *Prelude to Silence* (New York, 1944), pp. 47–8. Quoted by permission of Oxford University Press.
14. *Verfassungsausschuss der Nationalversammlung, Berichte und Protokolle* (Berlin, 1920), pp. 242 ff.
15. Theodor Heuss, *Friedrich Naumann* (Stuttgart, 1935), pp. 608–10.
16. *Ibid.*
17. The word used in the original is *sprengen*.—See Heuss, *op. cit.*, pp. 609–10.
18. *Ibid.*—On Professor Heuss' stand in regard to the electoral system after the Second World War, see F. A. Hermens, *Demokratie oder Anarchie? Untersuchung ueber die Verhaeltniswahl* (Frankfurt, 1951), Footnote 11, pp. 223–4. Heuss' reinterpretation of Naumann's views as contained in the second edition of his work, *Friedrich Naumann* (Stuttgart, 1949), p. 510, has been discussed

by Helmut Unkelbach, *Grundlagen der Wahlsystematik: Stabilitaetsbedingungen der parlamentarischen Demokratie* (Goettingen, 1956), pp. 56–7.

19. On the attitude of the Social Democrats toward electoral systems, see Donald J. Ziegler, "Proportional Representation in the Social and Political Conflict in Germany" (Ph.D. thesis, University of Nebraska, 1956), pp. 53–62.

20. *Ibid.*, p. 117. The SPD's decision was rational, of course, if the compromises with "bourgeois" elements which the majority system implied were to be rejected. The party had begun, however, to accept such compromises at the top, by supporting a government (that of Prince Max) which depended on other parties as well as itself, and it was soon to accept such coalitions as a matter of principle.

21. Baron de Montesquieu, *The Spirit of the Laws*, Hafner Library of Classics edn., trans. Thomas Nugent (New York, 1949), Bk. II, Chap. 2, p. 8.

22. Johannes Schauff, *Neues Wahlrecht* (Berlin, 1929), p. 150.

23. The "Democrats," a Left-Wing Liberal party, had 18.6 per cent of the total vote, but relatively few local strongholds. In constituencies where their candidates had little chance to win many Democrats would have supported Social Democrats. At that time, the Nationalists with 10.3 per cent of the votes and Stresemann's German People's party with 4.4 per cent would, under a majority system, have been a serious factor in only a small number of constituencies.

24. For the complete figures, see *Vierteljahrshefte zur Statistik des Deutschen Reichs; Erstes Ergaenzungsheft*, Vol. 28, p. 15, and F. A. Hermens, *Democracy or Anarchy? A Study of Proportional Representation* (Notre Dame, 1941), p. 219.

25. For the discussions leading to the election law of 1920 see Ziegler, *op. cit.*, pp. 151 ff.

26. Dr. Johannes Schauff, who was outstanding among them (Schauff, *op. cit.*) has made this observation repeatedly in conversation with this writer. In some respects, then, Oxenstierna is a more reliable guide to political reality than Karl Marx. Outright stupidity can, at times, have more to do with faulty political decisions than any economic, or other, interests.

27. Anton Erkelenz, "Ein unmoegliches Wahlgesetz," *Die Hilfe*, February 19, 1920.

28. See, in particular, the two articles by Father Grebe, a member of the Centrist group in the Prussian Diet, "Wahlkreis und Mandatsverteilung" ("Constituencies and Distribution of Seats"), and "Wahlrecht und Parteizersplitterung" ("The Election Law and Party Splintering") in the weekly *Die Allgemeine Rundschau,* March 23 and July 6, respectively.

29. This was to be done on the basis of the "automatic" rather than the d'Hondt system. For the details see H. G. Erdmannsdoerfer, *Wahlrecht in Gefahr* (Berlin, 1930), pp. 18 ff.

30. C. G. Hoag and G. H. Hallett, *Proportional Representation* (New York, 1926), pp. 134–5.

31. For details on all of these elections see Hermens, *Democracy or Anarchy?* . . . , pp. 221–31.

32. The party was close to bankruptcy most of the time between 1924 and 1930. Konrad Heiden—*Der Fuehrer* (Boston, 1944), p. 386—reported that "when highly deserving party comrades of the old guard came to the offices of the *Voelkischer Beobachter,* begging for ten marks in payment for an article which they had contributed, Rosenberg (the editor) was perfectly capable of kicking them downstairs." Quoted by permission of Houghton Mifflin Co.

With the onset of the depression the party found financial "angels" as well as voters, but before surrendering to the stereotype according to which all business men jumped on the Nazi bandwagon and financed it lavishly, it is well to study the sober analysis of the facts presented by Louis P. Lochner, *Tycoons and Tyrant: German Industry from Hitler to Adenauer* (Chicago,

1954), which shows that only a minority of the industrialists supported the Nazis; a larger number opposed them.

33. Arnold Brecht, *Prelude to Silence*, p. 130.

34. All of these figures apply for the period following the election of the first *Reichstag* under the Weimar Constitution. While the National Assembly was in session, the Social Democrats could easily form a majority by combining either with the Democrats or with the Centrists or with both. This majority of the so-called "Weimar Coalition" was, however, lost with the elections to the first *Reichstag*, never to return.

35. Count Westarp, *Am Grabe der Parteiherrschaft* (Berlin, 1932), p. 30.

36. Dr. Schauff has ascertained that, if the territory of the Reich is divided into 400 constituencies of approximately equal size, the Socialists secured pluralities in 225.—*Neues Wahlrecht*, p. 151. Their percentage of the total popular vote had, however, declined to 29.8, and their chances of securing a majority of the seats under a majority system would have depended upon the extent to which they could have attracted additional voters.

37. The author has done so on a previous occasion. See *Democracy or Anarchy?* . . . , pp. 257–72. What was said in those pages is an integral part of the above argument. Maurice Duverger charges the author with overlooking the fact that if the system of election changes, so does the distribution of the votes cast.—*Political Parties* (New York, 1954), p. 377. Actually, there are dozens of references to this fact in *Democracy or Anarchy?* The general aspects of the "dynamics" of systems of voting (their influence on the distribution of the popular vote) are discussed on pp. 9 ff., and the point is made specifically for almost every country and every election; for the German elections of 1930, see pp. 260 ff.

38. That this was partly due to the political uncertainty caused by the P.R. elections of September, 1930, is one of the points which Arthur Osenberg made brilliantly, and in considerable detail. See his "Ueber die dynamische Hierarchie der Rechts-Institutionen in der Weimarer Verfassung und die staatsrechtlichen Ursachen fuer den Zusammenbruch der Republik unter besonderer Beruecksichtigung des Wahlrechts" (Ph.D. thesis, University of Bonn, 1953). Dr. Osenberg's investigation is the most penetrating analysis of the effects of the electoral system during the Weimar Republic; it is much to be regretted that it is not available in print.

39. For the details see Clinton Rossiter, *Constitutional Dictatorship* (Princeton, 1948), pp. 41 ff.

40. *Ibid.*

41. George N. Shuster and Arnold Bergstraesser, *Germany: A Short History* (New York, 1944), pp. 185–6. Quoted by permission of W. W. Norton & Co., Inc.

42. Harold F. Gosnell, *Grass Roots Politics* (Washington, D.C., 1942), p. 28.

43. Konrad Heiden, *History of National Socialism* (New York, 1934), p. 129.

44. For the details see F. A. Hermens, *Der Staat und die Weltwirtschaftskrise* (Vienna, 1936), pp. 178–91.

45. This is one of the points made by Dr. Bruening in his highly informative "letter to the editor" of the *Deutsche Rundschau*, July, 1947, pp. 1–22.

46. For the details see Hermens, *Der Staat und die Weltwirtschaftskrise*, pp. 113 ff.

47. John Maynard Keynes, *Tract on Monetary Reform* (London, 1923).

48. See, for example, *Vierteljahrshefte zur Konjunkturforschung* (Berlin, 1933), X, Issue 1, p. 7.

49. S. L. W. Mellen, "The German People and the Post-war World," *The American Political Science Review*, August, 1943.

50. Dr. Joseph Goebbels, *Vom Kaiserhof zur Reichskanzlei* (Munich, 1934), pp. 195–230. See also Konrad Heiden, *Der Fuehrer* (Boston, 1944), pp. 485 ff. where these events are dealt with under the heading, "The Race with Catastrophe."

51. John W. Wheeler-Bennett, *Wooden Titan: Hindenburg in Twenty Years of German History, 1914–1934* (New York, 1936), p. 393.
52. *Ibid.*, pp. 393–4.
53. Heiden, *Der Fuehrer*, p. 351.
54. Goebbels' diaries (*op. cit.*, p. 200) contain this entry for November 11: "I receive a report concerning the financial condition of the Berlin organization. This is quite desperate (*trostlos*). Only low tide, debts and obligations, in addition the complete impossibility to raise money on a larger scale anywhere after this defeat." (Goebbels refers to the loss of votes in the preceding *Reichstag* elections.)
55. Emil Ludwig, *Hindenburg* (Amsterdam, 1935), p. 314.
56. Heiden, *Der Fuehrer*, pp. 539–40.
57. For the text see Ernst Forsthoff, *Deutsche Geschichte seit 1918 in Dokumenten* (Leipzig, 1935), pp. 156–62.
58. Wheeler-Bennett, *op. cit.*, p. 410.
59. Arnold Brecht, review of F. A. Hermens, *Democracy or Anarchy?* . . . , in *Social Research*, September, 1942, p. 412.

FOOTNOTES TO CHAPTER XVI

1. The term "Constitution" was avoided because not all of Germany was represented in the "Parliamentary Council" which drafted the new document; no representatives of the Russian zone of occupation or of the Saar territory were present. Besides, Western Germany was not sovereign when the deliberations of the Parliamentary Council took place. Therefore, the *Grundgesetz* concludes with the provision that it will cease to apply "on the day on which a Constitution becomes valid which has been determined upon by the German people in a free decision." (Art. 146)
2. Assuming that such blunders as the restrictions placed upon the right of parliamentary dissolution in the France of the Third and Fourth Republics are avoided.
3. The Weimar Constitution provided that the President could dissolve the *Reichstag*, but "only once for a particular reason." The ingenuity of the presidential draftsmen was put to considerable test when they had to invent a variety of reasons, where in reality there always was the same reason: lack of a coherent majority.
4. One half of the Deputies were to be elected under the plurality system and one half under P.R. Seats won under the plurality system were *not* to be deducted from a party's total.
5. *The Manchester Guardian Weekly* reported these events under the headline, "A Rebuff for Dr. Adenauer: Ex-Nazis Wreck a Cabinet," *The Manchester Guardian Weekly*, February 23, 1956.
6. For the details of the debate preceding the vote, the vote itself and the debate following the presentation of the new cabinet, see *Landtag Nordrhein-Westfalen*, 3. Wahlperiode, reports on the *Sitzungen*, February 16, February 29 and March 2, 1956, pp. 1013 ff.
7. Presumably, the President will take the Chancellor's advice to dissolve except under unusual circumstances. There exists, however, the possibility that the President will want to pursue a policy of his own, in particular if he belongs to a party different from that of the Chancellor. Article 68 opens the road to one of the few opportunities given the President along such lines.

8. For the considerations guiding its establishment, see John Brown Mason, "Federalism—The Bonn Model," in Arnold J. Zurcher, ed., *Constitutions and Constitutional Trends in World War II* (New York, 1951), pp. 134 ff., specifically pp. 144–6.

9. This was done on the basis of election laws differing from the general pattern. In the other *Laender* and in the Federation, as we shall see below, whatever seats one party gains by pluralities in single-member constituencies are deducted from the total, producing the overall effects of P.R. In these three *Laender* there was no such deduction. On the other hand, the votes cast for a party in a constituency in which it had secured a plurality were not all transferred to the "reserve list," but only those by which the vote for the victorious candidate exceeded the votes cast for his nearest rival. This type of election law contains genuine elements of a majority decision. On the other hand, it does not place that decision into the hands of the undecided voter in the doubtful constituencies. Given a multiple-party system any party substantially larger than its rivals may expect to secure a majority of the seats with a minority of the votes. It does not have to make the type of effort to obtain an overall majority of the votes which is needed under majority elections in single-member constituencies when, of course, the existence of one large political party tends to promote agreement on one candidate by its opponents. That these laws constituted a somewhat inorganic mixture of majority voting and P.R. is one of the reasons why they were abolished. Schleswig-Holstein and Hesse adopted election laws patterned on the Federal model. Hamburg chose the Weimar system with the whole *Land* constituting one constituency. No party could secure seats, however, unless it obtained at least five per cent of the total vote cast.

10. Karl Loewenstein, "The Government and Politics of Germany," in James T. Shotwell, ed., *Governments of Continental Europe* (rev. edn.; New York, 1952), p. 585.

11. For an evaluation of the law, as well as the Court's practice, see Guenther Willms, "Zur Reform des Bundesverfassungsgerichts," *Deutsche Richterzeitung*, June, 1955. On the mode of electing the judges see the article by the same author entitled "Kunstvolles Gleichgewicht? Zur Problematik der Richterwahl beim Bundesverfassungsgericht," *Neue Juristische Wochenschrift*, August 19, 1955.

12. They are embodied in the law entitled "Gesetz zur Aenderung des Gesetzes ueber das Bundesverfassungsgericht," of July 21, 1956.

12a. On these events see Joseph Dunner, "DANA or the Trojan Horse," *The New Leader*, May 25, 1946, and "American Innocents Abroad; Communists in Strategic Positions in German Radio and Press," *The New Leader*, June 8, 1946.

13. For the details see Office of the U.S. High Commissioner for Germany, *Elections and Political Parties in Germany, 1945–1952* (Bonn, 1952).

14. The movement towards the Nazis emanated with the rank and file of the Protestant voters rather than with their leaders; no outstanding Protestant was a member of the Nazi party's leadership.

15. Ludwig Bergstraesser, *Geschichte der Politischen Parteien in Deutschland* (7th ed.; Munich, 1952), pp. 293–4.

16. These founded the "Free Peoples Party" which later merged with the German Party.

17. For the details see F. A. Hermens, *Europe Between Democracy and Anarchy* (Notre Dame, 1951), pp. 182–92.

18. Hearings on the *Third Supplemental Appropriation Bill for 1948*, held before the Subcommittee of the Committee on Appropriations of the House of Representatives, p. 74.

19. Quoted from *Hochverrat und Staatsgefaehrdung, Urteile des Bundesgerichts-*

hofes, mit einem Vorwort von Bundesanwalt Dr. Walter Wagner (Karlsruhe, 1957), p. 288.

20. Hermens, *Democracy or Anarchy?* . . . , pp. 233–4.
21. Actually, one of the 202 votes was cast by a Deputy belonging to the Bavarian party.
22. Jack Raymond, "Adenauer Elected by a Single Vote," *The New York Times*, September 15, 1949.
23. The German abbreviation for *Der ueberfluesigste Bundesminister aller Zeiten*, a take-off on Hitler's claim to be "the greatest general of all time" (*der groesste Feldherr aller Zeiten*), which earned him the name *Groefaz*.
24. See his preface to the German edition of my book, *Democracy or Anarchy?— Demokratie oder Anarchie? Eine Entersuchung ueber die Verhaeltniswahl* (Frankfurt, 1951).
25. P. W. Wenger, "Im Weimar Express," *Rheinischer Merkur*, February 10, 1956.
26. For Erhard's views see his own formulation in his article, "Germany's Reconstruction," *Current History*, April, 1956.
27. For an analysis of the philosophy underlying this policy see Patrick Boarman, ed., *Der Christ und die soziale Marktwirtschaft* (Stuttgart, 1955).
28. On this subject see *Das deutsche Wahlwunder, 1953* (Frankfurt, 1953). This special issue of *Der Waehler*, the magazine published by the "German Voters Society" contains much interesting material on the subject, elucidated in a number of articles with points of view which have not always been taken into account in analyses published in the United States.
29. Theodor Heuss, *Friedrich Naumann* (Stuttgart, 1937), pp. 608–9.
30. In Ireland the two coalition governments collapsed in the end, and, characteristically, this collapse was brought about by the smallest coalition party, McBride's Republicans who, in the meantime, had imposed upon their country a course of action clearly not wanted by any majority. Premier Costello's Fine Gael, a party most definitely friendly to continued cooperation with England, had submitted to McBride's demand for the declaration of an Irish Republic. At that time, such action excluded further membership in the Commonwealth. The price, then, which the largest party of the coalition was willing to pay for staying in power was the abandonment of what was widely considered the major plank in its platform. There has been much criticism of this action in Ireland from the moral point of view; the only point at issue in this connection is that the fear of De Valera helped the partners of the coalition to overcome for a while differences which otherwise would have been fatal to the coalition at an early stage.
    Premier Costello's two periods of tenure were also characterized by a revival of border raids by the outlawed Irish Republican Army (IRA) against Northern Ireland. Mr. Costello undoubtedly regretted this fact, but he had to tolerate it both because his coalition was weak and because McBride's Republicans, on whose few votes he depended, would have opposed energetic action. It is interesting to note that, when De Valera returned to power in 1957, he immediately took action in this as well as in other matters. Lack of proportionality in the Irish election law had kept minor opposition groups off the ballot in large parts of the country, and made it possible for him to secure an absolute majority of the seats with a little less than a majority of the votes. De Valera demonstrated immediately how much more firmly a one-party majority cabinet can act than a coalition, even if he could not repair the psychological damage done by years of raids.
31. Typical of this tendency is Winfried Martini, *Das Ende Aller Sicherheit: Eine Kritik des Westens* (Stuttgart, 1954). According to this author the emotionalism inseparable from modern democracy has led to the end of all rational politics and of any real security.

32. Professor Karl Loewenstein has been one of the earliest, and most systematic, proponents of this concept; see his article, "Militant Democracy and Fundamental Rights," *The American Political Science Review*, issues of June and August, 1937.

33. Measures taken under provisions such as Article 21 of the Basic Law may also be too rigid. It is barely possible that, under the impact of such events as Khrushchev's speech to the Twentieth Congress of the Russian Communist party, and the Russian suppression of the Hungarian revolution, the pressures inside a particular Communist party might become strong enough to bring about a modification of its totalitarian character. The official banning of a Communist party, on the other hand, leads to a consolidation of what might be loosened up. It might be said that in Germany all that was needed was for the Federal Government not to ask the Constitutional Court to declare the KPD illegal. Such a course of action, however, would have meant disregarding the plain language of the Constitution, as the KPD was no less totalitarian than the SRP.

34. Guenther Willms, "Die Organisationsdelikte: Eine gesetzeskritische Betrachtung," *Neue Juristische Wochenschrift*, April 12, 1957; see, in particular, Section VI, p. 566.

35. See, for example, the article by H. R. Zimmermann, "Es geht nicht ohne politische Amnestie," *Stuttgarter Zeitung*, June 6, 1957.

36. Some of the aspects of Communist activity are criminal by any standard. They require not only close supervision aiming at preventing acts of espionage, sabotage, and of conspirational acts constituting a "clear and present danger" but also criminal prosecution. Communists always claim that since their aims are political they must be above the law even if they do things which are clearly illegal, such as, forging passports, and that anything done to combat such violations of the law of the land is "political persecution." It is as important not to be deceived by such claims as it is to have the proper political weapons available to handle the political aspects of Communist activities the way they should be handled.

37. In 1953 the CDU-CSU won its bare majority of the seats with 45.1 per cent of the votes cast for the party lists in the various *Laender*. The law gave each voter two votes, the first to be applied to the election of candidates in single-member districts, and the second to the election of candidates from the *Landeslisten*. The number of seats won in single-member constituencies was deducted, as in 1949, from the total due to a party on the basis of relative party strength in the *Laender*. For details, see James K. Pollock, "The West German Election Law of 1953," *The American Political Science Review*, March, 1955.

38. Rudolf Smend, *Verfassung und Verfassungsrecht*, here quoted from *Staatsrechtliche Abhandlungen* (Berlin, 1955), p. 151.

39. Zweiter Deutscher Bundestag, 4. Sitzung, Bonn, Mittwoch den 28. Oktober, 1953, p. 40.—Ollenhauer's speech (beginning on p. 35) clearly foreshadowed the moderate course which the party was to adopt during the campaign of 1957. It also contains some apt remarks on the illusions according to which stable political conditions can be taken for granted in Germany. Specifically, Ollenhauer called the expectation that Germany would develop a two-party system "premature." (p. 36)

40. On this issue see Dolf Sternberger, "Kommt das Zweiparteiensystem von selbst?" *Die Gegenwart*, January 15, 1955.

41. Its implications have been analyzed in Dolf Sternberger, *Lebende Verfassung*, (Meisenheim, 1956), pp. 101 ff.

42. For the results see "Die Sozialdemokraten staerkste Partei," *Frankfurter Allgemeine Zeitung*, October 30, 1956.

43. For all details, see Richard Schachtner, "Wahl zum Bayerischen Landtag vom 28, November, 1954," *Zeitschrift des Bayerischen Statistischen Landesamts,* 1955, pp. 146 ff.

44. For the details see "Neuer Kampf um das Wahlgesetz," *Die Welt,* January 17, 1957. See also the editorial entitled "Morgengabe" in the same issue.

45. Since, under the 1956 law, parties could secure seats from the *Landesliste* if they elected at least three Deputies in the single-member constituencies, there was an opportunity for a larger party to assist a smaller one by supporting the latter's candidates in certain districts. The CDU did this for the benefit of the DP in Lower Saxony and the SPD for the benefit of the Bavarian Party in Bavaria. The arrangement worked in the first case but not in the second. One reason was the overwhelming strength displayed by the Christian Democrats, which made their help more effective than that of the Social Democrats. Another reason may have been that while the CDU supported a party with tenets similar to its own the SPD asked its voters to cast their ballots for a party with radically different views. *The Manchester Guardian* commented: "It [The Bavarian Party] has made an electoral bargain with the SPD. The latter believe in socialism and centralisation: the Bavarians want a capitalist economy and increased right for the *Laender.* The Social Democrats desperately desire German reunification; the Bavarians do not care a jot for it."—"Two-Party Trend in West Germany," *The Manchester Guardian Weekly,* August 29, 1957.

46. As mentioned above, the desired relation in the strength of government and opposition would best be secured by increasing, for one term, the membership of the parliament in question and declare those opposition candidates elected who came closest to success in their constituencies.

FOOTNOTES TO CHAPTER XVII

1. For pre-Fascist Italian parliamentarism, see A. L. Lowell, *Government and Parties in Continental Europe* (New York, 1896), pp. 189 ff., in particular pp. 204 ff.; A. Malatesta, *Il Parlamento Italiano Da Cavour a Mussolini* (Milan, 1932); W. Hasbach, Die parlamentarische Kabinettsregierung (Stuttgart, 1919), pp. 200 ff.; H. Finer, *Mussolini's Italy* (New York, 1935), pp. 60 ff.
   A more detailed discussion of the general subject treated in this chapter, is in the author's *Democracy or Anarchy?. A Study of Proportional Representation* (Notre Dame, 1941), pp. 147–213 and *Europe Between Democracy and Anarchy* (Notre Dame, 1951), pp. 46–62 and pp. 160–181. It is to be considered an integral part of the above argument which had to be developed rather briefly.

2. Arnold Zurcher, "The Government and Politics of Italy," in James T. Shotwell, ed., *Governments of Continental Europe* (rev. ed.; New York, 1952), p. 224.

3. Hamilton Fish Armstrong, *We Or They* (New York, 1937), p. 88.

4. "Lectures on Post-War Italy," given at Harvard University, Lecture 2, p. 4, mimeo.

5. *Ibid.,* pp. 7–8.

6. *Camera dei Deputati, Discussioni,* Legislatura XXV, p. 19737.

7. Alesandro Schiavi, Come hanno votato gli electori italiani (Milan, 1914), p. 74. See also the author's *Democracy or Anarchy?,* pp. 151–3.

8. On the votes polled by the Italian Popular party, see Elio Caranti, "Il partito popolare nelle elezioni dell'altro dopoguerra," *Civitas*, September–October, 1956. For a discussion of the Christian Democratic movement as a whole, see Mario Einaudi and François Goguel, *Christian Democracy in Italy and France* (Notre Dame, 1955), pp. 1 ff.

9. For these elections, their background and their consequences, see Hermens, *Democracy or Anarchy?*, pp. 178 ff.

10. G. Volpe, *History of the Fascist Movement* (Rome, no year), p. 104.

11. H. Schneider, *Making the Fascist State* (New York, 1928), p. 80.

12. Luigi Sturzo, *Italy and Fascismo* (New York, 1928), p. 118.

13. G. Salvemini, *The Fascist Dictatorship in Italy* (New York, 1927), p. 113. Quoted by permission of Henry Holt & Co.

14. David Brown, "The Inside Story of Italy's Surrender," *The Saturday Evening Post*, September 9 and 16, 1944; General Eisenhower's reactions to the Italian armistice have been characterized as follows by Captain Butcher: "Ike feels that the terms of the agreement are unduly harsh. He suspects that our home government wants to make a propaganda Roman holiday by publicizing to the entire world the stern restrictions of the surrender . . ." Harry C. Butcher, *My Three Years with Eisenhower* (New York, 1946), p. 405. Quoted by permission of Simon and Schuster, Inc.

15. Sumner Welles, *Where Are We Heading?* (New York, 1946), p. 149.

16. See above p. 544, N. 63.

17. For a summary of Italian electoral legislation see Giovanni Schepis, *I. Sistemi Elettorali* (Empoli, 1955), pp. 6 ff. For bibliographic details see the literature quoted in Ferdinand A. Hermens, "Die Wahlrechtsentwicklung der Nachkriegszeit in Frankreich, Italien und Griechenland," *Jahrbuch des Oeffentlichen Rechts*, 1956, pp. 280 ff., in particular note 1 on p. 280.

18. G. Glisenti, Report published by NCWC News Service, dated June 30, 1947.

19. For its overall, as well as regional, strength, see Caranti, *op. cit.*

20. P. Luzzatto Fegiz, "Le caratteristiche demografiche e sociali dei simpatizzanti per i vari partiti," *Bollettino della Doxa*, December 28, 1953, pp. 268–69. Here quoted from Elio Caranti, *Sociologia e Statistica delle Elezioni Italiane nel Dopoguerra* (Rome, 1954), pp. 115–17.

21. Anne O'Hare McCormick, *The New York Times*, April 7, 1947.

22. This interpretation is not generally accepted. An influential school of thought holds that the power of dissolution is a presidential prerogative which could be exercised even in the absence of favorable advice on the part of the Prime Minister, although it is not easy to see how such a step would fit in with the requirements of parliamentary government.

23. Luigi Sturzo, "Significato del Voto Segreto," *Il Giornale d'Italia*, April 23, 1954.

24. In the preface to a collection of papers which he wrote during his presidency he stated: "I have, therefore, given to the norm of Article 95 according to which 'the President of the Council of Ministers directs the general policy of the government' an interpretation which, perhaps, is wider than the letter of the Constitution, but which I consider conform to the system wanted by the Constituent Assembly: the policy of the country belongs to the government which must have the confidence of Parliament, and not to the President of the Republic."—Luigi Einaudi, *Lo Scrittoio del Presidente, 1948–1955* (Turin, 1956), p. xiv.

25. On the general implications of the requirement of countersignature. see Luigi R. Letteri, *La Controfirma degli Atti del Presidente della Repubblica* (Rome, 1951), and on the office of President, Serio Galeotti, *La Pozitione Costituzionale del Presidente della Republica* (Milan, 1949).

26. "New President Asks Leftist Rule in Italy," *The New York Times*, May 12, 1955.

27. "Italian Government Blocks Gronchi Reply to Eisenhower Criticizing Policy of U.S.," *The New York Times,* April 5, 1957.
28. For a friendly interpretation of Gronchi's intentions, see C. L. Sulzberger, "Italy's President Seeks a New Political Role," *The New York Times,* July 6, 1957.
29. From a memorandum on the Italian presidency submitted to the author by Dr. Guglielmo Negri on November 12, 1956.
30. President Gronchi's activities on this occasion were the subject of a scholarly analysis of the functions of the President by Luigi Sturzo, a lifetime member of the Senate, in that body's session of June 27, 1927. For the text see *Senato della Repubblica, Discussioni,* issue of June 27, 1957, pp. 23311 ff. and, for a summary, the report in *Il Messagero di Roma,* issue of June 28, 1957.
31. Judicial review was one of the demands made by the Christian Democrats; see Mario Einaudi in: *Foreign Governments,* ed. Morstein Marx (New York, 1949), p. 251. Governments led by Christian Democrats were subsequently to be rather critical of the Court.
32. For all details on this and other matters see a memorandum by Dr. Guglielmo Negri, transmitted to the author on November 24, 1956; G. G. Stendarvi, *La Corte Costitutionale* (2nd rev. ed.; Milan, 1957); Roy Pryce, "Italy's Constitutional Court," *Parliamentary Affairs,* Spring, 1957.
33. Quoted from Daily Report, *Est-Ovest,* "Italy in 1956," p. 9.
34. Arnaldo Cortesi, *The New York Times,* February 17, 1948.
35. For an evaluation of these elections, see Mario Einaudi, "The Italian Elections of 1948," *The Review of Politics,* July 1948.
36. See Hermens, *Europe Between Democracy and Anarchy,* pp. 175–6.
37. See his letter to the editor of *Il Giornale d'Italia,* published in the issue of June 11, 1952, and for the more detailed reasons which caused his change of opinion, see his articles "Proporzionale e Governo," *L'Avvenire d'Italia,* January 24, 1954, and "Proporzionale, pura, corretta mista," *Il Giornale d'Italia,* February 9, 1954.
38. For the text see the daily, *Il Popolo,* issue of June 28, 1954.
39. *Camera dei Deputati, No. 984-A, Relazione della I Commissione permanente . . . sul Disegno di Legge . . . per La Elezione dei Consigli Comunali,* presentata alla presidenza il lo giugno 1950, p. 2.
40. *Stenographische Berichte, Deutscher Bundestag,* 254 Sitzung, Bonn, March 18, 1953, p. 12203.
41. These would have been all but inevitable, taking into consideration the political splintering which had developed in the country, and which, under a plurality system, might have led to results not always controllable to the extent that they should have been controlled. The ideal solution would have been run-off elections for one or two elections and the plurality system afterwards.
42. For the text of the memorandum see Luigi Einaudi, *op. cit.,* pp. 20–31; for the remarks on the alternative vote, pp. 27–31. The memorandum bears the date of December 22, 1933, and was not published until 1956, yet it seems likely that the President advanced these arguments during the discussions preceding the 1953 election law.
43. *Il Popolo,* June 28, 1954.
44. *Camera dei Deputati, N. 2971, Disegno di Legge presentato dal Ministro dell Interno* (Scelba); Seduta del 21 Ottobre 1952.
45. *Camera dei Deputati, N. 2971-A, Relazione . . . Sul Disegno di Legge Presentato dal Ministero dell Interno* (Scelba) *. . . Presentata alla Presidenza il 3 Diciembre,* 1952, p. 6.
46. *L'Opinione,* issue of September 22, 1952.
47. *Ministero dell' Interno, Elezione della Camera dei Deputati* (7 giugno 1953), Roma, 1953. The table will be found in the appendix.

48. For the basic figures see *Ministero dell' Interno, Elezione della Camera dei Deputati, 7 giugno 1953,* Risultati Complessivi e nei Communi Capoluoghi di Provincia, Rome, 1953.
For additional information the author is indebted to Professor Giovanni Schepis of the University of Rome, who made a detailed memorandum available under the date of October 27, 1954.
49. Quoted from Giorgio Tupini, *I Democratici Cristiani* (Milan, 1954), p. 312.
50. "O la borsa (Proporzionale) o la vita (del Governo)." "Proporzionale e Governo," *L'Italia,* January 16, 1954.
51. "Norme per la elezione della Camera dei Deputati," *Gazzetta Ufficiale della Repubblica Italiana,* Legge 16 maggio 1956, n. 493, Rome, 12 giugno, 1956, p. 2025. For the consolidated text of the legislation pertaining to Chamber elections see Decreto del Presidente della Repubblica 30 Marzo, 1957, n. 361: Approvazione del testo unico delle leggi recanti norme per la elezione della Camera dei Deputati, Supplemento ordinario alla Gazzetta Ufficiale del 3 giugno, 1957.
52. Hermens, *Democracy or Anarchy?,* pp. 395 ff.; *P.R., Democracy and Good Government* (Notre Dame, 1943), pp. 40 ff.
53. For the text see "Norme per la elezione dei Consigli Provinziali," *Gazzetta Ufficiale della Repubblica Italiana,* March 13, 1951.
54. Theoretically it is not a party but a group of candidates who filed a declaration that they intend to enter into a combination.
55. For the text of the modifications, see *Legge 23 Marzo,* 1956, No. 136, Supplemento Ordinario alla *Gazzetta Ufficiale,* No. 73 del 27 Marzo, 1956.
56. This is done in: Elio Caranti, "Le elezioni amministrative del 27 maggio," *Civitas,* December, 1956, p. 17, but not in other calculations, such as "Esame Critico delle Elezioni del 27 Maggio 1956," *Società Nuova,* June 30, 1956, and "Un primo bilancio delle elezioni ammistrative," *Mondo Economico,* June 9, 1956. The last two publications are the source for the above remarks.
57. For the details see "Esame Critico delle Elezioni del 27 Maggio 1956," *Societa Nuova,* issue of June 30, 1956, and "Un primo bilancio delle elezioni amministrative," *Mondo Economico,* issue of June 9, 1956.
58. On the Pella cabinet and its successors, see Muriel Grindrod, *The Rebuilding of Italy* (London, 1955), pp. 102 ff. and 140 ff.
59. For the text of Terracini's speech, see *Senato della Repubblica, Discussioni,* 27 giugno 1957, pp. 22303 ff. and for a summary, "Due Laboriose Sedute a Palazzo Madama," *Il Messagero di Roma,* issue of June 28, 1957.
60. For the original draft of the Vanoni Plan, see *Outline of Development Income and employment in Italy in the ten-year Period 1955–64,* Paris, OEEC, January, 1955. See also *Relazione Generale sulla Situazione Economica del Paese,* presentata dal Ministro del Bilancio Vanoni e dal Ministro del Tesoro Gava alla Presidenza il 22 Marzo 1955, Camera dei Deputati, Doc. VIII, N. 2.
The problems and prospects of the Italian economy are analysed intelligently in the *Italian Economic Survey,* a bimonthly published by the Association of Italian Joint Stock Companies. See, in particular, the articles, "1955 and the Development Plan," in the issue of May–June, 1956, and for the slow-down of expansion in 1956, "The Italian Economic Situation," issue of January–February, 1957.—In view of the fact that the break in Italian political developments took place in 1953, see the survey of conditions for that year in *Relazione Generale sulla Situazione Economica del Paese,* presentata dal Ministro del Bilancio Vanoni e dal Ministro del Tesoro Gava, alla Presidenza il 20 Marzo, 1954, Camera dei Deputati, Doc. VIII, N. 1. The essential parts of this report were presented in English in the March–June, 1954, issue of the *Italian Economic Survey.*
For a few remarks on overall economic developments, and their sociological

implications, see also my article, "Demokratie ohne Sicherheitsventil: Zur Nachkriegsgeschichte Italiens," *Zeitschrift fuer Zeitgeschichte,* April, 1955, pp. 158–63.

61. Michael Hoffman, "Italians Improve Life of Workers," *The New York Times,* September 28, 1954.
62. Few have dealt with these complications as lucidly as Mario Einaudi, to whose essay on "The Italian Land: Men, Nature and Government," *Social Research,* March, 1950, reference is made for details.
63. "Italy May Relax Oil Grant Terms, Gulf Company's Withdrawal and Pressure by Paris and Bonn Spur Review," *The New York Times,* February 26, 1957.
64. See his column entitled "Democracy's Crisis in Italy and France," *The New York Times,* June 24, 1957.
65. Erwin von Beckerath, *Politik und Wirtschaft: Moeglichkeiten und Grenzen einer rationalen Wirtschaftpolitik,* mimeographed.
66. Alcide De Gasperi, "Non Bisogna Esagerare," *La Discussione,* January 24, 1954.
67. Arnold Zurcher "Democracy's Declining Capacity to Govern," *Western Political Quarterly,* December, 1955.

FOOTNOTES TO CHAPTER XVIII

1. Charles A. Beard, *The Republic* (New York, 1943), p. 248.
2. Henry Hazlitt, *A New Constitution Now* (New York, 1942), pp. 59 ff.
3. Woodrow Wilson, *Congressional Government* (Boston, 1885). See the new Meridian Books edn. (New York, 1956). Wilson first stated his views in an article entitled "Cabinet Government in the United States," which was published in August, 1879, issue of *The International Review,* then edited by the young author's later enemy, Henry Cabot Lodge; it was reissued as a booklet with an introduction by Thomas K. Finletter (Stamford, Conn., 1947). Wilson also published an article entitled "Committee or Cabinet Government," *The Overland Monthly,* January, 1884. In 1908 his book on *Constitutional Government in the United States* appeared which, inspired by the Presidency of Theodore Roosevelt, contains what appears to be a reversal of his earlier views. The change, however, is more one of emphasis, as has been shown in detail by Irving Fasan, "Woodrow Wilson and the Separation of Powers" (Master's thesis, Univ. of Notre Dame, 1951).
4. Wilfred E. Binkley, *President and Congress* (New York, 1947), pp. 39 ff.
5. Walter Bagehot, *The English Constitution,* The World's Classics edn. (New York, 1928), pp. 14 ff. and 194 ff.
6. For Lippmann's comments on the reform proposals advanced by Wilson in *The Overland Monthly,* see his introduction to the paper-back edition of *Congressional Government,* pp. 14–15.
7. The vigorous controversy between Don K. Price and Harold Laski, which occurred in 1943 and 1944, proved to be the forerunner of extensive changes on the subject in American scholarly opinion. See Price, "The Parliamentary and Presidential System," *Public Administration Review,* Autumn (1943); Laski, "The Parliamentary and Presidential System," *Public Administration Review,* Autumn (1944); and "A Response to Mr. Laski," *Public Administration Review,* Autumn (1944). Price subsequently developed his opinions in the

pamphlet entitled "The New Dimension of Diplomacy" (New York, 1951), and in his book, *Government and Science* (New York, 1954). Arnold J. Zurcher was no less vigorous in his criticism of Wilson's original views in "The President, Congress and the Separation of Powers: A Reappraisal," *Western Political Quarterly*, March, 1950. See also Norman L. Stamps, "A Reappraisal of American Political Institutions," *The Southwestern Social Science Quarterly*, December, 1953. The report of the Committee on Political Parties of the American Political Science Association, entitled "Toward a More Responsible Two-Party System," Supplement to the *American Political Science Review*, September, 1950, took it for granted that the necessary reforms could be carried out within the general framework of the separation of powers. This was also the opinion of some of the members of a study group which analyzed American foreign policy for the Woodrow Wilson Foundation. Its report was published under the title, *United States Foreign Policy: Its Organization and Control* (New York, 1952). The volume reflects, however, equally the views of the chairman, Professor William Yandell Elliott, who was more inclined to think in terms of constitutional reform; see his earlier work, *The Need For Constitutional Reform* (New York, 1935), in particular pp. 182 ff.

8. Herman Finer, *The Theory and Practice of Modern Government* (rev. ed.; New York, 1949), pp. 94 ff., points out that Montesquieu's theory differs in essentials from that of any other writer, particularly Aristotle and John Locke. If any earlier writer is to be mentioned at all it should be Polybius, whose *Histories*, trans. Evelyn S. Schuckburgh (London, 1889) follows a trend of thought remarkably similar to the one in which any reasoned defense of the separation of powers, as contained in the American Constitution, would have to join.

9. A. T. Prescott, *Drafting the Constitution* (Baton Rouge, 1941), p. 446. Its role was emphasized by Sidney George Fischer, who wrote a book under the title *The Evolution of the Constitution of the United States: Showing that it is a Development of Progressive History and not an Isolated Document Struck off at a Given Time or an Imitation of English or Dutch Forms of Government* (Philadelphia, 1897). Fischer's sub-title refers to Gladstone's famous remark that "as the British Constitution is the most subtle organism which has proceeded from progressive history, so the American Constitution is the most wonderful work ever struck off at a given time by the brain and purpose of man."

10. In the words of Montesquieu: "Constant experience shows us that every man invested with power is apt to abuse it, and to carry his authority as far as it will go. Is it not strange, though true, to say that virtue itself has need of limits?

"To prevent this abuse, it is necessary from the very nature of things that power should be a check to power." *The Spirit of the Laws*, Hafner Library of Classics edn. (New York, 1941), p. 150.

"When the legislative and executive powers are united in the same person, or in the same body of magistrates, there can be no liberty; because apprehensions may arise, lest the same monarch or senate should enact tyrannical laws, to execute them in a tyrannical manner.

"Again, there is no liberty if the judiciary power be not separated from the legislative and executive. Were it joined with the legislative, the life and liberty of the subject would be exposed to arbitrary control; for the judge would then be the legislator. Were it joined to the executive power, the judge might behave with violence and oppression." *Ibid.*, pp. 151–2.

11. Sir William Blackstone, *Commentaries on the Laws of England*, ed. William Carey Jones (rev. ed.; San Francisco, 1916), Bk. II, Chap. II, Sec. II.

12. Prescott, *op. cit.*, pp. 816–17.

13. *Ibid.*, p. 313.

14. This is also done by Herman Finer, *Theory and Practice of Modern Government*, pp. 94 ff.
15. Montesquieu, *op. cit.*, Bk. XI, Chap. 6, p. 160.
16. Ernest F. Griffith, *Congress: Its Contemporary Role* (New York, 1951). See also the same author's *The American System of Government* (London, 1954).
17. *Organization of Congress*, Hearings before the Joint Committee on the Organization of Congress, 79th Congress, 1st session, Washington, 1945, p. 127.
18. Ed Flynn, *You Are the Boss* (New York, 1947), p. 181.
19. Bagehot, *op. cit.*, p. 164.
20. Wilfred E. Binkley, *President and Congress*, pp. 38–9.
21. A. Appadorai, *The Substance of Politics* (6th ed.; London, 1952), p. 460.
22. W. F. Willoughby, *The Government of Modern States* (rev. ed.; New York, 1936), pp. 238 ff. Willoughby treats the subject under the heading: "The English Government One of Separation of Powers Organically and Union of Powers Personally."
23. John Stuart Mill, *Considerations on Representative Government* (New York, 1862), pp. 97 ff.
24. On Jefferson, see Binkley, *President and Congress*, pp. 49 ff.; on Wilson see Binkley, pp. 202 ff.
25. For the details of the methods involved, see Pendleton Herring, *Presidential Leadership* (New York, 1940).
26. Thomas K. Finletter, *Can Representative Government Do the Job?* (New York, 1945), p. 65. Quoted by permission of Harcourt, Brace and Co., Inc.
27. W. Lippmann in the Meridian edn.'s introduction to Wilson's *Congressional Government*, p. 16.
28. Jerome Kerwin, "The Constitution Is at Fault," *America*, February 16, 1946. This article was followed by critical comments by various authors in the same issue as well as in the one of March 30, 1946, followed by Kerwin's concluding statement entitled "The Constitution Is Still at Fault,, *America*, April 27, 1946. See also his article "Checks and No Balances," *The Review of Politics*, April, 1944.
29. Montesquieu, *The Spirit of the Laws*, p. 150.
30. Prescott, *op. cit.*, p. 758.
31. *The Federalist*, Modern Library edn. (New York, n.d.), No. 51, p. 337.
32. It *was* the view of men such as Elbridge Gerry who did, indeed, look upon all power, including responsible power, in the same light as the power of a royal executive, which was not amenable to control by the colonial legislature. When Madison leans over backward in his defense of the separation of powers in Nos. 47–51 of *The Federalist*, he evidently does so because of the charge made by his opponents that the Constitution did not contain that principle explicitly enough.
      Naturally it was the very purpose of the movement for a new Constitution to establish a Federal Government with real control. Since Alexander Hamilton was so prominent in this movement, it is not surprising that he should have been more explicit in regard to both the anthropological premises and the political consequences of a reasonable grant of political power. Thus, as early as in 1775, he took exception to Hobbes' views concerning man's condition in a state of nature, emphasizing that men were always subject to the restraints of the (natural) moral law.—"The Farmer Refuted," here quoted from Caldwell, *The Administrative Theories of Hamilton and Jefferson* (Chicago, 1944), p. 10. In No. 26 of *The Federalist* papers (p. 159) he says: ". . . confidence must be placed somewhere," and in the New York Ratifying Convention he added: "Power must be granted, or civil society cannot exist."—Caldwell, p. 19. Hamilton was aware of the need to place checks on power but, as Professor Caldwell summarizes his views on that matter: "Power was best controlled, not by rigid limitations, but by the provision of channels for its responsible opera-

tion."—*Ibid.*, p. 20. Hamilton was more modern than his associates in assessing the nature of political parties and the function of an opposition as the major check on the government. What he says along these lines in No. 26 of *The Federalist* papers would logically form the starting point for considerations similar to those adduced above.

33. *The Federalist*, No. 49, p. 331.
34. Quoted from Thomas K. Finletter, *Can Representative Government Do the Job?*, pp. 46–7.
35. *Ibid.*, p. 47.
36. Turner Catledge, "Greasing the Ways for the President's Bills," *The New York Times Magazine*, February 28, 1937.
37. T. V. Smith and Robert A. Taft, *Foundations of Democracy*, A Series of Debates (New York, 1939), p. 57.
38. "Today and Tomorrow," *The Washington Post*, January 7, 1943.
39. Henry L. Stimson and McGeorge Bundy, *On Active Service in Peace and War* (New York, 1948), p. 562. Quoted by permission of Harper & Bros.
40. *Loc. cit.*
41. *Ibid.*, p. 564.
42. F. A. Hermens, *Der Staat und die Weltwirtschaftskrise* (Vienna, 1936), pp. 192 ff.
43. For the details see Raymond Moley, *After Seven Years* (New York, 1939), pp. 196 ff., and in particular p. 245.
44. *Loc. cit.*
45. *Ibid.*, pp. 248–9.
46. *Ibid.*, p. 250.
47. For the text see *ibid.*, pp. 259–60.
48. For the trend of thought behind the President's decision see James Harvey Rogers, *Capitalism in Crisis* (New Haven, 1938), pp. 69–72.
49. *Ibid.*, p. 211.
50. *Ibid.*, pp. 211–12.
50a. On the general significance of this fact, see Stephen D. Kertesz, "Reflections on Soviet and American Negotiating Behavior," *The Review of Politics*, January, 1957, pp. 30–1.
51. Joseph E. Davies, *Mission to Moscow*, Pocketbook edn. (New York, 1943), p. xi.
52. Issue of November 2, 1938. The title was "The Munich 'Timetable' and the Nobel Prize." See also Anne O'Hare McCormick's column in *The New York Times* of October 31, 1938.
53. Thomas K. Finletter, *op. cit.*, pp. 65–6.
54. Allen W. Dulles, *The German Underground* (New York, 1947), p. xii.
55. The details have been discussed in Herbert Feis, *Churchill, Roosevelt, Stalin: The War They Waged, The Peace They Sought* (Princeton, 1957), pp. 108–12. See also Robert E. Sherwood, *Roosevelt and Hopkins*, p. 696, and Winston S. Churchill, *The Second World War*, Vol IV, *The Hinge of Fate* (Boston, 1950), pp. 685–91.
56. *The Memoirs of Cordell Hull* (New York, 1948), II, 1570. Quoted by permission of The Macmillan Co.
57. The details have been reviewed by Hull, *Ibid.*, pp. 1570–82.
58. Harry C. Butcher, *My Three Years With Eisenhower* (New York, 1946), p. 518.
59. The Department of State, *Postwar Foreign Policy Preparation, 1939–1945*, Publication 3580, General Foreign Policy Series 15 (Washington, 1949), p. 244.
60. Cordell Hull, *op cit.*, p. 1606.
61. *Ibid.*, p. 1614.
62. Henry L. Stimson and McGeorge Bundy, *op. cit.*, p. 577.

63. It was, as is well known now, drawn up by Harry C. White, who drafted the memorandum which formed the basis of the Quebec negotiations. For the text of the memorandum see Henry Morgenthau Jr., *Germany Is Our Problem* (New York, 1945), pp. 1–4.

64. Drew Middleton, *The Struggle For Germany* (New York, 1949), p. 37. Quoted by permission of The Bobbs-Merrill Co., Inc.

65. Clinton L. Rossiter, *The American Presidency*, Signet Book edn. (New York, 1956), pp. 31 ff

66. Those listed above were preceded by Pendleton Herring, *The Politics of Democracy* (New York, 1940), in particular pp. 408 ff.

67. Hazlitt, *op. cit.*, p. 59.

68. "All Checks and No Balances," *The Review of Politics*, April, 1948.

69. Bagehot, *op. cit.*, pp. 125–6.

70. "The Constitution vs. the Peace," *The Yale Review*, Spring, 1944, p. 409.

71. Nor is the number of treaties rejected by the Senate small. As late as in 1944 Kenneth Colegrove found it appropriate to open his book on the subject—*The American Senate and World Peace* (New York, 1944)—with the well-known statement by John Hay: "A treaty entering the Senate is like a bull going into the arena. No one can say just how or when the final blow will fall. But one thing is certain—it will never leave the arena alive."

72. In England the conclusion and ratification of treaties is a prerogative of "the King in Council," in other words, the cabinet, but the very existence of the cabinet depends upon the confidence of the Commons.

73. Prescott, *op. cit.*, p. 462. Wilson later added: "If the majority cannot be trusted, it was proof, as observed by Mr. Gorham, that we were not fit for one society."—*Ibid.*, p. 463.

74. Nothing can be done about the fact that two Senate seats go to each state regardless of size, which favors the rural areas.

75. The various proposals for the reform of the electoral college were the subject of one of the most brilliant debates ever held in the United States Senate. See the Congressional Record of March 19, 20, 21, 22, 23, 26, and 27, 1956. Senator Kennedy, who organized the debate, centered his fire on the so-called Lodge-Gossett Amendment, which aimed at dividing the electoral vote cast in a state between the presidential candidates in proportion to the votes received by them. Senator Paul H. Douglas strongly defended what he considered the balance in the present system, with the preponderance given to the large and populous states by the unit rule tending to offset the discrimination to which they were subjected in both House and Senate. Senator Mundt presented a vigorous defense of the district system referred to above. The tactical situation was confused because the Lodge-Gossett Amendment and the Mundt-Goudert Amendment had been combined.

    For this writer's views on the subject, see his testimony in *Nomination and Election of President and Vice-President.* Hearings before a sub-committee of the Committee on the Judiciary, United States Senate, Washington, D.C., 1955, pp. 164 ff. and "Reform or Revolution," in *Nomination and Election of President and Vice-President.* Hearings before a Subcommittee of the Committee on the Judiciary on S.J., 2, Washington, D.C., 1949, pp. 203 ff.

76. The rights of these minority groups, some of which have very legitimate grievances, should, of course, in no way be slighted. On the other hand, their supporters should not have more rights than others. Ours is a system of persuasion, addressed to the individual voter. The unit vote introduces an element of possible coercion by minorities over majorities: In the same way in which a comparatively small amount of capital can dominate a holding company which, in its turn, can dominate a larger firm, organized minorities may first dominate the presidential vote in pivotal states, and through them the entire election.

77. George B. Galloway, *Congressional Reorganization Revisited* (College Park, Md., 1956). Quoted by permission of the Bureau of Governmental Research, University of Maryland.
78. *Ibid.*, p. 2.
79. "Towards a More Responsible Two-Party System," Supplement to *The American Political Science Review*, September, 1950.
80. See my comments on "Parties and Responsibility," *The Review of Politics*, January, 1951, pp. 116 ff.
81. Finletter, *op. cit.*, pp. 88 ff.
82. *Ibid.*, p. 93.
83. *Ibid.*, p. 93.
84. This does not mean that there are no strong arguments against the seniority rule. For a recent restatement, see Richard L. Neuberger, "A Senator's Case Against Seniority," *The New York Times Magazine*, April 7, 1957.
85. Finletter, *op. cit.*, pp. 106–7.
86. *Ibid.*, pp. 122–3.
87. *The President: Office and Powers* (34th ed.; New York, 1948), pp. 361 ff. Quoted by permission of New York University Press.
88. *Ibid.*, p. 362.
89. "Text of Explanation of U.S. Disarmament Policy Broadcast by Secretary Dulles," *The New York Times*, July 23, 1957. See also the comments by James Reston, "Education on Arms: A Commentary on Dulles' Broadcast to Nation on U.S. Disarmament Policy"—*ibid.*
90. Rossiter, *op. cit.*, p. 10.
91. It has been given, among others, brilliantly by Sidney Hyman, *The American President* (New York, 1954), pp. 309 ff. See also Eli F. Nobleman, "The Delegation of Presidential Functions: Constitutional and Legal Aspects," in *The Office of the American Presidency, The Annals* of the American Academy of Political and Social Science, ed. Sydney Hyman, September, 1956, pp. 134 ff.

FOOTNOTES TO CHAPTER XIX

1. The older generation of Indian Nationalists maintained friendly relations with the English Liberals, but these could hardly have achieved the same results as the close relation to Labour which developed during the quarter-century preceding independence.
2. Conditions in Ghana are, of course, far from being settled to the extent that they are in India. On some of the issues involved, see "A Grammar of Graft," *The Economist*, June 15, 1957.
3. The weight of the vote cast by members of state legislatures has been arranged in such a manner as to make the influence of each state roughly proportional to its population; see Articles 54 and 55 of the Constitution and, for a practical illustration, Alan Gledhill, *The Republic of India* (London, 1951), p. 98.
4. "The Council of States provides an opportunity for persons of capacity and experience of affairs, who are not disposed to partake in electioneering, to enter political life . . .

    "The Council of States is, however, intended to be less powerful and influential than the popular House. A defeat of the government in the Council of States will not involve the resignation of the Council of Ministers; its powers over finance are strictly limited. Its function is not to veto legislation, but to delay ill-considered proposals; it provides a calmer atmosphere in which speakers can debate controversial questions in a well-informed and objective manner, so that electors can consider and understand them"—*Ibid.*, p. 116.

5. That those members of the Council of States who are elected by state legislatures are elected by P. R. does not matter so long as these legislatures themselves are elected under the majority system.

6. For a summary of the arguments concerning the electoral systems in India, see Edward Robert O'Connor, "India and Democracy: An Analysis of the 1951–52 Elections and Their Political Impact" (Ph.D. thesis, Notre Dame, 1951), pp. 95 ff. This work (available on microfilm) attempts a systematic analysis of Indian society as well as of Indian political institutions.

7. *Constituent Assembly Debates*, Vol. I, December 17, 1946, pp. 98–99.

8. *Ibid.*, p. 1261.

9. In a lecture given in Munich during the winter, 1953–54.

10. For the details of the election law, and the election results, see, in addition to O'Connor (*op. cit.*), Margaret W. Fisher and Joan V. Bondurant, *The Indian Experience with Democratic Elections* (Berkeley, 1957), pp. 12 ff. and 47 ff. See also Richard L. Park, "Indian Election Results," *Far Eastern Survey*, May, 1952, and Irene Tinker and Mil Walker, "The First General Elections in India and Indonesia," *Far Eastern Survey*, July, 1956. The work entitled *Reports on the Indian General Elections, 1951–52*, edited by S. V. Kogekar and Richard L. Park (Bombay, 1956), appeared too late to be utilized in the text.

11. For a list, see Fisher and Bondurant, *op. cit.*, pp. 39–46.

12. What is usually referred to as the Hindu "communal" parties—a term not always accepted by those to whom it is applied—has been dealt with by Myron Weiner, *Party Politics in India: The Development of a Multi-Party System* (Princeton, 1957), pp. 164–222.

13. For an evaluation of both the first and second five-year plans, see W. S. Woytinski, "India's Five Year Plan," *The New Leader*, August 20, 1956.

14. See the book under that name by Peter Schmid (New York, 1955).

15. W. S. Woytinski, "Community Development in India," *The New Leader*, August 27, 1956. See also Chester Bowles, *Ambassador's Report* (New York, 1957), pp. 195 ff.

16. For a summary see "Community Projects in India," *The Hindu Weekly Review*, May 6, 1957. See also the comments in the editorial entitled "Community Projects: What Next"—*Ibid.*

17. "India Revisited: 'Spectacular Progress,'" *The New York Times Magazine* April 3, 1955.

18. Chester Bowles, "After Seven Years—Report on India," *The New York Times Magazine*, January 2, 1956.

19. Robert Trumbull, "Unhappy Resignation," *The Manchester Guardian Weekly* (February 10, 1955).

20. "India's Crisis of Ambition," *The Economist*, June 1, 1957.

21. "India Squeezes the Pips," *The Economist*, May 25, 1957.

22. William Henry Chamberlain, *Russia's Iron Age* (Boston, 1934).

23. Or, for that matter, from Puerto Rico's "Operation Bootstrap."

24. He claims that his views are pragmatic and flexible, and he has criticized the Indian Socialists for being doctrinaire; see Margaret W. Fisher and Joan V. Bondurant, *Indian Approaches to a Socialist Society* (Berkeley, 1956), pp. 31 ff. Mr. Nehru however remained quite inflexible when the second five-year plan produced the stresses which it was bound to produce, and when he was given the advice to "apply his mind to spring cleaning the plan."—Taya Zinkin, "India Faces Financial Crisis," *The Manchester Guardian Weekly*, June 27, 1957.

25. *The Economist,* June 1, 1957.
26. *The South Bend Tribune,* South Bend, Indiana, August 28, 1955.
27. Henry R. Lieberman, "India Acts to Ban Key Area Strikes," *The New York Times,* August 4, 1957.
28. Henry R. Lieberman, "Shift to Industry Is Straining India," *The New York Times,* May 9, 1957.
29. They are not limited to Socialists. See: "Nehru and Democracy," *The National Review,* February 22, 1956.
30. For the figures, and all other details, see James R. Roach, "India's 1957 Elections," *Far* Eastern Survey, May, 1957. G. S. Bhargava ("India After the Elections," *The New Leader,* May 13, 1957), who apparently did not have complete figures at his disposal (those given by Roach are not final, either) places the Congress party's vote at 42 per cent of the total. For the background, see also S. L. Poplai (ed.), *National Politics and 1957 Elections in India* (New Delhi, 1957).
31. G. S. Bhargava, "India's First Red State," *The New Leader,* May 27, 1957; Arthur Bonner, "Why the Communists Won in Kerala," *The Reporter,* May 2, 1957.
32. Margaret W. Fisher and Joan V. Bondurant, *The Indian Experience with Democratic Elections,* p. 63.
33. For the background see "Katholische Kommunisten in Indien?" *Der Volksbote* (a weekly published at Innsbruck, Austria), February 3, 1952.
34. G. S. Bhargava, "India's First Red State," *loc. cit.* (May 27, 1957).
34a. It is unlikely that the Communists could have achieved their victory with the second ballot or the alternative vote. In either case the Congress party should have picked up enough strength to prevail. Wherever the divisions within the electorate are so rigid that there is no adequate response to the invitation to unite on two major parties, which is the distinctive feature of the plurality system, the argument in favor of other types of majority voting is comparatively strong. In India there is, of course, good reason to be satisfied with the overall record of the plurality system, and to take the chance that results might develop locally as they did in Kerala, all the more since such results intensify the incentive to unite in later elections.
35. Nehru was adding his agreement to a statement by Aneurin Bevan, who had said that, if the Kerala Communists were to work out parliamentary democracy "theirs would be a socialist government with a communist label and not a communist government." See: "Kerala: Nehru on Election Results," *The Overseas Hindustan Times,* April 11, 1957.
36. For the details see Fisher and Bondurant, *The Indian Experience with Democratic Elections,* pp. 79 ff. These authors do not give percentages of the popular vote. Actually the Congress party with 39.2 per cent of the votes secured 61 per cent of the seats and the Communists with 30.9% of the votes, 7% of the seats.
37. Editorial entitled, "Famine Insurance for India," *The New York Times,* July 20, 1956.
38. *The Constitution of India,* London, 1950, quoted from a review in *The Manchester Guardian Weekly,* June 28, 1951.
39. For a background of the above discussion see Dorothy Woodman, *The Republic of Indonesia* (New York, 1955).
40. Rupert Emerson, *Representative Government in Southeast Asia* (Cambridge, 1955), pp. 18–19.
41. F. A. Hermens, *Democracy or Anarchy? A Study of Proportional Representation* (Notre Dame, 1941), pp. 339 ff.
42. Mochtar Lubis, "Party Confusion in Indonesia," *Far Eastern Survey,* October 29, 1952.
43. Rupert Emerson, *op. cit.,* p. 30.

44. Robert C. Bone, Jr., "Organization of the Indonesian Elections," *The American Political Science Review*, December, 1955, pp. 1076–77.
45. Irene Tinker and Mil Walker, "The First General Elections in India and Indonesia," Far Eastern Survey, July, 1956; Justus M. van der Kroef, "Indonesia's First National Election: A Sociological Analysis," *The American Journal of Economics and Sociology*, April and July, 1957.
46. Robert Alden, "Indonesia Holds a National Vote," *The New York Times*, September 29, 1955.
47. Bone, *op. cit.*, p. 1084.
48. Robert Alden, "Indonesia Is Found to Drift," *The New York Times*, August 30, 1956.
49. Bone, *loc. cit.*
50. Figures from estimates in *Report of the Committee on Elections to the Federal Legislative Council* (Kuala Lampur, 1954), Appendix VIII, p. 40. Quoted from the outstanding analysis of the first national elections in Malaya by Irene Tinker, "Malayan Elections: Electoral Pattern for Plural Societies?" *The Western Political Quarterly*, June, 1956.
51. *Ibid.*, p. 260.
52. *Ibid.*, p. 264.
53. "Malaya Prepares for Independence," *The Economist*, May 25, 1957.
54. Harold S. Quigley and John E. Turner, *The New Japan* (Minneapolis, 1956).
55. One small district elects only one deputy.
56. Burton Crane, "Japan's Reds Map Big Election Drive," *The New York Times*, December 27, 1948.
57. For comparisons of the 1946, 1947 and 1949 elections, see F. A. Hermens, *Europe Between Democracy and Anarchy* (Notre Dame, 1951), pp. 239–41.
58. New York, 1949, p. 57. Quoted by permission of The Macmillan Co.
59. For the results of these elections see Quigley and Turner, *op. cit.*, p. 279.
60. Chitoshi Yanaga, *Japanese People and Politics* (New York, 1956), p. 242.
61. *Ibid.*, p. 243.
62. So will the special interest groups to which the single non-transferable vote gives opportunities to send their representatives into the major parties which are similar to those provided by P.R. That is said to have applied to the interests connected with "history's oldest profession." When prostitution was made illegal, Robert Trumbull reported to *The New York Times* ("Prostitution Ban Scored in Japan," April 2, 1957): "Persons engaged in the proscribed field are highly organized throughout Japan in societies with paid officials and even with spokesmen in the Diet (Parliament)."
63. *Ibid.*, p. 244. On the relationship between this fact and the voting system, see Nobutaka Ike, *Japanese Politics* (New York, 1957), pp. 209–210.
64. Thus the arrangements against the majority system in single-member constituencies listed in Quigley and Turner (*op. cit.*, p. 249) can be explained only against the background of the pre-democratic period in Japanese politics, which is now definitely a matter of the past.
65. Even in the German case it must be borne in mind that the employment of the expellees was accompanied by extensive down-grading, a manager, for example, becoming a minor employee, or a gifted musician a farmhand. Furthermore, the expellees hold the most insecure positions in the country and are deathly afraid that in the case of a depression they would be the first ones to be dismissed.
66. C. M. Woodhouse, *Apple of Discord* (London, 1949), p. 12–13.
67. *Ibid.*, p. 14.
68. Karl Braunias, "Das parlamentarische Wahlrecht" (Berlin, 1932), I, 195.
69. On the Rally of the Greek People, see Bickham Sweet-Escott, *Greece: A Political and Economic Survey, 1939–53* (London, 1954), pp. 81–82.
70. Marc Marceau, "Victoire complète du Maréchal Papagos aux élections par-

tielles," *Le Monde*, April 4, 1953. For Greek government, pre-Papagos style, see Harold F. Alderfer, "Modern Greek Government, Part II, The Realities," *Journal of Central European Affairs*, April 1953.

71. Marc Marceau, "La Grèce en proie au doute," *Le Monde*, October 9, 1956, p. 7.
72. A. C. Sedgwick, "Living Standard Rising in Greece. Despite Gloomy Economic Statistics, People Seem More Prosperous," *The New York Times*, September 29, 1957.
73. William Hardy McNeill, *Greece: American Aid in Action, 1947–56* (New York, 1957), pp. 204 ff.
74. *Ibid.*, pp. 76–77.
75. See C. L. Sulzberger's column in *The New York Times*, February 18, 1956.
76. *Ibid.*, August 26, 1957.
77. *Ibid.*, February 18, 1956.
78. On the 1954 elections, see A. H. Hanson, "Democracy Transplanted: Reflections on a Turkish Election," *Parliamentary Affairs*, Winter (1955–56).
79. On Turkish economic policy see "Turkey in Transition, Part I: Pressing on Regardless," *The Economist*, June 15, 1957.
80. "Turkey in Transition, Part II: Democracy in Trouble," *loc. cit.*, June 22, 1957.
81. Ramón Infiesta, *Derecho Constitucional* (2nd ed.; Havana, 1954), pp. 409 ff.; see also his article entitled "Semi-Parlamentarismo," published in the daily, *El Mundo*, Jan. 15 and 18, 1957.
82. They can be circumvented; see William S. Stokes, "Parliamentary Government in Latin America," *The American Political Science Review*, June, 1945.
83. The electors composing an electoral college may, of course, be elected by P.R.
84. In Cuba, P.R. is taken for granted by most observers. When, however, in December, 1957, the author interviewed Cuban opposition leaders in Miami, two of them expressed strong opposition to P.R. They estimated that while an election in a single-member constituency might cost a candidate from 3,000 to 4,000 pesos (the peso is at a par with the dollar), from 60,000 to 80,000 pesos might be required to finance a P.R. campaign. The temptation, they added, was great to secure such funds through illicit means. Smaller parties in the Chamber of Representatives had, at times, simply "auctioned themselves off." Besides, the preferential vote, used in a manner similar to that followed in Italy, tended to disrupt parties, adding competition between the candidates appearing on the same ticket to the competition among parties.
Certain defects of P.R. are also quite noticeable in Chile, and they have not been absent in Uruguay. In Argentina, the Constituent Assembly elected under P.R. in 1957 proved to be so badly divided that it disbanded without having accomplished anything, even if the immediate reason for this outcome was the fact that the Radicals left it.
85. See, however, F. A. Hermens, *Europe between Democracy and Anarchy*, pp. 113 ff. and 116 ff. On Sweden, see Dankwart Rustow, *The Politics of Compromise* (Princeton, 1955), pp. 116 ff.

Conclusions

1. Ramón Infiesta's above-mentioned *Derecho Constitucional* indicates, however, a trend in the right direction; it avoids, above all, the legalism so widespread

among Latin writers who are inclined to treat the letter of the (constitutional) law as if it represented reality.

2. Rita Hinden, "The Outlook for Free Asia," *The Manchester Guardian Weekly*, July 11, 1957.

3. For an example, see Bruno Schlesinger, "Christopher Dawson and the Modern Political Crisis" (Ph.D. thesis, Notre Dame, 1949). (Printed)

4. For sobering thoughts on the subject, see Hans Kohn, "Some Reflections on Colonialism," *The Review of Politics*, July, 1956.

5. "Liberian Upholds Colonial Benefit: U. N. Envoy Explains Factors for Prosperity of Ghana Compared with Own Land," *The New York Times*, March 24, 1957.

6. On Ethiopia, see William H. Lewis, "The Ethiopian Empire: Progress and Problems," *Middle East Journal*, Summer 1956, pp. 257 ff.

7. The proponents of this school of thought take great care to emphasize their differences from what they call "the Palaeo-Liberals"; see C. J. Friedrich, "The Political Thought of Neo-Liberalism," *The American Political Science Review*, June, 1955.

8. *The Economist*, June 1, 1957.

9. For details see Gunnar Myrdal, *An International Economy* (New York, 1956).

10. The problems involved are social and educational as well as economic. For a good case study, see *Report on Cuba* (Baltimore, 1951), which contains the findings and recommendations of an Economic and Technical Mission organized by the International Bank for Reconstruction and Development in collaboration with the Government of Cuba in 1950. When it is emphasized (p. 4) that Cuba needs "A Strategy for Development" this holds equally for all other under-developed countries.

INDEX OF NAMES